PROFESSIONAL
RESPONSIBILITY

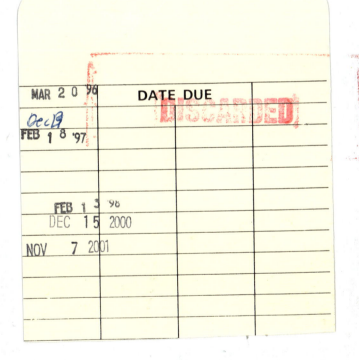

PROFESSIONAL RESPONSIBILITY

Third Edition

RONALD D. ROTUNDA

Professor of Law, University of Illinois College of Law

BLACK LETTER SERIES®

WEST PUBLISHING CO.
ST. PAUL, MINN.
1992

Black Letter Series and Black Letter Series design appearing on the
front cover are registered trademarks of West Publishing Co.
Registered in U.S. Patent and Trademark office.

COPYRIGHT © 1984, 1988 WEST PUBLISHING CO.
COPYRIGHT © 1992 By WEST PUBLISHING CO.
        50 West Kellogg Boulevard
        P.O. Box 64526
        St. Paul, MN 55164–0526

Library of Congress Cataloging-in-Publication Data

Rotunda, Ronald D.
    Professional responsibility / Ronald D. Rotunda. — 3rd ed.
      p.   cm. — (Black letter series)
    Includes index.
    ISBN 0–314–92146–X
    1. Legal ethics—United States. I. Title. II. Series.
    KF306.Z9R67 1992
    174'.3'0973—dc20   91–35299
                                      CIP

ISBN 0–314–92146–X

Rotunda—Prof.Resp. 3rd Ed. BLS

To
Nicholas and Florence

*

AUTHOR'S PREFACE

It is said that the future will bring us not only more change but also an increase in the rate of change. That has certainly been true in the area of legal ethics. Since the American Bar Association first proposed its Model Rules of Professional Conduct, in August of 1983, there have been several important additions to this model law, dealing with issues such as the sale of a law practice, government subpoenas of attorneys, and direct mail lawyer advertising. In addition, new court decisions and the American Law Institute's entrance into the world of legal ethics, with its proposed Restatement of the Law Governing Lawyers (parts of which are now in tentative draft form), have all conspired to make a new edition a necessity. The law of judicial ethics also has not stood still. In August of 1990 the ABA proposed a new Model Code of Judicial Conduct. And, of course, the case law and literature dealing with that topic has similarly increased. This edition is thus necessary, in order to keep pace with these new developments.

I am grateful that the previous two editions have been very successful, and have appealed to a diverse group of readers: law students studying for law courses in legal ethics and the bar examination in that same subject; practitioners who represent lawyers in malpractice cases and discipline proceedings, or who want to evaluate ethics issues that confront them in their daily practice; academics teaching in the area; and judges. I am particularly pleased that various judges have told me that they have found this book to be useful, and some have even cited it. E.g., *Pearson v. Parsons*, 541 So.2d 447, 452 (Miss.1989); *Attorney Grievance Commission v. Ficker*, 319 Md. 305, 312, 572 A.2d 501, 504 (Ct.App.1990). I hope that this new edition will be even more useful than the previous ones.

More than a few people have aided me in writing this new edition. I thank Ruth Manint, who carefully typed portions of the manuscript. (I also would like to add a brief note of thanks to me, for I also tackled several chapters, with much less good spirit than Ruth.) I appreciate the careful work of both Catherine A. Brunton, the Stuart N. Greenberger Research Assistant in Legal Ethics from the Class of '91, and Kathryn Firsching, the Stuart N. Greenberger Research Assistant in Legal Ethics, from the Class of '92. I am also indebted to Professor Jennifer G. Brown of Emory University, who read the entire manuscript, and Judge Noël Anketell Kramer, Superior Court of the District of Columbia, who read the chapter on Judicial Ethics. It is sometimes said that writing is a lonely business; I am afraid that has not been true in my case, thanks to my two children, Nora and Mark. I credit them for putting up with the disjointed schedule that necessarily greets the final days accompanying the completion of a book.

In any work such as this, it is almost inevitable that a few errors might creep in, in spite of my efforts, the efforts of my computer spelling check, and the efforts of West Publishing Company's editorial staff. If any gentle reader finds any such errors, I am hopeful that one or more of the people I mentioned in the previous paragraph will assume responsibility. And, in mitigation, I plead the words of Judge Henry de Bracton over 700 years ago:

> "I ask the reader, if he finds in this work anything superfluous or errone-
> ous, to correct and amend it, pass it over with eyes half closed, for to keep all in
> mind and err in nothing is divine rather than human."

2 H. de Bracton, *Bracton on the Laws and Customs of England* 20 (S. Thorne trans. 1968) (circ. 1250).

RONALD D. ROTUNDA

Champaign, Illinois
December, 1991

PUBLISHER'S PREFACE

This "Black Letter" is designed to help a law student recognize and understand the basic principles and issues of law covered in a law school course. It can be used both as a study aid when preparing for classes and as a review of the subject matter when studying for an examination.

Each "Black Letter" is written by experienced law school teachers who are recognized national authorities in the subject covered.

The law is succinctly stated by the author of this "Black Letter." In addition, the exceptions to the rules are stated in the text. The rules and exceptions have purposely been condensed to facilitate quick review and easy recollection. For an in-depth study of a point of law, citations to major student texts are given. In addition, a **Text Correlation Chart** provides a convenient means of relating material contained in the Black Letter to appropriate sections of the casebook the student is using in his or her law school course.

If the subject covered by this text is a code or code-related course, the code section or rule is set forth and discussed wherever applicable.

FORMAT

The format of this "Black Letter" is specially designed for review. (1) **Text.** First, it is recommended that the entire text be studied, and, if deemed necessary, supplemented by the student texts cited. (2) **Capsule Summary.** The Capsule Summary is an abbreviated review of the subject matter which can be used both before and after studying the main body of the text. The headings in the Capsule Summary follow the main text of the "Black Letter." (3) **Table of Contents.** The Table of Contents is in outline form to help you organize the details of the subject and the Summary of Contents gives you a final overview of the materials. (4) **Practice Examination.** The Practice Examination in Appendix B gives you the opportunity of testing yourself with the type of question asked on an exam, and comparing your answer with a model answer.

In addition, a number of other features are included to help you understand the subject matter and prepare for examinations:

Short Questions and Answers: This feature is designed to help you spot and recognize issues in the examination. We feel that issue recognition is a major ingredient in successfully writing an examination.

Perspective: In this feature, the authors discuss their approach to the topic, the approach used in preparing the materials, and any tips on studying for and writing examinations.

Analysis: This feature, at the beginning of each section, is designed to give a quick summary of a particular section to help you recall the subject matter and to help you determine which areas need the most extensive review.

Examples: This feature is designed to illustrate, through fact situations, the law just stated. This, we believe, should help you analytically approach a question on the examination.

Glossary: This feature is designed to refamiliarize you with the meaning of a particular legal term. We believe that the recognition of words of art used in an examination helps you to better analyze the question. In addition, when writing an examination you should know the precise definition of a word of art you intend to use.

We believe that the materials in this "Black Letter" will facilitate your study of a law school course and assure success in writing examinations not only for the course but for the bar examination. We wish you success.

THE PUBLISHER

SUMMARY OF CONTENTS

PART TEN. THE LAWYER'S OBLIGATIONS AS A JUDGE

APPENDICES

TABLE OF CONTENTS

PART FOUR. THE LAWYER'S OBLIGATION AS A MEMBER OF A FIRM

CAPSULE SUMMARY

PART ONE: DEFINING DISCIPLINABLE CONDUCT

I. THE DISTINCTION BETWEEN DISCIPLINABLE AND ASPIRATIONAL CONDUCT
The ethics rules distinguish between conduct to which a lawyer should aspire and conduct below which a lawyer may not go. Only failure to meet the latter subjects the lawyer to possible discipline.

II. THE "APPEARANCE OF IMPROPRIETY"
Language found in the Model Code and some court decisions refer to the lawyer's duty not to engage in conduct that has the appearance of impropriety. But the Model Code never intended this vague standard to be used as a test, and consequently the Model Rules nowhere even use such language.

III. DEFINING DISCIPLINABLE CONDUCT
A lawyer may be subject to discipline for violating any of the mandatory requirements of the ethics rules. In addition the lawyer may be subject to discipline for violation of certain other law. Some of these violations—those that have a functional relationship to the practice of law—are also disciplinable even if not engaged in while the lawyer acts in a legal capacity.

1

IV. THE LAWYER'S ROLE REGARDING JUDGES AND CANDIDATES FOR JUDICIARY

The lawyer may not, with scienter, falsely accuse a judge. Lawyers who are candidates for judicial office are under the same restrictions applied to incumbent judges.

PART TWO: THE LAWYER'S OBLIGATIONS TO SUPPORT BAR ADMISSIONS AND THE DISCIPLINARY SYSTEMS

I. APPLICANTS TO THE BAR

The ethics rules of a given jurisdiction govern only lawyers admitted to that bar. The rules do not apply to applicants to the bar, but if these applicants knowingly submit any materially false information they can be disciplined after they are later admitted. In addition, an applicant to the bar in State One, who is already a member of the bar in State Two, and who knowingly submits a materially false application to State One, is subject to discipline in State Two.

A Lawyer should not further the application of applicants known to be unqualified.

II. THE LAWYER'S ROLE REGARDING REPORTING DISCIPLINABLE VIOLATIONS OF LAWYERS

Lawyers have an affirmative "whistle-blowing" obligation to report other lawyers who violate the ethics rules, at least when the violations are serious and the lawyer's evidence to support the violation is substantial. This obligation, however, is subject to the reporting lawyer's duty of client confidentiality.

PART THREE: THE LAWYER'S OBLIGATION TO THE CLIENT

I. THE DUTY OF CONFIDENTIALITY

Lawyers must not disclose information gained in the professional relationship (1) that is protected as an evidentiary privilege, (2) that would otherwise be embarrassing or likely detrimental to the client, or (3) that the client has requested be kept secret.

Both the Model Code and the Model Rules prohibit the lawyer from using client information to the client's detriment, unless the client consents. The Code, unlike the Rules, also prohibits the lawyer, unless the client consents, from using client information to the lawyer's own (or a third party's) advantage, even if this information is not disclosed to anyone.

Notwithstanding this general requirement of nondisclosure, a lawyer may reveal such information if: (1) the client consents to disclosure, either expressly or impliedly; (2) other provisions of the ethics rules or other law allow disclosure; (3) disclosure is necessary to collect a fee or respond to charges of wrongful conduct; or (4) disclosure is necessary to prevent the client's criminal act that would be likely to result in death or substantial bodily harm. The Code, unlike the Rules, expands this last exception to include any crime by the client.

II. CONFLICTS OF INTEREST

Unless the client knowingly consents, a lawyer may not accept, or continue, employment by a client if the lawyer's exercise of professional judgment will reasonably be affected by the lawyer's own financial or personal interests or the interests of another client. The lawyer owes to each client a duty of zealous (but not over-zealous) representation, loyalty, and preservation of confidences. If fulfilling any of these duties to one client violates a duty to another client, there is a prohibited conflict.

In some cases, public policy demands that even client consent cannot waive the conflict.

If the lawyer is disqualified because of a conflict, typically this disqualification is imputed to every other lawyer in the same firm. If a lawyer leaves that firm and joins another, the lawyer's imputed knowledge (unlike a lawyer's actual knowledge) is not thereafter imputed to others in the new firm. Also, the Model Rules specifically provide that certain types of disqualifications are not imputed.

III. THE DUTY OF COMPETENCE AND THE SCOPE OF REPRESENTATION

The lawyer must perform services competently.

In general, the client has control both as to scope of the representation and the extent to which the lawyer may waive the client's substantive rights.

IV. FEES

The lawyer may not charge unreasonable fees. It is the better practice to put fee agreements in writing. The Rules require that contingent fees be in writing.

The lawyer may not charge a contingent fee in criminal cases. The Rules also prohibit contingent fees in divorce cases, while the Code only discourages such fee arrangements.

V. ACCEPTING, DECLINING, AND TERMINATING REPRESENTATION

Unless the court has appointed a lawyer to represent a client, a lawyer has no obligation to accept all clients in the order in which they walk in the door.

However, once the lawyer accepts a case, she is subject to various restrictions so that she has no general, absolute right of withdrawal.

VII. TRUST FUND ACCOUNTS

Client funds must be placed in trust fund accounts, and any interest earned on the accounts belongs to the client unless state bar rules provide otherwise.

PART FOUR: THE LAWYER'S OBLIGATIONS AS A MEMBER OF A FIRM

I. SUPERVISORY RESPONSIBILITY

The ethics rules do not govern the lay employees of a lawyer, but they do make it the lawyer's responsibility to assure that his employees act to protect client interests, such as the client's interests in confidentiality.

Lawyers also must exercise reasonable supervision over subordinate lawyers. The Rules make clear that a subordinate lawyer may defer to the reasonable judgment of the supervisory lawyer in ethical matters, but that otherwise there is no defense based simply on following orders.

II. SHARING FEES AND RESPONSIBILITY WITH LAY PEOPLE

Lawyers have broad authority to include nonlawyer employees in profit sharing or retirement plans, but lawyers may not share managerial responsibilities with lay people in matters relating to the lawyer's professional legal judgment.

III. UNAUTHORIZED PRACTICE OF LAW

What is the unauthorized practice of law is a legal question, the answer to which varies from one jurisdiction to another. In general, it may be said that the essence of the practice of law is to apply the general principles of law to specific factual circumstances.

Lawyers may not practice law in a jurisdiction unless they are admitted there. In addition, lawyers must not aid nonlawyers in unauthorized practice.

IV. AGREEMENTS TO RESTRICT THE RIGHT TO PRACTICE LAW

A lawyer may not be a party to an agreement that restricts his right to practice law, unless the restriction is part of a retirement benefits agreement, or is part of a valid agreement, authorized by the Model Rules, for the sale of a law practice.

PART FIVE: THE LAWYER'S OBLIGATIONS REGARDING ADVERTISING AND SOLICITATION

I.   ADVERTISING

Until the U.S. Supreme Court extended certain first amendment rights to lawyer's advertising, one could almost summarize the law of ethics in the sentence: Lawyers may not lie, cheat, steal, or advertise. Now, the Rules basically forbid advertising only if it is misleading. The Code has the same goal—no misleading advertising—but seeks to reach that goal by fairly detailed descriptions of the types of advertising that it allows.

II. SOLICITATION

Lawyers may not, in general, "solicit" clients for pecuniary gain in circumstances where the prospective client might be subjected to overreaching or, because of the emotional situation, have an impaired capacity for reasoned judgment. Beyond these extreme cases, efforts to prohibit solicitation may run afoul of the constitutional protections of free speech.

The Rules, amended to conform to Supreme Court decisional law, now do not treat direct mail advertising as improper solicitation, and only have a blanket prohibition of "in-person" (*i.e.,* face-to-face) or "live telephone" solicitation when a significant motive for the lawyer's actions is his pecuniary gain.

PART SIX: THE LAWYER'S OBLIGATIONS NOT TO MISUSE THE OFFICE OF GOVERNMENT

I.   THE PUBLIC OFFICIAL WHO IS ALSO A LAWYER

Lawyers may not abuse their public positions by, for example, accepting bribes, using their names in private law firms when they no longer practice law in that firm, or implying that they have the power to influence action corruptly.

II. THE REVOLVING DOOR

There are certain public benefits as well as possible disadvantages involved when lawyers for the government leave to enter private practice. In an effort to draw a clear and proper balance, the ethics rules forbid a lawyer in private practice from representing a client in a matter if that lawyer, while in the government, had personally and substantially participated in that matter, unless the appropriate government agency consents.

The former government lawyer's individual disqualification is not imputed to the entire firm if that lawyer is screened from the particular matter in question, is apportioned no part of the fee, and the law firm promptly gives written notice to the relevant government agency so that it can verify that the firm has complied with the provisions of this rule.

III. SPECIAL RESPONSIBILITIES OF A PUBLIC PROSECUTOR

The public prosecutor represents not only a governmental entity but also the public interest. Because the government is a particularly powerful client, the lawyer's duty of zealousness is tempered by the obligation to avoid harassing techniques and to refrain from instituting proceedings unsupported by probable cause.

PART SEVEN: THE LAWYER'S OBLIGATION AS AN ADVOCATE

Although the lawyer acts as an advocate, he or she must avoid taking frivolous positions. When appearing before a tribunal the lawyer must not mislead the tribunal, both as to law and to facts, avoid improper publicity that might reasonably prejudice the proceedings, avoid improper ex parte communications, and act with decorum. The lawyer must also treat third parties and opposing counsel with respect, and not mislead them.

PART EIGHT: THE LAWYER'S OBLIGATIONS AS ADVISER

The lawyer must give his client candid advice.

The lawyer may act as an intermediary between clients if all consent and the lawyer reasonably believes that she can perform this role impartially.

The lawyer may also evaluate a matter affecting a client for the benefit of a third party if the client consents and the lawyer believes that she can perform that role competently.

PART NINE: THE LAWYER'S OBLIGATIONS REGARDING PRO BONO ACTIVITIES

The ethics rules encourage, but do not require, the lawyer to volunteer to undertake pro bono activities. In addition, courts sometimes appoint lawyers to represent indigents, particularly in criminal cases.

The lawyer's obligations to his private clients do not prevent the lawyer from advocating his own personal views as to how the law should be reformed.

PART TEN: THE LAWYER'S OBLIGATIONS AS A JUDGE

I. INTRODUCTION
In 1990 the American Bar Association approved a comprehensive revision of judicial ethics, called the Model Code of Judicial Conduct. This Code replaced the Code of Judicial Conduct, adopted in 1972.

II. PERSONAL BEHAVIOR
The judge shall demonstrate judicial integrity and impartiality.

III. CONDUCT IN THE COURTROOM
The judge shall maintain courtroom decorum, not lend the prestige of judicial office to advance private interests, avoid improper ex parte communications, abstain from public comment about pending cases, and should not exercise the judicial power of appointment based on favoritism or nepotism. Judicial duties take precedence over all the judge's other activities. The judge shall perform judicial duties without improper bias or prejudice, and shall require judicial staff and lawyers in the proceedings to do likewise. And the judge shall not hold membership in any organization that practices invidious discrimination on the basis of race, sex, religion, or national origin.

IV. JUDICIAL DISQUALIFICATION
The judge shall hear and decide matters unless disqualification is required. Unless the parties consent, the judge should disqualify himself where his impartiality might reasonably be questioned, where he has actual bias or prejudice, where he is a material witness or had been a lawyer in the matter, or where he has more an a de minimis economic interest in the subject matter in controversy or party to the proceeding, or any other more than de minimis interest that could be substantially affected by the proceeding.

V. EXTRA-JUDICIAL ACTIVITIES
A judge may engage in extra-judicial activities if doing so does not cast doubt on the judge's capacity to decide impartially as a judge, does not demean the judicial office, and does not interfere with the proper performance of judicial duties.

VI. POLITICAL ACTIVITIES
A judge, including a candidate for election or selection to the bench, is subject to some limits in political activities so as to prevent inappropriate political activity.

VII. DEFINING WHO IS A JUDGE
All of the restrictions of the Code of Judicial Conduct apply only to full-time judges. Those restrictions that are functionally appropriate also apply to part-time judges, judges pro tempore, and retired judges.

*

PERSPECTIVE

Analysis

I. An Historical Introduction
II. Relationship With Other Courses
III. Preparing for a Professional Responsibility Examination
IV. Caveat

I. AN HISTORICAL INTRODUCTION

The present Model Rules of Professional Conduct has a long lineage. In 1836, when the legal profession was subject to virtually no regulation, David Hoffman, a professor of law at the University of Maryland, published for his students fifty "*Resolutions In Regard to Professional Deportment.*" Hoffman recommended that a lawyer's conscience be his "sole guide" (Resolution 33), and that a lawyer "espouse no man's cause out of envy, hatred or malice, toward his antagonist" (Resolution 2).

In 1854, Professor, and Judge, George Sharswood, turned to the issues raised by Hoffman and published "*A Compend of Lectures on the Aims and Duties of the Profession of Law.*" Sharswood's lectures greatly influenced the Alabama Bar Association, which published a "Code of Ethics" in 1887. Lawyers in other states followed Alabama's lead, and, on August 27, 1908, a nationwide voluntary bar association,the American Bar Association, approved 32 Canons, also based on the Alabama model.

Over the years various states adopted these Canons as positive law: The courts enforced these Canons, which were amended over time. In addition, the ABA purported to treat the Canons as private law governing those lawyers who chose to join that association. In 1940 it announced: "The Canons of this Association govern all its members, irrespective of the nature of their practice, and the application of the Canons is not affected by statutes or regulations governing certain activities of lawyers which may prescribe less stringent standards." ABA Formal Opinion 203 (Nov. 23, 1940) (patent lawyer may not advertise even though the U.S. Patent Office allows certain types of advertising).

In spite of the various amendments to the Canons, they were soon criticized as "generalizations designed for an earlier era." Stone,*The Public Influence of the Bar*, 48 Harv.L.Rev. 1, 10 (1934). But it was not until 1969 that the ABA adopted a completely revised set of rules, the Code of Professional Responsibility. In keeping with the view that the Code was "law" that governed ABA members regardless of state law, this Code, approved by the ABA House of Delegates on August 12, 1969, had an "effective date" of January 1, 1970. Until 1976, the membership form for the ABA also included a statement that the member promised to abide by the ABA Canons of Ethics and, later, by the ABA Code of Professional Responsibility.

The Antitrust Division of the Department of Justice, as well as other groups, noted serious antitrust problems when lawyers agree with each other to abide by certain purportedly "ethical" restrictions on, for example, advertising or fees. In 1978, in response to this criticism, the ABA formally acknowledged that its Code was really only a *Model* Code.

"The Canons of Professional Ethics and the succeeding Code of Professional Responsibility have been drafted, promulgated, and amended by agencies of the American Bar Association within the context of understanding that such codes might serve only as exemplars for the proper conduct of legal practitioners but that the power of disciplinary enforcement rests with the judiciary." ABA Informal Opinion 1420 (June 5, 1978).

To emphasize this change, the ABA retitled its Code of Professional Responsibility so it is called the *Model* Code of Professional Responsibility.

The ABA has been quite successful in persuading state and federal courts to adopt its Model Code as positive law. State courts also cite the Model Code as evidence of the law. Similarly, though the ABA Formal and Informal Opinions interpreting the Model Code are not law, courts have cited and relied on them as influential evidence of the law.

In 1977 the ABA took the first steps toward completely revamping the Model Code. It created a Commission on Evaluation of Professional Standards (initially chaired by the late Robert J. Kutak, and thus popularly referred to as the Kutak Commission). This Commission drafted the *Model Rules of Professional Conduct*, which the ABA adopted in August 1983. This time, the ABA House of Delegates specifically defeated a motion to set an effective date.

By the middle of 1991 more than two-thirds of the states have adopted or are near adopting the Model Rules, subject to various nonuniform amendments. In addition, the Model Rules are still evidence of the law and have already been cited as such in various court decisions, even when the states have not formally adopted a version of the Model Rules. The Model Rules are also a useful teaching tool to compare with the Model Code.

Note: For the sake of brevity, the Model Code and Model Rules will often be referred to as the Code or Rules. The Disciplinary Rules of the Code will be cited as "DR," as in DR 4–101. The Ethical Considerations of the Code will be cited as "EC," as in EC 2–21. The Model Rules will be cited as "Rule," as in Rule 1.6. The Comments will be cited by Rule number and paragraph number. The drafters of the Model Rules did not number the paragraphs of the Comments (or the Code Comparison, or the other divisions of the Rules), but, for ease of reference, we shall refer to them by number. Thus, a citation to Rule 1.6, Comment 15, refers to the fifteenth paragraph of the Comment to Rule 1.6; a citation to Rule 1.2, Code Comparison 5 refers to the fifth paragraph of the Code Comparison to Rule 1.2. The Appendices to this book reprint both the Model Code (which the ABA has not amended since it promulgated the Model Rules) and the latest ABA version of the Model Rules.

In 1986 the American Law Institute, a prestigious group of practicing lawyers, judges, and academics, began work drafting a *Restatement of the Law Governing Lawyers*. Although the ALI has never before tackled the law of lawyering, it has entitled this project, "Restatement of the Law Third." However, there is no Restatement Second, or Restatement Third. The ALI has chosen this title not out of a perverse desire to confuse law students and practicing lawyers (though that has been a not uncommon result) but to signify that the American Law Institute is now working on a third major series of Restatements, such as the Restatement, Third, of the Law of Unfair Competition, etc. Occasionally this book will refer to *tentative* drafts of the *Restatement Third of the Law Governing Lawyers*.

II. RELATIONSHIP WITH OTHER COURSES

The history of law, Maitland said, is a "seamless web." Maitland, *Prologue to a History of English Law,* 14 L.Q.R. 13 (1898). This observation is equally true of legal ethics. To write the first sentence is to make a tear in this unity. The lawyer's ethical duty to keep the client's confidences incorporates the law of evidence and the attorney-client privilege as well as the law of agency. The lawyer's duty of competence is related to the law of tort and the tort of malpractice. The lawyer's agreement with the client involves the law of contract, and take into account that the lawyer is a fiduciary of the client. The Model Code and Model Rules must also be interpreted in light of antitrust principles. And the state laws derived from either must be tested against constitutional principles, particularly those related to freedom of speech.

In addition to the relationship with other areas of substantive law, legal ethics is a branch of history and philosophy. "There is much more to it than rules of ethics. There is a whole atmosphere of life's behavior." Wigmore, *Introduction* xxiv, in, O. Carter, Ethics of the Legal Profession (1915). And this atmosphere exists whether or not the policeman is watching. Moreover, legal ethics is related to the interdisciplinary study of law and economics, and some of the present or past ethical violations are best understood as guild rules created by a cartel of lawyers. That is why George Bernard Shall once said that professions are "conspiracies against the laity." G.B. Shaw, Doctor's Dilemma (preface) (1911).

III. PREPARING FOR A PROFESSIONAL RESPONSIBILITY EXAMINATION

The "most fundamental legal skill consists of determining what kind of legal problems a situation may involve, a skill that necessarily transcends any particular specialized knowledge." Model Rules, Rule1.1, Comment 2.

However, in an examination of legal ethics, a little specialized knowledge would not hurt. The Model Code and Model Rules are a source of this specialized knowledge. The student should apply his or her traditional legal skills to the fact situation and evaluate how the Code or Rules (or other body of law) might deal with the problem. Sometimes these rules are too vague to be of much help; at other times they are quite specific, but one may think them to represent bad policy. A conclusion that a Rule represents bad policy is important, because the law is not static: what the law ought to be is very relevant, because the "ought" influences the "is." The fact that law is not static is what has required this new edition.

It is important to realize that the law of ethics advises the lawyer not only what one must or must not do, but also what one "should" do, or what one "may" do even if the client objects. Finally, whether or not conduct is consistent with the Code or Rules, that conduct may subject the lawyer to malpractice liability. The Multistate Professional Responsibility Examination recognizes these important distinctions in its specific definitions of several key phrases:

1. *Must* or *subject to discipline* asks whether the conduct referred to or described in the question subjects the attorney to discipline under the provisions of the Disciplinary Rules of the ABA Model Code of Professional Responsibility and the Model Rules of Professional Conduct.

2. *Should* asks whether the conduct referred to or described in the question at least conforms to the level of conduct expected of the attorney pursuant to the ABA Model Code of Professional Responsibility and the Model Rules of Professional Conduct, regardless of whether the obligation arises under the ethical considerations, comments, or disciplinary rules.

3. *May* or *proper* asks whether the conduct referred to or described in the question is professionally appropriate in that it:

   a. would not subject the attorney to discipline.

   b. is not inconsistent with the Ethical Considerations of the ABA Code of Professional Responsibility and the Preamble and Comments to the Model Rules of Professional Conduct.

   c. is not inconsistent with the ABA Model Code of Judicial Conduct.

4. *Subject to liability for malpractice* asks whether the conduct referred to or described in the question subjects the attorney to liability for damages for harm to the client resulting from that conduct. If a question refers to liability for malpractice, it should be answered according to generally accepted principles of law, and the relationship, if any, between being liable for malpractice and being subject to discipline.

IV. CAVEAT
A text limited in size necessarily restricts any full discussion of all the nuances of the ethics governing the practice of law. The black letter language

found throughout, and the capsule summary in particular, are intended to be (and in the nature of things can only be) summaries of the basic principles of legal ethics. For a more elaborate discussion, analysis, and research tool, see, e.g., C. Wolfram, *ModernLegal Ethics* (1986); ABA/BNA, *Lawyers' Manual on Professional Conduct* (multivolume loose leaf service); R. Underwood & W. Fortune, *Trial Ethics* (1988); G. Hazard & W. Hodes, *The Law of Lawyering: A Handbook on the Model Rules of Professional Conduct* (2d ed. 1990)(2 volumes); R. Hillman, *Law Firm Breakups: The Law and Ethics of Grabbing and Leaving* (1990). On the ABA Model Judicial Code, see, J. Shaman, S. Lubet, & J. Alfini, *Judicial Conduct and Ethics* (1990). On legal malpractice, see, R. Mallen & J. Smith, *Legal Malpractice* (3d ed. 1990)(2 volumes).

PART ONE

DEFINING DISCIPLINABLE CONDUCT

Analysis

I. THE DISTINCTION BETWEEN DISCIPLINABLE AND ASPIRATIONAL CONDUCT

A lawyer may only be disciplined for violating mandatory rules, but lawyers should strive to meet the aspirational goals.

A. ETHICAL CONSIDERATIONS

The Code distinguishes between Ethical Considerations ("EC") and Disciplinary Rules ("DR"). The Ethical Considerations are "aspirational" only. See Model Code, Preliminary Statement. Therefore, if conduct violates only an EC, it is not disciplinable. The EC's also aid in interpreting and explaining the policies underlying a DR. "They constitute a body of principles upon which the lawyer can rely for guidance in specific situations." See Model Code, Preliminary Statement.

Notwithstanding the fact that a violation of an EC is not disciplinable under the Code, in some cases courts have disciplined an attorney for violating an EC. See, *Committee on Professional Ethics and Conduct of State Bar Ass'n v. Behnke,* 276 N.W.2d 838, 840 (Iowa 1979) (violation of an EC, "standing alone," will support disciplinary action; in this case the violation was of EC 5–5). However, in most such instances, the fact that the conduct is prohibited can be derived from a DR, even though it might be expressed more clearly in the EC. Courts purporting to rely only on EC's may have failed to carefully and precisely interpret the Model Code. In short, one should not assume that if conduct expressly violates an EC, it does not also violate a more generally phrased DR.

B. DISCIPLINARY RULES

The Disciplinary Rules, unlike the Ethical Considerations, "are mandatory in character." They state "the minimum level of conduct below which no lawyer can fall without being subject to disciplinary action." See Model Code, Preliminary Statement. See also DR 1–102(A)(1) (misconduct to violate a disciplinary rule).

Some of the EC's and DR's are cast in terms of what the lawyer "may" do. E.g., DR 4–101(C) (when lawyer "may" reveal a client secret or confidence). In such cases the Code gives lawyers a power to be exercised in their sound discretion.

C. THE MODEL RULES

The Model Rules draw similar distinctions between what *must* be done, what *should* be done, and what *may* be done. When the black letter Rules use imperatives such as "shall" or "shall not," violations are disciplinable. See Model Rules, Scope 1. See Rule 8.4(a) (misconduct to violate or attempt to violate the Model Rules).

Like the Model Code, some of the Model Rules also use the term "may" in order to define areas of permissible lawyer discretion. Model Rules, Scope 1. E.g., Rule 1.6(b) (when lawyer "may" reveal client information). See also, Rule 6.1 ("A lawyer should render public interest legal service."); Rule 1.5(b) (basis of fee should be "preferably in writing").

Finally, many of the Comments to the Rules use the term "should." These Comments are comparable to the EC's of the Code. If a Comment uses the term "should," it does "not add obligations to the Rules but provides guidance for practicing in compliance with the Rules." Model Rules, Scope 1. The Comments also explain the Rules and provide interpretative guidance, though, of course, "the text of each Rule is authoritative." Rules, Scope 9. Therefore, while the black letter Rules control, one should not conclude that, because conduct violates an explicit aspirational Comment, it does not also violate a more broadly drafted Rule.

II. THE "APPEARANCE OF IMPROPRIETY"

Although the Code states that lawyers should avoid the "appearance of impropriety," this "appearance" provision is not a disciplinable standard and is also undefinable unless one first defines what is an "impropriety."

The title of Canon 9 states: "A Lawyer Should Avoid Even the Appearance of Impropriety." The titles of the Canons are not disciplinable rules themselves, but only titles of sections. They represent "axiomatic norms" (see Model Code, "Preliminary Statement"), not tests to determine when lawyers should be disciplined or disqualified. This "appearance of impropriety" standard may represent a reason behind a rule (see EC 9–3)—why, for example, some ethics rules are mechanical and absolute—but it is not a rule itself. It is significant that no Disciplinary Rule requires the lawyer to avoid the "appearance of impropriety."

Nonetheless, some courts have used this loose language as a standard of conduct. See, e.g., *Kramer v. Scientific Control Corp.,* 534 F.2d 1085 (3d Cir. 1976), cert. denied, 429 U.S. 830, 97 S.Ct. 90, 50 L.Ed.2d 94 (1976). Other courts, in contrast, have warned that use of such a broad test should not substitute for analysis to demonstrate why conduct does, or does not, fit within specific disciplinary rules. *International Electronics Corp. v. Flanzer,* 527 F.2d 1288, 1295 (2d Cir. 1975). As the court carefully noted in *Fund of Funds, Ltd. v. Arthur Andersen & Co.,* 567 F.2d 225, 227 (2d Cir. 1977): "When dealing with ethical principles . . . we cannot paint with broad strokes. The lines are fine and must be so marked. [T]he conclusion in a particular case can be reached only after painstaking analysis of the facts and precise application of precedent." In ABA Formal Opinion 342 (1975), the American Bar Association warned that if the "appearance of impropriety" language had been made a disciplinary rule, "it is likely that the determination of whether particular conduct violated the rule would have degenerated . . . into a determination on an instinctive, or even *ad hominem* basis. . . ."

The Rules reject the "appearance of impropriety" test. The drafters thought that it was too loose and vague; it gave no fair warning and it allowed, if not encouraged, instinctive judgments. Also, one can not begin to define "appearance of impropriety" unless one first defines "impropriety," and the purported "test" does neither. Rule 1.9, Comment 5. The Rules, at times, impose a bright line prohibition in order to avoid an "appearance of impropriety," but that phrase, by itself, is not a test; it is question-begging.

III. DEFINING DISCIPLINABLE CONDUCT

A lawyer may be disciplined for violating a mandatory requirement of the Code or Rules, or for engaging in conduct forbidden by other laws if such conduct demonstrates that the lawyer should not be entrusted with the confidence that clients normally place in a lawyer.

A. ACTS NOT DONE IN A LEGAL CAPACITY

A lawyer may be disciplined for wrongful conduct even though that person was not acting in his or her capacity as a lawyer when engaging in the wrong, *if* the conduct functionally relates to his or her capacity to practice law. ABA Formal Opinion 336 (June 3, 1974) concluded that any "illegal conduct involving moral turpitude," and any conduct "involving dishonesty, fraud, deceit, or misrepresentation" adversely affect the lawyer's capacity to practice law. See DR 1–102(A)(3), (4); Rule 8.4(b), (c).

Example: A lawyer knowingly makes a false statement of fact about a judicial candidate. DR 8–102(A); Rule 8.2(a). He has evidenced lack of trustworthiness and is subject to discipline.

In contrast to these rules, DR 7–107 and Rule 3.6, governing trial publicity, or DR 2–101, and Rule 7.2, governing advertising, relate to a lawyer only in her professional capacity.

B. CATEGORIES OF DISCIPLINABLE CONDUCT
1. Violating a Disciplinary Rule

It is, of course, disciplinable to violate a Disciplinary Rule. DR 1–102(A)(1); Rule 8.4(a). See generally Section I, B, supra. It is also disciplinable to assist or induce another to violate a Disciplinary Rule. DR 1–102(A)(2); Rule 8.4(a). The Rules add that it is disciplinable to "attempt to violate the Rules." Rule 8.4(a).

2. Criminal Acts

Not all illegal conduct is disciplinable. The Code only forbids crimes involving "moral turpitude." DR 1–102(A)(3).

The problem with the test of "moral turpitude" is that it is too vague and allows, or even invites, a court to discipline attorneys for acts that may be crimes in some states, although the crime is not connected or even relevant to the attorney-client relationship. See *Grievance Committee of Hartford County Bar v. Broder*, 112 Conn. 263, 152 A. 292 (1930) (extramarital relations with consenting person not a client; held, disciplinable).

It is not at all evident that the drafters of the Model Code intended to make disciplinable those crimes that are not functionally related to fitness to practice law, particularly because other provisions in the Code imply that such a functional relationship is necessary. See DR 1–102(A)(6), forbidding a lawyer from engaging in "any *other* conduct that adversely reflects on his fitness to practice law." (emphasis added).

In any event, the Rules adopt more precise language because "a lawyer should be professionally answerable only for offenses that indicate lack of those characteristics relevant to law practice." Rule 8.4, Comment 1. Rule 8.4(b) limits disciplinable crimes to those that reflect "adversely on the lawyer's honesty, trustworthiness or fitness as a lawyer in other respects." Discipline is inappropriate for violation of "personal morality" such as adultery. Rule 8.4, Comment 1.

> *Example:* Examples of disciplinable conduct include crimes of fraud or breach of trust; willful (rather than negligent) failure to file an income tax return; or "serious interferences with the administration of justice." Rule 8.4, Comment 1.

Rule 8.4, Comment 1 includes "violence" in the category of disciplinable crimes, even though violence does not necessarily indicate lack of trustworthiness or dishonesty: a drunken barroom brawl may only indicate a bad temper. Nonetheless, crimes of violence, particularly when the violence is quite serious, have been held disciplinable. E.G., *Matter of Webb*, 602 P.2d 408 (Alaska 1979) (first degree murder, accessory after the fact).

The Rules suggest that even a pattern of repeated minor offenses could be disciplinable if it indicates "indifference to legal obligation." Rule 8.4, Comment 1. The drafters give no examples, but repeated violations involving minor offenses may just as likely indicate an indifference only to a *particular* violation, e.g., a lawyer owns a grocery store that repeatedly is open on Sunday, in criminal violation of a local, generally unenforced, "blue law."

3. **Conduct Involving Dishonesty, Fraud, Deceit, or Misrepresentation**
    Conduct, whether or not a crime, that involves dishonesty, fraud, deceit, or misrepresentation, is disciplinable. DR 1–102(A)(4); Rule 8.4(c). Noncriminal fraud (for those states that have such an offense) would fall under this rubric. Similarly, violations of fiduciary obligations (whether or not undertaken in one's capacity as a lawyer) would be disciplinable.

    ABA Formal Opinion 337 (Aug. 10, 1974) relied on DR 1–102(A)(4) in order to hold that (except in the case of law enforcement that at least is in compliance with statutory and constitutional guidelines) a lawyer should not tape record conversations without the consent or prior knowledge of all parties involved. The secret nature of the recording, the Opinion reasoned, was a form of fraud, even if not a crime under the local jurisdiction.

4. **Other Conduct**
    The final version of the Rules (but *not* the Proposed Final Draft of May 30, 1981) makes it disciplinable to "engage in conduct that is prejudicial to the administration of justice." Rule 8.4(d). This vague and loose standard is also found in the Model Code. DR 1–102(A)(5). The Code offers another equally vague and loose catch-all standard: "any other conduct that adversely reflects on his fitness to practice law." DR 1–102(A)(5)(b). The Model Rules, however, do not continue this provision.

    The Model Rules, for unknown reasons, place in Rule 8.4 two further prohibitions that, more logically, could have been placed with the other substantive provisions in the Model Rules. Thus, a lawyer should not state or imply an ability to improperly influence a government agency or official, or to knowingly assist a judge to violate the Code of Judicial Conduct. Rule 8.4(e), (f). The Code has similar prohibitions, but they are placed in the body of the Code. See DR 9–101(c), which is almost identical to Rule 8.4(e), and DR 7–110(A), which is somewhat related to Rule 8.4(f).

IV. JURISDICTION

A. ACTS DONE OUTSIDE OF THE JURISDICTION
A state disciplinary authority has, in general, the power to discipline a person admitted to the bar in that jurisdiction even though the acts complained of occurred outside the jurisdiction.

1. **In General**

   Consider three cases: (1) Lawyer 1 is admitted in State *A,* yet practices in State *Y* after being admitted there *pro hac vice,* i.e., for purposes of this case only. (2) Lawyer 2 is admitted in State *A* and State *Y,* but practices only in State *Y,* outside the jurisdiction of State *A.* (3) Lawyer 3, admitted in State *A,* does not practice law at all, yet he engages in misconduct (in State *A* or *Y*) reflecting on his ability to practice law. (See section III, A, supra, on disciplinable misconduct engaged in by a person not acting in his or her capacity as a lawyer.) In all of these cases, State *A* has jurisdiction to discipline the lawyer, although the improper conduct occurred outside of State *A*'s jurisdiction. In addition, State *Y* also has jurisdiction to discipline Lawyer 1 for misconduct growing out of Lawyer 1's special appearance in State *Y.* E.g., *Kentucky Bar Ass'n v. Shane,* 553 S.W.2d 467 (Ky. 1977). Of course, because Lawyer 1 is not generally admitted in State *Y,* State *Y* cannot disbar him. However, State *Y* can revoke its permission for him to appear *pro hac vice* for that case and for future cases.

2. **Rationale**

   The rationale for the extraterritorial application of ethics rules is easy to understand. The purpose of lawyer discipline is not to punish but rather to "seek to determine the fitness of an officer of the court to continue in that capacity and to protect the courts and the public from the official ministration of persons unfit to practice." *In re Echeles,* 430 F.2d 347, 349 (7th Cir. 1970). If the lawyer engages in improper conduct outside the jurisdiction of State *A,* that conduct still reflects on the ability of the lawyer to practice in State *A.* It is the lawyer's admission to practice in State *A* (not the site of his improper act) that gives State *A* the jurisdiction to discipline. E.g. *State v. Pounds,* 525 S.W.2d 547 (Tex.Civ. App. 1975) (discipline of nonresident lawyer). See also, e.g., *Selling v. Radford,* 243 U.S. 46, 37 S.Ct. 377, 61 L.Ed. 585 (1917).

   The Code has no specific provision governing this jurisdictional question, though it is implicit in the definition of misconduct, DR 1–102, which, by its own terms, provides no jurisdictional limitations.

   The Rules explicitly codify the present law: "A lawyer admitted to practice in this jurisdiction is subject to the disciplinary authority of this jurisdiction although engaged in practice elsewhere." Rule 8.5.

3. **Choice of Law Problems**

   A lawyer may be admitted in two different jurisdictions, State *A,* and State *B.* This lawyer may engage in an act (either in State *A,* or *B,* or elsewhere) which is disciplinable in one State but not the other. Thus, State *A* may discipline a lawyer for engaging in conduct in State *B,* even though State *B* does not discipline such conduct, or punishes it less severely (e.g., private admonition, versus suspension for one year, versus disbarment). State *A* will no doubt contend that it has higher standards than State *B*. The situation is analogous to the case where two States adopt the multistate bar examination but one State sets a lower passing rate than the other.

Because a state can discipline a lawyer for conduct which is engaged in another jurisdiction, choice of law problems are inevitable. If a lawyer practices in two jurisdictions, it is quite conceivable that conduct *forbidden* in one jurisdiction is ethically *compelled* in another. For example, State *A* may demand disclosure of client confidences in a situation where State *B* may forbid it. The Model Rules provide: "Where the lawyer is licensed to practice law in two jurisdictions which impose conflicting obligations, applicable rules of choice of law may govern the situation." Rule 8.5, Comment 2. But this provision does little to solve the problem. If State *A* (like some states) has adopted all except the last clause of DR 7–102(B)(1), it may discipline a lawyer for refusing to disclose a client confidence in order to prevent a fraud on the court; however State *B* will discipline the same lawyer if he discloses the client confidence (if State *B* has adopted DR 7–102(B)(1) with the last clause). As states have adopted the Model Rules, there has been a great tendency to adopt nonuniform amendments. Thus, we may expect choice of law problems to increase.

B.   STATUTES OF LIMITATIONS
Neither the Code nor the Rules incorporate any statute of limitations for disciplinary actions.

Because the purpose of discipline is to protect the public rather than punish the attorney, *In re Echeles,* 430 F.2d 347, 349 (7th Cir. 1970), the time when the misconduct occurred is relevant only to the extent that it bears on the lawyer's present fitness to practice law. If the lawyer is accused of conduct that is also a civil tort or criminal wrong, the mere fact that the statute of limitations has run in either the civil or criminal case does not preclude disciplinary action. "Lawyer discipline and disability proceedings should not be subject to any statute of limitations." ABA Standards for Lawyer Discipline and Disability Proceedings § 4.6 (1979). "Staleness in a charge against an attorney might prevent its being considered, because an unreasonable delay in the presentation of a charge might make it impossible for an attorney to procure witnesses . . .; but the statute of limitations itself is no defense to such a proceeding." *In re Smith,* 73 Kan. 743, 745, 85 P. 584, 586 (1906). See also, *Anne Arundel County Bar Association, Inc. v. Collins,* 272 Md. 578, 325 A.2d 724 (1974).

V. REVIEW QUESTIONS

1. While the Model Code distinguishes between mandatory and aspirational conduct, the Model Rules abandon this distinction and only focus on mandatory conduct.

    _____ True _____ False

2. The "appearance of impropriety" test is:

    a. a useful litmus test found in both the Model Rules and the Model Code.

    b. a useful litmus test found only in the Model Rules.

    c. a generalized statement found only in the Model Code and abandoned in the Model Rules as too vague to be of assistance.

    d. a generalized statement created by the drafters of the Model Rules to guide the courts.

3. Lawyer, while driving home from a golf outing, was given a traffic ticket for speeding. In Lawyer's state, a traffic ticket is a criminal misdemeanor.

    Is Lawyer *subject to discipline*?

    a. No, because Lawyer was not acting in a professional capacity.

    b. No, because the crime does not involve moral turpitude.

    c. Yes, because the ticket shows a lack of respect for law.

4. E.X. was disbarred several years ago for theft of client funds. Subsequently, he rehabilitated himself and is about to be readmitted to practice. Lawyer, another lawyer, is thinking of hiring E.X. Lawyer likes E.X., thinks that E.X. is a good lawyer, and agrees with the bar authorities that E.X. is truly rehabilitated. However, he is concerned that if he hires E.X., influential members of the local business and legal community will look askance.

    Under the Model Code, Lawyer's *ethical obligation* is to:

    a. assist E.X. in being restored to his full right to practice law.

    b. refuse to hire E.X. if doing so would symbolize approval of E.X.'s earlier activities to influential members of the local business and legal community.

   c.   hire E.X. immediately, use him in his law office but give him the title of a "law clerk," so that E.X. is not technically considered to be practicing law, and then, after he is readmitted to the bar, give him the title of "lawyer."

   d.   refuse to hire E.X. if Lawyer believes that members of the general public would look askance.

5. Williams, an insurance adjuster, is a lawyer who has not practiced for years. He is still a member of the bar. When Friend, a good friend of his, suffered a house fire, Williams examined the premises, and greatly inflated his estimates of Friend's actual losses. Williams hoped to receive a kickback or rebate from Friend because of his actions, but Friend refused.

Is Williams *subject to discipline?*

   a.   No, because Williams did not engage in such conduct in his capacity as a lawyer.

   b.   No, because he received no kickback.

   c.   Yes, because he submitted a fraudulent insurance claim.

   d.   Yes, because he acted in a prohibited conflict of interest situation when he adjusted his friend's claim.

PART TWO

THE LAWYER'S OBLIGATION TO SUPPORT BAR ADMISSIONS AND THE DISCIPLINARY SYSTEM

Analysis

I. APPLICATION TO THE BAR

Both the applicant for admission and the lawyer who supplies an affidavit on behalf of an applicant or who responds to inquiries in a discipline matter may not make any false statements and must affirmatively correct any known misunderstandings. The lawyer or applicant retains any evidentiary or constitutional privileges.

A. APPLICABILITY TO APPLICANTS AND LAWYERS

Neither the Code nor the Rules purport to govern nonlawyers. However, if a nonlawyer, in his or her bar application, makes a materially false statement that would constitute "dishonesty" or a "fraud," that misstatement is disciplinable, DR 1–102(A)(4), even if the person was not a lawyer at the time. See Part I, section III, A, supra.

The Rules are more specific on this point. The applicant may not make a false statement in connection with the bar application. Rule 8.1(a). Though the applicant is not, at the time of the application, governed by the Rules of that jurisdiction, a violation of Rule 8.1(a) may form the basis of discipline if the applicant is already a member of the bar in one jurisdiction and seeking admission elsewhere, or is subsequently admitted and thus becomes subject to the jurisdiction of the Rules. Rule 8.1, Comment 1.

B. THE REQUIREMENTS OF NO MATERIAL FALSITY, CORRECTION OF MISAPPREHENSIONS, AND RESPONSE TO REQUESTED INFORMATION

1. No Material Falsity

The lawyer (or applicant, see supra, section I, A) may not knowingly make a *material* misstatement. Rule 8.1(a); DR 1–101(A). A statement is material if it has "the effect of inhibiting efforts of the bar to determine an applicant's fitness to practice law." *Grievance Commission v. Howe*, 257 N.W.2d 420 (N.D.1977). Moreover, the misstatement must be *knowingly* false when made. There is no violation if the misrepresentation was not deliberate. *Siegel v. Committee of Bar Examiners, State Bar of California*, 10 Cal.3d 156, 110 Cal.Rptr. 15, 514 P.2d 967 (1973).

2. Correction of Misapprehensions

The Code does not specifically compel the lawyer or applicant to correct a misapprehension that may have arisen on the part of the bar authorities. However, it might be considered, in some circumstances, to be a "fraud," DR 1–102(A)(4), not to correct misunderstandings of the bar authorities.

The Model Rules are, in contrast, quite clear on this point. The lawyer or applicant may *not* "*fail to disclose* a fact necessary to correct a misapprehension known by the person to have arisen in the matter . . . ." Rule 8.1(b) (emphasis added). What is less clear is whether the duty exists even if the misapprehension was not caused by something the lawyer or applicant said. The Comment supports a broad interpretation of the duty to correct misunderstandings. It says that the Rule "also requires affirmative clarification of *any misunderstanding* on the part of the admissions or disciplinary authority of which the person involved becomes aware." Rule 8.1, Comment 1 (emphasis added).

3. Requested Information

In the case of either an application for admission or a bar disciplinary matter, the bar authorities may request information. DR 1–103(B) specifically requires that the lawyer must reveal any "unprivileged knowledge" regarding another lawyer "upon proper request." This rule does not expressly apply to either the bar admission process or to a disciplinary investigation involving the lawyer's *own* conduct (though perhaps refusal to obey a lawful subpoena would be held to violate DR 1–102(A)(5)—conduct "prejudicial to the administration of justice"). The Rules specifically require a lawyer to cooperate with any "lawful demand for information" in any admissions or disciplinary investigation, including an investigation into the lawyer's own conduct. Rule 8.1(b).

Note that both the Code and the Rules only mandate obedience to a "proper request" or a "lawful demand." The lawyer or applicant, of course, has the right to claim any evidentiary or constitutional privilege, but "should do so openly and not use the right of nondisclosure as a justification for failure to comply . . ." Rule 8.1, Comment 2. See also, Rule 3.4(c) (requiring lawyer to obey rules of a tribunal "except for an open refusal").

The bar can discipline a lawyer or refuse to admit an applicant because the person unlawfully obstructs the investigation. *Konigsberg v. State Bar of California*, 366 U.S. 36, 81 S.Ct. 997, 6 L.Ed.2d 105 (1961) (Konigsberg II). However, because of free speech concerns, the bar cannot punish persons simply because they are or have been members of the Communist Party. *Schware v. Board of Bar Examiners of State of N.M.*, 353 U.S. 232, 77 S.Ct. 752, 1 L.Ed.2d 796 (1957). Nor may the bar violate a person's associational and privacy rights by charging perjury if one incorrectly answers *vague* inquiries about past associations. *Baird v. State Bar of Ariz.*, 401 U.S. 1, 91 S.Ct. 702, 27 L.Ed.2d 639 (1971) (bar threatens to punish applicant for perjury if she answers incorrectly—without a requirement of scienter—whether any of her past memberships, already disclosed, were in organizations that advocated the unlawful overthrow of the Government). However, a person may be refused admission if, with scienter, that person was a knowing member in an organization advocating the unlawful overthrow of the Government, and the applicant had the specific intent to further these unlawful goals of the organization. *Law Students Civil Rights Research Council, Inc. v. Wadmond*, 401 U.S. 154, 164–66, 91 S.Ct. 720, 727–28, 27 L.Ed.2d 749, 759–60 (1971). See generally,

3 R. Rotunda, J. Nowak, & J. Young, *Treatise on Constitutional Law: Substance and Procedure* § 20.44 (West Pub. Co. 1986).

C. FURTHERING THE APPLICATION OF CANDIDATES FOR THE BAR AND WHISTLE–BLOWING

Lawyers are often asked to supply character references for bar applicants. The Code requires that lawyers "shall not further," the admission of candidates to the bar whom the lawyer knows lack the required "character," "education," or "other relevant attribute." DR 1–101(B). The most natural reading of this section is that the lawyer should not file such references as to persons "known by him to be unqualified." DR 1–101(B). This interpretation is also supported by EC 1–3, which provides that, before recommending an applicant, the lawyer "should satisfy himself that the applicant is of good moral character." In other words, the lawyer need not become "a self-appointed investigator," EC 1–3, but he or she should not recommend an applicant if the lawyer has no basis for a recommendation (i.e., "should satisfy himself"), and definitely should not "further" the application of one known to be lacking the requisite characteristics.

Note: The last sentence of EC 1–6 affirmatively encourages lawyers to "assist" unqualified applicants to be licensed when the disqualification (e.g., mental or emotional stability) has terminated. Similarly, lawyers should assist suspended or disbarred lawyers to restore their right to practice law when their disqualifications have terminated.

Notwithstanding this interpretation, some have argued that the rule is phrased too broadly: "An attorney could 'further' the application of a person for admission to the bar by acting as his counsel in a bar admission proceeding." Weckstein, *Maintaining the Integrity and Competence of the Legal Profession,* 48 Tex.L.Rev. 267, 271 (1970). Consequently, the Rules do not contain any requirement similar to DR 1–101(B). A lawyer representing an applicant for admission is governed not by Rule 8.1 ("Bar Admission and Disciplinary Matters") but by the rules normally governing the attorney-client relationship. Rule 8.1, Comment 3. Any false affidavits given by an attorney on behalf of an applicant are prohibited under Rule 8.1(a).

No provisions of the Rules require (or even urge) a lawyer to *volunteer* unfavorable information about an applicant. However, a portion of EC 1–3 might be interpreted to encourage whistle-blowing. In context, however, EC 1–3 should not be so interpreted. EC 1–3 provides:

"Before recommending an applicant for admission, a lawyer should satisfy himself that the applicant is of good moral character. Although a lawyer should not become a self-appointed investigator or judge of applicants for admission, *he should report to proper officials all unfavorable information he possesses* relating to the character or other qualifications of an applicant" (emphasis added).

Some commentators rely on the portion of EC 1–3 italicized above to support, as an ethical aspiration, a lawyer's duty to volunteer unfavorable information to the bar authorities about an applicant.

DR 1–103(A) does contain a whistle-blowing provision that applies to already admitted lawyers. That provision is quite clear. One would think that if the drafters of the Code wanted to create a whistle-blowing obligation applying to applicants, they would have known how to write one, because they did so in DR 1–103(A).

A more natural reading of EC 1–3 is to regard the second sentence as modifying the first. In other words, if an applicant asks a lawyer to recommend him, before that lawyer files the affidavit, he or she should be satisfied that the applicant is of good moral character. It is not necessary for the lawyer, in order to be satisfied, to become a self-appointed investigator, but if the lawyer (who has been asked to recommend an applicant) happens to know or come across unfavorable information, then the lawyer should report it to the bar authorities. If the lawyer believes that the applicant is of good moral character notwithstanding the unfavorable information, the lawyer still must report the unfavorable information and let the bar authorities evaluate it.

Examples: Lawyer hired a summer Law Clerk in her law office. From that experience Lawyer, based on several incidents, believes that Law Clerk is mentally unstable. Law Clerk is now applying for admission to the bar, but does not ask Lawyer for a reference. Lawyer, after learning of Law Clerk's application, does nothing, though if the bar asks for a reference she intends to reply truthfully.

Lawyer has violated no provision of the Model Rules. Some argue that Lawyer has failed to meet the aspirational level of EC 1–3. Lawyer has violated no DR.

II. THE LAWYER'S ROLE REGARDING REPORTING DISCIPLINABLE VIOLATIONS OF LAWYERS

Lawyers have an obligation to volunteer information of another lawyer's disciplinable violations unless the information is privileged under the ethics rules.

A. THE GENERAL RULE

The Code requires, under threat of discipline, that a lawyer voluntarily report any disciplinable violation by another lawyer to the appropriate authority. DR 1–103(A); EC 1–4. This affirmative duty of whistle-blowing applies not only against a lawyer in another firm but also against a partner or associate in the reporting lawyer's own firm. ABA Informal Opinion 1203 (Feb. 9, 1972).

This DR has also been held to confer standing on a lawyer to report an alleged conflict of interest by an opposing counsel in litigation. The charge of conflict, if successful, could then lead to that opposing counsel's disqualification. See, e.g., *Estates Theatres, Inc. v. Columbia Pictures Industry, Inc.,* 345 F.Supp. 93, 98 (S.D.N.Y. 1972).

Note: DR 1–103(A) is supported by other provisions of the Model Code, which require the lawyer to report fraud perpetrated on a tribunal by "a person other than his client," DR 7–102(B)(2); to report improper conduct "by another towards" a juror, DR 7–108(G); and to reveal unprivileged knowledge of fraudulent or other illegal conduct "by a participant in a proceeding before a tribunal or legislative body . . ." EC 8–5. These sections require a lawyer to report improper conduct of any person. If the actor is a lawyer, failure of the duty to report would violate one or more of these other rules, as well as DR 1–103(A).

On its face, DR 1–103(A) applies to *all* disciplinable violations, whether, in the reporting lawyer's view, flagrant and substantial, or minor and technical. However, an element of judgment remains, because the lawyer need not (but may) report suspected violations that are not clear violations of the discipline rules. ABA Informal Opinion 1379 (Dec. 7, 1976). See also EC 1–4 (reporting conduct believed "*clearly* to be in violation of the Disciplinary Rules") (emphasis added).

DR 1–103(A) is largely unenforced, and lawyers rarely report other lawyers. See Note, *The Lawyer's Duty to Report Professional Misconduct,* 20 Ariz.L.Rev. 509 (1978); Marks & Cathcart, *Discipline Within the Legal Profession: Is it Self Regulation?,* 1974 U. of Ill.L.Forum 193. Until recently, in those rare cases where a court actually reprimanded a lawyer for failing to report another lawyer's wrongdoing, the lawyer was also disciplined for other wrongs. E.g., *Matter of Bonafield,* 75 N.J. 490, 383 A.2d 1143 (1978) (per curiam) (attorney disciplined for failing to report another and for aiding another lawyer's misconduct); *Attorney Grievance Commission of Maryland v. Kahn,* 290 Md. 654, 431 A.2d 1336 (1981)(attorney disciplined for failing to report another and for aiding unethical conduct of his law firm).

The Illinois Supreme Court, in 1988, became the first court where a disciplined lawyer (who was suspended for a year) was charged with nothing except failing to report another lawyer's misconduct, under circumstances where the client specifically told him not to report the other lawyer's conduct. *In re Himmel*, 125 Ill.2d 531, 127 Ill.Dec. 708, 533 N.E.2d 790 (1988). See, Rotunda, *The Lawyer's Duty to Report Another Lawyer's Unethical Violations in the Wake of Himmel*, 1988 U.Ill.L.Rev. 977. The Illinois court interpreted "unprivileged knowledge" in its version of DR 1–103(A) to mean only "confidence," the evidentiary privilege, and not "secret," the ethical privilege of DR 4–101(A). The ABA, in contrast, uses the term "privileged" in the Model Code to mean both "confidence" and "secret." ABA Formal Opinion 341 (1975). Cf. EC 4–4. It is unclear the extent to which other states will follow Illinois' lead.

The Rules continue the duty to report created by DR 1–103(A), but modify it so that the duty only covers conduct that raises a "substantial question" regarding the other lawyer's "honesty, trustworthiness or fitness as a lawyer." Rule 8.3(a). The drafters of the Rules, though agreeing that lawyers should initiate investigation of known violations of the Rules (Rule 8.3, Comment 1), also hoped that by limiting the obligation to report to only the more serious violations, the duty would be more realistic and therefore might be more enforceable. Rule 8.3, Comment 3.

The Rules define "substantial" to mean "a material matter of clear and weighty importance." Model Rules, Terminology, 10. Thus, "substantial" refers not to the amount of evidence of which the lawyer is aware, but to the "seriousness of the possible offense." Rule 8.3, Comment 3.

Note: Both the Code and the Rules call for an exercise of judgment in reporting violations. The Code requires the judgment to be exercised with respect to the quantum of evidence of violation. The Rules, in contrast, require the judgment to be exercised with regard to the seriousness of the violation.

B. THE APPLICABILITY OF THE RULE TO THE LAWYER'S OWN CONDUCT
1. Blowing the Whistle on Oneself

DR 1–103(A) requires a lawyer to report knowledge of unprivileged information of disciplinable conduct. Given the way in which it is drafted, DR 1–103(A) may be interpreted to require a lawyer to report his or her own misconduct. Failure to report would then be a separate disciplinable violation. This interpretation is supported by the contrasting language in DR 1–103(B), which specifically refers to "another lawyer." Of course, this interpretation would not require a lawyer to waive the fifth amendment privilege against self-incrimination because DR 1–103(A) only refers to "unprivileged knowledge or information." Thus, ABA Informal Opinion 1279 (Aug. 29, 1973) concluded:

"Does [DR 1–103(A)] require a lawyer to 'report' his knowledge that he has, himself, violated DR 1–102, in the situation where his unethical conduct is not privileged because, for example, he clearly cannot be exposed to criminal sanctions for having engaged in such unethical conduct? We construe DR 1–103(A) as requiring the lawyer to report himself in that situation."

In contrast, some commentators have argued, without discussion, that the "reporting provision of . . . DR 1–103(A) does not appear to apply to the lawyer's own conduct." 2 R. Mallen & J. Smith, Legal Malpractice § 19.6 at 162, note 20 (3d ed. 1989). On the other hand, at least one court has ruled that a lawyer must promptly notify a client of possible malpractice claims that a client may have against him. *Tallon v. Committee on Professional Standards, Third Judicial Dept., 86 A.D.2d 897, 447 N.Y.S.2d 50, 51 (3d Dept. 1982)(respondent suspended for six months for this and other violations).* On pre-Code law, see generally, Note, *The Lawyer's Duty of Candor and Fairness—A Duty to Confess,* 70 Yale L.J. 288 (1960).

The Rules do not raise this question of interpretation because the relevant provision explicitly refers to knowledge regarding "another lawyer." Rule 8.3(a).

2.   The Duty to Cooperate With Discipline Authorities
Both the Code and the Rules encourage a lawyer to cooperate with discipline authorities. Thus EC 1–4 says that, if requested, lawyers should serve and assist disciplinary committees. DR 1–103(A) and (B) also mandate cooperation. The lawyer not only must whistle-blow, DR 1–103(A), but must comply with the investigatory authority's "proper request" for information. DR 1–103(B). Accord, Rule 8.1(b) (a lawyer may not "fail to respond to a lawful demand for information from an admissions or disciplinary authority . . ."). Compare *State v. Weber,* 55 Wis.2d 548, 550, 200 N.W.2d 577, 580 (1972) (lawyer's deliberate refusal to cooperate is a grounds for sanction), with, *Committee on Legal Ethics of West Virginia State Bar v. Mullins,* 159 W.Va. 647, 226 S.E.2d 427, 431 (1976) (no separate violation because of refusal to cooperate).

If lawyer *# 1*'s client tells lawyer *# 1* that lawyer *# 2* has violated a disciplinary rule, that information may be privileged under Rule 1.6. Comment 2 of Rule 8.3 states that if lawyer *# 1*'s knowledge of lawyer *# 2*'s discipline violation is privileged client information, then lawyer *# 1* should encourage his client to waive the privilege if doing so will not "substantially prejudice the client's interests."

C.   APPLICABILITY OF PRIVILEGE
1.   Self–Incrimination
DR 1–103 restricts its application to "unprivileged knowledge" but does not define the term. Clearly the rule does not apply to knowledge protected by a constitutional privilege, such as the privilege against self-

incrimination; otherwise the rule would be unconstitutional. See ABA Informal Opinion 1279 (Aug. 29, 1973) (DR 1–103 does not require lawyer to engage in self-incrimination).

The Rules are not as clear on this point. The relevant sections refer to information "otherwise protected by Rule 1.6" (the confidentiality section); Rule 1.6 in turn does not refer to self-incrimination. See Rule 8.1(b), 8.3(c). However, to preserve the constitutionality of these Rules, the self-incrimination protection must be read into them. Comment 2 of Rule 8.1 so provides. Though the Comment to Rule 8.3 is silent on this issue, its interpretation should be similar.

As a constitutional matter, bar authorities cannot discipline or otherwise sanction a lawyer simply because he or she has asserted the privilege against self-incrimination. *Spevack v. Klein,* 385 U.S. 511, 87 S.Ct. 625, 17 L.Ed.2d 574 (1967). However, the attorney may be disciplined for refusing to testify if that testimony would not expose him to criminal prosecution. *Zuckerman v. Greason,* 20 N.Y.2d 430, 285 N.Y.S.2d 1, 231 N.E.2d 718 (1967).

Consequently, the state can grant a lawyer "use immunity"—i.e., a guarantee that the compelled testimony will not be used against the person in a criminal prosecution—and then use this testimony to disbar or otherwise discipline the lawyer. The justification for allowing the use of compelled testimony for bar discipline is that bar discipline is not a criminal matter. E.g., *Matter of Ungar,* 27 A.D.2d 925, 282 N.Y.S.2d 158 (1967); *Anonymous Attorneys v. Bar Ass'n of Erie County,* 41 N.Y.2d 506, 393 N.Y.S.2d 961, 362 N.E.2d 592 (1977); *In re Schwarz,* 51 Ill.2d 334, 282 N.E.2d 689 (1972); *In re Daley,* 549 F.2d 469 (7th Cir. 1977), cert. denied, 434 U.S. 829, 98 S.Ct. 110, 54 L.Ed.2d 89 (1977).

2. Client Confidences

DR 1–103 refers to "unprivileged knowledge" but does not explain if "privilege" includes only the attorney-client evidentiary privilege, or the much broader privilege protected by Canon 4. (On Canon 4 "confidences" and "secrets," see Part III, section I, A, 1). DR 7–102(B)(1), governing a different issue, also speaks of "a privileged communication." ABA Formal Opinion 341 (Sept. 30, 1975) interprets "privileged communication" in DR 7–102(B)(1) as referring to "those confidences and secrets that are required to be preserved by DR 4–101". This Formal Opinion found it undesirable to interpret "privileged" to mean only information protected as an evidentiary privilege because the lawyer's ethical duty would then vary from jurisdiction to jurisdiction, depending on the local rules of evidence. Also, the Formal Opinion argued, in some cases it might be difficult to determine which jurisdiction's evidence law should govern.

Because this interpretation of "privileged" under DR 7–102(B)(1) is equally applicable to DR 1–103, the same definition should also apply; that is, "unprivileged knowledge" or "evidence" under DR 1–103 means any information not protected by Canon 4.

The Rules opt for this same definition, and explicitly provide that the relevant Rules do not apply to information protected by Rule 1.6, which corresponds to Canon 4. See Rule 8.1(b), 8.3(c). Rule 1.6, of course, protects more than the attorney-client evidentiary privilege.

III. THE LAWYER'S ROLE REGARDING JUDGES AND CANDIDATES FOR THE JUDICIARY

A. THE DUTY TO CRITICIZE AND DEFEND JUDGES AND JUDICIAL CANDIDATES

1. Whistle–Blowing

While DR 1–103(A) mandates a whistle-blowing role for lawyers, see section II, supra, there is no analogous disciplinary rule mandating the lawyer to make an unsolicited report of misconduct by a judge. However, DR 1–103(A) would apply to judges who are also lawyers in the relevant jurisdiction.

Note: Not all judges fall in that category. There are approximately 14,000 nonlawyer judges in 44 states. See Time Magazine, Sept. 26, 1983, at 62, col. 1.

If a lawyer reported a judge's misconduct to the judicial discipline authority, which many states have created, that authority could impose sanctions on the judge.

As an ethical aspiration rather than a mandatory obligation, a lawyer should report to "appropriate authorities" (presumably including a judicial discipline commission) any fraudulent, deceptive, or otherwise illegal conduct of any "participant in a proceeding before a tribunal" if the information is not protected as a client confidence. EC 8–5. This language would apply to judges as well as lawyers and laypeople. The Code does explicitly provide that, "upon proper request," the lawyer must reveal unprivileged knowledge or evidence regarding a judge. DR 1–103(B).

In contrast, the Rules *require* a lawyer to whistle-blow, that is, to volunteer to the appropriate authorities any information (not protected as a client confidence) showing that the judge (whether or not a lawyer) violated the judicial rules if the conduct raises "a substantial question as to the judge's fitness for office . . . ." Rule 8.3(b)

Note: On the Code of Judicial Conduct, see Part X. On the definition of "substantial" see Part II, section II, A.

2. False Statements

If a lawyer makes any charges against a judge or judicial candidate the lawyer must not knowingly speak falsely or with "reckless disregard as to its truth or falsity." Rule 8.2(a); DR 8–102. Cf. *New York Times Co. v. Sullivan,* 376 U.S. 254, 279–80, 84 S.Ct. 710, 725–26, 11 L.Ed.2d 686, 706–07 (1964).

The Code prohibits knowingly making "false statements of fact," DR 8–102(A) and "false accusations," DR 8–102(B). The Rules do not follow this terminology and prohibit any knowingly false "statements" (or false statements made with reckless disregard as to their truth), when the statements relate to the judge's, or judicial candidate's qualifications or integrity. Rule 8.2(a). However, Comment 1 makes clear that it is important for lawyers to be able to improve the administration of justice by being able to express "honest and candid opinions." Thus, Rule 8.2 would approve of such cases as *State Bar v. Semaan,* 508 S.W.2d 429, 432 (Tex.Civ.App.1974), which found no disciplinable offense when an attorney expressed his opinion attacking a judge; because the criticism involved opinion, there was no statement of fact that could be tested as true or false. In contrast, the Rules would *not* approve of *In re Raggio,* 87 Nev. 369, 487 P.2d 499 (1971) (per curiam), which reprimanded an attorney for charging that a judicial opinion was "shocking."

3. Duty to Defend

The Code urges that lawyers defend judges and other adjudicatory officials against "unjust criticism" because these officials are not "wholly free to defend themselves." EC 8–6. See also *Rinaldi v. Holt, Rinehart & Winston, Inc.,* 42 N.Y.2d 369, 366 N.E.2d 1299, 397 N.Y.S.2d 943 (1977) (concurring opinion of Fuchsberg, J.), cert. denied, 434 U.S. 969, 98 S.Ct. 514, 54 L.Ed.2d 456 (1977) (arguing that lawyers have an affirmative duty to defend judges). Lawyers also should "be certain" of their criticisms of judges, "use appropriate language" and avoid "petty" and "unrestrained" criticism. EC 8–6.

On the other hand, the same ethical consideration urges lawyers to "protest earnestly against the appointment or election of those who are unsuited for the bench." EC 8–6. And lawyers "should avoid undue solicitude for the comfort or convenience of judge[s]." EC 7–36.

The Code thus points in two directions regarding the lawyer's duty to defend judges. The original draft of the Rules, in contrast, was much less protective of judges; it contained no express language that corresponded to that found in EC 8–6 regarding the lawyer's duty to defend judges. See,

Rule 8.2 (Proposed Final Draft, May 30, 1981). The final version, as approved by the House of Delegates, added a paragraph to the Comment that encourages lawyers "to continue traditional efforts to defend judges and courts unjustly criticized." Rule 8.2, Comment 3. However, there is no language (like the language found in EC 8–6) urging lawyers to be "certain" of the merits of their criticism. Rather, the Rules simply urge lawyers to express "honest and candid opinions." Rule 8.2, Comment 1.

B. CANDIDATES FOR JUDICIAL OFFICE

Judges running for retention or reelection are governed in their campaign activities by the ABA Model Code of Judicial Conduct (1990), see Part X, section VI, infra, as enacted by the individual states.

The Code and the Rules, in order to prevent lawyers campaigning for judicial office from having an unfair competitive advantage, similarly require that the lawyer-candidate comply with the applicable provisions of the Code of Judicial Conduct. DR 8–102(B); Rule 8.2(b).

The Model Code of Judicial Conduct places various restrictions on the judge's receipt of campaign contributions and other moneys or loans. See Part X, sections V & VI, infra. Lawyers are also prohibited from giving to judges that which the judges are not allowed to accept under the Model Code of Judicial Conduct. DR 7–110(A). See also Rule 8.4(f) (the lawyer should not "knowingly assist a judge" in "violation of applicable rules of judicial conduct or other law").

IV. REVIEW QUESTIONS

1. Attorney is a member of the bar and a practicing lawyer. One of his clients, Mary Smith, in the course of seeking legal advice, has just told Attorney that Smith has had financial reverses because her former lawyer (Former) has stolen money from her. Mary Smith told Attorney that she does not want Attorney to reveal this information because of her concern for her Former's sick wife, who is Smith's sister and who would be devastated if she knew of Former's financial dealings. Attorney told her: "Unless you are willing to let me reveal this information, there is little I can do. But I assure you, I will keep your secret."

Is Attorney *subject to discipline* if he does NOT reveal this information to the disciplinary authorities?

   a. Yes, because he must report such unfavorable information to the appropriate tribunal empowered to investigate it.

   b. No, unless the amount stolen is large.

    c.   Yes, if Smith's concerns for Former's wife is groundless.

    d.   No, because the information is privileged.

2. Lawyer is admitted to the practice of law in State First. She is presently arguing a case in the trial court of State Second, where she was admitted *pro hac vice*. The judge in State Second told her, in open court: "The other lawyer has accused you of destroying evidence. If that is true, and if you were a member of the bar in this jurisdiction, I would seek to have you disbarred."

Assuming that the accusation is true, is Lawyer *subject to discipline* in State First?

    a.   No, because her conduct did not occur in State First.

    b.   No, unless State Second first disciplines her.

    c.   Yes, because she should not practice law in State Second without a license.

    d.   Yes, because the discipline authorities in State First have jurisdiction over conduct engaged in elsewhere.

3. Lawyer is a real estate broker in State One and a member of the bar of State Two. In applying for a renewal for his real estate license in State One, Lawyer failed to disclose that he had just been charged with criminal fraud. This false answer to a specific question made his application materially false.

Is Lawyer, regarding this application, *subject to discipline* in State Two?

    a.   No, because he was not acting as a lawyer.

    b.   No, because he filed his application in State One.

    c.   Yes, because he acted dishonestly.

    d.   Yes, because as a lawyer he may not also be a real estate broker.

4. Lawyer reasonably believes that Judge is a drunk, both on the bench and off, and that therefore Judge lacks any proper judicial temperament. Judge is now running for reelection, and Lawyer, in response to a reporter's questions, states: "I will not support Judge's efforts for reelection because Judge is a drunk, and his drinking interferes with his work."

Is Lawyer *subject to discipline*?

a.   Yes, because Lawyer has cast the judicial system into disrepute.

b.   No, unless Lawyer supports Judge's opponent.

c.   Yes, because the statement was made during a reelection campaign.

d.   No, because Lawyer's beliefs were reasonable and his statements were not knowingly false.

*

PART THREE

THE LAWYER'S OBLIGATION TO THE CLIENT

Analysis

I. THE DUTY OF CONFIDENTIALITY

A. THE GENERAL RULE
The Attorney's obligation to protect a client's confidential information extends beyond the evidentiary privilege.

1. The Distinction Between the Evidentiary and the Ethical Privilege
An attorney is subject to discipline for violating the attorney-client evidentiary privilege. DR 4–101(A), (B); Rule 1.6(a). However, the attorney's duty goes beyond protection of the evidentiary privilege. The attorney is the agent of his client, the principal, and, as a general rule of agency law, the agent must neither use nor disclose "information confidentially given to him by the principal or acquired by him during the course of or on account of his agency. . . . " A.L.I., Restatement (Second) of Agency § 395. Both the Model Code and the Model Rules adopt this principle and offer protection much broader than the evidentiary privilege. The lawyer should not be "indiscreet" when discussing his client's affairs with people not in his law firm. EC 4–2. It is not necessary for a fee to be charged in order for the ethical or evidentiary privilege to attach.

The Code divides client information into two types: "confidence" and "secret." DR 4–101(A). A "confidence" is any information protected under the attorney client evidentiary privilege. A "secret" is any other information if: (1) the client has requested that it be held "inviolate;" or (2) disclosure would embarrass the client; or (3) disclosure would likely "be detrimental to the client."

Examples: Client asks Lawyer to represent Client in a transaction. In the course of this representation, Lawyer uncovers secret information. Pursuant to an investigation by the grand jury, Court later orders Lawyer to reveal this information to the grand jury on the grounds that it is not protected by the evidentiary privilege. Lawyer reveals this information in the grand jury room. Later reporters ask him: "Did you comply with the court order?" He answers: "Yes." Then they ask him: "What did you say to the grand jury?"

If Lawyer responds, Lawyer will commit a disciplinary violation by revealing a client's secret. In other words, virtually all information is initially within Canon 4, because the Code does not demand that the client's request (to hold the information "inviolate") be express. It may be implied. Also, it is not necessary that the source of the information be the client; it is only necessary that the information be "gained in the professional relationship." DR 4–101(A).

Note: The Code does not make clear whether "gained in" means "because of" the professional relationship, or the more broad, "during the course of" the professional relationship (e.g., in the course of seeking business advice, the client confides to the lawyer that the client is cheating on her husband). In any event, it is quite clear that it is unnecessary, under Canon 4, that the client be the source of the information.

Rule 1.6's basic definition of confidential information is at least as broad as the Code's. Rule 1.6 offers protection to *any* information "relating to representation of a client." All information of consequence is, at least initially, offered protection.

2. Rationale and Applicability to Information Generally Known

The purpose of this broad protection is to encourage the client to speak freely with the lawyer and to encourage the lawyer to obtain information beyond that offered by the client. EC 4–1; Rule 1.6, Comments 2, 3, 4, & 5.

Needless to say, this purpose would not be furthered if a lawyer would be forced to keep information confidential after it has become a matter of general knowledge. The general law of agency recognizes this exception (A.L.I., Restatement (Second) of Agency § 395), and the Rules adopt it in Rule 1.9(c)(1), which allows a lawyer to use, to the disadvantage of a *former* client, information otherwise protected by Rule 1.6, if the information is "generally known."

Note: A lawyer should not act to the detriment of a *present* client because of the duty of loyalty. This duty of loyalty extends beyond the need to protect client secrets. DR 5–101(A); Rule 1.7(a), (b).

The Code does not explicitly adopt the exception of Rule 1.9(c)(1) relating to client information that "has become generally known." In fact EC 4–4 states that the ethical duty to protect secrets exists "without regard" to "the fact that others share the knowledge." However, in context, EC 4–4 refers to *present* clients, and assumes that the secret nature of the conversation is not lost merely because the client has shared his secret with a *few* others besides the lawyer. Such sharing, beyond a strict "need to know basis," will mean the loss of the evidentiary privilege—see Proposed Federal Rule of Evidence 530(a)(4)—but not the loss of the ethical privilege. However, once the information is *generally known* (even though it once was a secret) its protection would not serve the purpose of the rule.

3. Extension of the Protection to Prospective and Former Clients

To fulfill the purpose of protection of client information, the ethical rules protect not only information that the lawyer learned from her clients but also secret information that she learned because a *prospective* client sought to (but did not) retain her. EC 4–1. Model Rule 1.6 does not make this point explicitly, but ABA Formal Opinion 90–358 (Sept. 13, 1990), reprinted in, *ABA/BNA Lawyers' Manual on Professional Conduct* (looseleaf service), at 901:132, concludes that information from a would-be client seeking representation is protected by Model Rule 1.6 even though the lawyer does not undertake representation of, or perform legal work for, the would-be client. See also, Model Rules, Scope 3 (some duties, like Rule 1.6 duty of confidentiality, "may attach when the lawyer agrees to consider whether a client-lawyer relationship shall be established.").

Protecting the confidences of the prospective client who does not retain the lawyer imposes an opportunity cost on the lawyer, who may be disqualified from later representing the opponent of the would-be client because the lawyer received confidences from the would-be client. ABA Formal Opinion 90–358 (Sept. 13, 1990) suggests several ways that the law firm may be able to limit these costs. It may institute procedures to identify as early as possible conflicts of prospective clients; it may limit information learned from the would-be client; it may secure, if practicable, waivers of confidentiality from the would-be client. The Formal Opinion also suggests that some courts might accept the law firm's screening of the lawyer who learned the confidential information "where the information disclosed by the would-be client is not extensive or sensitive. . . ." *ABA/BNA Lawyer's Manual,* at 901:137. The Model Rules, however, do not provide for screening except in the case of the movement of a lawyer between government and private practice, which is the topic of Model Rule 1.11. See, Model Rule 1.10, Comment 5, pointing out that different policy considerations justify screening in that situation that do not justify screening when lawyers move from one private firm to another.

The fact that the *former* client no longer employs a lawyer does not terminate the lawyer's obligation to preserve the former client's confidences and secrets. EC 4–6; Rule 1.6, Comment 21. See also, Rule 1.9.

4. Intrafirm Communications

Though a client may only deal with a few lawyers in a firm, the client really hires the firm. Partners and associates regularly discuss with each other the affairs of their clients and seek from each other advice regarding client affairs. EC 4–2; Rule 1.6, Comment 8. Such intrafirm communication is one of the reasons for the rule regarding imputation of attorney disqualifications. See Rule 1.10, Comment 1. See Part III, Section II, F.

Consequently, unless the client otherwise directs, a lawyer may disclose to other lawyers in the firm information protected by Canon 4 or Rule 1.6. See EC 4–2, Rule 1.6, Comment 8.

5. Controlling Subordinates

It is also reasonable in law practice to disclose client confidences to nonlawyer employees, such as secretaries, investigators, and paralegals. However, the Code and the Rules have no jurisdiction over these nonlawyer employees. See Rule 5.3, Comment 1. Therefore the ethics rules provide that the lawyer must exercise "reasonable care to prevent his employees or associates" from violating the obligation regarding client confidences or secrets. DR 4–101(D); EC 4–5. Rule 5.3.

A lawyer who fails in this duty of supervision violates these disciplinary rules even though no secrets are in fact disclosed, because the disciplinable violation is the failure to supervise. Similarly, a lawyer who adequately supervises has fulfilled his or her obligation, even though the employee nonetheless improperly discloses a client secret or confidence.

The lawyer may give "limited information from his files to an outside agency" for accounting or other legitimate purposes if the lawyer exercises due care in selecting the agency. EC 4–3; Rule 5.3, Comment 1 (referring to "independent contractors"). However, the lawyer may not transfer this information if the client chooses to forbid it. EC 4–3. Cf. Rule 1.6, Comment 8.

6. Applicability to Government Lawyers and Other Lawyers for an Entity

The obligations imposed by Canon 4 and Rule 1.6 apply not only to lawyers in private practice, but also to attorneys for the government (see Rule 1.6, Comment 6) and lawyers for any other entity, such as a corporation, or an association. Rule 1.6, Comment 16.

B. SPECIFIC PROHIBITIONS ON USING OR REVEALING CONFIDENTIAL OR SECRET INFORMATION

In general the lawyer must not reveal or use a client confidence or secret unless certain exceptions are applicable.

1. Revealing Client Information

The lawyer must not reveal client confidences except under certain circumstances. These situations, found in the Code or Rules or other law, are discussed more fully below.

2. Using Client Information to the Disadvantage of a Client

Both the Code and the Rules forbid using client secrets or confidences to the disadvantage of the client. DR 4–101(B)(2); Rule 1.8(b). This prohibition applies equally to protect a former client, *if* the information has not become generally known.   Rule 1.9(c)(1).   See EC 4–6.   See also, Part III, section I, A, 2, supra.

Note that a lawyer violates this rule of confidentiality even if the lawyer does not disclose the information to anyone.   What is relevant is that she *uses* the information to the client's detriment.   If the agent is allowed to use confidential information for purposes that cause injury to the principal, that would tend to harm the freedom of communication that should exist between principal and agent.

> ***Example:***   Lawyer learned, in confidence, that Client is planning to renew the lease on the building that Client now uses.   Lawyer then secretly visits Lessor and obtains the lease on Lawyer's own account but does not tell Lessor any Client information. Lawyer plans to raise the rent because she learned, in confidence, that this location is more important to Client than Lessor suspects.   Lawyer has committed a disciplinable violation.   Cf. A.L.I., Restatement (Second) of Agency § 395 & Illustration 1, which states that the agent "may be required to hold this lease as constructive trustee" for the principal.

3.   Using Client Information for the Advantage of the Lawyer or Third Person

Unless the client consents, the lawyer may not use a client confidence or secret for the lawyer's own advantage (or a third person's advantage). Under the Model Code, this rule is applicable whether or not the client suffers detriment.   DR 4–101(B)(3).

This prohibition on the use of client information is an old one.   See ABA Canons of Professional Ethics, Canon 11 (1908), and Canon 37 (1908), as amended.   E.g. *Healy v. Gray,* 184 Iowa 111, 119, 168 N.W. 222, 225 (1918): "[A]n attorney will not be permitted to make use of knowledge, or information, acquired by him through his professional relations with his client, or in the conduct of his client's business to his own advantage or profit."

It also reflects basic principles of agency law.   No agent, whether or not a lawyer, may use the principal's secret information to the agent's advantage even if there is no detriment to the principal and even if using the information does not require revealing it.   A.L.I., Restatement (Second) of Agency, § 388, and Comment c. The remedy in the law of agency for this breach of trust is that the agent must turn over any profits to the principal.

> ***Example:***   Where "a corporation has decided to operate an enterprise at a place where land values will be increased because of such

operation, a corporate officer who takes advantage of his special knowledge to buy land in the vicinity is accountable for the profits he makes, even though such purchases have no adverse effect upon the enterprise." Id. at Comment c. See also Id. at § 395, Comment e.

This rule is not applicable if the "information is a matter of general knowledge." Id. at § 395.

The theory behind the Code—and the law of agency, which the Code reflects—is that this confidential or secret information belongs to the client. The lawyer may not sell it or use it to the lawyer's own advantage unless the client consents.

The Rules, surprisingly, have *no* section corresponding to DR 4–101(B)(3). The drafters do not explain this oversight in the Comment.

Note: There also is no explanation in the "Research Notes" (which were not published with the final draft of Model Rules). In any event, these Research Notes "have not been adopted, do not constitute part of the Model Rules, and are not intended to affect the application or interpretation of the Rules or Comments." Model Rules, "Scope," 9. These Research Notes are reprinted in T. Morgan & R. Rotunda, 1983 Selected Standards Supplement 163–267 (1983).

Moreover, Rule 1.8, Comment 1 seems to negate the possibility that the Rules could be interpreted to incorporate the principle of DR 4–101(B)(3). That Comment says that "a lawyer may not exploit information relating to the representation *to the client's disadvantage*. For example, a lawyer who has learned that the client is investing in specific real estate may not, without the client's consent, seek to acquire nearby property *where doing so would adversely affect the client's plan for investment*." (emphasis added.) The negative implication is that there is no ethical problem if the lawyer's purchase of the land and use of the client's "insider" information does not harm the client.

It is quite clear that the conduct described in Rule 1.8, Comment 1 is improper under the Code even without the condition stated above in italics. Similarly, even if a jurisdiction would adopt the Rules instead of the Code, under the general Law of Agency a lawyer who used client information for the lawyer's advantage must account to the client for any profits made. The lawyer who turns to this section of the Model Rules for a safe harbor will find (when a court, pursuant to the law of agency, orders him to account to the client for any profits made) that this port is heavily mined. The lawyer may not use "on his own account" confidential information acquired from a former client.   A.L.I., Restatement (Second) of Agency, § 395, 396(b), (c).

C. EXCEPTIONS

1. Client Consent

Clients may always waive their confidentiality rights.   If the lawyer wants the client to consent to waive rights to confidentiality, this consent is effective only if the lawyer makes a full disclosure to the client.   DR 4–101(B)(3), (C)(1); Rule 1.6(a), 1.8(b).   In order that the consent be effective, the lawyer must communicate to the client enough information to permit the client to appreciate the significance of the waiver.   See Model Rules, Terminology 2.

The Code does not explicitly provide for implied consent, but its definition of "secret" is consistent with, and perhaps assumes, this possibility.   DR 4–101(A) in effect provides that the lawyer may reveal client information if: (1) it is not protected as an evidentiary privilege; (2) the client does not specifically request confidential treatment; (3) the information would not be embarrassing; *and* (4) the information is not likely to be detrimental.

The Rules explicitly recognize an implied consent, narrowly defined as "disclosures impliedly authorized in order to carry out the representation," Rule 1.6(a).   For example, the lawyer may disclose information in order to satisfactorily conclude a negotiation, or the lawyer in litigation may admit a fact that "cannot properly be disputed."   Rule 1.6, Comment 7.

2. When Other Provisions in the Disciplinary Rules Permit Disclosure

Other provisions of the ethics rules may permit or require disclosure in certain situations.   The lawyer should follow these other, more specific sections when they are applicable.   See Rule 1.6, Comment 20, referring to Rules 2.2, 2.3, 3.3, and 4.1.   See also DR 4–101(C)(2).   For example, a lawyer may be obligated to reveal client perjury.   See Part VII, section II, A, 3(c), discussing this issue, and Rule 3.3(a)(4) & (b), and DR 7–102(B).

The Code explicitly provides that other provisions of the Code may override the requirements of Canon 4, either by permitting, or requiring, disclosure.   See, e.g., DR 7–102(A)(3); *Matter of Kerr,* 86 Wash.2d 655, 662 n.2, 548 P.2d 297, 301 n.2 (1976).   See also DR 7–102(B)(2).   Although the Rules themselves have no such comparable section, there is such a provision in the Comments.   See Rule 1.6, Comment 20.   See also Rules 2.2, 2.3, & 3.3.

3. Challenging Court Orders Requiring Disclosure

The Code has an explicit provision allowing lawyers to reveal Canon 4 information when "required by law or court order."   DR 4–101(C)(2).   The

Proposed Final Draft of the Rules had a similar provision. The ABA House of Delegates explicitly deleted this provision from Rule 1.6 but left language in the Comment that makes the same point. See Rule 1.6, Comment 20.

The lawyer may challenge any court order requiring his testimony. However, there is no ethical requirement that the lawyer first suffer contempt before revealing client information in response to a court order. The lawyer may simply comply with the order and reveal the client secret rather than violate the order and challenge the contempt. See DR 4–101(C)(2), providing that the lawyer "*may* reveal" client information when "required" by court order. Cf., e.g., *Dike v. Dike*, 75 Wash.2d 1, 14–15, 448 P.2d 490, 498–499 (1968) (because it was proper for the lawyer to challenge the lower court order, the contempt order against the lawyer is vacated).

To be sure, Rule 1.6, Comment 19, does state that a "lawyer must comply" when the final orders of a court require the lawyer to "give information about the client." However, the requirement that the lawyer "*must* comply" should not be interpreted to forbid a challenge to the order of a trial court, because lawyers may, in good faith, challenge any law. Rule 1.2(d); cf. Rule 8.4, Comment 2. This challenge may necessitate disobedience to a law or the court's interpretation of it. Rule 1.2, Comment 9. However, once the lawyer has exhausted all appeals and the order is "final," the lawyer must obey it.

4. To Collect a Fee

The lawyer may reveal client confidences or secrets if necessary to establish or collect the lawyer's fee. DR 4–101(C)(4); Rule 1.6(b)(2). The purpose of this exception is to prevent the client, who is the "beneficiary of a fiduciary relationship," from exploiting that relationship to the detriment of the lawyer-fiduciary. Rule 1.6, Comment 18. For example, the client ought not be excused from a contractual obligation to pay a fee solely because the lawyer could not prove (unless he revealed a client confidence or secret) that services were in fact performed. See *Cannon v. United States Acoustics Corp.*, 532 F.2d 1118, 1120 (7th Cir. 1976) (per curiam). Similarly, the lawyer may use client confidences if necessary to collect the fee. *Nakasian v. Incontrade, Inc.*, 409 F.Supp. 1220, 1224 (S.D.N.Y. 1976) (lawyer, in effort to collect fee, may use client confidences to procure attachment order against client property). Accord, ABA Formal Opinion 250 (June 26, 1943).

This right to use confidences or secrets does not mean a right to blackmail the client. The lawyer may not state to the client: "Pay the fee or I will reveal to your employer your income tax problems." The lawyer may only exercise the right to reveal client information to the extent that it is reasonably *necessary* to establish or collect the fee. There should be no extortion or unnecessary disclosure. See Rule 1.6, Comment 18.

5. To Respond to a Charge of Wrongful Conduct

It has long been the rule that a lawyer is justified in disclosing client information if necessary to respond to a client's accusation of wrongful conduct. See ABA Formal Opinion 202 (May 25, 1940), relying on Canons of Professional Ethics, Canon 37 (1908, as amended). The original Canon 37 limited this exception to the case where the "lawyer is accused *by his client . . . .*" (emphasis added). The Code has no such limitation. The lawyer may reveal client information "if necessary" to respond to anyone's "accusation of wrongful conduct," though the lawyer should disclose only that which is "necessary" to establish a defense to the charge. DR 4-101(C)(4). Nor is it necessary that the accuser bring any formal proceedings or actually file any lawsuit against the lawyer. E.g., *Meyerhofer v. Empire Fire & Marine Ins. Co.,* 497 F.2d 1190, 1194–95 (2d Cir. 1974), cert. denied, 419 U.S. 998, 95 S.Ct. 314, 42 L.Ed.2d 272 (1974).

Originally the Rules limited this right of disclosure to cases where the client and the lawyer were involved in a lawsuit or where the lawyer had to use the client information to establish a defense to a civil or criminal claim based on conduct in which the client was involved. Draft Rule 1.7(C)(3), (Discussion Draft, Jan. 30, 1980), reprinted in T. Morgan & R. Rotunda, 1980 Selected National Standards Supplement 83 (1980). However, the Rules now are identical with the Code in this regard, though the wording is different. See Rule 1.6(b)(2).

Although Rule 1.6(b)(2) uses words such as "criminal charge," "civil claim," or "allegations in any proceeding," it is not necessary that the accuser initiate any formal proceedings before the lawyer may reveal client information. Moreover, the accuser may be someone other than the client. The Comment is quite clear on this point: "The lawyer's right to respond [to allegations of wrongful conduct] arises when an assertion of such complicity has been made. Paragraph (b)(2) *does not require the lawyer to await the commencement of an action* or a proceeding so that the defense may be established by responding *directly to a third party* who had made such an assertion." Rule 1.6, Comment 17 (emphasis added). See also Id. at Comment 18.

If it does not prejudice the lawyer's ability to establish a defense and if it is practicable to do so, "the lawyer should advise the client of the third party's assertion and request that the client respond appropriately." Id. at Comment 17. However, the client cannot prevent the lawyer from establishing the lawyer's innocence.

> ***Examples:*** A newspaper editorial accuses Lawyer of having won an acquittal in an important criminal case years ago by suborning her client's perjury. Lawyer responds by writing, to the newspaper, a letter that reveals that the Client had intentionally kept Lawyer in the dark about the perjury and that Lawyer never learned of it until years after the acquittal, when Client confessed to Lawyer on his death bed. Client, at that time, also told Lawyer never to reveal the perjury; then Client died. Lawyer also states that her version is confirmed by an associate in her office who was present during the conversation in question.

Under the Code and the Rules, Lawyer's disclosures are not disciplinable.

Note that while the Rules give attorneys liberal authority to violate client confidences or secrets in order to defend themselves, Rule 1.6 does not allow attorneys to reveal such information when necessary to prevent a substantial financial fraud by the client or to rectify the consequences of a client's criminal or fraudulent act in which the lawyer's services had been used. An earlier draft of the Rules would have allowed the lawyer to reveal such information—see Draft Rule 1.6(b)(2), (3) (Proposed Final Draft, May 30, 1981)—but the ABA House of Delegates, in 1983, deleted those sections. (In August of 1991 the ABA House of Delegates again refused to accept a similar proposal.) In 1983 the Delegates, ironically, approved a more liberal exception allowing the lawyer to intrude on client confidences where the lawyer believes it necessary for the lawyer's own defense.

6. When the Client Intends to Commit a Crime

The lawyer is the agent of the client, who is the principal. A basic principle of agency law is that:

> "An agent is privileged to reveal information confidentially acquired by him in the course of his agency in the protection of a superior interest of himself or a third person. Thus, *if the confidential information is to the effect that the principal is committing or about to commit a crime, the agent is under no duty not to reveal it.* However, an attorney employed to represent a client in a criminal proceeding has no duty to reveal that the client has confessed his guilt." A.L.I., Restatement (Second) of Agency, § 395, Comment f (emphasis added).

The Code codifies this common law rule (and the distinction it draws between confessions of past crimes and intentions to commit future ones). Thus the Code provides that the lawyer "may reveal" the client's intention "to commit a crime" as well as the information necessary to prevent it. DR 4–101(C)(3).

The Code does not distinguish between types of crimes—violation of a trivial offense versus premeditated murder—nor does the rule offer any guidelines to cabin the lawyer's exercise of discretion. We are only told that the attorney "may" reveal this information. However, a pre-Code ABA Formal Opinion, in considering the Canons of Professional Ethics, stated that if "the facts in the attorney's possession indicate beyond reasonable doubt that a crime will be committed," then disclosure of confidences is required. ABA Formal Opinion 314 (April 27, 1965). The Code quotes this portion of the Formal Opinion in the footnotes (see DR 4–101(C)(3) at note 16), and this disciplinary rule may be interpreted to adopt the test of the Formal Opinion. Thus, DR 4–103(C)(3) appears to permit a lawyer to reveal the client's intention to commit a crime and probably requires such disclosure if the lawyer knows, beyond a reasonable doubt, that the client will commit the crime.

An early version of the Rules made some effort to draw some useful distinctions not present in the Code. First, this early draft *required* the lawyer to reveal client information if "necessary to prevent the client from committing an act that would result in death or serious bodily harm to another person. . . . " Draft Rule 1.7(b) (Discussion Draft, Jan. 30, 1980). This mandatory disclosure proposal appears to reflect already existing tort law. See, e.g., *Tarasoff v. Regents of the University of California,* 17 Cal.3d 425, 131 Cal.Rptr. 14, 551 P.2d 334 (1976) (when psychotherapist knew of his patient's planned murder, the psychotherapist was liable in tort when he did not take steps reasonably necessary under the circumstances, such as notifying the police, or the victim).

The next draft of the proposed Rules eliminated this mandatory disclosure proposal, but *allowed* disclosure, inter alia, in order "to prevent the client from committing a criminal or fraudulent act that the lawyer believes is likely to result in death or substantial bodily harm, or substantial injury to the financial interests or property of another;" or "to rectify the consequences of a client's criminal or fraudulent act in the commission of which the lawyer's services had been used." Proposed Final Draft of Model Rules, Rule 1.6(b)(2), (3) (May 30, 1981), reprinted in T. Morgan & R. Rotunda, 1980 Selected Standards Supplement 113 (1980). This draft drew some interesting distinctions involving crimes or frauds causing serious harm and circumstances where the lawyer's services had unwittingly been used (actually, misused) by the client.

The final version of the Rules is significantly more protective of client information than either its predecessors or the Code. Present Rule 1.6 has no mandatory rule involving disclosure and, with respect to the fraud or crime issue, only permits disclosure to prevent the client "from committing a criminal act that the lawyer believes is likely to result in *imminent death or substantial bodily* harm." Rule 1.6(b)(1) (emphasis added).

In addition, when Rule 1.6(b)(1) gives the lawyer discretion to reveal client information, this discretion is intended to be absolute and unreviewable. See Rule 1.6, Comment 13: "A lawyer's decision not to take preventive action permitted by paragraph (b)(1) does not violate this Rule." See also, Rules, "Scope," 8: "The lawyer's exercise of discretion not to disclose information under Rule 1.6 should not be subject to reexamination." Given decisions like *Tarasoff,* supra, the efforts of the ABA House of Delegates to grant lawyers unreviewable discretion will not likely be successful, at least in a tort case. The Rules do admit that other law may mandate disclosure and thereby supersede Rule 1.6. See Rule 1.6, Comment 20.

May a lawyer reveal that her client has confessed to a crime for which an innocent person is about to be punished? This question is a "much mooted" one. C. Wolfram, *Modern Legal Ethics* 673 (1986). The lawyer's silence in such a case may permit a grave injustice to be done. In *State v. Macumber,* 112 Ariz. 569, 544 P.2d 1084 (1976), the court held that the trial judge in a murder case had properly excluded testimony by two attorneys that a third person, now deceased, had confessed to them that he had killed the people whom the state is charging the defendant with murdering. This third person confessed to the two attorneys who had represented him when he was tried in federal court for an unrelated murder. The state court ruled that the attorney-client privilege prevented this disclosure. The dissent argued that when this third person died, there was no chance of his prosecution for other crimes, and any privilege was merely a matter of property interest, which should not prevail over the constitutional right of the accused to introduce reliable hearsay declarations evidencing his innocence.

The proposed Restatement of the Law, Third, of the Law Governing Lawyers § 132, Illustration 4 (Tentative Draft No. 2, April 7, 1989) offered an illustration based on *Macumber.* At the May, 1989 annual meeting, various American Law Institute members objected to this illustration as "grotesque," "revolting," and "disgusting." It is not right, members said, that a lawyer may reveal privileged information in a fee dispute but not to prevent an innocent person from going to jail. By a vote of 164 to 65, the ALI members voted to strike the illustration.

7. **Filing a Notice of Withdrawal**
Both the Rules and Code agree that if the client will use a lawyer's services to further the client's "criminal or fraudulent conduct," then the lawyer must withdraw. Rule 1.6, Comment 14; Rule 1.16(a)(1); DR 2–110(B)(2); DR 7–102(A)(7). In some circumstances the fact of a lawyer's

withdrawal from representation may amount to a disclosure of client confidences or secrets. For example, if a lawyer withdraws in such a manner as to suggest that the client intends to commit fraud, then the lawyer will have disclosed information detrimental to the client. ABA Formal Opinion 314 (Apr. 27, 1965) recognized that in some instances "the very act of disassociation would have the effect of violating Canon 37." (Canon 37 of the ABA Canons of Professional Ethics (1908, as amended) is the predecessor to DR 4–101 of the Model Code.) Nonetheless the lawyer must withdraw. (*Different considerations apply if the perjured testimony or false evidence has been offered before a tribunal.* See Model Rule 3.3, and Part VII, Section II, A, 3 "Disclosure of Facts," infra.)

If a lawyer withdraws from representation of a client, the Model Code does not specifically deal with the question whether the lawyer may formally inform third parties that the lawyer is no longer in the case. None of the early drafts of the Rules talked of filing a *Notice of Withdrawal.* However, the final version contains a Comment on this new concept, created for the first time by the Rules.

The lawyer may file this Notice of Withdrawal even though its issuance may be a red flag that the client is up to no good. The relevant Comment provides:

> "After withdrawal the lawyer is required to refrain from making disclosure of the client's confidences, except as otherwise provided in Rule 1.6. Neither this Rule nor Rule 1.8(b) nor Rule 1.16(d) prevents the lawyer from giving notice of the fact of withdrawal and the lawyer may also withdraw or disaffirm any opinion, document, affirmation, or the like." Rule 1.6, Comment 15.

Rule 1.8(b), referred to in this Comment, provides that the lawyer shall not use client information to the disadvantage of the client, unless the client consents. Rule 1.16(d) states that after withdrawal the lawyer must take reasonable steps to protect a client's interests. Neither of these Rules, nor Rule 1.6 itself, limit the power discussed in Rule 1.6, Comment 15.

Note also that this Comment does not limit to whom the Notice of Withdrawal may be sent. The Notice may apparently be sent to third parties, not merely the opposing side.

Example: Lawyer learns, on the eve of closing, that the limited partnership agreement that Lawyer has prepared for her Client is a criminal fraud under the federal securities laws. Lawyer confronts Client, who states that he will go through with the deal and if Lawyer does not like it, Lawyer can resign. The lawyer must resign. Rule 1.16(a)(1); DR 2–110(B) (2). Under the Model Rules Lawyer may also send a Notice of Withdrawal to the other side and also to the Securities & Exchange Commission. Under the Model Code, the lawyer may reveal this information, under DR 4–101(C)(3).

Under the Rules, the lawyer may not, in these cases, blow the whistle, but the lawyer may waive the red flag. See generally, Rotunda, *The Notice of Withdrawal and the New Model Rules of Professional Conduct: Blowing the Whistle and Waiving the Red Flag,* 63 Oregon L.Rev. 455 (1984).

II. CONFLICTS OF INTEREST

A. THE BASIC RATIONALE
The rules governing conflict of interest derive, for the most part, from the need to protect client confidences and secrets, and the duty of client loyalty and zealous representation.

The rules dealing with conflicts of interest are found, primarily, in Canon 5 of the Code and Rules 1.7 through 1.13 of the Rules. All of these specific rules derive from several basic premises.

The first is the lawyer's duty to protect secret or confidential client information, discussed in section I, supra.

Example: A conflict may develop if Lawyer simultaneously represents Client *A* and Client *B,* or now represents Client *B* and used to represent Client *A.* Lawyer may know secret information about Client *A* (the present, or former, client) and this information would be useful to Client *B.* If Lawyer does not reveal the information to *B,* Lawyer violates his or her duty of zealous representation of *B.* If Lawyer does reveal the information to *B,* Lawyer violates his or her duty to *A* to keep *A*'s secrets.

Another basic premise is the lawyer's duty of loyalty to the client. This duty exists even if there is no breach of client secrets.

Example: Lawyer for Client *D* is paid by Insurer, who insures Client *D.* Insurer instructs Lawyer (who is defending *D* in a tort suit) not to dispute Plaintiff's charge that *D*'s tortious conduct was really intentional. If the jury believes that *D* acted intentionally, Insurer will not be liable. If Lawyer follows Insurer's instructions, Lawyer is violating the duty of loyalty to *D.*

Given these policies, there are various types of conflicts. There might be a conflict between the client and the lawyer's business or personal interests; between the client and another present or former client; or between the client and a person or group who may be paying for the client's legal assistance. This section will discuss all of these categories of conflicts.

Bear in mind that the client may be able to *waive* the conflict in some instances. When a conflicts rule is designed to protect only the client, little reason exists to prohibit a lawyer from engaging in the representation when a competent and informed client desires to waive that protection. In contrast, if the conflicts rule is designed to protect a systemic interest—an interest of the system of justice—client waiver should be ineffective. With respect to the different types of conflicts, we will consider when the client may desire to waive, and under what circumstances that waiver will be effective.

Finally, the Code and the Rules sometimes *impute* one lawyer's disqualifying conflict to all of the other lawyers in the same firm. We shall discuss when and why the Code and the Rules differ as to when a conflict is imputed. Because imputation applies even when the firm is very large, with branch offices in many states, the firm must adopt "reasonable procedures, appropriate for the size and type of firm and practice," to determine whether there are actual or potential conflicts, in both litigation and nonlitigative matters. Rule 1.7, Comment 1.

B. SIMULTANEOUS REPRESENTATION

1. Multiple Clients in the Same Matter

(a) In General

Very often the lawyer represents two or more clients in the same matter. For example, the lawyer may be asked to represent several clients in setting up a small corporation, or a husband and wife in a house closing, or the driver and owner-passenger of a car when both have been sued for injuries arising out of an automobile accident.

It is often in the best interest of clients to share the same lawyer. Such an arrangement reduces legal fees and saves time. On the other hand such an arrangement creates the potential for conflict, so the lawyer must "weigh carefully the possibility that his judgment may be impaired or his loyalty divided if he accepts or continues the employment." EC 5–15. The mere possibility of conflict "does not itself preclude the representation." Rule 1.7, Comment 4.

(b) In Litigation

The potential of conflict when representing multiple clients exists whether the representation involves litigation or counseling. However, disqualification is more likely in litigation because the lawyer acts primarily as an advocate. Cf. EC 7–4, 7–5; Rules 2.1, 3.1.

"A lawyer should never represent *in litigation* multiple clients with differing interests; and there are few situations in which he would be justified in representing *in litigation* multiple clients with potentially differing interests." EC 5–15 (emphasis added); Compare Rule 1.7, Comments 7 to 9 with Comments 11 to 14.

The lawyer may not represent both Client *A* and *B* in the case of *A v. B*. See Rule 1.7(a). E.g., *Jedwabny v. Philadelphia Transportation Co.*, 390 Pa. 231, 135 A.2d 252 (1957), cert. denied, 355 U.S. 966, 78 S.Ct. 557, 2 L.Ed.2d 541 (1958). Rule 1.7(a) speaks to the situation where the representation of a client is "*directly adverse*" to another client. Unfortunately, the Rule never defines what is "direct" or "indirect." However, it is the intent of Rule 1.7(a) to prohibit representation of "opposing parties in litigation." Rule 1.7, Comment 7. If a lawyer represents multiple clients in litigation who are all co-plaintiffs (or all co-defendants), Rule 1.7(b) is applicable. See Rule 1.7, Comment 7. The situation covered in Rule 1.7(b) is discussed in section II, B, 2, immediately following this section.

Waiver. The conflict illustrated by the case of *A v. B* should not even be cured by consent; that is, such a conflict may not be waived, because of the systemic interest—the interest in the system of justice—recognized in both DR 5–105(C) and Rule 1.7(a)(1) and Comment 5. DR 5–105(C) requires not only that there be consent after full disclosure of the risks involved, but also that it be "obvious that [the lawyer] can adequately represent the interest of each [client]." Comment 5 of Rule 1.7 offers, in the same spirit, a more specific test to determine when consent is ineffective: "when a disinterested lawyer would conclude that the client should not agree to the representation under the circumstances, the lawyer involved cannot properly ask for such agreement or provide representation on the basis of the client's consent." See also, Rule 1.7(a)(1).

In the case of *A v. B*, a lawyer could not determine that he or she could adequately represent both *A* and *B*. *A*'s and *B*'s consent, even though made after full disclosure, would not waive the conflict. The systemic interest in the fair administration of justice would prevail.

Simultaneously Representing Adverse Clients in Unrelated Matters. Not only may the lawyer not represent Clients *A* and *B* in the case of *A v. B*, but the lawyer may not sue *A* on behalf of *B*, while simultaneously representing *A* in another, *completely unrelated* matter.

Example: Lawyer represents Wife in a divorce suit against Husband while simultaneously representing Husband who is seeking to collect on his workman's compensation claim. *Memphis & Shelby County Bar Ass'n v. Sanderson,* 52 Tenn.App. 684, 378 S.W.2d 173 (1963) (lawyer disbarred).

Although the two cases—the divorce and the workman's compensation claim—are completely unrelated and create no danger of any use of confidences in one case that would or could be useful or relevant in the other case, there is a breach of loyalty. Rule 1.7, Comment 3. When an attorney represents one client in a suit against another, some adverse effect on the lawyer's exercise of independent judgment on behalf of a client may arise because of the lawyer's adversary posture towards that client in another matter. See, *I.B.M. Corp. v. Levin,* 579 F.2d 271 (3d Cir. 1978). For example, in the attorney's effort to please Client *A* (who is his long-standing client) there may be a "diminution in the rigor of his representation of the client in the other matter." 579 F.2d at 280. The lawyer might not—or it might appear that he might not—fight as vigorously for one of his clients as he otherwise would.

Waiver. It is unclear whether client consent is ever effective to allow such dual representation. Although the lawyer is not representing opposing parties in the same case, there is much authority that the duty of loyalty *always* prevents effective consent. The possible ineffectiveness of client consent is illustrated by *Matter of Kelly v. Greason,* 23 N.Y.2d 368, 374–79, 296 N.Y.S.2d 937, 942–46, 244 N.E.2d 456, 459–62 (1968). Two lawyers, Kelly and Whalen, were in a law partnership. Whalen was then employed as an insurance adjuster for the Nationwide Insurance Co. Whalen had no access to any Nationwide files other than those of claims assigned to him. Nonetheless the firm handled some claims against Nationwide. There was no proof that any of the Nationwide settlements were unreasonable or unfair to either the insurance carrier or the claimants. Nor was there any prejudice to any of Nationwide's claimants by the partnership's failure to bring a negligence liability claim against the carrier. Nonetheless the court held that "it was, prima facie, evidence of professional misconduct for the partnership to represent claimants, whether assured of Nationwide or not, in their claims against the carrier, while at the same time Whalen was also the carrier's employee." 23 N.Y.2d at 376, 296 N.Y.S.2d at 944, 244 N.E.2d at 461. The court found that discipline was appropriate unless, and *perhaps even if,* consent had been obtained from *both* clients after full disclosure.

A.B.A. Formal Opinion 112 (May 10, 1934) held that an attorney who represents an insurance company in workmen's compensation cases may not accept employment from a former general agent who is suing the insurance company. The Opinion expressly stated: "We assume that the insurance company has expressed no objection" to the lawyer's representation against the insurance company, "but that does not relieve lawyer *A* from his obligation to accept no employment from a new client in a case where fidelity to the new client may require examination of the motives and the good faith of the insurance company by which he has been and is employed in numerous other cases *and whose patronage he desires to continue."* (emphasis added). See also, H. Drinker, Legal Ethics 111 (1953); R. Wise, Legal Ethics 259 (2d ed. 1970).

The purpose of this simultaneous adverse representation rule is to protect the systemic interest in the fair administration of justice as well as to protect the clients' interest in loyalty. Thus there is a substantial question whether, even "with consent in such circumstances the attorney may profit from breach of the duty of loyalty." Fordham, *There are Substantial Limitations on Representation of Clients in Litigation Which are Not Obvious in the Code of Professional Responsibility*, 33 The Bus. Lawyer 1193, 1204 (Mar.1978).

These principles are, in general, reflected in DR 5–105 and Rule 1.7(a). "Thus, a lawyer ordinarily may not act as advocate against a person the lawyer represents in some other matter, even if it is wholly unrelated." Rule 1.7, Comment 3.

However, if a lawyer represents a large corporation, he or she may ordinarily represent another economic enterprise in a matter that is unrelated, even though one enterprise is competing with the other. For example, the lawyer is representing both *A* and *B* on two separate matters that are unrelated. Assume, for example, that the lawyer represents a major auto company on a securities matter. The lawyer is also representing another major auto company on a different, unrelated securities matter. Although *A* and *B* generally compete with each other, the lawyer is not suing either *A* or *B*. Nor is the lawyer giving legal advice to *A* that is to be used against *B* (or vice versa). Nor is there any violation of client confidences or secrets. In the words of the Model Rules, *A* and *B* are only "generally adverse" because they are merely competing economic enterprises; they are not "directly adverse." Rule 1.7, Comment 3. However, if the lawyer were suing Client *A* on behalf of Client *B* in one matter, the lawyer should not be able simultaneously to represent Client *A*, on a different matter, even if the two matters are completely unrelated. See, e.g., *IBM Corp. v. Levin*, discussed, supra. *As part of the duty of loyalty, a lawyer may not sue a present client.*

A Comment to the Rules appears to go well beyond present law and the Code when it states that "there are circumstances in which a lawyer may act as advocate against a client. For example, a lawyer representing an enterprise with diverse operations *may accept employment as an advocate against the enterprise* in an unrelated matter if doing so will not adversely affect the lawyer's relationship with the enterprise or conduct of the suit and if both clients consent upon consultation." Rule 1.7, Comment 8 (emphasis added). The Code nowhere approves of a lawyer suing a present client, whether or not the client is a large enterprise. See, *IBM Corp. v. Levin,* discussed supra. In any event, the circumstance hypothesized by Comment 8 assumes fact situations would seem to be few and far between, for the Comment requires both clients to consent upon consultation.

(c)   In Negotiation

A lawyer, while acting as an advocate, cannot represent the opposite side in negotiation. The Rules provide that a lawyer "may not represent multiple parties to a negotiation whose interests are fundamentally antagonistic to each other, but common representation is permissible where clients are generally aligned in interest even though there is some difference of interest among them." Rule 1.7, Comment 12. See also DR 5–105(A), EC 5–15. Thus a lawyer may represent several parties on the *same side* of a negotiation even though there is some difference among them. See Rule 1.7(b) (discussed below).

If a lawyer does seek to be a part of a situation involving fundamentally antagonistic multiple parties in negotiation, he should do so as a *mediator,* not as an advocate. See Rule 1.7, Comment 12; Rule 2.2, Comment 2; and Part VIII, section II, infra.

2.   Multiple Clients Not in Litigation or Negotiation Against Each Other

Rule 1.7(b) covers the situation where the lawyer represents codefendants or coplaintiffs in the same case, or where the same lawyer represents several parties on the same side in negotiation. See Rule 1.7(b), Comment 7; DR 5–105(B), (C). Rule 1.7(b) also covers the case where a lawyer's acceptance of employment from Client *A* may be limited by the lawyer's own interests or the lawyer's responsibilities to third parties or to other clients. Comments 4, 5. See also DR 5–105(A).

Basically Rule 1.7(b) tracks Rule 1.7(a) with two exceptions. First, Rule 1.7(a) requires that the client's interests "will be directly adverse to another client," but Rule 1.7(b) only requires that the lawyer's representation of one client "may be materially limited by the lawyer's responsibilities to another client or to a third person, or by the lawyer's own interests . . . "

Secondly, unlike Rule 1.7(a), Rule 1.7(b) covers cases where the lawyer represents co-plaintiffs or co-defendants, or co-parties in negotiation. In those cases, "[w]hen representation of multiple clients in a single matter is undertaken, the consultation shall include explanation of the implications of the common representation and the advantages and risks involved." Rule 1.7(b)(2). For example, the lawyer should normally explain that if two clients engage the same attorney to represent them in a matter, and each communicates separately with the attorney, then, as between the two clients, there are no confidences: "the communicating client, knowing that the attorney represents the other party also, would not ordinarily intend that the facts communicated should be kept secret from him." *McCormick's Handbook on the Law of Evidence* § 91 at 190 (E. Cleary, ed., 2d ed. 1972). If one of the co-clients wants relevant information kept from the other co-client, then each should obtain their own separate counsel to begin with.

3. **Special Problem Areas**

(a) Securing Consent

Before a lawyer may represent clients who are—or are reasonably likely to be—in conflict with each other, the lawyer must secure each client's consent. In order for the consent to be knowing, the lawyer must give each client "full disclosure." See DR 5–105(C); Rule 1.7 and "Terminology" 2 (definition of "consult"). In some cases, however, such "full disclosure" may include "secrets that the lawyer supposedly may not reveal" under Canon 4 or Rule 1.6. See G. Hazard, *Ethics in the Practice of Law* 24, 76 (1978). In such situations the lawyer cannot secure the adequate consent from Client *A* without violating his or her duty to keep confidential the secrets of Client *B*. Thus the lawyer cannot secure adequate consent and may not take on such representation. See Rule 1.7, Comment 5.

(b) The Organization as a Client

(i) Representing the Entity

Occasionally the lawyer represents an entity, such as a corporation, union, or a governmental unit. In such cases the lawyer owes his allegiance to the incorporeal entity and not to a "stockholder, director, officer, employee, representative, or other person connected with the entity." EC 5–18. This principle is stated somewhat differently in Rule 1.13(a), which provides that the lawyer "employed or retained by an organization *represents the organization* acting through its duly authorized constituents." (emphasis added). Cf. DR 5–107(B). Though the language used is distinct, there is no suggestion in the Code Comparison of the

Rules that any substantial change was intended. See Rule 1.13, Code Comparison 1.

> *Note:* One of the consultants to the ABA Commission, which drafted the Model Rules, has noted that often times the Commission rejected the language of the Model Code not because of any intent to change the meaning but only because of a preference for different phraseology. Sutton, *Professional Code Becoming Controversial Rules,* 35 Virginia L. Weekly 1, 4 col. 1 (Nov. 12, 1982).

The lawyer represents the "entity," but this legal entity can only act through its officers and other duly authorized agents. See Rule 1.13(a) and Comment 1.

The "entity" theory offers no Rosetta Stone to solve all corporate conflicts problems. It does offer some solutions. "[I]f a competitor sues a corporate client alleging an antitrust violation, it is easy to conclude that the corporate lawyer does not represent a shareholder of defendant who is also a shareholder of plaintiff; rather, the lawyer represents the corporation as an entity." Rotunda, *Law, Lawyers, and Managers,* in The Ethics of Corporate Conduct, 127, 129 (C. Walton, ed. 1977). But what of other, more difficult cases—where the shareholders of the corporation sue derivatively, alleging that the directors have not performed their legal obligations; or the lawyer for a corporation is asked to defend it from a hostile takeover, and yet a takeover may be in the best economic interests of the shareholders; or the corporate lawyer discovers that one of the officers is violating a law (e.g., engaging in price-fixing), which violation would be imputed to the entity but it "benefits" the corporation assuming that the corporation is not caught? Model Rule 1.13(b) & (c) provide a more useful analytical tool than the bare bones of EC 5–18.

(ii)   The Approach of the Model Code
The Code offers some assistance in the general principles of EC 5–18. The most specific guidance is found in EC 5–24, which states that the lawyer should make legal judgments but defer to the business judgment of the agents of the entity: directors and officers "necessarily have the right to make decisions of business policy [but] a lawyer must decline to accept direction of his professional judgment from any layman."

(iii) The Approach of the Model Rules

The Rules set up what basically is an "exhaustion of internal remedies requirement" in Rule 1.13(b) and (c). These subsections provide guidance as to when a lawyer must climb up the corporate ladder (or the chain of command of any other legal entity) in order to determine what the entity really "wants." Once that determination is made, the lawyer then is governed by the other Rules; that is, *Rule 1.13 is in addition to and does not replace other Rules,* such as Rule 1.6 (Confidentiality); Rule 1.8 (Conflicts); Rule 1.16 (Withdrawal); Rule 3.3 (Candor Towards the Tribunal); or Rule 4.1 (Truthfulness to Others). See Rule 1.13, Comment 6.

Rule 1.13(b) in part provides that if the lawyer for the entity learns that an agent of the entity is acting (or refuses to act) in a matter that is "related to the representation," *and:*

> "[(1)] is a violation of a legal obligation to the organization, *or* [(2)] a violation of law which reasonably might be imputed to the organization, *and* [(3)] is likely to result in substantial injury to the organization, [*then*] the lawyer shall proceed as is reasonably necessary in the best interest of the organization." (emphasis added)

Before determining what is in the "best interest" of the entity, it is well to point out several significant ambiguities. **First**, it is unclear whether clause (3)—"is likely to result in substantial injury to the organization"—modifies both clauses 1 and 2 or only clause 2. That is, must the agent's violation of a legal obligation to the entity result in substantial injury, or is the amount of injury relevant only if the agent's legal violation might be imputed to the entity? The language of Rule 1.13(b) does not number the clauses and grammatically allows either interpretation. **Second**, it is unclear whether the requirement of "substantial injury to the organization" means substantial "if discovered," or substantial "assuming that it is discovered." **Third**, what is "substantial"? If the violation of law imputed to the organization is a crime, but the criminal penalties are relative minor, is the violation "substantial"? 1 G. Hazard & W. Hodes, *The Law of Lawyering: A Handbook on the Model Rules of Professional Conduct* 416 (2d ed. 1990), argue that "[c]riminal matters must normally be considered per se 'substantial'. . . ." Unfortunately, neither the Comments nor the Black Letter Rule define "substantial" to mean any crime, though it would have been easy enough to do.

Example: Agent of Corporation engages in price-fixing on behalf of Corporation. If discovered, the violation of law will be imputed to Corporation and will result in substantial treble damages. But if it is not uncovered, Corporation will reap the profits of price-fixing, resulting in substantial profit to Corporation.

It is unclear how Rule 1.13(b) is intended to apply in this situation. It makes more sense to interpret this Rule to mean substantial "assuming that it is discovered." The alternative is to encourage constituents of the entity to cover-up wrongful activity and to give a premium to the attorney who, ostrich-like, sticks his head in the sand. Rule 1.13 obligates the attorney to find out what the entity wants so that he or she can act in its best interests. The attorney cannot make that determination unless he or she first discovers what is going on: if, e.g., the entity really "wants" to commit a crime (e.g., price-fixing) then the attorney may resign pursuant to Rule 1.13(d) or take other action pursuant to other applicable rules. Rule 1.13, Comment 6 ("Relation to Other Rules").

In any event, if the requirements of Rule 1.13(b) are met, the lawyer should proceed in the "best interest" of the entity. The lawyer must weigh the seriousness and consequences of the violation, the scope and nature of the lawyer's representation, the entity's responsibility, the apparent motivation of the person involved, the organization's policies concerning such matters, and anything else deemed relevant.

Depending on how the lawyer weighs such considerations, the lawyer may decide to (1) ask that the matter be reconsidered; (2) advise that a separate legal opinion be sought to present to the organization's appropriate authority; or (3) refer the matter to higher authority. Rule 1.13(b)(1), (2), (3). "Clear justification should exist for seeking review over the head of the constituent normally responsible for it." Rule 1.13, Comment 4.

If the highest authority of the organization (e.g., the Board of Directors) engages in action (or inaction) that is "clearly a violation of law *and* is likely to result in substantial injury to the organization" then the lawyer may resign, following the requirements of Rule 1.16. See Rule 1.13(c). Again, this subsection is ambiguous as to whether the requirement of "likely to result in substantial injury" means likely "only if revealed" or likely "assuming that it is discovered."

(iv) **Actual or Apparent Representation of the Organization and One or More of Its Constituents**

Occasionally the lawyer representing the organization will also have a relationship with the entity's employees, who may believe that the lawyer also represents their interests. The lawyer should then clarify his role and must "explain the identity of the client when it is apparent that the organization's interests are adverse to those of the constituents with whom the lawyer is dealing." Rule 1.13(d). See DR 7–104(A).

The lawyer may represent both the organization and one or more of its constituents if the normal requirements of knowing consent are met, and the potential conflict can be waived. See Rules 1.13(e); 1.7; DR 5–105(C). The organization's consent should be given by an appropriate person "other than the individual who is to be represented, or [it may be given] by the shareholders." Rule 1.13(e).

(v) **Derivative Suits**

In a derivative suit the shareholders sue on behalf of the corporation, which is unwilling to sue. In such cases the corporation may be aligned as a defendant and the other defendants may include corporate officers or directors. May the corporate counsel also defend these other corporate constituents against the claims of the corporate shareholders, or does such dual representation constitute an improper conflict of interests with the corporation? For example, if the shareholder/plaintiffs are successful, the individual defendants may have to pay a money judgment to the corporation. The corporate-defendant then is like a reluctant plaintiff; it benefits from the lawsuit brought against it and the other defendants. A typical case illustrating the modern trend is *Cannon v. United States Acoustics Corp.*, 398 F.Supp. 209, 219–20 (N.D.Ill. 1975), affirmed on this point, 532 F.2d 1118 (7th Cir. 1976) (per curiam), which held that "these two ethical considerations [EC 5–15, 5–18] convincingly establish that in a derivative suit the better course is for the corporation to be represented by *independent* counsel from the outset; even though [existing] counsel believes in good faith that no conflict exists." (emphasis added). This new counsel should then advise as to "the role the corporation will play in the litigation." Id. See also Note, *Independent Representation for Corporate Defendants in Derivative Suits*, 74 Yale L.J. 524 (1965).

The Rules reject any per se rule regarding this question. The Comment recognizes the issue but offers little guidance, for it only provides that if the claim "involves serious charges of wrongdoing by those in control of the organization," then a conflict "may arise" and then the general standards of Rule 1.7 will govern "who should represent the directors and the organization." Rule 1.13, Comment 12.

(vi) **The Lawyer as Director of the Corporate Client**
If a law firm does a substantial amount of work for a particular corporate client, it is not uncommon for one of the partners of the firm also to be a member of the corporation's board of directors. This dual membership has potential conflicts. For example, the lawyer on the board may also be a witness to certain events and thus later may be asked to be both an advocate in litigation and a prospective witness. The client may be confused as to when the lawyer is giving business advice (in her capacity as a director) or legal advice (in her capacity as counsel). If the corporation is sued, the lawyer who is also a director is more likely to find herself a named defendant.

The Code has no specific language dealing with this situation. The Rules acknowledge the problem but offer no concrete guidance except to advise that the lawyer should not wear these two hats if "there is a material risk that the dual role will compromise the lawyer's independence of professional judgment . . . ." Rule 1.7, Comment 14.

(vii) **Private Attorneys on the Board of Legal Services Organizations**
An attorney in a private law firm may also be a member, officer, or director of a legal services organization engaged in pro bono activities, including lawsuits against private parties represented by the attorney's private firm. Such a situation may raise a conflict. See Part IX, Section V, B, infra for a discussion of this issue.

(viii) **Corporate Family Issues**
Should affiliate corporate entities be treated the same for conflict purposes?

In the typical fact situation, Corporation X, a client of Law Firm, asks it to file suit against Corporation A; while Corporation A *is not a client of Law Firm*, Corporation B is, and Corporation A is a subsidiary of Corporation B. May Law Firm sue Corporation A while simultaneously representing its parent, Corporation B, on an unrelated matter? A Law Firm, of course, may not represent a client in one matter while suing it in another, even though the two matters are unrelated. Rule 1.7(a) and Comment 1. Should the parent and subsidiary (Corporations A and B) be treated as one client, or does the Law Firm only represent "the entity," that is, Corporation *B*?

Some cases have held that representing a corporation in one matter while undertaking a representation directly adverse to an affiliate of that corporation, such as a parent corporation, subsidiary, or sister corporation, is an improper conflict of interest. *Gould, Inc. v. Mitsui Mining & Smelting Co.*, 738 F.Supp. 1121 (N.D. Ohio 1990). Other cases have found that when the conflict is thrust upon the law firm (e.g., the conflict occurs because one corporation acquires another), there is no conflict mandating disqualification. *Pennwalt Corp. v. Plough, Inc.*, 85 F.R.D. 264 (D.Del. 1980).

One ethics opinion concludes that a lawyer who represents a parent corporation may also represent a party with interests adverse to a subsidiary of the parent corporation in an unrelated matter: *if* the lawyer does not have access to confidential information adverse to the subsidiary, there is no attorney-client relationship between the attorney and subsidiary, and the parent corporation's interests are not materially affected by action against the subsidiary. New York County Lawyers' Association, Committee on Professional Ethics, Opinion 684 (July 8, 1991). See also, California State Bar Standing Committee on Professional Responsibility and Conduct, Formal Opinion 1989–113 (July 6, 1990), concluding that a lawyer may undertake representation adverse to a wholly owned subsidiary of the existing corporate client so long as the parent corporation is not the alter ego of the subsidiary and the subsidiary has not revealed confidential information to the lawyer with the expectation that it would not be used adversely to the subsidiary. This Opinion advises: "The percentage of ownership of stock, while a factor to consider, is by no means itself determinative."

The lawyer should evaluate how separate the corporate entities really are. Are corporate formalities really observed? To what extent are the two entities really run separately? What is the nature of the charges filed against Corporation *A*? For example, does Corporation *X*'s lawsuit allege fraud or criminal conduct by Corporation *A*? Are the personnel with whom the lawyer must deal the same people? It would be difficult for the lawyer, on Day One, to call the general counsel of Parent Corporation, loyally advise her about the latest strategies on behalf of Subsidiary, and then, on Day Two, call the same general counsel and engage in tough negotiations on behalf of another client against Parent Corporation.

Note: Careful law firms will include parent-subsidiary information in their conflict of interest databases, so that they will be aware of possible conflict issues.

(c)   Attorney for the Insured and Insurer

The insurer, in a typical liability insurance policy, normally agrees to pay any liability within the policy limits, and to provide a lawyer to defend the insured. The insured, in turn, agrees to cooperate. Normally the insured and the insurer have a "community of interest," see ABA Formal Opinion 282 (May 27, 1950), because both wish to defend vigorously against the claim brought by plaintiff. However, conflicts may arise when the suit is for more than the policy limits and the insured is more anxious than the insurer to settle for an amount less than (or not much more than) the policy limits.

Example: Plaintiff offered to settle for $12,500 and the policy limit was $10,000. Insured was willing to add the additional $2500. Insurer initially authorized settlement of $9500. Lawyer for insured did not relay to the insured this relevant settlement information; nor did Lawyer inform insured that the settlement offer was rejected. After trial, the verdict was for $225,000. Attorney believed his sole duty as to settlement was to the insurer, but never so advised insured. Therefore Attorney could be personally liable for the judgment in excess of policy limits. *Lysick v. Walcom,* 258 Cal.App.2d 136, 65 Cal.Rptr. 406 (1968).

The lawyer's obligation to the insured requires that he respect the insured's confidences. Thus a "lawyer may not defend the insured and at the same time investigate the failure of the insured to give timely notice of the accident involved as required by the insurance policy. Nor may counsel reveal to the insurer the insured's confidential disclosure indicating that his earlier version of the accident is untrue, or that the case is not covered by the insurance policy." Aronson, *Conflict of Interest Problems of the Private Practitioner,* in Professional Responsibility: A Guide for Attorneys 91, 104 (ABA 1978).

The Code spots the issue, but gives little concrete guidance, noting simply that "[t]ypically recurring situations involving potentially differing interests" include cases where the lawyer represents "an insured and his insurer." EC 5–17.

The case law is not entirely clear, but the trend is to consider the lawyer in such cases to owe the duty of loyalty solely to the insured. Rather than treating such a lawyer as representing dual clients (the insured and insurer), some of the case law is best understood as treating the insured as the only client, while the insurer merely pays for the lawyer. DR 5–107(B) provides support for this view when it states that if another person pays the lawyer to render legal services for another, the lawyer may not permit that other person "to direct or regulate his professional judgment in rendering such legal services." Accord, Rule 1.8(f). The Rules also support this interpretation. See Rule 1.7, Comment 10.

(d) Positional Conflicts

A lawyer may represent Client *A*—in the case of *A vs. X*—seeking a particular legal result on one lawsuit (e.g., that the statute of limitations for tort should be tolled until the malpractice could reasonably have been discovered) and, at the same time, represent Client *B* in a completely different matter—the case of *Z vs. B*—raising the same general legal question. However, may the lawyer, on behalf of *B*, defend the contrary legal position?

The Code has no specific rule prohibiting a lawyer from taking different positions in different cases. Client *A* (or Client *B*) may object, but whether the lawyer responds to these objections is a business question, not an ethical one. The Code only speaks of such positional conflicts in the pro bono context, and in that context specifically allows positional conflicts. See EC 7–17 (lawyer may advocate law reform contrary to interest or desires of client); cf. EC 8–1. See also Fed.R.Civ.P., Rule 8(e)(2) (inconsistent pleadings in same case allowed).

The Rules raise a question about this practice but provide virtually no guidance in answering it. See Rule 1.7 Comment 9, which allows lawyers to advocate antagonistic positions on the same legal question in different cases "unless representation of either client would be adversely affected." Thus, says this Comment, it normally is proper to assert different positions "in cases pending in different trial courts, but it *may* be improper to do so in cases pending at the *same time* in an [the same?] appellate court." [emphasis added]

The ALI, Restatement of the Law Governing Lawyers, Third, § 209, Illustrations 5 and 6 (Tentative Draft No. 4, April 10, 1991) accept the notion of positional conflicts, but the two illustrations read like an ipse dixit. Illustration 5 allows an attorney to represent Client *A* and Client *B* in civil rights cases brought in two different federal district courts, where the lawyer will seek to introduce certain evidence in one trial and argue against its admissibility in the other trial. Even though "there is a substantial possibility" that the court's ruling in one case will be published and cited as persuasive authority in the other proceeding, the lawyer "may proceed with both representations without obtaining the consent of the clients involved." In contrast, consider Illustration 6. The facts are the same, except both cases are now before the U.S. Supreme Court, which will decide the common evidentiary question. This Illustration concludes that now there is a conflict and it is so great that it "is likely that even the consent of both Client *A* and Client *B* would be insufficient to cure [it]." Perhaps Clients *A* and *B* (when told of the conflict in Illustration 6) might be surprised to know that their common lawyer had no obligation to tell them when he planted the seed of the conflict in Illustration 5.

Nowadays, when it is not unusual for firms to have hundreds of members scattered among various cities, there are probably positional conflicts, like those in Illustration 5, going on all the time. It would be difficult for a conflicts check even to uncover these positional conflicts because legal arguments change all the time, even within the same case.

(e) Moving to Disqualify Opposing Counsel
If conflicts develop during litigation, counsel may move to disqualify opposing counsel. If the conflict is such that it "taints" the fact finding process or fairness of the trial, the courts should grant the motion. *Board of Education of City of New York v. Nyquist,* 590 F.2d 1241 (2d Cir. 1979). However, if the alleged ethical violation does not affect the fact finding process or the fairness of the trial (a claim by defendant that plaintiff's lawyer improperly solicited plaintiff), then the court should leave any enforcement of the alleged violation to the disciplinary process. See, *Lefrak v. Arabian American Oil Co.,* 527 F.2d 1136 (2d Cir. 1975). Moreover, counsel should not use this disqualification device as a "technique of harassment." Rule 1.7, Comment 15.

(f) Aggregate Settlements
The lawyer, on behalf of her multiple clients, may negotiate an aggregate settlement of the civil claims, or an agreement of guilty or nolo contendere pleas covering multiple clients in a criminal case. In such cases each client should consent after consultation, which must include "disclosure of the existence and nature of all the claims involved and of the participation of each person in the settlement." Rule 1.8(g). Accord, DR 5–106(A).

> ***Example:*** Attorney represents 18 individual plaintiffs who entered into a prior agreement that majority rule would govern acceptance of a settlement. Defendant offered $155,000 for distribution to the group, which voted 13–5 to accept it.

Notwithstanding the prior agreement, plaintiffs have a right to agree or refuse to agree once the settlement was made known to them. *Hayes v. Eagle–Picher Industries, Inc.,* 513 F.2d 892 (10th Cir. 1975).

C. SUCCESSIVE REPRESENTATION
A lawyer cannot represent a new client in a matter adverse to a former client if to do so results in a breach of loyalty or confidence to the former client.

The rule developed to determine conflicts in subsequent representation cases is really a judicial rule, incorporated into the Code only by inference in Canons 4, 5, and 9. Judge Weinfeld developed the basic test in the leading case of *T.C. Theatre Corp. v. Warner Brothers Pictures, Inc.,* 113 F.Supp. 265, 268–69 (S.D. N.Y. 1953):

> "[T]he former client need show no more than that the matters embraced within the pending suit wherein his former attorney appears on behalf of his adversary are *substantially related* to the matters or cause of action wherein the attorney previously represented him, the former client. The Court will assume that during the course of the former representation confidences were disclosed to the attorney bearing on the subject matter of the representation. It will not inquire into their nature and extent. Only in this manner can the lawyer's duty of absolute fidelity be enforced and the spirit of the rule relating to privileged communications be maintained." [emphasis added].

Judge Weinfeld's "substantial relationship" test for subsequent representation cases has been quoted, relied on, cited, and followed by a host of other court decisions. E.g., *Emle Industries, Inc. v. Patentex, Inc.,* 478 F.2d 562, 570–71 (2d Cir. 1973); *Schloetter v. Railoc of Indiana, Inc.,* 546 F.2d 706, 710–11 (7th Cir. 1976).

The Rules, unlike the Code, have an explicit section dealing with this problem. Rule 1.9 recognizes two interests that must be protected: loyalty and client confidences.

As a matter of client loyalty, whether or not the lawyer, in the case of *A vs. B,* learned from Client *A* secret or confidential information, that particular lawyer cannot now "switch sides" in the *same* matter and represent Client *B.* Rule 1.9(a), & Comments 1, 2, 11. "Thus, a lawyer could not properly seek to rescind on behalf of a new client a contract [that this lawyer had] drafted on behalf of the former client." Rule 1.9, Comment 1.

If the matter is not exactly the same, the lawyer still may not "switch sides" if the matters are "substantially related." *T.C. Theatre Corp.,* supra; Rule 1.9(a). To determine whether the matters are so related, is a question of degree. If the lawyer is involved in a "specific transaction" as opposed to a "recurrently handled type of problem," then the switching of sides is a direct breach of loyalty, and a conflict exists in the subsequent representation. In contrast, if the matter was a "recurrently handled type of problem," the lawyer may represent a new client "in a wholly distinct problem of that [general] type even though the subsequent representation involves a position adverse to the prior client." Rule 1.9, Comment 2.

> *Example:* Lawyer "L" has represented several banks over the years. However, a year ago he resigned from representing any of these banks when he changed law firms. He still practices in the same locality. He now plans to defend a debtor in a collection matter. "Since L no longer has any banker clients, and the new collection suit is a matter unrelated to his previous employment, his former clients may not prevent the new representation. L need not obtain the consent of his former clients nor even inform them of his plan." G. Hazard & W. Hodes, *The Law of Lawyering: A Handbook on the Model Rules of Professional Conduct* 184–85 (1985).

Both the Rules and Code also prohibit the lawyer from using confidential or secret information acquired from the former client on behalf of a new client. The case law, interpreting the Code, reaches this result by having the definition of "substantial relationship" turn on "the possibility, or appearance thereof, that confidential information might have been given to the attorney in relation to the subsequent matter in which disqualification is sought." *Westinghouse Electric Corp. v. Gulf Oil Corp.,* 588 F.2d 221, 224 (7th Cir. 1978). Rules 1.9(c)(1) reaches this same result by providing that the lawyer may not "use information relating to the representation to the disadvantage of the former client. . . ." See also, Rule 1.9(b)(2).

This protection of client confidences has some limits, or else a lawyer could never sue a former client. Thus it is not disqualifying if a lawyer had access to "*general information concerning the personality of a client,* which is always helpful in later suits against that client. . . ." *Unified Sewerage Agency of Washington County, Oregon v. Jelco Inc.,* 646 F.2d 1339, 1351 (9th Cir. 1981).

Similarly, there is no need to protect client information if that information has become "generally known," Rule 1.9(c)(1); or if the former client consents to the subsequent representation, Rule 1.9(a); or if the other exceptions to the normal rule protecting client confidences are applicable. See Rule 1.6; DR 4–101(C). Finally, Rule 1.9(b) provides there is also no need to limit the practice of a lawyer because of client secrets, when the lawyer has no actual (but only imputed) knowledge of those secrets. Thus, if Lawyer A leaves *Firm X* (which represents *Client # 1*) and then joins *Firm Y,* Lawyer A is not precluded from representing *Client # 2,* even though Client # 2's interests are materially adverse to *Client # 1, if* Lawyer A never acquired any confidential or secret information about *Client # 1* while Lawyer A was a member of *Firm X.* Cf. also, Rule 1.10(b). Otherwise, Lawyer A would be a Typhoid Mary, infecting any firm he joined with knowledge that he never actually has, but only knowledge that was imputed to him while he was with his original firm.

As to questions involving representation by the former government attorney against the government, see Part VI, section II, infra.

D. THE ATTORNEY'S PERSONAL AND FINANCIAL INTERESTS

1. Nonfinancial Interests—Lack of Belief in the Client's Cause

The mere fact that the lawyer does not believe in the justness of the client's cause is not disqualifying. Cf. EC 2–29; Rule 1.2(b) (lawyer's representation is not an endorsement of client's views). However, if the intensity of the lawyer's personal feelings is so great that he or she could not provide competent representation, the lawyer should not accept the case. EC 2–30; EC 5–1; DR 5–101(A); Rule 1.16(a).

2. Financial Interests

(a) Business Dealings With Others

The lawyer may be involved with business dealings with others, which may affect the lawyer's ability to represent the client. There is a conflict if these interests are significant and material enough to affect the lawyer's judgment. The lawyer in such cases should not accept the case unless he or she reasonably believes that the representation will not be adversely affected and the client consents. Rule 1.7(b); DR 5–101(A).

(b) Business Dealings With the Client

If the lawyer deals with the client in a business transaction, the lawyer may overreach the client, who may be relying on the lawyer's independent legal judgment. The Code and the Rules attempt to deal with this problem in slightly different ways.

The Code flatly forbids business relations with the client if two conditions exist: (1) the lawyer and client have differing interests, and (2) the client expects the lawyer to exercise his or her legal judgment for the protection of the client. DR 5–104(A). The client can nonetheless consent to the lawyer's involvement. Id.

On the nondisciplinable level, the Code also provides that lawyers should not "seek to persuade" their clients to permit them to invest in the client's business or undertaking. EC 5–3. Even if the lawyer's efforts at persuasion are unsuccessful, he has violated this ethical rule by attempting to persuade the client.

The Rules do not focus on the client's expectation that the lawyer will exercise professional judgment on behalf of the client. Rather, they allow client business dealings with the lawyer if: (1) the transaction is fair and reasonable to the client; (2) the terms of the transaction are given to the client *in writing* so that the client can understand them; (3) the client is given a reasonable opportunity to consult another lawyer (whether or not the client actually exercises that opportunity); and (4) the client consents *in writing*. Rule 1.8(a). Rule 1.8 does not specifically forbid the lawyer from seeking to invest in the client's enterprise.

(c) Gifts From the Client
    (i) That Do Not Require Instruments
        Because of the danger that the lawyer may overreach the client and abuse the fiduciary relationship, there are certain restrictions that a lawyer should observe when accepting client gifts.

Some gifts do not involve the drafting of any instruments. In contrast, a gift given by a will demands a legal instrument that needs to be drafted. A typical case involving no legal instrument occurs when the client, happy with the lawyer's work, decides to give a gift, which may be nominal (a basket of fruit) or substantial (e.g., a large amount of cash in addition to the agreed fee, or an expensive gold watch). The Code has no disciplinary rule dealing with such cases. On the ethical level the lawyer should, before accepting the gift, advise the client to secure "disinterested advice from an independent competent person who is cognizant of all the circumstances." EC 5–5. This other person need not be a lawyer. The client need not secure such advice but the lawyer should urge that course of action. Under EC 5–5, this review by this third person should take place regardless of whether the gift is substantial or nominal.

Because the Code draws no distinction between substantial versus nominal gifts, it probably goes too far in regulating client gifts. In contrast, the Rules do not go far enough, for they do not purport to regulate at all any client gifts that do not require the lawyer to prepare an instrument. Rule 1.8(c). The Comment goes beyond the Rule and advises that the lawyer may accept any gift that meets "general standards of fairness." Nominal gifts may simply be accepted. Rule 1.8, Comment 2.

If the gift is substantial, *and* if its effectuation requires that a legal instrument be drafted, then another lawyer should offer "detached advice." Rule 1.8 Comment 2. If the gift is substantial but does not require an instrument, then Rule 1.8(c) is inapplicable and Comment 2 offers no guidance except the "general standards of fairness" test.

(ii) That Require Instruments

If the effectuation of the gift requires an instrument, such as a will, the Code provides—on the ethical rather than disciplinable level—that another lawyer should prepare the instrument except in undefined "exceptional circumstances." EC 5–5.

The Rules raise this requirement to the disciplinable level, limit it to substantial gifts, and expand it to cover cases where the donee is not only the lawyer but the lawyer's parent, child, sibling, or spouse. Finally, the Rules do not regulate cases where the client/donor is related to the donee. Rule 1.8(c), Comment 2.

(d) Publication Rights

The situation where the lawyer negotiates with the client for publication rights to a particular matter before that matter has ended and while the lawyer is still in the employ of the client presents a problem. There is a danger that the lawyer, in bargaining with the client, may be able to overreach. For example, the client, needing the lawyer's services, may feel pressured to waive the attorney-client privilege so that the attorney can later write a more interesting book. Also, the lawyer, in his representation of the client, may be consciously or unconsciously influenced to "enhance the value of his publication rights to the prejudice of his client." EC 5–4. Accord, Rule 1.8, Comment 3.

The Code prohibits the lawyer from acquiring from the client an interest in publication rights relating to the subject matter "[p]rior to the conclusion of all aspects of the matter giving rise to his employment . . ." DR 5–104(B). Out of an overabundance of caution, this rule prohibits acquiring such rights if the matter giving rise to the employment still continues, even though another lawyer now represents the client and the first lawyer's employment regarding that matter has ended. EC 5–4. The Rules, in contrast, only prohibit acquiring such rights "[p]rior to the conclusion of representation of a client . . ." Rule 1.8(d).

The Code refers to "publication rights," but the Rules use a term that the drafters thought more expansive—"literary or media rights." Compare DR 5–104(A), with Rule 1.8(d); see Code Comparison 5.

Both DR 5–104(B) and Rule 1.8(d) exist not only to protect the client but to protect the interest of the judicial system in competent representation. Therefore neither the Code nor the Rules provide for client waiver of these restrictions. California, ignoring these systemic interests and basing its decision on the California Rules—which in this respect are not modeled on the Code or Rules—does allow client waiver. *Maxwell v. Superior Court of Los Angeles County,* 30 Cal.3d 606, 180 Cal.Rptr. 177, 639 P.2d 248 (1982).

If the lawyer represents the client in a dispute or other transaction concerning literary property, e.g., a copyright claim, the lawyer may contract for a reasonable contingent fee, that is, a reasonable share of the ownership of the literary property, assuming no other rules are violated. The prohibition on publication rights is not meant to cover this situation. Rule 1.8, Comment 3.

(e)   Financial Advances to the Client

When representing a client in a matter involving litigation the lawyer may not provide financial assistance to the client, but may advance or guarantee the expenses of litigation, such as the expenses of medical examination.

The Code has a specific requirement that the client must remain "ultimately liable," DR 5–103(B), but also advises (inconsistently) that the lawyer should not normally sue to collect his fee except to prevent fraud or gross imposition, EC 2–23, and that lawyers should charge the less fortunate clients less or no fee, EC 2–16.

The Rules are more straightforward on this point. They eliminate the requirement of client reimbursement and also allow the lawyer to pay directly an indigent's litigation expenses and court costs without the client remaining ultimately liable. Rule 1.8(e)(1), (2).

(f)   Limiting Malpractice Liability

The lawyer may not require the client to enter into an agreement *prospectively* limiting the lawyer's liability to that client for malpractice. DR 6–102(A); Rule 1.8(h). The Code does not explicitly use the word "prospectively," but this must be its intent. Cf. Rule 1.8, Code Comparison 10. Otherwise if the former client sued the lawyer for malpractice, the former client (who now is separately represented by new counsel) could not settle with, and release, the lawyer regarding that claim.

The Code has a provision, not found in the Rules, that allows a lawyer in a professional legal corporation to limit her *imputed* liability for her associates' malpractice, if other law permits. EC 6–6. This rule only applies if the law firm is organized as a professional legal corporation.

The Rules, on the other hand, allow the lawyer to limit her liability prospectively if the client is "independently represented in making the agreement . . ." Rule 1.8(h). The rationale must be that the purpose of the rule regarding malpractice liability is to prevent the attorney from overreaching the client, a fear that is unfounded if the client has separate counsel on this issue. Rule 1.8(h) also requires the lawyer who is being sued to advise the pro se litigant suing for malpractice that independent representation is appropriate before settlement, a requirement not found in the Code. See Section III, B, 2, infra. As a further protection for the pro se client or former client thinking of settling a malpractice claim, the lawyer's advice regarding the appropriateness of independent representation must be "in writing." The ABA Section on General Practice recommended this requirement and the ABA Commission accepted it without opposition. See The Legislative History of the Model Rules of Professional Conduct 60–64 (ABA, Center for Professional Responsibility 1987).

(g) Suing Parties Represented by the Lawyer's Relatives
Assume that Lawyer *A* represents *P* who is suing *D*. Lawyer *B* represents *D*. Is there any conflict if Lawyers *A* and *B*—both in different firms—are married to each other, or related as parent, child, or sibling?

The Code has no explicit provision dealing with this issue. ABA Formal Opinion 340 (Sept. 23, 1975), dealing with the husband/wife relationship, found no per se disqualification but otherwise offered little concrete guidance. It did state, however, that if one spouse is disqualified under DR 5–105(A), the entire firm is disqualified under DR 5–105(D).

The Rules have an explicit provision regarding such relationships. It forbids Lawyer *A* from representing Client *P* if Lawyer *B* is the spouse, parent, child, or sibling representing Client *D*, and *P* and *D* are "directly adverse" to each other, unless the client consents. Rule 1.8(i). However, this prohibition is *not imputed* to the other members of either *A* 's or *B* 's firm. See Rule 1.10. Thus, husband may not represent plaintiff while wife represents defendant (unless the clients knowingly consent), but husband's law firm may represent plaintiff while wife or wife's law firm represents defendant.

E. THE ADVOCATE AS WITNESS
Both the Code and the Rules regulate when an advocate may simultaneously act as a witness. The primary difference is that the Rules do not impute the disqualification to other members of the disqualified lawyer's firm.

Both the Code and the Rules treat the case where the advocate is asked to be a witness as an instance of conflict of interests. The Code places the relevant rules in Canon 5, the conflicts Canon—DR 5–101(B); DR 5–102—and the Rules specifically refer to the problem as a "conflict of interest." Rule 3.7, Comment 1.

The Code offers inconsistent rationales for the restrictions on the testifying advocate—e.g., such an advocate may be "more easily impeachable for interest" and simultaneously "the opposing counsel may be handicapped in challenging the credibility of the lawyer. . . ." EC 5–9.

The Rules offer as a primary rationale that the fact-finder may be confused if the person actually acting as an advocate before the fact-finder also offers testimony with his or her argument: "It may not be clear whether a statement by an advocate-witness should be taken as proof or as an analysis of the proof." Rule 3.7, Comment 2. The jury may be confused if the advocate gets up from counsel's chair and then sits in the witness box, and later addresses the jury in closing argument.

The Advocate–Witness rule is not any immunity from testifying; it is a limitation on advocacy. It basically provides that the advocate should withdraw if she is "likely to be called as a necessary witness" unless the testimony relates to an uncontested issue, or it relates to the nature and value of legal services in that case, or disqualification would work a "substantial hardship on the client." Rule 3.7(a)(1), (2), (3); DR 5–102(A). Nor should the lawyer accept employment if she "ought to be called as witness" unless one of these exceptions is applicable. DR 5–101(B). The Code also has a special, additional rule, which provides that if a lawyer, after accepting the case, is called as a witness "other than on behalf of the client," then the lawyer need not withdraw "until it is apparent" that the testimony may be "prejudicial" to the client. DR 5–102(B).

The Code explicitly imputes this disqualification to all lawyers in the firm, DR 5–101(B); DR 5–102(A), (B). Given the rationale of the Rules, discussed supra, the Rules do not impute the advocate-witness prohibition. Rule 3.7(b). Where the witness is a partner of another lawyer who is the advocate, there is no automatic imputation because there is no danger of confusing the fact–finder.

Given this rationale of confusion of the fact-finder—an interest of the judicial system rather than an interest of the client—nothing in either the Code or the Rules provides for client waiver of the advocate-witness rule. The California Rules of Professional Conduct, surprisingly, do provide for client waiver, though the case law makes no real attempt is made to justify a waiver. California Rule 5–210(C). There should be no waiver of the advocate witness rule, because that rule exists to protect systemic interests—the interests in the system of justice—and not merely to protect one of the parties. E.g., *Supreme*

Beef Processors, Inc. v. American Consumer Industries, Inc., 441 F.Supp. 1064, 1068 (N.D.Tex. 1977); *Draganescu v. First National Bank of Hollywood*, 502 F.2d 550, 552 (5th Cir. 1974). The party represented by the advocate-witness may seek to "waive" the disqualification because of bad advice from the advocate-witness who desires to remain on the case as a litigant. And the attorney for the other side "may avoid pressing for disqualification out of a desire to avoid clashing with opposing counsel or to obtain tactical advantages." Thus, where neither party moves for disqualification, the court should act *sua sponte*. *MacArthur v. Bank of New York*, 524 F.Supp. 1205, 1209 (S.D.N.Y. 1981).

If the advocate-witness rule is the only reason why a firm is disqualified, then the disqualified firm may consult with the party's substitute counsel and assist in preparing for trial. *MacArthur v. Bank of New York*, 524 F.Supp. 1205, 1211 n.3 (S.D.N.Y. 1981); *Jones v. Chicago*, 610 F.Supp. 350, 363 (N.D.Ill. 1984). None of the reasons offered for the advocate-witness rule (confusion of fact-finder, difficulty of challenging credibility of advocate-witness, etc.) justify prohibiting the disqualified advocate-witness from consulting with the new firm: for example, the disqualified lawyer will not impart any forbidden confidences or other improper information to the new lawyer, because the lawyer-witness was not disqualified for that reason; nor will the lawyer-witness, who is no longer a lawyer-advocate, be able to confuse the fact-finder.

Courts enforce the advocate-witness rule in the course of litigation. See, e.g., *Weil v. Weil*, 283 App.Div. 33, 35, 125 N.Y.S.2d 368, 370 (1953) (new trial granted because of violation of advocate-witness rule); *Supreme Beef Processors, Inc. v. American Consumer Industries, Inc.*, 441 F.Supp. 1064, 1069 (N.D.Tex. 1977) (judgment vacated because of violation of advocate-witness rule); *MacArthur v. Bank of New York*, 524 F.Supp. 1205 (S.D.N.Y. 1981) (mistrial because of violation of advocate-witness rule). This enforcement is proper, because a violation of the advocate-witness rule infects the truth-finding process by confusing the fact-finder, whether judge or jury.

F. VICARIOUS DISQUALIFICATION
1. Introduction

It has long been the general rule in all disqualification cases that if "a lawyer is required to decline employment or to withdraw from employment under a Disciplinary Rule, no partner or associate, or any other lawyer affiliated with him or his firm may accept or continue such employment." DR 5–105(D). One attorney's disqualification is imputed to all. E.g., *Consolidated Theatres v. Warner Brothers, Circuit Management Corp.*, 216 F.2d 920 (2d Cir. 1954). And if the lawyer actually disqualified as to a particular case moves to a new firm, his disqualification is normally imputed to all the lawyers of the new firm. Id.

The Code itself provides no explicit exceptions to this general rule, but in practice it has been interpreted to allow various exceptions. See, e.g., ABA Formal Opinion 342 (Nov. 24, 1975), dealing with the former government attorney, discussed in Part VI, section II, infra.

Model Rule 1.10 lays out the general rule for imputed disqualification. It is more narrowly drafted than DR 5–105(D). For the most part, it reflects the rule as it has actually been interpreted by the case law. Model Rule 1.10 is a good restatement of the law.

2. Application to Government and Former Government Lawyers

The disqualification principles of Rule 1.10 are more extensive than those provided by Rule 1.11 ("Successive Government and Private Employment"); Rule 1.10 does not apply to the problems involving the movement between private practice and government service. See Rule 1.10, Comment 5. These problems are considered elsewhere. See Part VI, section II, infra. The government is subject to different protections because of what public policy views as the special governmental interest in recruiting lawyers who will not be unduly burdened in seeking later private employment because of their former affiliation with the government. Similarly, because of the government's unusually broad legal relationships, it should not be unduly hampered when it recruits a lawyer from the private sector. Rule 1.10, Comment 5; Rule 1.11, Comment 3.

3. Waiver and Screening

Any affected client protected by the principles of Rule 1.10 may waive its protections if each client consents after consultation and the lawyer reasonably believes that his or her representation will not be adversely affected. Rule 1.10(c). Thus, a waiver is not effective unless: first, all parties knowingly consent after consultation; and second, the conflict is such that it can be waiver ("the lawyer reasonably believes. . . .").

If a lawyer is disqualified, and this disqualification is imputed to other members of the firm, Rule 1.10 does not provide for screening as a method of curing the disqualification. Rule 1.10 (unlike Rule 1.11) nowhere refers to a screen, and Comment 5 to Rule 1.10 emphasizes the obvious, that this failure was not inadvertent. Nonetheless, a few cases have suggested that a screen may be sufficient to remove the imputation of the disqualification. Sometimes this suggestion is dictum, or the court is faced with peculiar set of facts. E.g., *Nemours Foundation v. Gilbane, Aetna, Federal Ins. Co.,* 632 F.Supp. 418 (D.Del. 1986)(referring to a "cone of silence" and to Rule 1.11(a), which allows screening for the former *government* attorney). See also, ABA Formal Opinion 90–358 (Sept. 13, 1990), reprinted in, ABA/BNA Lawyers' Manual on Professional Conduct (loose leaf service), 901:132, 136–37 & n. 12 (noting that some cases have referred to screening in cases not involving the former government attorney).

Although Rule 1.10 does not itself provide for any screening mechanism—or what is sometimes called a "Chinese Wall"—around the affected attorney, the client may, if he so chooses, withhold consent, or agree to consent on the condition that the affected attorney is screened. Rule 1.10 does not preclude a client from knowingly waiving rights and allowing a screen.

The proposed Restatement, Third, of the Law Governing Lawyers (Tentative Draft No. 4, April 10, 1991), § 204(2) suggests a narrow role for screening. Section 204 is entitled: "Removing Imputation." Subsection (2) allows a lawyer's personal disqualification not to be imputed *if* "there is no reasonable prospect that confidential information of the former client will be used with material adverse effect on the former client" because: (a) the information is unlikely to be significant in the later case; (b) "[a]dequate screening measures are in effect to eliminate involvement by the personally-prohibited lawyer in the representation; and (c) [t]imely and adequate notice of the screening has been provided to all affected clients. . . ."

4. Defining the "Firm"

Rule 1.10 applies to lawyers associated together in a law "firm," a term intended to encompass not only private law firms but also corporate legal departments and legal service organizations. See, Terminology 3. Because the purpose of this rule is to protect client confidences and client loyalty (Rule 1.10, Comment 1) the definition of "firm" may vary. For example, while "firm" includes a legal aid office, it does "not necessarily include those [lawyers] employed in separate units [of the same legal aid organization]." Rule 1.10 Comment 3. When such lawyers are in different offices, the need to protect confidences of clients represented by different offices is lessened. The definition of "firm" for this purpose may also include co-counsel who are not members of the same firm but who are representing the same party *if* co-counsel have exchanged confidential information. In determining whether two or more lawyers should be treated as a "firm," it is relevant to know if the lawyers have mutual access to information concerning the clients that they serve.

Similarly the term may include lawyers who only share office space but who imply to the public that they are a partnership. Rule 1.10 Comment 1. Because these lawyers act as if they are partners, application of Rule 1.10 is necessary to protect client expectations of loyalty. But compare DR 2–102(D) (lawyers may not hold themselves out as partners "unless they are in fact partners."); Rule 7.5(d) (same).

5. Lawyers Currently Associated in a Firm

Rule 1.10(a) provides the basic imputation rule for lawyers *while* they are currently associated in the same firm. This Rule states that *only the disqualification principles of certain Rules*—Rule 1.7 ("Conflict of Interest: General Rule"); Rule 1.8(c) (prohibition of lawyers preparing for clients instruments that give the lawyer or his close relative substantial gifts); Rule 1.9 ("Conflict of Interest: Former Client"), and Rule 2.2 ("Intermediary")—*are imputed to all the other lawyers, and the imputation exists only while these other lawyers are currently associated in the same firm as the disqualified lawyer.*

Rule 1.10(a), unlike DR 5–105(D), does *not* impute to all the lawyers in the firm the disqualifications of all the other lawyers in the firm. Rather it imputes only those disqualifications specifically mentioned. Moreover, Rule 1.10(a) is not at all applicable to situations where one lawyer—either the one with the actual disqualification, or another lawyer with the imputed disqualification—leaves the first firm and joins another. Rule 1.10(b) and Rule 1.9 govern those situations.

Examples: Client asks Lawyer *A* to draft a will giving Lawyer *A*'s son a large sum of money. Lawyer *A* says: "I cannot draft this instrument, but my partner *B* can do it."

Lawyers *A* and *B* have violated Rule 1.10(a).

Lawyer *A* now leaves the firm and joins another one. When Client makes the same request Lawyer *A* says: "I cannot draft the will but my good friend and former law partner, Lawyer *B* can."

Lawyers *A* and *B* have not violated Rule 1.10(a).

6. When a Lawyer Moves From One Firm to Another

(a) Introduction

Imputed knowledge is not thereafter imputed to another.

If, for example, Lawyer # *1* represents Client *P* in a matter—*P v. D*—no Lawyer in Lawyer # *1*'s firm can also represent *D*. Rule 1.7(a). Such a representation would breach # *1*'s duty to *P*. Similarly, no member of # *1*'s firm could represent *D* because of the firm's duty of loyalty to *P*. **Rule 1.10(a)** & Comment 6. Assume now that Lawyer # *2* (a partner or associate in # *1*'s firm) leaves that firm and joins another firm. Lawyer # *2*'s representation of *D* against *P* does not breach *P*'s expectation of loyalty from Lawyer # *1* or # *1*'s firm. If the duty of loyalty prevented # *2* from litigating against *P*, then no lawyer could ever sue a former client, yet we know the rule is otherwise. See Rule 1.9.

On the other hand, if Lawyer # 2 had acquired confidential knowledge about P that would be helpful to D, then Lawyer # 2's representation of D would be improper because it would violate # 2's duty under Rule 1.6 to safeguard client information. **Rule 1.9(b)**.

If Lawyer # 2 did not *personally* represent Client P *and* did not acquire any material secrets or confidences from Client P, neither Lawyer # 2 nor # 2's new firm should be disqualified from representing Client D. **Rule 1.9(b)** & Comment 9. Otherwise mobility of the legal profession would be severely restricted, a burden not justified by any need to protect client loyalty or client information, neither one of which, by hypothesis, exists. Moreover, if the law imputed Lawyer # 2's imputed knowledge to # 2's new firm, then the imputed disqualification could exist *ad infinitum* when, for example, lawyer # 3 (# 2's new partner) leaves that firm and joins yet another: if lawyer # 2's imputed disqualification were imputed to lawyer # 3 is lawyer # 3's doubly imputed knowledge also imputed to the lawyers in lawyer # 3's new firm? The general rule is no. "[N]ew partners of a vicariously disqualified partner, to whom knowledge has been imputed during a former partnership, are not necessarily disqualified: they need only show that the vicariously disqualified partner's knowledge was imputed, not actual." *American Can Co. v. Citrus Feed Co.*, 436 F.2d 1125, 1129 (5th Cir. 1971). See also, e.g., *Gas–A–Tron of Arizona v. Union Oil Co. of California*, 534 F.2d 1322, 1325 (9th Cir. 1976) (per curiam), cert. denied, 429 U.S. 861, 97 S.Ct. 164, 50 L.Ed.2d 139 (1976).

(b)   When a Lawyer Joins a Firm
        Rule 1.9(a) & (b) governs the extent to which a lawyer who joins a new firm carries with him any disqualifications from the old firm.

Assume that lawyer Alpha is a member of Firm # 1. Firm # 1 represents Client P in a suit against Client D. Alpha herself was not involved in any representation of Client P, and Alpha has not acquired any secret or confidential information from Client P that is relevant to Client D. Alpha now leaves Firm # 1 and joins Firm # 2, which represents Client D.

Note that P's and D's interests are materially adverse to each other *and* Firm # 2 (Alpha's new firm) is representing D in a matter that is the same as (or substantially related to) the matter in which Firm # 1 (Alpha's old firm) is representing P. Nonetheless, both Firm # 2 and Alpha may properly represent D against P because Alpha acquired from Client *P* no material information protected by Rules 1.6 or 1.9(b). This same result would be reached either under Rule 1.9(b) or under the prior case law. See, e.g., *Silver Chrysler Plymouth, Inc. v. Chrysler Motors Corp.,* 518 F.2d 751, 757 (2d Cir. 1975) (a client cannot "reasonably expect to foreclose either all lawyers formerly at the firm or even those who have represented it on unrelated matters from subsequently representing an opposing party.").

> ***Example:*** Lawyer Gamma is a member of the firm of Alpha & Beta. Alpha represents *P* in the case of *P vs. D*. Gamma, while with the law firm of Alpha & Beta, did not work on the case of *P vs. D* and acquired no knowledge relating to client *P*. Gamma then leaves the firm and joins another firm, the "second firm." "[N]either the lawyer [Gamma] individually nor the second firm is disqualified from representing another client in the same or a related manner even though the interests of the two clients conflict." Rule 1.9, Comment 9.

Now assume the same facts in the previous hypothetical except that Alpha *personally* worked for *P* in the case of *P v. D* while Alpha was with Firm # 1. Alpha did not acquire any material client secrets or confidences, but she did work on that particular case. For example, she filed an appearance in court and asked for a continuance. By hypothesis, there is no need to protect the former client's secrets or confidences, but is there a need to protect any duty of loyalty owed to a former client?

Under the Code, it is likely that neither Alpha nor Firm # 2 (Alpha's new firm) could represent *D*. Alpha is personally disqualified because she personally represented *P*, and for her now to switch sides in the same case would be a breach of loyalty. See, e.g., H. Drinker, Legal Ethics 115 (1953). Because Alpha's disqualification is personal to her (not imputed to her), her disqualification is imputed to all the lawyers in her new firm, Firm # 2. See DR 5–105(D).

The approach of the Rules appears to be quite different. Unless the former client consents, Alpha is *personally* disqualified. **Rule 1.9(a)** provides that if Alpha formerly represented a client in a matter, she may not thereafter represent another person in the same or a substantially related matter, if that other person's interest is materially adverse to the interest of the former client (unless, or course, the former client consents). See also, Rule 1.9, Comment 2 ("When a lawyer has been directly involved in a specific transaction, subsequent representation of other clients with materially adverse interests clearly is prohibited.").

Now, is Alpha's disqualification imputed to the other lawyers in Firm # 2? Rule 1.9 Comment 11 states, Alpha's duty of loyalty to Client *P* requires Alpha's abstention from adverse representation against *P* in the same or substantially related matters. (To this extent the Code agrees.) But (and here the Rules diverge from the Code) this abstention by Alpha "does not properly entail abstention of other lawyers through imputed disqualification." Rule 1.9 Comment 11. Therefore Alpha cannot represent *D* against *P* in the case of *P v. D*, but the other lawyers in Alpha's new firm may represent *D*.

The problem with Rule 1.9, Comment 11 is that it contradicts Rule 1.10(a). Rule 1.10 is the general rule on imputation, and subsection (a) explicitly imputes *all* of Rule 1.9, not just Rules 1.9(b) & (c). This problem is probably the result of a drafting error by the American Bar Association. One would think that lawyers should know a lot about drafting, but drafting errors still occur, a fact of life that should serve to humble all of us. When the ABA House of Delegates, in February, 1989, amended and reorganized Rules 1.9 and 1.10, they moved Comment 15 of Rule 1.10 so that it became Comment 11 to Rule 1.9. Rule 1.10(b) was redrafted and became Rule 1.9(b). The ABA, it appears, forgot to clean up the imputation language of Rule 1.10(a).

(c)   When a Lawyer Leaves a Firm
Rule 1.10(b) governs the extent to which Firm *# 1* is still disqualified from handling a matter when Lawyer Alpha (the cause of the initial disqualification) has left Firm *# 1*. Basically Rule 1.10(b) states that, once Lawyer Alpha leaves Firm *# 1*, Firm *# 1* may then represent clients materially adverse to Firm *# 1*'s former clients who had been represented by Alpha when she was with Firm *# 1*, unless: the matter involved is the same as (or substantially related to) the matter in which Alpha (the formerly associated lawyer) had represented the client *and* any of the lawyers still with Firm *# 1* have knowledge of the former client's material secrets or confidences (i.e., client information protected by Rules 1.6 or 1.9(c)). In other words, if Lawyer Alpha was the sole lawyer who handled all of a client's affairs, and when Alpha left Firm *# 1* she took with her the client, and all confidential information about the client, then there is no need to preclude First *# 1* from taking matters adverse to that firm's former client.

Examples: Lawyer Alpha, a member of Firm *# 1*, represents Client *D* on various matters. Client *D* gives Alpha confidential information relating to a patent. Alpha did not relate any of the confidential information regarding the patent to any member of Firm # 1. Then Alpha leaves Firm # 1, takes Client *D* with him, and moves to Firm # 2.

Then Client *P* asks Firm # 1 to represent it in a patent infringement action against *D*. Alpha and Firm # 2 represent *D* in this patent suit. Firm # 1 may properly represent *P*. *Novo Terapeutisk Laboratorium A/S v. Baxter Travenol Laboratories, Inc.*, 607 F.2d 186 (7th Cir. 1979) (*en banc*). Accord, Rule 1.10, Comment 7.

(d) Burden of Proof

The application of Rule 1.9(b) and similar rules often turns on the question whether a lawyer had acquired material client information protected as client confidences or secrets. "In such an inquiry, the burden of proof should rest upon the firm whose disqualification is sought." Rule 1.9, Comment 8.

However, the fact that the firm must demonstrate that it is *not* the depository of material protected client information does not mean that the burden can never be met. "[I]t will not do . . . to make the standard for proof . . . unattainably high . . . particularly where . . . the attorney must prove a negative." *Laskey Bros. of W.Va., Inc. v. Warner Bros. Pictures, Inc.*, 224 F.2d 824, 827 (2d Cir. 1955). See *Gas–A–Tron of Arizona v. Union Oil Co. of California*, 534 F.2d 1322, 1325 (9th Cir. 1976) (per curiam), cert. denied, 429 U.S. 861, 97 S.Ct. 164, 50 L.Ed.2d 139 (1976): "[W]e are convinced that any initial inference of impropriety that arose from [Lawyer *B*'s] potential physical access to the files of Exxon and Shell and from his association with lawyers who did know confidential information about them was dispelled by evidence that he saw none of the files other than those relating to the cases assigned to him heretofore described and that he heard no confidences about Exxon and Shell from the lawyers with whom he was earlier associated." Rebuttal by attorney affidavit may also be allowed. *Silver Chrysler Plymouth, Inc. v. Chrysler Motors Corp.*, 518 F.2d 751, 756 (2d Cir. 1975).

G. SANCTIONS

If an attorney is involved in a conflict of interest, he may be subject to discipline, tort liability, and disqualification.

If an attorney violates one of the disciplinable rules relating to conflicts of interest, that attorney is subject to discipline by the bar authorities.

If the violation causes damage to the client, the lawyer may also be liable for damages for the tort of malpractice. E.g., *Arlinghaus v. Ritenour*, 622 F.2d 629 (2d Cir. 1980).

If the conflict occurs in the course of litigation, the court may also disqualify the attorney from further representation in that litigation, *if* the conflict is such that it may "taint" the fact-finding process. Compare *Board of Education of City of New York v. Nyquist*, 590 F.2d 1241 (2d Cir. 1979) (no disqualification when only claim is possible "appearance of impropriety" and "no claim that the trial will be tainted . . ."), with *Ceramco, Inc. v. Lee Pharmaceuticals*, 510 F.2d 268, 271 (2d Cir. 1975) ("the courts have not only the supervisory power but the duty and responsibility to disqualify counsel for unethical conduct prejudicial to his adversaries."). Thus, improper attorney solicitation of clients (see Part V, section II, infra) may merit discipline, but it does not taint or prejudice the fact finding process and hence the court supplies no remedy of disqualification. *Fisher Studio, Inc. v. Loew's Inc.*, 232 F.2d 199, 204 (2d Cir. 1956), cert. denied, 352 U.S. 836, 77 S.Ct. 56, 1 L.Ed.2d 55 (1956).

Appealability. When parties litigate attorney disqualification in the course of litigation, the question arises as to when adverse trial rulings (either granting or denying disqualification) are appealable prior to the conclusion of the main case. In the federal system, the Supreme Court has ruled that in a civil case a trial court decision denying or granting disqualification is not appealable as a final decision under 28 U.S.C.A. § 1291. *Firestone Tire & Rubber Co. v. Risjord*, 449 U.S. 368, 101 S.Ct. 669, 66 L.Ed.2d 571 (1981) (order denying disqualification motion not immediately appealable); *Richardson–Merrell, Inc. v. Koller*, 472 U.S. 424, 105 S.Ct. 2757, 86 L.Ed.2d 340 (1985) (order granting disqualification motion not immediately appealable).

The Court has also held that the granting of a disqualification motion in a *criminal* case is not immediately appealable. *Flanagan v. United States*, 465 U.S. 259, 104 S.Ct. 1051, 79 L.Ed.2d 288 (1984). We should expect it to reach a similar conclusion with respect to the denial of a disqualification motion in a criminal case. See *United States v. White*, 743 F.2d 488 (7th Cir. 1984) (criminal case; denial of disqualification motion not final order).

The courts do not preclude disqualification motions by applying overly strict notions of standing and laches; similarly, they do not easily find or imply client waiver of attorney conflicts. See generally, Hacker & Rotunda, *Standing, Waiver, Laches and Appealability in Attorney Disqualification Cases*, 3 Corp.L.Rev. 82 (1980). However, attorneys should not use motions to disqualify opposing counsel as a "technique of harassment. Rule 1.7, Comment 14.

III. THE DUTY OF COMPETENCE AND THE SCOPE OF REPRESENTATION

A. CLIENT CONTROL

The client has the authority to make major decisions—those affecting the merits of the case, or substantially prejudicing the client's rights.

The lawyer is the agent (not the guardian) of the client, who is the principal (not the ward). See *State v. Barley,* 240 N.C. 253, 81 S.E.2d 772 (1954); *Prate v. Freedman,* 583 F.2d 42, 48 (2d Cir. 1978). The lawyer must abide by his "client's decisions concerning the objectives of representation . . ." Rule 1.2(a). The Code and Rules therefore attempt to lay out basic guidelines to distinguish between those matters where the lawyer must secure client waiver and those where prior consent is unnecessary.

The lawyer is entitled to make her own decisions in matters "not affecting the merits of the cause or substantially prejudicing the rights of the client;" in other cases "the authority to make decisions is exclusively that of the client . . ." EC 7–7. See also Rule 1.2(a) (the client decides the "objectives of representation" and the lawyer must *consult* with the client "as to the means by which they are pursued."). However, as the Rules candidly admit, sometimes a "clear distinction . . . cannot be drawn." Rule 1.2, Comment 1. Terminology 2 defines "consult."

The ethics rules use examples in an effort to make the text more concrete. Thus, the client decides whether or not to accept a settlement offer or to plead guilty. EC 7–7; Rule 1.2(a). In criminal cases the client has the final say as to whether or not he will testify on his own behalf. Rule 1.2(a); ABA Standards of the Defense Function, Standard 4–5.2(a)(iii).

Cf. *Linsk v. Linsk,* 70 Cal.2d 272, 278–79, 74 Cal.Rptr. 544, 547–48, 449 P.2d 760, 763–64 (1969) (internal citations and paragraphing omitted):

> "An attorney may refuse to call a witness even though his client desires that the witness testify; may abandon a defense he deems to be unmeritorious, may stipulate that the trial judge could view the premises, that a witness, if called, would give substantially the same testimony as a prior witness, and that the testimony of a witness in a prior trial be used in a later action; and he may waive the late filing of a complaint. On the other hand, an attorney may not, by virtue of his general authority over the conduct of the action, stipulate that his client's premises constituted an unsafe place to work where such a stipulation would dispose of the client's sole interest in the premises, nor may he stipulate to a matter that would eliminate an essential defense. He may not agree to the entry of a default judgment against his client, may not compromise his client's claim, or stipulate that only nominal damages may be

awarded, and he cannot agree to an increase in the amount of the judgment against his client. Likewise an attorney is without authority to waive findings so that no appeal can be prosecuted, or agree that a judgement may be made payable in gold coin rather than in legal tender. An attorney is also forbidden without authorization to stipulate that the opposing party's failure to comply with a statute would not be pleaded as a defense. . . ."

While the Code and Rules offer examples of which conduct falls on which side of a not very bright line, these examples should not be regarded as negating all other instances. Thus, the Rules state that in a criminal case it is for the client to decide whether to waive a jury trial. Rule 1.2(a). Yet in a civil case as well the attorney may not waive the client's jury trial right without client consent. E.g., *Graves v. P.J. Taggares Co.,* 94 Wash.2d 298, 616 P.2d 1223 (1980).

Similarly, the ABA Defense Functions state that the "decisions on what witnesses to call, whether and how to conduct cross-examination, what jurors to accept or strike, *what trial motions should be made,* and all other strategic and tactical decisions are the *exclusive province of the lawyer* after consultation with the client." Standard 4–5.2(b) (emphasis added). However, if the trial motion relates to exclusion of evidence allegedly obtained in violation of the Constitution, the client should have the final say on that issue. Cf. *Henry v. Mississippi,* 379 U.S. 443, 85 S.Ct. 564, 13 L.Ed.2d 408 (1965).

Lawyers have a right to agree to "reasonable requests of opposing counsel which do not prejudice the rights of his client. . . ." DR 7–101(A)(1), such as "reasonable requests regarding court procedures, settings, continuances, waiver of procedural formalities, and similar matters which do not prejudice the rights of his client." EC 7–38. Accord Rule 1.3, Comment 1.

Examples: Defendant's Attorney asks Plaintiff's Attorney for a one week extension in the time allowed to file an Answer to the Complaint. The extension would not affect the merits of the case or prejudice Plaintiff. The ethics rules grant Plaintiff no right to forbid Plaintiff's Attorney from granting this request. EC 7–38; Rule 2(a). Rule 1.3, Comment 1.

Because the attorney is an agent of the client, the attorney and client have a great deal of power, within the law of contract, to change the division of lawyer/client responsibility. For example, client may properly tell lawyer: "Use your judgment as to whether or not to accept any settlement for at least $25,000." Though the Client has the sole power to accept or reject settlements, the client may give actual authority to the attorney to act on the client's behalf. The Client may also hire the lawyer only for a "specifically defined purpose." Rule 1.2, Comment 4.

Similarly, the lawyer may ask the client's permission to forego action that the lawyer believes is unjust, even though it is otherwise in the best interest of his client. EC 7–9. See also, Rule 1.2(c); Rule 1.2 Comment 4 (limitations on representation "may exclude objectives or means that the lawyer regards as repugnant or imprudent.").

The lawyer or client may also affect the extent of client control by terminating the relationship. That is, *the client can always fire the lawyer, who then must withdraw, even if the client seeks to terminate the lawyer for a less than noble reason.* Rule 1.16(a)(3); DR 2–110(B)(4). For example, if the client decides to fire the lawyer because the lawyer has hired a minority law associate, the lawyer still has no right to prevent the client from terminating the representation. The lawyer, in turn, *may* withdraw if the client insists on pursuing an objective that "the lawyer considers repugnant or imprudent," even though it is not illegal. Rule 1.16(b)(3). Cf. DR 2–110(C)(1)(a); cf. DR 7–101(B)(2). On withdrawal, see generally section V, B, infra.

The client's and lawyer's rights to control the scope of representation have some limits; that is, the power to contract may not be used to violate the ethical codes or other law. "Thus, the client may not be asked to agree to representation so limited in scope as to violate Rule 1.1 [requiring competence], or to surrender the right to terminate the lawyer's services or the right to settle litigation that the lawyer might wish to continue." Rule 1.2, Comment 5. Cf. DR 6–102(A). On the question of competence, see section III, B, infra.

Note: The ethics rules allow the attorney and client to agree that the attorney will present all nonfrivolous issues. And, as a matter of constitutional law, the indigent can compel appointed counsel to press a nonfrivolous appeal. *Anders v. California,* 386 U.S. 738, 87 S.Ct. 1396, 18 L.Ed.2d 493 (1967). However, as a matter of constitutional law, the indigent has no right to compel appointed counsel to present all nonfrivolous *issues* on appeal if the appointed lawyer's professional judgment is to forego certain issues. *Jones v. Barnes,* 463 U.S. 745, 103 S.Ct. 3308, 77 L.Ed.2d 987 (1983).

B. COMPETENCE
1. Defining Competence
Not only the law of malpractice but the law of ethics requires lawyers to be competent. DR 6–101(A); Rule 1.1. A lawyer is competent if he has "the legal knowledge, skill, thoroughness and preparation reasonably necessary for the representation." Rule 1.1.

The lawyer need not necessarily be experienced in a particular matter to be considered competent in that matter. Even a novice lawyer has training in the common denominator of all legal problems: legal method, the analysis of precedent and evidence, and legal drafting. Rule 1.1,

Comment 2. Cf. EC 6–1. On the other hand to develop other skills (e.g., trial practice, negotiation), training and close supervision are more important. Partners in law firms have the responsibility to make reasonable efforts to insure that all of the lawyers in the firm conform to the rules of professional conduct. Rule 5.1.

The lawyer also need not have the necessary degree of competence prior to accepting the employment. The lawyer may properly accept the matter and then acquire the necessary competence, through study, and preparation in a novel area of law. DR 6–101(A)(2). EC 6–4; Rule 1.1, Comment 2. The Code adds a specific caveat that this preparation should not result in "unreasonable delay or expense to his client." EC 6–3. This limitation is implicit in the requirement in the Rules that the preparation be "reasonable." Rule 1.1, Comment 4. Cf. Rule 1.1, Comment 5.

The lawyer has an ethical duty to engage in continuing legal education and study in order to maintain his or her competence. EC 6–2; Rule 1.1, Comment 6.

The lawyer may also establish the necessary competence by associating in the matter with another attorney who is already competent. DR 6–101(A)(1); Rule 1.1, Comment 2. Before any association is proper, the client must consent to it. EC 2–22, 6–3; Rule 1.5(e)(2). Cf. Rule 1.2(a).

Because what is "competent" is a function of reasonableness, a different standard of competence applies in an emergency. A lawyer in such cases may give advice reasonably necessary in the circumstances "where referral to or consultation with another lawyer would be impractical." Rule 1.1, Comment 3.

2. Waiving Malpractice Liability

The client has a right to expect competent representation. The Code nowhere permits the client to waive the lawyer's duty of competence. In fact the Disciplinary Rules explicitly forbid the lawyer from attempting "to exonerate himself from or limit his liability to his client for his personal malpractice." DR 6–102(A). Though the language of this Rule is not explicitly limited to prospective attempts, i.e., attempts before the malpractice actually occurs, such a limitation must be read into DR 6–102(A). Otherwise it would forbid the lawyer from agreeing to a settlement offer in which the client suing for malpractice released his claim.

The Model Code provides that the restriction on the lawyer's ability to reduce his malpractice liability is limited to cases regarding his "personal malpractice." DR 6–102(A). Thus, if other law permits, a lawyer in a professional legal corporation may limit his *imputed* liability for the malpractice of his associates. EC 6–6.

The Rules at one point also forbid the lawyer from asking the client to agree to incompetent representation. Rule 1.2, Comment 5. However, later the Rules make clear that, if other law permits, the lawyer may make an agreement "prospectively limiting the lawyer's liability to a client for malpractice" *if* the client "is independently represented in making the agreement. . . ." Rule 1.8(h). The rationale is that if the client is independently represented in making the decision to waive malpractice liability prospectively there is no danger of overreaching. This provision is logical, but as a practical matter it will be the unusual case where a client will hire a lawyer to represent him in negotiating an employment agreement with another lawyer where the client agrees to waive malpractice liability.

Rule 1.8(h) does not explicitly provide that this representation must be by another lawyer. Elsewhere it speaks of the client securing the advice of "independent counsel," Rule 1.8(a)(2), and so it is conceivable that Rule 1.8(h) only requires that the client, before waiving his malpractice rights, secure the disinterested advice of a "independent, competent person." Cf. EC 5–5. However, given the dangers of overreaching and the use of the term "represented," the Rules should be interpreted to mean the participation of another *lawyer.*

The Rules explicitly recognize that the lawyer may settle with her client a malpractice claim that the client has against her. Rule 1.8(h). If the client (or former client) is not separately represented in the settlement, the lawyer must advise him *in writing* that "independent representation is appropriate. . . ." Rule 1.8(h). The purpose of this provision is to give unrepresented people the right to settle malpractice claims, while guarding against overreaching on the part of the lawyer.

3. Neglect

Reasonable Communication. The "lawyer should fully and promptly inform his client of material developments in the matters being handled for the client," EC 9–2, and should keep his client informed of relevant considerations before the client makes decisions, EC 7–8. The Rules make clear that these requirements are not merely hortatory; to violate them is to violate a disciplinary rule. Rule 1.4(a), (b). However, these Rules are subject to a rule of reason. See Rule 1.4, Comment 2. In fact, the lawyer may even be justified in delaying the transfer of information to the client if the lawyer believes the client might react imprudently. Rule 1.4, Comment 3. Cf. Rule 1.14.

In addition to this duty of reasonable communication, the lawyer may not neglect a legal matter entrusted to him. DR 6–101(A)(3). The Rules use much more affirmative language: "A lawyer shall act with reasonable diligence and promptness in representing a client." Rule 1.3.

Neglect. Under the Code, a showing of neglect usually requires proof of a pattern of behavior. If a lawyer on one occasion forgot to file an answer to a complaint in time because of inadvertence, he could be guilty of civil malpractice if the client were damaged, but he would not be guilty of neglect. "Neglect involves indifference and a *consistent* failure to carry out the obligations which the lawyer has assumed to the client or a *conscious disregard* for the responsibility owed to the client." ABA Informal Opinion 1273 (Nov. 20, 1973). To demonstrate a violation of Rule 1.3 may not require such extensive proof, because it is probably true that "no professional shortcoming is more widely resented than procrastination," and unreasonable delay can cause a "needless anxiety" to a client. Rule 1.3, Comment 2.

Waiver. Nothing in the ethics rules permits the client to waive his right that his attorney act with reasonable promptness or diligence. Even the client's refusal to pay the lawyer's fee does not justify neglect. If the client deliberately disregards his obligation to pay his attorney, the attorney may withdraw only after taking reasonable steps to protect the client's interests. DR 2–110(A)(2) & (C)(1)(f); Rule 1.16(b)(4) & (d). If the matter is before a tribunal, then the lawyer may not even withdraw unless the tribunal permits. DR 2–110(A)(1); Rule 1.16(c). In any event, until the lawyer is able to withdraw in accordance with the requirements in the ethics rules, the lawyer may not neglect the client's case. E.g., *In re Pines,* 26 A.D.2d 424, 275 N.Y.S.2d 122, 123 (1st Dept. 1966) (per curiam) (client refusal to reimburse lawyer for expenses does not justify lawyer "in refraining from proceeding in the action for over three years. . . ."). Similarly, an attorney's heavy workload does not excuse his continued neglect of probate matters. *Matter of Loomos,* 90 Wash.2d 98, 579 P.2d 350 (1978).

C. CRIMES OR FRAUDS

The client's "ultimate authority to determine the purposes to be served by legal representation. . . ." (Rule 1.2, Comment 1) is limited by other law as well as by the ethics rules. Id. Thus, in general, the lawyer may not "counsel a client to engage, or assist a client, in conduct that the lawyer knows is criminal or fraudulent. . . ." Rule 1.2(d); See DR 7–102(A)(7); DR 7–102(A)(6).

Note: While the Rules use the term "criminal or fraudulent" the Code uses the broader term "illegal or fraudulent." DR 7–102(A)(7). The Code language is more vague and may even include violation of civil law, such as tortious conduct.

Neither the Code nor the Rules are as clear as we would like in defining "counsel" or "assist," though they make some effort to explain by example. In general, the lawyer may present an analysis of the legal aspects of questionable conduct but may not recommend "the means by which a crime or fraud might be committed with impunity." Rule 1.2, Comment 6. See EC 7-5. The lawyer must give his "honest opinion" about the "actual consequences" of the client's acts. Id. Accord, Rule 2.1, Comment 1. The fact that the client uses such advice to aid his crime or fraud "does not, of itself, make a lawyer a party to the course of action." Rule 1.2, Comment 1. However, assuming that the lawyer may not reveal such client information (see Part III, section I, supra, on confidences), the lawyer must avoid furthering the client's criminal or fraudulent purposes. The lawyer therefore may not suggest, for example, how the purpose might be concealed. Rule 1.2, Comment 7.

If the lawyer discovers that he has been unwittingly assisting the client in conduct that the lawyer then discovers is criminal or fraudulent, then the lawyer may have to withdraw. DR 2–110(C)(1)(b); Rule 1.2, Comment 7; Rule 1.16(b)(1), (2).

Note: Different considerations apply if perjured testimony or false evidence has been offered before a tribunal. See Model Rule 3.3(a)(2) ("A lawyer shall not knowingly fail to disclose a material fact to a tribunal when disclosure is necessary to avoid assisting a criminal or fraudulent act by the client."). See also, Rules 3.3(a)(4), 3.3(b). These issues are considered in Part VII, Section II, A, 3 ("Disclosure of Facts"), infra.

The Rules later announce that, in representing the client, a lawyer "shall not knowingly fail to disclose a material fact to a third person when disclosure is necessary to avoid assisting a criminal or fraudulent act by a client, *unless* disclosure is prohibited by Rule 1.6 [the confidentiality section]." Rule 4.1(b) (emphasis added). Rule 4.1(b) cannot mean that a lawyer may assist the client in a criminal or fraudulent act if failure to so assist would amount to a disclosure prohibited by Rule 1.6. If Rule 4.1(b) means that, it conflicts with Rule 1.2(d). In such a situation, in order to avoid violating either Rule 1.2(d) or 4.1(b), the lawyer would have to withdraw under Rule 1.16(a)(1). See Rule 1.6, Comment 14. When withdrawing, the lawyer *may waive a red flag* by filing a "notice of withdrawal." See Rule 1.6, Comment 15. The lawyer should also inform the client of the lawyer's obligations under the Model Rules. Rule 1.2(e). See generally Part III, Section I, C, 7, supra ("Filing a Notice of Withdrawal").

The lawyer may counsel or assist his client "to make a good faith effort to determine the validity, scope, meaning or application of the law." Rule 1.2(d). See also, DR 2–109(A)(2); DR 7–102(A)(2); EC 7–4; DR 7–106(A).

The lawyer may not agree to be general counsel for a criminal syndicate, but may agree to undertake "a criminal defense incident to a general retainer for legal services to a lawful enterprise." Rule 1.2, Comment 9; ABA Formal Opinion 281 (Mar. 11, 1952); ABA Defense Function Standards, Standard 4–3.7(c); *In re Abrams,* 56 N.J. 271, 266 A.2d 275 (1970).

D. THE INCOMPETENT CLIENT

The client may be under a mental disability, or the client's youth may impair his ability to render a considered judgment. In such cases the lawyer should endeavor, insofar as possible, to maintain a normal lawyer-client relationship. EC 7–12; Rule 1.14. Even if the client is under a legal disability, he or she might still be capable of understanding the matter. In that case, the lawyer should obtain "all possible aid" from the client. EC 7–12; Rule 1.14, Comment 1.

The client's mental incompetence may be such that the client lacks the legal capacity to discharge his attorney. Rule 1.16, Comment 6. The lawyer may not seek to have a guardian appointed for the client unless the lawyer "reasonably believes that the client cannot adequately act in the client's own interest." Rule 1.14(b). The lawyer, in such cases, should take into account that it may be traumatic or expensive for the client if such a legal representative is appointed. Rule 1.14, Comment 3. Cf. Rule 1.4, Comment 4 (lawyer may withhold client's psychiatric diagnosis if "examining psychiatrist indicates that disclosure would harm the client").

IV. FEES

A. BASIC PRINCIPLES

1. Reasonableness Requirement

Fees Must Be Reasonable.

Because the lawyer is a fiduciary of the client, the lawyer is subject to discipline if the fees are not "reasonable." Rule 1.5(a). The Code uses the term "clearly excessive," DR 2–106(A), but it really means "unreasonable." (It does not mean that a fee can be unreasonable, as long as it is not clearly so.) The Code itself goes on to define "clearly excessive" in terms of reasonableness: "a lawyer of ordinary prudence would be left with the definite and firm conviction that the fee is in excess of a reasonable fee." DR 2–106(B). See also, EC 2–17 ("A lawyer should not charge more than a reasonable fee;" "adequate compensation is necessary.").

Both the Code and the Rules list the same eight factors that are relevant in determining reasonableness. The ethics rules do not limit the determination of reasonableness to these eight factors; these are factors "to be considered."

Reasonableness is determined by considering how much time and labor are required, the novelty of the legal service, and how much skill is needed to perform it. DR 2–106(B)(1); Rule 1.5(a)(1). For many lawyers the hourly rate is the most important (or possibly even the sole) factor used to determine fees. Of course, a lawyer basing the fee on the hours expended may not engage in goldbricking, that is, employing wasteful procedures in an effort to increase the number of billable hours. Rule 1.5, Comment 3.

Taking one matter may well preclude lawyers from taking other legal work. The lawyer may consider this opportunity cost; if the client is not aware of this opportunity cost, the lawyer should tell him. DR 2–106(B)(2); Rule 1.5(a)(2).

The lawyer may also consider the fees customarily charged in the locality for similar legal services. DR 2–106(B)(3); Rule 1.5(a)(3). It would be a violation of the antitrust laws for the bar association to discipline a lawyer because he has charged less than a minimum (or more than a maximum) fee. *Goldfarb v. Virginia State Bar,* 421 U.S. 773, 95 S.Ct. 2004, 44 L.Ed.2d 572 (1975). However, the mere fact that all lawyers of similar quality charge the same, or approximately the same, fee for similar services is not evidence of price-fixing, because, in a perfectly competitive economy, the prices for similar services are also the same.

Note: While lawyers may not conspire to fix prices, the federal antitrust laws do not forbid the setting of prices by the state. Price-fixing by state action is exempt from the Sherman Act. See, e.g., *Gair v. Peck,* 6 N.Y.2d 97, 188 N.Y.S.2d 491, 160 N.E.2d 43 (1959), cert. denied, 361 U.S. 374, 80 S.Ct. 401, 4 L.Ed.2d 380 (1960) (maximum prices set by the court in contingent fee causes).

The lawyer may also take into account how much money is involved and how successful the attorney is in the particular matter. DR 2–106(B)(4); Rule 1.5(a)(4). It is not uncommon for a law firm to raise or lower a base hourly rate by a varying amount depending on the success of the negotiations, the size of the deal, and so forth. However, if the firm represented to the client that the fee would be based only on the numbers of hours worked, it should be unreasonable for the firm to retroactively change the basis of the fee.

The lawyer may adjust the bill if the circumstances or the client imposed special time limitations. DR 2–106(B)(5); Rule 1.5(a)(5). The nature and length of the relationship with the client is also relevant. DR 2–106(B)(6); Rule 1.5(a)(6). That is, special circumstances might make a lawyer more likely to reduce a bill for an old client, or to cut a bill as a "loss leader," in an effort to encourage a new client to continue to retain the lawyer in other matters.

The lawyer may also consider his own experience, reputation, and ability. DR 2–106(B)(7); Rule 1.5(a)(7). Lawyers who are twice as good are justified in charging twice as much.

Finally, the fee may be fixed or contingent. DR 2–106(B)(8); Rule 1.5(a)(8). Thus, a fee that looks large in retrospect, may not appear as large if one considers that the fee was contingent and that the lawyer risked receiving nothing.

If a lawyer's fee is alleged to be excessive, these various factors are used in determining what is an attorney's reasonable fee, what is the fair market value of his services. It is also certainly relevant if, for example, the attorney overreached the client, abused the relationship, or was not completely candid in discussing the elements of a fee. "Such a determination can never be reduced to a neat mathematical formula; it involves important matters of judgment." Berger, *Court Awarded Attorneys' Fees: What Is Reasonable,* 126 U.Pa.L.Rev. 281, 316 (1977).

Some commentators have claimed that "the nature of the lawyer's product and the bar's perception of its role in society combine to make rational valuation of the individual attorney's services practically impossible." R. Aronson, *Attorney–Client Fee Arrangements: Regulation and Review* 3 (Fed. Judicial Center 1980). That is a much too pessimistic view of the ability of the market place to value services. In addition, courts have not found it impossible to value attorney's fees, and have found some to be excessive. E.g., *The Florida Bar v. Moriber,* 314 So.2d 145 (Fla. 1975) (per curiam) (even though client may have been informed of fee of nearly $8,000 for collecting, on behalf of client, approximately $23,000 in an investor's variable payment fund, which had passed to client by operation of law, the fee was excessive). Cf. *United States v. Vague,* 697 F.2d 805, 806 (7th Cir. 1983) (Posner, J.) (even a fixed fee freely bargained by competent adults who do not complain about it may be excessive). See also, Brickman & Cunningham, *Nonrefundable Retainers: Impermissible Under Fiduciary, Statutory and Contract Law,* 57 Fordham L.Rev. 149 (1988); Fanning, *Fee–Busting,* Forbes, Sept. 7, 1987, at 64: "the IRS has recently begun examining estate returns to determine whether the fees charged by executor-attorneys, and the subsequent tax deductions, are too big."

Note: If the lawyer is paid in property, the fee may be subject to "special scrutiny" because the lawyer may have special knowledge of the value of the property. Rule 1.5, Comment 2.

Fee Shifting Statutes. To be distinguished from cases where the attorney and client bargain for a fee later challenged as excessive are the cases involving fee shifting statutes. In those cases, such as civil rights cases, the court is authorized to require the losing party to pay the attorney's fees of the prevailing party. Under the Civil Rights Attorney's Fee Awards Act of 1976, 42 U.S.C.A. § 1988, the prevailing plaintiff ordinarily should receive an attorney's fee; in contrast, the prevailing defendant may recover an attorney's fee only if the lawsuit was vexatious, frivolous, or brought to harass or embarrass the defendant. To determine what is a reasonable fee, the "critical inquiry" is generally the appropriate hourly rate multiplied by the number of hours reasonably expended on the litigation. 2 R. Rotunda, J. Nowak, & J. Young, *Treatise on Constitutional Law: Substance and Procedure* § 19.36 (1986).

2. Writing Requirement

A frequent cause of clients' disputes with their attorneys regarding fees is misunderstanding. The Code consequently advises that it "is usually beneficial to reduce [the fee arrangement] to writing. . . ." EC 2–19. The Rules raise this recommendation to the disciplinary level, but keep the precatory language, and limit it to new clients. Rule 1.5(b) ("preferably in writing"). Malpractice experts also recommend that the lawyer "confirm in writing the basis of the fee." 1 R. Mallen & J. Smith, *Legal Malpractice* § 2.9 (3d ed. 1989).

As to *contingent fees* the Code in particular urges a writing, EC 2–19, but the Rules *require* it. Rule 1.5(c). This writing must state how the fee is determined and whether expenses are deducted before or after the contingent fee is calculated. After the matter is concluded, the lawyer must also provide a detailed statement to the client. Rule 1.5(c). Cf. DR 2–101(B)(22) (*advertisements* of contingent fee rates must disclose whether percentages are computed before or after costs).

3. Price Discrimination

Both the Code and the Rules allow price discrimination. That is, the lawyer may lower a fee depending on who the client is. Because lawyers may charge less to the less wealthy, they, by necessary implication, may charge more for the same services offered to the more wealthy. See, e.g., EC 2–24, 2–25; Rule 1.5, Comment 3 ("it is proper to define the extent of services in light of the client's ability to pay"). Cf. EC 2–18 (it is "commendable" for lawyer to charge less to a "brother lawyer or member of his immediate family").

4. Suing to Collect Fees

On an aspirational level, the Model Code advised that lawyers should not sue the client to collect a fee "unless necessary to prevent fraud or gross imposition by the client." EC 2–23. If the bar has established a mediation or arbitration system, lawyers are encouraged to use them. Rule 1.5, Comment 5. Cf. EC 2–23.

B. CONTINGENT FEES

1. Writing Requirement

The Code encourages, and the Rules require, that all contingent fee arrangements be in writing. See section A, 2, supra.

2. Offering Alternatives

The lawyer has no right to impose a contingent fee on a client who desires another arrangement. Rule 1.5, Comment 3; cf. EC 2–20. In fact, the lawyer should volunteer alternative arrangements to clients if that is in the clients' best interest. Rule 1.5, Comment 3.

3. When Forbidden

Criminal Cases. Both the Code and the Rules forbid contingent fees in criminal cases because, it is said, of the lack of a *res* out of which the fee is to be paid. DR 2–106(C); EC 2–20; Rule 1.5(d)(2). However, in other areas of the law, litigation may produce no *res* and yet the attorney may be paid only if successful. E.g., *Mills v. Electric Auto–Lite Co.*, 396 U.S. 375, 90 S.Ct. 616, 24 L.Ed.2d 593 (1970) (in corporate derivative suit corporation must pay plaintiff's attorney on a "benefits conferred" theory, although victory produced no *res*). The reason for the rule prohibiting contingent fees in criminal cases probably rests on "historical accident, arising in earlier cases during a time when all contingent fee contracts were generally regarded with great suspicion. . . ." C. Wolfram, Modern Legal Ethics 536 (1986). Its continuation may result from the desire of criminal defense counsel to be paid by their clients in advance; the ethical prohibition thus gives lawyers a good excuse to reject the efforts of those clients who might insist on a contingent fee if that alternative were possible.

It would be contrary to public policy for the state to hire a *prosecutor* on a contingency fee basis, *i.e.,* the prosecutor gets paid only if he secures a criminal conviction. *Baca v. Padilla*, 26 N.M. 223, 190 P. 730 (1920) (contract is void and there can be no recovery on it). The rationale behind this prohibition is not difficult to find: the duty of a prosecutor is to do justice, not merely to convict. The state's interest "in a criminal prosecution is not that it shall win a case, but that justice shall be done." *Berger v. United States*, 295 U.S. 78, 88, 55 S.Ct. 629, 633, 79 L.Ed. 1314 (1935).

Domestic Relations Cases. The Code finds that contingent fees in domestic relations matters are "rarely justified," EC 2–20, but it does not raise this note of discouragement to the level of discipline. In contrast, the Rules flatly forbid fees in divorce matters contingent upon "the securing of a divorce or upon the amount of alimony or support or property settlement" achieved. Rule 1.5(d)(1). The Rules do not explain the purpose of its prohibition, but the reason behind it is easy to conceive. Because public policy does not encourage divorce, the lawyer's fee arrangements should not place the lawyer in a position where the lawyer might be encouraged to prevent any possible reconciliation of the parties. Moreover, the lawyer who charged a contingent fee would place himself in a conflict situation, for if the lawyer encouraged reconciliation, he would lose his fee.

Other Cases. Neither the Code nor the Rules forbid, as a matter of attorney discipline, contingent fees in other classes of cases. Typically contingent fees exist in personal injury litigation, but they are not limited to those cases. For example, contingent fees are proper in administrative agency proceedings. EC 2–20. The common justification of contingent fees is that they allow poorer litigants to hire competent lawyers and pay them out of the judgment won.

The Code does discourage (but does not forbid) a lawyer from accepting a contingent fee from a client who can afford a reasonable fixed fee: if such a client desires a contingent arrangement, then it is "not necessarily improper. . . ." EC 2–20. The Rules only say that if there is doubt that a contingent fee is in the client's best interest, the lawyer should offer alternatives and explain their implication. Rule 1.5, Comment 3.

Contingent fees raise a potential conflict of interest between the attorney and client. See EC 5–7. For example, the client may wish to settle litigation while the attorney would want to press on, or vice-versa. The ethics rules attempt to reduce such conflicts, and have specific provisions—in the conflicts of interest section—dealing with contingent fees. See DR 5–103(A); Rule 1.8(j). These provisions forbid a lawyer from acquiring a proprietary interest in the client's cause of action or subject matter except that: (1) he may acquire a lien to secure his fees or expenses if other law allows (see *Lien,* in the Glossary, Appendix I) and (2) he may "contract with a client for a reasonable contingent fee in a civil case." DR 5–103(A); Accord, Rule 1.8(j). *Exception 2 validates contingent fees.* However, the client may not assign to the attorney his cause of action; clients cannot waive their right to decide when to settle litigation. See EC 7–7; Rule 1.2, Comment 5.

Example: Client agrees to compensate Lawyer by giving him a one-fourth interest in certain real property and mining claims.

Ownership of these properties is disputed and Lawyer defends Client (and himself as well to the extent that the Lawyer's one-fourth interest is involved). Client becomes dissatisfied with Lawyer's services and tries to discharge Lawyer, who refuses to leave. Lawyer has violated DR 2–110(B)(4) and DR 5–103 because he has refused to accept discharge by the client. ABA Informal Opinion 1397 (Aug. 31, 1977).

C. FEE REFERRALS

A division of a fee "is a single billing to a client covering the fee of two or more lawyers who are not in the same firm." Rule 1.5, Comment 4. Such divisions are commonly called "referral fees" or "forwarding fees." *The Code and Rules do not regulate how lawyers divide legal fees within the same firm.*

The Code allows referral fees only if several conditions exist. First, the client consents to the employment of the other lawyer after "a full disclosure that a division of fees will be made." DR 2–107(A)(1). The Rules keep this restriction—though they use slightly different language, Rule 1.5(e)(1). The Rules also make clear that the client need not be told the share each lawyer will receive. The client must be told of the fact of a division but need not be told of the percentage of the fee each lawyer will receive. Rule 1.5, Comment 4.

Second, both the Rules and the Model Code also require that the total fee charged be reasonable. DR 2–107(A), (B).

It is with the third requirement—relating to the proportion of services performed—that the Rules and Code have significant differences. The Code requires that the division of fees be made "in proportion to the services performed *and* the responsibilities assumed by each." DR 2–107(A)(2) (emphasis added). If Lawyer # 1 referred a client to Lawyer # 2, whom Lawyer # 1 believed to be more competent, Lawyer # 2 could not therefore pay Lawyer # 1 a referral fee (e.g., one-third of Lawyer # 2's contingent fee) because the mere act of recommending Lawyer # 2 does not make Lawyer # 1 responsible for Lawyer # 2's actions. Also, the extent of Lawyer # 1's services was only to recommend Lawyer # 2.

Such restrictions do not give any financial incentive to Lawyer # 1 to refer the case to Lawyer # 2, even if referral is in the client's interest. Moreover, Lawyer # 1 can avoid the restrictions of DR 2–107(A)(2) by formally associating with Lawyer # 2. See DR 6–101(A)(1).

The Rules, in an effort to aid clients by encouraging referrals to other lawyers (see Rule 1.5, Comment 4), allow a division of fees if the client is advised and does not object to the participation of the lawyers involved, the total fee is reasonable, and the division is in "proportion to services performed by each lawyer *or*, by written agreement with the client, each lawyer assumes joint responsibility for the representation." Rule 1.5(e)(1) (emphasis added).

Many lawyers have objected to this change. See, e.g., National Law Jrl., (2/5/1979), at p. 18 (editorial). Oddly enough, the Rules on this point merely reinstate the rule existing under the old ABA Canons of Professional Ethics, Canon 37 (1908, as amended 1937), which allowed a division of fees with another lawyer "based upon a division of service *or* responsibility." (emphasis added).

The Rules do not specifically define "joint responsibility." According to Rule 1.5, Comment 4, it "entails," for that particular matter, the responsibility of a partner or supervisory lawyer as stated in Rule 5.1. The term "joint responsibility" should include more than that: to protect the client and to encourage referrals to competent attorneys, the assumption of joint responsibility should also require assumption of malpractice liability for the particular matter as if the lawyers were associated together. After all, that is what happens if a lawyer "associates" with another lawyer pursuant to DR 6–101(A)(1). "Entails" normally only means "include" or "involve." Thus Comment does not purport to state that Rule 5.1 supervision exhausts the meaning of the term "joint responsibility." As one commentator has noted: "The phrase 'joint responsibility' in the Rule is also susceptible to being read as a euphemism for assumption of joint and severable liability for legal malpractice purposes, as if the two lawyers were partners." C. Wolfram, Modern Legal Ethics 512 n. 9 (West, 1986). *Thus, a referral fee is proper under the Rules if Lawyer #1 assumes joint responsibility (i.e., malpractice liability and the supervisory responsibility imposed by Rule 5.1) with Lawyer #2 for the particular matter, the total fee is reasonable, and the Client is advised and does not object.*

V. ACCEPTING, DECLINING, AND TERMINATING REPRESENTATION

A. ACCEPTING AND DECLINING REPRESENTATION

The American lawyer, unlike the English barrister—or cab driver, bound to respond to the first hail—is not obligated to accept every client who walks through the door. But the lawyer may not reject a client because the client or the cause is unpopular. EC 2–27; Rule 6.2. See also 2–28, 2–29, 2–30. See generally Part IX, section III, infra. On the English "Taxicab Rule" for barristers, see W.W. Boulton, *A Guide to Conduct and Etiquette at the Bar of England and Wales* 17–33 (4th ed. 1965). This "Taxicab Rule" does not apply to solicitors.

A lawyer also may not accept a case if doing so will violate a disciplinary rule or other law, or if the lawyer cannot perform prompt and competent service. EC 2–30; Rule 1.16(a)(1), (2), Rule 1.16, Comment 1.

B. TERMINATING REPRESENTATION
1. Overriding Principles
The rules regarding withdrawal are more complex. One must first keep in mind several overriding principles.

First, if a matter is before a tribunal, the lawyer must follow that tribunal's rules, which typically require securing the tribunal's permission before withdrawing. If the tribunal does not grant permission, the lawyer must continue in the case even though the lawyer would otherwise have a right, or duty, to withdraw. DR 2–110(A)(1); Rule 1.16(c). If the tribunal asks the lawyer why he is seeking withdrawal, the lawyer's duty to keep client confidences may prevent the lawyer from responding. Rule 1.16, Comment 3. (However, the confidentiality rules do not prevent the attorney from filing a "notice of the fact of withdrawal" and withdrawing or disaffirming any opinion, document, affirmation, or the like. Rule 1.6, Comment 15. If the client discharges the lawyer and the tribunal does not permit the lawyer to withdraw, the lawyer must comply with the orders of the tribunal. Compare Rule 1.16(a) with Rule 1.16(c).

Second (assuming that the matter is not before a tribunal or that, if it is, the tribunal agrees), the client always "has a right to discharge a lawyer at any time, with or without cause, subject to liability for payment of the lawyer's services." Rule 1.16, Comment 4. In such a case, if the client fires the lawyer, the lawyer must withdraw. DR 2–110(B)(4); Rule 1.16(a)(3).

Agency law recognizes the concept of a "power coupled with an interest," such as the lender's power to sell the house when the mortgagor defaults. See, e.g., Sell on Agency § 229 (1975). But lawyers are not agents with a power coupled with an interest. No "lawyer can continue to represent a client who does not wish to be represented." ABA Informal Opinion 1397 (August 31, 1977). See also, Rule 1.16, Comment 4. Even a lawyer's contingent fee arrangement cannot be used to prevent the client from discharging the lawyer. Id. Cf. DR 5–103(A); Rule 1.8(j) (lawyer may not acquire a proprietary interest in client's cause of action). See *Richette v. Solomon,* 410 Pa. 6, 18–19, 187 A.2d 910, 917 (1963) (clause in retainer agreement prohibiting lawyer discharge is void).

Note: The power to discharge an attorney does not apply to cases controlled by other law, such as when a statute grants a term of office to a government attorney who cannot be fired except for cause. *Pillsbury v. Board of Chosen Freeholders of Monmouth*

County, 140 N.J.Super. 410, 356 A.2d 424 (1976) (per curiam), affirming, 133 N.J.Super. 526, 337 A.2d 632 (1975).

The client who discharges the lawyer is still liable for any fees earned, or for other contract or quasi-contract damages. See DR 2–110(A)(3); Rule 1.16(a)(3) and Comment 4. E.g., *Carlson v. Nopal Lines,* 460 F.2d 1209 (5th Cir. 1972). And the lawyer must return any fee advances not yet earned. DR 2–110(A)(3); Rule 1.16(d).

Third, the lawyer must make reasonable efforts to protect the client's interests, "such as giving reasonable notice to the client, surrendering papers and property to which the client is entitled. . . ." Rule 1.16(d). Accord DR 2–110(A)(2). This duty exists not only when the attorney resigns but also when he or she is discharged. E.g., *Dayton Bar Ass'n v. Weiner,* 40 Ohio St.2d 7, 317 N.E.2d 783 (1974), cert. denied, 420 U.S. 976, 95 S.Ct. 1400, 43 L.Ed.2d 656 (1975).

2. Mandatory and Permissive Withdrawal

Given these general principles, the Code and Rules divide withdrawal into two basic types—mandatory and permissive withdrawal. Both permissive and mandatory withdrawal are subject to the three overriding principles discussed above.

The lawyer must withdraw from a case if (1) continued employment would result in violating the disciplinary rules or other law; if (2) the lawyer's physical or mental condition results in a material adverse impact on the client; or (3) if the client discharges the attorney. DR 2–110(B); Rule 1.16(b).

The Rules provide that the lawyer may withdraw without any reason if doing so has no material adverse effect on the client. Rule 1.6(b). The Code has no such provision, but prior case law has recognized this right of an attorney, like any other agent. E.g., *Sterling v. Jones,* 255 La. 842, 846, 233 So.2d 537, 539 (1970). The Code does provide that the lawyer may withdraw if the lawyer and client freely assent to the termination. DR 2–110(C)(5).

The Code allows withdrawal if the client insists on presenting a frivolous claim; insists on pursuing an illegal course of conduct; insists that the lawyer violate the law or the disciplinary rules; makes it unreasonably difficult for the lawyer to perform effectively; insists (in a matter not in litigation) that the lawyer engage in conduct of which the lawyer disapproves; or refuses to pay the lawyer's fees or disbursements. DR 2–110(C)(1). The lawyer may also withdraw if continued employment is "likely" to result in violating a disciplinary rule; he is unable to work with co-counsel; his physical or mental condition make it difficult for him to continue; or he believes in good faith that the tribunal (in a matter before it) will find another good cause justifying withdrawal. DR 2–110(C) (2).

The Rules differ more in detail than in focus. Subject also to the three overriding principles discussed above, they permit withdrawal (even if it causes material adverse impact to the client) if the client: persists in using the lawyer's services in an action that the lawyer reasonably believes is a crime of fraud; has used the lawyer to perpetrate a crime or fraud; insists on conduct the lawyer believes is repugnant or imprudent; fails substantially to fulfill an obligation to the lawyer and the client has been warned; or has made representation unreasonably difficult. Rule 1.16(b)(1)–(5).

The Rules add a catch-all—when "other good cause" exists. This catch-all is not limited to cases where the *tribunal* finds good cause. Compare DR 2–110(C)(6) with Rule 1.16(b)(6). The Rules also add an entirely new reason: when "the representation will result in an unreasonable financial burden on the lawyer . . ." Rule 1.16(b)(5).

VI. TRUST FUND ACCOUNTS

A. ESTABLISHING TRUST FUND ACCOUNTS
Lawyers must be careful not to commingle a client's funds with the lawyer's own funds. The lawyer must hold client property as a fiduciary.

1. What Must Be Kept in Trust
The requirements of the Code and the Rules are substantially similar, but there are some interesting differences in detail. Under both provisions, the lawyer must keep separate, identifiable accounts of client funds. The law firm may not commingle the firm's (or lawyer's) own funds with these client funds. DR 9–102(A); Rule 1.15(a). For example, a law firm must not pay its debts by drawing a check on a client's trust fund account. The firm first should withdraw from that account any amount to which it is entitled. The firm then should place that amount in the firm's own account and draw a check on its own account. See, *Matter of Rabb*, 73 N.J. 272, 374 A.2d 461 (1977). The lawyer may not even temporarily borrow client funds. Such borrowing is really conversion.

Note: The trust fund rule prohibits commingling client funds with the lawyer's funds. The client's funds must be segregated from the lawyer's funds. There is no prohibition against the lawyer keeping one client's funds with one or more other clients' funds in one trust account so long as careful records of each client's interests are kept. However, "[s]eparate trust accounts may be warranted when administering estate monies or acting in similar fiduciary capacities." Rule 1.15, Comment 1. See also, Attorney Grievance Commission v. Boehm, 293 Md. 476, 446 A.2d 52, 53 n. 2 (1982).

The bank account should be maintained in the state where the law office is, unless the client consents to a different place. Also, the law firm must identify other client property as such, and safeguard it appropriately. DR 9–102(B)(2); Rule 1.15(a).

Example: Client gives Lawyer bearer bonds for safe-keeping while Client is in Europe on an extended vacation. Lawyer places these bonds in the office safe, but does not identify them as belonging to Client. Lawyer has committed a disciplinable violation.

The Rules apply these trust fund rules to property of third persons, who are not clients, when the property is in the lawyer's possession in connection with the representation of a client. Rule 1.15(a). This particular provision follows present practice. E.g., *Matter of Lurie,* 113 Ariz. 95, 546 P.2d 1126 (1976).

The Code *exempts* from the trust fund requirement any client funds paid as *advances for costs and expenses.* DR 9–102(A). There is no policy justification offered to support this exception, and the Rules do not continue it.

The Rules do *not* apply the trust fund rule to prepaid legal fees. (See Reporter's "Legal Background" to Rule 1.15 reprinted in T. Morgan & R. Rotunda, 1983 Selected Standards Supplement 210 (1983)). The rationale is that these unearned fees are not client funds; they are the lawyer's funds. The lawyer should deposit his funds in his own account. When the lawyer completes his services, he must return all prepaid fees that have not been earned, see Rule 1.16(d), but there is no requirement that, in the interim, these prepaid fees be separately maintained. The Code is unclear as to the status of prepaid, unearned legal fees, and the states differ, with some requiring trust fund treatment and some not. See, Note, *Attorney Misappropriation of Client Funds: A Study in Professional Responsibility,* 10 U.Mich.J. of L.Reform 415, 436 n. 135 (1977).

The lawyer must maintain "complete records" of all client property and "render appropriate accounts to his client regarding them." DR 9–102(B) (3). Rule 1.15(a), (b). The Rules add a requirement that these records be kept for a given number of years (the Rules recommend five years) after the legal representation has ended. Rule 1.15(a).

When the lawyer receives funds belonging in a trust fund account, the lawyer must promptly notify the client, DR 9–102(B)(1), or third party. Rule 1.15(b). The lawyer must then "promptly pay or deliver" to the client any trust funds or property that the client requests and to which the client is entitled. DR 9–102(B)(4).

Note: The Model Rules do not explicitly adopt the requirement of a "request" by a client or third party. See Rule 1.15(b).

2. Disputes Regarding Trust Fund Property

Occasionally the client and lawyer may have a dispute regarding trust fund property. For example, the settlement check for $90,000 may be deposited in the client account, and the lawyer would like to withdraw the agreed upon fee of one-third plus the amount to cover disbursements. But the client may claim that less than a third is due the lawyer, perhaps because of a dispute regarding whether one-third was reasonable under the circumstances, or because of a disagreement over disbursements.

The Rules and Code are in agreement that the lawyer may not withdraw the *disputed portion* until the dispute is resolved. DR 9–102(A)(2). Rule 1.15(c). The undisputed portion should be distributed; the lawyer may withdraw the undisputed portion of the funds from the trust fund account "when due." DR 9–102(A)(2). Rule 1.15(b). See also, Rule 1.15, Comment 2: "The undisputed portion of the funds shall be promptly distributed." The lawyer may not, in an effort to coerce the client to give up his claim, refuse to deliver to the client the money that is undisputedly the client's.

3. Audits of Trust Fund Accounts

Neither the Code nor the Rules require any spot or systematic auditing by the bar authorities of client trust funds.

Note: The ABA, in its Model Standards for Lawyer Discipline and Disability Proceedings recommended that bar discipline counsel should have "ready access" to records of the location and number of client trust fund accounts held by all of the lawyers in the state. Standard 3.11(i). However, bar counsel (the ABA recommended) should be able to verify the accuracy of these accounts only if there is "probable cause" that the funds have not been maintained properly or have been mishandled. Standard 13.3.

Notwithstanding the ABA's reluctance to require auditing, some states require spot checks. See Carpenter, *The Negligent Attorney Embezzler: Delaware's Solution,* 61 A.B.A.J. 338 (1975). Some Canadian provinces require accounting certificates of trust fund accounts. Id. at 339. Some commentators have proposed that all attorneys be bonded.

4. Interest Earned on Client Funds

Any interest earned on client trust fund accounts does not belong to the lawyer.

Neither the Code nor the Rules specifically deal with the question of the investment of client trust fund accounts. Usually, the funds are held for such a short time that the funds are kept in non-interest-bearing bank accounts. The administrative difficulty of apportioning to each of the clients their share of interest in a multi-client account with other clients' funds encourages non-interest bearing accounts. Although, with modern computers, the assumed burden imposed by administrative difficulty may be a thing of the past.

Normally a lawyer would be under no duty to invest client funds because he is usually keeping these funds in his capacity as a safeguarder, not an investor. However, in some cases the large amount of money and length of time involved may require the lawyer to secure from the client instructions regarding investments. ABA Formal Opinion 348 (July 23, 1982).

If funds are invested, the interest earned (whether small or large in amount) on the client's property belongs to the client, not to the lawyer. ABA Formal Opinion 348 (July 23, 1982). The original 1908 Canons of Professional Ethics made this point quite clearly. See Canon 11: Client funds should not "be commingled with [the lawyer's] own *or be used by him*" (emphasis added). Nor may the lawyer use interest earned to defray the expense of handling the agency account. ABA Informal Opinion 991 (July 3, 1967). However, the attorney may always bill the client separately for disbursements.

In recent years, the organized bar has created an exception to these basic rules. The organized bar has tried to collect, for its use, the interest from the pool of trust fund accounts. The bar would use this otherwise untapped resource to fund law-related public service projects such as indigent legal services. The nominal interest from many small accounts can quickly add up. The Law Foundation of British Columbia receives interest on Lawyer's trust fund accounts, and by 1976, interest income totalled over $2 million a year. See *In re Interest on Trust Accounts,* 356 So.2d 799, 804 (Fla. 1978).

In ABA Formal Opinion 348 (July 23, 1982), the ABA ruled that the Model Code does not stand in the way of such programs. Even without prior client consent or notice, the "interest earned on bank accounts in which are deposited client's funds, nominal in amount or to be held for short periods of time, under state-authorized programs providing for the interest to be paid to tax-exempt organizations" is not treated as funds of the client within the meaning of DR 9–102.

B. CLIENT SECURITY FUNDS

Some states have established client security trust funds in order to offer some protection to clients whose attorneys had misappropriated their money. These funds are typically funded by periodic assessments on the members of the bar.

Neither the Code nor the Rules require the establishment of such funds, but both urge the individual lawyers to participate in this effort of reimbursement. EC 9–7; Rule 1.15, Comment 5.

VII. REVIEW QUESTIONS

1. Lawyer represented Client in a lawsuit completed over a decade ago. Lawyer has not represented Client since. Plaintiff, who was not involved in the prior litigation with Client, seeks to retain Lawyer to sue Client in another matter that is distinct from the prior litigation, but ancillary to it, and involves in part the same facts and circumstances, some of which are confidential.

   It is *proper* for Lawyer to:

   a. Decline to represent Plaintiff.

   b. Refer the matter to his law partner, who was not involved in the prior litigation and who became associated with Lawyer only a year ago.

   c. Accept the representation after notifying Plaintiff and notifying Client.

   d. Refer the matter to Zeta, a lawyer in another firm, in exchange for a secret kickback of 10% of the fee that Zeta will charge Plaintiff.

2. Lawyer represents Plaintiff in a personal injury action. After successful negotiations, the case is settled. Defendant sends Lawyer a check for $30,000 payable to the order of Lawyer. One third of this amount represents Lawyer's undisputed fee. Consistent with Lawyer's ethical obligations, what may Lawyer do?

   I. Deposit the check in Plaintiff's trust fund account, inform Plaintiff, and forward a $20,000 check drawn on that account to Plaintiff.

   II. Deposit the check in Lawyer's personal bank account and send to Plaintiff Lawyer's personal check for $20,000.

III. Send the check directly to Plaintiff after having endorsed it, and then ask Client to pay the fee.

    a.   I & II only.

    b.   I & III only.

    c.   I, II, & III.

    d.   III only.

    e.   I only.

3. The same facts as Question 2. Who may keep any interest earned on the funds in the client's trust fund account?

    a.   The lawyer.

    b.   The client.

4. Plaintiff has hired Lawyer to represent him in a lawsuit against Defendant, who in turn has filed a counterclaim against Plaintiff. A great deal of personal hatred has developed over the years between Plaintiff and Defendant, so Plaintiff orders Lawyer to pursue a hard line in the suit against Defendant. "I shall not settle," he says. "And I shall show him no mercy. I want to teach him a lesson."

Assuming that the lawsuit is not frivolous, Lawyer plans:

I. to refuse to accede to Defendant's reasonable request for a continuance because Client refuses to consent.

II. to refuse to waive Client's affirmative defense to Defendant's counterclaim because Client refuses to consent.

    a.   Neither I nor II are *proper.*

    b.   Only II is *proper.*

    c.   Only I is *proper.*

    d.   Both I and II are *proper.*

5. Williams is one of over 200 victims of an airline disaster case. The carrier has admitted liability and the only question remaining is the amount of damages. A few similar cases have already gone to trial with jury verdicts returned between $225,000 and $250,000 per victim. Williams asked Attorney to represent her in settlement negotiations with the carrier, which has announced that it will settle cases similar to Williams' for $235,000, a figure that is satisfactory to Williams. Therefore Williams asks Attorney to work for a reasonable hourly fee. She believes that Attorney's role will be primarily formal. Attorney, however, wants a standard one-third contingent fee.

If Williams eventually agrees to Attorney's condition, was it *proper* for Attorney to insist upon a one-third contingent fee as a condition to taking the case?

a. Yes, because Williams did not have to agree to the fee but could have selected another lawyer.

b. No, unless a one-third contingent fee is customary in accident cases in the area where Attorney practices.

c. No, if under the circumstances, an hourly fee would have been more advantageous to Williams.

d. Yes, because a successful prosecution of the claim produces a *res* out of which the fee can be paid.

6. John Doe requested that Attorney defend him in a murder charge. Attorney told Doe that he usually restricted his practice to civil matters, so he gave Doe the names of three good criminal lawyers. As Doe was leaving, and in an effort to persuade Attorney to reconsider his decision, he told Attorney the facts leading to his arrest, including an admission that he shot the deceased. Doe then asked Attorney what his reactions were. Attorney briefly discussed temporary insanity as a defense. Attorney still refused to take the case. Doe subsequently hired another lawyer. Attorney did not charge Doe any fee.

The prosecutor learned of Doe's conversation with Attorney and has subpoenaed Attorney to appear as a witness in Doe's trial.

Is it *proper* for Attorney to testify that Doe admitted shooting the deceased?

a. Yes, because Attorney–Client relationship was never formed between Doe and Attorney.

b. Yes, because an Attorney did not charge Doe any fee.

c. No, because a lawyer may not disclose the confidence or secrets of a prospective client.

d.   Yes, because Attorney told Doe that Attorney did not usually handle criminal matters.

e.   No, because Attorney's testimony would be hearsay.

7. Attorney was an assistant state's attorney at the time the case of *State v. Criminal* was awaiting trial. The state Public Defender represented Criminal. Attorney could have obtained access to the file in that case but did not. Attorney, in fact, did not participate at all in this matter except once, when Public Defender moved for a continuance, and Attorney consented.

Attorney subsequently left that employment and now practices in a private law firm. Criminal has asked Attorney to represent him on the appeal from his criminal conviction in the case of *State v. Criminal.* Is it *proper* for Attorney to represent Criminal on the appeal?

a.   No, because Attorney had appeared on behalf of the prosecutor in the matter.

b.   No, because Attorney is now, in effect, suing his former employer.

c.   Yes, unless Attorney acquired confidential information concerning the case while in the prosecutor's office.

d.   Yes, because Attorney had no substantial responsibility in the matter while in the prosecutor's office.

e.   Both *c* and *d.*

8. Adam Advocate represents 22 plaintiffs who were victims of the same bus accident. He has negotiated with the bus company and the engine manufacturer a settlement that he reasonably believes is beneficial to all of the plaintiffs. Each plaintiff will receive between $35,000 and $250,000 in damages, the amount received being a function of the damages sustained. The defendants have stated quite clearly that they will not settle any of the 22 claims unless all 22 are settled. Adam is worried that if he reveals all of the details of the settlement to each of the 22 plaintiffs, there is a danger that the entire settlement will be upset.

If Adam reveals the entire settlement details to each of the 22 participants, is he *subject to discipline*?

a.   No, but he would be engaged in a violation of his ethical aspirations.

b.   Yes, because to do so might upset the entire settlement.

c.   Yes, because he would violate client secrets.

d. No, because unless he advises each of the individuals of the participation of each person in the settlement, they cannot provide informed consent.

9. Larry Lawyer engages extensively in counseling and advising clients with respect to tax matters and transactions that are largely tax-motivated. If the client-taxpayer's treatment of the transaction is not challenged by the Internal Revenue Service or if any challenge by the IRS is not sustained either on IRS review or by the courts, the transaction may result in a substantial reduction in taxes to the client. If, on the other hand, the transaction is not sustained, the taxpayer will at least be required to pay the tax he had hoped to avoid plus an interest and possibly a negligence penalty.

In advising a client on such a transaction with doubtful consequences, consider the following fee arrangements, none of which involve a criminal case:

I. Larry Lawyer and Client agree that the client will be charged a fixed fee, which includes not only the planning of the transaction but also covers representation of the client in the event the client's return is selected for audit, both before the Internal Revenue Service and in possible litigation before the Tax Court. If either the audit or the Tax Court litigation did not ensue, the lawyer would still keep the fee.

II. Larry Lawyer and Client agree on a contingent fee where Larry Lawyer is only to be paid if he accomplishes a tax saving for the client.

III. Larry Lawyer and Client agree on a fixed fee coupled with a contingency on the outcome of the case providing it is also understood that the fixed fee applies irrespective of the outcome and that the contingency applies only to the tax saving effected.

IV. Larry Lawyer and Client agree that Client will be charged for the legal services on an hourly basis.

Is Larry Lawyer *subject to discipline* for any of these fee arrangements, assuming that the fee is not "clearly excessive?"

a. Yes, as to I, II, & IV.

b. I only.

c. II only.

d. III only.

e. IV only.

f. I, II, III, & IV are all permitted.

10. In a city of 200,000 Attorney Alpha represents Client Adams in the purchase of a residence. The representation was commenced in August and will continue until December, producing a fee of $300. In October, Client Brewer comes to Alpha and wishes to bring a $200,000 personal injury case against Client Adams on a contingent fee basis. (The statute of limitations of the claim runs in November). Under the *disciplinary rules:*

   a. Alpha should have another lawyer in his office handle the personal injury claim.

   b. Alpha should transfer Brewer to another law firm but may claim a referral fee of ⅓ of the net fee, even if Brewer does not know of the referral fee.

   c. Alpha may accept Brewer's case, if he makes a full disclosure to Brewer and Brewer consents.

   d. Alpha may ethically represent Brewer, but for practical reasons should not do so.

   e. Alpha cannot represent Brewer.

11. Which of the following "fee schedules" are permitted after *Goldfarb v. Virginia State Bar*?

   I. The state legislature sets a fee of 5% of the gross estate in probate cases.

   II. The state Supreme Court sets a fee ranging from 10% to 20% in personal injury cases.

   III. The local, voluntary bar mandates a minimum fee of $150 for an uncontested divorce.

   IV. The state voluntary bar surveys every member of its association, and reports that in one downstate county, lawyers charge from $175 to $295 for an uncontested adoption.

      a. Neither I, II, III, nor IV.

      b. Only I & II.

      c. Only I, II & IV.

      d. All are permitted.

PART FOUR

THE LAWYER'S OBLIGATION AS A MEMBER OF A FIRM

Analysis

I. INTRODUCTION

Part 5 of the Rules has a specific section dealing with "Law Firms and Associations." Many of these provisions have no explicit counterpart in the Code. For the most part, however, Part 5 of the Rules does not change the law. Rather, it recodifies and amplifies provisions found in scattered sections of the Code and elaborates on topics already implicit in the law of agency and tort.

II. SUPERVISORY RESPONSIBILITY OVER OTHER LAWYERS OR NONLAWYER EMPLOYEES

A. LAWYERS

The partners in a law firm have the duty to make reasonable efforts to assure that all of the lawyers in the firm comply with the ethics rules. Rule 5.1(a). Cf. DR 4–101(D); EC 4–5. This duty similarly applies to other lawyers with general supervisory powers, such as the head of a corporate law department, the head of a government agency, or the shareholders of a professional legal corporation. Rule 5.1, Comment 1. The Rules do not specify what are the appropriate procedural safeguards. Whether the measures are reasonable depends on all the facts and the measures may vary depending on the size of the firm. Rule 5.1, Comment 2.

Even if a lawyer is not a partner or other general supervisor, he or she may have direct supervisory authority over another lawyer. Rule 5.1(b). For example, a senior associate may have some authority over a junior associate. Such a supervisor has the same responsibility as a partner or manager to assure compliance with the ethical rules by those lawyers under her direct supervisory authority. Rule 5.1(b). While the partner's or general manager's responsibilities relate to *all* lawyers in the firm, the supervisory lawyer's responsibilities relate only to those lawyers under her direct supervisory authority. Rule 5.1(b).

Finally, as a general principle, a lawyer may not knowingly assist another to violate the ethics rules or to violate those rules through the acts of another. Rule 8.4(a); DR 1–102(A)(2). Consequently, a lawyer is responsible for another lawyer's ethics violation if the first lawyer orders the second to engage in misconduct, or knowingly ratifies the second lawyer's misconduct. Rule 5.1(c) (1). The supervisory lawyer is also responsible for the other lawyer's ethical misconduct if the supervisory lawyer fails to take reasonable remedial action to avoid or mitigate the misconduct. Rule 5.1(c)(2). Cf. DR 1–103(A). For example, "if a supervisory lawyer knows that a subordinate misrepresented a matter to an opposing party in negotiation, the supervisor as well as the subordinate has a duty to correct the resulting misapprehension." Rule 5.1, Comment 4.

Wrongful Discharge. In recent years attorneys who have been fired by their clients or their law firm for refusal to engage in unethical activity have brought wrongful discharge suits, even though they are employees at will. The courts have split on this issue, but the trend appears to favor such a cause of action. See, Wilbur, *Wrongful Discharge of Attorneys: A Cause of Action to Further Professional Responsibility*, 92 Dick. L.Rev. 777 (1988). The fact that a client or a law firm has the right to fire an attorney for no reason does not imply a right to fire for the wrong reason. Of course, because clients can always fire their counsel at any time, with or without cause (Rule 1.16, Comment 4) the remedy for wrongful discharge would not be reinstatement but damages.

Comparing Tort and Ethical Liability. One should keep in mind the distinction between Rule 5.1 and tort liability, as well as the distinction, within Rule 5.1, between the failure to supervise and the ordering or ratifying of unethical conduct.

Example 1:   Lawyer *A* is the supervisor of Lawyer *B*. Neither the firm nor Lawyer *A* exercises any care to assure that Lawyer *B* will protect client confidences. Nonetheless, Lawyer *B* in fact has not violated any confidences. Lawyer *A* has violated Rule 5.1(b), but not Rule 5.1(c). Lawyer *A* is also not liable to the client in tort, because there are no damages.

Example 2:   Assume, in the above example, that Lawyer *A* does exercise reasonable supervisory care over Lawyer *B*, but Lawyer *B* nonetheless violates a client's confidences, causing the client monetary damage. Lawyer *A* has not violated Rule 5.1(b) or 5.1(c), but is liable in tort under a theory of vicarious liability.

Example 3:   Assume, in Example 2, that Lawyer *A* discovers Lawyer *B*'s breach of confidence in time to prevent it, but Lawyer *A* acts unreasonably and fails to take any remedial action. Lawyer *A* has not violated Rule 5.1(b) but has violated Rule 5.1(c)(2), and is also liable in tort, under a theory of vicarious liability.

B.   NONLAWYER EMPLOYEES
A lawyer's responsibility over nonlawyer employees parallels that over subordinate lawyers. See Rule 5.3. Cf. DR 4–101(D); EC 4–5; DR 7–107(J).

III. RESPONSIBILITY OF A LAWYER SUBJECT TO SUPERVISION BY ANOTHER LAWYER

A lawyer cannot escape responsibility for ethical misconduct merely by claiming that he followed orders. Rule 5.2(a). See also, e.g., *In re Knight,* 129 Vt. 428, 430, 281

A.2d 46, 48 (1971) (per curiam) ("inexperienced attorney" under "domination" of experienced practitioner suspended for ethical violation; he could not "assign to another his duty to his oath").

On the other hand, if the ethical violation is not clear, the subordinate lawyer may defer to the judgment of the supervisory attorney. The subordinate does not violate his ethical duties if he follows the supervisor's "reasonable resolution of an arguable question of professional duty." Rule 5.2(b). Cf. Rule 1.13(b)(2) (in resolving ethical problem, lawyer for organization may advise that outside counsel supply separate legal opinion). See Rotunda, *Law, Lawyers and Managers,* in, The Ethics of Corporate Conduct 135–36 (C. Walton, ed. 1977).

IV. SHARING FEES AND RESPONSIBILITY WITH LAYPEOPLE

A. SHARING FEES

The general rule is that a lawyer or law firm cannot "share legal fees with a nonlawyer. . . ." Rule 5.4(a); DR 3–102(A). However, several significant limitations swallow much of the prohibition.

One important exception allows lawyers to include nonlawyer employees in a compensation or retirement plan "even though the plan is based in whole or in part on a profit-sharing arrangement." DR 3–102(A)(3); Rule 5.4(a)(3).

> *Example:* At the end of the year Law Firm gives each secretary a bonus because the firm just settled a significant case on very favorable terms. The firm's actions do not constitute a prohibited sharing of fees.

In addition, a law firm may agree to pay money to the estate of a deceased lawyer (or to other specified persons) for a reasonable period of time after the lawyer's death. Rule 5.4(a)(1); DR 3–102(A)(2).

More importantly, the Model Rules (since 1990) allow a lawyer to sell her law practice to another lawyer. Rule 1.17. To conform to that principle, the ABA added Rule 5.4(a)(2), which provides that if a lawyer (e.g., Lawyer A) purchases the law practice of "a deceased, disabled, or disappeared lawyer," (e.g., Lawyer B), then Lawyer A may agree to pay the purchase price to the estate or other representative of Lawyer B. The sale of a law practice is discussed at the end of this chapter, at section VI, B, below.

> *Note:* If a lawyer retires from a law firm, the restrictions of Rule 5.4(a)(1) & (a)(2) and DR 3–102(A)(1) & (A)(2) are inapplicable. The deceased lawyer obviously cannot exercise any continuing oversight or be available for consultation regarding the legal matters. A retired lawyer, however, can. Thus, these rules do not apply to sharing fees

with *lawyers*, a topic governed elsewhere. See DR 2–107(B); DR 2–108(A); Rule 1.5(e); Rule 5.6(a). See Part III, Section IV, C, *supra*, regarding sharing fees with lawyers.

B. SHARING RESPONSIBILITY

Although lawyers may include lay employees in a profit-sharing arrangement, the lawyer may not give these people managerial control. Thus, lay people cannot be partners in law firms. See, e.g., Rule 5.4(b): "A lawyer shall not form a partnership with a nonlawyer if any of the activities of the partnership consist of the practice of law." Accord, DR 3–103(A). Perhaps some day the Model Rules will change, and Sears will be allowed to own a law firm. It is interesting to note that on January 1, 1991, Washington, D.C. became the first jurisdiction to amend its Rule 5.4(b) and allow nonlawyers to become partners in law firms, subject to various conditions (the effect of which is to prohibit Sears from owning a law firm).

Similarly, if the lawyer is practicing law in the form of a professional legal corporation, no lay person may be a director or officer, or control the lawyer's legal judgment, or own any financial interest (except that a deceased lawyer's fiduciary representative may hold the lawyer's interest for a reasonable period of time during the administration of the estate). Rule 5.4(d); DR 5–107(C).

If someone other than the client pays for the client's legal services, the lawyer's obligations are still to the client. The lawyer may not allow the third party (who is paying for the services or who recommended the lawyer) to interfere with the lawyer's professional judgment. Rule 5.4(c); DR 5–107(B). Cf. Rule 1.8(f).

C. ANCILLARY BUSINESSES

Someday, Sears may be able to own a law firm. In the meantime, may a law firm own and operate a department store? May it own an ancillary business, such as patent consulting? In August of 1991, the ABA House of Delegates narrowly approved a new rule to deal with this question, Model Rule 5.7, "Provision of Ancillary Services."

Ancillary Services are non-legal services that relate to the practice of law, such as title insurance, trust services, and patent consulting. Rule 5.7, Comment 1. Also, "a presumption that a service is 'ancillary to the practice of law' should exist if the service is normally provided by nonlawyers in discrete professions or occupations, e.g., doctors, architects, engineers, real estate brokers, investment bankers or financial consultants." Comment 8. Services such as owning a restaurant, or providing copying services incidental to the practice of law are not considered non-legal ancillary services because "they do not pose serious ethical problems in the lawyer client relationship . . . ." Comment 7. Lawyers may also have a passive financial interest in a separate entity that provides non-legal ancillary services, such as an investment banking firm, so long as the interest "is not a controlling one." Comment 9.

Various law firms, particularly in the Washington, D.C. area, have created subsidiaries to perform these services. Customers may include clients and nonclients. The existence of such subsidiaries raises various ethical issues mainly relating to conflicts of interest and attorney-client privilege. In Rule 5.7 the ABA attempts to restrict the growth of such businesses by making it unethical for law firms to offer non-legal services to customers who are not also clients of the law firm. The ancillary services must be "incidental to, in connection with and concurrent to" the law firm's provision of legal services to its clients; the services must be provided by employees of the law firm, and not by a subsidiary of the law firm; and the law firm must disclose in writing to the clients the firm's interest in providers of the ancillary services and inherent potential conflicts. Rule 5.7(b) & Comment 15. In "appropriate circumstances," the firm should recommend that the client seek the advice of independent counsel or independent providers of non-legal services. Comment 15.

It is unclear the extent to which jurisdictions will adopt this proposed rule, given its broad prohibitions. It may be that some jurisdictions will be content to rely on existing Rule 1.8(a), which already governs business transactions with a client.

V. UNAUTHORIZED PRACTICE OF LAW

What constitutes the unauthorized practice of law is a matter of state law. The Model Code and Model Rules merely incorporate by reference these local rules, and provide that if a lawyer violates state law regarding unauthorized practice, that violation is also disciplinable. DR 3–101(A); Rule 5.5. See also EC 3–5; Rule 5.5, Comment 1.

Typically state laws provide that it is a defense to a lawsuit for the payment of fees that the party seeking fees engaged in the unauthorized practice of law. The unauthorized practice of law may also be a criminal violation. For example, in June, 1991, a paralegal in Green Bay, Wisconsin, was sentenced to nine months in jail for helping people file petitions in federal bankruptcy court in Madison. He was released on probation after 30 days. Wall St.Jrl., Aug. 28, 1991, at B4, col. 6 (midwest ed.).

The state law definitions of unauthorized practice are varied and often confused. See Rhode, *Policing the Professional Monopoly: A Constitutional and Empirical Analysis of Unauthorized Practice Prohibitions*, 34 Stan.L.Rev. 1 (1981). And, to some extent unauthorized practice rules can represent guild rules, efforts to protect a cartel and prevent reform that might lead to competition from nonlawyers. The late Professor Arthur Sutherland once remarked that one "can scarcely imagine a speaker at a meeting of a county medical society discussing the possible elimination of some disease by public health measures, and then qualifying his observations by the statement that many practitioners make a living out of treating the disease in question; and that unless the physicians are vigilant to prevent the adoption of such measures, this source of business will be taken from them. Yet speakers at bar association meetings are frequently heard to make similar observations about the effects of proposed reforms." Quoted in, M. Mayer, *The Lawyers* 28 (1967).

In general it may be said that a person practices law when he *applies the law to the facts of a particular case.* "Functionally, the practice of law relates to the rendition of service for others that call for the professional judgment of a lawyer. The essence of the professional judgment of the lawyer is his educated ability to relate the general body of and philosophy of law to a specified legal problem of a client. . . ." EC 3–5. See, e.g., *State v. Winder,* 42 A.D.2d 1039, 348 N.Y.S.2d 270 (1973) (no unauthorized practice in distribution of do-it-yourself divorce kits with forms and instructions because kit did not contain personalized advice applied to a particular person).

Thus, if a police officer tells you that the speed limit is 55 m.p.h., or the court clerk tells you that reply briefs should be printed on blue-backed paper, these people use the law, but they are not practicing the law. EC 3–5. If a lawyer instructs these people (or similar people, such as a claims adjuster) in the law, the lawyer is not normally engaging in the unauthorized practice of law because these people, the recipients of the lawyers' aid, do not practice law.

The lawyer may delegate various tasks to secretaries, law clerks, or paralegals, and, so long as the lawyer supervises the delegated work and is responsible for it, there is no unauthorized practice. EC 3–6; Rule 5.5, Comment 1.

The rule against unauthorized practice only applies to a person seeking to represent another. A lay person may represent himself, even if doing so requires that the lay person appear in court and otherwise practice law. EC 3–7. In fact, in criminal cases defendants have a constitutional right to defend themselves. *Faretta v. California,* 422 U.S. 806, 95 S.Ct. 2525, 45 L.Ed.2d 562 (1975).

If a lay person wishes to proceed *pro se,* a lawyer may assist him. This assistance does not violate the rule against aiding a lay person in the unauthorized practice of law because the lay person, while practicing law, is not engaged in the *unauthorized* practice of law. A nonlawyer may represent himself. Rule 5.5, Comment 1.

While an individual may represent himself, the typical rule is that corporations may not appear *pro se.* Because a corporation is a separate legal entity, this incorporeal entity can only appear through others. These others must be lawyers if the representation involves the practice of law. E.g., *Simbraw, Inc. v. United States,* 367 F.2d 373 (3d Cir. 1966) (per curiam).

The fact that a person is a graduate of a law school does not make him authorized to practice law unless he is admitted to the bar of the relevant jurisdiction. "Authority to engage in the practice of law conferred in any jurisdiction is not per se a grant of the right to practice elsewhere, and it is improper for a lawyer to engage in practice where he is not permitted by law or by court order to do so." EC 3–9. See DR 3–101(B); Rule 5.5(a).

The Code encourages members of the bar, as well as the organized bar itself, to remove unnecessary restrictions on interstate practice. See EC 3–9. Accord, EC 8–3. The Rules, interestingly, do not have any corresponding exhortation in favor of removing needless barriers to entry.

VI. AGREEMENTS TO RESTRICT THE RIGHT TO PRACTICE LAW

A. RESTRICTIVE COVENANTS

Both the Code and Rules prohibit a law firm from requiring (or a lawyer agreeing to accept) an employment contract restricting a lawyer's right to practice law after termination of the relationship created by the agreement. However, such a requirement may be imposed as a condition to the payment of retirement benefits. DR 2–108(A); Rule 5.6(a).

Such restrictive covenants violate the discipline rules even if they are limited to a stated period and geographic area. ABA Formal Opinion 300 (Aug. 7, 1961). Moreover, courts do not enforce such agreements. *Cohen v. Lord, Day & Lord,* 75 N.Y.2d 95, 551 N.Y.S.2d 157, 550 N.E.2d 410 (1989)(law firm partnership agreement that conditions payment of earned but uncollected partnership revenues upon a withdrawing partner's obligation to refrain from the practice of law in competition with the former law firm restricts the practice of law in violation of New York's DR 2–108(A) "and is unenforceable in these circumstances as against public policy.").

Similarly, lawyers may not restrict this right to practice as part of the settlement of a client's controversy. DR 2–108(B); Rule 5.6(b). Clients always have a right to discharge their lawyers at any time and hire new counsel. (See Part III, Section V.) If lawyers were forced to (or forced others to) agree to restrictive covenants, then there would be restraints not only on the lawyer's professional autonomy but also on the client's freedom to choose a lawyer. Rule 5.6, Comment 1.

Rule 5.6 is virtually identical to DR 2–108, which in turn reflects pre-Code authority. See, e.g., ABA Formal Opinion 300 (Aug. 7, 1961). Some lawyers have vigorously attacked Rule 5.6 without appreciating its very traditional origins. See Jackson & Atlas, *The Ethics of Stealing Clients,* 69 A.B.A.J. 706, 707 (1983) ("Firms are being bled and even destroyed [but Rule 5.6 does] nothing to protect the attorney who has built a law practice.").

B. SALE OF LAW PRACTICE

The Model Code prohibits a lawyer from "selling" the law practice (EC 4–6) because, it is said that "clients are not merchandise." ABA Formal Opinion 266 (June 2, 1945). However, the Code does not concern itself with division of fees among lawyers within the same firm. DR 2–107. Thus, a firm could always add another lawyer as a partner in the firm, and have that new partner purchase equity in the firm. This equity typically includes not only cost of physical assets like law books and desks, but also "good will," that is, the expectation of continued business. Thus, under the Model Code there was a disparity of treatment between the sole practitioners, who were forbidden from selling "good will." Cf. *O'Hara v. Ahlgren, Blumenfeld & Kempster,* 127 Ill.2d 333, 130 Ill.Dec. 401, 537 N.E.2d 730 (1989), holding that a sole practitioner may not sell good will.

California responded to such concerns by adopting a new rule allowing for the sale of a law practice by a living or deceased lawyer. Rule 2–300, California Rules of Professional Conduct (operative on May 27, 1989). The California State Bar urged the ABA to adopt a similar rule, and it did so in February, 1990, when it added Rule 1.17, "Sale of Law Practice."

Comment 1 to Rule 1.17 reaffirms that "[c]lients are not commodities that can be purchased and sold at will." However, the remainder of that Comment, and the ones that follow, explain the proper way to sell the law practice as a going concern. The Rule imposes various restrictions.

First, the seller must cease to engage in the practice of law in the jurisdiction (or a particular geographic area) [the state court adopting Rule 1.17 is to choose one of these alternatives], unless the seller returns to private practice because of unanticipated circumstances Rule 1.17 & Comment 1. In addition, a seller who becomes in-house counsel, or works for the Government, or a legal services entity is not considered to be returning to private practice. Comment 2.

Second, the seller must sell the entire practice to a single purchaser (subject to client consent, and assuming that there is no disqualifying conflict). The reason this rule prohibits piecemeal sale of a practice is to protects clients "whose matters are less lucrative and who might find it difficult to secure other counsel if the sale could be limited to substantial fee-generating matters." Comment 5. It is ironic that the ABA, which has objected to "too much litigation" [see, Rotunda, *Lawyers and Professionalism: A Commentary on the Report of the American Bar Association Commission on Professionalism,* 18 Loyola U. of Chicago L.Rev. 1149, 1159 (1987)] drafted Rule 1.17 so that it forces the purchaser to subsidize those clients with the less lucrative cases, including clients with cases that the purchaser candidly evaluates should not have been brought to begin with. The purchaser cannot avoid accepting the clients with the less lucrative cases by trying to raise their fees, because Rule

1.17(d) prohibits raising any fees because of the sale. Although the purchaser can charge these new clients higher fees than the seller had charged, these new fees must be the same that he already charges his other clients for substantially similar services. Rule 1.17(d) & Comment 9. The purpose behind these restrictions is to prevent the seller from financing the sale by increasing fees from the new clients.

Third, the sale of a law practice raises questions of client confidentiality, for the purchaser is not the lawyer with whom the clients contracted and in whom they confided. Consequently, each of the seller's clients must receive written notice of the proposed sale, the terms of any proposed fee changes, and notice that each client retains the right to retain other counsel and to take possession of his file. Rule 1.17(c)(1), (2), & (3). (Even after the sale, a client may always transfer the representation to another lawyer. Comment 8.) Of course, not all clients will likely respond to this notice. Thus, it is significant that Rule 1.17(c)(4) provides that the client should also be notified that the client's consent to the sale is presumed, *if* the client does not respond within 90 days. If the client cannot be given notice, the purchaser must secure a court order authorizing the transfer. To protect the client's confidentiality, the seller may disclose to the court *in camera* information about the proposed representation only to the extent necessary to obtain this order.

Recall that if a lawyer divides fees with another lawyer in a different law firm, each lawyer must assume joint responsibility for the representation. Rule 1.5(e)(1). Rule 1.17 does not refer to that section; in fact, Comment 15 to Rule 1.17 specifically provides that this Rule does not apply to the transfer of legal representation unrelated to the sale of a practice. On the other hand, one would think, as a logical matter, that the responsibilities assumed under Rule 1.17 should be no less than those assumed pursuant to Rule 1.5(e)(1). Rule 1.17, Comment 11 notes that the seller has the obligation to exercise competence in identifying a qualified purchaser. While the seller cannot exercise continuing supervision (he has, after all, left the practice), it does not appear unreasonable to make him share joint malpractice liability (as if they were partners) with the person whom he picked to buy his practice. Such a rule would assure that the seller picked carefully. And it does not appear any more onerous than the burden placed by Rule 1.5(e)(1). However, except for Comment 11, Rule 1.17 does not provide for any seller's liability.

VII. REVIEW QUESTIONS

1. Thomas is an attorney who specializes in plaintiff tort cases. He has employed James, an employee of the law firm. James is an investigator who is not a lawyer. They have the following financial arrangement: for every case James works on that Thomas wins for a client, James will receive fifteen

percent of the award or settlement: if Thomas' client loses, James will receive nothing.

Is this fee arrangement *permitted by the disciplinary rules?*

a. No, unless the client consents after full disclosure.

b. Yes, because lawyers may include nonlawyer employees in a compensation plan based on a profit sharing arrangement; investigators have to get paid and their pay in fact comes out of clients' fees. Thomas' arrangement simply recognizes that economic fact.

c. No, because it involves James in the unauthorized practice of law.

d. Yes, this arrangement does not violate the disciplinary rules but it is discouraged by the ethical aspirations.

e. No, because an attorney may not divide his legal fees with a non-attorney.

2. Lawyer Able entered into a partnership with Accountant Baker and Insurance Agent Clark. The name of the partnership is Able, Baker and Clark. The partnership maintains its offices in a building owned by Lawyer Able and carries on its business in a suite of offices composed of a waiting room, law and tax book library, and offices. Each member of the partnership has a private office for himself and his secretary that is adjacent to the waiting room and library. They have a small, dignified sign on the door that says "Able, Baker, and Clark; Lawyer, Accountant and Insurance." All of the monies received by any partner goes into the common bank account and all expenses are paid therefrom and the remaining monies or profits are divided equally: one-third ($\frac{1}{3}$) to each of the partners.

Is Lawyer Able *subject to discipline?*

 I. Yes, because Able has shared his legal fees with a non-lawyer.

 II. Yes, because a lawyer shall not form a partnership with a nonlawyer if any of the activities of the partnership consist in the practice of law.

The best answer is:

a. Both I and II.

b. Neither I nor II.

c. I only.

d. II only.

3. Attorney Jones is the majority shareholder of Collection Agency, Inc. If Collection Agency's collection efforts have not been successful, Jones has authorized Collection Agency's Manager, who has graduated from law school but is not admitted to the bar, to use his (Manager's) best judgment to write an appropriate collection letter. The letter is on Jones' legal letterhead. The letter may, if Manager so decides, contain a statement that the matter has been referred to Attorney Jones and that suit will be filed in five days if payment is not received. Manager is authorized to sign Attorney Jones' name to the letter. Jones does not personally review each letter before it is sent.

Is Attorney Jones *subject to discipline?*

a. Yes, because Attorney may not threaten suit to gain advantage in a civil case.

b. Yes, because the letter is a threat.

c. Yes, because Collection Agency, through Manager, is engaging in the unauthorized practice of law.

d. No, because Manager is authorized to act as Jones' agent.

4. Attorney asks Secretary to file a copy of Client's confidential papers. Attorney then leaves the office early. Attorney's instructions are quite clear, and Secretary in the past has followed them. But that night, Secretary is rushed, and Secretary leaves the confidential papers on the top of the conference table. Later that night, some clients in a different matter meet at the firm with another attorney in the firm. These other clients use the conference table, see the confidential documents, express surprise, and tell the firm's attorney, who locks up the papers.

Is Attorney *subject to discipline?*

a. No, because she reasonably supervised Secretary.

b. No, because Attorney is not responsible for Secretary.

c. Yes, under a theory of vicarious liability.

d. Yes, because the other clients saw the confidential documents.

PART FIVE

THE LAWYER'S OBLIGATIONS REGARDING ADVERTISING AND SOLICITATION

Analysis

I. LAWYER ADVERTISING AND SOLICITATION

A. INTRODUCTION

1. Historical and Constitutional Background

The Canons of Ethics of 1908 originally allowed lawyers to advertise. Publication of business cards in newspapers and directories as well as advertisements of a lawyer's specialty were then quite common. Some of the advertisements created problems. For example, one 1911 lawyer's ad in the Los Angeles Daily Times included the following (in all capital letters): "WE GET THE COIN." See, Oliver, *Lawyer Advertising*, Calif. Lawyer, July, 1987, at 29. By 1937 a complete redraft of Canon 27 severely restricted lawyer advertising. See ABA Formal Opinion 276 (Sept. 20, 1947). The organized bar maintained this virtual prohibition until the 1970's when consumer groups, attorneys, and others began actively opposing the bar's position.

The Supreme Court opened the door to legal advertising in *Bates v. State Bar of Arizona,* 433 U.S. 350, 97 S.Ct. 2691, 53 L.Ed.2d 810 (1977), when the Court held that the first amendment protects truthful newspaper advertising of availability and fees for routine legal services. The Court allowed the states to subject such advertising to reasonable restrictions on time, place and manner, and to prohibit false or misleading advertising.

In *Ohralik v. Ohio State Bar Association,* 436 U.S. 447, 98 S.Ct. 1912, 56 L.Ed.2d 444 (1978), the Court turned to the question of solicitation and held that a state may constitutionally discipline a lawyer who solicits clients in-person under circumstances likely to create undue pressure on the client. *Ohralik* thus answered a question left open in *Bates* regarding the greater potential for overreaching when the attorney solicits business face to face rather than through the media.

In a companion case, *In re Primus,* 436 U.S. 412, 98 S.Ct. 1893, 56 L.Ed.2d 417 (1978), the Court recognized that certain types of solicitation are entitled to special protection. *Primus* involved an American Civil Liberties Union (ACLU) lawyer who, through a letter, offered free legal services to a woman allegedly deprived of her civil rights. The Court extended the first amendment's protection for free speech and association to the lawyer's activities and struck the state's efforts to reprimand the ACLU lawyer for solicitation.

In *In re R.M.J.,* 455 U.S. 191, 102 S.Ct. 929, 71 L.Ed.2d 64 (1982) a unanimous Supreme Court invalidated additional restrictions on lawyer advertising. Missouri reprimanded R.M.J. because he had deviated from the precise listing of certain areas of practice included in the state's Rule 4. For example, R.M.J.'s advertisement listed "real estate" but Rule 4 used the term "property;" R.M.J. listed "contracts" but Rule 4 did not list that term at all. Because the state could neither demonstrate that R.M.J.'s listing was deceptive nor show that its restrictions promoted any substantial interests, the U.S. Supreme Court found the state limitations unconstitutional. The Court also invalidated a part of Rule 4 that prohibited a lawyer from identifying the jurisdictions in which he is licensed to practice.

R.M.J. had also emphasized in large, boldface type that he was a member of the U.S. Supreme Court bar. Justice Powell, for the Court, acknowledged that this fact was "relatively uninformative," but held that R.M.J. could not constitutionally be disciplined for advertising it: the record did not show that it was misleading, and Rule 4 did not specifically identify it as misleading, nor place a limitation on its type size, nor require any explanatory disclaimer explaining the significance (or lack thereof) of U.S. Supreme Court bar admission.

In *Zauderer v. Office of Disciplinary Counsel of Supreme Court of Ohio,* 471 U.S. 626, 105 S.Ct. 2265, 85 L.Ed.2d 652 (1985) the Court held that a state may not discipline an attorney who ran newspaper advertisements containing nondeceptive illustrations (in this case, a drawing of a Dalkon Shield Intrauterine Device) and legal advice (in this case, the advice that product liability tort claims may not yet be time barred by the statute of limitations). However, the Court explained, the state could discipline a lawyer for failure to include in his advertisements information reasonably necessary to make his advertisement not misleading. In this case the lawyer advertised that he would represent clients on a contingent fee basis and "if there is no recovery, no legal fees are owed by our clients." The lawyer did not disclose that the client might still be liable for litigation costs. The state has broader power to mandate disclosure than it has to prohibit advertising. The lawyer's "constitutionally protected interest in *not* providing any particular factual information in his advertising is minimal." (emphasis in original).

In *Shapero v. Kentucky Bar Association,* 486 U.S. 466, 108 S.Ct. 1916, 100 L.Ed.2d 475 (1988), the Court held that free speech guarantees preclude the states from imposing blanket bans on direct mail advertising.

In *Peel v. Attorney Registration and Disciplinary Commission of Illinois,* 495 U.S. ___, 110 S.Ct. 2281, 110 L.Ed.2d 83 (1990), the Court (with no majority opinion) ruled that the First Amendment limited Illinois' power to censure a lawyer for truthfully stating that he was "certified as a civil trial specialist by the National Board of Trial Advocacy," a bona fide private organization.

2. **The Bar's Response to *Bates***

The American Bar Association (ABA) immediately responded to *Bates* by amending Canon 2, which now lists the information that an attorney may include in an advertisement. DR 2–101. The new rule prohibits anything that is not expressly permitted. The Model Rules, in contrast, take the opposite approach: anything not expressly prohibited is allowed. Rule 7.1 broadly prohibits "false or misleading statements." Subject to the requirements of this Rule, Rule 7.2 permits a lawyer to advertise through a broad spectrum of media.

The constitutionality of any law restricting truthful lawyer advertising is uncertain after *Bates* and its offspring. Consequently, some of the Code's or Rules' specific restrictions, either on their face or as applied, may, in the future, fall to constitutional challenges.

B. **USE OF THE MEDIA**

1. **The Model Code**

The Code regulations on use of the media begin with a general prohibition of "false, fraudulent, misleading, deceptive, self-laudatory or unfair" statements or claims. DR 2–101(A). The Code then lists 25 categories of information that may be advertised, subject to the requirement of DR 2–101(B) that any communication be presented "in a dignified manner." DR 2–101(B) (1–25).

(a) Scope

The Code permits advertising through both print and broadcast media. DR 2–101(B). *Bates* had reserved the question as to the extent of constitutional protection in light of the possible "special problems of advertising on the electronic broadcast media."

The Code also provides that the advertising may cover only the geographic area in which the lawyer resides, maintains offices, or where a "significant part" of the lawyer's clients reside. DR 2–101(B).

(b) Content

A lawyer may present biographical information such as the lawyer's name, DR 2–101(B)(1), schools attended, DR 2–101(B)(5), and foreign language ability, DR 2–101(B)(14). Advertisements may also include office information such as hours, DR 2–101(B)(19) and fee information, DR 2–101(B)(20–25). If contingent fees are advertised, the publicity must include a statement that the percentage is computed before or after deduction of costs. DR 2–101(B)(22).

As a general rule, the Code prohibits lawyers from identifying themselves in their advertisements as specialists in a particular field of law. DR 2–102(A); DR 2–105; EC 2–14. This rule is subject to several exceptions. First, the Code recognizes the traditional exception for patent lawyers. DR 2–105(A)(1).

Note: EC 2–14 also includes the fields of admiralty and trademark. This EC is contrary to DR 2–105(A)(1). It appears that the ABA House of Delegates amended DR 2–105(A)(1) in 1977 (eliminating admiralty and trademark) and forgot to amend the corresponding EC.

Second, the Code permits lawyers to advertise their specialty *if* certified by the appropriate state agency, DR 2–105(A)(3). Furthermore, lawyers may indicate that their practice is limited to certain areas only by using state-designated terms. DR 2–105(A)(2).

These restrictions regarding advertising of truthful information raise constitutional concerns. If a lawyer only handles real estate matters, should he not be able to so advertise, whether he uses state designated terms or not? See *In re R.M.J.,* discussed in section I, A, 1, supra.

The Code provides that any person wishing to advertise information not on the "approved list" may apply to the appropriate state agency for an expansion of the Code. If the agency grants relief, the Code should be amended to reflect it. DR 2–101(C).

(c) Other Regulations

The Code regulates other aspects of lawyer advertising besides mode, range, and content. If a lawyer uses the broadcast media, the lawyer must pre-record the advertisement and retain a copy. DR 2–101(D). And, if a lawyer advertises a specific service for a set fee, the Code requires the lawyer to render the service for such fee for a reasonable time after the advertisement appears. DR 2–101(E), (F), & (G).

2. The Model Rules

(a) Scope

The Model Rules, like the Model Code, recognize the public's need to know about the availability and quality of legal services. *See, e.g.,* Rule 7.2, Comment 1; EC 2–10. The Rules, however, approach regulation of lawyer advertising more liberally and less technically than the Code. The Rules recognize that "[t]he interest in expanding public information about legal services ought to prevail over considerations of tradition." Rule 7.2, Comment 1. Thus, the Rules permit truthful advertising through any medium except "in-person solicitation," which is narrowly defined and governed by Rule 7.3. See section II, infra. Furthermore, unlike the Code, the Rules do not restrict the advertisement's geographic reach.

(b) Content

The Rules ban false or misleading communications about a lawyer's services. Such prohibited statements include those likely to create unjustified expectations about results the lawyer expects to achieve. Rule 7.1(b). A typical example would be an advertisement of a lawyer's *past* jury awards, because each case is fact-bound. Rule 7.1, Comment 1. Just because a lawyer secured a million dollar fee in one personal injury case does not mean that such a victory will be repeated. The new plaintiff may well have a different set of facts or be subject to different law. This Comment adds that advertisements containing client endorsements similarly may create unjustified expectations. This Rule also forbids factually unsubstantiated statements that compare one lawyer's services with another's. Rule 7.1(c). And it forbids any material misrepresentation of law or fact, or any *omission* of "a fact necessary to make the statement considered as a whole not materially misleading." Rule 7.1(a). Cf. Securities & Exchange Commission Rule 10b–5. *Zauderer v. Office of Disciplinary Counsel of Supreme Court of Ohio,* 471 U.S. 626, 653 n. 15, 105 S.Ct. 2265, 2283 n.15, 85 L.Ed.2d 652 (1985) upholds the constitutionality of such a disclosure rule as long as it is not "unduly burdensome" and not too vague.

The Rules also regulate the communication of fields of practice. A lawyer may communicate through advertising that the lawyer's practice is limited to (or excludes) particular fields of law. Rule 7.4. The Rules, unlike the Code, do not require that the lawyer use certain designations (specifically approved by the state regulatory authority) in order to describe these fields. See DR 2–105(A)(2).

Prior to February, 1989, the Comment to Rule 7.4 had provided that the lawyer may not state that his practice "is limited to" or is "concentrated in" a particular area. Now, there is no such restriction. In light of the modern lawyer advertising cases, the pre–1989 version would probably be unconstitutional, unless the state could meet the difficult burden of demonstrating that the use of language such as "is limited to" is misleading (while "is not limited to" is not misleading).

The Rules also provide that one may not call himself a "specialist" unless he is admitted to the United States Patent and Trademark Office, or he is a patent attorney, a proctor in admiralty, or he has complied with his state's procedures for certifying or recognizing specialists (assuming that the state has such procedures). The Comment to Rule 7.4 argues that the term "specialist," has acquired a "secondary meaning" that implies some type of formal recognition by the state as a specialist. Rule 7.4, Comment 1.

However, such a restriction may well be precluded by *Peel v. Attorney Registration and Disciplinary Commission of Illinois*, 495 U.S. ___, 110 S.Ct. 2281, 110 L.Ed.2d 83 (1990), where a divided Court ruled that free speech guarantees prohibited Illinois from disciplining an attorney who had stated on his letterhead that the National Board of Trial Advocacy had certified him as a "Certified Civil Trial Specialist." Stevens, J., joined by Brennan, Blackmun, and Kennedy, JJ., concluded that Peel's statement was neither potentially nor actually misleading (the National Board of Trial Advocacy was a bona fide organization that had made a reasonable inquiry into Peel's fitness), and that the state did not have a sufficient interest to justify a categorical ban on the use of such statements (even though the state argued that Peel's representation was potentially misleading). The plurality noted that terms like "air conditioning specialist" or "foreign car specialist" are common, and the public does not think that they imply a claim of formal recognition by the state. In addition, although Illinois does not recognize any specialities and does not certify, its ethics rules allow the use of the titles "Proctor in Admiralty" and "Registered Patent Attorney," a fact that undermined Illinois' argument that there was a need for a "complete prophylactic against any claim of speciality. . . ."

The Rules (unlike the Code) require that any advertising contain the name of at least one lawyer responsible for its content. Rule 7.2(d).

(c) Other Regulations

Like the Code, the Rules require the lawyer who uses broadcast media to retain a copy of the advertisement. Rule 7.2(b). The Rules require that the copy or recording be kept for two years. Rule 7.2(b). The Code has no time limit. DR 2–101(D) (" . . . shall be retained. . . .").

C. FIRM NAMES, LETTERHEADS, AND OTHER PERSONAL PUBLICITY
1. Trade Names and Firm Names
(a) Trade Names

The Code prohibits lawyers in private practice from practicing under a trade name, such as "The 47th Street Law Office," whether or not it is misleading. DR 2–102(B). The Rules, however, prohibit the use of trade names in private practice only if the name is either misleading or implies a connection with a government agency or public legal services organization. Rule 7.5(a).

Note: It is constitutional for the state to have a blanket prohibition of trade names. *Friedman v. Rogers*, 440 U.S. 1, 99 S.Ct. 887, 59 L.Ed.2d 100 (1979). However, there may be constitutional problems when the state bans one type of trade name ("the

44th Street Clinic") but not another ("Jones & Smith"—when Jones is no longer with the firm because he is dead); then, the asserted justification is undercut by the state's own actions. Cf. *Allegheny Pittsburgh Coal Co. v. County Commission of Webster County, W.Va.*, 488 U.S. 336, 109 S.Ct. 633, 102 L.Ed.2d 688 (1989)(disparate assessments on real property violate the Equal Protection Clause when they do not reflect any distinctions found in state law).

A firm name that uses the name of a deceased partner is really a form of trade name. Rule 7.5, Comment 1, recognizes this fact. The Code pretends that such names are not trade names and consequently the Code permits them without trying to distinguish them from other trade names. See section (b), infra.

(b) Firm Names

Lawyers may not, under the Code, practice under a name that is misleading as to the identity of the lawyers practicing under such a name. DR 2–102(B). Thus, firm names may not contain names other than those of the lawyers in the firm; however, the Code permits (where otherwise lawful) firm names to contain the names of deceased or retired members of the firm, in a continuing line of succession. DR 2–102(B). The Code apparently recognizes that a well known firm name develops value and good will, over the years. Also, the Code specifically allows professional corporations to use certain initials ("P.C." or "P.A.") to indicate the nature of the organization. DR 2–102(B).

The Rules take a more liberal position with respect to firm names. The Rules prohibit only misleading firm names. Thus it allows trade names (unless they falsely imply a connection with a governmental or charitable agency), Rule 7.5(a); similarly, the Rules also allow the use of the name of a deceased or retired member in a continuing line of succession. Rule 7.5, Comment 1.

Leaving aside the question of deceased or retired partners, only a member of a law firm actively and regularly practicing with that firm may be named in a firm name. Consequently the names of lawyers acting in judicial, executive, or administrative capacities may not appear in firm names or on professional notices during the period in which the lawyer is serving in that capacity, unless that lawyer is still actively and regularly practicing law with the firm. DR 2–102(B). See also Rule 7.5(c) (prohibiting the use of the name of a lawyer serving in public office during any substantial period in which the lawyer is not regularly practicing with the firm).

Both the Rules and the Code permit a lawyer to state or imply that such lawyer is a member of a partnership or organization only where such is in fact the case. Rule 7.5(d); DR 2–102(D).

2. Professional Cards, Signs, Letterheads

The Code, unlike the Rules, has quite specific and detailed regulations governing professional cards, signs, and letterheads. The Code begins with a general prohibition against the use of professional cards, office signs, letterheads, and other similar types of personal publicity. DR 2–102(A). However, as exceptions to this prohibition, the Code permits several types of personal publicity that serve to assist clients in locating and identifying an attorney. The Code permits lawyers to use such personal publicity if it is in "dignified form." DR 2–102(A).

The Code allows a lawyer to use a professional card that carries only the lawyer's name, profession, telephone number, and the name of the lawyer's law firm, the names of the firm's members or associates, and limitations on practice to the extent that DR 2–105 approves of those limits. DR 2–102(A)(1). A lawyer may use such cards for identification. DR 2–102(A)(1). DR 2–102 also creates a limited exception for the use of "brief" professional announcement cards, DR 2–102(A)(2), office signs, DR 2–102(A)(3), and letterheads, DR 2–102(A)(4).

The Code does not permit partnerships among lawyers licensed in different jurisdictions unless each lawyer's jurisdictional limitations are indicated on the letterhead and on other permissible publicity. DR 2–102(D). Rule 7.5(b) governs this situation and is substantially similar to the Code.

The Rules, unlike the Code, do not engage in such regulatory detail. Rule 7.5(a) simply prohibits the use of a "firm name, letter or other professional designation that violates Rule 7.1," which bans misleading or false statements.

3. Lawyer Identification

(a) The Model Code

The Code has a special provision allowing the "limited and dignified" identification of a lawyer's name and profession in certain circumstances. DR 2–101(H). These circumstances include political advertisements (if germane), public notices (if germane), announcements of business, civic, professional or political organizations if the lawyer in an officer or director, legal documents, legal textbooks prepared by the identified lawyer, or in public notices whenever the identification is reasonably pertinent to some purpose "other than the attraction of clients." Where it is proper to identify a lawyer as a lawyer and the author of a book, it is also proper to identify the author as a lawyer in dignified advertisements for the book. DR 2–101(H)(5).

(b) The Model Rules

The Rules, in contrast, make no special exception for such lawyer identification because its less restrictive regulatory scheme does not prohibit truthful identification of a lawyer as a lawyer.

II. SOLICITATION

A. INTRODUCTION

Solicitation is a form of advertising on a retail, rather than a wholesale level. The Code, which has strict rules against most solicitation, makes a distinction between general media advertising and improper "in-person" solicitation, which involves contact with specific prospective clients motivated by pecuniary gain. EC 2–2, 2–3 & 2–4. In contrast, the Rules, as they have been amended in response to various Supreme Court decisions, now make a distinction that forbids "in-person [*i.e.,* face to face] or live [*i.e.,* non-prerecorded] telephone contact" where the lawyer engages in such actions because his "pecuniary gain" is a "significant motive". Rule 7.3(a).

B. DIRECT CONTACT WITH CLIENT

The Code and Rules both restrict two types of solicitation. The first type involves direct contact between a lawyer and a prospective client. The second involves a lawyer's effort to obtain a recommendation or client referral from a third party.

Under the Code, lawyers may not recommend their services or those of their partners to a prospective client unless that person initiated the consultation. DR 2–103(A). Similarly, lawyers who render unsolicited advice to prospective clients may not usually accept employment arising from such advice. DR 2–104(A). A lawyer may, however, accept employment resulting from unsolicited advice to a close friend or relative. Unsolicited advice to a former client in order to secure business is also permitted if the advice is germane to a matter the lawyer formerly handled for such client. DR 2–104(A)(1). Similarly, a lawyer may accept employment resulting from participation in educational activities sponsored by a qualified legal services organization. DR 2–104(A)(2). The Code generally permits a lawyer to accept employment resulting from a lawyer's spoken or written legal scholarship, so long as he does not tout his own professional qualifications. DR 2–104(A)(4).

Under the Code a lawyer may not accept employment from a client who seeks that lawyer's services as a result of prohibited solicitation. DR 2–103(E). Consequently, a lawyer may not accept employment if the lawyer knows the client has been solicited by the lawyer's employee, partner, or other lawyer affiliated with such lawyer. Cf. DR 1–102(A)(2).

The Rules' restrictions are expressed in much less detail, and have been amended over the years to respond to Supreme Court decisions that have protected, under the First Amendment, various forms of advertising. The

Rules now prohibit solicitation by "in-person of live telephone contact" of a prospective client with whom the lawyer has no prior professional or family relationship when "a significant motive" is the lawyer's pecuniary gain. Rule 7.3(a).

The Rules used to distinguish mass mailings (which were allowed) from direct, targeted mail (which were not), claiming "[d]irect mail solicitation cannot be effectively regulated by means less drastic than outright prohibition." See, former Comment 5 to Rule 7.3 (1988 version). However, targeted mailing does not involve face-to-face contact, and the recipient can simply throw the mail away. Targeted mailing is really only a more efficient form of advertising than a mass mailing. Indeed, in *Bates v. State Bar of Arizona*, 433 U.S. 350, 402 n.5, 97 S.Ct. 2691, 2718 n.12, 53 L.Ed.2d 810 (1977), Powell, J., concurring in part and dissenting in part, joined by Stewart, J., admitted that there was no "principled basis" to distinguish advertisements in newspapers from "handbills, and mail circulations."

In February of 1987 two ABA entities initially proposed that Rule 7.3 be amended to allow targeted mailing, but they withdrew this proposal after the ABA Board of Governors opposed it. Then, in *Shapero v. Kentucky Bar Association*, 486 U.S. 466, 108 S.Ct. 1916, 100 L.Ed.2d 475 (1988), the Court ruled that, pursuant to the First Amendment, states may not categorically prohibit lawyers from seeking business by sending truthful, nondeceptive letters to potential clients known to face particular legal problems.

In February, 1989, the ABA responded to *Shapero* by amending Rule 7.3, which now allows direct mail or prerecorded telephone contact unless the recipient has indicated that he or she does not wish to be solicited by the lawyer, or the solicitation involves coercion, duress, or harassment. Any written solicitation must include the words "Advertising Material" on the outside envelope" and at the beginning and ending of any recorded message. The touchstone of the new Rule is to protect the prospective client from direct, personal encounters or live telephone persuasion from a lawyer because those situations are fraught with the possibility of "undue influence, intimidation, and over-reaching." Rule 7.3, Comment 1. In addition, in light of the possibility of direct mail or prerecorded telephone advertising, there is no real need for such personal encounters. The direct mailing can always invite the prospective client to call the lawyer's office if the recipient wishes more information.

C. OBTAINING RECOMMENDATIONS OR CLIENT REFERRALS

The Code prohibits a lawyer from paying a person or organization for a recommendation or giving a reward for such a recommendation. DR 2–103(B). A lawyer may, however, pay reasonable and customary fees or dues to a legal service organization that recommends the lawyer's services. DR 2–103(B). The Code prohibits a lawyer from requesting a person or organization to recommend the lawyer's services. DR 2–103(C). The Code permits, however, a lawyer to pay media advertisers, for their services, but not to pay for professional publicity in a news item. DR 2–101(I). The lawyer may also request referrals from bar association-sponsored lawyer referral services, DR 2–103(C)(1), and legal service organizations, DR 2–103(C)(2), and pay them usual and reasonable dues and fees.

Rule 7.2(c) similarly forbids a lawyer from giving anything of value in exchange for a recommendation, except that a lawyer may pay media advertising and the "usual charges" of not-for-profit lawyer referral services or legal service organizations. She may also purchase a law practice pursuant to Rule 1.17. See, Rule 7.2(c)(3). Otherwise, a lawyer may not pay someone for channeling professional work. Rule 7.2, Comment 6.

D. LEGAL SERVICES ORGANIZATIONS

The Code, in DR 2–103(D), specifically and in great detail, defines the types of legal service organizations from which a lawyer may accept a recommendation or client referral. DR 2–103(D) authorizes referrals from public defender, military legal assistance, and bar association referral services. The Code specifically requires that the recommending or referring organization exert no influence nor interfere with the lawyer's exercise of independent professional judgment on behalf of a client. DR 2–103(D). The Code extensively regulates other legal services organizations such as employee or union legal benefits plans. DR 2–103(D)(4)(a–g). This set of complicated rules draws various distinctions involving for-profit and not-for-profit plans; open and closed plans; plans where the organization "bears ultimate liability of its member" (i.e., a typical insurance plan where the insurer bears liability and chooses the attorney to defend the insured); and plans that the lawyer initiated. DR 2–103(D)(4).

The Rules, in contrast, do not have such a Byzantine set of rules, though they do have the general rule requiring a lawyer to guarantee his professional independence (Rule 5.4), and the general restrictions regarding solicitation, Rule 7.3. Comment 8 to Rule 7.3 makes clear that Rule 7.3(d) allows an attorney to participate in (but not own or direct) a prepaid legal service plan even though the plan uses personal contact to solicit potential members generally (but does not target particular persons who are known to need legal services in a particular matter).

ABA Formal Opinion 87–355 (Dec. 14, 1987) reaffirms that the Model Rules approve of a lawyer participating in a for-profit prepaid legal service plan if the plan allows the lawyer to exercise independent judgment on behalf of the clients, to keep client confidences, and to practice competently. The participating lawyer must ensure that the plan involves neither improper advertising, nor improper solicitation, nor improper fee sharing, and must be in compliance with other applicable law.

III. REVIEW QUESTIONS

1. George Uncle, the uncle of Attorney Beta, asked her to lecture to a retired persons' association. Attorney Beta selected the topic, "You need an attorney to plan your estate." In her talk, she does not tout her professional reputation and engages in no direct, private communications. Consistent with Beta's responsibilities under the Model Code and Model Rules, select the most accurate statement:

    a. The topic *is improper* because a lawyer should not give advice to laypeople that they need a lawyer.

    b. The topic *is improper* unless Beta refuses to accept employment from the advice, except she may accept employment from Uncle.

    c. It *is proper* for Beta to accept employment at the meeting from those attending because she does not tout her own professional reputation and only engages in general advertising, not direct private contact.

    d. The topic *is proper only if* Beta refuses to accept employment from the advice, including employment from Uncle.

2. *A & B*, both attorneys, assumed duties as officers and directors of the First National Bank. Before and after banking hours they maintained a partnership engaged in the private practice of law. The law partnership was in a separate office in a section of the bank building rented to various offices, including other law offices. There was no evidence showing that there had been any solicitation of law business stemming from the banking activities nor was there any advertising by the bank that directly or indirectly benefitted *A* and *B* in the practice of Law.

    I. *A* and *B* are aiding in the unauthorized practice of law.

    II. *A* and *B* are involved in an inherent conflict of interest between their banking interests and their legal interests.

    III. *A* and *B* have violated no disciplinary rules.

    The best answer is:

    a. I only

    b. II only

    c. I and II

    d. III only

3. *A*, *B*, & *J* are attorneys whose sole professional relationship is that they are full-time salaried employees of *C* Corporation and constitute its Legal Department. The President of *C* Corporation has requested *A*, *B*, & *J*, in corresponding with third parties, to use letterheads that do not disclose that the signatories are members of the Legal Department of the corporation. Much of the correspondence would be to warn the addressees of possible violations by the addressees of contracts with *C* Corporation. The President of the corporation feels that a letterhead that does not identify the signatory as a member of the Legal Department of the corporation would tend to sound more impressive to the recipients. The letterhead would read:

> A, B, & J
> Attorneys at Law
> [Street address]
> [telephone number]

I. The letterhead is a *violation of the disciplinary rules* unless the Board of Directors authorized it, because the corporate attorneys owes his obligation to the corporate entity and not any member thereof.

II. The letterhead *is proper* because it represents customary advertising.

III. The letterhead *is proper* under the disciplinary rules *if* A, B, & J shared the same offices.

IV. The letterhead *is improper* because A, B, & J are not in fact partners.

The best answer is:

    a.   I and IV

    b.   II only

    c.   I only

    d.   III only

    e.   IV only

4. The Supreme Court in *Bates v. State Bar of Arizona*, 433 U.S. 350, 97 S.Ct. 2691, 53 L.Ed.2d 810 (1977) held, inter alia, that:

I. The state may regulate legal advertising in order to assure its truthfulness.

II. Legal advertising on radio and television are subject to the same restraints as those on the print media.

III. In-person solicitation is constitutionally protected.

IV. Advertising the quality of legal services is constitutionally protected.

The best answer is:

    a.   Neither I, II, III, nor IV.

    b.   I, II, & IV, only.

    c.   I only.

    d.   I and IV only.

5. Attorney practices largely in the areas of tax, wills and estates, and trusts. Attorney learned of a new Internal Revenue Service regulation that may affect provisions in a will she prepared for Former Client two years ago. Attorney has not heard from Former Client since she drew the will.

Is Attorney *subject to discipline* if she advises Former Client of the new IRS ruling?

    a.   No, unless Attorney's motive is to secure employment by Former Client.

    b.   No, because Attorney believes that the new rules may affect Former Client's will.

    c.   Yes, because Former Client is no longer a client.

    d.   Yes, because Attorney would be soliciting legal business.

6. Attorney, the only adjunct (i.e., part-time) faculty member at Law School, asked that the following statement be included in the law school catalog.

"Each adjunct member of our faculty is a certified practicing specialist in the subject which he or she teaches."

Is Attorney *subject to discipline* if the statement is included in Law School's catalog?

    a.   No, if Attorney limits her practice to the subjects she teaches.

    b.   No, if Attorney is in fact experienced in the subjects she teaches.

    c.   Yes, because the designation of Attorney as a specialist appears in a publication intended for persons other than members of the bar.

    d.   Yes, unless Attorney is certified as a specialist in the subjects she teaches.

PART SIX

THE LAWYER'S OBLIGATION NOT TO MISUSE THE OFFICE OF GOVERNMENT

Analysis

I. THE PUBLIC OFFICIAL WHO IS ALSO A LAWYER

Lawyers holding public office may not use their public positions in order to obtain improper advantage for their clients.

A. FIRM NAMES

In many instances a lawyer may hold a public position and be allowed to practice law or another occupation. For example, a part-time mayor, state legislator, or city council member typically is allowed to continue the practice of law.

In such cases the lawyer's law firm may continue to use the lawyer's name in the firm name as long as that lawyer engages in active and regular practice with the firm. DR 2–102(B); Rule 7.5(c). If the lawyer is not so engaged, to allow the firm to continue to use his name in firm communications is misleading because it may imply a connection that no longer exists. See ABA Informal Opinion 1205 (Feb. 9, 1972).

B. USING A PUBLIC POSITION TO OBTAIN SPECIAL ADVANTAGE

The lawyer-legislator may be in an advantageous position to offer legislation, in her capacity as a legislator, in order to benefit her private client. Canon 8 of the Model Code specifically considers this problem. The Rules do not directly address it, though some of the general Rules are applicable.

The lawyer-legislator may accept private clients but he is prohibited from using his public position to obtain a "special advantage in legislative matters for himself or for a client" only in those cases "where he knows or *it is obvious* that such action is not in the public interest." DR 8–101(A)(1) (emphasis added).

This section is not so much a meaningful prohibition as it is a license, because of the difficulty of meeting any test using the phrase: "it is obvious." Thus, there is no *per se* prohibition against a lawyer accepting a retainer from a private client who is likely to be affected by proposed legislation. ABA Informal Opinion 1182 (Dec. 5, 1971). The requirement of "special advantage" means "a direct and peculiar advantage." The "not in the public interest" standard means legislation "clearly inimical to the best interests of the public as a whole." Id.

However, this license does not mean that a lawyer-legislator may ethically receive from a private client anything of value *in exchange for* introducing or voting for legislation. In such a case the transaction amounts to a bribe and is directly prohibited by DR 8–101(A)(3). Cf. Rules 3.5(a); 8.4(b). DR 8–101(A)(3) prohibits the lawyer-legislator (or similar person) from accepting anything of value from anyone if the lawyer "knows or it is *obvious* that the offer is for the purpose of influencing his action as a public official." DR 8–101(A)(3) (emphasis added).

This prohibition applies whether or not the lawyer fulfills his part of the bargain, i.e., whether the lawyer in fact uses, or attempts to use, his influence corruptly, in violation of DR 8–101(A)(3). It also applies if the bargain is only implicit.

Example: Thus, *In re D'Auria*, 67 N.J. 22, 24, 334 A.2d 332, 333 (1975) held that it is improper for a judge handling worker's compensation matters to accept numerous "free" lunches from lawyers or insurance companies who had cases then pending before the judge. Though there was no explicit evidence proving the corrupt intent of those who offered the "free" lunch, the facts and setting probably convinced the court that the purpose of the offer was "obvious." As economists would say, "There is no such thing as a free lunch."

Where the factual background is less compelling, the result should be different. Cf. ABA Informal Opinion 1182 (Dec. 5, 1971) (no per se violation of DR 8–101(A)(3) when facts only show that a lawyer-legislator represented in legal matters a person also affected by contemplated legislation).

Though the Rules have no direct counterpart to DR 8–101(A)(3), a fact situation that meets the stiff requirements of that DR probably also meets the general prohibitions of Rule 8.4(c) or (d), prohibiting dishonesty and conduct prejudicial to the administration of justice.

Just as the lawyer-official may not accept anything of value offered to influence her own actions as a public official, neither may a lawyer seek to influence a public official (or juror) improperly. Rule 3.5(a); Cf. EC 7–35; DR 9–101(C).

C. ATTEMPTS TO INFLUENCE A TRIBUNAL

A lawyer may not use his public position in order to gain a corrupt advantage for himself or his client. DR 8–101(A)(2); Rule 3.5(a). The basic question is whether the effort to influence the tribunal was corrupt.

Example: A lawyer-legislator appears before the state commerce commission to urge a rate increase on behalf of a private client. This lawyer-legislator is also on the state house committee that oversees the state commerce commission and sets the administrators' salaries. Such circumstantial facts alone do not show anything improper. The lawyer-legislator must also have actually engaged in an overt attempt to exert improper influence over the state commerce commission. ABA Informal Opinion 1182 (Dec. 5, 1971). See also *State ex rel. Nebraska State Bar Ass'n v. Holscher*, 193 Neb. 729, 738, 230 N.W.2d 75, 80 (1975).

D. IMPLYING THE POWER TO INFLUENCE IMPROPERLY

A lawyer, whether or not a public official, may not state "or imply" to anyone that he or she has the power to influence a public official or agency on improper or irrelevant grounds. DR 9–101(C); Rule 8.4(e).

This prohibition applies whether or not the lawyer actually exercises the influence and whether or not the lawyer could, in fact, exercise such influence.

Example: Lawyer tells Client: "You are lucky you hired me. The judge hearing your case is my old college roommate and good friend. He'll do what he can to help me." Lawyer has violated DR 9– 101(C) and Rule 8.4(e) whether or not the judge even knows of Lawyer.

The rationale for this rule is that such suggestions by lawyers serve no valid purpose and undermine public confidence in the legal system, even if the implication is false. EC 9–4. See, Rotunda, *Ethical Problems in Federal Agency Hiring of Private Attorneys,* 1 Georgetown J. Legal Ethics 85, 121–22 (2987).

See, *Matter of Sears*, 71 N.J. 175, 364 A.2d 777 (1976), where the attorney wrote an official of his company/client implying that the attorney would or could improperly influence a federal judge in connection with an S.E.C investigation of that company. Though there was no evidence that the attorney communicated *ex parte* with the judge, the attorney wrote an official of the corporate client as follows:

> "When you talk to Bob [Vesco], will you please tell him that I have made contact re the above and have done all that I can properly be done [sic] under the circumstances."

The Ethics Committee found that this letter was referring to Vesco's earlier request that the lawyer approach the federal judge. The lawyer characterized the letter "as merely 'rain-making'—that is, an effort to mollify a client who had been pressuring him to undertake a specific action." The state supreme court found a violation of DR 9–101(C):

> "In the instant case, the Vesco request was aimed at influencing the S.E.C. suit and was highly improper. By fostering the impression that he had satisfied or could satisfy that request, respondent's conduct fell directly within the ambit of DR 9–101(C)."

71 N.J. at 191, 364 A.2d at 785.

II. THE REVOLVING DOOR

A. THE FORMER GOVERNMENT LAWYER

When a lawyer who works for the Government leaves that position and accepts private employment, the commentators talk about the "revolving door" between governmental service and private employment. The goal of the rules in this area is to limit potential abuses—e.g., the risk of improper use of confidential government information or the risk that the government lawyer might use that position to benefit a future private employer—without unduly restricting the ability of the government to attract lawyers. See Rule 1.11, Comment 3. There are public advantages to having the door between government service and private practice revolve.

The basic Code provision is DR 9–101(B):

> "A lawyer shall not accept *private* employment in a *matter* in which he had *substantial responsibility* while he was a *public employee*." (Emphasis added).

The meaning of the italicized words explain the breadth and limitations of this rule, which must be read in connection with DR 5–105(D). DR 5–105(D) imputes the disqualification of DR 9–101(B) to every other lawyer in the firm.

ABA Formal Opinion 342 (Nov. 24, 1975), which has been very influential in the application of this rule, addressed the following issues:

1. Private Employment

"Private employment" means work "as a private practitioner." If a lawyer in private practice has accepted, as one of his clients, a government agency, that lawyer is accepting *private* employment from the government agency. E.g., *General Motors Corp. v. City of New York*, 501 F.2d 639 (2d Cir. 1974) (private lawyer accepts contingent fee case from New York City). This term, however, does not cover the situation where one government agency recruits a lawyer presently employed by another agency because there is no realistic danger that a lawyer will abuse his government office for private gain merely because he moves from one salaried government position to another salaried government position.

2. Matter

This term refers to "a discrete and isolatable transaction or set of transactions between identifiable parties."

Example 1: Lawyer represents Government in suing Widget, Inc. for a strip-mining violation. The Lawyer leaves the Government and represents Widget, Inc. in defending against this suit. Or, Lawyer represents a class action plaintiff suing Widget for pollution damage growing out of the same facts. The various suits involve the same "matter."

Example 2: Lawyer for a congressional committee helps draft a new law governing the coal industry and establishing requirements for returning the land back to its natural form after strip mining. Lawyer then leaves the congressional committee and begins work for Coal Co., Inc. involving the same point of *law*. The two situations are not the same "matter" because there is no discrete transaction between identifiable parties in a particular situation. Drafting a law for the government does not disqualify a lawyer from later private employment involving the same point of law.

3. Substantial Responsibility

A government lawyer does not have "substantial responsibility" over a matter if she only gives perfunctory approval or disapproval. The lawyer should have "had such a heavy responsibility for the matter in question that it is unlikely he did not become personally and substantially involved in the investigative or deliberative processes regarding that matter."

4. Public Employee

This term encompasses every capacity in which the lawyer is employed by the government. It is not necessary that the employment be in one's capacity as a lawyer.

5. Imputation

ABA Formal Opinion 342 concluded that there was no pressing public need, under DR 5–105(D), to apply an inflexible imputation of the DR 9–101(B) disqualification. Such inflexibility is costly. It would restrict government recruitment and limit a client's choice of lawyers. Thus, the former government lawyer's disqualification is not imputed to the other lawyers in his new firm if the former government lawyer is "screened, to the satisfaction of the government agency concerned, from participation in the work and compensation of the firm on any matter over which as a public employee he had substantial responsibility."

6. The Approach of the Model Rules

Rule 1.11 is in many respects substantially similar to DR 9–101(B), as that rule has been interpreted. However, Rule 1.11 is more specific. First, it expressly incorporates the requirements of other law, such as government conflict of interest law.

The Rule also requires that a firm screening a disqualified lawyer notify "promptly" the governmental *agency* in writing, so that the agency may assure itself that the firm has complied with the requirements of this rule.. Rule 1.11(a)(2). "Promptly" means only "as soon as practicable." Rule 1.11, Comment 6. While the lawyer must notify the government agency, there is *no* requirement that any notice be given to any adverse *private party* to enable it to ascertain that there has been compliance with this Rule. Compare Rule 1.11(b), with Rule 1.11(a)(2).

Note: Because part of Formal Opinion 342 speaks of the need to permit "the one protected by DR 9–101(B) to waive" its protection, the question may arise as to whether a government agency may unreasonably refuse to "waive," e.g., to withhold its waiver only for tactical reasons. See *Kesselhaut v. United States,* 555 F.2d 791, 794 (Ct.Cl. 1977) (per curiam) (government's unjustified withholding of consent to a screening not binding on the court). The Model Rules avoid this issue and reach the result in *Kesselhaut* by not requiring any government consent as to screening. The government must receive notice so that it can ascertain that the screening is effective; however, it has no power to withhold consent to a proper screening. However, the former government lawyer does need consent from the government if that former government lawyer wants to be able *personally* to represent a private client in a matter in which he had participated earlier personally and substantially as a government official. Rule 1.11(a)[first sentence].

Rule 1.11(a)(1) also provides that the screened lawyer must be "apportioned no part of the fee" from the disqualifying matter. This rule may be less restrictive than Formal Opinion 342. The Rule explicitly allows the screened lawyer to receive "a salary or partnership share established by prior independent agreement." The Rule only prohibits "*directly* relating the attorney's compensation to the fee" in the disqualifying matter. Rules 1.11, Comment 5 (emphasis added).

Rule 1.11(b) has a special provision regarding confidential government information. "Confidential government information" is defined as information obtained pursuant to government authority and not available to the public. See Rule 1.11(e). The former government attorney cannot use such confidential information about a person to the "material disadvantage of that person." Rule 1.11(b). This special restriction on the former government lawyer is also not imputed to other members of the firm if the former government lawyer is screened from the matter in question and is apportioned no part of the fee from that matter.

The lawyer in government service also must not negotiate for private employment with a party who is involved in a matter in which the government lawyer is then participating, personally and substantially. Rule 1.11(c)(2).

> *Note:* Law clerks seeking private employment are treated differently. See the next section, C(1), infra.

B. THE PRIVATE LAWYER MOVING INTO GOVERNMENT PRACTICE

A lawyer for the government may not take a case in which she had personal and substantial participation while in private practice, unless under substantive law that lawyer is subject to a nondelegable duty to act. Rule 1.11(c)(1).

The disqualification imposed on the former private practitioner now in government service is not imputed to any other lawyers within the government. See Rule 1.10. To impute would place a tremendous cost on the government—a cost not justified by public policy. The lawyer cannot ethically reveal her former client's secrets to her new colleagues. See Canon 4; Rule 1.6. And, there is little incentive to breach this Chinese Wall because a salaried government lawyer has no "financial interest in the success of departmental representation that is inherent in private practice." The duty of a government lawyer is "to seek just results rather than the results desired by a client." ABA Formal Opinion 342 (Nov. 25, 1975). This government official should, however, be screened from participation in the particular matter. Id.

C. THE FORMER JUDGE
1. The General Rule

A *former judge* may not accept private employment in a matter if she acted in a judicial capacity, on the merits of that case. DR 9–101(A); Rule 1.12(a) ("participated personally and substantially"). This disqualification rule applies not only to judges but to other persons who have acted in a "judicial capacity," such as a hearing officer, special master, or referee. Rule 1.12(a), Comment 1. *Powers v. State Dept. of Social Welfare,* 208 Kan. 605, 493 P.2d 590 (1972) (DR 9–101(A) applies to referee in social welfare department). See also EC 5–20 (impartial mediator or arbitrator).

If the judge's *law clerk* "personally and substantially" participated with the judge on the case, then the law clerk is also disqualified from later representing anyone in the same matter. Rule 1.12(a). The judge's law clerk may, however, negotiate for employment with a party or attorney who is involved in a matter—even though the clerk is participating personally and substantially on that matter—so long as the clerk notifies the judge. Rule 1.12(b).

A *partisan arbitrator—i.e.,* the partisan member of a multimember arbitration panel—is not disqualified from later representing a party to the arbitration because that type of arbitrator did not serve, in that matter, as an impartial decision-maker. Rule 1.12(d).

2. Waiver

The general rule requiring disqualification of the former judge is for the protection of the parties. Consequently, the parties may knowingly waive this protection. Rule 1.12(a). Cf. Model Code of Judicial Conduct, Canon 3F (1990), which provides for waiver of certain disqualifications by a sitting judge.

3. Imputation and Screening

The disqualification of the former judge is *not* imputed to any other lawyer in the former judge's new law firm if two conditions exist: first, the former judge should be screened from the disqualifying matter and be apportioned no part of the fee from it; and, second, the law firm should promptly give written notice to the appropriate tribunal so that it can determine that the screening is adequate. Rule 1.12(c). This screening and notice provision parallels the rule regarding the former government lawyer. See Rule 1.11(a).

III. SPECIAL RESPONSIBILITIES OF A PUBLIC PROSECUTOR

The duty of the public prosecutor "is to seek justice, not merely to convict." EC 7–13; Rule 3.8, Comment 1. From this principle, there have developed certain limitations that modify the duty of zealous behavior.

A. CRIMINAL CASES

A prosecutor may not institute charges if he knows that they are not supported by probable cause. DR 7–103(A); Rule 3.8(a). Ordinarily a lawyer may bring any nonfrivolous action. See DR 2–109(A); 7–102(A)(1); Rule 3.1.

The prosecutor must inform the accused of the existence of evidence of which the prosecutor knows if that evidence tends to negate the guilt of the accused or mitigate the punishment. DR 7–103(B); Rule 3.8(d). The prosecutor should not intentionally fail to follow certain leads because he believes the information secured might damage his case. EC 7–13.

The prosecutor must also inform the sentencing tribunal of all mitigating information not covered by a protective order or otherwise privileged. Rule 3.8(d). Whenever the prosecutor is proceeding *ex parte,* as in a grand jury hearing, he should offer the tribunal "all material facts" whether or not adverse. Rule 3.3(d). See Rule 3.8, Comment 1.

The prosecutor should give the accused a reasonable opportunity to obtain counsel, and should not urge an unrepresented accused to waive important pretrial rights, such as the right to a preliminary hearing. Rule 3.8(b), (c). Cf. DR 7–104(A)(2). However, if the accused has decided to appear *pro se,* the government attorney must negotiate directly with the accused. Rule 3.8, Comment 2. Cf. EC 3–7.

The Model Rules now place ethical limits on a prosecutor who seeks to subpoena an attorney.

In recent years, the Government has appeared to increase its subpoenas of criminal defense lawyers to testify before the grand jury. In the District of Massachusetts, for example, the Federal Government, during most of the 1980's, subpoenaed attorneys in approximately 10% to 32% of the criminal cases. *United States v. Klubock,* 832 F.2d 649, 658 (1st Cir. 1987)(amended panel opinion), affirmed by equally divided en banc court, 832 F.2d 664 (1st Cir. 1987). The Government often seeks information on the amount of the fee paid to the attorney, whether it was paid in cash, whether the client or a third party paid it. The answers to these questions are relevant in light of various federal laws such as the Racketeer Influenced and Corrupt Organizations Act, 18 U.S.C.A. §§ 1961—1968 and the Continuing Criminal Enterprise Statute, 21 U.S.C.A. §§ 848—853. The fee information may be useful in determining whether any fee is subject to forfeiture because it was acquired through certain criminal activity, or is evidence of a criminal enterprise. E.g., Brickey, *Tainted Assets and the Right to Counsel—The Money Laundering Conundrum,* 66 Wash. U.L.Q. 47 (1988).

An attorney, just like any other witness who is called to testify before the grand jury, can always raise any applicable privilege, such as the attorney/ client evidentiary privilege. However, these attorneys have typically argued that they should not even be subpoenaed unless there is first an adversary hearing before a judge, who is to determine that the information is not privileged, the evidence is "essential," and that there is "no other feasible alternative" to secure this evidence. After most courts rejected this position, *e.g., United States v. Perry,* 857 F.2d 1346 (9th Cir. 1988), the ABA (in February, 1990) added new Rule 3.8(f) & Comment 4, which imposes such a requirement on the prosecutor as a matter of legal ethics.

The full effect of new Rule 3.8(f) remains to be seen. The ABA Standing Committee on Ethics and Professional Responsibility, which proposed Rule 3.8(f), filed a Report suggesting that Rule 3.8(f) should have very broad scope. This Report complained, for example, that the attorney/client evidentiary privilege does not offer enough protection because it does not cover client "secrets," as defined in DR 4–101(A) and 1.6(a) & Comment 5. "Similarly," the Report protested, "an attorney in possession of documents received from a client in the course of a case may be compelled by subpoena to produce those documents assuming that the client personally could be compelled to produce the documents were they in the client's hands." Of course, one wonders why a client should be able to avoid a subpoena for documents by the simple expedient of turning them over to his or her attorney for safe-keeping.

Compare, Norton, *Ethics and the Attorney General*, 74 Judicature 203 (Dec.-Jan. 1991), with Thornburgh, *Ethics and the Attorney General: the Attorney General Responds*, 74 Judicature 290 (April–May 1991).

In *United States v. Klubock*, 832 F.2d 649 (1st Cir. 1987)(*en banc*), an equally divided court approved a state rule and a federal rule similar to Rule 3.8(f). However, other courts have disagreed. E.g., *Baylson v. Disciplinary Board of Supreme Court of Pennsylvania*, 764 F.Supp. 328 (E.D.Pa. 1991), holding that a state rule patterned after Rule 3.8(f) cannot be enforced against federal prosecutors. The rule "distorts evidentiary privileges, disrupts existing subpoena practice, and compromises the authority and function of the modern grand jury."

B. CIVIL CASES

The government lawyer's special duty to seek justice extends to civil or administrative proceedings. The lawyer should not use her position or the government's economic power to "harass parties," or to cause "unjust settlements or results." EC 7–14. If the government lawyer believes that litigation is unfair, she should use her discretionary power not to proceed, or offer such a recommendation to her superiors. EC 7–14.

IV. REVIEW QUESTIONS

1. While working for the Department of Justice, Attorney had the major responsibility for initiating a suit against Cosmetic Co. for an antitrust violation. Attorney then left the Department of Justice and went into private practice in the capital city of her home state. The State Attorney General now is seeking to hire Attorney (for a contingent fee) as a special prosecutor to help in a case against Cosmetic Co. based on the same facts in the Department of Justice suit. Attorney will continue her private practice.

   Is it *proper* for Attorney to accept the employment?

   a. Yes, unless attorney will be required to take a position on behalf of the State that is adverse to the Department of Justice interests.

   b. Yes, if Cosmetic Co. consents after full disclosure.

   c. No, because Attorney had substantial responsibility for this matter while she was a public employee.

   d. No, because it gives the appearances of impropriety for Attorney to accept various clients when all of them seek to sue the same defendant.

   e. Yes, because her new employer, for this case, is also a governmental unit.

2. Attorney Doe has tried many contested cases before Judge. Doe believes Judge lacks judicial temperament and is not too bright and that Attorney Roe would make an excellent judge. Doe wishes to defeat Judge and assist Roe in getting elected.

    Is Doe *subject to discipline* if he tells the local reporter?

    "I support candidate Roe because I believe Judge is not too bright."

    a. Yes, because Doe practices before Judge.

    b. Yes, because Doe is attacking a sitting judge.

    c. No, because Doe believes that she is telling the truth.

    d. No, unless the reporter publishes the comment.

3. State's Attorney seeks an indictment against Deft for extortion. State's Attorney knows that there is no probable cause to support the indictment, but believes that he can use the indictment as a bargaining chip with Deft in order to secure Deft's testimony against others.

    Is State's Attorney *subject to discipline?*

    a. No, because State's Attorney has a duty to prosecute zealously.

    b. No, if State's Attorney has acted in good faith with no personal vindictiveness against Deft.

    c. Yes, unless the Grand Jury in fact indicts.

    d. Yes, because there is no probable cause.

4. Lawyer is a practicing attorney and also a member of a Special Commission appointed by the Governor to recommend law reform. Client, a divorced husband, has asked Lawyer to handle a legal problem regarding child custody. Lawyer researches the law and finds that it is, in her view, unjust toward husbands. Her view is shared by many, but not all, experts. Lawyer asks the Commission to recommend a change in the law to correct the problem. Lawyer, with Client's consent, discloses to the Commission her relationship with Client. The new bill, if enacted, would greatly strengthen Client's case.

Is Lawyer *subject to discipline?*

a. Yes, because she misused her public office to help a private client.

b. Yes, because the bill is not necessarily for the public good, given the objections of some experts.

c. No, because Lawyer did not act obviously against the public interest.

d. No, because her duty of zealous representation of client required Lawyer to act the way she did even if the bill is contrary to the public interest.

*

PART SEVEN

THE LAWYER'S OBLIGATION AS AN ADVOCATE

Analysis

I. FRIVOLOUS AND DILATORY POSITIONS

Lawyers may not assert frivolous positions.

Lawyers may not assert frivolous positions, claims, defenses, or motions. DR 7–102(A); DR 2–109(A); Rule 3.1. Thus a lawyer can be disciplined for filing a "frivolous" lawsuit, *In re Sarelas*, 360 F.Supp. 794 (N.D.Ill. 1973) (attorney suspended and fined for filing frivolous immigration appeals), or asserting "baseless" defenses. *In re Bithoney*, 486 F.2d 319 (1st Cir. 1973). See also Rule 3.4(a), (d) (prohibiting frivolous discovery requests or failure to make reasonably diligent effort to comply with discovery request).

However, the mere fact that a legal position is "creative" or contrary to existing law does not make that position frivolous. The existing law often has ambiguities and always has potential for change. Rule 3.1, Comment 1. Therefore a lawyer may make a "good faith argument for an extension, modification or reversal of existing law." Rule 3.1. Accord, DR 2–109(A)(2); DR 7–102(A)(2). See also Rule 3.4(c) (lawyer should not knowingly disobey tribunal unless there is "open refusal based on an assertion that no valid obligation exists.") Accord, DR 7–106(A).

The duty to refrain from asserting frivolous claims includes pursuing dilatory tactics, which are not permissible even in criminal cases. *State v. Darnell*, 14 Wash.App. 432, 542 P.2d 117, 120 (1975). See also, Rule 3.2; DR 7–102(A)(1). However, the duty to avoid frivolous claims does not preclude the attorney from putting the state to its burden of proof in a criminal case. The government, in every criminal case, has the constitutional duty to prove every element of the charge if defendant pleads not guilty. The government cannot constitutionally shift the burden to defendant. *Mullaney v. Wilbur*, 421 U.S. 684, 95 S.Ct. 1881, 44 L.Ed.2d 508 (1975). The Rules explicitly recognize this principle in Rule 3.1.

Note: The language of the Rules regarding dilatory motions is phrased more affirmatively than that of the Model Code. Rule 3.2 requires the lawyer to make "reasonable efforts to expedite litigation consistent with the interests of the client," while DR 7–102(A)(1) and DR 2–109(A)(1) forbid a lawyer from delaying when the lawyer "*knows* or it is *obvious* that such action would serve *merely to harass* or maliciously injure another." (emphasis added).

Whether the case is civil or criminal, the lawyer need not first fully substantiate the facts before making a claim. Nor does the claim become frivolous merely because the lawyer believes that the client will not prevail. The lawyer may expect to develop vital evidence by discovery. Rule 3.1, Comment 2. Discovery, after all, normally comes after the complaint is filed, not before. But, "if the pleading or oral representation when made is without any reasonable basis and is designed merely to embarrass or [for] . . . some other ill-conceived or improper motives, such a pleading or oral representation would clearly be subject to disciplinary action." *State v. Anonymous (1974–5)*, 31 Conn.Sup. 179, 326 A.2d 837, 838 (1974).

Note: The drafters of the Model Rules claim that, unlike DR 7–102(A)(1), the test of Rule 3.1 is "an objective test." See Rule 3.1, Code Comparison 1. However, this "objective" test defines "not frivolous" in terms of a "good faith argument" for a change or modification in the law. Rule 3.1. In addition, Rule 3.1, Comment 2, states that an action is frivolous if "taken *primarily for the purpose of* harassing or maliciously injuring a person" or if made in bad faith (emphasis added). Such a test is virtually identical to that found in DR 7–102(A) and DR 2–109(A). This test, defined in part in terms of motivation, is hardly objective.

The New Rule 11. In 1983, Rule 11 of the Federal Rules of Civil Procedure was amended to provide that every pleading, motion, or other paper must be signed by an individual lawyer; this signature certifies that she has read the paper, that to the best of her knowledge "formed after reasonable inquiry" it is well grounded in fact and is warranted by existing law or good faith argument to extend, modify, or reverse existing law, and that it is not filed for any improper purpose. For violation of this rule the court may sanction the party *or the attorney*. The sanction may include reasonable attorney fees for the opposing party.

Rule 11 has spawned a great deal of controversy over its scope, meaning, procedures, and application. Opponents claim that it has chilled lawyers' enthusiasm over pursuing novel legal theories; that it is biased against plaintiffs, particularly against plaintiffs in civil rights suits; that it has also not reduced but has increased satellite litigation and the attendant expenses. Since adoption of Rule 11 in 1983 there have been approximately 3000 decisions dealing with Rule 11 sanctions; in one case alone the lawyers spent $100,000 to reverse a $3,000 sanction. Judge Wiggins of the Ninth Circuit has expressed concern at the "vicious attitude" of some lawyers in their Rule 11 motions; he urged that sanctions should be imposed only in egregious cases after the lawyer had been warned. In contrast, Judge Schwarzer of the Northern District of California, an advocate of Rule 11, claims that Rule 11 has not unnecessarily increased the expenses of prefiling investigation, and that it only requires a lawyer to do what a responsible lawyer should do anyway. In some circuits, a very few judges are responsible for a disproportionate number of Rule 11 sanctions. E.g., 3 ABA/BNA Lawyers' Manual on Professional Conduct 266–67 (Aug. 19, 1987); Rotunda, *Learning the Law of Lawyering,* 136 U.Pa.L.Rev. 1761, 1773–75 (1988); Rule 11 in Transition: The Report of the Third Circuit Task Force on Federal Rule of Civil Procedure 11 (Am. Judicature Society 1989) (Stephen B. Burbank, Reporter); *Interim Report of the Committee on Civility of the Seventh Federal Judicial Circuit* 20–21, 44–45 (1991); Kramer, *Viewing Rule 11 as a Tool to Improve Professional Responsibility,* 75 Minn.L.Rev. 793 (1991). The Advisory Committee on the Federal Rules of Civil Procedure is now reevaluating Rule 11 and may suggest changes. Samborn, *Rule 11 Sanctions Examined,* 13 National Law Journal 1, 14–15, 20 (May 20, 1991).

The U.S. Supreme Court has decided a handful of cases involving Rule 11. *Pavelic & LeFlore v. Marvel Entertainment Group*, 493 U.S. 120, 110 S.Ct. 456, 107 L.Ed.2d 438 (1989) held that Rule 11 sanctions may be imposed only on the individual attorney who signs the pleading or other papers, not on the attorney's law firm. It is then up to the law firm to absorb these costs if it wishes.

Cooter & Gell v. Hartmarx Corp., 496 U.S. ___, 110 S.Ct. 2447, 110 L.Ed.2d 359 (1990) ruled that (1) the district court could impose Rule 11 sanctions on a plaintiff and its lawyer even though the plaintiff voluntarily dismissed the action; (2) the appellate court should apply a deferential abuse-of-discretion standard in reviewing all aspects of a Rule 11 determination (and that a district court "would necessarily abuse its discretion if it based its ruling on an erroneous view of the law or a clearly erroneous view of the evidence"); and (3) Rule 11 does not authorize a district court to award attorney's fees incurred because of an appeal from a Rule 11 sanction (but Rule 38 of the Federal Rules of Appellate Procedure authorizes the appellate court to award expenses because of a frivolous appeal). Justice O'Connor, for the Court, also noted, ominously, for attorneys seeking to appeal Rule 11 sanctions: "[B]ecause the district court has broad discretion to impose Rule 11 sanctions, appeals of such sanctions may frequently be frivolous." 496 U.S. at ___, 110 S.Ct. at 2462. Stevens, J., concurring in part and dissenting in part objected that the Court was creating a federal common law of malicious prosecution inconsistent with the limited mandate of the Rules Enabling Act. One might also wish to note that if the litigant's activities were so frivolous, one wonders why the appellate court must defer to the trial court; the frivolous nature of the litigant's actions should be obvious even if the appellate court had a de novo review.

Business Guides, Inc. v. Chromatic Communications Enterprises, Inc., 498 U.S. ——, 111 S.Ct. 922, 112 L.Ed.2d 1140 (1991) concluded that Rule 11 imposed an objective standard of reasonable inquiry on represented parties who signed papers or pleadings, whether the signatures were voluntary or mandated. Kennedy, J., dissenting (joined by Marshall & Stevens, JJ. and Scalia, J., in part) objected that sanctions will now "apply quite often to those so uninformed that they sign a paper without necessity."

II. RESPONSIBILITIES TOWARD THE TRIBUNAL

A. CANDOR
1. Disclosure of Representative Capacity
A lawyer appearing before a tribunal may not mislead the tribunal regarding the fact that the lawyer appears in a representative capacity.

The identity of the lawyer's client is rarely privileged. See, e.g., *Colton v. United States*, 306 F.2d 633, 637 (2d Cir. 1962). Even when it is, the lawyer may not mislead the tribunal—whether it be judicial, administrative, or legislative—regarding the fact that the lawyer appears in a representative capacity. It is not misleading for a lawyer to disclose that she appears on behalf of another, whose name is privileged; it is misleading for the lawyer to pretend that she appears pro se when in fact she does not. DR 7–106(B)(2); DR 1–102(A)(4); Rule 8.4(c); cf. Rule 3.9.

Typically, the identity of the client is not privileged. In judicial as well as nonadjudicative proceedings (such as those involving lobbying), the government has a legitimate need to know "who is being hired, and who is putting up the money, and how much." *United States v. Harriss*, 347 U.S. 612, 625, 74 S.Ct. 808, 816, 98 L.Ed. 989, 1000 (1954) (upholding disclosure provisions of Federal Lobbying Act, 2 U.S.C.A. § 261 et seq.). Accord, Rule 3.9; DR 7–106(B)(2). This principle has long been settled. See, e.g., ABA Canons of Professional Ethics (1908, as amended), Canon 26: "[I]t is unprofessional for a lawyer [appearing before legislative or other bodies] to conceal his attorneyship. . . ."

2. Disclosure of Adverse Legal Authority

A lawyer is subject to discipline if he knowingly makes a false statement of law to a tribunal. DR 7–102(A)(5); Rule 3.3(a)(1).

A lawyer must also disclose to a tribunal any legal authority in the controlling jurisdiction that he knows is directly adverse to his client's position and that opposing counsel has not disclosed. DR 7–106(B)(1). Accord, Rule 3.3(a)(3). This rule applies whether or not the tribunal is judicial, legislative, or administrative. Rule 3.9.

This rule does not require the lawyer to make "a disinterested exposition of the law. . . ." Rule 3.3, Comment 3. The lawyer is engaged in advocacy, not a seminar discussion. But this advocate may not fail to disclose pertinent, adverse legal authority in the controlling jurisdiction. Of course, after disclosing these decisions he may seek to distinguish them, or challenge their soundness, "or present reasons which he believes would warrant the court in not following them in the pending case." ABA Formal Opinion 146 (July 17, 1935).

Note that the rule does not speak of "controlling authorities." It is broader and refers to "legal authority in the controlling jurisdiction." The ABA Formal Opinion 280 (June 18, 1949) rejects the narrow view that the lawyer must only cite decisions that are decisive of the pending case. Rather, the disclosure rule applies to—

"a decision directly adverse to any proposition of law on which the lawyer expressly relies, which would reasonably be considered important by the judge sitting on the case. . . . The test in every case should be: Is the decision which opposing counsel has overlooked one which the court should clearly consider in deciding the case? Would a reasonable judge properly feel that a lawyer who advanced, as the law, a proposition adverse to the undisclosed decision was lacking in candor and fairness to him? Might the judge consider himself misled by an implied representation that the lawyer knew of no adverse authority."

Case law has adopted the ABA test. See, *In re Greenberg*, 15 N.J. 132, 137, 104 A.2d 46, 49 (1954) ("limiting it, however, to decisions of the courts of this State and, with respect to federal questions, to decisions of the courts of the United States").

The Rules extend the duty to disclose adverse legal authority until the proceedings are concluded "even if compliance requires disclosure of information otherwise protected by Rule 1.6." Rule 3.3(b).

3.   Disclosure of Facts
  (a)   Affirmative Misrepresentation
         The general principle is that a lawyer may not make any misrepresentation or engage in any dishonest, fraudulent or deceitful conduct. DR 1–102(A)(4); Rule 8.4(c). A specific corollary of this principle is that a lawyer may not make a false statement of fact to a tribunal. DR 7–102(A)(5); Rule 3.3(a)(1). The lawyer also may not offer evidence that he knows to be false. DR 7–102(A)(4); Rule 3.3(a)(4). In addition, the Rules give the lawyer discretion to refuse to offer evidence he or she "reasonably believes is false." Rule 3.3(c). Similarly the lawyer may not falsify evidence or aid in its creation or preservation "if he knows, or it is obvious that the evidence is false." DR 7–102(A)(6). See also, Rule 3.4(b).

  (b)   Misrepresentations by Omission
         It is not always necessary, or even permissible, to volunteer adverse facts when appearing before a tribunal. However, in some circumstances, the "failure to make a disclosure is the equivalent of an affirmative misrepresentation." Rule 3.3, Comment 2. Because lawyers may not affirmatively misrepresent—DR 1–102(A)(4); Rule 8.4(c)—they must make the necessary disclosures in such circumstances.

         Rule 3.3(a)(2) thus provides explicitly that the lawyer shall not knowingly "fail to disclose a material fact to a tribunal *when disclosure is necessary to avoid assisting a criminal or fraudulent act by the client*." (emphasis added). This principle is implicit in the Model Code; if the lawyer remained silent in such circumstances he would be assisting his client's fraudulent or criminal act. DR 7–102(A)(7). Cf. DR 7–102(A)(3) and Rule 3.3, Code Comparison 2.

(c) Remedial Measures

Commentators have long debated the degree of disclosure appropriate when the lawyer discovers that he or she has submitted material, false evidence, e.g., that the client or a witness has lied. Some have argued, particularly in criminal cases, that keeping client confidences must prevail. See, e.g., M. Freedman, *Lawyers' Ethics in an Adversary System* (1975); M. Freedman, Understanding Lawyers' Ethics 109–41 (1990). Others have rejected that conclusion. E.g., Rotunda, *Book Review of Lawyers' Ethics in an Adversary System*, 89 Harv.L.Rev. 622 (1976). See generally, Rule 3.3, Comments 4 to 14. The Rules have clearly come down on the side of disclosure.

If the lawyer has offered material evidence and later learns of its falsity, under the Rules the lawyer "must take reasonable remedial measures." Rule 3.3(a)(4). This duty applies "even if compliance requires disclosure of information otherwise protected" by the confidentiality requirements of Rule 1.6. See Rule 3.3(b). Similarly, the lawyer's duty continues "to the conclusion of the proceeding" even though "compliance requires disclosure of information otherwise protected by Rule 1.6." Rule 3.3(b).

The Rules do not specifically define when the proceedings have concluded. In a criminal case, a verdict of acquittal should conclude the proceedings, given that the double jeopardy clause prevents the state from retrying the defendant. In a civil case, the proceedings should probably be treated as concluded when the time for appeal has passed. In a criminal case where the defendant was nonetheless convicted, the defendant may wish to appeal to secure a new trial or an outright reversal; the defendant should not be able to benefit from his earlier perjury, and so the proceeding should probably not be treated as "concluded" until at least the time for direct appeal (as opposed to collateral attack via a writ of habeas corpus) has passed.

The lawyer may even have to reveal the fact that his client committed perjury in order to comply with the candor requirements of Rule 3.3. First, of course, the lawyer should seek to persuade the client to correct the falsehood. Rule 3.3, Comment 5. The lawyer should "remonstrate with the client confidentially" (Rule 3.3, Comment 11) and, if the client is still adamant, the lawyer "should seek to withdraw if that will remedy the situation. If withdrawal will not remedy the situation or is impossible, the advocate should make disclosure to the court." It is not enough for the lawyer, like Pontius Pilate, to wash his hands of the situation. If withdrawal will not remedy the situation, the lawyer must disclose the relevant information to the court. The lawyer's obligation is to take reasonable remedial measures. The court then decides what to do next: (1) make a statement to the trier of fact; (2) order a mistrial; (3) "or perhaps nothing." Id. See, Rotunda, *Client Fraud: Blowing the Whistle, Other Options,* 24 TRIAL Magazine 92 (Nov. 1988).

Note: If the lawyer discloses client perjury to the court, and the client disputes the charge, the Comments tell us that "the lawyer cannot represent the client in resolution of th[is factual] issue and a mistrial may be unavoidable. An unscrupulous client might in this way attempt to produce a series of mistrials and thus escape prosecution. However, a second such encounter could be construed as a deliberate abuse of the right to counsel and as such a waiver of the right to further representation." Rule 3.3, Comment 11.

There is constitutional support for the proposition (embraced by the Comment) that the client may lose the right to counsel. Cf. *Illinois v. Allen,* 397 U.S. 337, 90 S.Ct. 1057, 25 L.Ed.2d 353 (1970) (defendant's courtroom disruption justifies conducting trial without defendant's presence). However, rather than speak of "waiver of the right to further representation," the Model Rules should more precisely speak of "forfeiture." See, Westen, *Away from Waiver: A Rationale for the Forfeiture of Constitutional Rights in Criminal Procedure,* 75 Mich.L.Rev. 1214 (1977).

The Code is less clear regarding the duty to remedy lack of candor towards a tribunal. It appears to draw a distinction between client fraud and fraud by those who are not clients, such as witnesses. DR 7–102(B)(2) provides that if the lawyer "clearly" learns that someone "other than the client has perpetrated a fraud upon a tribunal," then the lawyer "shall promptly reveal the fraud to the tribunal." However, if the client "in the course of representation" has "perpetrated a fraud upon a person or tribunal," then the lawyer must "promptly call upon his client to rectify" it. If his client refuses or is unable to do so, the lawyer must "reveal the fraud to the affected person or tribunal, *except when the information is protected as a privileged communication.*" DR 7–102(B)(1) (emphasis added). The ABA added the italicized language in 1974. Many states have refused to adopt this 1974 amendment.

In ABA Formal Opinion 341 (Sept. 30, 1975), "privileged" was interpreted to include both "confidences" or "secrets" within the meaning of Canon 4. The drafters of ABA Formal Opinion 341 may have thought that this interpretation made DR 7–102(B)(1) a bar to disclosure. However, by incorporating Canon 4, Formal Opinion 341 also incorporated all of Canon 4's exceptions, including the exception for disclosure necessary to prevent "crimes" such as fraud. These exceptions are "broad enough to engulf the new rule promulgated by Opinion 341." Rotunda, *When the Client Lies: Unhelpful Guides from the ABA*, 1 Corp.L.Rev. 34, 39 (1978). Under this interpretation of DR 7–102(B)(1), the lawyer has a duty to disclose the perjury. Rule 3.3, Code Comparison 4.

The Commentary to Rule 3.3 acknowledges that if a jurisdiction requires, as a constitutional matter, that the lawyer present the accused as a witness, then if the accused wishes to testify "even if counsel knows the testimony will be false," the lawyer must follow the constitutional requirement. Rule 3.3, Comment 12. In *Nix v. Whiteside*, 475 U.S. 157, 106 S.Ct. 988, 89 L.Ed.2d 123 (1986) the Supreme Court, with no dissent, held that there is no violation of the Sixth Amendment right to effective assistance of counsel when the lawyer refuses to cooperate with the criminal defendant in presenting perjured testimony at the trial. In that case the lawyer told the defendant Whiteside that if he (Whiteside) insisted on committing perjury, then "it would be my duty to advise the Court of what he [Whiteside] was doing and that I felt he was committing perjury; also, that I probably would be allowed to impeach that particular testimony." The lawyer also said that he would seek to withdraw from further representation. Whiteside, to buttress his self-defense claim in a murder charge, wanted to testify that he had seen something "metallic" in the victim's hand. In fact, until a week before trial Whiteside had consistently stated that he had not actually seen the victim with a gun. When asked about the change in testimony, Whiteside said: "If I don't say I saw a gun I'm dead."

At trial Whiteside testified and admitted that he had not actually seen a gun in the defendant's hand. Whiteside was convicted and claimed ineffective assistance of counsel because his counsel's admonition had prevented his giving false testimony. The Eighth Circuit actually granted habeas relief to Whiteside but the Supreme Court reversed, relying in part on Model Rule 3.3.

ABA Formal Opinion 87–353 (April 20, 1987) advises that the disclosure obligation of Rule 3.3 is "strictly limited" to the case where "the lawyer *knows* that the client has committed perjury. The lawyer's suspicions are not enough." (emphasis in original). If the lawyer cannot dissuade the client from testifying perjuriously, and if the lawyer cannot withdraw from representation, the lawyer either should not call the client as a witness (when the lawyer knows "that the only testimony the client would offer is false"), or call the client and question him only on those matters that would not produce perjury. If the client does testify falsely, the lawyer must disclose the false testimony under Rule 3.3(a)(2), (4). The lawyer cannot avoid this responsibility by having the client testify in a narrative form, without questioning. ABA Formal Opinion 87–353 concludes that the Model Code rejects the narrative approach outlined in Proposed ABA Defense Function Standard 4–77 (1979). A lawyer "can no longer rely on the narrative approach to insulate him from a charge of assisting a client's perjury."

(d) Ex Parte Proceedings

The Model Rules place upon the lawyer a special affirmative duty in ex parte proceedings: the obligation to disclose all material facts (whether or not thought to be adverse) to enable the tribunal to make an informed decision. Rule 3.3(d). In an ex parte proceeding, one cannot rely on the adversary system to uncover the truth. Because the lawyer cannot rely on the other side to balance her presentation, she has this broader affirmative duty. Rule 3.3, Comment 15.

There is no similar provision in the Model Code, but the principle of Rule 3.3(a) finds support in the case law. Cf. *Precision Instrument Mfg. Co. v. Automotive Maintenance Machinery Co.*, 324 U.S. 806, 818, 65 S.Ct. 993, 999, 89 L.Ed. 1381, 1388 (1945) (patent applicant must report to the Patent Office all facts concerning possible fraud or inequities underlying patent application).

B. TRIAL PUBLICITY

Both DR 7–107 and Rule 3.6 attempt to balance the right of free speech with the right to a fair trial. For the most part they strike the same balance with the difference more in particulars than in basics.

Note: Any limits on a lawyer's right to comment raise questions regarding possible unconstitutional restrictions on the lawyer's first amendment rights. Several courts have found various first amendment problems with DR 7–107. See *Chicago Council of Lawyers v. Bauer*, 522 F.2d 242 (7th Cir.1975), cert. denied sub nom., *Cunningham v. Chicago Council of Lawyers*, 427 U.S. 912, 96 S.Ct. 3201, 49 L.Ed.2d 1204 (1976); *Markfield v. Association of the Bar of City of New York*, 49 A.D.2d 516, 370 N.Y.S.2d 82 (1975), appeal dismissed, 37 N.Y. 2d 794, 375 N.Y.S.2d 106, 337 N.E.2d 612 (1975); *Hirschkop v. Snead*, 594 F.2d 356 (4th Cir. 1979) (per curiam). In *Gentile v. State Bar of Nevada*, 501 U.S. ___, 111 S.Ct. 2720, 115 L.Ed.2d 888 (1991), a very divided Supreme Court held that a Nevada Supreme Court Rule governing a lawyer's pretrial statements about a case (a Rule almost identical to Model Rule 3.6) incorporated a standard that was consistent with the First Amendment, but was void for vagueness as interpreted. Different majorities of the Court supported each holding. Justice Kennedy, for the Court, concluded that the "notwithstanding" language [which is found in Model Rule 3.6(c)] purports to create a safe harbor, listing statements that can be made (e.g., the general nature of the claim or defense, information contained in a public record) without fear of discipline. Nevada's decision to discipline Gentile in spite of this purported safe harbor provision raised concerns of vagueness and selective enforcement. The Rule misled petitioner to believe that he could make statements on those issues at a press conference, even if he knows or reasonably should know that these statements will have a substantial likelihood of prejudicing an adjudicative proceeding.

Both Rule 3.6 and DR 7–107 distinguish between criminal and civil cases by providing a bit more restriction of speech in criminal cases. DR 7–107(F) also applies the restrictions of criminal cases to professional discipline proceedings and juvenile proceedings. However, the Code provides that none of the restrictions on trial publicity—whether in a civil or criminal case—apply if the lawyer is (1) replying to charges of misconduct publicly made against the lawyer or (2) participating in any proceeding of any legislative, administrative, or other investigative body. DR 7–107(I).

Rule 3.6(a) adopts a general test restricting speech if the extrajudicial statement "will have a substantial likelihood of materially prejudicing an adjudicative proceeding." The Code has no such general test, though it at times uses a test even more protective of the fair trial interests and less protective of the free speech interests: "reasonably likely to interfere with a fair trial" or similar proceeding. See DR 7–107(D), (F), (G)(5), & (H)(5).

DR 7–107(C)(7) allows the attorney to describe, at the time of seizure, physical evidence seized except for a confession, admission, or statement. Rule 3.6 does not allow such announcements, viewing them as "substantially prejudicial. . . ." Rule 3.6, Code Comparison 1.

DR 7–107 states specifically what attorneys may or may not publicly disclose. Rule 3.6, in contrast, treats these specifics as illustrations of conduct that will usually meet the "substantial likelihood" test of Rule 3.6(a).

Finally, whether the case is civil or criminal, with or without a jury, it is important to remember the matters as to which extrajudicial statements are allowed, including inter alia, information contained in a public record, a request for assistance, a warning of the danger concerning an individual, the scheduling or results of any steps in litigation, the general nature of the claim, or the general scope of an investigation. DR 7–107(B), (G); Rule 3.6(c).

C. DECORUM AND EX PARTE COMMUNICATIONS
1. Disruption of the Tribunal
Both the Code and the Rules forbid the lawyer to disrupt the tribunal. DR 7–106(C)(6), Rule 3.5(c). *In the Matter of McAlevy,* 69 N.J. 349, 354 A.2d 289 (1976), the court severely reprimanded an attorney who, at a side bar

conference, threatened (in vulgar terms) physical violence to the Deputy Attorney General, and who, later attacked the Deputy Attorney General during a conference in the judge's chambers. When the judge and his law clerk tried to separate the two men now locked in combat, they were drawn into the fight and at one point all four men were rolling on the floor. The judge suffered minor injuries. See generally, Rotunda, *The Litigator's Professional Responsibility,* 25 TRIAL Magazine 98 (Mar. 1989).

The lawyer, however, may disobey a tribunal's order if there is an "*open refusal based on an assertion that no valid obligation exists. . . .*" Rule 3.4(c) (emphasis added). See also DR 7–102(A).

2. Ex Parte Communications
Both the Code and Rules forbid improper ex parte communications with jurors or prospective jurors, DR 7–108; Rule 3.5(b), or with judges. DR 7–110(B); Rule 3.5(b). Similarly, both forbid improper efforts to influence judges, jurors, prospective jurors, or other officials. DR 7–108(A); DR 7–110(A); Rule 3.5(a). The main difference in this instance between the two sets of rules—and a typical difference that exists throughout the two codes—is that the Rules simply incorporate the requirements of other law. Rule 3.5(a), (b). The Code, on the other hand, is much more specific in describing the forbidden conduct.

3. Arguments During Trial
During the trial the lawyer may not "allude" to any matter not reasonably believed to be relevant, or admissible. Nor may he, in closing argument or otherwise, assert his personal opinion or knowledge regarding facts at issue, unless he is actually testifying as a witness. DR 7–106(C) (1), (3), (4); Rule 3.4(e). However, he may argue for any position or conclusion based on his analysis of the evidence. DR 7–106(C)(4).

Example 1: In closing argument Lawyer states: "How can you believe Witness? I've seen many people testify over the years, and in my experience, Witness is lying. I don't believe him, can you?" Lawyer's action is improper, even if Lawyer really believes that Witness is lying.

Example 2: In closing argument Lawyer states: "How can you believe Witness? His testimony contradicts the sworn testimony of three other people who, unlike Witness, have no financial interest in this case." Lawyer's action is proper.

III. RESPONSIBILITIES TOWARD OPPOSING COUNSEL AND OTHER PERSONS

A. CANDOR

Lawyers have certain affirmative obligations of candor to a tribunal, e.g., to disclose material adverse legal authority, see Section II(A), supra. However, with respect to opposing parties or third parties, the lawyer's duty is more limited. The fundamental principle is that lawyers may not knowingly misrepresent either a material fact or law to opposing parties or other persons. DR 7–102(A)(5); DR 7–102(A)(4); Rule 4.1(a); Rule 8.4(c). This principle applies whether the lawyer is involved in litigation or negotiation. While the Code (unlike the Rules) does not specifically use the term "material," it is probably an implicit requirement.

Note: The Model Rules provide in the Comments: "Under generally accepted conventions in negotiation, certain types of statements ordinarily are not taken as statements of material fact. Estimates of price or value placed on the subject of a transaction and a party's intentions as to an acceptable settlement of a claim are in this category, and so is the existence of an undisclosed principal except where nondisclosure of the principal would constitute fraud." Rule 4.1, Comment 2. While the Model Code would probably exclude "puffing" or immaterial misstatements, nothing in the Model Code specifically approves of the exceptions found in Rule 4.1, Comment 2. Cf. ABA Informal Opinion 1283 (Nov. 20, 1973) (unethical in settlement negotiations to represent that class action will be brought if this intention is false).

A corollary to this prohibition against material misrepresentation is that a lawyer may not unlawfully obstruct access to, alter, or conceal evidence, or conceal a witness, or encourage a witness to testify falsely. DR 7–109(A), (B), (C); DR 7–106(C)(7); Rule 3.4(a), (b).

Note: The Code specifically prohibits a lawyer from paying a witness any money contingent on the outcome of the case. DR 7–109(C). The lawyer may advance, guarantee, or acquiesce in the payment of (1) a witness' expenses in attending or testifying; (2) compensation for the witness' loss of time because of his or her attending or testifying and (3) a reasonable fee for an expert witness' professional services. DR 7–109(C). The Rules have no such explicit provision, but a Comment contends that the "common law rule in most jurisdictions is that it is improper to pay an occurrence witness any fee for testifying and that it is improper to pay an expert witness a contingent fee." Rule 3.4, Comment 3.

Rule 4.1(b) provides that a lawyer shall not knowingly "fail to disclose a material fact *to a third person* when disclosure is necessary to avoid assisting a criminal or fraudulent act by a client, *unless* disclosure is prohibited by Rule 1.6." (emphasis added). Rule 1.6 governs client confidences. As explained elsewhere (see Part III, Section III, C, supra) Rule 4.1(b) does not require a lawyer to assist a client in a crime or fraud even if failure to assist would amount to a disclosure prohibited by Rule 1.6. Rather, the lawyer must not assist, must withdraw, and may also file a notice of withdrawal. If the failure to disclose a material fact involves a tribunal, Rule 3.3(a)(2)—not Rule 4.1(b)— is applicable; the lawyer's remedy in such a case is provided by Rule 3.3(a)(4). This remedy may require disclosure of the perjury to the tribunal because of the lawyer's duty of candor. See Part VII, Section II, A, supra.

B.   COMMUNICATIONS
1.   Persons Represented by Counsel
If a lawyer for a client (Lawyer # 1) knows that another person is represented by his own attorney (Lawyer # 2), then Lawyer # 1 may not communicate with the person represented by Lawyer # 2 in that matter unless Lawyer # 2 consents. DR 7–104(A)(1); Rule 4.2. The obvious reason for this requirement is to prevent lawyers from overreaching the person contacted. DR 7–104(A)(1); Rule 4.2.

While both DR 7–104(A)(1) and Rule 4.2 refer to a "party" represented by counsel, if a nonparty (e.g., a witness) is represented by counsel, the requirements of these rules are still applicable. Rule 4.2, Comment 2 makes clear that the requirement of counsel consent "also covers any person, whether or not a party to a formal proceeding, who is represented by counsel concerning the matter in question." See also EC 7–18 (also using the word "person").

This extension of the requirement to all persons is quite consistent with the rationale of preventing overreaching.

The requirement of this Rule is inapplicable if *other law* authorizes Lawyer *# 1* to communicate directly with a person about the subject of the representation. For example, the law may authorize a party in a controversy with a government agency to speak to government officials about the matter. Rule 4.2, Comment 1. Or, in a class action, defense attorneys may secure a court order allowing communication with members of the plaintiff class in appropriate circumstances.

In criminal cases the prosecutor may wish to secure evidence from a suspect covertly (by wiring an undercover agent or informant) without seeking permission from the suspect's counsel. Defense attorneys in some criminal cases have argued that such investigative techniques violate Rule 4.2 and DR 7–104(A)(1), and that courts should enforce these rules by suppressing any evidence acquired by their violation. E.g., Norton, *Ethics and the Attorney General*, 74 Judicature 203 (Dec.-Jan.1991). Attorney

General Thornburgh obviously disagrees and argues that prosecutors are authorized "by law" to make such contacts directly or through agents. Thornburgh, *Ethics and the Attorney General: The Attorney General Responds,* 74 Judicature 290 (April–May 1991).

The requirements of Rule 4.2 are, of course, inapplicable if the communication does not concern the subject of representation but rather another, separate matter.

In addition, "parties to a matter may communicate directly with each other. . . . " Rule 4.2, Comment 1. This Rule was not intended to prohibit lawyers from advising principals to speak directly with their counterparts. However, this Rule in connection with Rule 8.4(a) (lawyer may not violate a Rule "through the acts of another") does preclude a lawyer from "using an intermediary to carry a message from the lawyer to the opposing party. . . ." The Legislative History of the Model Rules of Professional Conduct 148 (ABA, 1987).

If a corporation or other entity is represented by counsel, then alter egos of that organization are also treated as persons represented by that counsel for purposes of the rule restricting communications to persons represented by counsel. ABA Informal Opinion 1410 (Feb. 14, 1978). As this Informal Opinion makes clear, "If the officers and employees that [the lawyer proposes] to interview *could commit the corporation* because of their authority as corporate officers or employees or for some other reason the law cloaks them with authority, then they, as the alter egos of the corporation, are parties for purposes of DR 7–104(A)(1)." (emphasis added). In addition, Rule 4.2 should be interpreted to protect the attorney-client privilege. During the ABA debates on Rule 4.2, the Reporter for the Model Rules said that "the purpose of Rule 4.2 was to protect the lawyer-client relationship against breach by a lawyer representing another." The Legislative History of the Model Rules of Professional Conduct 148(ABA, 1987). This Rule does not otherwise preclude the lawyer from interviewing the other party's intended witnesses.

The Rules adopt the alter ego test but also appear to expand it:

> "In case of an organization, this Rule [4.2] prohibits communications by a lawyer for one party concerning the matter in representation with persons [1] having a managerial responsibility on behalf of the organization, and [2] with any other person whose act or omission in connection with that matter may be imputed to the organization for purposes of civil or criminal liability or [3] whose statement may constitute an admission on the part of the organization." Rule 4.2, Comment 2.

If clause [2] is an independent test, it may appear to cover every employee-witness in some cases. But see, Rule 4.2, Code Comparison 1. ("This Rule substantially is identical to DR 7–104(A)(1).") Otherwise, a lawyer could not interview corporate employees for whom the organization may have vicarious liability unless corporate counsel agreed. Others have argued for a narrower interpretation, stating that the purpose of Rule 4.2 and DR 7–104(A)(1) "is to prevent improvident settlements and similarly major capitulations of legal position on the part of a momentarily uncounseled, but represented, party and to enable the corporation's lawyer to maintain an effective lawyer-client relationship with members of management. Thus, in the case of corporate and similar entities, the anticontact rule should prohibit contact with those officials, *but only those*, who have the legal power to bind the corporation in the matter or who are responsible for implementing the advice of the corporation's lawyer, or any member of the organization whose own interests are directly at stake in a representation." C. Wolfram, *Modern Legal Ethics* 613 (1986) (emphasis added). Thus Professor Wolfram concludes that if an employee's only relation to a case is as a holder of factual information the employee "should be freely accessible to either lawyer." Id. See also, ABA Formal Opinion 117 (1934).

On behalf of his client, the lawyer may always *request* an unrepresented nonclient witness to refrain from voluntarily giving relevant information to another party *if* the witness is the client's relative, employee, or agent whose interests will not be adversely affected if this request is honored. Rule 3.4(f). The lawyer, however, cannot forbid such witnesses from being interviewed. Whether they are in fact interviewed is up to them. They can always insist on being subpoenaed and then deposed.

In addition, if the witness is merely a low level corporate employee who does not fit these tests, then the interviewing lawyer need not secure any permission from the party's lawyer. If this nonparty witness (whether an occurrence witness or expert witness) has independent representation, the lawyer seeking the interview should secure the permission of the witness' personal lawyer for this matter but *need not secure any permission from the opposing party's lawyer.* See generally, Hacker & Rotunda, *Ethical Restraints on Communications with Adverse Expert Witnesses,* 5 Corp.L.Rev. 348 (1982). See, also, *In re Investigation of FMC Corporation,* 430 F.Supp. 1108 (S.D.W.Va. 1977).

Neither Rule 4.2 nor its Comments require a lawyer representing a client in a matter adverse to a corporation to seek permission of that corporation's attorney before interviewing *former employees* of the corporate party about the subject of the representation. Courts have split on this issue, but ABA Formal Opinion 91–359 (March 22, 1991) made clear that neither the text nor the Comments cover former employees.

Any other reading of Rule 4.2 is very unnatural. Moreover, to so interpret the Rule would greatly inhibit a lawyer from obtaining information about her case.

2. Persons Not Represented by Counsel

DR 7–104(A)(2) and Rule 4.3 restrict the lawyer's communications with unrepresented persons. Though Rule 4.3 is phrased differently than DR 7–104(A)(2), Rule 4.3 generally reflects the interpretation of DR 7–104(A)(2). If a person is not represented by counsel, the lawyer may neither state nor imply that the lawyer is disinterested. If the unrepresented person does not understand the lawyer's role, the lawyer should try to correct the misunderstanding.

> *Example:* Attorney for Employer prepares settlement papers in a workman's compensation case. Employee, who signs these papers, is not represented. Attorney does not advise or mislead Employee as to the law or Lawyer's role in this matter. Lawyer also advises the court, which must approve the settlement, that Employee is appearing pro se. Lawyer's actions are proper. ABA Formal Opinion 102 (Dec. 15, 1933).

C. HARASSING TECHNIQUES

A lawyer's duty to represent a client competently and effectively does not allow a lawyer to harass another person, to violate another's legal rights or to use means that serve no substantial purpose but to "embarrass, delay, or burden a third person. . . ." Rule 4.4. See also, DR 7–102(A)(1); DR 7–106(C)(2); DR 7–108(D), (E).

> *Note:* The Code also forbids a lawyer from threatening to present or presenting "criminal charges solely to obtain an advantage in a civil matter." DR 7–105(A). See also EC 7–21. *The Rules have no such provision.* If the lawyer's threats amount to criminal extortion under state law, then Rule 8.4(b) would apply. See Model Penal Code § 223.4 (1962) (crime of theft by extortion to accuse anyone of criminal offense in order to obtain property not honestly claimed as indemnification for harm caused by conduct relating to the accusation).

IV. REVIEW QUESTIONS

1. The State's Attorney of Blanke County, has an office practice of forwarding a copy to the defendant of the letter sent to his counsel containing an offer to plea bargain. This letter is sent before indictment. The form letter basically states that if the defendant will plead guilty to a lesser crime (e.g., attempted robbery) the government will not proceed on charges of a greater crime (e.g., robbery).

Are State's Attorney's actions *proper?*

a. State's Attorney has an ethical obligation to plea bargain and sending a copy of the letter offering a bargain helps fulfill this duty.

b. State's Attorney may not send a copy of the plea bargain letter to the defendant unless the state's attorney in good faith believes that defense counsel will not inform defendant of the plea bargain.

c. State's Attorney must not send a copy of the plea bargain letter to defendant unless defense counsel consents.

d. State's Attorney must send a copy of the plea bargain letter to fulfill his duty to assure that defendant is kept informed on all of those matters in which the decisions are exclusively for the client.

2. In closing arguments, Attorney makes the following statements.

  I. "The evidence indicates that the witness is a liar."

  II. "I know for a fact that the road was slick when the accident occurred."

  III. "In my opinion the defendant is liable for the accident."

Is Attorney *subject to discipline?*

a. Yes, because of II & III, only.

b. Yes, because of II, only.

c. Yes, because of I & II, only.

d. No.

e. Yes, because of I, II, & III.

3. Attorney is asked by his regular client, Millionaire, to file a suit against the United States, and "take it to the Supreme Court if necessary" to have the progressive income tax declared unconstitutionally confiscatory as applied to him. Attorney advised Millionaire that the suit is baseless, but Attorney finally agreed to file the suit on receipt of a $10,000 retainer.

Is Attorney *subject to discipline?*

a.   Yes, because no portion of the fee was earned when Attorney accepted the retainer.

b.   Yes, because it is unethical to present a claim not warranted under existing law unless it can be supported by a good faith argument for reversal, or modification, or extension of existing law.

c.   No, because Attorney fully advised Millionaire that the suit was baseless and Millionaire paid the retainer with full knowledge.

d.   No, if a fee in these circumstances is not excessive.

4. Decedent's last will left her estate to a trust to be used to improve the public schools of the district in which she lived throughout her lifetime.

Niece and Nephew, Decedent's only surviving relatives, are contesting Decedent's will. The case will be heard before a judge and jury. Attorney, who represents the estate is contacted by a newspaper reporter shortly before the trial begins.

Assuming the statements are true, it is *proper* for Attorney to tell the reporter:

I.   "We have a lot of evidence to show that Niece and Nephew did not visit Decedent a single time during the last lonely year of her life in Twilight Time Nursing Home."

II.   "Our answer states that just before the will was drafted, Decedent discussed with several persons the possibility of leaving her estate to her church and/or public schools. Decedent specifically stated to said persons that she did not want to leave anything to Niece and Nephew."

III.   "In my opinion, Niece and Nephew don't have a leg to stand on."

IV.   "I have no comment whatsoever."

a.   IV only.

b.   II or IV, but not I and III.

c.   I and II, but not III.

d.   I, II and III or IV.

5. The defendant corporation has three witnesses who will testify at trial. Assume the corporate client agrees to reimburse all monies advanced by the lawyer. *Under the disciplinary rules*, on behalf of this corporate client:

   I. The attorney may pay travel expenses for a witness who must come from a distant city.

   II. The attorney may pay a witness $48 for lost wages for spending one day at trial (the witness is normally employed at $6 an hour for an 8 hour day).

   III. The attorney may pay $2500 to an expert for his testimony, if that fee is a reasonable one.

   IV. The attorney may guarantee an expert witness a fee of $400 to $3500, depending on the outcome of the case.

    a.   Only actions I and II are nondisciplinable.

    b.   Only actions I and III are nondisciplinable.

    c.   Only actions I, II and III are nondisciplinable.

    d.   All four actions are permitted.

PART EIGHT

THE LAWYER'S OBLIGATIONS AS ADVISER

Analysis

I. ADVISER VERSUS ADVOCATE

When the client consults the attorney as advocate, the attorney may urge upon the courts any nonfrivolous interpretation of the law that favors the client; when the client consults the attorney as adviser, the attorney should give the client his or her good faith opinion on how the courts will likely rule, and the full effects of such a decision.

When the client asks the lawyer to represent him in litigation, the lawyer may urge the tribunal to adopt any permissible construction of the law. A permissible construction would include any nonfrivolous position, such as a good faith argument for extension, modification, or reversal of existing law. EC 7–4; DR 7–102(A)(1), (2); DR 2–109(A); Rule 3.1.

When the client asks the lawyer to supply legal advice, the lawyer must render his candid opinion of what the court is likely to do. He should also inform the client of the practical effects of such a ruling. EC 7–5; Rule 2.1. The lawyer's efforts to comfort the client cannot limit the duty to give an honest assessment of unpleasant facts. Rule 2.1, Comment 1.

In offering legal advice, the lawyer need not limit his comments to purely technical legal considerations but may refer to economic, political, social and moral considerations. The lawyer may offer his judgment as to what effects are morally just as well as legally permissible. EC 7–8, 7–9; Rule 2.1. The lawyer who couches his advice too narrowly ill-serves the client. Rule 2.1, Comment 2. However, the client, not the lawyer, ultimately must make the final decision whether to accept the lawyer's judgment based on nonlegal considerations. EC 7–8.

The client may ask the lawyer, either expressly or impliedly, to limit his advice to only technical legal matters. The lawyer should follow this limitation, unless the inexperience of the client indicates to the lawyer that he must say more. Rule 2.1, Comment 3. Normally the lawyer need not give unsought advice, but the lawyer "may initiate advice to a client when doing so appears to be in the client's interest." Rule 2.1, Comment 5. See EC 7–8 ("lawyer ought to initiate this decision-making process").

II. MEDIATION AMONG MULTIPLE CLIENTS

The lawyer may represent multiple clients with potentially conflicting interests in order to mediate these differences if the clients knowingly consent.

There is no explicit reference in the Model Code to the concept of the lawyer as intermediary between clients. DR 5–105(B) recognizes that the lawyer may represent multiple clients with differing interests if, under DR 5–105(C), the clients consent and it is "obvious" that the lawyer can represent each adequately. See also, EC 5–20, concerning the lawyer as "impartial arbitrator or mediator."

Because clients often desire mediation to save costs and time, it is "common practice" for attorneys to act "for both partners in drawing articles of copartnership or drawing agreements for the dissolution of copartnership, in acting for both the grantor and the grantee in the sale of real property, in acting for both the seller and purchaser in the sale of personal property, in acting for both the lessor and the lessee in the leasing of property, and in acting for both the lender and borrower in handling a loan transaction . . . " *Lessing v. Gibbons,* 6 Cal.App.2d 598, 606, 45 P.2d 258, 261 (1935).

In such cases the lawyer is mediating between his own clients. Rule 2.2, which deals explicitly with this common occurrence, is designed to protect the lawyer's clients and does not cover cases of formal arbitration where the lawyer is selected by parties who are *not* his clients. See Rule 2.2, Comment 2; cf. Rule 1.12.

The clients must give knowing consent. Therefore the lawyer must inform each client of the effects of such group representation on the attorney client privilege. Rule 2.2(a)(1). See Rule 2.2, Comment 6 (generally "as between commonly represented clients the privilege does not attach"). The clients should understand that the lawyer will not act in a partisan role on behalf of one of the clients to the detriment of the others. Id. at Comment 8.

The lawyer must believe, not only that the matter can be resolved in all of the clients' best interests, but also that it is unlikely that any client will be materially prejudiced if the mediation falls through. Rule 2.2(a)(2). The lawyer must also believe that she can act impartially. Rule 2.2(a)(3). For example, if she has served one client for many years, and expects that relationship to continue, and the other client is a very recent one, the lawyer might find it difficult to act impartially as between the two. Rule 2.2, Comment 7.

Throughout the mediation the lawyer should consult with each client, Rule 2.2(b), and withdraw if any client insists, or if the conditions for proper mediation no longer exist. Rule 2.2(c). After withdrawal the lawyer should not represent any of the clients concerning the matter being mediated. Rule 2.2(c); Cf. EC 5–20.

III. THE LAWYER AS EVALUATOR

Clients may sometimes hire the lawyer to evaluate a matter for the benefit of third parties.

The Rules have a provision explicitly governing a role that lawyers, particularly in recent times, have undertaken—the lawyer as evaluator for the benefit of a third party. Rule 2.3. At least one major New York law firm has found this practice so lucrative that it now has a special team to conduct such investigations. Many courts will tend to dismiss shareholder suits against officials found to be without blame after such an investigation, and companies often believe that they can avoid more extensive government inquiries by showing that they are willing to clean their own house. Cohen, *Firms Faulted for "Independent" Inquiries,* Wall St. Journal, June 14, 1989, at B1, col. 4–6 (midwest ed.).

The lawyer is an evaluator, for example, when she issues a legal opinion "concerning the title of property rendered at the behest of a vendor for the information of a prospective purchaser, or . . . an opinion concerning the legality of the securities registered for sale under the securities laws." Rule 2.3, Comment 1. See also, ABA Formal Opinion 335 (1974). Another example of the lawyer as evaluator occurs when the lawyer for a corporation responds to an auditor's request for information. Id. at Comment 6. Or, a government agency may ask its lawyer to furnish an opinion on the legality of contemplated action. If the opinion is to be made public, the agency may seek to use that opinion to justify its action. The lawyer is then an evaluator, governed by Rule 2.3, See also id. at Comment 2. If the agency asks for confidential advice, then the lawyer is an adviser, governed by Rule 2.1.

Evaluation for the benefit of a third party should be distinguished from investigation for the benefit of a client. A prospective purchaser may retain a lawyer to do a title search on property that the purchaser is planning to purchase. The lawyer's client is the purchaser, not the vendor, and the lawyer's duty of loyalty is only to his client. In contrast, if the vendor retains a lawyer to furnish a title opinion that the vendor plans to show to the purchaser to bolster his claim that the title is a good one, then the lawyer is retained by the client to *evaluate* the property for the benefit of a nonclient. Rule 2.3, Comment 3. The lawyer's duty of loyalty is to the client, id., but the lawyer may also have legal obligations to the third parties who rely on the evaluation. Restatement (Second) of Torts § 552.

To protect the clients, and to take into account the needs of third parties, Rule 2.3 places some restrictions on "evaluations." The lawyer must reasonably believe that conducting an evaluation is compatible with other aspects of the lawyer's relationship with the client. Rule 2.3(a)(1). For example, if the lawyer had been an advocate defending the client on charges of fraud, it would usually not be compatible for the lawyer to conduct an evaluation of the same or related transaction. Id. at Comment 4. See also, Fuld, *Lawyers' Standards and Responsibilities in Rendering Opinions,* 33 Bus.Lawyer 1295, 1310–11 (1978).

The client should also knowingly consent to this arrangement. Rule 2.3(a)(2). In order for the consent to be knowing, the client should know that the lawyer will not act as a typical partisan because of the lawyer's responsibilities to third persons. Id. at Comment 4.

The client may place limits on the scope of an evaluation, e.g., by excluding certain issues, or placing time constraints. Id. at Comment 5. Or, some persons may simply refuse to cooperate. Id. The lawyer's evaluation should disclose in the evaluation all material limits. Id.

To the extent that the evaluation is shown to third parties, there can be no client confidences. But otherwise, all information relating to the evaluation is confidential because of the lawyer-client relationship. Rule 2.3(b). See also, *Diversified Industries, Inc. v. Meredith,* 572 F.2d 596 (8th Cir. 1977).

IV. REVIEW QUESTIONS

1. Lawyer represents Bank, which asks him to examine some old mortgage papers. Lawyer discovers that several of these old mortgages, though carrying low interest rates, allow Bank to reset the rates every five years. Therefore Bank could now raise the mortgage rate several points. None of the Bank officers apparently had understood that the Bank could raise the mortgage rate on some of these old mortgages. Attorney also believes that if the Bank actually raises the rates suddenly and dramatically, the Bank's reputation will suffer.

   a. Attorney *may* simply refuse to tell the Bank officers about the old mortgage papers unless they ask him a specific question about them.

   b. Attorney *must* inform the Bank officers about the old mortgage papers but *may* also advise them that any sudden increase in the old mortgage loans might hurt the goodwill of Bank.

   c. Attorney *must* inform the Bank officers about the old mortgage papers but *may not* also give them nonlegal, moral or business advice because he is a lawyer, not a business adviser.

   d. Attorney *must not* inform the Bank officers about the old mortgage papers if he reasonably believes that they will act in a way that will hurt the Bank shareholders by damaging the goodwill of Bank.

2. Husband and Wife came to Attorney's office together. They told him they were separated and both wanted a divorce. The spouses were in agreement that Wife should have custody of the two children but had been unable to agree on the amounts of spousal support and child support. They asked if Attorney would be willing to serve as impartial mediator in an attempt to help them reach a reasonable agreement. Attorney said "Yes" and with his help, the spouses reached an agreement that Attorney reduced to writing and the parties signed. Shortly thereafter Husband changed his mind about custody, discharged Attorney, and hired Alpha to represent him in an attempt to get immediate custody of the two children. Attorney, at Wife's request, then filed a petition for divorce.

   Without Husband's consent, Attorney represented Wife at the hearing on temporary custody.

Was Attorney's conduct proper?

a.   No, because after acting as an impartial mediator, a lawyer should not represent either of the parties in the dispute.

b.   No, because a lawyer's proper role is that of an advocate, not a mediator.

c.   Yes, because the divorce was pending.

d.   Yes, because Husband voluntarily discharged Attorney and hired new counsel.

e.   Attorney's conduct is not encouraged but he is not subject to discipline.

PART NINE

THE LAWYER'S OBLIGATIONS REGARDING PRO BONO ACTIVITIES

Analysis

I. ENGAGING IN PRO BONO ACTIVITIES

Both the Model Code and the Model Rules encourage, but do not require, lawyers to engage in pro bono activities.

A. DEFINITIONS
1. Representing Clients
Pro Bono Publico means, "for the public good," or for the welfare of the whole. As applied to the work of lawyers, it usually refers to work that lawyers do for no fee or for a reduced fee for litigants who are otherwise too poor to hire private counsel. Lawyers may also represent charitable organizations, such as the Y.M.C.A., the Boy Scouts, the A.C.L.U., and the N.A.A.C.P. on a no fee or reduced fee basis.

If a lawyer represents a client on a pro bono basis, it does not imply that the client is necessarily right, or that the public interest is served only if the client's claim is vindicated. Rather, it means that the public interest is served because that client's views are represented. The client then has his or her day in court.

2. Representing Causes
Law reform activities are also considered pro bono. That is, for no fee a lawyer represents a cause rather than a client. Such activities may include:

> (1) testifying before legislative or administrative hearings urging law reform;

> (2) lobbying for law reform in the selection and retention of judges;

> (3) participating in bar association activities.

Again, the fact that the lawyer engages in law reform activities does not imply that the lawyer's view of law reform is correct. Rather, the public is served because lawyers offer their services, judgment, and experience, to promote causes that they, in good faith, believe promote law reform.

B. ENCOURAGED BUT NOT REQUIRED
1. The Individual Lawyer
Neither the Code nor the Rules require a lawyer to engage in pro bono activities. In fact, in the Code, no disciplinary rule even deals with this issue. Only in the ethical considerations do we find the concern expressed that persons who are unable to pay "all or a portion of a reasonable fee" still should be able to obtain "necessary legal services," and that, consequently, "lawyers should support and participate in ethical activities designed to achieve that objective." EC 2–16.

Though the Code says that it is an "obligation" of each lawyer to render "free legal services to those unable to pay reasonable fees" (EC 2–25), failure to meet his "obligation" is not disciplinable.

The Rules, unlike the Code, refer to pro bono services in the Black Letter (Model Rule 6.1) as well as the Comments. However, Rule 6.1 is the only Black Letter Rule that never uses the word "shall" and only uses the word "should." (Rule 1.5(b) does use the word "preferably.") Though Rule 6.1 is not enforced though the disciplinary process (Rule 6.1, Comment 1), it does have symbolic importance. The drafters of the Model Rules believed that a reference to pro bono activities should at least be made in the Black Letter Rules, even though they were unable to secure acceptance of a mandatory pro bono requirement.

2. Legal Aid Organizations

Some lawyers are more forthcoming than others in offering free (or reduced fee) legal services to those unable to pay the normal fee. In addition, in an effort to provide more representation for those unable to hire private lawyers, the state and federal governments, and some foundations, fund various legal service organizations, which hire lawyers to represent the poor. These organizations take the form of legal aid offices, state public defender offices (for the defense of criminal cases), and bar-sponsored lawyer referral services. Lawyers "should support all proper efforts" of these programs. EC 2–25; EC 2–16; EC 2–33. Accord, Rule 6.1, Comment 3.

II. FEES

In order to be engaged in pro bono work, it is not necessary that the lawyer charge no fee. The lawyer may charge a reduced fee.

A. INDIGENTS VERSUS THE MIDDLE CLASS

If the client in a pro bono case cannot afford to pay a fee, the lawyer should charge no fee. EC 2–24, 2–25; Rule 6.1, Comment 1. However, often a person of moderate means can afford some fee, but—because of the complexity of the matter—cannot afford the lawyer's customary fee. Then the lawyer should charge a reduced fee. EC 2–16, 2–24. Rule 6.1, Comment 1.

B. PRICE DISCRIMINATION

The Model Code does not set a minimum fee—to do so would violate the antitrust laws, see Part III, Section IV, A, 1—but it recognizes that "adequate compensation is necessary in order to enable the lawyer to serve his client effectively and to preserve the integrity and independence of the profession." EC 2–17.

A lawyer, therefore, may charge a "reasonable fee" of clients able to afford it. Those clients who only can afford less, should be charged a lesser fee. The Code and Rules therefore, in effect, approve of price discrimination: a lawyer may charge one client less (or more) than another client is charged, based on the clients' ability to pay. If one charges a client less because the client is less wealthy, the other side of the coin must be that one is charging another client more because that client is more wealthy. Compare EC 2–18, which explicitly approves of price discrimination in a special circumstance (it provides that it is appropriate to charge less to a fellow lawyer or members of a fellow lawyer's immediate family).

Example: Attorney represents Client *A,* another lawyer, in the purchase of a home. Attorney charges $50 per hour for her services. Attorney also represents Client *B,* a wealthy manufacturer, in the purchase of his home. Attorney charges $90 per hour for her services. Client *C,* an indigent, asks Attorney to represent him in reviewing his rental contract with Landlord in a low income housing project. Attorney charges nothing. Finally, Client *D,* a person of moderate means, asks attorney to represent him in the purchase of his moderate cottage. Attorney charges $40 per hour for her services, which is all that *D* can afford. Assuming that none of these charges is unreasonably high, Attorney has done nothing improper.

III. THE DECISION TO ACCEPT A PRO BONO CASE

A lawyer need not accept every client who walks in the office, but the lawyer should not refuse a case because the cause or client is unpopular. Nor should the lawyer lightly turn down appointed cases.

A. PROPER AND IMPROPER REASONS TO REJECT PRO BONO EMPLOYMENT

The lawyer is not like the cab driver waiting at a taxi stand. The lawyer need not accept every client who walks through the door. However, it is improper for a lawyer to refuse a case for the wrong reason. To achieve the goal of making legal services fully available, a lawyer "should not lightly decline proffered employment," a principle that "requires" that a lawyer accept "his share of tendered employment which may be unattractive both to him and to the bar generally." EC 2–26.

For example, a lawyer must refuse a case because he is too busy to give it his competent attention. EC 2–30; DR 6–101(A)(1); Rule 1.1; Rule 6.2, Comment 2. A lawyer also must refuse a case if the client seeks to maintain a frivolous action or one brought only to harass another. EC 2–30; DR 2–109(A); DR 7–102(A)(1); Rule 3.1.

On the other hand, a lawyer should not decline representation merely because the client, or the client's cause, is unpopular (EC 2–27, Rule 6.2, Comment 1), or because influential members of the community oppose the lawyer's involvement. EC 2–28.

In addition, a lawyer need not refuse a case merely because he or she does not believe in the merits of a client's case, or believes, in a criminal case, that the client is guilty. EC 2–29. However, if the lawyer's personal feelings are so intense that his effective representation is impaired, then he must not take the case. Model Rule 6.2(c) & Comment 2; EC 2–30.

B. APPOINTED CASES

A lawyer should not refuse a court appointment to handle a pro bono case except for "compelling reasons." EC 2–29; Rule 6.2(a). In addition, the Rules allow a lawyer to refuse a pro bono case if taking it would result in "an unreasonable financial burden. . . ." Rule 6.2(b).

The Code has no such specific provision, but earlier case law has allowed this excuse when the burden is truly unreasonable rather than merely minor. Compare *People ex rel. Conn v. Randolph*, 35 Ill.2d 24, 219 N.E.2d 337 (1966) (State paid fee in excess of statutory maximum allowed in appointed case in order to prevent an unconstitutional taking of property when the financial burden was staggering), with *People v. Sanders*, 58 Ill.2d 196, 317 N.E.2d 552 (1974) (only $250 statutory maximum awarded in capital punishment case because financial burden in this instance is not unreasonable), and *Brown v. Board of County Commissioners of Washoe County*, 85 Nev. 149, 451 P.2d 708 (1969) (minor loss of income should be borne by attorney).

While courts have held that there is no constitutional right to compensation for compelled jury service, *Maricopa County v. Corp*, 44 Ariz. 506, 39 P.2d 351 (1934) (per curium), the difference between compelled jury service and compelled legal representation is not only in the amount of time and effort typically required, but also in the nature of the limited and discrete class burdened. The burden of uncompensated criminal defense representation is borne only by trial lawyers while the burden of jury service does not single out any discrete class of individuals. A purpose of the just compensation clause is to prevent the majority from requiring discrete classes of people to bear special burdens without just compensation. Thus the Alaska Supreme Court held that, under the state Constitution, the court could not compel a private attorney to represent an indigent criminal defendant unless the state paid just compensation, defined as, "the compensation received by the average competent attorney operating in the open market." *DeLisio v. Alaska Superior Court*, 740 P.2d 437, 443 (Alaska 1987) (overruling prior cases).

While it is improper for a lawyer to refuse a case because the client is unpopular, EC 2–27, the lawyer should not take a case if his or her own personal feelings against the client or cause are so strong that the lawyer could not do a competent job. EC 2–30 (" . . . the intensity of his personal feeling, as distinguished from a community attitude. . . ."). Accord, Rule 6.2(c).

Caveat: The Code says that "[c]ompelling reasons [not to take a case] do not include such factors as the repugnance of the subject matter . . ." EC 2–29. In contrast, Rule 6.2(c) states that a proper reason to refuse to accept an appointed case is that "the client or the cause is so repugnant . . ." to the lawyer. See also Rule 6.2, Comment 1 ("A lawyer ordinarily is not obliged to accept a client whose character or cause the lawyer regards as repugnant."). These two sections are not really in conflict. EC 2–30 explains that a lawyer should decline representation if "the intensity of his personal feelings" may "impair his effective representation . . .," and Comment 1 to Rule 6.2 qualifies the reference to repugnancy by explaining that it is modified by the lawyer's responsibility to provide pro bono service.

IV. MANDATORY PRO BONO SERVICE

A. PROPOSALS

The ABA Model Code and Model Rules do not presently require that lawyers engage in mandatory pro bono service, but the idea has been often proposed and justified under various theories.

It is settled that in individual cases the courts have the power to compel attorneys to accept appointment to cases before the court. "Attorneys are officers of the court, and are bound to render service when required by such an appointment." *Powell v. Alabama,* 287 U.S. 45, 73, 53 S.Ct. 55, 65, 77 L.Ed. 158, 172 (1932). Less certain is the extent to which counsel must assume this burden with little or no compensation. See section III, B, supra.

A related question is the extent to which a state bar association or the state disciplinary machinery can or should require mandatory pro bono representation in civil, rather than criminal cases, and mandatory pro bono counseling and advice in nonlitigative situations.

In California, for example, the state legislature considered, and defeated, a bill requiring active members of the bar to engage in a minimum of 40 hours per year of mandatory pro bono work for no fee or a "substantially reduced" fee. Assembly Bill No. 4050 (1976).

Thomas Ehrlich, the first President of the Legal Services Corporation, was also a member of the ABA Commission that drafted the Model Rules. He argued, "with enthusiasm" that the Rules should mandate (not merely encourage) pro bono activities by private attorneys to help the poor. Ehrlich, *Rationing Justice,* 34 The Record of the Association of the Bar of the City of New York 729, 743 (Dec. 1979).

The Model Rules initially proposed:

> "A lawyer *shall* render unpaid public interest legal service . . . [and] shall make an annual report concerning such service to the appropriate regulatory authority." Proposed Rule 8.1, Discussion Draft (Jan. 30, 1980), reprinted in T. Morgan & R. Rotunda, 1980 Selected National Standards Supplement 142 (1980).

There was much opposition, however, from ABA members, and the Commission withdrew its proposal.

B. RATIONALE

Proponents of mandatory pro bono offer various rationales. The former President of the Legal Services Corporation argued that lawyers, but not medical doctors, are obliged to offer free service because "lawyers are an essential part of the public justice system, with monopolistic access to the workings of the system. With that monopoly comes a public obligation to help ensure the sound workings of the system—otherwise the rationing of justice becomes warped in ways that are dangerous not only to poor people, who are denied an opportunity to use the system, but also to the public generally, which is denied a legal system that works fairly." Ehrlich, *Rationing Justice,* 34 Record of the Association of the Bar of the City of New York 729, 743 (Dec. 1979).

Others reply that while lawyers have a legal monopoly to the practice of law, medical doctors have a legal monopoly over the practice of medicine. Thus, the President of the California State Bar once proposed that medical doctors, lawyers, and dentists all should be obligated to contribute one-half day per month of free services. San Jose Mercury, Nov. 29, 1976, at 26, col. 1. In 1987, the ABA Journal and the Journal of the American Medical Association each published an editorial advocating that "all doctors and all lawyers, as a matter of ethics and good faith, should contribute a significant percentage of their total professional efforts without expectation of financial remuneration." They said that 50 hours a year was "an appropriate minimum amount." 73 A.B.A.J. 55 (Dec. 1, 1987).

In reply, some have argued that the fact that there is a legal monopoly proves little: if the monopoly is bad, it should be eliminated; if the monopoly is good and needed, then its existence adds little to the pro bono debate. The local utility company has a monopoly and does not have to provide free electricity.

The ABA Commission that drafted the Model Rules and initially proposed a mandatory pro bono requirement did not rely on any theory of legal monopoly. The ABA Commission relied on "the lawyer's commitment to the law's idea of equal justice." Proposed Model Rule 8.1, Comment 1 (Discussion Draft, Jan. 30, 1980), reprinted in T. Morgan & R. Rotunda, 1980 Selected National Standards Supplement 142 (1980).

Others argue that to say that free legal services to the poor and less advantaged will promote justice does not lead to the conclusion that it is an individual lawyer's duty to provide such services for free. These people argue that it is society's duty to fund services and pay the lawyers who perform them. See, e.g., *State v. Green,* 470 S.W.2d 571, 573 (Mo.1971), where the court said that it "will not *compel* the attorneys . . . to discharge *alone* a 'duty which constitutionally is the burden of the State' " (emphasis in original); *State ex rel. Scott v. Roper,* 688 S.W.2d 757 (Mo.1985) (en banc) (extensive historical discussion and holding that court does not have power to appoint counsel in civil cases without compensation). See also Shapiro, *The Enigma of the Lawyer's Duty to Serve,* 55 N.Y.U.L.Rev. 735, 738–39 (1980): "Although frequently urged as rooted in the firmest of traditions, the 'duty to serve' in fact has a history shrouded in obscurity, ambiguity, and qualification, and this murkiness is reflected in recent struggles of courts and commentators to deal rationally with the issues. Imposition of a duty by the state. . . . raises substantial constitutional issues and is perhaps even more vulnerable on economic and other policy grounds."

C. MANDATORY PRO BONO AND ALTERNATIVE SERVICE

Some proposals for mandatory pro bono provide forms of alternative service. For example, if Lawyer Alpha is appointed by the court to represent an indigent, can Alpha, a partner in a large firm, fulfill this responsibility by assigning the case to one of the young associates? Lawyers in solo practice or in small firms often believe that this opt out in effect places a proportionately heavier burden on them, because it is easier for the larger firms to find a less expensive associate in their office. Moreover, when the firms are large enough and there is always a supply of young associates who do not have any client base yet, the marginal cost to the larger firm (of assigning a young associate to a pro bono activity) may be close to zero.

Alternatively, can lawyer Alpha fulfill his pro bono responsibility by paying another lawyer in a different firm to do the work? Can Alpha simply buy out of this obligation? Such a buy out is equally available to solo practitioners as well as members of the larger firms. The burden, however, is relatively greater for the poorer lawyer.

If Alpha can simply buy out, then mandatory pro bono is really a tax, and, as such, some argue that it is better for the state legislature to tax each lawyer directly and use that money to hire attorneys to staff legal aid offices. This tax could be made progressive.

Others reply that what is needed is not just the lawyer's money but the lawyer's time. "The responsibility for pro bono service should be borne *by each lawyer individually.*" Proposed Model Rule 8.1, Comment 1 (Discussion Draft, Jan. 30, 1980) (emphasis added), reprinted in T. Morgan & R. Rotunda, 1980 Selected National Standards Supplement 142 (1980). There is support for this view in some language of the Model Code and Model Rules. See EC 2–25: "*[P]ersonal involvement* in the problems of the disadvantaged can be one of the most rewarding experiences in the life of a lawyer" (emphasis added). Accord, Rule 6.1, Comment 3 (same).

Yet, some contend that if the real purpose of pro bono work is to help the poor, the poor would be better helped by a legal service lawyer specializing in their problems rather than a municipal bond lawyer who was forced to learn about the law of evictions. Contra, Ehrlich, *Rationing Justice,* 34 Record of the Association of the Bar of the City of New York 729, 744 (Dec. 1979): "But many legal aid programs have found that, with relatively modest amounts of training, even bond indenture lawyers can re-emerge from their specialist shells."

The Model Rules specifically allow an attorney to render pro bono service "by financial support for organizations that provide legal services to persons of limited means." This provision in Rule 6.1 was added a few months before the final version of the Model Rules was adopted. The Commission on the Model Rules did not oppose the change.

V. LAW REFORM ACTIVITIES AFFECTING PRIVATE CLIENTS

For reasons of public policy, it is not generally considered a conflict of interest for a lawyer to engage in pro bono activities even though such activities are adverse to the interests of the lawyer's private clients.

A. THE LAWYER'S PERSONAL VIEWS
1. Law Reform Activities Adverse to a Private Client's Interests
A lawyer only represents a client in the lawyer's professional capacity. It is not necessary that the lawyer agree with, adopt, or support his or her client's views. "The obligation of loyalty to his client applies only to a lawyer in the discharge of his professional duties and implies no obligation to adopt a personal viewpoint favorable to the interests or desires of his client." EC 7–17. Accord, Rule 1.2(b). Lawyers who abhor cigarettes may represent tobacco companies without taking up the smoking habit.

In fact, the Code specifically provides that a lawyer "may take positions on public issues and espouse legal reforms he favors without regard to the individual views of any client." EC 7–17. The Rules are not as specific in this respect, though their general tenor supports the principle expressed in EC 7–17. The first sentence of Model Rule 6.4 states that a lawyer may be a director, officer, or member of a group involved in law reform activities "notwithstanding that the reform may affect the interests of a client of the lawyer." If there is no breach of loyalty when the lawyer is a member of an organization advocating law reform contrary to a client's interest, there should be little argument that there is a breach of loyalty when the lawyer speaks out on his own behalf. Cf. EC 8–4. In both cases the Code and Rules conclude that the benefits to clients because of the conflicts rules are outweighed by the social costs of using these rules to prohibit lawyers from engaging in law reform efforts, either individually or through bar associations, legal service organizations, the A.C.L.U., and similar groups.

The client may not like the fact that the lawyer is publicly advocating law reform views contrary to the client's private interests. The client may always fire the lawyer, DR 2–110(B)(4); Rule 1.16(a)(3), but the client may not properly charge that the lawyer acted unethically in taking the contrary position. In practice, of course, the client often does not discharge the lawyer because lawyers are not fungible.

Example: Attorney normally represents corporations defending against charges of job discrimination brought by the Equal Employment Opportunity Commission. Attorney is also a member of the NAACP and NOW. Attorney publicly endorses the lobbying activities of both organizations in their efforts to strengthen the power of the EEOC to fight racial and gender discrimination in employment. It might be adverse to the interests of Attorney's corporate clients if the powers of the EEOC are increased. Attorney has, nonetheless, acted properly.

2. Law Reform Activities Supportive of a Private Client

The Client's interest and the personal law reform interests of the lawyer may coincide. If the lawyer is representing a private client while, for example, appearing before a legislative committee and asking for law reform, the lawyer may not mislead the committee as to the true identity of the client. DR 7–106(B); Rules 3.9 & 4.1(a). If the attorney is representing XYZ Corp., she may not pretend to be representing her own views. If the identity of the client is privileged, the lawyer should at least alert the committee that she is representing a private client whose identity cannot be revealed. Id. Cf. Rule 6.4.

If the lawyer personally believes in an item of law reform and his own belief coincides with the interest of his client, it is unclear under the Model Code whether the lawyer must nonetheless disclose that fact even if such disclosure does not identify the client. See EC 8–4, which only states that if the lawyer purports to act on behalf of the public, then the lawyer should conscientiously believe in the position advocated.

Rule 6.4 is much more specific. "When the lawyer knows that the interests of a client may be materially benefitted by a decision in which the lawyer participates, the lawyer shall disclose that fact but need not identify the client." The disclosure of the fact of representation helps to preclude the suspicion that the lawyer exercised improper influence on behalf of a client.

B. MEMBERSHIP ON A LEGAL SERVICE BOARD

Often attorneys are members of the Board of Directors of a Legal Services Organization. In fact, after Congress established the federal Legal Services Corporation in 1974, see 42 U.S.C.A. § 2996b, in order to offer noncriminal legal services to indigents, the relevant regulations required that at least 60% of the local governing bodies should be attorneys admitted in that state and supportive of the delivery of quality legal services to the poor. 45 C.F.R. § 1607.3(b) (1982).

If an attorney in private practice is on a legal services board, in a matter of time it may be almost inevitable that the staff members of the legal services organization, on behalf of an indigent client, will file suit against one of the private attorney's private clients, or defend the indigent against suit brought by the private client. There is, however, no conflict of interest because the private attorney who is a member of the Board does not have an attorney-client relationship with the Legal Service Organization's clients. ABA Formal Opinion 345 (July 12, 1979); Rule 6.3, Comment 1. The individual legal service clients do not confer with the Board members; nor do they place any confidences or secrets with these Board members, ABA Formal Opinion 334 (Aug. 10, 1974). "The Board's role is restricted solely to establishment of broad policy for the Program, and not the management of or the direct participation in Program client representation." ABA Formal Opinion 345 (July 12, 1979). See also 45 C.F.R. § 1607.4(b) (1982) (same). Cf. DR 5–107(B) (lawyer should not permit person who employs him to render services for another to direct his professional judgment); Rule 5.4(c) (same). See also ABA Formal Opinion 334 (Aug. 10, 1974) (same). Finally, public policy favors having active practitioners involved in the activities of legal service organizations. ABA Formal Opinion 345 (July 12, 1979); Rule 6.3, Comment 1.

ABA Formal Opinion 345, supra, based on the Model Code, concludes, nonetheless, that there remains a problem when a Board member represents a client adverse to the client of a legal services program. Perhaps, said the

Opinion, one of the counsel might feel self-restrained in exercising zeal. Or, a client (particularly an indigent one) may acquiesce only because he believes that he has no choice in the matter. ABA Formal Opinion 345 (July 12, 1979).

Consequently, Formal Opinion 345 concluded that the clients on both sides must be made aware of the Board member's role. The lawyers and clients on either side should "feel comfortable," and "if, in the course of the representation, it becomes apparent that independent representation is not being afforded on both sides or one or the other of the clients perceives that it is not afforded, *no matter what the reality,* then the lawyers should assist in change of counsel for one or both clients." Id. (emphasis added). If the Board member's law firm is large enough, the Opinion continued, a lawyer other than the Board member should represent the firm's clients in disputes with the legal services program, so that the Board member is not directly involved. The ABA Ethics Committee, in this Opinion, "urges" that the Board member's law firm provide "screening procedures." Id. Cf. Rule 1.11. Finally, because of the "extreme value" of having active lawyers serve as Board members, the legal services staff lawyer "should not seek unfairly to gain advantage for their clients by disqualification of the Board member or his firm." ABA Formal Opinion 345 (July 12, 1979).

The approach of the Model Rules is somewhat different. The Rules try to solve the problem of any perceived conflicts by selectively screening the private lawyer from the decision-making process of the legal services organization. If the private lawyer is also a member, director, or officer of the legal services organization, then the private lawyer should not "knowingly" participate in any decision or action of the legal services organization if such participation would be inconsistent with the lawyer's obligation, under Rule 1.7, to his or her private clients. (Rule 1.7 is the general rule governing conflicts of interest.) Similarly, the private lawyer should not knowingly participate in a decision on behalf of the legal services organization if the decision could have a "material adverse effect" on a legal services' client whose interests are adverse to the lawyer's private client. The private lawyer, then, is not disqualified from serving on the Board; that lawyer is disqualified from participating in certain Board decisions.

The legal services organization is also encouraged to establish written policies regarding the role of the legal services decision-making process in order to enhance the credibility of the assurances that it gives to its indigent clients. Model Rule 6.3, Comment 2.

VI. REVIEW QUESTIONS

1. Hiram Lawyer is an attorney with great prestige in the legal community. He has been asked by the court to represent an accused burglar who is indigent. Hiram:

   a. *Should* refuse to take the case if he has read about the case in newspapers and believes the defendant is probably guilty.

   b. *May* refuse to take the case if doing so would hurt his reputation, because a lawyer's reputation is his stock in trade.

   c. *Should not* take the case if the intensity of his personal feeling may impair the effective representation of the prospective client.

   d. *Should* take the case unless it requires him to align himself against influential members of the community.

2. Lloyd Smith is a local attorney who is also a member of the State Bar Committee on Corporate Law. That Committee is considering whether to propose changes in the state's corporate statutes in order to allow directors to hold meetings and take binding votes by telephone. One of Smith's clients is very supportive of the new proposed law and asks Smith to vote for the proposed law in the Committee. Is it *proper* for Smith to support the proposed law?

   a. Yes, if Smith discloses the fact that one of his clients would benefit and if he espouses only those changes in the law that he conscientiously believed to be in the public interest.

   b. Yes, because he owes duty to his client to fight zealously for that client's interests and must do so even if he personally does not agree with the proposed changes.

   c. No, because Smith was involved in a conflict of interest in representing this private client and also being a member of the state bar committee dealing with matters that impinged on the client's interests.

   d. No, because Smith must disqualify himself, even if Smith would have supported the proposed law without the client's request.

3. Delta, a lawyer and the head of the state disciplinary authority, has asked Alpha, also a lawyer, to sit on one of the state hearing boards responsible for hearing charges of disciplinary violations. The board is normally composed of two lawyers and one lay person. The state pays no compensation for such services.

Alpha *should:*

a.   sit on the board because in doing so he can assist in the administration of the Disciplinary Rules, but he will not be disciplined if he refuses.

b.   refuse to sit unless the state pays reasonable compensation, because in so doing he can assist in improving the enforcement of the Disciplinary Rules.

c.   refuse to sit so long as there is a lay member of the board.

PART TEN

THE LAWYER'S OBLIGATIONS AS A JUDGE

Analysis

I. AN INTRODUCTORY NOTE

A. A SHORT HISTORY

In 1924 the ABA House of Delegates promulgated the first judicial code of ethics, called the Canons of Judicial Ethics. An important catalyst to the 1924 Canons of Judicial Ethics was the scandalous revelation, in the early 1920's, that Kenesaw Mountain Landis, a federal judge, was engaging in private employment and supplementing his federal salary of $7,500 with a more generous yearly salary of $42,500 for being the major league baseball commissioner. The ABA adopted a resolution of censure of the judge. Armstrong, *The Code of Judicial Conduct*, 26 Southwestern L.J. 708, 709 (1972); C. Wolfram, *Modern Legal Ethics* 965 n.72 (Practitioner's Edition 1986). Even though Chief Justice Taft was chairman of the ABA Committee that drafted the 1924 Judicial Canons, many states did not adopt them, with their "curious mixture of generalized, hortatory admonitions and specific rules of standards of proscribed conduct." Sutton, *A Comparison of the Code of Professional Responsibility with the Code of Judicial Conduct*, 1972 Utah L.Rev. 355, 255–56. Nearly a half century later, the ABA House of Delegates replaced these Canons with the Code of Judicial Conduct (1972), written in more conventional statutory form. This Judicial Code, as well, was, at least in part, a reaction to the scandal that led to Justice Fortas's resignation from the Supreme Court and the uproar relating to the financial and other disclosures that came about when the U.S. Senate rejected President Nixon's nomination of Federal Circuit Judge Haynsworth, and then Judge Circuit Judge Carswell. Wolfram, supra, at 966 n.79. Many states widely adopted the 1972 Code (subject, of course, to various nonuniform amendments). The United States Judicial Conference adopted a version as well. 101 F.R.D. 389 (1984). In 1990, the ABA House of Delegates approved a comprehensive revision, called the Model Code of Judicial Conduct.

B. SOME GENERAL COMPARISONS BETWEEN THE 1990 JUDICIAL CODE AND THE 1972 JUDICIAL CODE

The 1990 Model Code is in the same format as the 1972 Code, but many of the sections are renumbered and reorganized. The 1990 Code has 5 Canons, while the 1972 Code has 7.

The 1990 Code, unlike the 1972 Code, is gender neutral. The drafters of the 1990 Code also intended to offer clearer standards than those offered by the 1972 Code. But sometimes they did not succeed.

C. TERMINOLOGY

The 1972 Code used the term "should" in the Canons and text and, as a consequence, some jurisdictions thought that "should" only expressed an aspirational standard. (Although the Preface to the 1972 Code indicated it intended mandatory standards, some jurisdictions omitted the Preface). The 1990 Code eliminates this confusion by using the term *"shall"* in the text and "*must*" in the Commentary to indicate that a standard is mandatory, and violation of that standard subjects the judge to discipline. The 1990 Code uses "*may*" in to indicate that the judge has permissible discretion. "*Should*" or "*should not*" is intended to be hortatory.

D. THE STRUCTURE OF THE 1990 JUDICIAL CODE

The 1990 Code has a *Preamble,* which explains that the Code is divided into a series of *Canons,* which are broad statements. Specific rules under each Canon are called *Sections.* After this Preamble, there is a section called *Terminology,* which puts in one place all of the terms of art used in the 1990 Code. When these terms appear in the body of the 1990 Code, an asterisk (*) accompanies them, indicating to the reader to turn to the Terminology section. At the end of the 1990 Code is an *Application Section,* which discusses what types of persons are covered by the 1990 Code. The Canons, the Sections, Terminology, and Application Section are authoritative. The *Commentary* (which follows various Sections) is intended to provide guidance, but it is not intended to be a statement of additional rules.

E. INTERPRETING THE 1990 JUDICIAL CODE

The Preamble explains that the 1990 Code is not intended to be a basis for civil or criminal liability. The text of the Canons and Sections is intended to govern the conduct of, and be binding on, judges, but not "every transgression will result in disciplinary actions." Preamble 5. The Preamble also cautions that the 1990 Code is not intended to be an exhaustive guide, and the standards that it offers are to be interpreted as *rules of reason,* a point that the Preamble makes several times. Preamble 3, 5. A "minor violation of a rule need not invariably result in discipline." *ABA's Standing Committee Report on 1990 Code, Legislative Draft* 2 (1990). Lawyers are not supposed to invoke these Canons for "mere tactical advantage," Preamble 4, a principal that should prove difficult to enforce, because the adversary system, by its very nature, gives many incentives to lawyers to use laws, rules, and precedent for "mere tactical advantage."

Note: Because the ABA has replaced the 1972 Code with the 1990 Code, this chapter will focus, in the main, on the 1990 Code, *not* the 1972 Code. Because the 1990 Model Judicial Code is new, it has not been subject to case law interpretation. However, much case law decided under the 1972 Code is still relevant under the 1990 Code because much of the substantive provisions are basically unchanged (although many of the sections are renumbered). The drafters of the 1990 Code did not write on a clean slate. Hence we will refer to appropriate cases decided under the 1972 Code. *You should assume that any citation to a Code section is to the 1990 Code, unless the text indicates otherwise.* During the course of this chapter, we will compare differences between the two Codes when such a comparison is useful.

II. PERSONAL BEHAVIOR

A. CANON ONE
A judge shall uphold the integrity and independence of the judiciary.

1. Purpose of Canon One
Canon 1 sets the tone for the rest of the Model Code of Judicial Conduct (1990). The public must not only have confidence in the reliability of judicial procedures, but also in the integrity of the judges. The basic purpose of the Code is to "assure that judges will be worthy of . . . independence and deserving of . . . confidence." See *New Standards of Judicial Conduct,* 46 Fla.B.J. 268, 269 (1972) (Quoting R. Traynor, Chairman of the ABA Special Committee on Standards of Judicial Conduct). Canon 1 introduces the parameters of that goal.

2. Judicial Independence
Canon 1 maintains that an independent judiciary is an indispensable element of justice, and that judges must strive to see that the independence of the judiciary is preserved.

The rationale of Canon 1 is to preserve an independent judiciary and thereby ensure a free society. Risks of conflicts would arise if a judge, under the *control* of the government, were called upon to decide a case in which the government is a party. Similarly, if judges were and remained members of the legislature, they might not be able to apply impartially the laws they passed. See E. Thode, *Reporter's Notes to [1972] Code of Judicial Conduct* 45–46 (1973) [hereinafter cited as *Reporter's Notes [1972]*].

3. Judicial Integrity
The drafters explain that a judge cannot be disciplined for violating the first clause of the second sentence of Canon 1A, which provides that the judge "*should* participate in maintaining and enforcing high standards of conduct" (emphasis added). *ABA's Standing Committee Report on 1990 Code, Legislative Draft* (1990), at 8. Nonetheless, this hortatory statement is evidence of the Code's goal of assuring public confidence in the judiciary.

Courts generally do not rely on Canon 1 as the sole basis for disciplinary action. Note that the second clause of the second sentence provides that judges "*shall* personally observe" high standards of conduct. (emphasis added). Courts do, however, refer to Canon 1 in their opinions when the judge's conduct constitutes a separate violation of a more specific section of the Code. Because any violation of the Judicial Code impairs the "integrity" of the judiciary, this Canon is often cited, though never primarily relied upon. E.g., *In re Larkin*, 368 Mass. 87, 333 N.E.2d 199 (1975) (judge's repeated attempts to give illegal campaign contributions to the governor violated Canons 1, and other sections). Courts prefer to rely on the specific language of other Canons rather than the general language found in Canon 1.

> *Note:* The Code of Judicial Conduct is a *Model* Code and is not enforceable in any jurisdiction unless officially adopted by that jurisdiction. (The title to 1972 Code does not include the word "Model," although it is a "model" or proposed code of conduct for judges. The 1990 Code incorporates "model" as part of its title.) The basis for discipline in *In re Larkin* was Massachusetts' adoption of the ABA Model Judicial Code as its own standards of judicial conduct. Any future citation of a case indicates that the jurisdiction has adopted a version of the applicable Canon as its own.

ABA Informal Opinion 1452 (March 20, 1980) offers an example of conduct that it concludes might impair the integrity of the judiciary and violate Canon 1. The issue concerned the propriety of an appellate court bargaining with a union that represented the court's secretaries where the union was also a frequent litigant before the court. The ABA concluded that the integrity of the court could be compromised because the secretaries were privy to nonpublic information related to undecided cases in which the union was a litigant, and therefore interpreted Canon 1 to prohibit the judge from bargaining with the union. With whom, then, are the secretaries to bargain? "We observe," the Informal Opinion concludes, some laws pertaining to collective bargaining "exclude from coverage confidential employees." Thus, apparently, the Judicial Code, in effect, prevents judges' secretaries from having a union! A peculiar result, some might say, and not necessarily compelled by the vague language of Canon 1.

4. Duty to Report Violations

Canon 1 implicitly requires a judge to report any known violations of the Code to the proper disciplinary authority, because, as the Comment to Canon 1 explains, judges "must comply with the law, including the provisions of this Code." No court or disciplinary authority, however, has needed to cite Canon 1 when disciplining judges for failure to report violations of the Judicial Code because the Code contains an explicit duty to report in Canon 3D(1),(2), discussed infra.

B. CANON TWO

A judge shall avoid impropriety and the appearance of impropriety in all of the judge's activities.

1. **Applies Whether Judge Is on or Off the Bench**

Canon 2 compels a judge to observe high standards of conduct whether on the bench or off the bench because public esteem for the judiciary is affected by the judge's behavior in either situation. Comment 2 to Canon 2A explicitly notes that the duty to avoid impropriety or its appearance "applies to both the professional and personal conduct of a judge." Thus, a judge was publicly reprimanded for openly engaging in sexual acts while in an automobile parked in a public parking lot. *In re Lee,* 336 So.2d 1175 (Fla. 1976). Some courts, however, take a more liberal attitude toward out-of-court behavior, and hold that such conduct is not punishable unless it affects the judicial role. See, e.g., *Matter of Dalessandro,* 483 Pa. 431, 397 A.2d 743 (1979) (judge not disciplined for having open adulterous relationship; the acts of adultery, however, were not committed in the open, nor in a parking lot). The cases in this area of sexual misconduct "are nearly impossible to reconcile." S. Lubet, *Beyond Reproach: Ethical Restrictions on the Extrajudicial Activities of State and Federal Judges* 40 (1984).

"Off-bench" conduct more likely affects the judicial role if the conduct is illegal. The court in *Dalessandro* emphasized that the judge's adulterous relationship was not contrary to Pennsylvania law. Illegal conduct was the basis for disciplining "off-bench" behavior in *Matter of Sawyer,* 286 Or. 369, 594 P.2d 805 (1979). *Sawyer* disciplined a judge for teaching part-time in a state college in violation of a state constitutional provision. The court suspended the judge from office during the period of time that he was a teacher.

Note: If otherwise allowed by law, Canon 4A and Canon 4B (discussed below) permit a judge to teach on subjects concerning the law, the legal system, and the administration of justice; Canon 4B also allows a judge to teach nonlegal subjects if teaching does not demean the judicial office or interfere with the performance of judicial duties.

2. **Appearance of Impropriety and the Standard of Review**

Although the Model Rules of Professional Conduct reject the "appearance of impropriety" standard as too vague to be a useful test, Model Rule 1.5, Comment 5 (discussed in Part I, § 2, supra), the Model Judicial Code adopts it in the introductory sentence to Canon 2: "A judge shall avoid impropriety and the appearance of impropriety in all of the judge's activities." Canon 2A, Comment 2, admits that this standard "is necessarily cast in general terms," and offers this test:

"whether the conduct would create in reasonable minds a perception that the judge's ability to carry out judicial responsibilities with integrity, impartiality and competence is impaired."

Given this purported test, judicial conduct under this Canon should be scrutinized objectively. The standard is whether the conduct would appear to a reasonable person to demonstrate partiality or prejudice public esteem for the judicial office. "The guiding consideration is that the administration of justice should reasonably appear to be disinterested as well as be so in fact." *Public Utilities Commission of District of Columbia v. Pollak,* 343 U.S. 451, 467, 72 S.Ct. 813, 823, 96 L.Ed. 1068, 1079 (1952) (separate statement of Frankfurter, J.), quoted in, *School District of Kansas City, Missouri v. Missouri,* 438 F.Supp. 830, 835 (W.D.Mo. 1977).

"Impropriety" is, at best, a very vague standard. After all, we cannot begin to define "appearance of impropriety" unless we know what is an "impropriety." Thus, cases disciplining a judge for engaging in impropriety typically rely on a more specific standard found elsewhere in the Code. But the court, after relying on a more specific section, will often add the violation of this more general standard, perhaps as a makeweight.

The following cases and ABA opinions are examples of conduct violative of other sections of the Judicial Code or other statutory or common law standards of conduct; in all instances the conduct was also held to violate Canon 2 and thus they help explain, by way of example, the meaning of "impropriety" or "appearance" thereof.

Spruance v. Commission on Judicial Qualifications, 13 Cal.3d 778, 119 Cal. Rptr. 841, 532 P.2d 1209 (1975). The judge conducted court in a "bizarre and unjudicial manner" by treating attorneys in a cavalier and rude manner, subjecting an attorney to an improper cross-examination when he took the stand in support of a motion to disqualify the judge, demeaning the deputy district attorney in open court and placing him under physical restraint because the deputy appealed the judge's disposition of another case, expressing disbelief in the defendant's testimony by creating a sound commonly referred to as a "raspberry," and giving the defendant "the finger" for coming in late in a traffic matter.

In *School District of Kansas City, Missouri v. Missouri,* 438 F.Supp. 830 (W.D.Mo. 1977), the trial judge recused himself in a case where his former law firm represented the plaintiff, even though the firm's personnel had changed over the years during which the judge had been on the bench. The judge denied the defendant's motion for disqualification based on 28 U.S.C.A. § 455, but then disqualified himself for reasons based in part on Canon 2 principles.

The judge in *School District* believed the overriding consideration favoring recusal was the avoidance of the appearance of impropriety. Therefore he transferred the case to a judge completely removed from any charge of partiality. It must be remembered that the judge recused himself on his own motion; under Canon 3E(1)(b), disqualification is not mandatory when the presiding judge's former law firm merely represents a party in the case. Canon 3E(1)(b) compels disqualification in such a case only when the judge had been á member of the firm *while* the firm was representing the party in the very matter now pending before the judge.

3. Compliance With the Law

(a) When Acting in a Judicial Capacity

Canon 2A provides that the judge shall "comply with the law," and "the law" is defined to include not only "court rules" but also "statutes, constitutional provisions, and decisional law." Terminology 9. In *Sawyer,* supra, the judge failed to comply with a state constitutional restriction. *Matter of Cieminski,* 270 N.W.2d 321 (N.D. 1978) the court ruled that a judge violated Canon 2A when he failed to follow a state rule of criminal procedure that mandated a verbatim record of the initial appearance and arraignment of the defendants. Such conduct was improper even though the judge did not have a court reporter or tape recorder readily available. In *United States v. Long,* 656 F.2d 1162 (5th Cir. 1981), a defendant's sentence of life imprisonment was overturned because the trial judge failed to consider a presentence report before sentencing in violation of Federal Rule of Criminal Procedure 32. Although this case did not involve a disciplinary proceeding, the appellate court relied in part on Canon 2A's "compliance with the law" requirement in ordering that the case be sent to another judge on remand. Because the trial judge had stated that no presentence report could change his mind, he in effect had stated that he would not comply with the law and therefore could not make an impartial decision with respect to the defendant's sentence.

Aside from the self-evident requirement that a judge comply with statutory and procedural law, a judge violates Canon 2 if he interferes with other judicial orders or proceedings.

Example: *Matter of Conda,* 72 N.J. 229, 370 A.2d 16 (1977) (per curiam) censured a surrogate for altering the designation of bank depositories set forth in orders by the county court judges. Apparently, the surrogate believed the county court had no authority to designate the banks where settlements of minors should be deposited. The New Jersey Supreme Court held that even if the county court lacked authority to designate the bank, altering the order without the consent of the signatory judge was inexcusable. The surrogate also violated Canon 2 by using the office facilities and employees for personal political purposes in violation of a New Jersey Supreme Court rule.

(b) When Not Acting in a Judicial Capacity

A judge must respect and comply with the law even when not acting in a judicial capacity. Thus, a judge was removed from office when he unlawfully entered a neighbor's house and ransacked the house while searching for a gun in response to the neighbor's threat that she would use the gun to "blow the brains out" of members of the judge's family. This violation of law was held to be a violation of Canon 2A as well, and was in itself sufficient grounds for removal. *Matter of Duncan*, 541 S.W.2d 564 (Mo. 1976).

Another example is *In re Conduct of Roth*, 293 Or. 179, 645 P.2d 1064 (1982) (per curiam). In *Roth*, a judge discovered his estranged wife together with Allen, a male friend, in a parked car. The judge proceeded to hit the car with his own car, thereby injuring Allen. The court in *Roth* relied on the "compliance with the law" language found in Canon 2A in censuring the judge. The judge argued that there must be a prior conviction before a judge can be disciplined for not "complying with the law." The court, however, held that no prior conviction was necessary because the court could determine for itself whether the judge had committed a crime, using the "clear and convincing evidence" standard of proof. Thus, although the judge had not been convicted of any crime, sufficient evidence existed for the court to determine that the judge did not comply with the law.

4. Independence of Judgment

Canon 2B provides that *a judge should not allow family, social, political, or other relationships to influence the judge's judicial conduct or judgment.* See *Cuyahoga County Board of Mental Retardation v. Association of Cuyahoga County Teachers of Trainable Retarded*, 47 Ohio App.2d 28, 351 N.E.2d 777 (1975) (judge required, under Canons 2B and 3E(1)(d)(i) of the 1990 Code [that is, Canon 3C(1)(d)(i) of the 1972 Code], to disqualify himself where his brother was a member of the Board of Mental Retardation, a party to the proceedings). See also, *Matter of Del Rio*, 400 Mich. 665, 256 N.W.2d 727 (1977), appeal dismissed, 434 U.S. 1029, 98 S.Ct. 759, 54 L.Ed.2d 777 (1978) (judge demonstrates improper influence when he "fixes" a ticket for a friend).

The 1990 Code added the reference to "political" relationships to highlight the need for judges to be immune to influence by political relationships. *ABA's Standing Committee Report on 1990 Code, Legislative Draft* 9 (1990).

A judge should also not allow "other relationships to influence his judicial conduct or judgment." This principle prohibited a judge from giving legal advice to a person outside of the courtroom where that person later brought suit based on the judge's advice and the case came before the same judge. *Scogin v. State,* 138 Ga.App. 859, 227 S.E.2d 780 (1976).

Note: Although not discussed by the court, this conduct also may have violated Canon 4G's prohibition against a judge practicing law, discussed below.

However, a judge may provide a pro se litigant with a legal memorandum explaining procedural requirements, provided the other party also receives the memorandum. ABA Informal Opinion 1311 (March11, 1975). This Informal Opinion implies that if both parties were represented by counsel, then offering the memorandum to one party would be unnecessary and would probably demonstrate partiality.

5. Preserving the Prestige of Office
A judge shall not lend the prestige of judicial office to advance her private interests or the private interests of another person, nor should she convey the appearance that others are in a special position to influence her.

One ABA Informal Opinion forbids a full time judge from being an honorary director of a bank, even though he has only advisory powers and no power to vote. ABA Informal Opinion 1385 (Feb. 17, 1977). The Opinion held that this situation conveyed the impression that others are in a position of influence and lent the prestige of the judicial office to the advancement of the private ventures. This Informal Opinion emphasizes that even the *appearance* of lending prestige is a violation of Canon 2. The propriety of a judge as an officer or director of a business is more fully discussed *infra,* in examining Canon 4D(1)(a) of the 1990 Code [which is Canon 5C of the 1972 Code, on which this Opinion also relied].

The judge also conveys the impression that others are in a position to influence him when the judge "fixes" traffic tickets at the request of a police chief, even though the judge has good intentions and wants to alleviate a heavy court calendar. *Matter of Holder,* 74 N.J. 581, 379 A.2d 220 (1977).

Examples: Judge writes a letter, using judicial stationery, to the City Council complaining about a proposal to widen the street in front of Judge's house. Judge has acted improperly because he used judicial letterhead for her personal business. Canon 2B, Comment 1.

Judge # 1 writes a letter to Judge # 2, who is sentencing a former business associate of Judge # 1. Judge # 1 urges Judge # 2 to take into account the former business associate's ill health. Judge # 1 has acted improperly because he *initiated* the communication. Canon 2B, Comment 3. Judge *# 1,* however, may reply to a formal request from Judge *# 2.*

A part-time judge should be held to violate this standard where—in a jurisdiction where the judge is permitted to practice law—the judge has his private law office receptionist answer his telephone with: "Judge X's office, may I help you?" ABA Informal Opinion 1473 (July 20, 1981).

6.   The Judge as Witness
(a)   Testifying as to Factual Matters
A judge arguably lends his prestige to advance the interests of others when he testifies as a witness on behalf of one party. The judge, of course, is not presiding, but the fact finder, knowing that the witness is also a judge, may feel the judge should know the best position in a given case because of the authority and legal knowledge associated with the judicial office. On the other hand, the judicial office should not excuse the judge from offering eyewitness or other factual information, any more than the prestige of a Bishop would immunize the holder of that office from offering relevant factual testimony.

Thus a judge may testify as an eyewitness. In one case, the judge who was to preside over a criminal matter was approached by an attorney regarding the timing of the trial. The attorney claimed that at this ex parte meeting he spoke only of the *timing* of the trial, and did not state any concern for the *outcome* of the trial. The judge said that he had cautioned the attorney not to talk about any of his assigned cases, but that nonetheless the attorney talked not only about the timing of the case but his interest in the outcome. The judge then wrote to the parties of his meeting and recused himself. At the trial, to establish that this attorney (whom defendants called as a witness) had an interest in the case, the new presiding judge allowed the Government to call the former presiding judge to testify as to his version of the meeting in order to attack the credibility of the other witness. *United States v. Frankenthal,* 582 F.2d 1102 (7th Cir. 1978).

Frankenthal explicitly declined to adopt any rule that a judge who is *not* presiding in a case may never testify in a criminal case. There is no federal rule generally exempting a nonpresiding judge from the normal obligation to respond as a witness when he has information material to a criminal or civil proceeding. *Dennis v. Sparks,* 449 U.S. 24, 101 S.Ct. 183, 66 L.Ed.2d 185 (1980). This principle is also generally true in the state courts. See 97 C.J.S., Witnesses § 16. A nonpresiding judge does not violate any Canon of the Code of Judicial Conduct by testifying as to factual matters.

Note: Rule 605 of the Federal Rules of Evidence prohibits a *presiding* judge from testifying at the trial.

(b) Testifying as a Character Witness
Canon 2 prohibits a judge from "voluntarily" testifying as a character witness. The judge shall not exploit the dignity and prestige of judicial office by testifying voluntarily as a character witness. On the other hand, a judge does not have any privilege to refuse to testify, however, if a party has officially subpoenaed him.

If a party wishes a judge to testify as a character witness, the party must subpoena the judge. The judge then must obey the subpoena. If the party asks the judge to appear voluntarily as a character witness, the judge must refuse.

A judge, however, may ask to be subpoenaed as illustrated by the Fifth Circuit opinion in *United States v. Callahan,* 588 F.2d 1078 (5th Cir. 1979), cert. denied, 444 U.S. 826, 100 S.Ct. 49, 62 L.Ed.2d 33 (1979). In that case, the defendant's attorney called a judge as a character witness in a prosecution for tax evasion. The attorney subpoenaed the judge, but the district court questioned the purpose of the subpoena. The trial court claimed that if the judge/witness was really a voluntary witness, and the subpoena was a mere technical strategy to comply with the Code, then the judge might still violate the Code by being in effect a "voluntary" character witness. The district court allowed the judge to decide for himself whether he would testify, and the following day the judge/witness refused to testify.

On appeal the circuit court concluded that the district court was in error. The trial court had no power to bar the judge/witness from testifying under a legally valid subpoena, even if the judge/witness, in order to comply with the rule, had asked for the subpoena. The Fifth Circuit, however, argued that the error in this case was harmless because the witness had—the court claimed—himself decided not to testify after having heard the trial judge's gratuitous and erroneous lecture on the Judicial Code.

The Fifth Circuit's conclusion in *Callahan,* that the district court erred, is sound because the Code specifically bars only voluntary, i.e., nonsubpoenaed, testimony. If a subpoena is issued, then the testimony is no longer voluntary. Any other result would open to question all character witness testimony by a judge and would erode the Code's policy of *permitting* testimony by judicial witnesses who are subject to subpoena. The Commentary to this section explicitly states that the judge may "testify when properly summoned." Canon 2B, Comment 5. This section offers no privilege against testifying. Any other rule would permit the judge to create an immunity merely by stating that the summons was "welcomed." On the other hand, Comment 5 of Canon 2B adds an ambiguous sentence that did not exist in the 1972 Code: "Except in unusual circumstances where the demands of justice require, a judge should discourage a party from requiring the judge to testify as a character witness."

7. Membership in Organizations That Practice Invidious Discrimination

Canon 2C mandates that a "judge shall not hold membership in any organization that practices invidious discrimination on the basis of race, sex, religion or national origin."

In August of 1984 the ABA added a Comment to Canon 2 dealing with the judge holding membership in a group that invidiously discriminates. In the 1990 Code the ABA moved this issue from the Comments into the black letter standard, which not prohibits such membership. Notice that Canon 2C uses the term, "shall."

This issue has generated a lot of controversy over the years. Some judges have complained that they should not be second class citizens. The Model Rules of Professional Conduct, after all, place no such restriction on lawyers. On the other hand, judges (unlike lawyers) decide cases, including civil rights issues, and, as Comment 1 to Canon 2C explains, the judge's membership in discriminatory organizations creates perceptions of impartiality.

Comment 1 recognizes that it may be difficult to decide if an organization practices "invidious" discrimination, for the mere fact that no member of a minority race is a member of a club does not necessarily mean that the club discriminates on the basis of race. The drafters, however, specifically rejected the alternative of leaving "to each individual's judge's conscience the determination of whether an organization practices invidious discrimination." *ABA's Standing Committee Report on the 1990 Code, Legislative Draft* 5 (1990).

An organization may discriminate on a basis relating to race, sex, religion, or national origin, but that such discrimination is not necessarily "invidious." In that case, Canon 2C does not prohibit membership in such groups. Similarly, Canon 2C, Comment 2 explains that it is inapplicable to groups whose membership limitations could not be constitutionally proscribed.

Example: Judge belongs to a church as well as to a church-related fraternal organization. Membership in both organizations is limited to those who are church members. Judge has not violated Canon 2C's prohibition against discrimination on the basis of religion, because the organizations are "dedicated to the preservations of religious, ethnic or cultural values of legitimate common interest to its members. . . ." Canon 2C, Comment 1.

Canon 2C limits its scope to invidious discrimination on the basis of race, sex, religion, or national origin, because these have received special protection in the constitutional case law. *ABA's Standing Committee Report on 1990 Code, Legislative Draft* 14 (1990). However, if the law of the judge's jurisdiction prohibits discrimination on another basis, for example, sexual preference, for the judge to violate that law "also violates Canon 2 and Section 2A and gives the appearance of impropriety." Canon 2C, Comment 2.

Example: Judge belongs to an organization that practices invidious discrimination on the basis of sexual preference. The jurisdiction has no law prohibiting such discrimination. Judge has not violated Canon 2C. If the jurisdiction banned such discrimination, Judge would be violating Canon 2 and Canon 2A.

If the judge is not a member of an invidiously discriminatory club, the judge is still subject to discipline, if he or she regularly uses such a club, or arranges for meeting there. The judge's conduct does not violate Canon 2C, but it violates Canon 2 ("appearance of impropriety") and Canon 2A ("diminishes public confidence in the integrity and impartiality of the judiciary"). Canon 2C, Comment 3.

Comment 2 to Canon 2C also states that a judge who publicly manifests a "knowing approval of invidious discrimination" also violates Canon 2 and 2A.

Note: To the extent that this Comment seeks to discipline a judge for what he or she says as opposed to what he or she does, it raises free speech problems, particularly when the judge's comments are made while not on the bench. As one noted judge has remarked: a judge's off-bench comments should deserve full First Amendment protection even if the remarks are "discourteous, offensive, vile, insulting, degrading, humiliating, ill-mannered and boorish." Mosk, *Judges Have First Amendment Rights*, 2 Calif. Lawyer 30, 76 (No. 9, Oct. 1982). See also, Westin, *Out–of–Court Commentary by U.S.*

Supreme Court Justices, 1790–1962: Of Free Speech and Judicial Lockjaw, 62 Colum.L.Rev. 633 (1961).

Time Limits. A judge who learns that he or she belongs to a club that engages in invidious discrimination under Canon 2C (or the judge's participation is prohibited by Canons 2 and 2A) should either resign, or take "immediate efforts" to have the group stop discriminating. While the judge is engaged in this effort, he or she *must* suspend participation in the club. If the club has not stopped its invidious discrimination within one year after the judge first learned of its practices, the judge must then resign.

III. CONDUCT IN THE COURTROOM

Canon 3 of the Code of Judicial Conduct provides that a judge shall perform the duties of the judicial office impartially and diligently.

A. DEFINING "JUDICIAL DUTIES"

Canon 3A declares that a judge's "judicial duties" take precedence over *all* the judge's other activities. This declaration is significance in light of the nonjudicial duties permitted by Canon 4 (governing extra-judicial duties), discussed below. The judge must always be aware that her nonjudicial duties, whether or not specifically authorized by Canon 4 are subordinate to her judicial duties.

The 1990 Code drafters adopted (with minor changes) this section from the 1972 Code. The task of defining "judicial duties" proved illusive to the 1972 Code's drafters. See *Reporter's Notes [1972]* at 50–51. "Judicial duties," besides obviously including the traditional adjudicative duties such as presiding in court, might also include other duties that are not adjudicative but nevertheless essential to an efficient judicial system. Such duties could include administrative duties or appointing members of local boards or agencies. The ABA decided to define "judicial duties" as "all the duties of . . . office prescribed by law." This definition includes duties provided by constitution, statute, rule, regulation, or common law. "If the activity is one that is prescribed in a judge's jurisdiction as a duty of the judicial office, it is a judicial duty for the purposes of the *Code.*" Id.

B. ADJUDICATIVE RESPONSIBILITIES
1. Affirmative Duty to Hear Cases

Canon 3B(1) is new in the 1990 Code. It provides that a judge has an affirmative duty to hear a case ("shall hear and decide"), *unless* the judge is required to be disqualified ("except those [matters] in which disqualification is required"). Thus it should be improper for a judge, out of an abundance of caution, always to grant a party's motion seeking the judge's disqualification, when disqualification is not really required. (If Canon 3E, "Disqualification," discussed below, requires disqualification, then, of course the judge must disqualify herself.) The drafters added Canon 3B(1) "to emphasize *the judicial duty to sit* and to minimize potential abuse of the disqualification process." *ABA's Standing Committee on 1990 Code, Legislative Draft* 15 (1990).(emphasis added) *Public policy forbids a judge to disqualify himself for frivolous reasons that would delay the proceedings, overburden other judges, and encourage improper judge-shopping.*

Prior to the 1974 amendment to 28 U.S.C.A. § 455, federal courts generally held that a judge had a "duty to sit" in cases where there was no technical violation of the disqualification statute, although there may have been a "question" of impartiality. The amended section 455 modifies the "duty to sit" rule by requiring disqualification if there is a *reasonable* question as to the judge's impartiality. The test is objective: would a "reasonable person" knowing all the circumstances come to the conclusion that the judge's "impartiality might reasonably be questioned." Thus, judges still should not disqualify themselves merely to avoid difficult or controversial cases. *See* e.g., H.R. Rep.No.1453, 93d Cong., 2d Sess. 5 (1974).

2. **Faithful to the Law, Maintaining Professional Competence, and Unswayed by Fear of Criticism**
Faithful to the Law. Canon 3B(2) places three main duties on judges. First, it states that a judge should be "faithful to the law." (The "law" is defined broadly in Terminology 9.) This phrase reminds a judge that he is part of a system that places limits and obligations on him.

The Michigan Supreme Court discussed those limits in *Matter of Hague*, 412 Mich. 532, 315 N.W.2d 524 (1982). A trial judge had discussed several complaints filed under the city's firearm control ordinance. The judge, in dismissing the complaints, held the firearm control ordinance unconstitutional on the basis of the state's preemption doctrine. These dismissals were then reversed on appeal. The trial judge thereafter dismissed similar complaints, again holding the firearm control ordinance unconstitutional; this time he based his decisions on the Second Amendment to the United States Constitution. Again, his dismissals were reversed on appeal. Undaunted by the appellate court, the judge continued to dismiss similar complaints using the same rationales that the appellate court had consistently rejected in the previous cases. For this conduct, and other alleged violations of the Judicial Code, the state's disciplinary tribunal recommended that the judge be suspended from office for 60 days without pay.

The state supreme court accepted the recommendation. As to the dismissals of the firearm control complaints, the court remarked that failure to follow stare decisis is not per se judicial misconduct. The court noted, however, that a judge must be "faithful to the law" as required by Canon 3B(2), and cannot impose his personal view of an issue simply to thwart the law clearly and repeatedly announced by an appellate court.

The conduct in this case presented an easy fact situation for the supreme court. The trial judge had stated publicly that the appellate court did not make the law in the state and that he did not have to follow any appellate decision. Judges do not necessarily violate Canon 3B(2) merely by deciding cases contrary to appellate decisions. The Michigan Supreme Court emphasized that the dismissals involved in *Hague* were not the result of reasoned judgment, but rather the product of personal prejudices. If the judge frames his decision in the context of reasoned decision making, a decision contrary to the apparent state of the law should not violate the "faithful to the law" standard of Canon 3B(2).

The Reporter's Notes to the 1972 Code offer another example of the limits and obligations placed upon judges under Canon 3B(2) of the 1990 Code [Canon 3A(1) of the 1972 Code]. The ABA Committee drafting the Judicial Code had received complaints that some judges did not uphold the attorney-client relationship between attorneys and their indigent clients, and that the judges applied substantive legal standards to indigent litigants that were different from those applied to nonindigent litigants. See *Reporter's Notes [1972]* at 51. The ABA Committee decided not to define a specific standard to address this problem, believing that the phrase "faithful to the law" means that, whatever the standard involved, it should be administered whether the litigant is indigent or not. Id. The ABA's conclusion gained judicial recognition in *Matter of Bennett,* 403 Mich. 178, 267 N.W.2d 914 (1978), where the Court held that a judge violated Canon 3 when he improperly sought to terminate the appointment of public defenders and appointed substitute counsel in their places. The terminations were improper because the judge interfered with the attorney-client relationship by cutting off the indigent defendants from their counsel without request or explanation. In addition, the terminations were "further evidence of a lack of judicial temperament. It gave the appearance not of a judiciously reasoned decision, but rather of an arbitrary exercise of judicial power." 267 N.W.2d at 921.

Maintain Professional Competence. Canon 3B(2) also states that a judge should maintain professional competence in the law. This aspiration presumably encourages judges to keep abreast of recent developments and changes in the law. In full compliance with the spirit of the Judicial Code, the Board of Governors of the New Hampshire Judges Association relied on this Canon in adopting a resolution requiring judges to attend a minimum of one judicial education conference each calendar year, unless excused for good cause. *In re Proposed Rule Relating to Continuing Education for District and Municipal Court Judges,* 115 N.H. 547, 345 A.2d 394 (1975).

"Unswayed by Partisan Interests, Public Clamor, or Fear of Criticism." Canon 3B(2)'s statement that a judge should be unswayed by partisan interests, public clamor, or fear of criticism reemphasizes the requirement of judicial independence earlier articulated in Canon 1, discussed above.

3. Courtroom Decorum

Canon 3B(3) requires a judge to maintain order and decorum in the courtroom. Thus a judge was found to have violated Canon 3B(3) when he held criminal arraignments in his chambers in circumstances where the procedures created security problems, crowded the courtroom, and were therefore inconsistent with the proper conduct of the court. The judge was censured for this violation and other violations of the Code. *In re Dwyer,* 223 Kan. 72, 572 P.2d 898 (1977).

In another case, the "maintaining order and decorum" standard justified a judge ordering the defendant to be quiet when the defendant was conversing with his attorney in a loud voice that could be heard by others in the courtroom. *State v. Lovelace,* 227 Kan. 348, 607 P.2d 49 (1980). The defendant in that case asserted on appeal that the judge's comments prejudiced the jury. The appellate court did not agree, citing Canon 3B(3) as authority justifying the judge's actions.

Canon 3B(3) also grants judges the power to preserve or restore order in the courtroom by temporarily ejecting disruptive and disorderly persons, including attorneys. *Matter of Hague,* 412 Mich. 532, 315 N.W.2d 524 (1982). A judge may not, however, have attorneys removed from the courtroom merely because of a professional or personal disagreement with the attorney.

4. Judicial Patience and Temperament

Although the Code requires judges to maintain order and decorum in court proceedings, judges must balance this duty with Canon 3B(4), which provides that a judge "shall be patient, dignified, and courteous to litigants, jurors, witnesses, lawyers, and others with whom the judge deals in his official capacity." However, the duty to hear proceedings with patience "is not inconsistent with the duty to dispose promptly of the business of the court." Canon 3B, Comment 1; Canon 3B(8). This Canon also requires the judge to require similar conduct of the lawyers and of staff and others subject to the judge's direction and control.

A proper judicial temperament is probably one of the most, if not the most, important qualities of a judge. That rare breed of lawyer, the trial litigator, often expresses admiration for those judges who by inclination or careful self-control exhibit the proper judicial character, who treat all parties with patience and with fairness, and who handle the case load with reasonable dispatch. See, Rotunda, *Remembering Judge Walter R. Mansfield,* 53 Brooklyn L.Rev. 271 (1987).

The "patience and dignity" standard of Canon 3B(4) speaks in broad and ambiguous terms not susceptible to precise definition. The following are examples of behavior that courts have found violative of Canon 3B(4).

Matter of Ross, 428 A.2d 858 (Me. 1981) (per curiam) involved a judge who used abusive and vulgar language against persons appearing before him. For example, in one such case, the judge told a defendant, "[T]he Court could really be a 'dink'," and, "Young man, you will remember that the likes of you I chew up and spit out before breakfast, and I never have breakfast until 8:00 o'clock at night." The court noted that intemperate language is on occasion understandable, but vile, obscene, and abusive language is inexcusable. The judge was suspended for 90 days without pay.

In re Rome, 218 Kan. 198, 542 P.2d 676 (1975) involved a judge who granted a convicted prostitute two years probation. In granting probation, the judge wrote a humorous opinion in poetic verse. The local newspaper reprinted the opinion, and the prostitute became the primary topic of conversation around town. Although neither the prostitute nor her parents complained, the judge was censured by the disciplinary commission. The court upheld the censure, not because the opinion was written in verse, but because the prostitute was portrayed in a "ludicrous or comical situation."

Note: The judge contended that the First Amendment protected his conduct. The state supreme court held that the judge's right to free speech was limited by the Code of Judicial Conduct, and First Amendment rights do not exempt a judge from discipline for proven judicial misconduct. *See, also, Halleck v. Berliner,* 427 F.Supp. 1225, 1241 (D.D.C. 1977) ("The need for public confidence in and respect for the judiciary requires some reasonable limits on the freedom of a judge to say what he pleases from the bench . . . ."). On the other hand, other judges, without being subjected to discipline, have written opinions in verse that appear to make light of someone's problems. E.g., *Fisher v. Lowe,* 122 Mich.App. 418, 333 N.W.2d 67 (1983) (opinion and West headnotes in verse).

In re Jordan, 290 Or. 303, 314, 622 P.2d 297, 308 (1981). At the defendant's sentencing, the judge told the defendant, "I know why you won't tell me why you've been drinking. It's because you're chicken shit." The judge was removed from office for this remark and other violations of the Code.

Canon 3B(4) also states that a judge should require his staff, court officials, and others subject to his discretion and control to conform to the same standards of patience and dignity required of the judge.

This requirement does not mean, however, that the judge must be the "keeper" of his staff or attorneys appearing in his courtroom. Thus, a judge does not violate Canon 3A(3) if his staff is rude or undignified toward others if the judge does not have knowledge of such instances of rudeness; if he had knowledge, he is not liable if he acted reasonably in trying to correct the problem, even though his efforts were to no avail. *Matter of Kohn,* 568 S.W.2d 255 (Mo. 1978).

Judges can help fulfill their responsibilities to require lawyers and staff under their jurisdiction to refrain from sexual harassment by being a good role models themselves. Comment 2 to Canon 3B(4) explains that the judge personally "must refrain from speech, gestures or other conduct that could reasonably be perceived as sexual harassment. . . ." Judges engaged in sexist behavior have been disciplined in such circumstances.

Matter of Del Rio, 400 Mich. 665, 256 N.W.2d 727 (1977), appeal dismissed, 434 U.S. 1029, 98 S.Ct. 759, 54 L.Ed.2d 777 (1978). The judge, who was suspended for five years without pay for his behavior, constantly subjected attorneys, spectators, litigants, and witnesses appearing before him to discourtesy, harassment, unjust criticism, and abuse. In one bench trial, the judge persisted in talking on the telephone during critical testimony from the complainant and another witness. When the prosecutor requested the judge's attention, the judge ordered him into chambers where he gave the prosecutor an insulting tongue-lashing. The judge also boasted about his sex life to female attorneys, and asked them for dates. When the attorneys refused, they were often treated with disdain when later appearing professionally before the judge. The same judge had ordered an 11–year–old youngster to be locked up alone for one half hour in the "bullpen" for causing a disturbance in the courtroom during a field trip.

The Illinois Courts Commission reprimanded a judge for disparaging remarks directed to three women defense lawyers. He told one pregnant lawyer, for example, that "if your husband had kept his hands in his pockets, you would not be in the condition you are in." He told another, "Ladies should not be lawyers." *In re Circuit Judge Arthur J. Cieslik, 2*

Ill. Courts Commission 111 (1987). See generally, Angel, *Sexual Harassment by Judges*, 45 U.Miami L.Rev. 817 (1991).

Geiler v. Commission on Judicial Qualifications, 10 Cal.3d 270, 110 Cal. Rptr. 201, 515 P.2d 1 (1973), *cert. denied*, 417 U.S. 932, 94 S.Ct. 2643, 41 L.Ed.2d 235 (1974) removed the judge for "willful misconduct," and conduct prejudicial to the administration of justice." The judge, among other things, approached the court commissioner from behind in a public corridor and grabbed his testicles, made lustful references to female clerks, used vulgar and profane language in conversations with clerks, and invited two female attorneys into his chambers where he discussed the salacious nature of evidence in several rape cases using profane terms to describe bodily functions.

5. Performing Judicial Duties Without Bias or Prejudice

Canon 3B(5) requires the judge to perform judicial duties "without bias or prejudice." While performing judicial duties, the judge, by words or conduct "shall not" display "bias or prejudice based upon race, sex, religion, national origin, disability, age, sexual orientation or socioeconomic status, and shall not permit staff, court officials and others subject to the judge's direction and control to do so."

Notice that this litany the types of bias which the judge must guard against is broader than the list in Canon 2C. However, Canon 2C governs the off-bench behavior, *i.e.*, the types of organizations that the judge must not join. Canon 3B(5) governs the judge "in the performance of judicial duties." Because the judge must perform these duties impartially and fairly, any manifestation of bias "impairs the fairness of the proceeding and brings the judiciary into disrepute." Canon 3B(5), Comment 1. The judge must also guard against facial expression and body language that might communicate an appearance of bias.

6. Requiring Lawyers Before the Judge to Refrain From Manifesting Improper Bias

Canon 3B(6) provides that the judge "shall require lawyers in proceedings before the judge to refrain from manifesting by words or conduct, bias or prejudice based upon race, sex, religion, national origin, disability, age, sexual orientation or socio-economic status, against parties, witnesses, counsel or others." However, this section does not preclude "legitimate advocacy" when those factors are at issue.

Lawyers are officers of the court, and so judges have the power—and Canon 3B(6) gives judges the duty—to prevent attorneys from manifesting improper prejudice. The judge's duty to "require" means that the judge must exercise "reasonable direction and control over the conduct of those persons subject to the judge's direction and control." Terminology 18.

7. Avoidance of Ex Parte Communications

(a) Right to Be Heard

Canon 3B(7) requires a judge to accord every person "who has a legal interest in a proceeding" (or that person's lawyer) full right to be heard according to law. Thus a judge violates Canon 3B(7) when he denies the state an opportunity to be heard in a criminal case. In *Matter of Edens,* 290 N.C. 299, 226 S.E.2d 5 (1976), the defendant's guilty plea was not given in open court in the presence of the assistant district attorney or prosecuting officer; the guilty plea was accepted without prior notice to the assistant district attorney; and the judge signed the judgment in the court clerk's office, out of the presence of (and without notice to) the assistant district attorney.

> *Note:* If Canon 3(B)(7) requires the presence of, or notice to, a party, if that party is represented by counsel, it is counsel who is to be present or to whom notice shall be given. Rule 3B(7), Comment 3.

A judge violates Canon 3B(7) if he imposes sentence without affording the defendant the hearing to which he is entitled by law. *Matter of Ross,* 428 A.2d 858 (Me. 1981). See also *In re Conduct of Jordan,* 290 Or. 669, 672, 624 P.2d 1074, 1076 (1981) (per curiam) (judge disciplined because, inter alia, he began criminal trial and entered a finding of "guilty" in the absence of defendant).

> *Notes:* This ethical requirement is supported by the due process requirement embodied in the United States Constitution. Cf. e.g., *Board of Regents v. Roth,* 408 U.S. 564, 92 S.Ct. 2701, 33 L.Ed.2d 548 (1972).
>
> Although ex parte communications are generally not permitted, Canon 3B(7)(e) permits ex parte communications that are "expressly authorized by law." Many states, for example, have enacted domestic abuse statutes, authorizing ex parte protective orders for the protection of the petitioners. See Note, *Domestic Abuse Legislation in Illinois and Other States: A Survey and Suggestions for Reform,* 1983 U.Ill.L.Rev. 261.

(b) Ex Parte Communications

(i) Introduction

Canon 3B(7) prohibits a judge from initiating or considering ex parte communications concerning a pending or impending proceeding unless the communication: is about scheduling, or for administrative purposes, or emergencies that do not deal with substantive issues, and the judge promptly notifies all the other parties, Canon 3B(7)(a) & (a)(i), (a)(ii); falls within the "disinterested expert on the law" exception, Canon 3B(7)(b), as discussed *infra;* is with court personnel, Canon 3B(7)(c), discussed *infra;* the parties consent to the judge conferring separately in an effort to mediate or settle the case, Canon 3B(7)(d); or is authorized by law, Canon 3B(7)(e), discussed *supra. In re Conduct of Jordan,* 290 Or. 669, 671, 624 P.2d 1074, 1075 (1981) (per curiam) (judge disciplined when—at the conclusion of a preliminary hearing—he talked privately to a potential witness about her testimony at a future trial). Cf. Canon 3B(7), Comment 6 (judge must not independently investigate facts in a case).

Note: The "impending proceeding" limitation in tended to discourage forum shopping by a party or lawyer who tries to assess the judge's predilections on a particular fact situation before a claim is filed. See *Reporter's Notes [1972]* at 54.

Even if the ex parte communication does not concern a pending proceeding, the judge should be aware that if a proceeding related to the communication subsequently comes before her, that earlier communication may require her disqualification under Canon 3E(1) because her "impartiality might reasonably be questioned." Thus, recusal was required when a person merely explained her legal problem to the judge, the judge gave advice, and that case later came before the judge. *Scogin v. State,* 138 Ga.App. 859, 227 S.E.2d 780 (1976).

A judge clearly violates the ex parte communication prohibition if he considers ex parte communications on substantive matters [Canon 3B(7)(a)] from a party or lawyer in a pending proceeding, or initiates such communications. *See In re Dekle,* 308 So.2d 5 (Fla. 1975) (per curiam). In that case, after oral argument before the state supreme court, the attorney for one party handed Justice Dekle a legal memorandum. Dekle erroneously thought the memorandum was a duly filed amicus submission because the attorney mentioned that he had already presented the memo to another justice for use in preparing the majority opinion. When the justice originally assigned to write the majority opinion decided to join the dissent, Justice Dekle was assigned to write for the majority. In drafting his opinion, he relied on the memorandum that had not been filed. The use of the memorandum violated Canon 3B(7)(a) even though Justice Dekle thought, erroneously, that the memo had been duly filed. The court found that Dekle's conclusion was not reasonable. Therefore, judging Dekle by objective and not subjective intent, the court held that the misconduct warranted judicial discipline. The court, in effect, concluded that Justice Dekle should have known the memo was beyond his power to consider. Even if there is no actual harm to any party, a judge who intentionally commits an act that he knew or should have known was beyond his power is guilty of misconduct. The court reprimanded the judge, adding in dicta that removal would be proper if there was a clear showing of corrupt motive or a deliberate wrong.

One court has even held that a judge also violates Canon 3B(7) if he attends a public meeting when he should have known that its purpose was to raise money for criminal defendants whose cases were then pending before the superior court where the judge sat, but *not* before this particular judge, who was the chief judge. *Matter of Bonin*, 375 Mass. 680, 378 N.E.2d 669 (1978). The public meeting included a lecture by Gore Vidal on "Sex and Politics in Massachusetts." The defendants in the criminal case were indicted for alleged sexual acts between men and boys. The judge, by attending the meeting, exposed himself to ex parte statements and arguments on matters pending before his court, the court reasoned.

Note: Judges are human beings who cannot divorce themselves from the real world, public discussions, newspapers, and the like. Canon 4A, Comment 1. The Massachusetts Court acknowledged that normally "any judge would be entirely free to attend a public lecture about sex and politics whether or not sponsored by a 'gay' group." Yet the Court said that Judge Bonin's actions were different because the lecture concerned cases pending in the Superior Court where he sat and of which he was chief justice. The Massachusetts Court showed little sensitivity to First Amendment concerns. Judge Bonin had not been assigned to hear the case and would make no ruling regarding it, so the reference to hearing "one sided argumentation" was not too relevant. When he was on the bench, he made no comment concerning the case. And when he was off of it (when he was at the large meeting), he also made no remarks or statements about the case. "While it is true that his attendance at the meeting might cause some to infer his support for the cause, it is at least equally likely that it would be interpreted as being motivated by curiosity or interest in the remarks of the well-known featured speaker." S. Lubet, *Beyond Reproach: Ethical Restrictions on the*

Extrajudicial Activities of State and Federal Judges 44 (1984).

In *State v. Valencia*, 124 Ariz. 139, 602 P.2d 807 (1979), the trial judge had sentenced the defendant to death but the court reversed because of an ex parte communication between the victim's brother and the trial judge prior to sentencing. The victim's brother told the judge that the family wanted the death penalty imposed. The court reversed even though the judge had not committed himself to a position after his conversation with the victim's brother; the judge merely stated that he had a difficult decision to make and would consider all the facts. Although the appellate court did not specifically rely on Canon 3B(7) in its holding, it was cited in support of reversal.

(ii)   Disinterested Expert Exception
       Canon 3B(7)(b) provides: *"A judge may obtain the advice of a disinterested expert on the law applicable to a proceeding before the judge if the judge gives notice to the parties of person consulted and the substance of the advice, and affords the parties reasonable opportunity to respond."* The rule permitting ex parte communications if there is notice to the parties applies only to disinterested experts on the law; a judge cannot absolve any other ex parte communication from impropriety merely by giving notice to the parties and an opportunity for them to respond. When the judge seeks a disinterested expert on the law, the judge does not need to secure the parties' consent in such circumstances. Nor does the requirement of "notice" mean "prior notice." The judge only must tell the parties the name of the person consulted and the substance of the advice, and give the parties a reasonable opportunity to respond. This exception recognizes both the judge's interest in seeking expert legal advice to help her decide complex questions of law and the interest of the parties in the adversary system.

This rule, by its own terms, only applies to experts *on the law*, not to all experts. See *E.I. du Pont de Nemours & Co. v. Collins*, 432 U.S. 46, 57, 97 S.Ct. 2229, 2235, 53 L.Ed.2d 100, 110 (1977) (Error for Court of Appeals to employ Professor of Business Administration to assist in understanding the record in the case, including economic observations, even though parties had an opportunity to respond; Canon 3B(7)(b) was not cited.).

The restrictions on ex parte communications include communications from law teachers and other lawyers, unless an exception applies. Canon 3B(7), Comment 1.

An appropriate and desirable procedure for obtaining the advice of a disinterested expert is to have the expert file an amicus curiae brief. Canon 3B(7), Comment 4. The filing of such a brief, however, is not a prerequisite for compliance with the Code. In fact, the *Reporter's Notes [1972]* suggest that the ex parte advice need not even be in writing; the advice could be received in a telephone conversation. See *Reporter's Notes [1972]* at 54.

(iii) Court Personnel Exception

Canon 3B(7)(c) makes clear that this Canon does notpreclude a judge from consulting with "court personnel whose function is to aid the judge in carrying out the judge's adjudicative responsibilities or with other judges." Thus, in general a judge may communicate with his law clerks, other judges, and other court personnel who aid him in carrying out his adjudicative responsibilities. It is not necessary for the judge in such cases to give the parties either notice or an opportunity to respond.

ABA Informal Opinion 1346 (Nov. 26, 1975) examines the scope of the phrase "court personnel." The judge wanted to obtain answers to specific criminal law issues through law students working in the law school's legal information center. The Opinion concluded that "court personnel" refers only to immediate employees of the court over whose activities the judge exercises supervision. Therefore, the judges could only obtain and use the answers in a pending proceeding if the judge gave notice to the parties of the person who was consulted and the substance of the advice received, and then afforded the parties a reasonable opportunity to respond.

While Canon 3B(7)(c), broadly authorizes the judge to consult "with other judges," Comment 9 to this Canon advises: "[i]f communication between the trial judge and the appellate court with respect to a proceeding is permitted, a copy of any written communication or the substance of any oral communication should be provided to all parties." This statement is new to the 1990 Code, and it will be interesting to see how this principle will be interpreted in practice, particularly in jurisdictions where appellate and trial judges are in the same building, and often eat and socialize together.

Prior case law recognizes that there must be at least some limitations to communications *on particular cases* between trial and appellate judges. See, *Matter of Cunningham,* 57 N.Y.2d 270, 273, 456 N.Y.S.2d 36, 37, 442 N.E.2d 434, 435 (1982), where the court censured an appellate judge who wrote two letters to a trial judge that referred to several pending cases by name; the appellate judge, among other things, assured the trial judge that there "is no way I would ever change a sentence that you had imposed. You can do whatever you want to whenever you want to and I'll agree with you . . . I take the position that you know the case and as sentencing judge you can do whatever you damn well please." He also wrote: if "I catch the appeal, I will affirm as always, on a judge's discretion."

Although a judge can converse with his law clerks regarding a pending matter, certain communications are still prohibited under Canon 3B(7), because the "judge must not independently investigate the facts in a case and must consider only the evidence presented." Canon 3B(7), Comment 6. The judge must make reasonable efforts to supervise law clerks and other personnel on the judge's staff. Id. at Comment 9. *Price Brothers Co. v. Philadelphia Gear Corp.*, 629 F.2d 444 (6th Cir. 1980), cert. denied, 454 U.S. 1099, 102 S.Ct. 674, 70 L.Ed.2d 641 (1981), illustrates a case where the judge's law clerk became a factual witness. In that case, the trial judge's law clerk visited the plaintiff's manufacturing plant to view some machines alleged to be malfunctioning in breach of the defendant's warranties. The defendant's attorney requested the judge to amend his findings of fact to reflect the visit by the law clerk. The judge refused the request without commenting on whether his clerk actually made the trip. The appellate court reversed and remanded, ordering the district court to consider whether there was any ex parte communication in violation of Canon 3B(7). The trial court was to determine (1) whether the clerk had visited the plant, (2) whether the trip had been at the direction of the judge, (3) whether the clerk had conversations with the plaintiff's employees, (4) whether any observations had been made at the plant, (5) whether the information had been reported to the judge, and (6) when the defense counsel had learned of the trip and whether the defendant had expressly or tacitly approved of the trip.

In *Kennedy v. Great Atlantic and Pacific Tea Co.*, 551 F.2d 593 (5th Cir. 1977), the judge's law clerk, without the judge's knowledge, went to the defendant's store after a rainstorm to determine whether the floor was wet at the place the plaintiff alleged that he had fallen. The floor was indeed wet, and when the judge learned of his clerk's discovery, he instructed his clerk to inform the defendant's lawyer to foster a settlement. The parties did not settle, and at trial the judge informed the plaintiff's lawyer of the clerk's observation. The plaintiff's counsel subsequently called the judge's clerk as a witness, and judgment was rendered in favor of the plaintiff.

The appellate court vacated the judgment because the clerk's visit to the site of the accident was an ex parte "communication" that "infected" the jury, who must have thought that the clerk's observation had some special importance if the clerk had taken the trouble to visit the property.

8. Prompt Disposition of Business

Canon 3B(8) states that a judge "shall dispose of all judicial matters promptly, efficiently, and fairly. This Canon is the ABA's response to reports of judges who procrastinated in deciding proceedings ripe for decision, judges with heavy dockets who were very irregular in their court appearances, and judges who, by regularly arriving late to court, unreasonably delayed jurors, witnesses, parties, and lawyers. See *Reporters Notes* at 54.

"Prompt disposition" means that the judge must devote "adequate time to judicial duties," and be "punctual in attending court and expeditious in determining matters under submission." The judge must also insist on similar conduct by court officials, litigants, and their lawyers. Canon 3B(8), Comment 2. The duty of prompt disposition of judicial business is not inconsistent with the duty to be patient and deliberate. Canon 3B(4), Comment 1. Rotunda, *Remembering Judge Walter R. Mansfield,* 53 Brooklyn L.Rev. 271, 274–76 (1987).

If a judge fails to conclude matters within a statutorily prescribed time limit, he is not disposing of business promptly, within the meaning of Canon 3B(8). *Matter of Anderson,* 312 Minn. 442, 252 N.W.2d 592 (1977). This Canon is not limited, however, to statutorily prescribed limits, as made clear by the Commentary and *Reporter's Notes [1972].* What constitutes "adequate" time and being "punctual," or "expeditious," however, are issues resolvable only in the context of a particular proceeding.

9. Public Comments

Under **Canon 3B(9),** a judge shall not, while a proceeding is pending or impending *in any court,* make any public comment that might reasonably be expected to affect it outcome or impair its fairness. In addition, the judge must not make any *nonpublic* comment "that might substantially interfere with a fair trial or hearing." The judge is also obligated to require similar abstention on the part of court personnel subject to his direction and control.

Note: "Court personnel" do not include attorneys who are in the proceeding before the judge. Terminology 4. DR 7–107 and Model Rule 3.6 regulate their conduct. Canon 3B(9), Comment 1.

When the public comment prohibition is applicable, it extends to comments about proceedings in any court, not just proceedings before the judge making the comments.

Canon 3B(9), of course, allows judges to make public statements "in the course of their official duties . . ." and to explain court procedures to the public. However, this provision gives a judge no *carte blanche* authority. A "judge is strictly prohibited from public comment on the merits of a pending case. On the other hand, a judge is encouraged to explain a pending case in abstract terms. Obviously, judges walk a fine line between the duties and prohibitions of Canon 3A(6) [of the 1972 Code, Canon 3B(9) of the 1990 Code]." *Matter of Sheffield*, 465 So.2d 350, 355 (Ala. 1984). In this case the court suspended a judge for two months without pay for, among other things, making some comments to a reporter (who had called him in the evening before a hearing) about the merits of a case.

Cf., State ex rel. *Commission on Judicial Qualifications v. Rome*, 229 Kan. 195, 623 P.2d 1307 (1981) (per curiam), where the court removed a judge from office for various violations, including writing a memorandum decision that stated as conclusions various factual matters that were being contested in two criminal cases, and then trying to get these statements publicized by hand-delivering a copy of the memorandum to one reporter and mailing another copies to two news stations.

The Reporter's Notes to the 1972 Code suggest that, consistent with the Judicial Code, court personnel may be authorized, pursuant to established guidelines, to release certain information regarding a pending or impending proceeding. See *Reporter's Notes [1972]* at 55–56. Presumably this practice is allowed under the provision allowing judges (and therefore, court personnel) to make "public statements in the course of their official duties," or to explain "for public information the procedures of the court."

Judge sued in personal capacity. This section does not apply to a judge who is a litigant in a *personal* capacity. Such a judge is treated like any other litigant, and any comments the judge makes about the case are not made in his capacity as a judge. But this section applies to judges sued in their official capacity, such as by writ of mandamus. Canon 3B(9), Comment 1.

10. Media in the Courtroom

When the ABA first published the Judicial Code in 1972, it contained a Canon 3A(7), which was an almost absolute prohibition of the broadcast media in the courtroom. The Canon first stated the general rule that a "judge should prohibit broadcasting, televising, recording, or taking photographs in the courtroom and areas immediately adjacent thereto during sessions of court or recesses between sessions . . ." The Canon then delineated several narrow exceptions. In *Chandler v. Florida*, 449 U.S. 560, 101 S.Ct. 802, 66 L.Ed.2d 740 (1981), the United States Supreme Court held that there is no per se constitutional prohibition against media coverage in the courtroom, and each case must be viewed on its own facts. See generally, 3 R. Rotunda, J. Nowak, J. Young, *Treatise on Constitutional Law: Substance and Procedure* § 20.25 (1986).

In reaction to *Chandler*'s rejection of a per se approach to the prohibition of media in the courtroom, the ABA amended Canon 3A(7) on August 11, 1982. The revised version, like its previous counterpart, begins with a general prohibition of media coverage in the courtroom. However, the revised version contains a more expansive exception to the general prohibition.

Finally, when the ABA adopted the 1990 Code, it eliminated any reference to the issue of media in the courtroom. The drafters of the 1990 Code explained that they deleted former Canon 3A(7) "because it addresses a matter of court administration, not judicial ethics, that is more appropriately regulated by separate court rules." *ABA's Standing Committee Report on 1990 Code, Legislative Draft* 22 (1990).

11. Criticism of Jurors

Canon 3B(10) instructs judges not to criticize or commend jurors for their verdict other than in a court order or opinion in a proceeding, but they may express appreciation to jurors for their service to the judicial system and the community.

The purpose of this section, which is new, is to "protect jurors from improper influence by judges and to preserve the appearance of fairness in judicial decision-making." *ABA's Standing Committee Report on 1990 Code, Legislative Draft* 22 (1990).

12. Judicial Use of Nonpublic Information

Canon 3B(11) provides that judges shall not disclose or use nonpublic information acquired in a judicial capacity for any purpose unrelated to judicial duties.

Nonpublic information is information that, by law, is not available to the public, such as information offered in grand jury proceedings, presentence reports, dependency cases, psychiatric reports, and information sealed by court order, impounded, or communicated in camera. Terminology 13.

C. ADMINISTRATIVE RESPONSIBILITIES
1. Sound Judicial Administration

Canon 3C(1) *provides that a judge "shall" diligently discharge administrative responsibilities "without bias or prejudice and maintain professional competence in judicial administration. . . ."*

Thus, a judge was suspended without pay for one month when he flagrantly and persistently disregarded a local rule requiring judges to compile and file accurate and complete records on pending matters. *Matter of Carstensen*, 316 N.W.2d 889 (Iowa 1982). A judge does not have to violate administrative rules, however, to violate Canon 3C. A judge also violates Canon 3C(1) if she fails to supervise her staff, infrequently attends court, or fails to maintain court records in a manner that would maintain professional competence and facilitate the performance of administrative responsibilities. *Matter of Briggs*, 595 S.W.2d 270 (Mo. 1980). A judge also violates Canon 3C if he charges traffic violators more money to be paid as a fine than the amount officially reported as paid to the county. *In re Anderson*, 412 So.2d 743 (Miss.1982) (judge removed from office). (It is amazing, is it not, what some people try to get away with.)

Canon 3C(1) also provides that a judge "should" cooperate with other judges and court officials in administrating court business. A judge violated this requirement when he refused his administrative superior's order to file weekly and monthly reports of his activities; obstinacy was the only apparent reason for his conduct. *In re McDonough*, 296 N.W.2d 648 (Minn. 1979). The judge in *McDonough* also violated Canon 3C(1) by failing to get along with his administrative superior to the extent necessary to carry out judicial duties. The judge apparently accused his superior of lying, making false assumptions, and being grossly ignorant, and also cursed at and was generally disrespectful to his superior.

Canon 3C(2) mandates that judges require their staff and those court officials subject to their control to observe the standards of "fidelity and diligence" that apply to the judge and "to refrain from manifesting bias or prejudice in the performance of their official duties." Canon 3C(2). A judge violated this Canon when he refused to take action against his clerk after learning that the clerk illegally granted a limited driving privilege to her brother-in-law and reduced traffic fines without authority to do so. *Matter of Briggs*, 595 S.W.2d 270 (Mo. 1980).

Canon 3C(3) governs judges with supervisory power over other judges. Supervisory judges "shall take reasonable measures" to assure that other judges promptly dispose of matters before them and they properly perform their other judicial responsibilities. This section is new to the 1990 Code.

2. Making Appointments

Under Canon 3C(4), a judge shall not make unnecessary appointments to employment positions, and shall appoint impartially, only on the basis of merit, avoiding nepotism and favoritism. Appointees include assigned counsel, referees, commissioners, special masters, receivers, guardians, and personnel such as clerks, secretaries, and bailiffs. Canon 3C(4), Comment 1. It is no defense that the parties to the case consent to the appointment of, for example, the assigned counsel. Id.

A judge violated Canon 3C(4) when he overwhelmingly appointed his friends and political supporters to represent indigent defendants in criminal cases. *Spruance v. Commission on Judicial Qualifications*, 13 Cal. 3d 778, 119 Cal.Rptr. 841, 532 P.2d 1209 (1975) (44% of cases appointed to the judge's two friends; the remaining 56% of appointments were received by 22 other attorneys, no one of whom received more than 3 appointments; however, a public defender's office was able to afford legal representation; and the judge should have known the proper procedures required in appointing counsel). The problem in *Spruance* was not that the judge appointed people he knew; it was that he did not appoint impartially and on the basis of merit. A judge may properly appoint someone (other than a close relative) whom he knows well, "if the appointment itself is necessary and the person objectively merits the appointment." *ABA's Standing Committee Report on 1990 Code, Legislative Draft* 24 (1990).

Difficult cases thus arise where a judge appoints someone on the basis of merit, yet there is also evidence of favoritism. A divided court refused to censure a judge who appointed his lover as chief cashier because the appointee was "well qualified for the appointment." *Matter of Dalessandro*, 483 Pa. 431, 397 A.2d 743, 759 (1979) (per curiam).

A judge cannot evade Canon 3C(4) by laundering judicial appointments. Thus, in *Spector v. State Commission on Judicial Conduct*, 47 N.Y.2d 462, 418 N.Y.S.2d 565, 392 N.E.2d 552 (1979), the court cited Canon 3C(4) in admonishing a judge who appointed other judges' sons to represent defendants, knowing that those judges would in return appoint his son.

A judge obviously violated Canon 3C(4) where he made sexual relations a condition of employment, terminated one employee for refusing to continue having sex with him, and terminated another employee for refusing to have sex with him. *In re Hammond*, 224 Kan. 745, 585 P.2d 1066 (1978) (judge censured, although he would have been removed if ill health had not already forced his retirement).

A judge also shall not approve compensation beyond the fair value of services rendered. Canon 3B(4). If the compensation is excessive, it is no defense that the parties consent to the award of compensation. Canon 3C(4), Comment 1.

D. Duty to Report Unethical Conduct of Others

Canon 3D governs the judge's disciplinary responsibilities. It is divided into three parts. The first part governs judges reporting judges; the second part governs judges reporting lawyers; and the third part provides that no judges may be subject to civil liability because have they discharged their disciplinary responsibilities, an activity for which they are "absolutely privileged."

This Canon reemphasizes the Canon 1 duty to enforce high standards of conduct. This section is intended to be analogous to the lawyer's duty to report under Rule 8.3 of the Model Rules of Professional Conduct.

Canon 3D(1). A judge who receives information that indicates "a substantial likelihood that another judge" has violated the Judicial Code "*should* take appropriate action." If the judge has "knowledge" that another judge has committed a violation of the Judicial Code and that violation "raises a substantial question" as to the other judge's fitness for office, the judge "*shall* inform the *appropriate authority*." (emphasis added)

The Commentary explains that "*appropriate action*" may include direct communication with the judge or lawyer in question, or other direct action, or reporting a lawyer's misconduct to the "appropriate authority." Canon 3D, Comment 1. The "*appropriate authority*" is the "authority with responsibility for initiation of disciplinary process with respect to the violation to be reported." Terminology 1. "*Knowledge*" means "actual knowledge of the fact in question." A person's knowledge "may be inferred from circumstances." Terminology 8.

Canon 3D(2). This section parallels Canon 3D(1), but it applies to judges reporting lawyers. The judge "should" take "appropriate action" if the judge has "information indicating a substantial likelihood" that the lawyer has violated the state's version of the Model Rules or Model Code. If the judge has "knowledge" that the lawyer has committed a violation that "raises a substantial question as to the lawyer's honesty, trustworthiness or fitness as a lawyer in other respects," the judge "shall" inform the "appropriate authority."

Although a judge violates the Judicial Code—at least in theory—if she does not report misconduct within the requirements of Canon 3B(3), judges rarely bring violations of the lawyers' or judges' ethical codes to the attention of the proper authorities. Statistics indicate that lay persons file the greatest percentage of disciplinary complaints, not lawyers or other judges. See Thode,

The Code of Judicial Conduct—The First Five Years in the Courts, 1977 Utah L.Rev. 395, 401.

In light of these statistics, the drafters of the 1990 Judicial Code have tried to encourage more reporting. The rule regarding reporting was changed specifically from the 1972 Judicial Code to require judges to report to a disciplinary authority "significant misconduct of lawyers and other judges, thus diminishing the number of instances in which judges take it upon themselves to impose sanctions for professional misconduct without such reporting." *ABA's Standing Committee on 1990 Code, Legislative Draft* 25 (1990). This new rule also encourages judges to take other remedial steps, such as referring, in appropriate cases, a lawyer or judge to a bar-sponsored substance abuse treatment agency. Id.

Canon 3D(3). To encourage reporting, Canon 3D(3) provides that judicial activities under Canon 3D(1) & (2) are "absolutely privileged" and there shall be "no civil action" against the judge for such reporting.

If a judge does refer a lawyer's unethical conduct to the proper disciplinary authority, the judge does not necessarily have to recuse himself from hearing the post-conviction motions of the attorney's client, particularly where that attorney no longer represents the client. *Honneus v. United States*, 425 F.Supp. 164 (D.Mass.1977).

IV. JUDICIAL DISQUALIFICATION

A. AN INTRODUCTORY NOTE

Canon 3E of the 1990 Judicial Code (Canon 3C of the 1972 Judicial Code) governs judicial disqualification, which is perhaps the most litigated area of the Code of Judicial Conduct. Canon 3E shares many similarities with 28 U.S. C.A. § 455, reprinted in the Appendix. (There are, as well, a few important differences, discussed below). See, e.g., *Laird v. Tatum*, 409 U.S. 824, 825, 93 S.Ct. 7, 8, 34 L.Ed.2d 50, 51 (1972) (Memorandum of Rehnquist, J., denying recusal motion and stating that ABA Judicial Conduct Standards not "materially different" from standards in federal statute). Consequently, in an effort to analyze and illustrate Canon 3E, we will refer not only to state cases but also federal cases when those cases use provisions of 28 U.S.C.A. § 455 that are similar (or were similar, at the time of decision) to Canon 3E. It may be assumed that the applicable language in the Code and federal statute are substantially identical unless otherwise indicated.

Note: Two additional federal disqualification statutes of interest include: 28 U.S.C.A. § 47, which prohibits a judge from hearing an appeal in any case over which he presided as a trial judge; and, 28 U.S.C.A. § 144, which disqualifies district court judges for actual bias or prejudice as alleged in a party's affidavit.

Waiver. Canon 3F provides a procedure where the parties may waive any disqualification imposed by Canon 3E. The federal statute only allows waiver if the judge is disqualified because his or her impartiality might reasonably be questioned. 28 U.S.C.A. § 455(e). We shall discuss the waiver issue later.

B. DISQUALIFICATION WHERE IMPARTIALITY MIGHT REASONABLY BE QUESTIONED
1. Introduction

Canon 3E(1)—and 28 U.S.C.A. § 455(a)—provide generally that a judge "shall disqualify himself or herself in any proceeding in which the judge's impartiality might reasonably be questioned. . . ." Subsequent subsections add specific instances where the judge must be disqualified, but those instances are *in addition* to any other case where the judge's impartiality might reasonably be questioned.

The judge should disclose on the record information that the parties or their lawyers "might consider relevant" to the disqualification issue, even if the judge believes that there is no real basis for disqualification. Canon 3E(1), Comment 2. This disclosure should be "broad" to assure that the parties are aware of the relevant facts. *ABA's Standing Committee Report on 1990 Code* 26 (1990).

2. Objective Test

Prior to the 1974 amendment to 28 U.S.C.A. § 455, federal courts generally held that a judge had a "duty to sit" in cases where there was no technical violation of the disqualification statute, although there may have been a "question" of impartiality. The amended section 455 modifies the "duty to sit" rule by requiring disqualification if there is a *reasonable* question as to the judge's impartiality. The test is objective: would a "reasonable person" knowing all the circumstances come to the conclusion that the judge's "impartiality might reasonably be questioned." Thus, judges still should not disqualify themselves merely to avoid difficult or controversial cases. *See* e.g., H.R. Rep.No.1453, 93d Cong., 2d Sess. 5 (1974).

Similarly, the test of Canon 3E(1) is also objective. It requires that the judge's partiality "might *reasonably* be questioned." (emphasis added). Canon 3B(1), a new section added to the 1990 Code, reaffirms this principle. It requires judges to decide matters "except those in which disqualification is required." The drafters added this section "to emphasize the judicial duty to sit and to minimize potential abuse of the disqualification process." *ABA's Standing Committee on 1990 Code, Legislative Draft* 15 (1990). *Public policy forbids a judge to disqualify himself for frivolous reasons that would delay the proceedings, overburden other judges, and encourage improper judge-shopping.*

3. The Rule of Necessity

Canon 3E(1), Comment 3, is new, and it recognizes that Courts have created an exception to the disqualification provisions: no judge is required to disqualify himself if the basis for disqualification would require every judge to disqualify himself. This "rule of necessity" was created to give every person effective redress in the courts.

For example, *United States v. Will,* 449 U.S. 200, 101 S.Ct. 471, 66 L.Ed. 2d 392 (1980), considered whether Congress could repeal or modify a statutorily defined formula for annual cost-of-living increases in the salary of federal judges. Every federal judge, from the district court level to the Supreme Court, had a financial interest in the outcome of the proceeding. The Court held that the "rule of necessity" precluded disqualification. "The declared purpose of § 455 is to guarantee litigants a fair forum in which they can pursue their claims. Far from promoting this purpose, failure to apply the Rule of Necessity would have a contrary effect, for without the Rule, some litigants would be denied their right to a forum." 449 U.S. at 217, 101 S.Ct. at 481, 66 L.Ed.2d at 407.

In some cases the judge who is disqualified may be the only person who is available at the moment to handle the matter (such as a temporary restraining order) on an emergency basis. That judge then must disclose the disqualifying facts on the record, and use "reasonable efforts" to transfer the matter. Canon 3E(1), Comment 3.

4. Generally Questioning the Impartiality of the Judge

The catch-all disqualification provision in Canon 3E(1)—where the judge's "impartiality might reasonably be questioned"—while measured according to an objective standard of conduct, is still subject to the particular circumstances of each case. Canon 3E(1), Comment 1 offers one example— where the judge was thinking of leaving the bench and negotiating for employment with a law firm, and that firm was appearing before the judge in a matter.

The following cases offer other examples where a judge disqualified himself or herself, or a higher court held that the judge should be disqualified on the grounds that the judge's impartiality might reasonably be questioned, or where the judge or higher court found no reasonable question of impartiality and therefore no disqualification.

5. Judge's Prior or Present Connection With Attorney

Rinden v. Marx, 116 N.H. 58, 351 A.2d 559 (1976) involved an attorney who was a defendant before the judge on drunken driving charges. Previously, the attorney *qua* attorney had served a complaint on the judge because the judge was a clerk of a corporate defendant and was the person authorized to receive service of process. The corporate defendant was covered by liability insurance, so there was no chance that the judge would be personally liable for any adverse judgment. In the absence of actual bias or prejudice, the judge did not have to disqualify himself. The disposition of the drunken driving charges against the attorney would have no effect on the civil suit.

Contrast *Smith v. State*, 239 Ga. 477, 238 S.E.2d 116 (1977), where the Supreme Court of Georgia reversed the defendant's conviction of theft and selling marijuana because of the trial judge's refusal to disqualify himself. During the trial, a deputy struck the defense counsel, who then moved for a postponement stating that, because of the beating, he was unable to represent his client on that day. The trial judge denied the motion, and even sympathized with the deputy because the deputy had earlier been subjected to defense counsel's derogatory questioning concerning sexual activities with an informer in the case. The state supreme court held that a judge has a duty to protect counsel for either party, and where the judge fails to perform this duty after knowledge of the attack and shows that his sympathies are with the attackers, his impartiality might reasonably be questioned.

In ABA Informal Opinion 1477 (Aug. 12, 1981), the ABA recommended that a judge recuse himself when a party is represented by the judge's own attorney, whether that attorney is representing the judge in a personal matter or in a matter pertaining to the judge's official position or conduct. It is irrelevant whether or not the lawyer charges a fee. Furthermore, disqualification is required even if it is the lawyer's partner or associate who is the one appearing before the judge. Accord, e.g., *Texaco, Inc. v. Chandler*, 354 F.2d 655 (10th Cir.1965) (trial judge disqualified because counsel for a party had recently represented judge in unrelated case against judge for civil damages because of judge's official activity).

6. Judge's Intemperate Remarks

In *Nicodemus v. Chrysler Corp.*, 596 F.2d 152 (6th Cir. 1979), the plaintiff sought reinstatement in an unfair employment practices suit. The judge, who granted the plaintiff's preliminary injunction, had stated:

> "This thing is the most transparent and the most blatant attempt to intimidate witnesses and parties that I have seen in a long time. I

don't believe anything that anybody from Chrysler tells me because there is nothing in the record that is before me and in my experience in dealing with this case that gives me reason to believe that they are not worthy of credence by anybody. They are a bunch of villains and they are interested only in feathering their own nests at the expense of everybody they can, including their own employees, and I don't intend to put up with it.

The trial judge also said that he was awarding $1000 in attorney fees "not necessarily because the employment laws allow it but because I believe" that the company is trying to "defy the court." Because these and similar remarks were hardly temperate and were "unsupported by the record," the appellate court reversed the preliminary injunction and disqualified the trial judge from further considering the case. The Court of Appeals noted that "this is not our first encounter with intemperate language by this particular district judge."

Contrast *In re International Business Machines Corp.*, 618 F.2d 923 (2d Cir. 1980). IBM claimed that the trial judge was biased because 86% of 10,000 oral motions made and 74 out of 79 written motions were decided against IBM and in favor of the government. The appellate court held that adverse rulings alone do not create the appearance of impartiality. "A trial judge must be free to make rulings on the merits without the apprehension that if he makes a disproportionate number in favor of one litigant, he may have created the impression of bias." 618 F.2d at 929. See also, *Lazofsky v. Sommerset Bus Co.*, 389 F.Supp. 1041 (E.D.N.Y. 1975) (judge does not demonstrate partiality merely because his rulings in a proceeding favor one party over the other).

7. Judge's Religion

Idaho v. Freeman, 507 F.Supp. 706 (D.Idaho 1981) involved a judge hearing a case concerning the constitutionality of Congress' extension of the ratification period for the Equal Rights Amendment. The Mormon Church generally opposed the ERA, and the judge was a Mormon and a regional representative of that Church. However, he was never required nor requested to promote the church's position, and his duties as a representative did not relate to the ERA. The judge concluded that his religious affiliation did not require him to disqualify himself. (The trial judge later held that the extension was unconstitutional, a ruling that the Supreme Court dismissed as moot.)

8. Where a Party, Witness, or Attorney Is Known to the Judge

As a general rule, the judge's obligation to disqualify herself where her "impartiality might reasonably be questioned" does not mean that a judge must automatically recuse herself simply because someone she might know casually is involved in litigation before her, either as a party, a witness, or as an attorney. In a small town, in particular, a judge may have a casual acquaintance with many people who become involved in some way with a trial. For example, in *Commonwealth v. Perry*, 468 Pa. 515, 364 A.2d 312 (1976), a murder trial, the judge was acquainted with the victim, a police officer, who "had oftentimes appeared here in court" as a witness. The judge had also attended the victim's funeral. The defendant sought reversal of his conviction because the judge did not recuse himself. The divided court held that, in the absence of actual prejudice, the judge did not have to disqualify himself merely because of this personal acquaintance with the victim; judges do not live in a vacuum and a contrary rule could result in a judge being disqualified in many cases. The majority reasoned that a judge should be permitted to form social relationships and society should not reasonably expect judges to be prejudiced merely because of the fact of that relationship. Any other result would deter many qualified persons from seeking a judicial office.

However, there are certain circumstances where a judge's personal acquaintance requires disqualification. *In re Conduct of Jordan*, 290 Or. 669, 624 P.2d 1074 (1981) (per curiam) involved a defendant who served on a library board with the judge. The judge stated that he could not believe that the defendant had committed the alleged acts. Therefore, the judge's impartiality might reasonably be questioned, for if there is a conflict in the evidence, a reasonable person would expect the judge to be inclined to believe the testimony offered on behalf of the defendant.

Even if the case is tried to a jury, a judge's personal bias in favor of, or against, a litigant should require disqualification. Neither the ABA Model Code of Judicial Conduct nor the federal statute draws any distinction based on the possibility of a jury or bench trial, perhaps recognizing that the judge's bias regarding a party can infect the entire proceeding, may be tacitly or implicitly communicated to the jury, and might affect the judge's actions in a host of discretionary rulings (e.g., whether to grant a continuance or judgment N.O.V., whether to rule that a damage verdict in a civil case is "excessive," or whether to impose a more severe sentence in a criminal case).

9. **When Judge's Former Law Clerk Represents a Party**
A judge is not automatically disqualified from presiding over a case because her former law clerk represents a party in the litigation. Because many clerks continue to practice law in the jurisdiction where they served as clerks, an absolute disqualification rule would deter highly qualified people from serving as law clerks.

No specific Code provision creates a *per* se rule prohibiting a judge from hearing a case where the judge's former law clerk is participating as a lawyer. Canon 3E(1)(b) does not apply because the law clerk was not a "lawyer" with whom the judge had previously practiced law. Canon 3E(1)(d)(ii) is also inapplicable unless the former law clerk is also the judge's spouse or a person within the third degree of relationship to either the judge or her spouse.

Note: However, *there are ethical restrictions on the former law clerk because of that former clerk's prior association with the judge.* Model Rule 1.12(c), Model Rules of Professional Conduct, does not allow a lawyer to represent anyone in connection with a matter in which the lawyer "participated personally and substantially as a . . . law clerk to [a judge], unless all parties to the proceeding consent after consultation." If a lawyer is disqualified under this section, no other lawyer in the firm may handle the matter unless the former law clerk is effectively screened, pursuant to Model Rule 1.12(c)(i), & (2). See also, Model Rule 1.12(b)(law clerk for judge may negotiate for employment with law firm that has a case before the judge in which the judicial clerk is participating personally and substantially "but only after" the judicial clerk first notifies the judge). See generally, Jones, *Some Ethical Considerations for Judicial Clerks,* 4 Georgetown J. Legal Ethics 771 (1991).

In certain circumstances, however, a judge may have to disqualify himself under the catch-all provision of Canon 3E(1) [or 28 U.S.C.A. § 455(a)] if his impartiality might reasonably be questioned because of his former law clerk's participation in the case. Consider the following cases.

In *Simonson v. General Motors Corp.,* 425 F.Supp. 574 (E.D.Pa. 1976), a law student worked one day per week as a judicial intern and was also employed by a local law firm. In one case before the judge, the defendant was represented by the same law firm that employed the intern. The plaintiff moved to reassign the case to another judge alleging that the intern's dual responsibilities created the "appearance of impropriety." The judge denied the motion and instituted the following procedures to insure that the judge's impartiality could not be reasonably questioned: (1) instructed the student not to participate in the litigation as a judicial intern, (2) instructed the law clerks not to give the student any assignments related to the litigation, or discuss the case with him, and (3) instructed the student to make arrangements with his law firm not to perform legal services on this particular case. This case, in effect, presaged Model Rule 1.12(b) & (c).

Fredonia Broadcasting Corp. v. RCA Corp., 569 F.2d 251 (5th Cir. 1978), reversed the trial judge because he did not disqualify himself when his former law clerk was an associate in the law firm representing one of the parties. The law clerk was on the judge's staff *during* the first trial and belonged to the law firm when the case was again before the judge on remand. The court of appeals required disqualification because the former law clerk "had been exposed to the trial judge's innermost thoughts about the case," and therefore the party represented by the clerk's law firm had an unfair advantage in the case. The court emphasized, however, that it was not holding that a former law clerk could never practice before the judge, but in this particular case the law clerk was "actively involved as counsel for a party in a case in which the law clerk participated during his clerkship." Id. at 256. If this fact situation would occur now, the judge could avoid disqualification if his former law clerk would be screened in accordance with Model Rule 1.12(c).

10. Where Judge Participated in Prior Related Case

Parties often seek to disqualify a judge on the basis of the judge's prior participation in a case involving the same party or the same facts. Absent some showing of hostility or actual bias, however, a judge should not be disqualified merely because of earlier judicial contacts with the party. This principle is really no different than the situation where the judge knows of damaging evidence that he later excludes at trial. The judge, even in a bench trial, is presumed to be able to screen out the excluded evidence.

For example, a judge is not required to disqualify himself in a criminal action because of a decision adverse to the party in a prior criminal case involving different and unrelated criminal charges. *State v. Cabiness*, 273 S.C. 56, 254 S.E.2d 291 (1979). Similarly, a sentencing judge is not automatically disqualified from hearing a habeas corpus motion that claims that the trial was unfair. *Panico v. United States*, 412 F.2d 1151 (2d Cir. 1969), cert. denied, 397 U.S. 921, 90 S.Ct. 901, 25 L.Ed.2d 102 (1970). A judge is also not disqualified from hearing a case if an appellate court reverses the judge's ruling and remands the case back to the trial court. *Mayberry v. Maroney*, 558 F.2d 1159 (3d Cir. 1977).

In *State v. Beshaw*, 134 Vt. 347, 359 A.2d 654 (1976), the defendant, convicted of burglary, asserted on appeal that the judge should have disqualified himself because, in a prior proceeding, the judge had cited the defendant for contempt for kicking a metal stand at the judge. Because the contempt proceeding was not material to the present case and had occurred 19 months earlier, the Vermont Supreme Court held that the judge did not abuse his discretion in refusing to disqualify himself. Though the court affirmed the judge, it did suggest that perhaps the judge should have disqualified himself under Canon 3C(1) because his impartiality might reasonably have been questioned.

The plaintiffs in *Meeropol v. Nizer*, 429 U.S. 1337, 97 S.Ct. 687, 50 L.Ed.2d 729 (1977), were sons of Julius and Ethel Rosenberg. The Rosenbergs were executed in 1953 following their convictions for conspiracy to commit espionage. The Meeropols sued attorney Louis Nizer for libel, invasion of privacy, and infringement of copyright. They also filed a motion before U.S. Supreme Court Justice Marshall, as Circuit Justice, to designate judges from other circuits to sit as appellate judges because the Second Circuit judges were associates, friends, or consultants of judges who had presided over the previous trial of the Meeropols' parents. Fourteen years earlier, Justice Marshall had been a member of the second circuit panel that denied post-conviction relief to Morton Sobell, the Rosenbergs' codefendant. Raising the disqualification issue *sua sponte*, Justice Marshall did not feel disqualification was necessary because he did not believe his " 'impartiality' to decide the extent of a circuit justice's powers under § 291(a) 'might reasonably be questioned' in light of this participation in a case not related to the present action." 429 U.S. at 1338 n.2, 97 S.Ct. at 689 n.2, 50 L.Ed.2d at 731 n.2. Justice Marshall then ruled that he had no authority to disqualify all of the judges on the appeals panel or to transfer the appeals to another circuit.

However, in *Rice v. McKenzie*, 581 F.2d 1114 (4th Cir. 1978), a judge was required to disqualify himself under 28 U.S.C.A. § 455 where, as a federal judge reviewing a habeas corpus petition, he was required to consider a case that he had helped to decide as chief justice of the state supreme court. The court recognized that generally a judge is not precluded from presiding in a case because of an earlier decision in which he participated. In this case, however, the judge's impartiality could reasonably be questioned because, as a district judge, the judge was reviewing the constitutionality of what he previously approved as chief justice of the state supreme court.

Note: 28 U.S.C.A. § 47 prohibits a judge from sitting on an appellate panel to review a case that he had decided as a trial judge. Section 47 did not apply to this case, however, because the judge had not been the trial judge on the case.

C. DISQUALIFICATION FOR PERSONAL BIAS OR PREJUDICE
1. Introduction
Canon 3E(1) first provides that a judge should disqualify herself whenever her impartiality might reasonably be questioned, "including but not limited to [specified] instances.. . . ." The Code then delineates specific instances where the judge's impartiality *would* be questioned. One of those instances, of course, is where a judge has actual bias or prejudices.

Canon 3E(1)(a) and 28 U.S.C.A. § 455(b)(1) thus provide that a judge must disqualify herself where she has *"a personal bias or prejudice concerning a party, or a party's lawyer, or personal knowledge of disputed evidentiary facts concerning the proceeding."*

Note: 28 U.S.C.A. § 455, unlike Canon 3E(1), does not categorize the specific instances requiring disqualification as examples where a judge's impartiality might reasonably be questioned. Section 455(b) begins, "He shall also disqualify himself in the following circumstances." The language change was not intended to alter application of the federal statute from situations where Canon 3E would require disqualification.

2. Extrajudicial Bias

Both Canon 3E(1)(a) and 28 U.S.C.A. § 455(b)(1) require disqualification only if there is bias concerning a *party*, as distinguished from bias concerning an issue in the case. This distinction reflects the Code's intent that a judge need not disqualify himself if bias arises from his beliefs as to the *law* that applies to a case. A judge may have fixed beliefs about principles of law that would not mandate disqualification. Otherwise, a judge could not write books or articles or speak on legal subjects, activities expressly permitted under Canon 4B. Indeed, after deciding cases and creating precedent for years, if would be incredible if the judge did not form some fixed ideas about the law. E.g., *Samuel v. University of Pittsburgh*, 395 F.Supp. 1275 (W.D.Pa. 1975).

In *Papa v. New Haven Federation of Teachers*, 186 Conn. 725, 444 A.2d 196 (1982), the trial judge was presiding over an attempt to enjoin teachers from striking. Seeking to disqualify the judge, the defendants asserted the judge was biased because of a speech he had earlier given criticizing teachers' strikes in general. This speech was given before the case arose and did not specifically address the case. Although the judge's statements were extrajudicial in nature, the state supreme court analogized the judge's statements to judicial expressions of opinion about specific laws, the obligation to obey those laws, and the consequences of disobedience. If disqualification is not required for judicial expressions of opinion about the law, noted the court, then extrajudicial opinions on points of law should not require disqualification as long as the comments do not raise a reasonable question that the judge will prejudge a pending or impending case. The judge in this case was disqualified, however, for giving another interview to a reporter concerning the pending proceeding. That interview violated Canon 3A(6) of the 1972 Code [Canon 3B(9) of the 1990 Code]. See also, *In the Matter of Sheffield,* 465 So.2d 350 (Ala. 1984), which suspended a judge for two months, without pay, because he (among other things) had a telephone interview with a reporter where the judge commented on the merits of a pending case.

The Extra–Judicial Source Rule. Even if the judge becomes biased against a party, such a bias is not normally considered improper and grounds for disqualification if the bias is based on *facts* learned about a party during the very proceeding at which the judge sits. The judge, after all, is supposed to make judgements and decisions based learned at the hearing. Similarly, courts generally also hold that a judge's participation over separate jury trials of codefendants does not constitute reasonable grounds for questioning the judge's impartiality in a subsequent jury trial involving a remaining codefendant. See *United States v. Cowden*, 545 F.2d 257 (1st Cir. 1976), cert. denied, 430 U.S. 909, 97 S.Ct. 1181, 51 L.Ed.2d 585 (1977).

In examining the reasons for the "extrajudicial source" rule, the court in *United Nuclear Corp. v. General Atomic Co.*, 96 N.M. 155, 249, 629 P.2d 231, 325 (1980), quoting *In re International Business Machines Corp.*, 618 F.2d 923, 930 (2d Cir. 1980) explained:

> "[A] judge is not merely a passive observer. He must . . . shrewdly observe the strategies of the opposing lawyers, perceive their efforts to sway him by appeals to his predilections. He must cannily penetrate through the surface of their remarks to their real purposes and motives. He has an official obligation to become prejudiced in that sense. Impartiality is not gullibility. Disinterestedness does not mean child-like innocence. If the judge did not form judgements of the actors in those court-house dramas called trials, he could never render decisions."

However, the situation is different, if the source of this bias as to facts was an "extrajudicial source." *United States v. Grinnell Corp.*, 384 U.S. 563, 86 S.Ct. 1698, 16 L.Ed.2d 778 (1966). "The alleged bias and prejudice to be disqualifying must stem from an extrajudicial source and result in an opinion on the merits on some basis other than what the judge learned from his participation in the case." 384 U.S. at 583, 86 S.Ct. 1710.

Although a judge generally does not have to disqualify himself if he acquires knowledge through his judicial duties, the fact that a judge's remarks or behavior take place in the judicial context does not exclude them from scrutiny and from requiring recusal if they reflect such pervasive bias and prejudice as would constitute bias against one of the parties.

Thus, in *State v. Harry*, 311 N.W.2d 108 (Iowa 1981), the judge was required to recuse himself for prejudicial statements made in a judicial context. According to the affidavit of the defendant's attorney, the judge accused the defendant's attorney of delaying tactics and informed the attorney that if the attorney allowed an innocent man to go on trial because of the defendant's silence, the judge would make it difficult for the defendant at his own trial. The prosecution claimed the judge should not recuse himself because the statements did not arise from an extrajudicial source. The state supreme court did not rely on Canon 3E(1) (a), but rather required disqualification because of a violation of Canon 3A(3) of the 1972 Code [Canon 3B(4) of the 1990 Code], which required the judge to be patient, dignified, and courteous to litigants, lawyers, and others.

3. Actual Bias or Prejudice in General

Instances of actual bias or prejudice, like the appearance of impartiality, are often fact-bound and should therefore be examined on a case-by-case basis. The following cases explore several situations where courts have found actual bias or prejudice, or the lack thereof.

In *Commonwealth v. Leventhal*, 364 Mass. 718, 307 N.E.2d 839 (1974), the defendant moved for a new trial, asserting that the trial judge was biased for numerous reasons. The defendant alleged the judge had an "intimate relationship" with the chief prosecution witness. This "intimate relationship" only amounted to the judge's having taught the witness in a bar review course 35 years previously, and having written a letter of recommendation for admission to the bar. The court dismissed this ground as frivolous. The defendant also asserted that the judge made prejudicial remarks during the trial, displaying to the jury that the judge believed the defendant was guilty. The court held that these remarks did not demonstrate bias, for the judge normally has a great deal of discretion in commenting on the trial to the jury. Finally, the defendant claimed the judge was biased because the judge was a defendant in a civil suit that the defendant had brought against the judge. The court noted that a lawsuit between a judge and a party may require disqualification in certain circumstances, but a party cannot disqualify a judge simply by bringing a separate action against him after the principal suit has commenced. It would then be too easy for a litigant, by creating a "conflict," to go judge shopping.

Department of Revenue v. Golder, 322 So.2d 1 (Fla. 1975). The issue in the underlying case was the constitutionality of an estate tax statute. At the time of the statute's enactment, the justice writing the opinion in the case was special tax counsel to the Florida House of Representatives and prepared a preliminary memorandum of law supporting the constitutionality of the proposed statute. The judge's prior involvement with the statute did not constitute bias because the views expressed in the memorandum were developed independently of any particular controversy or party. Also, the views as to the constitutionality of the statute were not extrajudicial. See also *Laird v. Tatum*, Memorandum of Justice Rehnquist, 409 U.S. 824, 93 S.Ct. 7, 34 L.Ed.2d 50 (1972). Justice Rehnquist refused to disqualify himself in this case: his previous participation was limited to testifying on similar legal issues before a Senate Subcommittee; although the *Laird* case itself was then in the lower courts, and Rehnquist did briefly refer to the case in Senate testimony, he never was counsel of record, did not even consult on that case, and was not otherwise involved with it.

Note: 28 U.S.C.A. § 455(b)(3) now requires a judge to disqualify himself "[w]here he has served in government employment and in such capacity participated as counsel, adviser or material witness concerning the proceeding or expressed an opinion concerning the merits of the particular case in controversy." The Model Judicial Code, in contrast, has a less broad provision requiring disqualification when the judge served as a lawyer or was a material witness in the matter in controversy. Canon 3E(1)(b). (28 U.S.C.A. § 455(b)(2) corresponds to this less broad prohibition.) These provisions are discussed in the following section.

In *State v. Linsky*, 117 N.H. 866, 379 A.2d 813 (1977) the state sought to enjoin the defendants from demonstrating at a nuclear powerplant. The defendants alleged the judge had prejudged the issues because of certain statements he made at the arraignment. The court held the judge was not biased because the judge subsequently had stated that he was not prejudging the defendants' guilt and would reach a verdict only on the evidence. The defendants also claimed the judge had personal knowledge of disputed evidentiary facts through newspapers, radio, and a meeting between the judge and defense counsel, thereby creating the possibility that the judge could be called as a witness. The court held that such knowledge did not require disqualification because the facts of which the judge had knowledge would probably not be material at trial and the evidence could be obtained from other sources. One might also add that if knowledge gathered from news media mandated disqualification, then only judges who never read newspapers or listened to the radio or television could hear cases. The court noted also that information learned at the judge's meeting with defense counsel probably was not "material" to any trial. Finally, the court held that it would be inappropriate for defense counsel to object to his own meeting with the judge; if defense counsel had not wanted the meeting, he should not have had it. To hold otherwise would allow any counsel to create the grounds for disqualification.

In *State v. Ahearn*, 137 Vt. 253, 403 A.2d 696 (1979) the defendant was charged with assault and robbery with a deadly weapon. The defendant appeared pro se and physically attacked the judge during the trial. The appellate court noted that "much of the defendant's conduct was intended to harass the court and generally disrupt the judicial process." The defendant sought reversal of his conviction because of an unfair trial. One of the grounds asserted was the judge's failure to disqualify himself because of the physical attack. The court held that the defendant's attack did not require disqualification because it was a "scheme to drive [the] judge out of the case." The defendant also argued that his harsh sentence demonstrated the judge's bias. The court noted that the judge probably should have recused himself because his impartiality might reasonably be questioned. But the sentence itself did not demonstrate actual bias in light of the defendant's crimes and his twelve previous felony convictions. The failure to disqualify, therefore, was within the trial judge's discretion and was not reversible error.

Commonwealth v. Boyle, 498 Pa. 486, 447 A.2d 250 (1982) held that bias did not exist just because a trial judge's rulings in a former trial were similar to rulings in a pretrial proceeding. "If the rulings at the second trial constituted a fair exercise of discretion, the fact that a trial judge had previously ruled in a similar manner under similar circumstances is to be expected." 498 Pa. at 491, 447 A.2d at 252. Similarly, a judge does not demonstrate partiality merely because his rulings in a proceeding tend to favor one party over the other. *Lazofsky v. Sommerset Bus Co.,* 389 F.Supp. 1041 (E.D.N.Y.1975).

United States v. Poludniak, 657 F.2d 948 (8th Cir. 1981). The judge in this case was presiding over a case where a U.S. Senator was an extortion victim. In a previous newspaper article, the judge had stated that he hoped to talk with senators to obtain additional funds to hire more marshals for courthouse security. Because the Senator involved in the case was a victim, not a party, the judge did not have to disqualify himself.

Contrast, *United States v. Brown,* 539 F.2d 467 (5th Cir. 1976). In this case, it was learned that the trial judge had mentioned at a swimming pool that he was going to preside over the defendant's trial and that he was "going to get that nigger." The court reversed defendant's conviction on appeal because the judge's statement did not "comport with the appearance of justice" and demonstrated the judge's personal bias, and "it could not be said from the record alone that appellant received a fair trial."

United States v. Holland, 655 F.2d 44 (5th Cir. 1981). In the first trial of this case, the judge, after consent of all counsel, had an unrecorded conversation with the jury in the jury room. The defendant asserted the judge's conduct as error on appeal and won a right to a new trial. The same trial judge stated that because of the defendant's appeal, he was going to increase the defendant's sentence. The court held that the judge's remarks demonstrated actual bias and also the appearance of partiality. The judge was disqualified from presiding over further proceedings in the case.

D. DISQUALIFICATION WHEN THE JUDGE IS A FORMER LAWYER OR MATERIAL WITNESS

Canon 3E(1)(b) requires disqualification where (1) a judge served as a lawyer in the matter in controversy, (2) a lawyer, with whom the judge previously practiced law, served as a lawyer during such association in the matter now pending before the judge, or (3) the judge has been a material witness concerning the matter in controversy.

Note: While the Judicial Code refers to a "lawyer in the matter", 28 U.S.C.A. § 455(b)(2) refers to judges who had served as a lawyer while in "private practice." However, the drafters of the federal statute added a new subsection, § 455(b)(3), which provides that a judge is disqualified "[w]here he has served in *governmental* employment and in such capacity participated as counsel, adviser or material witness concerning the proceeding or expressed an opinion concerning the merits of the particular case in controversy." (emphasis added). A judge should disqualify himself, for example, if he acted as an Assistant U.S. Attorney in the case before he became a judge. *Mixon v. United States*, 608 F.2d 588 (5th Cir. 1979). This very broad disqualification provision, § 455(b)(3), also provides that judges who previously served in a governmental capacity (whether or not they served as lawyers) are disqualified if, in that capacity, they advised on, were a material witness concerning, or expressed any opinion about the merits of a *particular* case. *See* H.R.Rep. No. 1453, 93d Cong., 2d Sess. 6 (1974).

Canon 3E(1)(b), Comment 1 discusses the application of this disqualification provision to prior governmental employment. A "lawyer in a governmental agency does not ordinarily have an association with other lawyers employed by that agency" within the meaning of this subsection. The drafters used the word "ordinarily" to indicate that "disqualification does not usually result from these relationships." *ABA's Standing Committee Report on 1990 Code, Legislative Draft* 27 (1990).

Thus, a judge who was formerly employed by the Securities and Exchange Commission would not have to disqualify himself under Canon 3E(1)(b) simply because another former or present member of the SEC brings a case before the judge. However, the judge must still disqualify himself under the catch-all provision of Canon 3E(1), *if* the fact situation is such that his impartiality might reasonably be questioned. Furthermore, a judge would have to disqualify himself under Canon 3E(1)(b) if the SEC matter before him were one in which he had personally served as a lawyer with the SEC.

In *Matter of O'Brien*, 437 N.E.2d 972 (Ind. 1982) (per curiam), a part-time judge (who was also authorized to practice law) represented the husband in a dissolution of marriage proceeding. The judge prepared the petition and served the summons on the wife. At the hearing on the matter, the regular judge was absent, and the judge who represented the husband was selected as judge *pro tempore.* The judge then entered the dissolution decree and approved the property settlement. Even though the parties consented to the judge/lawyer acting as judge *pro tempore,* the judge's conduct still violated Canon 3E(1)(b), as well as DR 9–101(A) and DR 1–102(A)(5). The judge was reprimanded and admonished.

Canon 3E(1)(b) requires disqualification only if the judge acted as a lawyer in the *matter in controversy.* Thus, a judge did not disqualify himself when he was passing on the constitutionality of an estate tax statute even though, three years earlier—when he was special tax counsel to the state legislature—he had written a preliminary memorandum concluding that the statute was constitutional. *Department of Revenue v. Golder,* 322 So.2d 1 (Fla. 1975). Canon 3E(1)(b) requires disqualification only if the bias is based upon prior contacts with a *proceeding,* and not simply because of familiarity with a legal issue.

Note: If this case had involved a federal judge, then 28 U.S.C.A. § 455(b)(3) would have been applicable. It requires disqualification of the judge who, when she was a government employee, had "expressed an opinion concerning the merits of the particular *case* in controversy." (emphasis added.) Because the judge had not expressed an opinion about the merits of the particular case, the federal statute also should not require disqualification.

The second clause of Canon 3E(1)(b) (as well as § 455(b)(2) of 28 U.S.C.A.) requires judicial disqualification when a judge's former law partner or associate has served as a lawyer in the matter, but only if the lawyer served as counsel *while* the judge was also practicing law with the lawyer. In other words, a judge should not participate in a case that his former law firm handled, even though the firm is no longer involved, if the judge was a member of the firm when it was acting as counsel. Thus, in *Hall v. Hall,* 242 Ga. 15, 247 S.E.2d 754 (1978), a judge did not have to disqualify himself in a divorce proceeding where the wife's counsel was the judge's former law partner in the absence of proof that the wife's representation began before the judge left his legal practice. (Of course, one must always bear in mind that, depending on the fact situation, the judge may still have to recuse himself under the catch-all provision of Canon 3E(1) where there is a reasonable question as to the judge's impartiality. The longer the judge is on the bench, the less likely the need for disqualification under the general provisions of Canon 3E(1).)

E. DISQUALIFICATION FOR FINANCIAL INTERESTS OR INTERESTS THAT COULD BE SUBSTANTIALLY AFFECTED BY THE OUTCOME OF THE PROCEEDING

1. Introduction

Canon 3E(1)(c) mandates disqualification when a judge "knows" that he or she, "individually or as a fiduciary," has an "economic interest" (that is not "de minimis") in the subject matter in controversy or in a party to the proceeding, or has any other more than "de minimis" interest that could be substantially affected by the proceeding. Canon 3E(1)(c) also mandates disqualification if the judge "knows" that his or her spouse, parent or child (no matter where they are residing), or any other "member of the judge's family residing in the judge's household" has a similar "economic interest" (that is not "*de minimis*") or any other more than "*de minimis*" interest that could be substantially affected by the proceeding.

Introductory Definitions. This rule uses various terms of art defined in the Terminology section. In the order in which they are used in this Canon, **"knows"** means "actual knowledge of the fact in question." However, a person's knowledge "may be inferred from circumstances." Terminology 8. **"Fiduciary"** includes such relationships as "executor, administrator, trustee, and guardian." Terminology 8. (Note that Canon 4E prohibits a judge from acting as a fiduciary except for the estate, trust, or person of a member of his family, and only if such service will not interfere with the proper performance of his judicial duties.) **"Member of the judge's family residing in the judge's household"** means "any relative of the judge, by blood or marriage, or a person treated by the judge as a member of the judge's family, who resides in the judge's household." Terminology 12.

"Economic interest" is a lengthy definition, which will be discussed below. Subject to a few exceptions, it means a legal or equitable interest that is "*more than a de minimis*," or a relationship such "as officer, director, advisor or other active participant in the affairs of a party." Terminology 6. Note that any legal or equitable interest in a party is, by definition, a disqualifying "economic interest" only if it is more than de minimis. If the judge is an officer, director, etc. in a party, that is automatically disqualifying, and the issue of "*de minimis*" is not applicable. The drafters used the term "economic interest" instead of "financial interest" (which is what the 1972 Code used) in order to emphasize that an economic interest included a *relationship,* such as officer or director of a party. **"De minimis"** means "an insignificant interest that could not raise reasonable question as to a judge's impartiality." Terminology 5.

2. Economic Interests

(a) Legal or Equitable Interest

Unless the economic interest is a relationship such as an officer or director, the economic interest must be legal or equitable in nature before it is disqualifying. Terminology 6. (This "economic interest"— unless it is a relationship—must also be, by definition, more than "de minimis," a term discussed below.)

For example, *In re Virginia Electric & Power Co.*, 539 F.2d 357 (4th Cir. 1976) involved VEPCO, a public utility, attempting to recover damages caused by defective pump supports for its nuclear powerplant. Because of a fuel adjustment clause, VEPCO was permitted to charge its customers directly for the amount that VEPCO claimed as damages. If VEPCO won its suit, it might be required to return to its customers that part of the award representing the surcharge. Customers could receive a $70 to $100 refund. The presiding judge was a VEPCO customer. The court upheld the judge's refusal to disqualify himself under this section because the judge merely had a contingent interest in the litigation, not a legal or equitable financial interest. VEPCO customers would only receive a refund if the Virginia State Corporation Commission authorized a return of the surcharge. The court also held that the judge did not have any other interest that would be substantially affected by the outcome of the case. *See also, Dacey v. Connecticut Bar Association*, 170 Conn. 520, 368 A.2d 125 (1976) (judge did not have legal or equitable financial interest in case where plaintiff was suing the state bar association for libel and any judgment adverse to the bar association could raise bar dues).

Similarly, a judge's interest as a ratepayer or taxpayer should not be a "legal or equitable" economic interest. Such interests, however, could require disqualification if it is "any other" interest that is "more than de minimis" and could be "substantially affected" by the outcome of the proceeding. Canon 3E(1)(c).

Although the judge's economic interest must be legal or equitable before the judge will be disqualified, this interest need not have the traditional indicia of ownership, such as a title or other physical representation of ownership. In *Taylor v. Public Convalescent Service*, 245 Ga. 805, 267 S.E.2d 242 (1980), a pauper was appealing a default judgment that had been entered in the justice of the peace court. Before the pauper could perfect his appeal, the justice of the peace had to determine the validity of the pauper's affidavit, claiming that he could not pay court costs. Under local rules, approval of the pauper's affidavit could deny (or, at least delay) the justice of the peace from receiving a portion of his income, because the justice of the peace received court costs as fees. The state supreme court required disqualification in this case because the justice of the peace had a direct economic interest in whether or not the pauper would succeed on his affidavit. Such a structural set-up is defective because it gives the judge a financial interest in the controversy.

(b) The Subject Matter in the Controversy

In order for Canon 3E(1)(c) to be applicable, the judge's economic interest must be "in the subject matter in controversy." *Commonwealth v. Keigney,* 3 Mass.App.Ct. 347, 329 N.E.2d 778 (1975) addressed this issue. In this case, the defendant pled guilty to armed robbery while masked, larceny of a motor vehicle, and unlawfully carrying a revolver in a motor vehicle. The presiding judge, a former stockholder and board member of the bank named in the indictment, was an accommodation maker for a friend's $1,500 note held by the bank. In the defendant's motion for a new sentencing trial, he argued that the judge should have disqualified himself because of his past pecuniary relationship with the bank. The court held that in the absence of actual bias or prejudice, the judge was not required to disqualify himself. The disposition of the indictment could not have resulted in the judge having to pay the note.

(c) A *"De minimis"* Interest"

The 1972 Code. The 1972 Judicial Code required the judge to disqualify himself if he (or spouse or minor child in his household) had a "financial interest" in the subject matter in controversy. See, Canons 3C(1)(c) & 3D (1972 Judicial Code). The 1972 Code, in general, defined "financial interest" to mean legal or equitable interest *"however small."* Canon 3C(3)(b) (1972 Judicial Code). However, the parties and their lawyers could waive this disqualification. Thus, under the 1972 Code, a judge will be disqualified from a case where International Business Machines is a party, if she owns even one share of IBM stock, and even if the value of the stock will be unaffected by the litigation (unless there is a proper waiver). J. Shaman, S. Lubet, & J. Alfini, *Judicial Conduct and Ethics* § 5.20 at 138 (1990).

The drafters of the 1972 Judicial Code thought that it would be too difficult to interpret an ambiguous concept such as "substantial" financial interest. If the substantiality test were applied to financial interests, it would not be clear whether the judge's financial interest should be compared to the total of all financial interests of others in the party, or the total of all the judge's financial interests. *See Reporter's Notes [1972]* at 65. In either case, judges would have to expose the value of their entire stock portfolio to the parties in order to determine whether the judge's economic interest was "substantial."

Many judges did not want to reveal that much information about their financial affairs.

The "however small" qualification to the financial interest conflict could lead to some anomalous results. For example, in *In re Cement Antitrust Litigation (Mdl No. 296),* 688 F.2d 1297 (9th Cir. 1982), affirmed, 459 U.S. 1191, 103 S.Ct. 1173, 75 L.Ed.2d 425 (1983) (per curiam), the judge's wife owned some stock in several of the plaintiff class members. The judge recused himself at the defendants' request, but the plaintiffs sought to have the judge reappointed because of the complicated nature of the case. After concluding that unnamed class members were parties within the meaning of 28 U.S.C.A. § 455(d)(4)—which also defines "financial interest" to include "a legal or equitable interest, however small"—, the appellate court upheld the judge's decision to recuse himself. The Ninth Circuit's disdain for this result is reflected in the following statement: "[A]fter five years of litigation, a multi-million dollar lawsuit of major national importance, with over 200,000 class plaintiffs, grinds to a halt over Mrs. Muecke's $29.70." 688 F.2d at 1313. On the other hand, one might point out that whenever one draws a bright line, there will always be cases close to the line that some argue should go the other way. The alternative to a bright line is a vague one, and vagueness leads to more litigation, not less.

Note: In *Union Carbide Corp. v. United States Cutting Service, Inc.,* 782 F.2d 710 (7th Cir. 1986), a divided panel held that, at least in some cases—in this case, in the midst of a large antitrust class action—a judge could "cure" the disqualification resulting from her husband's ownership of stock by selling the stock. Congress, in 1988, subsequently codified this result in § 455(f).

The 1990 Code. The drafters of the 1990 Code provide that when "economic interest" refers to ownership, it means "ownership of more than a de minimis legal or equitable interest. . . ." Terminology 6. And they, in turn, define "de minimis" to mean "an insignificant interest that could not raise reasonably question as to a judge's impartiality." Terminology 5. Judges, thus, are not required to disqualify themselves under Canon 3E(1)(c) unless that have more than a de minimis legal or equitable ownership in the subject matter in controversy or in a party to the proceeding. In addition, they must disqualify themselves if there is any other interest that is "more than de minimis" and "that could be substantially affected by the proceeding." Canon 3E(1)(c).

Note: Given the punctuation in Canon 3E(1)(c), the more natural reading is that if the judge (or relevant family member) **has a relationship such as an officer,** director, etc. in a party, or has **more than a de minimis economic interest** in the subject matter in controversy or a party to the proceeding, then the judge must be disqualified. However, if the judge (or relevant family member) has **any other interest,** then this other interest must satisfy two criteria: *first,* it must be **more than de minimis,** and *second,* this interest is such that it **could be substantially affected by the proceeding.**

The drafters of the 1990 Judicial Code are exceedingly pithy in explaining this significant new requirement that the interest be more than de minimis. They simply announce that they added this requirement "to obviate the need for disqualification where a judge's financial interest is de minimis and would not affect impartiality." *ABA's Standing Committee Report on 1990 Code, Report,* at 6 (1990). See also, *ABA's Standing Committee on 1990 Code, Legislative Draft,* at 5 (1990)("more than de minimis" was included "to preclude disqualification based on any de minimis legal or equitable interest. . . ."). Moser, *The 1990 ABA Code of Judicial Conduct,* 4 Georgetown J. of Legal Ethics 731, 752 & n. 82 (1991), also merely repeats the definition in the Terminology section.

Unfortunately, the drafters offer no test to determine when an interest if "de minimis." Obviously, a judge will not be disqualified under the 1990 Judicial Code if she owns one share of I.B.M. stock and I.B.M. is a party. But what if she owns 100 shares, with a tax basis of over $10,000? Is that de minimis? What if she owns 50 shares, but her entire net worth is only $75,000? Does one compare her I.B.M shares to her total stock portfolio, or to her net worth, or to some absolute standard? What if she has a stock portfolio with a tax basis of over $3 million, so that the I.B.M. is only .33% of her portfolio. Is the amount de minimis as to her? Does the answer change if the market value (as opposed to tax basis) of I.B.M. stock is $15,000, and the market value of her portfolio is $4 million, so that I.B.M. comprises .375% of her portfolio? What if her net worth if $6 million.

Many judges like to keep their financial information private. Canon 4I, Comment 1, recognizes that a "judge has the rights of any other citizen, including the right to privacy of the judge's financial affairs, except to the extent that limitations established by law are required to safeguard the proper performance of the judge's duties." While proclaiming an interest in the privacy of a judge's financial affairs, the drafters have ironically drafted a rule that should give litigants the right to learn a lot more about a judge's financial affairs. The "de minimis" rule makes such information material, for in order to learn whether a financial interest is "de minimis," the litigants will normally need to have a complete picture of the judge's net worth.

(d)   The Judge's Family

Canon 3C(1)(b) extends the net of disqualification to cases where the judge's family own disqualifying interests. If either the spouse, parent, or child (no matter where they are residing), or any other "member of the judge's family residing in the judge's household" (an expression defined in Terminology 11) has an economic interest or other interest that would disqualify the judge if the judge had that interest, then that interest is, in effect, imputed to the judge, who them must disqualify himself. However, this disqualification provision only applies *if* the judge knows of the interest. Thus, let us turn to the question of "knowledge."

(e)   Knowledge of Economic Interests

Canon 3E(1)(c)—as well as 28 U.S.C.A. § 455(b)(4)—requires disqualification only if the judge "knows" of the disqualifying economic interest. Canon 3E(2)—and 28 U.S.C.A. § 455(c)—thus require that a judge inform himself about his own financial interests. If the judge does not keep himself so informed, he would be subject to sanctions for violating the Code. Otherwise the Judicial Code would place a premium on ignorance. But ignorance is not always bliss. This requirement of knowledge *precludes the use of a "blind trust"* to avoid disqualification. See *Reporter's Notes to 1972 Judicial Code,* at 64–65.

Although a judge *shall* keep informed of his or her own *personal and fiduciary* economic interests, the judge need only make a "reasonable effort" to learn of the personal economic interests of his or her spouse and minor children residing in his household. The Canons realistically recognize that there may be limits to what a judge can do to require others to keep him or her informed of all financial dealings. The *Reporter's Notes to the 1972 Judicial Code* list the following relevant factors to determine whether a reasonable effort has been made: "Did the interest of the spouse or child come from the judge or from another source? Does the spouse or child know the nature of the interest, or is he or she the beneficiary of a blind trust? Has the spouse's or child's financial interest been supervised by the judge in the past, or has the judge not been involved in the handling of the interest?" *Reporter's Notes to 1972 Judicial Code* at 68.

As to other members of the judge's family who do not fall under Canon 3E(2), Canon 3E(1)(c) requires the judge to disqualify herself only if she has actual knowledge of the financial interest of such persons. The simple reality is that such persons often act independently of the judge, and so this section pragmatically does not require her to exert an effort to gain knowledge of such persons' economic interests.

(f) Exceptions to Economic Interest Disqualification
The definition of "Economic Interest" excludes several types of economic interest. Terminology 6. Cf. 28 U.S.C.A. § 455(d)(4).

(i) Mutual Funds
A judge must disqualify himself if he has an economic interest (i.e., more than a de minimis interest) in a mutual fund that is a party to the proceeding before him. He need not disqualify himself, however, simply because he owns shares in a mutual fund that directly owns shares in a party that appears before him, *unless* the judge participates in the management of the fund. In other words, if the judge owns more than a de minimis amount of shares in Fidelity Magellan Mutual Fund, and Fidelity Magellan Mutual Fund is a party before the judge, he has a disqualifying interest. However, if I.B.M. is a party before him, the fact that he owns shares in Fidelity Magellan Mutual Fund (which, in turn, owns shares in I.B.M.) is not disqualifying, *unless* the judge (1) participates in the management of the fund, or (2) "a proceeding pending or impending before the judge could substantially affect the value of the interest."

> *Note:* The drafters tell us that this second clause was added "to cover situations such as an investment club where the outcome of a proceeding involving the club might affect the value of the judge's interest." *ABA's Standing Committee Report on 1990 Code, Legislative Draft* 5 (1990). However, one would think that if the judge was a member of an investment club, that situation is already covered by the language [in Terminology 6(i)] including the judge who holds investments in, and participates in the management of, a "common investment fund."

In any event, the rule regarding mutual funds is easy to justify. The judge lacks control over the fund's investment decisions. Moreover, it is not easy to find out at any given time what are the components of a mutual fund's portfolio, which is constantly changing. In addition, judges have a need for some types of nondisqualifying investments.

(ii)   Civic Organizations
Terminology 6(ii) provides that if the judge or her spouse, parent or child hold an office in an educational, religious, charitable, fraternal, or civic organization, that does not create any "economic interest" in securities held by the organization. Thus, if she is an officer in her local church, and the church owns 100 shares of IBM stock, the judge need not disqualify herself simply whenever IBM is a party before her. However, if the church is a party before her, and she is an officer of her church, she must disqualify herself because "economic interest" includes the relationship of officer, director, advisor, or other active participant in the affairs of a party."

(iii) Financial Institutions and Mutual Insurance Companies
Terminology 6(iii) explains that the interest of a policy holder in a mutual insurance company, or the deposit in a mutual savings association, or credit union, or similar proprietary interest, is an "economic interest" only if the pending or impending proceeding could substantially affect the value of the interest.

(iv)   Government Bonds
Finally, Terminology 6(iv) provides that ownership of government securities is not an "economic interest" in the issuer (e.g., the State of Illinois) unless the proceeding could substantially affect the value of the bonds. In other words, simply because a judge owns a certain number of municipal bonds of Chicago does not mean that he must disqualify himself in every case where Chicago is a party. Similarly, merely because a judge owns $5,000 (or $500,000) of U.S. Bonds does not require her to disqualify herself in every case where the U.S. Government is a party.

However, if an issue concerning the bonds themselves were the subject of the litigation before the judge (e.g., was it legal for the state to extend the time when the bonds were due), and the judge owned these bonds, then the judge has a disqualifying economic interest if the proceeding before the judge could substantially affect the value of the securities.

(g) Other Interests
In addition to disqualification for economic interests in the subject matter in controversy, a judge will be disqualified for "any other more than de minimis interest" *if* that interest "could be substantially affected by the outcome of the proceeding." Canon 3C(1)(c) and 28 U.S.C.A. § 455(b)(4).

F. DISQUALIFICATION BASED ON FAMILY RELATIONSHIPS
1. Introduction

Canon 3E(1)(d) provides that a judge will be disqualified if the judge, the judge's spouse, a person "within the third degree of relationship" to either of them judge, or spouses of any of the foregoing persons, is a party, or officer, director or trustee of a party, is a lawyer in the proceeding, "is known by the judge to have more than a de minimis interest that could be substantially affected by the proceeding," or is likely to be a material witness. This disqualification provision is so expansive because the Code's drafters felt "that to maintain the appearance of impartiality the disqualification standard should encompass all persons within the third degree of relationship to a judge or his spouse even though the relationship arises only through marriage." *Reporter Notes to 1972 Judicial Code* at 67–68.

The degree of relationship, referred to in Canon 3E(1)(d) is measured according to the civil law system. The civil law system counts as one degree each person in the chain from the judge to the common ancestor and from the common ancestor to the person whose relationship raises the issue. Happily, we do not have to remember all that, because Terminology 19 defines the third degree of relationship to be the following persons: great-grandparent, grandparent, parent, uncle, aunt, brother, sister, child, grandchild, great-grandchild, nephew, or niece. Of course, even if the judge's or his spouse's relative does not fall within the third degree of relationship, the judge still may be disqualified under the general impartiality standard of Canon 3E(1). See, e.g., *Gray v. Barlow*, 241 Ga. 347, 245 S.E.2d 299 (1978) (judge disqualified where relatives were related in the 6th degree but also held security interests in the parties' property in case where plaintiff sought removal of obstruction to his property).

2. Party to the Proceeding

Canon 3E(1)(d)(i) [and 28 U.S.C.A. § 455(b)(5)(i)] requires disqualification where any of the parties covered under this disqualification provision is a party to the proceeding or an officer, director, or trustee of a party. For example, in *Cuyahoga County Board of Mental Retardation v. Association of Cuyahoga County Teachers of Trainable Retarded*, 47 Ohio App.2d 28, 351 N.E.2d 777 (1975), a judge was obligated to recuse himself when his brother was a member of the plaintiff/board.

3. Acting as Lawyer in the Proceeding

Canon 3E(1)(d)(ii) [and 28 U.S.C.A. § 455(b)(5)(ii)] requires disqualification if a person falling within that section—the judge's spouse or any third degree relative (or spouse of such a relative) of either the judge or the judge's spouse—is a lawyer in the proceeding.

Note: Recall that Canon 3E(1)(b) [cf. 28 U.S.C.A. § 455(b)(2) & (3)] also requires a judge to disqualify himself if he had acted as a lawyer in the matter in controversy.

The Commentary to Canon 3E(1)(d)(ii) explains an important caveat to this disqualification provision.   Canon 3E(d)(ii) does not automatically disqualify a judge simply because a lawyer in the proceeding is a member of the law firm with which a relative of the judge is affiliated.   In other words, the disqualification caused by the relative's personal appearance in the action is *not imputed* to the members of that relative's firm.   The judge may still be disqualified under the catch-all provision of Canon 3E(1), however, if his impartiality might reasonably be questioned.   A judge may also be disqualified under Canon 3E(1)(d)(iii) if the lawyer-relative is known by the judge to have an interest in the law firm that could be substantially affected by the outcome of the proceeding."

Consider, for example, in *Potashnick v. Port City Construction Co.*, 609 F.2d 1101 (5th Cir. 1980).   The judge's father was the senior partner in the law firm representing the plaintiffs.   The judge's father, however, was not participating in the case.   The court held that the judge was not disqualified under 28 U.S.C.A. § 455(b)(5)(ii) [which corresponds to Canon 3E(1)(d)(ii)], but then held that he was disqualified under § 455(b)(5)(iii) [which corresponds to Canon 3E(1)(d)(iii)].   The judge's father received a 1% share of the firm's income.   Although the fee in this case could not be affected by the outcome of the decision because the fee was based on an hourly fixed rate, the court held that disqualification is required even if the lawyer-relative's interest has a mere potential to be affected by the outcome of the case.   The case could have been handled on a contingent fee basis, or a favorable result may have justified a higher fee. Furthermore, the decision in the case could affect the firm's reputation, its relationship with its clients, and its ability to attract new clients.   The court concluded, therefore, that the judge's father had interests that could substantially be affected by the outcome of the case.

In contrast, in *United States ex rel. Weinberger v. Equifax, Inc.*, 557 F.2d 456 (5th Cir. 1977), the judge's son was an associate in the law firm representing the defendant but the son did not personally participate in the case.   The judge was therefore not disqualified under 28 U.S.C.A. § 455(b)(5)(ii).   The court also held the judge was not disqualified under § 455(b)(5)(iii) because as an associate the son did not have an interest that could be substantially affected by the outcome ofthe case.   Regarding the impartiality standard under 28 U.S.C.A. § 455(a), the court held that the judge did not abuse his discretion in concluding that his impartiality could not reasonably be questioned.

In *SCA Services, Inc. v. Morgan,* 557 F.2d 110 (7th Cir. 1977), the Seventh Circuit interpreted the disqualification provisions broadly, to favor disqualification. The judge's brother was a partner in the law firm representing one of the parties, but he did not directly participate in the case, thereby precluding disqualification under 28 U.S.C.A. § 455(b)(5)(ii). Nonetheless, the court required disqualification under both § 455(b)(5)(iii) and § 455(a) because the brother would share in the fees generated by the case. Furthermore, the court argued that the judge's impartiality could be reasonably questioned because it is reasonable to assume that brothers enjoy a close personal and family relationship and would probably support each other's interests.

S.J. Groves & Sons Co. v. International Brotherhood of Teamsters, Chauffeurs, Warehousemen and Helpers of America, Local 627, 581 F.2d 1241 (7th Cir. 1978) is another case where the judge's brother was a partner in the law firm representing one of the parties. In this case, however, the law firm withdrew from the case before the judge had made any discretionary rulings. The court held the judge did not abuse his discretion in refusing to disqualify himself where the firm had no continuing interest in the case and there was no evidence that the judge forced the firm's withdrawal through delay or other means. The court noted, however, that it probably would be better for a judge to recuse himself in such circumstances to avoid hardship on the parties.

McCuin v. Texas Power & Light Co., 714 F.2d 1255 (5th Cir. 1983) added an important qualification to the situation where the judge's close relative is a lawyer in the firm representing one of the parties. In that case, six years after the plaintiffs filed a discrimination suit, defendant added as co-counsel the trial judge's brother-in-law. In a companion case another defendant added the brother-in-law shortly after it filed its answer. The court was concerned that a litigant could disrupt preparation for trial and disqualify a judge whose rulings are expected to be unfavorable by "the simple expedient of finding one of the judge's relatives who is willing to act as counsel. . . ." Congress, however, has not given federal litigants the right of preemptory challenge to a judge. Thus the court interpreted § 455 to mean that "counsel may not be chosen solely or primarily for the purpose of disqualifying the judge." The district court threatened with such maneuvers "need not confine itself to grievance proceedings against errant counsel." The judge who was initially assigned to the case and who is threatened with disqualification should disqualify himself as soon as he became aware that his brother-in-law had been enrolled as counsel. The Fifth Circuit then simply announced that if the new judge thought the employment of the brother-in-law was "stratagem" or a "sham," the new judge should then disqualify counsel. The case would then be reassigned to the first judge.

4. An Interest That Could Be Substantially Affected by the Outcome

Canon 3E(1)(d)(iii) mandates disqualification where a person covered under this section "is known by the judge to have more than a de minimis interest that could be substantially affected by the outcome of the proceeding." This interest could be a non-economic as well as an economic interest. Furthermore, in order for this section to apply, the interest must be both (1) more than "de minimis" (a term vaguely defined in the Terminology section), and (2) this more than "de minimis" interest is something that "could be substantially affected by the proceeding." [Note that 28 U.S.C.A. § 455(b)(5)(iii) is analogous to Canon 3E(1)(d)(iii) except the federal statute does not allow even de minimis interests.]

The judge has no affirmative duty to become aware of the interests of his relatives under this subsection unless the relative is a spouse or minor child residing in his household. Canon 3E(2).

5. Material Witness in the Proceeding

Canon 3E(1)(d)(iv). The last circumstance enumerated in Canon 3E(1)(d) [and 28 U.S.C.A. § 455(b)(5)] requires the judge's disqualification whenever a person covered in this section "is to the judge's knowledge likely to be a material witness in the proceeding." Note that it is not enough that the relative will likely be a witness, but the testimony also must be "material" before the judge is required to disqualify himself. Parties cannot mandate judicial disqualification by calling a judicial relative as a witness for a nonmaterial matter. The Judicial Canons do not explain what is meant by "material," but the standard is probably somewhat analogous to that of Model Rule 3.7, of the Model Rules of Professional Conduct (the advocate-witness rule).

G. REMITTAL OF JUDICIAL DISQUALIFICATION

Note: The waiver of disqualification provisions in the ABA Code of Judicial Conduct and the federal disqualification statute differ significantly. The two disqualification provisions will therefore be treated separately.

1. Canon 3F

If the judge is disqualified by the Canon 3E, Canon 3F permits the parties to waive disqualification unless the basis for disqualification is the judge's personal bias or prejudice concerning a party.

Canon 3F describes clearly the procedure for waiver. To secure a proper waiver, the judge discloses on the record the basis for the disqualification, and then (assuming that the basis is not personal bias or prejudice) asks the parties and lawyers, to consider, *outside of the presence of the judge,* whether to waive disqualification. If the parties and lawyers, *without participation by the judge,* all agree that the judge should not be disqualified, then the judge may participate. (Canon 3F states that the judge may participate if "the judge is then willing to participate," but one would think that the judge would not have asked the parties to waive the disqualification to begin with if he had not been willing to participate.) The agreement regarding this waiver "shall be incorporated in the record of the proceeding."

This question of waiver of disqualification, the Code emphasizes, must be made independently of the judge. Thus, if one of the parties rejects waiver, the judge is not supposed to know who it is. A judge "must not solicit, seek or hear comment on possible" waiver "unless the lawyers jointly propose remittal after consultation as provided in the rule." Canon 3F, Comment 1. It is all right if a party acts through counsel "if counsel represents on the record that the party has been consulted and consents." Id.

The 1972 Judicial Code required that the waiver be reduced to a writing, signed by all the parties and their lawyers, and be incorporated in the record of the proceeding. Canon 3D, 1972 Judicial Code. The 1990 Judicial Code inexplicably omits this important safeguard for the parties, and then, in the last sentence of the Comment to Canon 3F advises: "As a practical matter, a judge may wish to have all parties and sign the remittal agreement."

Even under the 1972 Judicial Code, some courts were lax in requiring a written waiver. E.g., *Haire v. Cook,* 237 Ga. 639, 229 S.E.2d 436 (1976), stating that: "A waiver of disqualification of a judge may be effected expressly by agreement, or impliedly by proceeding without objection with the trial of the case with knowledge of the disqualification."

The wisdom of such cases is open to question. Of course we do not want the parties to plant error by not waiving in writing and then raising the writing requirement if the trial decision on the merits is not to their liking. But judges can easily foreclose this possibility by simply requiring a writing. The purpose of imposing the writing requirement on both the lawyers *and* the parties "independently of the judge's participation" is to prevent the judge from cajoling the parties and their lawyers to waive important rights. It is also to make sure that lawyers consult their clients outside of the judge's presence. Some lawyers, after all, may be sycophants, falling over themselves in an effort to please the judge, and thus too willing to waive their clients' rights. Judges should not be able to pressure a waiver of disqualification by figuratively cloaking the judge's fist in a velvet glove. The writing procedure minimizes the chance that a party or lawyer will feel coerced into an agreement.

2. 28 U.S.C.A. § 455(e)

The federal disqualification statute permits waiver of disqualification only where the judge would be disqualified under § 455(a), when "his impartiality might reasonably be questioned." This provision of the statute was changed from the Code because the drafters believed that "confidence in the impartiality of federal judges is enhanced by a more strict treatment of waiver." H.R.Rep. No. 1453, 93d Cong., 2d Sess. 7 (1974). Thus there can be no waiver of any ground of disqualification set out in § 455(b). The only procedural requirement set out in the statute for waiver of disqualification is that the basis for disqualification be disclosed on the record.

The federal statute, § 455(e), is silent regarding the requirement of a waiver in writing by the parties and the attorneys, but the Judicial Conference of the United States, by rule, has adopted such a requirement. See 101 F.R.D. 373, 392–93 (1980). Unfortunately, in practice many federal judges do not know of the Judicial Conference Requirement, and so there are many unreported decisions where the writing requirement is often ignored.

V. EXTRA–JUDICIAL ACTIVITIES

Canon 4 requires the judge to conduct extra-judicial activities so as to minimize the risk of conflict with judicial obligations.

A. AN INTRODUCTORY NOTE

The 1972 Judicial Code has three separate Canons dealing with a judge's extrajudicial activities. Canon 4 of the 1972 Code states: "A judge may engage in activities to improve the law, the legal system and the administration of justice." Canon 5 of the 1972 Code provides: "A judge should regulate his extra-judicial activities to minimize the risk of conflict with his judicial duties." And Canon 6 of the 1972 Code created a reporting section: "A judge should regularly file reports of compensation received for quasi-judicial and extra-judicial activities." All three of these Canons deal with the same general subject: a judge's extra-curricular activities. Moreover, under the 1972 Judicial Code, whether an organization is governed by Canon 4 or Canon 5 is very important, because Canon 5 places significantly more limitations on a judge's participation than does Canon 4 of the 1972 Code. Unfortunately, the 1972 Judicial Code is ambiguous in distinguishing between these two types of organizations.

Happily, the 1990 Code has eliminated the confusion between a Canon 4 and a Canon 5 organization by lumping together these two Canons, along with Canon 6. They now are all part of Canon 4 of the 1990 Code.

Canon 3A of the 1990 Code states that a judge's judicial duties take precedence over all the judge's other activities. Yet Canon 4, Comment 1 advises that a "judge should not become isolated from the community in which the judge serves." To completely separate a judge from extra-judicial activities "is neither possible nor wise." Hence, Canon 4A permits a judge to engage in certain quasi-judicial activities so long as these activities do not cast reasonable doubt on his capacity to act impartially as a judge; do not demean the judicial office, and do not interfere with the proper performance of his judicial duties.

Note: The drafters explained that they used the phrase "demean the office" instead of "detract from the dignity of his office" to indicate injurious conduct, not merely undignified conduct, "as the latter might in some cases not be proscribed." *ABA's Standing Committee on 1990 Code, Legislative Draft* 34 (1990).

The Commentary to Canon 4 recognizes that a judge's legal experience places him "in a unique position" to improve the law. Public policy encourages judges to engage in quasi-judicial activities either alone or through bar associations, judicial conferences, or other such organizations. That the judge publicly advocates her opinions on the law, that she has prejudged the law, does not imply that she will prejudge the facts of a case. If, as Judge Frank acknowledged, "bias" and "partiality" are defined to mean "the total absence of preconceptions in the mind of the judge, then no one has ever had a fair trial and no one ever will. The human mind, even at infancy, is no blank piece of paper. We are born with predispositions; and the process of education, formal and informal, creates attitudes in all men which affect them in judging situations, attitudes which precede reasoning in particular cases and which, therefore, by definition, are prejudices." *In re J.P. Linahan, Inc.,* 138 F.2d 650, 651 (2d Cir. 1943). Moreover, as a practical matter, whether or not the judge participates in such activities, she will have definite views on the law and what it should be. "Proof that a Justice's mind at the time he joined the Court was a complete *tabula rasa* in the area of constitutional adjudication would be evidence of lack of qualification, not lack of bias." *Laird v. Tatum,* 409 U.S. 824, 835, 93 S.Ct. 7, 14, 34 L.Ed.2d 50 (1972) (memorandum of Rehnquist, J.). For this reason, a judge was not required to disqualify himself in a homicide case simply because he was a member of the Criminal Law Revision Commission that drafted the criminal code under which the defendant was convicted. *State v. McKenzie,* 186 Mont. 481, 608 P.2d 428 (1980) (relying on Canon 4 of the 1972 Judicial Code). [Later, defendant sought habeas relief, on other grounds. McKenzie v. Risley, 915 F.2d 1396 (9th Cir. 1990).]

On the other hand, if the judge indicates bias, even during off-bench behavior, that may "cast reasonable doubt" on the judge's ability to act with impartiality. Canon 4A, Comment 1. Even "jokes or other remarks demeaning individuals on the basis of race, sex, religion, national origin, disability, age, sexual orientation or socioeconomic status" fall in this category. Id.

B. SPEAKING, WRITING, AND TEACHING

Canon 4B broadly provides that a judge may speak, write, lecture, teach, and participate in other extra-judicial activities concerning the law, the legal system, and administration of justice, *and non-legal subjects as well,* unless such activities violate other sections of the Judicial Code. Canon 4B, Comment 2. Thus a judge may teach a law course, write law review articles, and publish his judicial philosophy, without being required to disqualify himself. Nor does the fact that a judge has published his views prior to his confirmation affect his ability to sit on a case raising a similar legal issue. Thus Justice Jackson participated in the decision of one case that raised an issue on which he had earlier written an opinion as Attorney General. *McGrath v. Kristensen,* 340 U.S. 162, 71 S.Ct. 224, 95 L.Ed. 173 (1950). Jackson, by the way, concurred in the opinion of the Court even though it was contrary to his opinion as Attorney General. Compare 340 U.S. at 176, 71 S.Ct. at 233 with 39 Op.Atty.Gen. 504 (1940). Jackson quoted Lord Westbury who had earlier stated (when his Lordship repudiated one of his previous opinions): "I can only say that I am amazed that a man of my intelligence should have been guilty of giving such an opinion." 340 U.S. at 178, 71 S.Ct. at 178.

Judges may seek improvement in the law, both procedurally and substantively, and they "may express opposition to the persecution of lawyers and judges in other countries because of their professional activities." Canon 4B, Comment 1.

C. GOVERNMENTAL, CIVIC OR CHARITABLE ACTIVITIES
1. Public Hearings and Consultations

Under **Canon 4C(1)**, a judge may testify at public hearings before a legislative or administrative body, or "otherwise consult with, an executive or legislative body or official," on any legal matters, whether they are substantive or procedural, and whether or not they relate to court organization. The judge may also testify or consult in matters affecting the judge's interests or when the judge is acting pro se. The 1972 Judicial Code drew various distinctions between public hearings and private consultations. The 1990 Code draws no such distinctions.

2. Extra-Judicial Appointments

Canon 4C(2) provides that a judge shall not accept appointment to a governmental position that is concerned with issues of fact or policy on matters "other than the improvement of the law, the legal system, or the administration of justice." The Commentary suggests that the reasons for this prohibition are to conserve judicial manpower and to protect the courts from involvement in extra-judicial matters that may be controversial. Canon 4C(2), Comment 1. A judge, however, may represent units of government on ceremonial occasions or in connection with historical, educational, and cultural activities. There is nothing wrong when a judge cuts the "blue ribbon."

Canon 4C(2) disapproves of other governmental appointments of judges to nonjudicial duties, including, for example, President Johnson's appointment of Chief Justice Earl Warren to preside over the Commission investigating President John Kennedy's assassination, or President Roosevelt's appointment of Justice Robert Jackson to be the Chief American Prosecutor at the Nuremberg trials. See Acheson, *Removing the Shadow Cast on the Courts,* 55 A.B.A.J. 919, 920 (1969).

Canon 4C(2) only governs governmental appointments, not non-governmental appointments. Thus, for example, a judge may not accept appointment to serve on the Board of Trustees of the State University, because that is a governmental appointment. He or she can accept appointment to serve on the Board of Trustees of a State Law School, because a law school is a governmental agency devoted to the improvement of law, the legal system, or the administration of justice. And, under Canon 4C(3), discussed immediately below, the judge may accept appointment to the Board of Trustees of a Private University, because Canon 4C(3) says so. Such an appointment is not a governmental appointment because the university is private. See, Canon 4C(2), Comment 2. (Remember, whenever we draw bright lines, items that are close to the line could, perhaps, be just as comfortably on the other side of the line. Remember, also, that judges had a lot of input into the drafting of the Judicial Code, and so, at least to some extent, it allows what many judges like to do, and prohibits what many judges do not want to do.)

3.   Charitable and Civic Organizations

Canon 4C(3) provides that a judge may serve as an officer, director, trustee or nonlegal advisor of an organization or governmental agency devoted to the improvement of the law, the legal system or the administration of justice or of an educational, religious, charitable, fraternal or civil organization not conducted for profit," subject to various restrictions, and assuming that the appointment does not violate some other section of the Judicial Code.

Notice that Canon 4C(3) provides that the educational, civic, etc. organization must not be conducted "for profit." The 1972 Judicial Code required that such civic organizations not be conducted "for the economic or political advantage of its members." (See, Canon 5B of the 1972 Code.) The reason the change is that the drafters wanted to make clear that judges may participate in nonprofit judicial organizations even though they support increases in judicial compensation, an activity that is intended to benefit the members. *ABA's Standing Committee Report on 1990 Code, Legislative Draft* 38 (1990).

The requirement that membership in such fraternal, civic, etc. organizations is subject to other requirements of the Judicial Code simply emphasizes the obvious: while there is no per se rule against the judge serving on the board of such an organization, in particular cases it may violate another provision of the Judicial Code. For example, the judge cannot be on the board of an organization that practices invidious discrimination against race, sex, religion, or national origin, in violation of Canon 2C. In addition, service on the board of some organizations may cast doubt on the judge's capacity to act impartially, in violation of Canon 4A(1).

Canon 4C(3)(a). Recall that Canon 3E(1)(c) requires judges to disqualify themselves if they have an economic interest in a party to a proceeding. "Economic interest" is defined to include a "relationship such as officer, director or other active participant in the affairs of a party. . . ." Terminology 6. Thus, if the judge is, for example, an officer of a fraternal organization, and that organization is involved in a lot of litigation, the judge would find that he or she must be disqualified in a lot of cases. Hence, Canon 4C(3)(a) provides that the judge "shall not serve" as an officer, director, etc. of the organization (civic, fraternal, etc.) if: (1), the organization is likely to be engaged in proceedings that would ordinarily come before the judge [Canon 4C(3)(a)(1)]; or (2), it is likely to be engaged frequently in adversary proceedings before the court of which the judge is a member, or any court subject to the appellate jurisdiction of the court of which the judge is a member [Canon 4C(3)(a)(2)]. The judge, in other words, must arrange her extra-judicial affairs so that she does not put herself in a position where she must frequently disqualify herself.

Canon 4C(3)(b). Canon 4C(3)(b) places additional restrictions on membership solicitation and fund raising solicitation that applies not only to the judge who is an officer, director, etc. of the organization (civic, fraternal, etc.), but also to one *who is merely a member*. The basic theme behind these specific restrictions is that the judge must not use (or appear to use) the prestige of judicial office to raise funds in a coercive manner. Canon 4C(3)(b), Comment 1. The specific rules and comments are all elaborations of this theme. Thus Canon 4C(3)(b)(iv) explains, the judge "shall not use or permit the use of the prestige of judicial office for fund raising or membership solicitation."

For example, the judge "shall not personally participate" in fund-raising activities, *but may* solicit funds from other judges over whom the judge does not exercise supervisory or appellate authority. Canon 4C(3)(b)(1). The reason for this exception is to allow judges to solicit funds for judicial organizations. Moreover, the dangers of overreaching are nil because the soliciting judge cannot solicit in cases where he or she might exert improper influence. Similarly, the judge may solicit other persons for membership "if neither those persons nor persons with whom they are affiliated are likely ever to appear before the court on which the judge serves. . . ." Canon 4C(3)(b), Comment 1. The judge who is an officer of such an organization may send a general membership solicitation over the judge's signature. Id.

Even in cases where the judge shall not personally participate, he or she may assist in planning fund-raising events and may participate in management and investment of funds. Canon 4C(3)(b)(1). Similarly, the judge may attend an organizations's fund-raising event, but may not be the speaker or guest of honor. Comment 3.

D. FINANCIAL ACTIVITIES

1. Financial and Business Dealings

Canon 4D(1) *provides that a judge shall not engage in financial and business dealings that "may reasonably be perceived to exploit" the judicial office or involve the judge in frequent transactions or continuing business relationships with "lawyers or other persons likely to come before the court on which the judge serves."* Judges should never foster the appearance that patronizing a judge's business will benefit a litigant, or that failure to patronize will work to the litigant's disadvantage.

Thus a judge may not use confidential information learned while a judge for private gain. Canon 4D(1), Comment 2. And the judge "should discourage" family members from engaging in dealings that "would reasonably appear to exploit the judge's judicial position."

A judge "exploited" his judicial position and was involved in transactions with persons before him in violation of Canon 4D(1) where the judge charged parties more for legal notices required in probate matters than the expenses the judge incurred in securing the notices. *In re Douglas*, 135 Vt. 585, 382 A.2d 215 (1977). This conduct also violated Canons 1 and 2 of the Code.

Canon 4D(2) permits a judge to hold and manage investments of the judge and the judge's family, including real estate. This Canon does not limit the judge to passive investment activity, for it specifically allows the judge to engage "in other remunerative activity," unless, of course, these activities contravene some other provision of the Judicial Code.

Canon 4D(3) limits an expansive reading of Canon 4D(2), because Canon 4D(3) prohibits a judge from serving as an officer, director, manager, general partner, advisor, or employee of "any business entity," except for a family business (assuming, of course, that no other provision of the Judicial Code is violated). That is, the judge may "manage and participate in" a closely held business of the judge or members of the judge's family, or a business entity "primarily engaged in investment of the financial resources of the judge or members of the judge's family."

For example, a judge is prohibited from being even an "honorary" director of a bank, a position allowing the judge to attend meetings and express his opinion concerning bank matters, but not giving him a vote. ABA Informal Opinion No. 1385 (Feb. 17, 1977). There was also a danger that the arrangement might appear to exploit the judicial office or favoritism. Similarly, a judge "must avoid participating in a closely-held family business if the judge's participation would involve misuse of the prestige of judicial office." Canon 4D(3), Comment 2.

Canon 4D(4) requires the judge to manage his investments and other financial investments so as to minimize the number of cases in which he is disqualified. If some investment or financial investment requires the judge to be disqualified frequently, then the judge should to divest himself of that investment as soon as he can do so "without serious financial detriment."

2. Receiving Gifts

Canon 4D(5) establishes a general prohibition on a judge from accepting a gift, bequest, favor, or loan from anyone subject to various exceptions noted below. (Note this provision does not cover campaign contributions, which are governed by Canon 5.) The drafters adopted this general prohibition of noncampaign gifts to avoid the appearance of impropriety and possible actual impropriety by the judge accepting such a gift or loan. Of course, the donor might wish to avoid this restriction by bestowing the gift on someone in the judge's family residing in the judge's household. Thus, the judge is instructed to urge such family members not to receive such bequests, though the Code recognizes that, as a practical matter, the judge cannot be expected to know of control all the financial and business dealings of family members, even those residing in the household.

> *Note:* Terminology 12 broadly defines "member of the judge's family residing in the judge's household" as "any relative of a judge by blood or marriage, or a person treated by a judge as a member of the judge's family, who resides in the judge's household."

Canon 4D(5) then lists several important exceptions to the general prohibition on receiving gifts.

Canon 4D(5)(a). The first exception relates to a gift incident to a public testimonial; or complementary books, or tapes, or "other resource materials" supplied by publishers for official use; or an invitation to the judge and "spouse or guest" to attend a bar-related function or activity devoted to the improvement of the law, the legal system, or the administration of justice. The public testimonial gift must not come from a donor organization whose members comprise or frequently the same side in litigation (Comment 2), for such acceptance could raise an appearance of impropriety.

Also, one should keep in mind a distinction as to who pays for functions. As Comment 1 notes: subsection 4D(5)(a) governs a judge's acceptance of an invitation to a law-related function; in contrast, the judge' acceptance of an invitation that an individual lawyer or group of lawyers pay for is governed by Canon 4D(5)(h), discussed below.

Canon 4D(5)(b). This second group of exceptions covers gifts, awards, or benefits incident to the business or profession of the judge's spouse or family member residing in the judge's household. This exception reflects the fact that the judge's spouse may have an independent professional life. It is permissible that the benefit is for the use of both the spouse (or family member) and the judge. However, the purpose of this exception is not to allow the donor to launder the gift by using the spouse or other family member, so this rule requires that the benefit could not reasonably be understood as intending to influence the judge in the performance of judicial duties.

Canon 4D(5)(c). The provision allows acceptance of "ordinary social hospitality." Judges may accept "ordinary social hospitality even from lawyers who practice before them." J. Shaman, S. Lubet, & J. Alfini, *Judicial Conduct and Ethics* § 7.28 at 201 n. 226 (1990). There are common sense limits to this exception, which are discussed below.

The *Reporter's Notes to the 1972 Code* state that the drafters had difficulty determining what social hospitality to permit. *Reporter's Notes [1972]* at 84. The drafters adopted the "ordinary social hospitality" standard, thus permitting the type of social hospitality to vary from place to place according to local customs.

Example: A month at the mountain cabin of a lawyer-friend who practices in the judge's court is *not* ordinary social hospitality and would be prohibited. See *Reporter's Notes [1972]* at 84–85.

Canon 4D(5)(d) allows acceptance of a gift from a relative or friend for a special occasion, such as a wedding or birthday. However, the gift must be "commensurate with the occasion and the relationship." The gift must not be "excessive in value. . . ." Canon 4D(5)(d), Comment 1.

Note: Canon 4D(5)(d) does not simply allows the judge to accept all wedding gifts. There may be circumstances where doing so might appear to exploit the judicial office. For example, if the judge, getting married while in office, invited many lawyers practicing before the judge to the wedding (even though these lawyers were not personal friends), the lawyers might feel coerced into offering gifts. The gift must be commensurate not only with the occasion but also with the relationship. The Judicial Code implies that wedding invitations must be bona fide, and non-bona fide invitations really "exploit the judge's judicial position. . . ." Canon 4D(1)(a).

Canon 4D(5)(e) allows acceptance of a gift, loan, etc. from a relative or close friend whose "appearance or interest in a case would in any event require disqualification" under Canon 3E. The judge's acceptance of such a gift from such a person does not create any possibility that the judge might be exploiting the judicial office. The acceptance is a moot point, for the judge will have to disqualify herself anyway.

Canon 4D(5)(f) allows acceptance of a loan from a lending institution in its regular course of business on the same terms generally available to persons who are not judges.

In re McDonough, 296 N.W.2d 648 (Minn. 1979), addressed the problem of a judge receiving a loan from a financial institution. In that case, the judge received preferential treatment from a bank in the form of an unsecured loan of over $20,000 and a large number of uncharged overdrafts on his wife's checking account. The loan was used to pay family and medical expenses beyond the judge's control. The court held that the judge did not violate what is now Canon 4D(5)(f) because there was no evidence that the bank's treatment of the judge was motivated by the fact he was a judge. In other words, other persons who were (like the judge) good credit risks could receive similar treatment. The court felt that it was common knowledge that financial institutions take community reputation and professional stature into consideration when extending credit or assessing fees. (The court suggested, however, that the judge should give security for the loan or perhaps refinance through another bank. The court additionally warned the judge that he should not sit on cases involving the bank either as a party, guardian, or trustee.)

Canon 4D(5)(g) permits acceptance of "a scholarship or fellowship awarded on the same terms applied to other applicants."

These listed exceptions are quite realistic and logical. Judges, like everyone else, may need to secure a mortgage from the bank, or the judge's child may win a scholarship. The judge may get married and the judge's friends will want to send wedding gifts. None of these loans or gifts are, or normally should be, prohibited.

Canon 4D(5)(h) offers the last exception to the general prohibition on gifts found in Canon 4D(5). This provision permits acceptance of "any *other* gift, bequest, favor, or loan *only if* the donor is not a party or other person" whose interests have come or are likely to come before the judge. (emphasis added). If such a gift, bequest, favor, or loan exceeds $150, the judge must report it in the same manner he or she reports compensation under Canon 4H, discussed below.

> *Example:* A judge violated Canon 4D(5)(h) when he borrowed money regularly from attorneys who appeared before him, even though he always paid back the loans. *Matter of Anderson,* 312 Minn. 442, 252 N.W.2d 592 (1977) (judge suspended without pay for 3 months for this and other violations of the Judicial Code).

A judge must also be aware of the general propriety standard of Canon 2B. For example, in *Matter of Bonin,* 375 Mass. 680, 378 N.E.2d 669 (1978), the court held that a judge's activities did not violate Canon 5D(5)(h), but his activities did violate Canon 2B. When the judge was an Assistant Attorney General, he had performed legal services for an insurance agency and obtained jobs for relatives of the company's president. The company paid for the judge's reception when he was sworn in, and also paid his rental payments for a leased automobile. The judge had filed a report disclosing these gifts and thus had not violated Canon 4H. In addition, there was no indication that the insurance company or its affiliate or officers had any cases pending in the court where the judge sat. The court held, however, that receipt of the leased automobile as a gift created the appearance of impropriety because the judge had appointed relatives of the company's president to staff positions while he had been an Assistant Attorney General.

E. FIDUCIARY ACTIVITIES

Canon 4E. The drafters, concerned about the judicial "appearance of impropriety," placed limits on a judge when acting in a fiduciary capacity. **Canon 4E(1)** generally prohibits a judge from serving as an executor, administrator or other personal representative, trustee, guardian, attorney in fact, or other fiduciary. A judge violated this prohibition when he handled personal checking accounts on behalf of persons who were having difficulty managing their own finances. *Matter of Cieminski,* 270 N.W.2d 321 (N.D. 1978) (judge censured for this and other violations of the Judicial Code).

A judge may act in such capacity, however, for the estate, trust, or person of a member of his or her family, *but only if* such service will not interfere with the proper performance of judicial duties. Note that a member of the judge's family is defined as a judge's "spouse, child, grandchild, parent, grandparent, or other relative or person with whom the judge maintains a close familial relationship." Terminology 10 & 11. It is not necessary that the family member reside in the household.

Note: Under the Effective Date of Compliance section of the Judicial Code, if a new judge was serving as a fiduciary when selected as a judge, the new judge may continue to act as a fiduciary, but only for the period of time to avoid "serious adverse consequences to the beneficiary of the fiduciary relationship," and, in no event, longer than one year. See, Application of the Code of Judicial Conduct, § F, Comment 1.

Canon 4E(2) provides that a judge shall not serve as a fiduciary if it is "likely" that the judge, as fiduciary, would be engaged in proceedings that would ordinarily come before him. The judge is also disqualified if the estate, trust, or ward, in fact becomes involved in adversary proceedings in the court on which he serves or one under its appellate jurisdiction.

Canon 4E(3) provides that a judge, when acting as a fiduciary, is subject to the same restrictions on financial activities that apply to a judge acting in her personal capacity. The Commentary suggests that a judge should resign as trustee under this provision if her duties as a judge violated her duties as a fiduciary.

Example: If it would result in detriment to the trust to divest it of holdings, but retention of those holdings would place the judge in violation of Canon 4D(4), then the judge should resign as trustee.

F. ARBITRATION AND THE PRACTICE OF LAW
1. Arbitration and Mediation

Canon 4F prohibits a judge from acting as an arbitrator or mediator or otherwise perform judicial functions in a private capacity, unless expressly authorized by law. The *Reporter's Notes to the 1972 Code of Judicial Conduct* at 89, suggest various reasons to justify the prohibition:

(1) the arbitration proceeding could come before the court on which the judge sits;

(2) the court could be drawn into social and political controversies in which a judge acted as an arbitrator;

(3) the judicial office might be exploited by those seeking to use its dignity and prestige in support of an arbitration award; and

(4) judicial time could be diverted in a case in which a judge's fee as arbitrator would be large.

The drafters of the 1990 Code continue these restrictions.

2. Practice of Law

Canon 4G. In order to avoid the appearance of impropriety and conflicts of interest Canon 4G prohibits a judge from practicing law. The drafters left the definition of "practice of law" to the law of each jurisdiction.

This prohibition is quite natural. One who is a full time judge in name, should also be a full time judge in fact. Thus, a probate judge cannot continue to draft deeds, wills, contracts, and other legal instruments, or act as an attorney for executors, administrators, or guardians. ABA Informal Opinion 1294 (June 17, 1974). A judge can, however, continue to practice law if his election to judicial office is being contested, so long as he has not actually assumed his office by taking the prescribed oath. *Reed v. Sloan*, 475 Pa. 570, 381 A.2d 421 (1977). But once a judge actually assumes his office he may not continue to practice law, even on matters he had started before becoming a judge. *In re Ryman*, 394 Mich. 637, 232 N.W.2d 178 (1975); *In re Piper*, 271 Or. 726, 534 P.2d 159 (1975).

The prohibition against the practice of law does not apply to the judge who is acting *pro se*. In addition, a judge may give uncompensated legal advice and even draft documents to members of the judge's family.

G. Compensation, Reimbursements, and Reporting

Introductory Note: Canon 4I provides that the Judicial Code does not require a judge to disclose his income, debts, investments, or other assets except as provided in Canons 3E [disqualification] and 3F [remittal of disqualification], this Canon [Canon 4], and other law. The Comment to this section emphasizes that judges have the same rights as other citizens to privacy of financial affairs "except to the extent that limitations established by law are required to safeguard the proper performance of judicial duties."

1. Canon 4H Generally

Canon 4H(1) provides that a judge may receive not only reimbursement of expenses, but also compensation for extra-judicial activities permitted by the Judicial Code, provided that the source of the payments does not give the appearance of impropriety or of influencing the judge in performing judicial duties. Canon 4H then adds other restrictions on a judge's receipt of compensation or reimbursement.

2. Compensation

Canon 4H(1)(a) limits the amount of compensation that judges may receive for non-judicial duties. The amount must be reasonable and should not be more than what a person who is not a judge would receive for the same activity.

3. Expense Reimbursement

Canon 4H(1)(b) limits expense reimbursement to the "actual cost" of travel, food, and lodging. Furthermore, these expenses must be "reasonably incurred" by the judge. A judge may also be reimbursed for the expenses of the judge's "spouse or guest" if that person's presence is "appropriate to the occasion." Any amount reimbursed over those expenses reasonably incurred is considered compensation. This distinction is important because compensation for non-judicial duties must be publicly reported under Canon 4H(2), while reimbursement for expenses need not be.

4. Public Reports

Canon 4H(2) sets out the manner for reporting compensation. The judge must report the date, place, and nature of any activity for which compensation was received, the name of who paid the compensation, and the amount received.

Notes: Canon 4D(5)(h) requires a similar report for gifts over $150. Reports must be made at least once a year and should be filed as a public document in the court clerk's office or other office designated by rule of court.

Compensation or income of a spouse attributed to the judge by operation of community property law is not considered the judge's income, and thus is not subject to these requirements.

VI. POLITICAL ACTIVITIES

A. INTRODUCTION

Canon 5 of the ABA Model Code of Judicial Conduct, concerning political activity, requires judges and judicial candidates to refrain from inappropriate political activity. Canon 5 is divided into several sections—Section A, governing the general political conduct of all judges and candidates for judicial office; Section B, dealing with candidates seeking appointment to judicial office or a judge seeking appointment to another governmental office; Section C, governing judges and candidates subject to public election; Section D, dealing with incumbent judges, and Section E, governing applicability. Canon 5, in short, applies as a model code whether judges are selected in a public election or by a merit selection (appointive) system.

B. GENERAL POLITICAL CONDUCT

Canon 5A places broad restrictions on the political activity of a judge or a candidate for election to judicial office, subject to various exceptions. The purpose of this section is to limit the active participation of a judge (or candidate for judicial office) in the election process of any other political candidate

Note: There may be practical problems in enforcing the Judicial Code against those who are not judges. If the candidate is successful and becomes a judge, he or she would then be subject to appropriate sanctions for any misdeeds as a candidate. In addition, if the candidate is a lawyer, DR 8–103(A) and Model Rule 8.2(b) require the lawyer to follow these provisions of the Judicial Code. Canon 5E.

Note also: A "candidate" is defined in Terminology 2. In general, it refers to anyone seeking selection or election to judicial office. The term has the same meaning when applied to elected or appointed judges.

Canon 5A(1)(a) prohibits a judge or candidate from acting as a "leader" of, or holding any office in, a political organization. **Canon 5A(1)(b)** prohibits such persons from making speeches for a political organization or candidate, or from publicly endorsing another candidate for public office. However, public endorsement requires more than mere public association. Thus, Comment 5 to Canon 5A(1) makes clear that a candidate for judicial office does not publicly endorse another candidate for public office merely by having the candidate's name on the same ticket.

Canon 5A(1)(a),(b),(c),(d), & (e) prohibits the judge or candidate from making speeches on behalf of a political organization, attending political gatherings, or soliciting funds or making contributions to a political organization or to another political candidate, attending political gatherings, or purchasing tickets for political party dinners or other functions. However, the judge or candidate may vote. [Yes indeed, Comment 1 to Canon 5A(1) explicitly states that the judge or candidate retains the right to participate as a voter.] A judge or judicial candidate also retains the right to respond to false information concerning a judicial candidate. The judge or judicial candidate may "privately" express his or her views on judicial candidates or other candidates for office. (Yes, the drafters thought it necessary for Comment 4 to make this caveat. Another other rule would raise very serious first amendment concerns.) And, an "office in a political organization" means exactly that: a candidate who is a county prosecutor, for example, does not hold an office in a "political" organization. Comment 4.

Canon 5A(1) explicitly provides that Canons 5B(2), 5C(1), and 5C(3) are authorized exceptions to the limitations of Canon 5A. These exceptions consume much of the restrictions that Canon 5A(1) impose. Thus, **Canon 5B(2)** allows a candidate for *appointment* to judicial office, or a judge seeking appointment to another judicial office, to communicate with the appointing authority and its agents, to seek support from other appropriate organizations and individuals. **Canon 5C(1)** allows judges and candidates subject to public election to be involved in a great deal of political activity (unless otherwise prohibited by law); they may purchase tickets and attend political gatherings, identify themselves as members of a political party, and contribute to a political organization. And, **Canon 5C(3)** allows candidates for judicial election to be listed on election materials with the names of other candidates and to appear in promotions of the ticket. The ABA, in short, prefers merit selection of judges. But, not all states have merit selection, and if judges and candidates must campaign in partisan elections, then the Model Code of Judicial Conduct realistically acknowledges that it is difficult to take the politics out of politics.

Canon 5A(2) requires a judge to resign from judicial office if she is a candidate for a *non*-judicial office either in a party primary or in a general election. However, this prohibition does not apply to a judge who is serving as a delegate or running as a candidate for delegate to a state constitutional convention (if otherwise permitted by law).

C. CAMPAIGN CONDUCT

1. Generally

Canon 5A(3)(a) requires candidates for judicial office to maintain appropriate dignity. Although a member of the judge's family are free to do things forbidden a judicial candidate, the judicial candidate "shall encourage" his family members to adhere to the same political activity standards of Canon 5 applicable to judicial candidates. It is difficult to seek how the requirement to "encourage" will be subject to any realistic enforcement mechanism.

Canon 5A(3)(b) provides that a candidate shall prohibit public officials or employees "who serve at the pleasure of the candidate" from doing that which the judicial candidate is prohibited from doing under Canon 5. In addition, the candidate "shall discourage" other employees or officials who are "subject to the candidate's direction and control" from doing that which the candidate must not do under Canon 5. Finally, the candidate "shall not authorize or knowingly permit any other person" to do for the candidate what the candidate is prohibited from doing. **Canon 5A(3)(c).**

Canon 5A(3)(d) regulates the type of campaign that a candidate for judicial office can conduct. A candidate shall not make pledges or promises of conduct in office other than the faithful and impartial performance of the duties of the office; make statements that commit or appear to commit the candidate regarding cases or issues likely to come before the court; or misrepresent his (or his opponent's) identity, qualifications, present position, or other fact. However, **Canon 5A(3)(e)** allows the candidate to respond to personal attacks or attacks on his record [assuming that this response does not violate Canon 5A(3)(d)].

The rules intended to help protect candidates from improper questioning in opinion polls, interviews, or questionnaires. They do not prevent a candidate from promising to improve court administration. And an incumbent judge may make "private statements" to other judges or court personnel in performance of judicial duties. In any public statement, a candidate "should emphasize" the candidate's duty to uphold the law regardless of one's personal views. Canon 5A(3)(d), Comment 1.

> *Example:* The judicial candidate (whether seeking election or appointment) may not properly state: "Elect me, and I will favor high verdicts in personal injury lawsuits."

2. Solicitation of Campaign Funds

Candidates for *appointive* judicial office are not permitted to engage in the fund-raising activities permitted other judicial candidates. **Canon 5B(1).**

Although a judicial candidate subject to public election may not personally solicit or accept campaign contributions, or "personally solicit publicly stated support," he can establish committees to conduct campaigns, solicit and accept "reasonable campaign contributions," manage the expenditure of funds for his campaign, as well as to obtain public statements of support and "reasonable campaign contributions" for the candidacy (even from lawyers). **Canon 5C(2).**

> *Note:* This campaign committee provision is an explicit exception to Canon 5A(3)(c)'s prohibition on third persons performing those things that judges are prohibited from doing.

The Judicial Code also requires each jurisdiction to place time limits on the solicitation of campaign funds. Canon 5C(2). Each jurisdiction may specify its own time limits, but the Judicial Code suggests that a campaign committee should solicit funds no earlier than one year before an election [the 1972 Judicial Code proposed 90 days] and no later than 90 days after the last election in which a candidate participates during the election year. To solicit campaigns after the election may smell of tribute. On the other hand, judges who run for election have campaign expenses, and soliciting contributions after the election has proven to be a useful means of securing necessary contributions. This Judicial Canon also prohibits the use of campaign contributions for the private benefit of the candidate or others.

Note: The 1972 Code prohibited the campaign committee from revealing the names of the contributors to the candidate unless the candidate was required by law to file a list of his campaign contributors. The 1990 Code does not have such a restriction. First, most jurisdictions now require the candidates to disclose the names of the contributors, so a secrecy provision is unrealistic. Second, the judge should know the names of contributors in order to determine whether recusal is advisable. Canon 5C(2), Comment 1 notes: "Though not prohibited, campaign contributions of which a judge has knowledge, made by lawyers or others who appear before the judge, may be relevant to disqualification under Section 3E."

Solicitation of campaign funds raises a problem with no easy solution. Judges who run in elections need money. Unless the state provides the money, candidates must raise it, and the most likely source of funds are those most interested in judicial elections—the lawyers. Yet financial gifts by lawyers raise questions of partiality. In the multi-billion dollar *Pennzoil v. Texaco* case, the Texas state trial court judge received a $10,000 contribution from Pennzoil's chief trial attorney, "[w]ithin days of being assigned the Pennzoil case. . . ." The trial judge described it as a "princely sum." Petzinger & Solomon, *Texaco Case Spotlights Questions on Integrity of the Courts in Texas*, Wall Street Journal, Nov. 4, 1987, at 1, 20 column 2. See also, *More of the Same*, Forbes, Sept. 7, 1987 at 8 (in the last 3½ years all nine members of the Texas Supreme Court "openly accepted campaign contributions from lawyers with cases pending before them," which Texas law allows). See generally, Anderson, *Ethical Problems of Lawyers and Judges in Election Campaigns*, 50 A.B.A.J. 819 (1964).

VII. APPLICATION OF THE JUDICIAL CODE: DEFINING WHO IS A JUDGE

A. INTRODUCTION

The final section of the ABA Model Code of Judicial Conduct, "Application of the Code of Judicial Conduct," defines who is a judge and what sections of the Judicial Code are inapplicable to part-time judges or judges *pro tempore*.

The Judicial Code is intended to apply to all persons who perform "judicial functions," whether or not they are lawyers. Application A. It is surprising but true that not all judges in the United States are lawyers. Cf. *North v. Russell*, 427 U.S. 328, 96 S.Ct. 2709, 49 L.Ed.2d 534 (1976). To perform a "judicial function" it is not necessary that the person be a judge of a court of general jurisdiction. For example, a referee in bankruptcy, special master, court commissioner, or magistrate is a judge for the purposes of this Code.

All persons who fall in this category of "judge" should comply with the Judicial Code, subject to four exceptions: (1) Retired Judge subject to recall; (2) Continuing Part-time Judge; (3) Periodic Part-time Judge; and (4) Pro Tempore Part-time Judge. All these types of judges (except for retired judge subject to recall) are defined in the Terminology section of the Model Judicial Code.

B. RETIRED JUDGE

A retired judge who is subject to being recalled as a judge, and who is not allowed to practice law, is not ever required to comply with Canon 4E (dealing with fiduciary activities), and is only required to comply with Canon 4F (service as an arbitrator or mediator) while he is serving as a judge.

Retired judges *not* subject to recall to judicial service are not mentioned in § B of "Application," because, by implication, they are not governed by the Judicial Code.

C. CONTINUING PART-TIME JUDGE

A judge is classified as continuing part-time if he serves repeatedly on a part-time basis by election or under a continuing appointment. This definition includes a retired judge subject to recall who is permitted to practice law. Terminology 3.

> *Example:* Alpha is a judge in a court of general jurisdiction who receives the same salary as other judges in that capacity. She is forbidden from engaging in any other occupation but only works every other morning because she works fast and her docket is up-to-date. She is a full-time judge required to comply with all provisions of the Judicial Code.

If one is a continuing part-time judge, then that person need not comply with Canon 3B(9) (dealing with public comments on pending or impending cases) except while serving as a judge. This person, however, is not ever required to comply with Canons 4C(2), 4D(3), 4E(1), 4F, 4G, 4H, 5A(1), 5B(2), and 5D. A part-time judge who is practicing law part-time shall not do so in the court on which he serves or in any court subject to the appellate jurisdiction of the court on which he serves. Application, § C(2). In addition, he should not act as a lawyer in any proceeding or related proceeding in which he had served as judge. Id.

D. PERIODIC PART-TIME JUDGE

A periodic part-time judge is a judge who serves or expects to serve repeatedly on a part-time basis but under a separate appointment for each limited period of service. Terminology 14. Such a person need not comply with Canon 3B(9) except while serving as a judge. This person does not ever have to comply with Canons 4C(2), 4C(3)(a), 4D(1)(b), 4D(3), 4D(4), 4D(5), 4E, 4F, 4G, 4H, 5A(1),

5B(2), and 5D. Application, § D(1). In addition, a part-time judge who is practicing law part-time shall not do so in the court on which she serves or in any court subject to the appellate jurisdiction of the court on which she serves. Application, § D(2). In addition, she should not act as a lawyer in any proceeding or related proceeding in which she had served as judge. Id.

E. PRO TEMPORE PART-TIME JUDGE

A pro tempore part-time judge is someone who serves or expects to serve as a judge once or only sporadically one a part-time basis under separate appointment for each period of service or case heard. While acting as a judge, he is excused from Judicial Canons 2A, 2B, 2B(9), and 4C(1), except while serving as a judge. In addition, this type of judge is not required to comply at any time with Canons 2C, 4C(2), 4C(3)(a), 4C(3)(b), 4D(1)(b), 4D(3), 4D(4), 4D(5), 4E, 4F, 4G, 4H, 5A(1), 5A(2), 5B(2), and 5D. A pro-tempore part-time judge must not act as a lawyer in any proceeding or related proceeding in which he had served as a judge, except as otherwise permitted by the adopting state's version of Model Rule 1.12(a), of the Model Rules of Professional Conduct.

VIII. REVIEW QUESTIONS

1. State Governor is on trial for federal tax fraud. He plans to call Judge, his life-long friend, as a character witness. Governor had appointed Judge to the State Supreme Court several years ago.

    When Governor asked Judge to testify on his behalf, Judge responded: "You know, under our rules, you must subpoena me. I cannot appear voluntarily, but after I receive an official summons I will be pleased to testify on your behalf."

    Is Judge *subject to discipline?*

    a. Yes, if he responds to the official summons.

    b. No, if he responds to an official summons.

    c. No, because Governor had appointed him to the state supreme court.

2. Judge First is on a panel of state appellate judges who are ruling on an issue of comparative fault. In trying to interpret the application of a new statute, he asked the advice of Clerk (who is his law clerk), and Judge Second, another appellate judge who was not on his panel and Judge Third, an appellate judge who is on the same panel as Judge First. He never informed counsel of any of these conversations.

Are Judge First's actions *proper*?

a. No, because he initiated *ex parte* communications concerning a pending proceeding.

b. No, because Judge Second was not on the same appellate panel.

c. No, because Clerk is not another judge.

d. Yes, because there are no restrictions on a judge's communications with experts on the law.

e. Yes, because First and Second are other judges, and Clerk is a court employee.

3. In the case of *P. vs. D.*, the Chief Justice of the State Supreme Court announced at the beginning of oral argument: "I own 100 shares of the stock of D., Inc., worth $19,000. I'll recuse myself from this case and we'll bring in another judge, unless you have no problem." Counsel for P. and for D. turned to each other, briefly discussed the matter privately, and then each said on the record: "We have no problem, your Honor." The Chief Justice then declared the disqualification waived. The Chief Justice believed that her financial interest is substantial.

Did Chief Justice act *properly*?

a. No, because the judge did not secure a proper waiver of the parties and lawyers.

b. No, because the parties cannot waive such a disqualification.

c. Yes, because any disqualification was waived.

d. No, because the Chief Justice should not have threatened to recuse himself when her financial interest was so minor.

4. Judge, while a practicing attorney, represented class action plaintiffs in a complex consumer fraud case. Judge, in that case acquired no relevant client confidences or secrets because he was only involved a various legal questions rather than factual issues: he was then an associate, and he worked on some legal background memos regarding some venue issues. The senior partners in his firm worked substantially on the case.

Several years have passed and Judge is now a judge, and this same class action suit has now been brought before him. He has been asked to rule on several substantive issues of law having nothing to do with his earlier work on the venue matters.

Is it *proper* for Judge to so rule?

a.   Yes, if the attorneys each exercise a waiver of disqualification.

b.   Yes, because Judge acquired no relevant confidences or secrets in the prior representation.

c.   No, because Judge had served as a lawyer in the controversy now before him.

d.   No, unless his former law firm is no longer involved in representing any of the parties.

5. Judge is getting married and has invited Lawyer to his wedding. He and Lawyer are very close friends and Lawyer, an active litigator, appears before Judge. Lawyer plans to buy Judge a wedding gift costing $500. Under the circumstances, the cost of this gift is not surprising, given the occasion and the relationship between Judge and Lawyer.

Is it *proper* for Judge to accept this gift?

a.   No, because Lawyer appears in Judge's court often.

b.   Yes, because the gift is a wedding gift.

c.   Yes, but only if Judge reports the gift as compensation.

d.   No, because the gift cost was more than $100.

6. Judge, the Chief Justice of the State Supreme Court, is planning to run for his party's nomination for Governor.

When should Judge *resign* his judgeship?

a.   When he first becomes a candidate in his party's primary.

b.   After the primary, if he wins it.

c.   After the general election, if he wins it.

7. A judge who is disqualified from hearing a case by reason of some provision of the Code of Judicial Conduct—

a. may nevertheless hear the case, whatever the nature of the disqualification, if the parties and their lawyers independently agree that the judge may participate in the proceedings.

b. may not hear the case involving the disqualification, whatever its nature and without regard to any purported waivers by the clients or lawyers.

c. may nevertheless hear the case if the reason for the disqualification is based on the judge's economic interests and the parties and their lawyers independently agree that the judge may participate in the proceedings and that the judge's interest is insubstantial.

d. may nevertheless hear the case if the reason for the disqualification is based on the fact that the judge is a material eye witness to the transaction that is the subject of the trial, but the parties and their lawyers independently agree that the judge may participate in the proceedings, and that his capacity as a witness will not affect his objectivity.

8. Judge is presently serving on her state's trial court. In several opinions she has refused to provide any protection to state prison inmates who are disciplined by prison authorities for violating the prison's rules of conduct. Judge is now running for election to her state's supreme court. She is vigorously opposed by several organizations concerned with the conditions under which prisoners are incarcerated in the state's prison. In an interview, the local reporter has asked her about her attitude on the subject of prisoners' rights.

Judge says:

I. "I promise always to act impartially."

II. "In my opinion, incarceration for the commission of a crime carries with it a loss of civil liberties in prison discipline proceedings. I will not change my view, even with respect to the *Jones* case, which is now before the court and raises the same issue that was involved in my previous prisoner rights cases, and that's why the people should elect me to the supreme court."

III. "I am convinced I was right in those cases and will make the same decision in the *Jones* case, a case quite similar to the earlier cases you mentioned."

Were Judge's statements *proper*?

a.   Yes, as to I only.

b.   Yes, as to II only.

c.   Yes, as to I & II only.

d.   Yes, as to I, II, & III.

ANSWERS TO REVIEW QUESTIONS

PART I

1. **False.** While the Model Rules do not use the term "ethical consideration," both the Model Code and the Model Rules guide a lawyer as to what must, may, and should be done in different circumstances.

2. **c.**

3. **b.** The answer is the same under the Model Code and Model Rules, though the latter does not use the "moral turpitude" language. See Model Rule 8.4(b).

4. **a.** See EC 1–6.

5. **c.** See DR 1–102(A)(4); Model Rule 8.4(c).

PART II

1. **d.** DR 1–103(A); Model Rule 8.3(a) & (c). *In re Himmel,* 125 Ill.2d 531, 533 N.E.2d 790 (1988) should not change this answer because the information, at this point, is still covered by the attorney/client evidentiary privilege.

2. *d.* DR 1–102(A)(4); Model Rule 8.5.

3. *c.* DR 1–102(A)(4); Model Rules 8.4(c) & 8.5. Note that Lawyer has only been *charged* with criminal fraud. He has not been convicted (at least, not yet). But Lawyer falsely failed to disclose that he had been charged with criminal fraud. His dishonesty is his present failure to disclose, *i.e.,* his false answer to a specific question.

4. *d.* DR 8–102(A); Model Rule 8.2(a).

PART III

1. *a.* See DR 2–107(A); DR 4–101; Model Rules 1.5(e) & 1.9(b). Note that it is not enough, in "c", to inform the parties; they must consent and waive the conflict.

2. *b.* See DR 9–102; Model Rule 1.15. N.B. It would be the unusual lawyer who would choose option III, but it is an ethically permissible option.

3. *b.* See Part II, section VII, B, supra.

4. *b.* EC 7–7, 7–8; Model Rule 1.2(a), Comments 1 & 4.

5. Under the Model Code the answer is c. See EC 5–7; 2–20. Under the Model Rules, the answer is also c. See Rule 1.5, Comment 3.

6. *c.* See EC 4–1; DR 4–101(A); Model Rules, Scope 3 (some duties, like confidentiality, "may attach when the lawyer agrees to consider whether a client-lawyer relationship shall be established."). Cf. Model Rule 1.6(a).

7. *e.* DR 9–101(B); Rule 1.11(a). If Attorney had acquired confidential information, he would be disqualified under Canon 4 or Rule 1.9(b).

8. *d.* DR 5–106; Model Rule 1.8(g).

9. *f.* DR 2–106(C); Rule 1.5(d).

10. *e.* DR 5–105(C); Model Rule 1.7(a). Note, consent only by Brewer is not enough. Note also that the referral fee referred to in alternative *b* is not even permitted by the more liberal Model Rules. See, Rule 1.5(e)(1).

11. *c.* I & II are state action. IV is not setting a fee.

PART IV

1. *b.* DR 3–102(A)(3); Model Rule 5.4(a)(3). Note: if the investigator were a lawyer in another office, then DR 2–107(A) and Model Rule 1.5(e) would be applicable.

2. *a.* DR 3–102(A) & (B); Model Rule 5.4(a) & (b).

3. *c.* DR 3–101(A); EC 3–5; Model Rule 5.5(b). The manager is making an unsupervised judgment that the letter should contain a threat of suit.

4. *a.* DR 4–101(D); Model Rule 5.3.

PART V

1. *c.* DR 2–104(A)(4); Model Rule 7.3.

2. *d.*

3. *e.* DR 2–102(C); Model Rule 7.5(d).

4. *c.*

5. *b.* DR 2–104(A)(1); Model Rule 7.3.

6. *d.* DR 2–105(A); Model Rule 7.4.

PART VI

1. *c.* DR 9–101(B); Model Rule 1.11(a) & Comment 4. See Section II, A(1) of Part VI.

2. *c.* DR 8–102(A); Rule 8.2(a).

3. *d.* DR 7–103(A); Model Rule 3.8(a).

4. *c.* DR 8–101(A)(1). The Model Rules do not have a provision corresponding exactly to DR 8–101(A)(1). However, Model Rule 6.4 seems to be applicable, because Lawyer is a member of an organization involved in law reform. Lawyer made the necessary disclosures and so is not violating Rule 6.4.

PART VII

1. *c.* DR 7–104(A); Model Rule 4.2.

2. *a.* DR 7–106(C)(3); Model Rule 3.4(e).

3. *b.* DR 7–102(A)(1), (2); DR 2–109(A); Model Rule 3.1.

4. *b.* DR 7–107(G); Model Rules 3.6(b)(1), (5), & (c)(2).

5. Under the Model Code the answer is c. See DR 7–109(C). Under the Model Rules the answer is less clear. Rule 3.4(b), Comment 3 suggests that c remains the correct answer in a typical jurisdiction.

PART VIII

1. *b.* EC 7–8; 7–9; DR 7–101(A)(1); Model Rule 2.1, Comments 1 & 2.

2. *a.* DR 5–105(A) & (C); EC 5–20; Model Rule 2.2(c).

PART IX

1. *c.* EC 2–27; EC 2–29; EC 2–30; Model Rule 6.2.

2. *a.* EC 8–1; EC 8–4; Model Rule 6.4.

3. *a.* EC 1–4; Model Rule 6.1.

PART X

1. *a.* Model Judicial Code, Canon 2B. Note that, while the last sentence of Canon 2B states simply that "A judge shall not testify voluntarily as a character witness," the last sentence of Canon 2B, Comment 5 advises (on an aspirational level) that "[e]xcept in unusual circumstances where the demands of justice require, a judge *should* discourage a party from requiring the judge to testify as a character witness." (emphasis added)

2. *e.* Model Judicial Code, Canon 3B(7)(c) and Comment 9.

3. *a.* We know that the judge's ownership of stock in a party is a disqualifying interest, under Model Judicial Code, Canon 3E(1)(c) if the ownership is not de minimis. Terminology 5, 6. We don't know enough to conclude that the judge is wrong in her assessment that the stock ownership is not de minimis, so we shall assume that she is correct. Model Judicial Code, Canon 3F requires that the judge ask the lawyers *and* the parties to consider a waiver *out of the presence of the judge*. That was not done here.

4. *c.* Model Judicial Canon 3E(1)(b). While this disqualification can be waived, the waiver is not proper unless the lawyers *and* the parties agree to waive it. Canon 3F.

5. *b.* Model Judicial Code, Canon 4D(5)(d).

6. *a.* Model Judicial Canon 5A(2). Judge is clearly now a candidate. Terminology 2.

7. *c.* Model Judicial Code, Canon 3E & 3F. The judge cannot waive a disqualification if its basis is the judge's personal bias or prejudice concerning a party.

8. *a.* Code of Judicial Conduct, Canon 5A(3)(d), and Comment 1.

*

APPENDIX B

A SAMPLE EXAMINATION

INSTRUCTIONS

This examination consists of three questions. You are to answer all of them in light of the relevant ABA codes, supplemented where appropriate by other materials and considerations discussed in this course.

If any facts that you think are necessary to answer a question are missing, make appropriate assumptions and alternative assumptions of fact. Identify what assumptions you made and explain why you believe such assumptions were required. Each question is weighted in proportion to the suggested time. You have a total of 3½ hours.

QUESTION ONE
(Forty–Five Minutes)

Plaintiff is an individual seeking to prosecute a class action involving construction of a standard life insurance policy. Plaintiff has asked Attorney to file a class action. Attorney would advance the needed funds, and Plaintiff agreed to remain liable for all costs of the litigation; that is, Plaintiff will pay for all costs out of any recovery. However, if the litigation were unsuccessful, and there is no recovery,

Plaintiff would not have sufficient funds to repay Attorney. Is Attorney engaged in an improper conflict of interest if Attorney, in effect, finances the law suit?

Would it affect the conflicts issue if Plaintiff were a legal secretary employed by Attorney's law office?

For a discussion of these issues, see *Janicik v. Prudential Ins. Co.*, 451 A.2d 451, 458–60 & nn. 9–12 (Pa.Super.1982).

QUESTION TWO
(Ninety Minutes)

Closed, Inc. was a close corporation dominated by Pres, its chief executive officer. Pres and members of his family owned the stock. Law Firm did both the corporate legal representation of Closed, Inc. and the personal legal work for Pres and his family, but all legal services were billed to Closed, Inc. regardless of whether the work performed was corporate or private.

Pres had a falling out with his family members, who were continually at odds with each other. The members of Pres' family formed a voting trust; Law Firm did not prepare this trust. However, Law Firm continued to advise Pres and the other members of the board regarding their problems. Pres thought that Law Firm's actions were a display of disloyalty to him.

Pres reconciled with Wife; then Wife sued the other family members, and the board of directors of Closed, Inc. in order to break the voting trust that Wife had earlier joined. Partner of Law Firm represented the board members in defending this suit. Wife objected, so Partner withdrew and had an associate in Law Firm handle the defense.

Finally, Pres regained control of Closed, Inc. and fired all the people whom he felt had been disloyal. These terminated employees formed a new corporation, called New Corp., to compete with Closed. Pres also fired Law Firm. New Corp. hired Law Firm to represent it. Law Firm, now in the employ of New Corp., advised it that the non-competition contracts that New Corp.'s employees had signed with Closed, Inc. (before the employees had been fired by Closed, Inc.) were, for the most part, invalid. Law Firm, when it had been working for Closed, Inc., had handled litigation for Closed, Inc. regarding these contracts. Though Law Firm had not originally drafted them, Law Firm had, from time to time, suggested changes in their format. Partner in Law Firm was also a stockholder and investor in New Corp., Inc.

Are Partner and Law Firm subject to discipline?

For a discussion of these issues, see *In re Banks*, 283 Or. 459, 584 P.2d 284 (1978) (per curiam).

QUESTION THREE
(Forty–Five Minutes)

Utility is suing Defendant for damages in a complex case involving the manufacture of pump supports for a nuclear power station. Utility is the utility providing power in the area. Trial Judge is a customer of Utility. In fact, all judges in the state are customers of Utility. Pursuant to a fuel adjustment clause, all of Utility's customers have been directly surcharged an amount that Utility now claims as an element of damages. If Utility is successful, it may have to refund to its customers, including Trial Judge, a part of its damage award. This refund to Trial Judge would amount to between $70 and $100. Judge thought that his interest in the hypothetical $100 might require him to recuse himself. He told the parties about his problem. Four months later, after many pleadings in the case, Defendant moved to disqualify Trial Judge. Defendant did not allege any personal bias on the part of Trial Judge.

Should Trial Judge disqualify himself under ABA Model Code of Judicial Conduct 3E or under 28 U.S.C.A. § 455?

For a discussion of these issues, see *In re Virginia Electric & Power Co.*, 539 F.2d 357 (4th Cir. 1976).

QUESTION FOUR
(Thirty Minutes)

The Government is investigating XYZ Corp. for alleged violations of the criminal law. Corp. is complaining that the Government is interviewing XYZ Corp.'s agents and employees without first obtaining the permission of the general counsel of XYZ Corp. Some of the agents and employees of XYZ Corp. are hourly employees. Others are salaried. None have personal counsel. The Government has brought suit only against the corporate entity.

Is it ethical for the Government to interview the agents and employees without first securing the consent of XYZ Corp.'s general counsel? Are there any restrictions as to different types of employees or agents? If the Government is or may be acting improperly, what, if anything, can a court do? Or is the matter solely for the attorney disciplinary commission?

For a discussion of these issues, see *In re Investigation of FMC Corp.*, 430 F.Supp. 1108 (S.D.W.Va.1977).

APPENDIX C

AMERICAN BAR ASSOCIATION MODEL CODE OF PROFESSIONAL RESPONSIBILITY

As Amended

PREAMBLE AND PRELIMINARY STATEMENT

Preamble

The continued existence of a free and democratic society depends upon recognition of the concept that justice is based upon the rule of law grounded in respect for the dignity of the individual and his capacity through reason for enlightened self-government. Law so grounded makes justice possible, for only through such law does the dignity of the individual attain respect and protection. Without it, individual rights become subject to unrestrained power, respect for law is destroyed, and rational self-government is impossible.

Lawyers as guardians of the law, play a vital role in the preservation of society. The fulfillment of this role requires an understanding by lawyers of their relationship with and function in our legal system. A consequent obligation of lawyers is to maintain the highest standards of ethical conduct.

In fulfilling his professional responsibilities, a lawyer necessarily assumes various roles that require the performance of many difficult tasks. Not every situation which he may encounter can be foreseen, but fundamental ethical principles are always present to guide him. Within the framework of these principles, a lawyer must with courage and foresight be able and ready to shape the body of the law to the ever-changing relationships of society.

The Code of Professional Responsibility points the way to the aspiring and provides standards by which to judge the transgressor. Each lawyer must find within his own conscience the touchstone against which to test the extent to which his actions should rise above minimum standards. But in the last analysis it is the desire for the respect and confidence of the members of his profession and of the society which he serves that should provide to a lawyer the incentive for the highest possible degree of ethical conduct. The possible loss of that respect and confidence is the ultimate sanction. So long as its practitioners are guided by these principles, the law will continue to be a noble profession. This is its greatness and its strength, which permit of no compromise.

Preliminary Statement

In furtherance of the principles stated in the Preamble, the American Bar Association has promulgated this Code of Professional Responsibility, consisting of three separate but interrelated parts: Canons, Ethical Considerations, and Disciplinary Rules. The Code is designed to be adopted by appropriate agencies both as an inspirational guide to the members of the profession and as a basis for disciplinary action when the conduct of a lawyer falls below the required minimum standards stated in the Disciplinary Rules.

Obviously the Canons, Ethical Considerations, and Disciplinary Rules cannot apply to non-lawyers; however, they do define the type of ethical conduct that the public has a right to expect not only of lawyers but also of their non-professional employees and associates in all matters pertaining to professional employment. A lawyer should ultimately be responsible for the conduct of his employees and associates in the course of the professional representation of the client.

The Canons are statements of axiomatic norms, expressing in general terms the standards of professional conduct expected of lawyers in their relationships with the public, with the legal system, and with the legal profession. They embody the general concepts from which the Ethical Considerations and the Disciplinary Rules are derived.

The Ethical Considerations are aspirational in character and represent the objectives toward which every member of the profession should strive. They constitute a body of principles upon which the lawyer can rely for guidance in many specific situations.

The Disciplinary Rules, unlike the Ethical Considerations, are mandatory in character. The Disciplinary Rules state the minimum level of conduct below which no lawyer can fall without being subject to disciplinary action. Within the framework of fair trial, the Disciplinary Rules should be uniformly applied to all lawyers, regardless of the nature of their professional activities. The Code

makes no attempt to prescribe either disciplinary procedures or penalties for violation of a Disciplinary Rule, nor does it undertake to define standards for civil liability of lawyers for professional conduct. The severity of judgment against one found guilty of violating a Disciplinary Rule should be determined by the character of the offense and the attendant circumstances. An enforcing agency, in applying the Disciplinary Rules, may find interpretive guidance in the basic principles embodied in the Canons and in the objectives reflected in the Ethical Considerations.

CANON 1

A Lawyer Should Assist in Maintaining the Integrity and Competence of the Legal Profession

ETHICAL CONSIDERATIONS

EC 1–1 A basic tenet of the professional responsibility of lawyers is that every person in our society should have ready access to the independent professional services of a lawyer of integrity and competence. Maintaining the integrity and improving the competence of the bar to meet the highest standards is the ethical responsibility of every lawyer.

EC 1–2 The public should be protected from those who are not qualified to be lawyers by reason of a deficiency in education or moral standards or of other relevant factors but who nevertheless seek to practice law. To assure the maintenance of high moral and educational standards of the legal profession, lawyers should affirmatively assist courts and other appropriate bodies in promulgating, enforcing, and improving requirements for admission to the bar. In like manner, the bar has a positive obligation to aid in the continued improvement of all phases of pre-admission and post-admission legal education.

EC 1–3 Before recommending an applicant for admission, a lawyer should satisfy himself that the applicant is of good moral character. Although a lawyer should not become a self-appointed investigator or judge of applicants for admission, he should report to proper officials all unfavorable information he possesses relating to the character or other qualifications of an applicant.

EC 1–4 The integrity of the profession can be maintained only if conduct of lawyers in violation of the Disciplinary Rules is brought to the attention of the proper officials. A lawyer should reveal voluntarily to those officials all unprivileged knowledge of conduct of lawyers which he believes clearly to be in violation of the Disciplinary Rules. A lawyer should, upon request, serve on and assist committees and boards having responsibility for the administration of the Disciplinary Rules.

EC 1–5 A lawyer should maintain high standards of professional conduct and should encourage fellow lawyers to do likewise. He should be temperate and dignified, and he should refrain from all illegal and morally reprehensible conduct. Because of his position in society, even minor violations of law by a lawyer may tend to lessen public confidence in the legal profession. Obedience to law exemplifies respect for law. To lawyers especially, respect for the law should be more than a platitude.

EC 1–6 An applicant for admission to the bar or a lawyer may be unqualified, temporarily or permanently, for other than moral and educational reasons, such as mental or emotional instability. Lawyers should be diligent in taking steps to see that during a period of disqualification such person is not granted a license or, if licensed, is not permitted to practice. In like manner, when the disqualification has terminated, members of the bar should assist such person in being licensed, or, if licensed, in being restored to his full right to practice.

DISCIPLINARY RULES

DR 1–101 Maintaining Integrity and Competence of the Legal Profession.

(A) A lawyer is subject to discipline if he has made a materially false statement in, or if he has deliberately failed to disclose a material fact requested in connection with, his application for admission to the bar.

(B) A lawyer shall not further the application for admission to the bar of another person known by him to be unqualified in respect to character, education, or other relevant attribute.

DR 1–102 Misconduct.

(A) A lawyer shall not:

(1) Violate a Disciplinary Rule.

(2) Circumvent a Disciplinary Rule through actions of another.

(3) Engage in illegal conduct involving moral turpitude.

(4) Engage in conduct involving dishonesty, fraud, deceit, or misrepresentation.

(5) Engage in conduct that is prejudicial to the administration of justice.

(6) Engage in any other conduct that adversely reflects on his fitness to practice law.

DR 1–103 Disclosure of Information to Authorities.

(A) A lawyer possessing unprivileged knowledge of a violation of DR 1–102 shall report such knowledge to a tribunal or other authority empowered to investigate or act upon such violation.

(B) A lawyer possessing unprivileged knowledge or evidence concerning another lawyer or a judge shall reveal fully such knowledge or evidence upon proper request of a tribunal or other authority empowered to investigate or act upon the conduct of lawyers or judges.

CANON 2

A Lawyer Should Assist the Legal Profession in Fulfilling Its Duty to Make Legal Counsel Available

ETHICAL CONSIDERATIONS

EC 2–1 The need of members of the public for legal services is met only if they recognize their legal problems, appreciate the importance of seeking assistance, and are able to obtain the services of acceptable legal counsel. Hence, important functions of the legal profession are to educate laymen to recognize their problems, to facilitate the process of intelligent selection of lawyers, and to assist in making legal services fully available.

Recognition of Legal Problems

EC 2–2 The legal profession should assist laypersons to recognize legal problems because such problems may not be self-revealing and often are not timely noticed. Therefore, lawyers should encourage and participate in educational and public relations programs concerning our legal system with particular reference to legal problems that frequently arise. Preparation of advertisements and professional articles for lay publications and participation in seminars, lectures, and civic programs should be motivated by a desire to educate the public to an awareness of legal needs and to provide information relevant to the selection of the most appropriate counsel rather than to obtain publicity for particular lawyers. The problems of advertising on television require special consideration, due to the style, cost, and transitory nature of such media. If the interests of laypersons in receiving relevant lawyer advertising are not adequately served by print media and radio advertising, and if adequate safeguards to protect the public can reasonably be formulated, television advertising may serve a public interest.

As amended in 1977.

EC 2–3 Whether a lawyer acts properly in volunteering in-person advice to a layperson to seek legal services depends upon the circumstances. The giving of advice that one should take legal action could well be in fulfillment of the duty of the legal profession to assist laypersons in recognizing legal problems. The advice is proper only if motivated by a desire to protect one who does not recognize that he may have legal problems or who is ignorant of his legal rights or obligations. It is improper if motivated by a desire to obtain personal benefit, secure personal publicity, or cause legal action to be taken merely to harass or injure another. A lawyer should not initiate an in-person contact with a non-client, personally or through a representative, for the purpose of being retained to represent him for compensation.

As amended in 1977.

EC 2–4 Since motivation is subjective and often difficult to judge, the motives of a lawyer who volunteers in-person advice likely to produce legal controversy may well be suspect if he receives professional employment or other benefits as a result. A lawyer who volunteers in-person advice that one should obtain the services of a lawyer generally should not himself accept employment, compensation, or other benefit in connection with that matter. However, it is not improper for a lawyer to volunteer such advice and render resulting legal services to close friends, relatives, former clients (in regard to matters germane to former employment), and regular clients.

As amended in 1977.

EC 2–5 A lawyer who writes or speaks for the purpose of educating members of the public to recognize their legal problems should carefully refrain from giving or appearing to give a general solution applicable to all apparently similar individual problems, since slight changes in fact situations may require a material variance in the applicable advice; otherwise, the public may be mislead and misadvised. Talks and writings by lawyers for laypersons should caution them not to attempt to solve individual problems upon the basis of the information contained therein.

As amended in 1977.

Selection of a Lawyer

EC 2–6 Formerly a potential client usually knew the reputations of local lawyers for competency and integrity and therefore could select a practitioner in whom he had confidence. This traditional selection process worked well because it was initiated by the client and the choice was an informed one.

EC 2–7 Changed conditions, however, have seriously restricted the effectiveness of the traditional selection process. Often the reputations of lawyers are not sufficiently known to enable laypersons to make intelligent choices. The law has become increasingly complex and specialized. Few lawyers are willing and competent to deal with every kind of legal matter, and many laypersons have difficulty in determining the competence of lawyers to render different types of legal services. The selection of legal counsel is particularly difficult for transients, persons moving into new areas, persons of limited education or means, and others who have little or no contact with lawyers. Lack of information about the availability of lawyers, the qualifications of particular lawyers, and the expense of legal representation leads laypersons to avoid seeking legal advice.

As amended in 1977.

EC 2–8 Selection of a lawyer by a layperson should be made on an informed basis. Advice and recommendation of third parties—relatives, friends, acquaintances, business associates, or other lawyers—and disclosure of relevant information about the lawyer and his practice may be helpful. A layperson is best served if the recommendation is disinterested and informed. In order that the recommendation be disinterested, a lawyer should not seek to influence another to recommend his employment. A lawyer should not compensate another person for recommending him, for influencing a prospective client to employ him, or to encourage future recommendations. Advertisements and public communications, whether in law lists, telephone directories, newspapers, other forms of print media, television or radio, should be formulated to convey only information that is necessary to make an appropriate selection. Such information includes: (1) office information, such as, name, including name of law firm and names of professional associates; addresses; telephone numbers; credit card acceptability; fluency in foreign languages; and office hours; (2) relevant biographical information; (3) description of the practice, but only by using designations and definitions authorized by [the agency having jurisdiction of the subject under state law], for example, one or more fields of law in which the lawyer or law firm practices; a statement that practice is limited to one or more fields of law; and/or a statement that the lawyer or law firm specializes in a particular field of law practice, but only by using designations, definitions and standards authorized by [the agency having jurisdiction of the subject under state law]; and (4) permitted fee information. Self-laudation should be avoided.

As amended in 1978.

Selection of a Lawyer: Lawyer Advertising

EC 2–9 The lack of sophistication on the part of many members of the public concerning legal services, the importance of the interests affected by the choice of a lawyer and prior experience with unrestricted lawyer advertising, require that special care be taken by lawyers to avoid misleading the public and to assure that the information set forth in any advertising is relevant to the selection of a lawyer. The lawyer must be mindful that the benefits of lawyer advertising depend upon its reliability and accuracy. Examples of information in lawyer advertising that would be deceptive include misstatements of fact, suggestions that the ingenuity or prior record of a lawyer rather than the justice of the claim are the principal factors likely to determine the result, inclusion of information irrelevant to selecting a lawyer, and representations concerning the quality of service, which cannot be measured or verified. Since lawyer advertising is calculated and not spontaneous, reasonable regulation of lawyer advertising designed to foster compliance with appropriate standards serves the public interest without impeding the flow of useful, meaningful, and relevant information to the public.

As amended in 1977.

EC 2–10 A lawyer should ensure that the information contained in any advertising which the lawyer publishes, broadcasts or causes to be published or broadcast is relevant, is disseminated in an objective and understandable fashion, and would facilitate the prospective client's ability to compare the qualifications of the lawyers available to represent him. A lawyer should strive to communicate such information without undue emphasis upon style and advertising strategems which serve to hinder rather than to facilitate intelligent selection of

counsel. Because technological change is a recurrent feature of communications forms, and because perceptions of what is relevant in lawyer selection may change, lawyer advertising regulations should not be cast in rigid, unchangeable terms. Machinery is therefore available to advertisers and consumers for prompt consideration of proposals to change the rules governing lawyer advertising. The determination of any request for such change should depend upon whether the proposal is necessary in light of existing Code provisions, whether the proposal accords with standards of accuracy, reliability and truthfulness, and whether the proposal would facilitate informed selection of lawyers by potential consumers of legal services. Representatives of lawyers and consumers should be heard in addition to the applicant concerning any proposed change. Any change which is approved should be promulgated in the form of an amendment to the Code so that all lawyers practicing in the jurisdiction may avail themselves of its provisions.

As amended in 1977.

EC 2–11 The name under which a lawyer conducts his practice may be a factor in the selection process. The use of a trade name or an assumed name could mislead laypersons concerning the identity, responsibility, and status of those practicing thereunder. Accordingly, a lawyer in private practice should practice only under a designation containing his own name, the name of a lawyer employing him, the name of one or more of the lawyers practicing in a partnership, or, if permitted by law, the name of a professional legal corporation, which should be clearly designated as such. For many years some law firms have used a firm name retaining one or more names of deceased or retired partners and such practice is not improper if the firm is a bona fide successor of a firm in which the deceased or retired person was a member, if the use of the name is authorized by law or by contract, and if the public is not misled thereby. However, the name of a partner who withdraws from a firm but continues to practice law should be omitted from the firm name in order to avoid misleading the public.

As amended in 1977.

EC 2–12 A lawyer occupying a judicial, legislative, or public executive or administrative position who has the right to practice law concurrently may allow his name to remain in the name of the firm if he actively continues to practice law as a member thereof. Otherwise, his name should be removed from the firm name, and he should not be identified as a past or present member of the firm; and he should not hold himself out as being a practicing lawyer.

EC 2–13 In order to avoid the possibility of misleading persons with whom he deals, a lawyer should be scrupulous in the representation of his professional status. He should not hold himself out as being a partner or associate of a law firm if he is not one in fact, and thus should not hold himself out as partner or associate if he only shares offices with another lawyer.

EC 2–14 In some instances a lawyer confines his practice to a particular field of law. In the absence of state controls to insure the existence of special competence, a lawyer should not be permitted to hold himself out as a specialist or as having official recognition as a specialist, other than in the fields of admiralty, trademark, and patent law where a holding out as a specialist historically has been permitted. A lawyer may, however, indicate in permitted advertising, if it is factual, a limitation of his practice or one or more particular areas or fields of law in which he practices using designations and definitions authorized for that purpose by [the state agency having jurisdiction]. A lawyer practicing in a jurisdiction which certifies specialists must also be careful not to confuse laypersons as to his status. If a lawyer discloses areas of law in which he practices or to which he limits his practice, but is not certified in [the jurisdiction], he, and the designation authorized in [the jurisdiction], should avoid any implication that he is in fact certified.

As amended in 1977.

EC 2–15 The legal profession has developed lawyer referral systems designed to aid individuals who are able to pay fees but need assistance in locating lawyers competent to handle their particular problems. Use of a lawyer referral system enables a layman to avoid an uninformed selection of a lawyer because such a system makes possible the employment of competent lawyers who have indicated an interest in the subject matter involved. Lawyers should support the principle of lawyer referral systems and should encourage the evolution of other ethical plans which aid in the selection of qualified counsel.

Financial Ability to Employ Counsel: Generally

EC 2–16 The legal profession cannot remain a viable force in fulfilling its role in our society unless its members receive adequate compensation for services rendered, and reasonable fees should be charged in appropriate cases to clients able to

pay them. Nevertheless, persons unable to pay all or a portion of a reasonable fee should be able to obtain necessary legal services, and lawyers should support and participate in ethical activities designed to achieve that objective.

Financial Ability to Employ Counsel: Persons Able to Pay Reasonable Fees

EC 2–17 The determination of a proper fee requires consideration of the interests of both client and lawyer. A lawyer should not charge more than a reasonable fee, for excessive cost of legal service would deter laymen from utilizing the legal system in protection of their rights. Furthermore, an excessive charge abuses the professional relationship between lawyer and client. On the other hand, adequate compensation is necessary in order to enable the lawyer to serve his client effectively and to preserve the integrity and independence of the profession.

EC 2–18 The determination of the reasonableness of a fee requires consideration of all relevant circumstances, including those stated in the Disciplinary Rules. The fees of a lawyer will vary according to many factors, including the time required, his experience, ability, and reputation, the nature of the employment, the responsibility involved, and the results obtained. It is a commendable and long-standing tradition of the bar that special consideration is given in the fixing of any fee for services rendered a brother lawyer or a member of his immediate family.

As amended in 1974.

EC 2–19 As soon as feasible after a lawyer has been employed, it is desirable that he reach a clear agreement with his client as to the basis of the fee charges to be made. Such a course will not only prevent later misunderstanding but will also work for good relations between the lawyer and the client. It is usually beneficial to reduce to writing the understanding of the parties regarding the fee, particularly when it is contingent. A lawyer should be mindful that many persons who desire to employ him may have had little or no experience with fee charges of lawyers, and for this reason he should explain fully to such persons the reasons for the particular fee arrangement he proposes.

EC 2–20 Contingent fee arrangements in civil cases have long been commonly accepted in the United States in proceedings to enforce claims. The historical bases of their acceptance are that (1) they often, and in a variety of circumstances, provide the only practical means by which one having a claim against another can economically afford, finance, and obtain the services of a competent lawyer to prosecute his claim, and (2) a successful prosecution of the claim produces a *res* out of which the fee can be paid. Although a lawyer generally should decline to accept employment on a contingent fee basis by one who is able to pay a reasonable fixed fee, it is not necessarily improper for a lawyer, where justified by the particular circumstances of a case, to enter into a contingent fee contract in a civil case with any client who, after being fully informed of all relevant factors, desires that arrangement. Because of the human relationships involved and the unique character of the proceedings, contingent fee arrangements in domestic relation cases are rarely justified. In administrative agency proceedings contingent fee contracts should be governed by the same consideration as in other civil cases. Public policy properly condemns contingent fee arrangements in criminal cases, largely on the ground that legal services in criminal cases do not produce a *res* with which to pay the fee.

EC 2–21 A lawyer should not accept compensation or any thing of value incident to his employment or services from one other than his client without the knowledge and consent of his client after full disclosure.

EC 2–22 Without the consent of his client, a lawyer should not associate in a particular matter another lawyer outside his firm. A fee may properly be divided between lawyers properly associated if the division is in proportion to the services performed and the responsibility assumed by each lawyer and if the total fee is reasonable.

EC 2–23 A lawyer should be zealous in his efforts to avoid controversies over fees with clients and should attempt to resolve amicably any differences on the subject. He should not sue a client for a fee unless necessary to prevent fraud or gross imposition by the client.

Financial Ability to Employ Counsel: Persons Unable to Pay Reasonable Fees

EC 2–24 A layman whose financial ability is not sufficient to permit payment of any fee cannot obtain legal services, other than in cases where a contingent fee is appropriate, unless the services are provided for him. Even a person of moderate means may be unable to pay a reasonable fee which is large because of the complexity, novelty, or difficulty of the problem or similar factors.

EC 2–25 Historically, the need for legal services of those unable to pay reasonable fees has been met in part by lawyers who donated their services or

accepted court appointments on behalf of such individuals. The basic responsibility for providing legal services for those unable to pay ultimately rests upon the individual lawyer, and personal involvement in the problems of the disadvantaged can be one of the most rewarding experiences in the life of a lawyer. Every lawyer, regardless of professional prominence or professional workload, should find time to participate in serving the disadvantaged. The rendition of free legal services to those unable to pay reasonable fees continues to be an obligation of each lawyer, but the efforts of individual lawyers are often not enough to meet the need. Thus it has been necessary for the profession to institute additional programs to provide legal services. Accordingly, legal aid offices, lawyer referral services, and other related programs have been developed, and others will be developed, by the profession. Every lawyer should support all proper efforts to meet this need for legal services.

Acceptance and Retention of Employment

EC 2–26 A lawyer is under no obligation to act as advisor or advocate for every person who may wish to become his client; but in furtherance of the objective of the bar to make legal services fully available, a lawyer should not lightly decline proffered employment. The fulfillment of this objective requires acceptance by a lawyer of his share of tendered employment which may be unattractive both to him and the bar generally.

EC 2–27 History is replete with instances of distinguished and sacrificial services by lawyers who have represented unpopular clients and causes. Regardless of his personal feelings, a lawyer should not decline representation because a client or a cause is unpopular or community reaction is adverse.

EC 2–28 The personal preference of a lawyer to avoid adversary alignment against judges, other lawyers, public officials, or influential members of the community does not justify his rejection of tendered employment.

EC 2–29 When a lawyer is appointed by a court or requested by a bar association to undertake representation of a person unable to obtain counsel, whether for financial or other reasons, he should not seek to be excused from undertaking the representation except for compelling reasons. Compelling reasons do not include such factors as the repugnance of the subject matter of the proceeding, the identity or position of a person involved in the case, the belief of the lawyer that the defendant in a criminal proceeding is guilty, or the belief of the lawyer regarding the merits of the civil case.

EC 2–30 Employment should not be accepted by a lawyer when he is unable to render competent service or when he knows or it is obvious that the person seeking to employ him desires to institute or maintain an action merely for the purpose of harassing or maliciously injuring another. Likewise, a lawyer should decline employment if the intensity of his personal feeling, as distinguished from a community attitude, may impair his effective representation of a prospective client. If a lawyer knows a client has previously obtained counsel, he should not accept employment in the matter unless the other counsel approves or withdraws, or the client terminates the prior employment.

EC 2–31 Full availability of legal counsel requires both that persons be able to obtain counsel and that lawyers who undertake representation complete the work involved. Trial counsel for a convicted defendant should continue to represent his client by advising whether to take an appeal and, if the appeal is prosecuted, by representing him through the appeal unless new counsel is substituted or withdrawal is permitted by the appropriate court.

EC 2–32 A decision by a lawyer to withdraw should be made only on the basis of compelling circumstances, and in a matter pending before a tribunal he must comply with the rules of the tribunal regarding withdrawal. A lawyer should not withdraw without considering carefully and endeavoring to minimize the possible adverse effect on the rights of his client and the possibility of prejudice to his client as a result of his withdrawal. Even when he justifiably withdraws, a lawyer should protect the welfare of his client by giving due notice of his withdrawal, suggesting employment of other counsel, delivering to the client all papers and property to which the client is entitled, cooperating with counsel subsequently employed, and otherwise endeavoring to minimize the possibility of harm. Further, he should refund to the client any compensation not earned during the employment.

EC 2–33 As a part of the legal profession's commitment to the principle that high quality legal services should be available to all, attorneys are encouraged to cooperate with qualified legal assistance organizations providing prepaid legal services. Such participation should at all times be in accordance with the basic tenets of the profession: independence, integrity, competence and de-

votion to the interests of individual clients. An attorney so participating should make certain that his relationship with a qualified legal assistance organization in no way interferes with his independent, professional representation of the interests of the individual client. An attorney should avoid situations in which officials of the organization who are not lawyers attempt to direct attorneys concerning the manner in which legal services are performed for individual members, and should also avoid situations in which considerations of economy are given undue weight in determining the attorneys employed by an organization or the legal services to be performed for the member or beneficiary rather than competence and quality of service. An attorney interested in maintaining the historic traditions of the profession and preserving the function of a lawyer as a trusted and independent advisor to individual members of society should carefully assess such factors when accepting employment by, or otherwise participating in, a particular qualified legal assistance organization, and while so participating should adhere to the highest professional standards of effort and competence.

Added in 1974; amended in 1975.

DISCIPLINARY RULES

DR 2–101 Publicity.

(A) A lawyer shall not, on behalf of himself, his partner, associate or any other lawyer affiliated with him or his firm, use or participate in the use of any form of public communication containing a false, fraudulent, misleading, deceptive, self-laudatory or unfair statement or claim.

(B) In order to facilitate the process of informed selection of a lawyer by potential consumers of legal services, a lawyer may publish or broadcast, subject to DR 2–103, the following information in print media distributed or over television or radio broadcast in the geographic area or areas in which the lawyer resides or maintains offices or in which a significant part of the lawyer's clientele resides, provided that the information disclosed by the lawyer in such publication or broadcast complies with DR 2–101(A), and is presented in a dignified manner:

(1) Name, including name of law firm and names of professional associates; addresses and telephone numbers;

(2) One or more fields of law in which the lawyer or law firm practices, a statement that practice is limited to one or more fields of law, or a statement that the lawyer or law firm specializes in a particular field of law practice, to the extent authorized under DR 2–105;

(3) Date and place of birth;

(4) Date and place of admission to the bar of state and federal courts;

(5) Schools attended, with dates of graduation, degrees and other scholastic distinctions;

(6) Public or quasi-public offices;

(7) Military service;

(8) Legal authorships;

(9) Legal teaching positions;

(10) Memberships, offices, and committee assignments, in bar associations;

(11) Membership and offices in legal fraternities and legal societies;

(12) Technical and professional licenses;

(13) Memberships in scientific, technical and professional associations and societies;

(14) Foreign language ability;

(15) Names and addresses of bank references;

(16) With their written consent, names of clients regularly represented;

(17) Prepaid or group legal services programs in which the lawyer participates;

(18) Whether credit cards or other credit arrangements are accepted;

(19) Office and telephone answering service hours;

(20) Fee for an initial consultation;

(21) Availability upon request of a written schedule of fees and/or an estimate of the fee to be charged for specific services;

(22) Contingent fee rates subject to DR 2–106(C), provided that the statement discloses whether percentages are computed before or after deduction of costs;

(23) Range of fees for services, provided that the statement discloses that the specific fee within the range which will be charged will vary depending upon the particular matter to be handled for each client and the client is entitled without obligation to an estimate of the fee within the range likely to be charged. In print size equivalent to the largest print used in setting forth the fee information;

(24) Hourly rate, provided that the statement discloses that the total fee charged will depend upon the number of hours which must be devoted to the particular matter to be handled for each client and the client is entitled to without obligation an estimate of the fee likely to be charged, in print size at least equivalent to the largest print used in setting forth the fee information;

(25) Fixed fees for specific legal services,* the description of which would not be misunderstood or be deceptive, provided that the statement discloses that the quoted fee will be available only to clients whose matters fall into the services described and that the client is entitled without obligation to a specific estimate of the fee likely to be charged in print size at least equivalent to the largest print used in setting forth the fee information.

(C) Any person desiring to expand the information authorized for disclosure in DR 2–101(B), or to provide for its dissemination through other forums may apply to [the agency having jurisdiction under state law]. Any such application shall be served upon [the agencies having jurisdiction under state law over the regulation of the legal profession and consumer matters] who shall be heard, together with the applicant, on the issue of whether the proposal is necessary in light of the existing provisions of the Code, accords with standards of accuracy, reliability and truthfulness, and would facilitate the process of informed selection of lawyers by potential consumers of legal services. The relief

---

* The agency having jurisdiction under state law may desire to issue appropriate guidelines defining "specific legal services."

granted in response to any such application shall be promulgated as an amendment to DR 2–101(B), universally applicable to all lawyers.**

(D) If the advertisement is communicated to the public over television or radio, it shall be pre-recorded, approved for broadcast by the lawyer, and a recording of the actual transmission shall be retained by the lawyer.

(E) If a lawyer advertises a fee for a service, the lawyer must render that service for no more than the fee advertised.

(F) Unless otherwise specified in the advertisement if a lawyer publishes any fee information authorized under DR 2–101(B) in a publication that is published more frequently than one time per month, the lawyer shall be bound by any representation made therein for a period of not less than 30 days after such publication. If a lawyer publishes any fee information authorized under DR 2–101(B) in a publication that is published once a month or less frequently, he shall be bound by any representation made therein until the publication of the succeeding issue. If a lawyer publishes any fee information authorized under DR 2–101(B) in a publication which has no fixed date for publication of a succeeding issue, the lawyer shall be bound by any representation made therein for a reasonable period of time after publication but in no event less than one year.

(G) Unless otherwise specified, if a lawyer broadcasts any fee information authorized under DR 2–101(B), the lawyer shall be bound by any representation made therein for a period of not less than 30 days after such broadcast.

(H) This rule does not prohibit limited and dignified identification of a lawyer as a lawyer as well as by name:

(1) In political advertisements when his professional status is germane to the political campaign or to a political issue.

(2) In public notices when the name and profession of a lawyer are required or authorized by law or are reasonably

pertinent for a purpose other than the attraction of potential clients.

(3) In routine reports and announcements of a bona fide business, civic, professional, or political organization in which he serves as a director or officer.

(4) In and on legal documents prepared by him.

(5) In and on legal textbooks, treatises, and other legal publications, and in dignified advertisements thereof.

(I) A lawyer shall not compensate or give any thing of value to representatives of the press, radio, television, or other communication medium in anticipation of or in return for professional publicity in a news item.

As amended in 1974, 1975, 1977 and 1978.

DR 2–102 Professional Notices, Letterheads and Offices.

(A) A lawyer or law firm shall not use or participate in the use of professional cards, professional announcement cards, office signs, letterheads, or similar professional notices or devices, except that the following may be used if they are in dignified form:

(1) A professional card of a lawyer identifying him by name and as a lawyer, and giving his addresses, telephone numbers, the name of his law firm, and any information permitted under DR 2–105. A professional card of a law firm may also give the names of members and associates. Such cards may be used for identification.

(2) A brief professional announcement card stating new or changed associations or addresses, change of firm name, or similar matters pertaining to the professional offices of a lawyer or law firm, which may be mailed to lawyers, clients, former clients, personal friends, and relatives. It shall not state biographical data except to the extent reasonably necessary to identify the lawyer or to explain the change in his association, but it may state the

---

** The agency having jurisdiction under state law should establish orderly and expeditious procedures for ruling on such applications.

immediate past position of the lawyer. It may give the names and dates of predecessor firms in a continuing line of succession. It shall not state the nature of the practice except as permitted under DR 2–105.

(3) A sign on or near the door of the office and in the building directory identifying the law office. The sign shall not state the nature of the practice, except as permitted under DR 2–105.

(4) A letter head of a lawyer identifying him by name and as a lawyer, and giving his addresses, telephone numbers, the name of his law firm, associates and any information permitted under DR 2–105. A letterhead of a law firm may also give the names of members and associates, and names and dates relating to deceased and retired members. A lawyer may be designated "Of Counsel" on a letterhead if he has a continuing relationship with a lawyer or law firm, other than as a partner or associate. A lawyer or law firm may be designated as "General Counsel" or by similar professional reference on stationary of a client if he or the firm devotes a substantial amount of professional time in the representation of that client. The letterhead of a law firm may give the names and dates of predecessor firms in a continuing line of succession.

(B) A lawyer in private practice shall not practice under a trade name, a name that is misleading as to the identity of the lawyer or lawyers practicing under such name, or a firm name containing names other than those of one or more of the lawyers in the firm, except that the name of a professional corporation or professional association may contain "P.C." or "P.A." or similar symbols indicating the nature of the organization, and if otherwise lawful a firm may use as, or continue to include in, its name the name or names of one or more deceased or retired members of the firm or of a predecessor firm in a continuing line of succession. A lawyer who assumes a judicial, legislative, or public executive or administrative post or office shall not permit his name to remain in the name of a law firm or to be used in professional no-

tices of the firm during any significant period in which he is not actively and regularly practicing law as a member of the firm, and during such period other members of the firm shall not use his name in the firm name or in professional notices of the firm.

(C) A lawyer shall not hold himself out as having a partnership with one or more other lawyers or professional corporations unless they are in fact partners.

(D) A partnership shall not be formed or continued between or among lawyers licensed in different jurisdictions unless all enumerations of the members and associates of the firm on its letterhead and in other permissible listings make clear the jurisdictional limitations on those members and associates of the firm not licensed to practice in all listed jurisdictions; however, the same firm name may be used in each jurisdiction.

(E) Nothing contained herein shall prohibit a lawyer from using or permitting the use of, in connection with his name, an earned degree or title derived therefrom indicating his training in the law.

As amended in 1976, 1977, 1979 and 1980.

DR 2–103 Recommendation of Professional Employment.

(A) A lawyer shall not, except as authorized in DR 2–101(B), recommend employment as a private practitioner, of himself, his partner, or associate to a layperson who has not sought his advice regarding employment of a lawyer.

(B) A lawyer shall not compensate or give anything of value to a person or organization to recommend or secure his employment by a client, or as a reward for having made a recommendation resulting in his employment by a client, except that he may pay the usual and reasonable fees or dues charged by any of the organizations listed in DR 2–103(D).

(C) A lawyer shall not request a person or organization to recommend or promote the use of his services or those of his partner or associate, or any other lawyer affiliated with him or his firm, as a private practitioner, except as authorized in DR 2–101, and except that

(1) He may request referrals from a lawyer referral service operated, sponsored, or approved by a bar association and may pay its fees incident thereto.

(2) He may cooperate with the legal service activities of any of the offices or organizations enumerated in DR 2–103(D)(1) through (4) and may perform legal services for those to whom he was recommended by it to do such work if:

    (a) The person to whom the recommendation is made is a member or beneficiary of such office or organization; and

    (b) The lawyer remains free to exercise his independent professional judgment on behalf of his client.

(D) A lawyer or his partner or associate or any other lawyer affiliated with him or his firm may be recommended, employed or paid by, or may cooperate with, one of the following offices or organizations that promote the use of his services or those of his partner or associate or any other lawyer affiliated with him or his firm if there is no interference with the exercise of independent professional judgment in behalf of his client:

(1) A legal aid office or public defender office:

    (a) Operated or sponsored by a duly accredited law school.

    (b) Operated or sponsored by a bona fide nonprofit community organization.

    (c) Operated or sponsored by a governmental agency.

    (d) Operated, sponsored, or approved by a bar association.

(2) A military legal assistance office.

(3) A lawyer referral service operated, sponsored, or approved by a bar association.

(4) Any bona fide organization that recommends, furnishes or pays for legal services to its members or beneficiaries provided the following conditions are satisfied:

    (a) Such organization, including any affiliate, is so organized and operated that no profit is derived by it from the rendition of legal services by lawyers, and that, if the organization is organized for profit, the legal services are not rendered by lawyers employed, directed, supervised or selected by it except in connection with matters where such organization bears ultimate liability of its member or beneficiary.

    (b) Neither the lawyer, nor his partner, nor associate, nor any other lawyer affiliated with him or his firm, nor any non-lawyer, shall have initiated or promoted such organization for the primary purpose of providing financial or other benefit to such lawyer, partner, associate or affiliated lawyer.

    (c) Such organization is not operated for the purpose of procuring legal work or financial benefit for any lawyer as a private practitioner outside of the legal services program of the organization.

    (d) The member or beneficiary to whom the legal services are furnished, and not such organization, is recognized as the client of the lawyer in the matter.

    (e) Any member or beneficiary who is entitled to have legal services furnished or paid for by the organization may, if such member or beneficiary so desires, select counsel other than that furnished, selected or approved by the organization for the particular matter involved; and the legal service plan of such organization provides appropriate relief for any member or beneficiary who asserts a claim that representation by counsel furnished, selected or approved would be unethical, improper or inadequate under the circumstances of the matter involved and the plan provides an appropriate procedure for seeking such relief.

    (f) The lawyer does not know or have cause to know that such organization is in violation of applicable laws, rules of court and other legal requirements that govern its legal service operations.

(g) Such organization has filed with the appropriate disciplinary authority at least annually a report with respect to its legal service plan, if any, showing its terms, its schedule of benefits, its subscription charges, agreements with counsel, and financial results of its legal service activities or, if it has failed to do so, the lawyer does not know or have cause to know of such failure.

(E) A lawyer shall not accept employment when he knows or it is obvious that the person who seeks his services does so as a result of conduct prohibited under this Disciplinary Rule.

As amended in 1974, 1975 and 1977.

DR 2–104 Suggestion of Need of Legal Services.

(A) A lawyer who has given in-person unsolicited advice to a layperson that he should obtain counsel or take legal action shall not accept employment resulting from that advice, except that:

(1) A lawyer may accept employment by a close friend, relative, former client (if the advice is germane to the former employment), or one whom the lawyer reasonably believes to be a client.

(2) A lawyer may accept employment that results from his participation in activities designed to educate laypersons to recognize legal problems, to make intelligent selection of counsel, or to utilize available legal services if such activities are conducted or sponsored by a qualified legal assistance organization.

(3) A lawyer who is recommended, furnished or paid by a qualified legal assistance organization enumerated in DR 2–103(D)(1) through (4) may represent a member or beneficiary thereof, to the extent and under the conditions prescribed therein.

(4) Without affecting his right to accept employment, a lawyer may speak publicly or write for publication on legal topics so long as he does not emphasize his own professional experience or reputation and does not undertake to give individual advice.

(5) If success in asserting rights or defenses of his client in litigation in the nature of a class action is dependent upon the joinder of others, a lawyer may accept, but shall not seek, employment from those contacted for the purpose of obtaining their joinder.

As amended in 1974, 1975 and 1977.

DR 2–105 Limitation of Practice.

(A) A lawyer shall not hold himself out publicly as a specialist, as practicing in certain areas of law or as limiting his practice permitted under DR 2–101(B), except as follows:

(1) A lawyer admitted to practice before the United States Patent and Trademark Office may use the designation "Patents," "Patent Attorney," "Patent Lawyer," or "Registered Patent Attorney" or any combination of those terms, on his letterhead and office sign.

(2) A lawyer who publicly discloses fields of law in which the lawyer or the law firm practices or states that his practice is limited to one or more fields of law shall do so by using designations and definitions authorized and approved by [the agency having jurisdiction of the subject under state law].

(3) A lawyer who is certified as a specialist in a particular field of law or law practice by [the authority having jurisdiction under state law over the subject of specialization by lawyers] may hold himself out as such, but only in accordance with the rules prescribed by that authority.

As amended in 1977.

DR 2–106 Fees for Legal Services.

(A) A lawyer shall not enter into an agreement for, charge, or collect an illegal or clearly excessive fee.

(B) A fee is clearly excessive when, after a review of the facts, a lawyer of ordinary prudence would be left with a definite and firm conviction that the fee is in excess of a reasonable fee. Factors to be considered as guides in determining the reasonableness of a fee include the following:

(1) The time and labor required, the novelty and difficulty of the questions involved, and the skill requisite to perform the legal service properly.

(2) The likelihood, if apparent to the client, that the acceptance of the particular employment will preclude other employment by the lawyer.

(3) The fee customarily charged in the locality for similar legal services.

(4) The amount involved and the results obtained.

(5) The time limitations imposed by the client or by the circumstances.

(6) The nature and length of the professional relationship with the client.

(7) The experience, reputation, and ability of the lawyer or lawyers performing the services.

(8) Whether the fee is fixed or contingent.

(C) A lawyer shall not enter into an arrangement for, charge, or collect a contingent fee for representing a defendant in a criminal case.

DR 2–107 Division of Fees Among Lawyers

(A) A lawyer shall not divide a fee for legal services with another lawyer who is not a partner in or associate of his law firm or law office, unless:

(1) The client consents to employment of the other lawyer after a full disclosure that a division of fees will be made.

(2) The division is made in proportion to the services performed and responsibility assumed by each.

(3) The total fee of the lawyers does not clearly exceed reasonable compensation for all legal services they rendered the client.

(B) This Disciplinary Rule does not prohibit payment to a former partner or associate pursuant to a separation or retirement agreement.

DR 2–108 Agreements Restricting the Practice of a Lawyer.

(A) A lawyer shall not be a party to or participate in a partnership or employment agreement with another lawyer that restricts the right of a lawyer to practice law after the termination of a relationship created by the agreement, except as a condition to payment of retirement benefits.

(B) In connection with the settlement of a controversy or suit, a lawyer shall not enter into an agreement that restricts his right to practice law.

DR 2–109 Acceptance of Employment.

(A) A lawyer shall not accept employment on behalf of a person if he knows or it is obvious that such person wishes to:

(1) Bring a legal action, conduct a defense, or assert a position in litigation, or otherwise have steps taken for him, merely for the purpose of harassing or maliciously injuring any person.

(2) Present a claim or defense in litigation that is not warranted under existing law, unless it can be supported by good faith argument for an extension, modification, or reversal of existing law.

DR 2–110 Withdrawal from Employment.

(A) In general.

(1) If permission for withdrawal from employment is required by the rules of a tribunal, a lawyer shall not withdraw from employment in a proceeding before that tribunal without its permission.

(2) In any event, a lawyer shall not withdraw from employment until he has taken reasonable steps to avoid foreseeable prejudice to the rights of his client, including giving due notice to his client, allowing time for employment of other counsel, delivering to the client all papers and property to which the client is entitled, and complying with applicable laws and rules.

(3) A lawyer who withdraws from employment shall refund promptly any part of a fee paid in advance that has not been earned.

(B) Mandatory withdrawal.

A lawyer representing a client before a tribunal, with its permission if required by its rules, shall withdraw from employment, and a lawyer representing a client in other matters shall withdraw from employment, if:

(1) He knows or it is obvious that his client is bringing the legal action, conducting the defense, or asserting a position in the litigation, or is otherwise having steps taken for him, merely for the purpose of harassing or maliciously injuring any person.

(2) He knows or it is obvious that his continued employment will result in violation of a Disciplinary Rule.

(3) His mental or physical condition renders it unreasonably difficult for him to carry out the employment effectively.

(4) He is discharged by his client.

(C) Permissive withdrawal.

If DR 2–110(B) is not applicable, a lawyer may not request permission to withdraw in matters pending before a tribunal, and may not withdraw in other matters, unless such request or such withdrawal is because:

(1) His client:

    (a) Insists upon presenting a claim or defense that is not warranted under existing law and cannot be supported by good faith argument for an extension, modification, or reversal of existing law.

    (b) Personally seeks to pursue an illegal course of conduct.

    (c) Insists that the lawyer pursue a course of conduct that is illegal or that is prohibited under the Disciplinary Rules.

    (d) By other conduct renders it unreasonably difficult for the lawyer to carry out his employment effectively.

    (e) Insists, in a matter not pending before a tribunal, that the lawyer engage in conduct that is contrary to the judgment and advice of the lawyer but not prohibited under the Disciplinary Rules.

    (f) Deliberately disregards an agreement or obligation to the lawyer as to expenses or fees.

(2) His continued employment is likely to result in a violation of a Disciplinary Rule.

(3) His inability to work with co-counsel indicates that the best interests of the client likely will be served by withdrawal.

(4) His mental or physical condition renders it difficult for him to carry out the employment effectively.

(5) His client knowingly and freely assents to termination of his employment.

(6) He believes in good faith, in a proceeding pending before a tribunal, that the tribunal will find the existence of other good cause for withdrawal.

CANON 3

A Lawyer Should Assist in Preventing the Unauthorized Practice of Law

ETHICAL CONSIDERATIONS

EC 3–1 The prohibition against the practice of law by a layman is grounded in the need of the public for integrity and competence of those who undertake to render legal services. Because of the fiduciary and personal character of the lawyer-client relationship and the inherently complex nature of our legal system, the public can better be assured of the requisite responsibility and competence if the practice of law is confined to those who are subject to the requirements and regulations imposed upon members of the legal profession.

EC 3–2 The sensitive variations in the considerations that bear on legal determinations often make it difficult even for a lawyer to exercise appropriate professional judgment, and it is therefore essential that the personal nature of the relationship of client and lawyer be preserved. Competent professional judgment is the product of a trained familiarity with law and legal processes, a disciplined, analytical approach to legal problems, and a firm ethical commitment.

EC 3–3 A non-lawyer who undertakes to handle legal matters is not governed as to integrity or legal competence by the same rules that govern the conduct of a lawyer. A lawyer is not only subject to that regulation but also is committed to high standards of ethical conduct. The public interest is best served in legal matters by a regulated profession committed to such standards. The Disciplinary Rules protect the public in that they prohibit a lawyer from seeking employment by improper overtures, from acting in cases of divided loyalties, and from submitting to the control of others in the exercise of his judgment. Moreover, a person who entrusts legal matters to a lawyer is protected by the attorney-client privilege and by the duty of the lawyer to hold inviolate the confidences and secrets of his client.

EC 3–4 A layman who seeks legal services often is not in a position to judge whether he will receive proper professional attention. The entrustment of a legal matter may well involve the confidences, the reputation, the property, the freedom, or even the life of the client. Proper protection of members of the public demands that no person be permitted to act in the confidential and demanding capacity of a lawyer unless he is subject to the regulations of the legal profession.

EC 3–5 It is neither necessary nor desirable to attempt the formulation of a single, specific definition of what constitutes the practice of law. Functionally, the practice of law relates to the rendition of services for others that call for the professional judgment of a lawyer. The essence of the professional judgment of the lawyer is his educated ability to relate the general body and philosophy of law to a specific legal problem of a client; and thus, the public interest will be better served if only lawyers are permitted to act in matters involving professional judgment. Where this professional judgment is not involved, non-lawyers, such as court clerks, police officers, abstracters, and many governmental employees, may engage in occupations that require a special knowledge of law in certain areas. But the services of a lawyer are essential in the public interest whenever the exercise of professional legal judgment is required.

EC 3–6 A lawyer often delegates tasks to clerks, secretaries, and other lay persons. Such delegation is proper if the lawyer maintains a direct relationship with his client, supervises the delegated work, and has complete professional responsibility for the work product. This delegation enables a lawyer to render legal service more economically and efficiently.

EC 3–7 The prohibition against a non-lawyer practicing law does not prevent a layman from representing himself, for then he is ordinarily exposing only himself to possible injury. The purpose of the legal profession is to make educated legal representation available to the public; but anyone who does not wish to avail himself of such representation is not required to do so. Even so, the legal profession should help members of the public to recognize legal problems and to understand why it may be unwise for them to act for themselves in matters having legal consequences.

EC 3–8 Since a lawyer should not aid or encourage a layman to practice law, he should not practice law in association with a layman or otherwise share legal fees with a layman. This does not mean, however, that the pecuniary value of the interest of a deceased lawyer in his firm or practice may not be paid to his estate or specified persons such as his widow or heirs. In like manner, profit-sharing retirement plans of a lawyer or law firm which include non-lawyer office employees are not improper. These limited exceptions to the rule against sharing legal fees with laymen are permissible since they do not aid or encourage laymen to practice law.

EC 3–9 Regulation of the practice of law is accomplished principally by the respective states. Authority to engage in the practice of law conferred in any jurisdiction is not per se a grant of the right to practice elsewhere, and it is improper for a lawyer to engage in practice where he is not permitted by law or by court order to do so. However, the demands of business and the mobility of our society pose distinct problems in the regulation of the practice of law by the states. In furtherance of the public interest, the legal profession should discourage regulation that unreasonably imposes territorial limitations upon the right of a lawyer to handle the legal affairs of his client or upon the opportunity of a client to obtain the services of a lawyer of his choice in all matters including the presentation of a contested matter in a tribunal before which the lawyer is not permanently admitted to practice.

DISCIPLINARY RULES

DR 3–101 Aiding Unauthorized Practice of Law.

(A) A lawyer shall not aid a non-lawyer in the unauthorized practice of law.

(B) A lawyer shall not practice law in a jurisdiction where to do so would be in violation of regulations of the profession in that jurisdiction.

DR 3–102 Dividing Legal Fees with a Non–Lawyer.

(A) A lawyer or law firm shall not share legal fees with a non-lawyer, except that:

(1) An agreement by a lawyer with his firm, partner, or associate may provide for the payment of money, over a reasonable period of time after his death, to his estate or to one or more specified persons.

(2) A lawyer who undertakes to complete unfinished legal business of a deceased lawyer may pay to the estate of the deceased lawyer that proportion of the total compensation which fairly represents the services rendered by the deceased lawyer.

(3) A lawyer or law firm may include non-lawyer employees in a compensation or retirement plan, even though the plan is based in whole or in part on a profit-sharing arrangement providing such plan does not circumvent another disciplinary rule.

As amended in 1980.

DR 3–103 Forming a Partnership with a Non–Lawyer.

(A) A lawyer shall not form a partnership with a non-lawyer if any of the activities of the partnership consist of the practice of law.

CANON 4

A Lawyer Should Preserve the Confidences and Secrets of a Client

ETHICAL CONSIDERATIONS

EC 4–1 Both the fiduciary relationship existing between lawyer and client and the proper functioning of the legal system require the preservation by the lawyer of confidences and secrets of one who has employed or sought to employ him. A client must feel free to discuss whatever he wishes with his lawyer and a lawyer must be equally free to obtain information beyond that volunteered by his client. A lawyer should be fully informed of all the facts of the matter he is handling in order for his client to obtain the full advantage of our legal system. It is for the lawyer in the exercise of his independent professional judgment to separate the relevant and important from the irrelevant and unimportant. The observance of the ethical obligation of a lawyer to hold inviolate the confidences and secrets of his client not only facilitates the full development of facts essential to proper representation of the client but also encourages laymen to seek early legal assistance.

EC 4–2 The obligation to protect confidences and secrets obviously does not preclude a lawyer from revealing information when his client consents after full disclosure, when necessary to perform his professional employment, when permitted by a Disciplinary Rule, or when required by law. Unless the client otherwise directs, a lawyer may disclose the affairs of his client to partners or associates of his firm. It is a matter of common knowledge that the normal operation of a law office exposes confidential professional information to non-lawyer employees of the office, particularly secretaries and those having access to the files; and this obligates a lawyer to exercise care in selecting and training his employees so that the sanctity of all confidences and secrets of his clients may be preserved. If the obligation extends to two or more clients as to the same information, a lawyer should obtain the permission of all before revealing the information. A lawyer must always be sensitive to the rights and wishes of his client and act scrupulously in the making of decisions which may involve the disclosure of information obtained in his professional relationship. Thus, in the absence of consent of his client after full disclosure, a lawyer should not associate another lawyer in the handling of a matter; nor should he, in the absence of consent, seek counsel from another lawyer if there is a reasonable possibility that the identity of the client or his confidences or secrets would be revealed to such lawyer. Both social amenities and professional duty should cause a lawyer to shun indiscreet conversations concerning his clients.

EC 4–3 Unless the client otherwise directs, it is not improper for a lawyer to give limited information from his files to an outside agency necessary for statistical, bookkeeping, accounting, data processing, banking, printing, or other legitimate purposes, provided he exercises due care in the selection of the agency and warns the agency that the information must be kept confidential.

EC 4–4 The attorney-client privilege is more limited than the ethical obligation of a lawyer to guard the confidence and secrets of his client. This ethical precept, unlike the evidentiary privilege, exists without regard to the nature or source of information or the fact that others share the knowledge. A lawyer should endeavor to act in a manner which preserves the evidentiary privilege; for example, he should avoid professional discussions in the presence of persons to whom the privilege does not extend. A lawyer owes an obligation to advise the client of the attorney-client privilege and timely to assert the privilege unless it is waived by the client.

EC 4–5 A lawyer should not use information acquired in the course of the representation of a client to the disadvantage of the client and a lawyer should not use, except with the consent of his client after full disclosure, such information for his own purposes. Likewise, a lawyer should be diligent in his efforts to prevent the misuse of such information by his employees and associates. Care should be exercised by a lawyer to prevent the disclosure of the confidences and secrets of one client to another, and no employment should be accepted that might require such disclosure.

EC 4–6 The obligation of a lawyer to preserve the confidences and secrets of his client continues after the termination of his employment. Thus a lawyer should not attempt to sell a law practice as a going business because, among other reasons, to do so would involve the disclosure of confidences and secrets. A lawyer should also provide for the protection of the confidences and secrets of his client following the termination of the practice of the lawyer, whether termination is due to death, disability, or retirement. For example, a lawyer might provide for the personal papers of the client to be returned to him and for the papers of the lawyer to be delivered to another lawyer or to be destroyed. In determining the method of disposition, the instructions and wishes of the client should be a dominant consideration.

DISCIPLINARY RULES

DR 4–101 Preservation of Confidences and Secrets of a Client.

(A) **"Confidence" refers to information protected by the attorney-client privilege under applicable law, and "secret" refers to other information gained in the professional relationship that the client has requested be held inviolate or the disclosure of which would be embarrassing or would be likely to be detrimental to the client.**

(B) **Except when permitted under DR 4–101(C), a lawyer shall not knowingly:**

(1) **Reveal a confidence or secret of his client.**

(2) **Use a confidence or secret of his client to the disadvantage of the client.**

(3) **Use a confidence or secret of his client for the advantage of himself or of a third person, unless the client consents after full disclosure.**

(C) **A lawyer may reveal:**

(1) **Confidences or secrets with the consent of the client or clients affected, but only after a full disclosure to them.**

(2) **Confidences or secrets when permitted under Disciplinary Rules or required by law or court order.**

(3) **The intention of his client to commit a crime and the information necessary to prevent the crime.**

(4) **Confidences or secrets necessary to establish or collect his fee or to defend himself or his employees or associates against an accusation of wrongful conduct.**

(D) **A lawyer shall exercise reasonable care to prevent his employees, associates, and others whose services are utilized by him from disclosing or using confidences or secrets of a client, except that a lawyer may reveal the information allowed by DR 4–101(C) through an employee.**

CANON 5

A Lawyer Should Exercise Independent Professional Judgment on Behalf of a Client

ETHICAL CONSIDERATIONS

EC 5–1 The professional judgment of a lawyer should be exercised, within the bounds of the law, solely for the benefit of his client and free of compromising influences and loyalties. Neither his personal interests, the interests of other clients, nor the desires of third persons should be permitted to dilute his loyalty to his client.

Interests of a Lawyer That May Affect His Judgment

EC 5–2 A lawyer should not accept proffered employment if his personal interests or desires will, or there is a reasonable probability that they will, affect adversely the advice to be given or services to be rendered the prospective client. After accepting employment, a lawyer carefully should refrain from acquiring a property right or assuming a position that would tend to make his judgment less protective of the interests of his client.

EC 5–3 The self-interest of a lawyer resulting from his ownership of property in which his client also has an interest or which may affect property of his client may interfere with the exercise of free judgment on behalf of his client. If such interference would occur with respect to a prospective client, a lawyer should decline employment proffered by him. After accepting employment, a lawyer should not acquire property rights that would adversely affect his professional judgment in the representation of his client. Even if the property interests of a lawyer do not presently interfere with the exercise of his independent judgment, but the likelihood of interference can reasonably be foreseen by him, a lawyer should explain the situation to his client and should decline employment or withdraw unless the client consents to the continuance of the relationship after full disclosure. A lawyer should not seek to persuade his client to permit him to invest in an undertaking of his client nor make improper use of his professional relationship to influence his client to invest in an enterprise in which the lawyer is interested.

EC 5–4 If, in the course of his representation of a client, a lawyer is permitted to receive from his client a beneficial ownership in publication rights relating to the subject matter of the employment, he may be tempted to subordinate the interests of his client to his own anticipated pecuniary gain. For example, a lawyer in a criminal case who obtains from his client television, radio, motion picture, newspaper, magazine, book, or other publication rights with respect to the case may be influenced, consciously or unconsciously, to a course of conduct that will enhance the value of his publication rights to the prejudice of his client. To prevent these potentially differing interests, such arrangements should be scrupulously avoided prior to the termination of all aspects of the matter giving rise to the employment, even though his employment has previously ended.

EC 5–5 A lawyer should not suggest to his client that a gift be made to himself or for his benefit. If a lawyer accepts a gift from his client, he is peculiarly susceptible to the charge that he unduly influenced or over-reached the client. If a client voluntarily offers to make a gift to his lawyer, the lawyer may accept the gift, but before doing so, he should urge that his client secure disinterested advice from an independent, competent person who is cognizant of all the circumstances. Other than in exceptional circumstances, a lawyer should insist that an instrument in which his client desires to name him beneficially be prepared by another lawyer selected by the client.

EC 5–6 A lawyer should not consciously influence a client to name him as executor, trustee, or lawyer in an instrument. In those cases where a client wishes to name his lawyer as such, care should be taken by the lawyer to avoid even the appearance of impropriety.

EC 5–7 The possibility of an adverse effect upon the exercise of free judgment by a lawyer on behalf of his client during litigation generally makes it undesirable for the lawyer to acquire a proprietary interest in the cause of his client or otherwise to become financially interested in the outcome of the litigation. However, it is not improper for a lawyer to protect his right to collect a fee for his services by the assertion of legally permissible liens, even though by doing so he may acquire an interest in the outcome of litigation. Although a contingent fee arrangement gives a lawyer a financial interest in the outcome of litigation, a reasonable contingent fee is permissible in civil cases because it may be the only means by which a layman can obtain the services of a lawyer of his choice. But a lawyer, because he is in a better position to evaluate a cause of action, should enter into a continent fee arrangement only in those instances where the arrangement will be beneficial to the client.

EC 5–8 A financial interest in the outcome of litigation also results if monetary advances are made by the lawyer to his client. Although this assistance generally is not encouraged, there are instances when it is not improper to make loans to a client. For example, the advancing or guaranteeing of payment of the costs and expenses of litigation by a lawyer may be the only way a client can enforce his cause of action, but the ultimate liability for such costs and expenses must be that of the client.

EC 5–9 Occasionally a lawyer is called upon to decide in a particular case whether he will be a witness or an advocate. If a lawyer is both counsel and witness, he becomes more easily impeachable for interest and thus may be a less effective witness. Conversely, the opposing counsel may be handicapped in challenging the credibility of the lawyer when the lawyer also appears as an advocate in the case. An advocate who becomes a witness is in the unseemly and ineffective position of arguing his own credibility. The roles of an advocate and of a witness are inconsistent; the function of an advocate is to advance or argue the cause of another, while that of a witness is to state facts objectively.

EC 5-10 Problems incident to the lawyer-witness relationship arise at different stages; they relate either to whether a lawyer should accept employment or should withdraw from employment. Regardless of when the problem arises, his decision is to be governed by the same basic considerations. It is not objectionable for a lawyer who is a potential witness to be an advocate if it is unlikely that he will be called as a witness because his testimony would be merely cumulative or if his testimony will relate only to an uncontested issue. In the exceptional situation where it will be manifestly unfair to the client for the lawyer to refuse employment or to withdraw when he will likely be a witness on a contested issue, he may serve as advocate even though he may be a witness. In making such decision, he should determine the personal or financial sacrifice of the client that may result from his refusal of employment or withdrawal therefrom, the materiality of his testimony, and the effectiveness of his representation in view of his personal involvement. In weighing these factors, it should be clear that refusal or withdrawal will impose an unreasonable hardship upon the client before the lawyer accepts or continues the employment. Where the question arises, doubts should be resolved in favor of the lawyer testifying and against his becoming or continuing as an advocate.

EC 5-11 A lawyer should not permit his personal interests to influence his advice relative to a suggestion by his client that additional counsel be employed. In like manner, his personal interests should not deter him from suggesting that additional counsel be employed; on the contrary, he should be alert to the desirability of recommending additional counsel when, in his judgment, the proper representation of his client requires it. However, a lawyer should advise his client not to employ additional counsel suggested by the client if the lawyer believes that such employment would be a disservice to the client, and he should disclose the reasons for his belief.

EC 5-12 Inability of co-counsel to agree on a matter vital to the representation of their client requires that their disagreement be submitted by them jointly to their client for his resolution, and the decision of the client shall control the action to be taken.

EC 5-13 A lawyer should not maintain membership in or be influenced by any organization of employees that undertakes to prescribe, direct, or suggest when or how he should fulfill his professional obligations to a person or organization that employs him as a lawyer. Although it is not necessarily improper for a lawyer employed by a corporation or similar entity to be a member of an organization of employees, he should be vigilant to safeguard his fidelity as a lawyer to his employer, free from outside influences.

Interests of Multiple Clients

EC 5-14 Maintaining the independence of professional judgment required of a lawyer precludes his acceptance or continuation of employment that will adversely affect his judgment on behalf of or dilute his loyalty to a client. This problem arises whenever a lawyer is asked to represent two or more clients who may have differing interests, whether such interests be conflicting, inconsistent, diverse, or otherwise discordant.

EC 5-15 If a lawyer is requested to undertake or to continue representation of multiple clients having potentially differing interests, he must weigh carefully the possibility that his judgment may be impaired or his loyalty divided if he accepts or continues the employment. He should resolve all doubts against the propriety of the representation. A lawyer should never represent in litigation multiple clients with differing interests; and there are few situations in which he would be justified in representing in litigation multiple clients with potentially differing interests. If a lawyer accepted such employment and the interests did become actually differing, he would have to withdraw from employment with likelihood of resulting hardship on the clients; and for this reason it is preferable that he refuse the employment initially. On the other hand, there are many instances in which a lawyer may properly serve multiple clients having potentially differing interests in matters not involving litigation. If the interests vary only slightly, it is generally likely that the lawyer will not be subjected to an adverse influence and that he can retain his independent judgment on behalf of each client; and if the interests become differing, withdrawal is less likely to have a disruptive effect upon the causes of his clients.

EC 5-16 In those instances in which a lawyer is justified in representing two or more clients having differing interests, it is nevertheless essential that each client be given the opportunity to evaluate his need for representation free of any potential conflict and to obtain other counsel if he so desires. Thus before a lawyer may represent multiple clients, he should explain fully to each client the implications of the common representation and should accept or continue employment only if the clients consent. If there are present other circumstances that might cause any of the multiple clients to question the undivided loyalty of the lawyer, he should also advise all of the clients of those circumstances.

EC 5–17 Typically recurring situations involving potentially differing interests are those in which a lawyer is asked to represent co-defendants in a criminal case, co-plaintiffs in a personal injury case, an insured and his insurer, and beneficiaries of the estate of a decedent. Whether a lawyer can fairly and adequately protect the interests of multiple clients in these and similar situations depends upon an analysis of each case. In certain circumstances, there may exist little chance of the judgment of the lawyer being adversely affected by the slight possibility that the interests will become actually differing; in other circumstances, the chance of adverse effect upon his judgment is not unlikely.

EC 5–18 A lawyer employed or retained by a corporation or similar entity owes his allegiance to the entity and not to a stockholder, director, officer, employee, representative, or other person connected with the entity. In advising the entity, a lawyer should keep paramount its interests and his professional judgment should not be influenced by the personal desires of any person or organization. Occasionally a lawyer for an entity is requested by a stockholder, director, officer, employee, representative, or other person connected with the entity to represent him in an individual capacity; in such case the lawyer may serve the individual only if the lawyer is convinced that differing interests are not present.

EC 5–19 A lawyer may represent several clients whose interests are not actually or potentially differing. Nevertheless, he should explain any circumstances that might cause a client to question his undivided loyalty. Regardless of the belief of a lawyer that he may properly represent multiple clients, he must defer to a client who holds the contrary belief and withdraw from representation of that client.

EC 5–20 A lawyer is often asked to serve as an impartial arbitrator or mediator in matters which involve present or former clients. He may serve in either capacity if he first discloses such present or former relationships. After a lawyer has undertaken to act as an impartial arbitrator or mediator, he should not thereafter represent in the dispute any of the parties involved.

Desires of Third Persons

EC 5–21 The obligation of a lawyer to exercise professional judgment solely on behalf of his client requires that he disregard the desires of others that might impair his free judgment. The desires of a third person will seldom adversely affect a lawyer unless that person is in a position to exert strong economic, political, or social pressures upon the lawyer. These influences are often subtle, and a lawyer must be alert to their existence. A lawyer subjected to outside pressures should make full disclosure of them to his client; and if he or his client believes that the effectiveness of his representation has been or will be impaired thereby, the lawyer should take proper steps to withdraw from representation of his client.

EC 5–22 Economic, political, or social pressures by third persons are less likely to impinge upon the independent judgment of a lawyer in a matter in which he is compensated directly by his client and his professional work is exclusively with his client. On the other hand, if a lawyer is compensated from a source other than his client, he may feel a sense of responsibility to someone other than his client.

EC 5–23 A person or organization that pays or furnishes lawyers to represent others possesses a potential power to exert strong pressures against the independent judgment of those lawyers. Some employers may be interested in furthering their own economic, political, or social goals without regard to the professional responsibility of the lawyer to his individual client. Others maybe far more concerned with establishment or extension of legal principles than in the immediate protection of the rights of the lawyer's individual client. On some occasions, decisions on priority of work may be made by the employer rather than the lawyer with the result that prosecution of work already undertaken for clients is postponed to their detriment. Similarly, an employer may seek, consciously or unconsciously, to further its own economic interests through the action of the lawyers employed by it. Since a lawyer must always be free to exercise his professional judgment without regard to the interests or motives of a third person, the lawyer who is employed by one to represent another must constantly guard against erosion of his professional freedom.

EC 5–24 To assist a lawyer in preserving his professional independence, a number of courses are available to him. For example, a lawyer should not practice with or in the form of a professional legal corporation, even though the corporate form is permitted by law, if any director, officer, or stockholder of it is a non-lawyer. Although a lawyer may be employed by a business corporation with non-lawyers serving as directors or officers, and they necessarily have the right to make decisions of business policy, a lawyer must decline to accept direction of his professional judgment from any layman. Various types of legal aid offices are administered by boards of directors composed of lawyers and laymen. A lawyer should not accept employment from such an organization unless the board sets only broad policies and there is no interference in the relationship of the lawyer and the individual client he serves. Where a lawyer is employed by an organization, a written agreement that defines the relationship between him and the organization and provides for his independence is desirable since it may serve to prevent misunderstanding as to their respective roles. Although other innovations in the means of supplying legal counsel may develop, the responsibility of the lawyer to maintain his professional independence remains constant, and the legal profession must insure that changing circumstances do not result in loss of the professional independence of the lawyer.

DISCIPLINARY RULES

DR 5–101   Refusing Employment When the Interests of the Lawyer May Impair His Independent Professional Judgment.

(A) Except with the consent of his client after full disclosure, a lawyer shall not accept employment if the exercise of his professional judgment on behalf of his client will be or reasonably may be affected by his own financial, business, property, or personal interests.

(B) A lawyer shall not accept employment in contemplated or pending litigation if he knows or it is obvious that he or a lawyer in his firm ought to be called as a witness, except that he may undertake the employment and he or a lawyer in his firm may testify:

   (1) If the testimony will relate solely to an uncontested matter.

   (2) If the testimony will relate solely to a matter of formality and there is no reason to believe that substantial evidence will be offered in opposition to the testimony.

   (3) If the testimony will relate solely to the nature and value of legal services rendered in the case by the lawyer or his firm to the client.

   (4) As to any matter, if refusal would work a substantial hardship on the client because of the distinctive value of the lawyer or his firm as counsel in the particular case.

DR 5–102   Withdrawal as Counsel When the Lawyer Becomes a Witness.

(A) If, after undertaking employment in contemplated or pending litigation, a lawyer learns or it is obvious that he or a lawyer in his firm ought to be called as a witness on behalf of his client, he shall withdraw from the conduct of the trial and his firm, if any, shall not continue representation in the trial, except that he may continue the representation and he or a lawyer in his firm may testify in the circumstances enumerated in DR 5–101(B)(1) through (4).

(B) If, after undertaking employment in contemplated or pending litigation, a lawyer learns or it is obvious that he or a lawyer in his firm may be called as a witness other than on behalf of his client, he may continue the representation until it is apparent that his testimony is or may be prejudicial to his client.

DR 5–103   Avoiding Acquisition of Interest in Litigation.

(A) A lawyer shall not acquire a proprietary interest in the cause of action or subject matter of litigation he is conducting for a client, except that he may:

   (1) Acquire a lien granted by law to secure his fee or expenses.

   (2) Contract with a client for a reasonable contingent fee in a civil case.

(B) While representing a client in connection with contemplated or pending litigation, a lawyer shall not advance or guarantee financial assistance to his client, except that a lawyer may advance or guarantee the expenses of litigation, including court costs, expenses of investigation, expenses of medical examination, and costs of obtaining and presenting evidence, provided the client remains ultimately liable for such expenses.

DR 5–104　Limiting Business Relations with a Client.

(A) A lawyer shall not enter into a business transaction with a client if they have differing interests therein and if the client expects the lawyer to exercise his professional judgment therein for the protection of the client, unless the client has consented after full disclosure.

(B) Prior to conclusion of all aspects of the matter giving rise to his employment, a lawyer shall not enter into any arrangement or understanding with a client or a prospective client by which he acquires an interest in publication rights with respect to the subject matter of his employment or proposed employment.

DR 5–105　Refusing to Accept or Continue Employment if the Interests of Another Client May Impair the Independent Professional Judgment of the Lawyer.

(A) A lawyer shall decline proffered employment if the exercise of his independent professional judgment in behalf of a client will be or is likely to be adversely affected by the acceptance of the proffered employment, or if it would be likely to involve him in representing differing interests, except to the extent permitted under DR 5–105(C).

(B) A lawyer shall not continue multiple employment if the exercise of his independent professional judgment in behalf of a client will be or is likely to be adversely affected by his representation of another client, or if it would be likely to involve him in representing differing interests, except to the extent permitted under DR 5–105(C).

(C) In the situations covered by DR 5–105(A) and (B), a lawyer may represent multiple clients if it is obvious that he can adequately represent the interest of each and if each consents to the representation after full disclosure of the possible effect of such representation on the exercise of his independent professional judgment on behalf of each.

(D) If a lawyer is required to decline employment or to withdraw from employment under a Disciplinary Rule, no partner or associate, or any other lawyer affiliated with him or his firm may accept or continue such employment.

As amended in 1974.

DR 5–106　Settling Similar Claims of Clients.

(A) A lawyer who represents two or more clients shall not make or participate in the making of an aggregate settlement of the claims of or against his clients, unless each client has consented to the settlement after being advised of the existence and nature of all the claims involved in the proposed settlement, of the total amount of the settlement, and of the participation of each person in the settlement.

DR 5–107　Avoiding Influence by Others Than the Client.

(A) Except with the consent of his client after full disclosure, a lawyer shall not:

　(1) Accept compensation for his legal services from one other than his client.

　(2) Accept from one other than his client any thing of value related to his representation of or his employment by his client.

(B) A lawyer shall not permit a person who recommends, employs, or pays him to render legal services for another to direct or regulate his professional judgment in rendering such legal services.

(C) A lawyer shall not practice with or in the form of a professional corporation or association authorized to practice law for a profit, if:

　(1) A non-lawyer owns any interest therein, except that a fiduciary representative of the estate of a lawyer may hold the stock or interest of the lawyer for a reasonable time during administration;

　(2) A non-lawyer is a corporate director or officer thereof; or

　(3) A non-lawyer has the right to direct or control the professional judgment of a lawyer.

CANON 6

A Lawyer Should Represent a Client Competently

ETHICAL CONSIDERATIONS

EC 6–1 Because of his vital role in the legal process, a lawyer should act with competence and proper care in representing clients. He should strive to become and remain proficient in his practice and should accept employment only in matters which he is or intends to become competent to handle.

EC 6–2 A lawyer is aided in attaining and maintaining his competence by keeping abreast of current legal literature and developments, participating in continuing legal education programs, concentrating in particular areas of the law, and by utilizing other available means. He has the additional ethical obligation to assist in improving the legal profession, and he may do so by participating in bar activities intended to advance the quality and standards of members of the profession. Of particular importance is the careful training of his younger associates and the giving of sound guidance to all lawyers who consult him. In short, a lawyer should strive at all levels to aid the legal profession in advancing the highest possible standards of integrity and competence and to meet those standards himself.

EC 6–3 While the licensing of a lawyer is evidence that he has met the standards then prevailing for admission to the bar, a lawyer generally should not accept employment in any area of the law in which he is not qualified. However, he may accept such employment if in good faith he expects to become qualified through study and investigation, as long as such preparation would not result in unreasonable delay or expense to his client. Proper preparation and representation may require the association by the lawyer of professionals in other disciplines. A lawyer offered employment in a matter in which he is not and does not expect to become so qualified should either decline the employment or, with the consent of his client, accept the employment and associate a lawyer who is competent in the matter.

EC 6–4 Having undertaken representation, a lawyer should use proper care to safeguard the interests of his client. If a lawyer has accepted employment in a matter beyond his competence but in which he expected to become competent, he should diligently undertake the work and study necessary to qualify himself. In addition to being qualified to handle a particular matter, his obligation to his client requires him to prepare adequately for and give appropriate attention to his legal work.

EC 6–5 A lawyer should have pride in his professional endeavors. His obligation to act competently calls for higher motivation than that arising from fear of civil liability or disciplinary penalty.

EC 6–6 A lawyer should not seek, by contract or other means, to limit his individual liability to his client for his malpractice. A lawyer who handles the affairs of his client properly has no need to attempt to limit his liability for his professional activities and one who does not handle the affairs of his client properly should not be permitted to do so. A lawyer who is a stockholder in or is associated with a professional legal corporation may, however, limit his liability for malpractice of his associates in the corporation, but only to the extent permitted by law.

DISCIPLINARY RULES

DR 6–101 Failing to Act Competently.

(A) A lawyer shall not:

(1) Handle a legal matter which he knows or should know that he is not competent to handle, without associating with him a lawyer who is competent to handle it.

(2) Handle a legal matter without preparation adequate in the circumstances.

(3) Neglect a legal matter entrusted to him.

DR 6–102 Limiting Liability to Client.

(A) A lawyer shall not attempt to exonerate himself from or limit his liability to his client for his personal malpractice.

CANON 7

A Lawyer Should Represent a Client Zealously Within the Bounds of the Law

ETHICAL CONSIDERATIONS

EC 7–1 The duty of a lawyer, both to his client and to the legal system, is to represent his client zealously within the bounds of the law, which includes Disciplinary Rules and enforceable professional regulations. The professional responsibility of a lawyer derives from his membership in a profession which has the duty of assisting members of the public to secure and protect available legal rights and benefits. In our government of laws and not of men, each member of our society is entitled to have his conduct judged and regulated in accordance with the law; to seek any lawful objective through legally permissible means; and to present for adjudication any lawful claim, issue, or defense.

EC 7–2 The bounds of the law in a given case are often difficult to ascertain. The language of legislative enactments and judicial opinions may be uncertain as applied to varying factual situations. The limits and specific meaning of apparently relevant law may be made doubtful by changing or developing constitutional interpretations, inadequately expressed statutes or judicial opinions, and changing public and judicial attitudes. Certainty of law ranges from well-settled rules through areas of conflicting authority to areas without precedent.

EC 7–3 Where the bounds of law are uncertain, the action of a lawyer may depend on whether he is serving as advocate or adviser. A lawyer may serve simultaneously as both advocate and adviser, but the two roles are essentially different. In asserting a position on behalf of his client, an advocate for the most part deals with past conduct and must take the facts as he finds them. By contrast, a lawyer serving as adviser primarily assists his client in determining the course of future conduct and relationships. While serving as advocate, a lawyer should resolve in favor of his client doubts as to the bounds of the law. In serving a client as adviser, a lawyer in appropriate circumstances should give his professional opinion as to what the ultimate decisions of the courts would likely be as to the applicable law.

Duty of the Lawyer to a Client

EC 7–4 The advocate may urge any permissible construction of the law favorable to his client, without regard to his professional opinion as to the likelihood that the construction will ultimately prevail. His conduct is within the bounds of the law, and therefore permissible, if the position taken is supported by the law or is supportable by a good faith argument for an extension, modification, or reversal of the law. However, a lawyer is not justified in asserting a position in litigation that is frivolous.

EC 7–5 A lawyer as adviser furthers the interest of his client by giving his professional opinion as to what he believes would likely be the ultimate decision of the courts on the matter at hand and by informing his client of the practical effect of such decision. He may continue in the representation of his client even though his client has elected to

pursue a course of conduct contrary to the advice of the lawyer so long as he does not thereby knowingly assist the client to engage in illegal conduct or to take a frivolous legal position. A lawyer should never encourage or aid his client to commit criminal acts or counsel his client on how to violate the law and avoid punishment therefor.

EC 7–6 Whether the proposed action of a lawyer is within the bounds of the law may be a perplexing question when his client is contemplating a course of conduct having legal consequences that vary according to the client's intent, motive, or desires at the time of the action. Often a lawyer is asked to assist his client in developing evidence relevant to the state of mind of the client at a particular time. He may properly assist his client in the development and preservation of evidence of existing motive, intent, or desire; obviously, he may not do anything furthering the creation or preservation of false evidence. In many cases a lawyer may not be certain as to the state of mind of his client, and in those situations he should resolve reasonable doubts in favor of his client.

EC 7–7 In certain areas of legal representation not affecting the merits of the cause or substantially prejudicing the rights of a client, a lawyer is entitled to make decisions on his own. But otherwise the authority to make decisions is exclusively that of the client and, if made within the framework of the law, such decisions are binding on his lawyer. As typical examples in civil cases, it is for the client to decide whether he will accept a settlement offer or whether he will waive his right to plead an affirmative defense. A defense lawyer in a criminal case has the duty to advise his client fully on whether a particular plea to a charge appears to be desirable and as to the prospects of success on appeal, but it is for the client to decide what plea should be entered and whether an appeal should be taken.

EC 7–8 A lawyer should exert his best efforts to insure that decisions of his client are made only after the client has been informed of relevant considerations. A lawyer ought to initiate this decision-making process if the client does not do so. Advice of a lawyer to his client need not be confined to purely legal considerations. A lawyer should advise his client of the possible effect of each legal alternative. A lawyer should bring to bear upon this decision-making process the fullness of his experience as well as his objective viewpoint. In assisting his client to reach a proper decision, it is often desirable for a lawyer to point out those factors which may lead to a decision that is morally just as well as legally permissible. He may emphasize the possibility of harsh consequences that might result from assertion of legally permissible positions. In the final analysis, however, the lawyer should always remember that the decision whether to forego legally available objectives or methods because of non-legal factors is ultimately for the client and not for himself. In the event that the client in a non-adjudicatory matter insists upon a course of conduct that is contrary to the judgment and advice of the lawyer but not prohibited by Disciplinary Rules, the lawyer may withdraw from the employment.

EC 7–9 In the exercise of his professional judgment on those decisions which are for his determination in the handling of a legal matter, a lawyer should always act in a manner consistent with the best interests of his client. However, when an action in the best interest of his client seems to him to be unjust, he may ask his client for permission to forego such action.

EC 7–10 The duty of a lawyer to represent his client with zeal does not militate against his concurrent obligation to treat with consideration all persons involved in the legal process and to avoid the infliction of needless harm.

EC 7–11 The responsibilities of a lawyer may vary according to the intelligence, experience, mental condition or age of a client, the obligation of a public officer, or the nature of a particular proceeding. Examples include the representation of an illiterate or an incompetent, service as a public prosecutor or other government lawyer, and appearances before administrative and legislative bodies.

EC 7–12 Any mental or physical condition of a client that renders him incapable of making a considered judgment on his own behalf casts additional responsibilities upon his lawyer. Where an incompetent is acting through a guardian or other legal representative, a lawyer must look to such representative for those decisions which are normally the prerogative of the client to make. If a client under disability has no legal representative, his lawyer may be compelled in court proceedings to make decisions on behalf of the client. If the client is capable of understanding the matter in question or of contributing to the advancement of his interests, regardless of whether he is legally disqualified from performing certain acts, the lawyer should obtain from him all possible aid. If the disability of a client and the lack of a legal representative compel the lawyer to make decisions for his client, the lawyer should consider all circum-

stances then prevailing and act with care to safeguard and advance the interests of his client. But obviously a lawyer cannot perform any act or make any decision which the law requires his client to perform or make, either acting for himself if competent, or by a duly constituted representative if legally incompetent.

EC 7–13 The responsibility of a public prosecutor differs from that of the usual advocate; his duty is to seek justice, not merely to convict. This special duty exists because: (1) the prosecutor represents the sovereign and therefore should use restraint in the discretionary exercise of governmental powers, such as in the selection of cases to prosecute; (2) during trial the prosecutor is not only an advocate but he also may make decisions normally made by an individual client, and those affecting the public interest should be fair to all; and (3) in our system of criminal justice the accused is to be given the benefit of all reasonable doubts. With respect to evidence and witnesses, the prosecutor has responsibilities different from those of a lawyer in private practice: the prosecutor should make timely disclosure to the defense of available evidence, known to him, that tends to negate the guilt of the accused, mitigate the degree of the offense, or reduce the punishment. Further, a prosecutor should not intentionally avoid pursuit of evidence merely because he believes it will damage the prosecutor's case or aid the accused.

EC 7–14 A government lawyer who has discretionary power relative to litigation should refrain from instituting or continuing litigation that is obviously unfair. A government lawyer not having such discretionary power who believes there is lack of merit in a controversy submitted to him should so advise his superiors and recommend the avoidance of unfair litigation. A government lawyer in a civil action or administrative proceeding has the responsibility to seek justice and to develop a full and fair record, and he should not use his position or the economic power of the government to harass parties or to bring about unjust settlements or results.

EC 7–15 The nature and purpose of proceedings before administrative agencies vary widely. The proceedings may be legislative or quasi-judicial, or a combination of both. They may be *ex parte* in character, in which event they may originate either at the instance of the agency or upon motion of an interested party. The scope of an inquiry may be purely investigative or it may be truly adversary looking toward the adjudication of specific rights of a party or of classes of parties. The foregoing are but examples of some of the types of proceedings conducted by administrative agencies. A lawyer appearing before an administrative agency, regardless of the nature of the proceeding it is conducting, has the continuing duty to advance the cause of his client within the bounds of the law. Where the applicable rules of the agency impose specific obligations upon a lawyer, it is his duty to comply therewith, unless the lawyer has a legitimate basis for challenging the validity thereof. In all appearances before administrative agencies, a lawyer should identify himself, his client if identity of his client is not privileged, and the representative nature of his appearance. It is not improper, however, for a lawyer to seek from an agency information available to the public without identifying his client.

EC 7–16 The primary business of a legislative body is to enact laws rather than to adjudicate controversies, although on occasion the activities of a legislative body may take on the characteristics of an adversary proceeding, particularly in investigative and impeachment matters. The role of a lawyer supporting or opposing proposed legislation normally is quite different from his role in representing a person under investigation or on trial by a legislative body. When a lawyer appears in connection with proposed legislation, he seeks to affect the lawmaking process, but when he appears on behalf of a client in investigatory or impeachment proceedings, he is concerned with the protection of the rights of his client. In either event, he should identify himself and his client, if identity of his client is not privileged, and should comply with applicable laws and legislative rules.

EC 7–17 The obligation of loyalty to his client applies only to a lawyer in the discharge of his professional duties and implies no obligation to adopt a personal viewpoint favorable to the interests or desires of his client. While a lawyer must act always with circumspection in order that his conduct will not adversely affect the rights of a client in a matter he is then handling, he may take positions on public issues and espouse legal reforms he favors without regard to the individual views of any client.

EC 7–18 The legal system in its broadest sense functions best when persons in need of legal advice or assistance are represented by their own counsel. For this reason a lawyer should not communicate on the subject matter of the representation of his client with a person he knows to be represented in the matter by a lawyer, unless pursuant to law or rule of court or unless he has the consent of the lawyer for that person. If one is not represented by counsel, a lawyer representing another may have to deal directly with the unrepresented person; in such an instance, a lawyer should not undertake to give advice to the person who is attempting to represent himself, except that he may advise him to obtain a lawyer.

Duty of the Lawyer to the Adversary System of Justice

EC 7–19 Our legal system provides for the adjudication of disputes governed by the rules of substantive, evidentiary, and procedural law. An adversary presentation counters the natural human tendency to judge too swiftly in terms of the familiar that which is not yet fully known; the advocate, by his zealous preparation and presentation of facts and law, enables the tribunal to come to the hearing with an open and neutral mind and to render impartial judgments. The duty of a lawyer to his client and his duty to the legal system are the same: to represent his client zealously within the bounds of the law.

EC 7–20 In order to function properly, our adjudicative process requires an informed, impartial tribunal capable of administering justice promptly and efficiently according to procedures that command public confidence and respect. Not only must there be competent, adverse presentation of evidence and issues, but a tribunal must be aided by rules appropriate to an effective and dignified process. The procedures under which tribunals operate in our adversary system have been prescribed largely by legislative enactments, court rules and decisions, and administrative rules. Through the years certain concepts of proper professional conduct have become rules of law applicable to the adversary adjudicative process. Many of these concepts are the bases for standards of professional conduct set forth in the Disciplinary Rules.

EC 7–21 The civil adjudicative process is primarily designed for the settlement of disputes between parties, while the criminal process is designed for the protection of society as a whole. Threatening to use, or using, the criminal process to coerce adjustment of private civil claims or controversies is a subversion of that process; further, the person against whom the criminal process is so misused may be deterred from asserting his legal rights and thus the usefulness of the civil process in settling private disputes is impaired. As in all cases of abuse of judicial process, the improper use of criminal process tends to diminish public confidence in our legal system.

EC 7–22 Respect for judicial rulings is essential to the proper administration of justice; however, a litigant or his lawyer may, in good faith and within the framework of the law, take steps to test the correctness of a ruling of a tribunal.

EC 7–23 The complexity of law often makes it difficult for a tribunal to be fully informed unless the pertinent law is presented by the lawyers in the cause. A tribunal that is fully informed on the applicable law is better able to make a fair and accurate determination of the matter before it. The adversary system contemplates that each lawyer will present and argue the existing law in the light most favorable to his client. Where a lawyer knows of legal authority in the controlling jurisdiction directly adverse to the position of his client, he should inform the tribunal of its existence unless his adversary has done so; but, having made such disclosure, he may challenge its soundness in whole or in part.

EC 7–24 In order to bring about just and informed decisions, evidentiary and procedural rules have been established by tribunals to permit the inclusion of relevant evidence and argument and the exclusion of all other considerations. The expression by a lawyer of his personal opinion as to the justness of a cause, as to the credibility of a witness, as to the culpability of a civil litigant, or as to the guilt or innocence of an accused is not a proper subject for argument to the trier of fact. It is improper as to factual matters because admissible evidence possessed by a lawyer should be presented only as sworn testimony. It is improper as to all other matters because, were the rule otherwise, the silence of a lawyer on a given occasion could be construed unfavorably to his client. However, a lawyer may argue, on his analysis of the evidence, for any position or conclusion with respect to any of the foregoing matters.

EC 7–25 Rules of evidence and procedure are designed to lead to just decisions and are part of the framework of the law. Thus while a lawyer may take steps in good faith and within the framework of the law to test the validity of rules, he is not justified in consciously violating such rules and he should be diligent in his efforts to guard against his unintentional violation of them. As examples, a lawyer should subscribe to or verify only those pleadings that he believes are in compliance with applicable law and rules; a lawyer should not make any prefatory statement before a tribunal in regard to the purported facts of the case on trial unless he believes that his statement will be supported by admissible evidence; a lawyer should not

ask a witness a question solely for the purpose of harassing or embarrassing him; and a lawyer should not by subterfuge put before a jury matters which it cannot properly consider.

EC 7–26 The law and Disciplinary Rules prohibit the use of fraudulent, false, or perjured testimony or evidence. A lawyer who knowingly participates in introduction of such testimony or evidence is subject to discipline. A lawyer should, however, present any admissible evidence his client desires to have presented unless he knows, or from facts within his knowledge should know, that such testimony or evidence is false, fraudulent, or perjured.

EC 7–27 Because it interferes with the proper administration of justice, a lawyer should not suppress evidence that he or his client has a legal obligation to reveal or produce. In like manner, a lawyer should not advise or cause a person to secrete himself or to leave the jurisdiction of a tribunal for the purpose of making him unavailable as a witness therein.

EC 7–28 Witnesses should always testify truthfully and should be free from any financial inducements that might tempt them to do otherwise. A lawyer should not pay or agree to pay a non-expert witness an amount in excess of reimbursement for expenses and financial loss incident to his being a witness; however, a lawyer may pay or agree to pay an expert witness a reasonable fee for his services as an expert. But in no event should a lawyer pay or agree to pay a contingent fee to any witness. A lawyer should exercise reasonable diligence to see that his client and lay associates conform to these standards.

EC 7–29 To safeguard the impartiality that is essential to the judicial process, veniremen and jurors should be protected against extraneous influences. When impartiality is present, public confidence in the judicial system is enhanced. There should be no extrajudicial communication with veniremen prior to trial or with jurors during trial by or on behalf of a lawyer connected with the case. Furthermore, a lawyer who is not connected with the case should not communicate with or cause another to communicate with a venireman or a juror about the case. After the trial, communication by a lawyer with jurors is permitted so long as he refrains from asking questions or making comments that tend to harass or embarrass the juror or to influence actions of the juror in future cases. Were a lawyer to be prohibited from communicating after a trial with a juror, he could not ascertain if the verdict might be subject to legal challenge, in which event the invalidity of a verdict might go undetected. When an extrajudicial communication by a lawyer with a juror is permitted by law, it should be made considerately and with deference to the personal feelings of the juror.

EC 7-30 Vexatious or harassing investigations of veniremen or jurors seriously impair the effectiveness of our jury system. For this reason, a lawyer or anyone on his behalf who conducts an investigation of veniremen or jurors should act with circumspection and restraint.

EC 7-31 Communications with or investigations of members of families of veniremen or jurors by a lawyer or by anyone on his behalf are subject to the restrictions imposed upon the lawyer with respect to his communications with or investigations of veniremen and jurors.

EC 7-32 Because of his duty to aid in preserving the integrity of the jury system, a lawyer who learns of improper conduct by or towards a venireman, a juror, or a member of the family of either should make a prompt report to the court regarding such conduct.

EC 7-33 A goal of our legal system is that each party shall have his case, criminal or civil, adjudicated by an impartial tribunal. The attainment of this goal may be defeated by dissemination of news or comments which tend to influence judge or jury. Such news or comments may prevent prospective jurors from being impartial at the outset of the trial and may also interfere with the obligation of jurors to base their verdict solely upon the evidence admitted in the trial. The release by a lawyer of out-of-court statements regarding an anticipated or pending trial may improperly affect the impartiality of the tribunal. For these reasons, standards for permissible and prohibited conduct of a lawyer with respect to trial publicity have been established.

EC 7-34 The impartiality of a public servant in our legal system may be impaired by the receipt of gifts or loans. A lawyer, therefore, is never justified in making a gift or a loan to a judge, a hearing officer, or an official or employee of a tribunal, except as permitted by Section C(4) of Canon 5 of the Code of Judicial Conduct, but a lawyer may make a contribution to the campaign fund of a candidate for judicial office in conformity with Section B(2) under Canon 7 of the Code of Judicial Conduct.

As amended in 1974.

EC 7-35 All litigants and lawyers should have access to tribunals on an equal basis. Generally, in adversary proceedings a lawyer should not communicate with a judge relative to a matter pending before, or which is to be brought before, a tribunal over which he presides in circumstances which might have the effect or give the appearance of granting undue advantage to one party. For example, a lawyer should not communicate with a tribunal by a writing unless a copy thereof is promptly delivered to opposing counsel or to the adverse party if he is not represented by a lawyer. Ordinarily an oral communication by a lawyer with a judge or hearing officer should be made only upon adequate notice to opposing counsel, or, if there is none, to the opposing party. A lawyer should not condone or lend himself to private importunities by another with a judge or hearing officer on behalf of himself or his client.

EC 7-36 Judicial hearings ought to be conducted through dignified and orderly procedures designed to protect the rights of all parties. Although a lawyer has the duty to represent his client zealously, he should not engage in any conduct that offends the dignity and decorum of proceedings. While maintaining his independence, a lawyer should be respectful, courteous, and above-board in his relations with a judge or hearing officer before whom he appears. He should avoid undue solicitude for the comfort or convenience of judge or jury and should avoid any other conduct calculated to gain special consideration.

EC 7-37 In adversary proceedings, clients are litigants and though ill feeling may exist between clients, such ill feeling should not influence a lawyer in his conduct, attitude, and demeanor towards opposing lawyers. A lawyer should not make unfair or derogatory personal reference to opposing counsel. Haranguing and offensive tactics by lawyers interfere with the orderly administration of justice and have no proper place in our legal system.

EC 7-38 A lawyer should be courteous to opposing counsel and should accede to reasonable requests regarding court proceedings, settings, continuances, waiver of procedural formalities, and similar matters which do not prejudice the rights of his client. He should follow local customs of courtesy or practice, unless he gives timely notice to opposing counsel of his intention not to do so. A lawyer should be punctual in fulfilling all professional commitments.

EC 7-39 In the final analysis, proper functioning of the adversary system depends upon cooperation between lawyers and tribunals in utilizing procedures which will preserve the impartiality of tribunals and make their decisional processes prompt and just, without impinging upon the obligation of lawyers to represent their clients zealously within the framework of the law.

DISCIPLINARY RULES

DR 7–101 Representing a Client Zealously.

(A) A lawyer shall not intentionally:

   (1) Fail to seek the lawful objectives of his client through reasonably available means permitted by law and the Disciplinary Rules, except as provided by DR 7–101(B). A lawyer does not violate this Disciplinary Rule, however, by acceding to reasonable requests of opposing counsel which do not prejudice the rights of his client, by being punctual in fulfilling all professional commitments, by avoiding offensive tactics, or by treating with courtesy and consideration all persons involved in the legal process.

   (2) Fail to carry out a contract of employment entered into with a client for professional services, but he may withdraw as permitted under DR 2–110, DR 5–102, and DR 5–105.

   (3) Prejudice or damage his client during the course of the professional relationship except as required under DR 7–102(B).

(B) In his representation of a client, a lawyer may:

   (1) Where permissible, exercise his professional judgment to waive or fail to assert a right or position of his client.

   (2) Refuse to aid or participate in conduct that he believes to be unlawful, even though there is some support for an argument that the conduct is legal.

DR 7–102 Representing a Client Within the Bounds of the Law.

(A) In his representation of a client, a lawyer shall not:

   (1) File a suit, assert a position, conduct a defense, delay a trial, or take other action on behalf of his client when he knows or when it is obvious that such action would serve merely to harass or maliciously injure another.

   (2) Knowingly advance a claim or defense that is unwarranted under existing law, except that he may advance such claim or defense it if can be supported by good faith argument for an extension, modification, or reversal of existing law.

   (3) Conceal or knowingly fail to disclose that which he is required by law to reveal.

   (4) Knowingly use perjured testimony or false evidence.

   (5) Knowingly make a false statement of law or fact.

   (6) Participate in the creation or preservation of evidence when he knows or it is obvious that the evidence is false.

   (7) Counsel or assist his client in conduct that the lawyer knows to be illegal or fraudulent.

   (8) Knowingly engage in other illegal conduct or conduct contrary to a Disciplinary Rule.

(B) A lawyer who receives information clearly establishing that:

   (1) His client has, in the course of the representation, perpetrated a fraud upon a person or tribunal shall promptly call upon his client to rectify the same, and if his client refuses or is unable to do so, he shall reveal the fraud to the affected person or tribunal, except when the information is protected as a privileged communication.

   (2) A person other than his client has perpetrated a fraud upon a tribunal shall promptly reveal the fraud to the tribunal.

As amended in 1974.

DR 7–103 Performing the Duty of Public Prosecutor or Other Government Lawyer.

(A) A public prosecutor or other government lawyer shall not institute or cause to be instituted criminal charges when he knows or it is obvious that the charges are not supported by probable cause.

(B) A public prosecutor or other government lawyer in criminal litigation shall make timely disclosure to counsel for the defendant, or to the defendant if he has no counsel, of the existence of evidence, known to the prosecutor or other government lawyer, that tends to negate the guilt of the accused, mitigate the degree of the offense, or reduce the punishment.

DR 7–104 Communicating With One of Adverse Interest.

(A) During the course of his representation of a client a lawyer shall not:

(1) Communicate or cause another to communicate on the subject of the representation with a party he knows to be represented by a lawyer in that matter unless he has the prior consent of the lawyer representing such other party or is authorized by law to do so.

(2) Give advice to a person who is not represented by a lawyer, other than the advice to secure counsel, if the interests of such person are or have a reasonable possibility of being in conflict with the interests of his client.

DR 7–105 Threatening Criminal Prosecution.

(A) A lawyer shall not present, participate in presenting, or threaten to present criminal charges solely to obtain an advantage in a civil matter.

DR 7–106 Trial Conduct.

(A) A lawyer shall not disregard or advise his client to disregard a standing rule of a tribunal or a ruling of a tribunal made in the course of a proceeding, but he may take appropriate steps in good faith to test the validity of such rule or ruling.

(B) In presenting a matter to a tribunal, a lawyer shall disclose:

(1) Legal authority in the controlling jurisdiction known to him to be directly adverse to the position of his client and which is not disclosed by opposing counsel.

(2) Unless privileged or irrelevant, the identities of the clients he represents and of the persons who employed him.

(C) In appearing in his professional capacity before a tribunal, a lawyer shall not:

(1) State or allude to any matter that he has no reasonable basis to believe is relevant to the case or that will not be supported by admissible evidence.

(2) Ask any question that he has no reasonable basis to believe is relevant to the case and that is intended to degrade a witness or other person.

(3) Assert his personal knowledge of the facts in issue, except when testifying as a witness.

(4) Assert his personal opinion as to the justness of a cause, as to the credibility of a witness, as to the culpability of a civil litigant, or as to the guilt or innocence of an accused; but he may argue, on his analysis of the evidence, for any position or conclusion with respect to the matters stated herein.

(5) Fail to comply with known local customs of courtesy or practice of the bar or a particular tribunal without giving to opposing counsel timely notice of his intent not to comply.

(6) Engage in undignified or discourteous conduct which is degrading to a tribunal.

(7) Intentionally or habitually violate any established rule of procedure or of evidence.

DR 7–107 Trial Publicity.

(A) A lawyer participating in or associated with the investigation of a criminal matter shall not make or participate in making an extrajudicial statement that a reasonable person would expect to be disseminated by means of public communication and that does more than state without elaboration:

(1) Information contained in a public record.

(2) That the investigation is in progress.

(3) The general scope of the investigation including a description of the offense and, if permitted by law, the identity of the victim.

(4) A request for assistance in apprehending a suspect or assistance in other matters and the information necessary thereto.

(5) A warning to the public of any dangers.

(B) A lawyer or law firm associated with the prosecution or defense of a criminal matter shall not, from the time of the filing of a complaint, information, or indictment, the issuance of an arrest warrant, or arrest until the commencement of the trial or disposition without trial, make or participate in making an extrajudicial statement that a reasonable person would expect to be disseminated by means of public communication and that relates to:

(1) The character, reputation, or prior criminal record (including arrests, indictments, or other charges of crime) of the accused.

(2) The possibility of a plea of guilty to the offense charged or to a lesser offense.

(3) The existence or contents of any confession, admission, or statement given by the accused or his refusal or failure to make a statement.

(4) The performance or results of any examinations or tests or the refusal or failure of the accused to submit to examinations or tests.

(5) The identity, testimony, or credibility of a prospective witness.

(6) Any opinion as to the guilt or innocence of the accused, the evidence, or the merits of the case.

(C) DR 1–107(B) does not preclude a lawyer during such period from announcing:

(1) The name, age, residence, occupation, and family status of the accused.

(2) If the accused has not been apprehended, any information necessary to aid in his apprehension or to warn the public of any dangers he may present.

(3) A request for assistance in obtaining evidence.

(4) The identity of the victim of the crime.

(5) The fact, time, and place of arrest, resistance, pursuit, and use of weapons.

(6) The identity of investigating and arresting officers or agencies and the length of the investigation.

(7) At the time of seizure, a description of the physical evidence seized, other than a confession, admission, or statement.

(8) The nature, substance, or text of the charge.

(9) Quotations from or references to public records of the court in the case.

(10) The scheduling or result of any step in the judicial proceedings.

(11) That the accused denies the charges made against him.

(D) During the selection of a jury or the trial of a criminal matter, a lawyer or law firm associated with the prosecution or defense of a criminal matter shall not make or participate in making an extra-judicial statement that a reasonable person would expect to be disseminated by means of public communication and that relates to the trial, parties, or issues in the trial or other matters that are reasonably likely to interfere with a fair trial, except that he may quote from or refer without comment to public records of the court in the case.

(E) After the completion of a trial or disposition without trial of a criminal matter and prior to the imposition of sentence, a lawyer or law firm associated with the prosecution or defense shall not make or participate in making an extra-judicial statement that a reasonable person would expect to be disseminated by public communication and that is reasonably likely to affect the imposition of sentence.

(F) The foregoing provisions of DR 7–107 also apply to professional disciplinary proceedings and juvenile disciplinary proceedings when pertinent and consistent with other law applicable to such proceedings.

(G) A lawyer or law firm associated with a civil action shall not during its investigation or litigation make or participate in making an extra-judicial statement, other than a quotation from or reference to public records, that a reasonable person would expect to be disseminated by means of public communication and that relates to:

(1) Evidence regarding the occurrence or transaction involved.

(2) The character, credibility, or criminal record of a party, witness, or prospective witness.

(3) The performance or results of any examinations or tests or the refusal or failure of a party to submit to such.

(4) His opinion as to the merits of the claims or defenses of a party, except as required by law or administrative rule.

(5) Any other matter reasonably likely to interfere with a fair trial of the action.

(H) During the pendency of an administrative proceeding, a lawyer or law firm associated therewith shall not make or participate in making a statement, other than a quotation from or reference to public records, that a reasonable person would expect to be disseminated by means of public communication if it is made outside the official course of the proceeding and relates to:

(1) Evidence regarding the occurrence or transaction involved.

(2) The character, credibility, or criminal record of a party, witness, or prospective witness.

(3) Physical evidence or the performance or results of any examinations or tests or the refusal or failure of a party to submit to such.

(4) His opinion as to the merits of the claims, defenses, or positions of an interested person.

(5) Any other matter reasonably likely to interfere with a fair hearing.

(I) The foregoing provisions of DR 7–107 do not preclude a lawyer from replying to charges of misconduct publicly made against him or from participating in the proceedings of legislative, administrative, or other investigative bodies.

(J) A lawyer shall exercise reasonable care to prevent his employees and associates from making an extra-judicial statement that he would be prohibited from making under DR 7–107.

DR 7–108   Communication with or Investigation of Jurors.

(A) Before the trial of a case a lawyer connected therewith shall not communicate with or cause another to communicate with anyone he knows to be a member of the venire from which the jury will be selected for the trial of the case.

(B) During the trial of a case:

(1) A lawyer connected therewith shall not communicate with or cause another to communicate with any member of the jury.

(2) A lawyer who is not connected therewith shall not communicate with or cause another to communicate with a juror concerning the case.

(C) DR 7–108(A) and (B) do not prohibit a lawyer from communicating with veniremen or jurors in the course of official proceedings.

(D) After discharge of the jury from further consideration of a case with which the lawyer was connected, the lawyer shall not ask questions of or make comments to a member of that jury that are calculated merely to harass or embarrass the juror or to influence his actions in future jury service.

(E) A lawyer shall not conduct or cause, by financial support or otherwise, another to conduct a vexatious or harassing investigation of either a venireman or a juror.

(F) All restrictions imposed by DR 7–108 upon a lawyer also apply to communications with or investigations of members of a family of a venireman or a juror.

(G) A lawyer shall reveal promptly to the court improper conduct by a venireman or a juror, or by another toward a venireman or a juror or a member of his family, of which the lawyer has knowledge.

DR 7–109   Contact with Witnesses.

(A) A lawyer shall not suppress any evidence that he or his client has a legal obligation to reveal or produce.

(B) A lawyer shall not advise or cause a person to secrete himself or to leave the jurisdiction of a tribunal for the purpose of making him unavailable as a witness therein.

(C) A lawyer shall not pay, offer to pay, or acquiesce in the payment of compensation to a witness contingent upon the content of his testimony or the outcome of the case.

But a lawyer may advance, guarantee, or acquiesce in the payment of:

(1) **Expenses reasonably incurred by a witness in attending or testifying.**

(2) **Reasonable compensation to a witness for his loss of time in attending or testifying.**

(3) **A reasonable fee for the professional services of an expert witness.**

DR 7–110   Contact with Officials.

(A) **A lawyer shall not give or lend any thing of value to a judge, official, or employee of a tribunal, except as permitted by Section C(4) of Canon 5 of the Code of Judicial Conduct, but a lawyer may make a contribution to the campaign fund of a candidate for judicial office in conformity with Section B(2) under Canon 7 of the Code of Judicial Conduct.**

(B) **In an adversary proceeding, a lawyer shall not communicate, or cause another to communicate, as to the merits of the cause with a judge or an official before whom the proceeding is pending, except:**

(1) **In the course of official proceedings in the cause.**

(2) **In writing if he promptly delivers a copy of the writing to opposing counsel or to the adverse party if he is not represented by a lawyer.**

(3) **Orally upon adequate notice to opposing counsel or to the adverse party if he is not represented by a lawyer.**

(4) **As otherwise authorized by law, or by Section A(4) under Canon 3 of the Code of Judicial Conduct.**

As amended in 1974.

CANON 8

A Lawyer Should Assist in Improving the Legal System

ETHICAL CONSIDERATIONS

EC 8–1 Changes in human affairs and imperfections in human institutions make necessary constant efforts to maintain and improve our legal system. This system should function in a manner that commands public respect and fosters the use of legal remedies to achieve redress of grievances. By reason of education and experience, lawyers are especially qualified to recognize deficiencies in the legal system and to initiate corrective measures therein. Thus they should participate in proposing and supporting legislation and programs to improve the system, without regard to the general interests or desires of clients or former clients.

EC 8–2 Rules of law are deficient if they are not just, understandable, and responsive to the needs of society. If a lawyer believes that the existence or absence of a rule of law, substantive or procedural, causes or contributes to an unjust result, he should endeavor by lawful means to obtain appropriate change in the law. He should encourage the simplification of laws and the repeal or amendment of laws that are outmoded. Likewise, legal procedures should be improved whenever experience indicates a change is needed.

EC 8–3 The fair administration of justice requires the availability of competent lawyers. Members of the public should be educated to recognize the existence of legal problems and the resultant need for legal services, and should be provided methods for intelligent selection of counsel. Those persons unable to pay for legal services should be provided needed services. Clients and lawyers should not be penalized by undue geographical restraints upon representation in legal matters, and the bar should address itself to improvements in licensing, reciprocity, and admission procedures consistent with the needs of modern commerce.

EC 8–4 Whenever a lawyer seeks legislative or administrative changes, he should identify the capacity in which he appears, whether on behalf of himself, a client, or the public. A lawyer may advocate such changes on behalf of a client even though he does not agree with them. But when a lawyer purports to act on behalf of the public, he should espouse only those changes which he conscientiously believes to be in the public interest.

EC 8–5 Fraudulent, deceptive, or otherwise illegal conduct by a participant in a proceeding before a tribunal or legislative body is inconsistent with fair administration of justice, and it should never be participated in or condoned by lawyers. Unless constrained by his obligation to preserve the confidences and secrets of his client, a lawyer should reveal to appropriate authorities any knowledge he may have of such improper conduct.

EC 8–6 Judges and administrative officials having adjudicatory powers ought to be persons of integrity, competence, and suitable temperament. Generally, lawyers are qualified, by personal observation or investigation, to evaluate the qualifications of persons seeking or being considered for such public offices, and for this reason they have a special responsibility to aid in the selection of only those who are qualified. It is the duty of lawyers to endeavor to prevent political considerations from outweighing judicial fitness in the selection of judges. Lawyers should protest earnestly against the appointment or election of those who are unsuited for the bench and should strive to have elected or appointed thereto only those who are willing to forego pursuits, whether of a business, political, or other nature, that may interfere with the free and fair consideration of questions presented for adjudication. Adjudicatory officials, not being wholly free to defend themselves, are entitled to receive the support of the bar against unjust criticism. While a lawyer as a citizen has a right to criticize such officials publicly, he should be certain of the merit of his complaint, use appropriate language, and avoid petty criticisms, for unrestrained and intemperate statements tend to lessen public confidence in our legal system. Criticisms motivated by reasons other than a desire to improve the legal system are not justified.

EC 8–7 Since lawyers are a vital part of the legal system, they should be persons of integrity, of professional skill, and of dedication to the improvement of the system. Thus a lawyer should aid in establishing, as well as enforcing, standards of conduct adequate to protect the public by insuring that those who practice law are qualified to do so.

EC 8–8 Lawyers often serve as legislators or as holders of other public offices. This is highly desirable, as lawyers are uniquely qualified to make significant contributions to the improvement of the legal system. A lawyer who is a public officer, whether full or part-time, should not engage in activities in which his personal or professional interests are or foreseeably may be in conflict with his official duties.

EC 8–9 The advancement of our legal system is of vital importance in maintaining the rule of law and in facilitating orderly changes; therefore, lawyers should encourage, and should aid in making, needed changes and improvements.

DISCIPLINARY RULES

DR 8–101 Action as a Public Official.

(A) A lawyer who holds public office shall not:

    (1) Use his public position to obtain, or attempt to obtain, a special advantage in legislative matters for himself or for a client under circumstances where he knows or it is obvious that such action is not in the public interest.

    (2) Use his public position to influence, or attempt to influence, a tribunal to act in favor of himself or of a client.

    (3) Accept any thing of value from any person when the lawyer knows or it is obvious that the offer is for the purpose of influencing his action as a public official.

DR 8–102 Statements Concerning Judges and Other Adjudicatory Officers.

(A) A lawyer shall not knowingly make false statements of fact concerning the qualifications of a candidate for election or appointment to a judicial office.

(B) A lawyer shall not knowingly make false accusations against a judge or other adjudicatory officer.

DR 8–103 Lawyer Candidate for Judicial Office.

(A) A lawyer who is a candidate for judicial office shall comply with the applicable provisions of Canon 7 of the Code of Judicial Conduct.

Added in 1974.

CANON 9

A Lawyer Should Avoid Even the Appearance of Professional Impropriety

ETHICAL CONSIDERATIONS

EC 9–1 Continuation of the American concept that we are to be governed by rules of law requires that the people have faith that justice can be obtained through our legal system. A lawyer should promote public confidence in our system and in the legal profession.

EC 9–2 Public confidence in law and lawyers may be eroded by irresponsible or improper conduct of a lawyer. On occasion, ethical conduct of a lawyer may appear to laymen to be unethical. In order to avoid misunderstandings and hence to maintain confidence, a lawyer should fully and promptly inform his client of material developments in the matters being handled for the client. While a lawyer should guard against otherwise proper conduct that has a tendency to diminish public confidence in the legal system or in the legal profession, his duty to clients or to the public should never be subordinate merely because the full discharge of his obligation may be misunderstood or may tend to subject him or the legal profession to criticism.

When explicit ethical guidance does not exist, a lawyer should determine his conduct by acting in a manner that promotes public confidence in the integrity and efficiency of the legal system and the legal profession.

EC 9–3 After a lawyer leaves judicial office or other public employment, he should not accept employment in connection with any matter in which he had substantial responsibility prior to his leaving, since to accept employment would give the appearance of impropriety even if none exists.

EC 9–4 Because the very essence of the legal system is to provide procedures by which matters can be presented in an impartial manner so that they may be decided solely upon the merits, any statement or suggestion by a lawyer that he can or would attempt to circumvent those procedures is detrimental to the legal system and tends to undermine public confidence in it.

EC 9–5 Separation of the funds of a client from those of his lawyer not only serves to protect the client but also avoids even the appearance of impropriety, and therefore commingling of such funds should be avoided.

EC 9–6 Every lawyer owes a solemn duty to uphold the integrity and honor of his profession; to encourage respect for the law and for the courts and the judges thereof; to observe the Code of Professional Responsibility; to act as a member of a learned profession, one dedicated to public service; to cooperate with his brother lawyers in supporting the organized bar through the devoting of his time, efforts, and financial support as his professional standing and ability reasonably permit; to conduct himself so as to reflect credit on the legal profession and to inspire the confidence, respect, and trust of his clients and of the public; and to strive to avoid not only professional impropriety but also the appearance of impropriety.

EC 9–7 A lawyer has an obligation to the public to participate in collective efforts of the bar to reimburse persons who have lost money or property as a result of the misappropriation or defalcation of another lawyer, and contribution to a clients' security fund is an acceptable method of meeting this obligation.

DISCIPLINARY RULES

DR 9–101 Avoiding Even the Appearance of Impropriety.

(A) A lawyer shall not accept private employment in a matter upon the merits of which he has acted in a judicial capacity.

(B) A lawyer shall not accept private employment in a matter in which he had substantial responsibility while he was a public employee.

(C) A lawyer shall not state or imply that he is able to influence improperly or upon irrelevant grounds any tribunal, legislative body, or public official.

DR 9–102 Preserving Identity of Funds and Property of a Client.

(A) All funds of clients paid to a lawyer or law firm, other than advances for costs and expenses, shall be deposited in one or more identifiable bank accounts maintained in the state in which the law office is situated and no funds belonging to the lawyer or law firm shall be deposited therein except as follows:

(1) Funds reasonably sufficient to pay bank charges may be deposited therein.

(2) Funds belonging in part to a client and in part presently or potentially to the lawyer or law firm must be deposited therein, but the portion belonging to the lawyer or law firm may be withdrawn when due unless the right of the lawyer or law firm to receive it is disputed by the client, in which event the disputed portion shall not be withdrawn until the dispute is finally resolved.

(B) A lawyer shall:

(1) Promptly notify a client of the receipt of his funds, securities, or other properties.

(2) Identify and label securities and properties of a client promptly upon receipt and place them in a safe deposit box or other place of safekeeping as soon as practicable.

(3) Maintain complete records of all funds, securities, and other properties of a client coming into the possession of the lawyer and render appropriate accounts to his client regarding them.

(4) Promptly pay or deliver to the client as requested by a client the funds, securities, or other properties in the possession of the lawyer which the client is entitled to receive.

DEFINITIONS*

As used in the Disciplinary Rules of the Code of Professional Responsibility:

(1) "Differing interests" include every interest that will adversely affect either the judgment or the loyalty of a lawyer to a client, whether it be a conflicting, inconsistent, diverse, or other interest.

(2) "Law firm" includes a professional legal corporation.

(3) "Person" includes a corporation, an association, a trust, a partnership, and any other organization or legal entity.

(4) "Professional legal corporation" means a corporation, or an association treated as a corporation, authorized by law to practice law for profit.

(5) "State" includes the District of Columbia, Puerto Rico, and other federal territories and possessions.

(6) "Tribunal" includes all courts and all other adjudicatory bodies.

(7) "A Bar association" includes a bar association of specialists as referred to in DR 2–105(A)(1) or (3).

(8) "Qualified legal assistance organization" means an office or organization of one of the four types listed in DR 2–103(D)(1)–(4), inclusive that meets all the requirements thereof.

As amended in 1974.

---

* "Confidence" and "secret" are defined in DR 4–101(A).

*

APPENDIX D

AMERICAN BAR ASSOCIATION MODEL RULES OF PROFESSIONAL CONDUCT

**Annotated to Reflect Amendments and Prior Text of the Model Rules in Footnotes.
Adopted August 1983, as Amended to August, 1991.**

[Less than a decade after the Model Code of Professional Responsibility was promulgated in 1969, the ABA established a commission to create another code of ethics for the legal profession. Between 1977 to 1983 the Kutak Commission, named after its chairman Robert Kutak, proceeded to write several drafts of a new code of conduct for lawyers. In 1983, the ABA enacted the Model Rules of Professional Conduct based upon the work of the Kutak Commission. The Model Rules were a response to criticisms about the Model Code's focus on litigation and its three tier structure of canons, ethical considerations, and disciplinary rules. The Model Rules follow Restatement-like approach by placing the rule of professional responsibility in text and including elaborative material in the comments. However, unlike the Restatements, the Model Rules provide no illustrations or hypotheticals. Since its adoption in 1983, the ABA has amended the Model Rules several times, and thus this version of the Model Rules is annotated to indicate in footnotes the manner in which the ABA has amended the Model Rules since the original adoption in 1983. Although the current ABA version is important, the original version of the Model Rules is more likely to form the basis for the state adoptions of the Model Rules. When studying a case or an ethics opinion in the various states, one should examine whether the decision is based upon the current version of the Model Rules or a prior version. Additionally, the comments to the Model Rules are numbered sequentially under each Model Rule provision to facilitate citation of a particular comment. Ed.]

CONTENTS

PREAMBLE, SCOPE, AND TERMINOLOGY

Preamble: A Lawyer's Responsibilities

[1] * A lawyer is a representative of clients, an officer of the legal system and a public citizen

---

* Editors' Note: The ABA Model Rules do not number the paragraphs of the Comments. However, for ease of reference and citation, we have supplied bracketed numbers. Thus, a citation to Rule 1.6, Comment 15 refers to the fifteenth paragraph of the Comment to Model Rule 1.6; a citation to Rule 1.2, Code Comparison 5 refers to the fifth paragraph of the Code Comparison to Model Rule 1.2.

having special responsibility for the quality of justice.

[2] As a representative of clients, a lawyer performs various functions. As advisor, a lawyer provides a client with an informed understanding of the client's legal rights and obligations and explains their practical implications. As advocate, a lawyer zealously asserts the client's position under the rules of the adversary system. As negotiator, a lawyer seeks a result advantageous to the client but consistent with requirements of honest dealing with others. As intermediary between clients, a lawyer seeks to reconcile their divergent interests as an advisor and, to a limited extent, as a spokesperson for each client. A lawyer acts as evaluator by examining a client's legal affairs and reporting about them to the client or to others.

[3] In all professional functions a lawyer should be competent, prompt and diligent. A lawyer should maintain communication with a client concerning the representation. A lawyer should keep in confidence information relating to representation of a client except so far as disclosure is required or permitted by the Rules of Professional Conduct or other law.

[4] A lawyer's conduct should conform to the requirements of the law, both in professional service to clients and in the lawyer's business and personal affairs. A lawyer should use the law's procedures only for legitimate purposes and not to harass or intimidate others. A lawyer should demonstrate respect for the legal system and for those who serve it, including judges, other lawyers and public officials. While it is a lawyer's duty, when necessary, to challenge the rectitude of official action, it is also a lawyer's duty to uphold legal process.

[5] As a public citizen, a lawyer should seek improvement of the law, the administration of justice and the quality of service rendered by the legal profession. As a member of a learned profession, a lawyer should cultivate knowledge of the law beyond its use for clients, employ that knowledge in reform of the law and work to strengthen legal education. A lawyer should be mindful of deficiencies in the administration of justice and of the fact that the poor, and sometimes persons who are not poor, cannot afford adequate legal assistance, and should therefore devote professional time and civic influence in their behalf. A lawyer should aid the legal profession in pursuing these objectives and should help the bar regulate itself in the public interest.

[6] Many of a lawyer's professional responsibilities are prescribed in the Rules of Professional Conduct, as well as substantive and procedural law. However, a lawyer is also guided by personal conscience and the approbation of professional peers. A lawyer should strive to attain the highest level of skill, to improve the law and the legal profession and to exemplify the legal profession's ideals of public service.

[7] A lawyer's responsibilities as a representative of clients, an officer of the legal system and a public citizen are usually harmonious. Thus, when an opposing party is well represented, a lawyer can be a zealous advocate on behalf of a client and at the same time assume that justice is being done. So also, a lawyer can be sure that preserving client confidences ordinarily serves the public interest because people are more likely to seek legal advice, and thereby heed their legal obligations, when they know their communications will be private.

[8] In the nature of law practice, however, conflicting responsibilities are encountered. Virtually all difficult ethical problems arise from conflict between a lawyer's responsibilities to clients, to the legal system and to the lawyer's own interest in remaining an upright person while earning a satisfactory living. The Rules of Professional Conduct prescribe terms for resolving such conflicts. Within the framework of these Rules many difficult issues of professional discretion can arise. Such issues must be resolved through the exercise of sensitive professional and moral judgment guided by the basic principles underlying the Rules.

[9] The legal profession is largely self-governing. Although other professions also have been granted powers of self-government, the legal profession is unique in this respect because of the close relationship between the profession and the processes of government and law enforcement. This connection is manifested in the fact that ultimate authority over the legal profession is vested largely in the courts.

[10] To the extent that lawyers meet the obligations of their professional calling, the occasion for government regulation is obviated. Self-regulation also helps maintain the legal profession's independence from government domination. An independent legal profession is an important force in preserving government under law, for abuse of legal authority is more readily challenged by a profession whose members are not dependent on government for the right to practice.

[11] The legal profession's relative autonomy carries with it special responsibilities of self-government. The profession has a responsibility to assure that its regulations are conceived in the public interest and not in furtherance of parochial or self-interested concerns of the bar. Every lawyer is responsible for observance of the Rules of Professional Conduct. A lawyer should also aid in securing their observance by other lawyers. Neglect of these responsibilities compromises the independence of the profession and the public interest which it serves.

[12] Lawyers play a vital role in the preservation of society. The fulfillment of this role requires an understanding by lawyers of their relationship to our legal system. The Rules of Professional Conduct, when properly applied, serve to define that relationship.

Scope

[1] The Rules of Professional Conduct are rules of reason. They should be interpreted with reference to the purposes of legal representation and of the law itself. Some of the Rules are imperatives, cast in the terms "shall" or "shall not." These define proper conduct for purposes of professional discipline. Others, generally cast in the term "may," are permissive and define areas under the Rules in which the lawyer has professional discretion. No disciplinary action should be taken when the lawyer chooses not to act or acts within the bounds of such discretion. Other Rules define the nature of relationships between the lawyer and others. The Rules are thus partly obligatory and disciplinary and partly constitutive and descriptive in that they define a lawyer's professional role. Many of the Comments use the term "should." Comments do not add obligations to the Rules but provide guidance for practicing in compliance with the Rules.

[2] The Rules presuppose a larger legal context shaping the lawyer's role. That context includes court rules and statutes relating to matters of licensure, laws defining specific obligations of lawyers and substantive and procedural law in general. Compliance with the Rules, as with all law in an open society, depends primarily upon understanding and voluntary compliance, secondarily upon reinforcement by peer and public opinion and finally, when necessary, upon enforcement through disciplinary proceedings. The Rules do not, however, exhaust the moral and ethical considerations that should inform a lawyer, for no worthwhile human activity can be completely defined by legal rules. The Rules simply provide a framework for the ethical practice of law.

[3] Furthermore, for purposes of determining the lawyer's authority and responsibility, principles of substantive law external to these Rules determine whether a client-lawyer relationship exists. Most of the duties flowing from the client-lawyer relationship attach only after the client has requested the lawyer to render legal services and the lawyer has agreed to do so. But there are some duties, such as that of confidentiality under Rule 1.6, that may attach when the lawyer agrees to consider whether a client-lawyer relationship shall be established. Whether a client-lawyer relationship exists for any specific purpose can depend on the circumstances and may be a question of fact.

[4] Under various legal provisions, including constitutional, statutory and common law, the responsibilities of government lawyers may include authority concerning legal matters that ordinarily reposes in the client in private client-lawyer relationships. For example, a lawyer for a government agency may have authority on behalf of the government to decide upon settlement or whether to appeal from an adverse judgment. Such authority in various respects is generally vested in the attorney general and the state's attorney in state government, and their federal counterparts, and the same may be true of other government law officers. Also, lawyers under the supervision of these officers may be authorized to represent several government agencies in intragovernmental legal controversies in circumstances where a private lawyer could not represent multiple private clients. They also may have authority to represent the "public interest" in circumstances where a private lawyer would not be authorized to do so. These Rules do not abrogate any such authority.

[5] Failure to comply with an obligation or prohibition imposed by a Rule is a basis for invoking the disciplinary process. The Rules presuppose that disciplinary assessment of a lawyer's conduct will be made on the basis of the facts and circumstances as they existed at the time of the conduct in question and in recognition of the fact that a lawyer often has to act upon uncertain or incomplete evidence of the situation. Moreover, the Rules presuppose that whether or not discipline should be imposed for a violation, and the severity of a sanction, depend on all the circumstances, such as the willfulness and seriousness of the violation, extenuating factors and whether there have been previous violations.

[6] Violation of a Rule should not give rise to a cause of action nor should it create any presumption that a legal duty has been breached. The Rules are designed to provide guidance to lawyers and to provide a structure for regulating conduct through disciplinary agencies. They are not designed to be a basis for civil liability. Furthermore, the purpose of the Rules can be subverted when they are invoked by opposing parties as procedural weapons. The fact that a Rule is a just basis for a lawyer's self-assessment, or for sanctioning a lawyer under the administration of a disciplinary authority, does not imply that an antagonist in a collateral proceeding or transaction has standing to seek enforcement of the Rule. Accordingly, nothing in the Rules should be deemed to augment any substantive legal duty of lawyers or the extradisciplinary consequences of violating such a duty.

[7] Moreover, these Rules are not intended to govern or affect judicial application of either the attorney-client or work product privilege. Those privileges were developed to promote compliance with law and fairness in litigation. In reliance on the attorney-client privilege, clients are entitled to expect that communications within the scope of the privilege will be protected against compelled disclosure. The attorney-client privilege is that of the client and not of the lawyer. The fact that in exceptional situations the lawyer under the Rules has a limited discretion to disclose a client confidence does not vitiate the proposition that, as a general matter, the client has a reasonable expectation that information relating to the client will not be voluntarily disclosed and that disclosure of such information may be judicially compelled only in accordance with recognized exceptions to the attorney-client and work product privileges.

[8] The lawyer's exercise of discretion not to disclose information under Rule 1.6 should not be subject to reexamination. Permitting such reexamination would be incompatible with the general policy of promoting compliance with law through assurances that communications will be protected against disclosure.

[9] The Comment accompanying each Rule explains and illustrates the meaning and purpose of the Rule. The Preamble and this note on Scope provide general orientation. The Comments are intended as guides to interpretation, but the text of each Rule is authoritative. Research notes were prepared to compare counterparts in the ABA Model Code of Professional Responsibility (adopted 1969, as amended) and to provide selected references to other authorities. The notes have not been adopted, do not constitute part of the Model Rules, and are not intended to affect the application or interpretation of the Rules and Comments.

Terminology

[1] "Belief" or "Believes" denotes that the person involved actually supposed the fact in question to be true. A person's belief may be inferred from circumstances.

[2] "Consult" or "Consultation" denotes communication of information reasonably sufficient to permit the client to appreciate the significance of the matter in question.

[3] "Firm" or "Law firm" denotes a lawyer or lawyers in a private firm, lawyers employed in the legal department of a corporation or other organization and lawyers employed in a legal services organization. See Comment, Rule 1.10.

[4] "Fraud" or "Fraudulent" denotes conduct having a purpose to deceive and not merely negligent misrepresentation or failure to apprise another of relevant information.

[5] "Knowingly," "Known," or "Knows" denotes actual knowledge of the fact in question. A person's knowledge may be inferred from circumstances.

[6] "Partner" denotes a member of a partnership and a shareholder in a law firm organized as a professional corporation.

[7] "Reasonable" or "Reasonably" when used in relation to conduct by a lawyer denotes the conduct of a reasonably prudent and competent lawyer.

[8] "Reasonable belief" or "Reasonably believes" when used in reference to a lawyer denotes that the lawyer believes the matter in question and that the circumstances are such that the belief is reasonable.

[9] "Reasonably should know" when used in reference to a lawyer denotes that a lawyer of reasonable prudence and competence would ascertain the matter in question.

[10] "Substantial" when used in reference to degree or extent denotes a material matter of clear and weighty importance.

MODEL RULES OF PROFESSIONAL CONDUCT

CLIENT–LAWYER RELATIONSHIP

RULE 1.1 Competence

A Lawyer shall provide competent representation to a client. Competent representation requires the legal knowledge, skill, thoroughness and preparation reasonably necessary for the representation.

COMMENT:

Legal Knowledge and Skill

[1] In determining whether a lawyer employs the requisite knowledge and skill in a particular matter, relevant factors include the relative complexity and specialized nature of the matter, the lawyer's general experience, the lawyer's training and experience in the field in question, the preparation and study the lawyer is able to give the matter and whether it is feasible to refer the matter to, or associate or consult with, a lawyer of established competence in the field in question. In many instances, the required proficiency is that of a general practitioner. Expertise in a particular field of law may be required in some circumstances.

[2] A lawyer need not necessarily have special training or prior experience to handle legal problems of a type with which the lawyer is unfamiliar. A newly admitted lawyer can be as competent as a practitioner with long experience. Some important legal skills, such as the analysis of precedent, the evaluation of evidence and legal drafting, are required in all legal problems. Perhaps the most fundamental legal skill consists of determining what kind of legal problems a situation may involve, a skill that necessarily transcends any particular specialized knowledge. A lawyer can provide adequate representation in a wholly novel field through necessary study. Competent representation can also be provided through the association of a lawyer of established competence in the field in question.

[3] In an emergency a lawyer may give advice or assistance in a matter in which the lawyer does not have the skill ordinarily required where referral to or consultation or association with another lawyer would be impractical. Even in an emergency, however, assistance should be limited to that reasonably necessary in the circumstances, for ill considered action under emergency conditions can jeopardize the client's interest.

[4] A lawyer may accept representation where the requisite level of competence can be achieved by reasonable preparation. This applies as well to a lawyer who is appointed as counsel for an unrepresented person. See also Rule 6.2.

Thoroughness and Preparation

[5] Competent handling of a particular matter includes inquiry into and analysis of the factual and legal elements of the problem, and use of methods and procedures meeting the standards of competent practitioners. It also includes adequate preparation. The required attention and preparation are determined in part by what is at stake; major litigation and complex transactions ordinarily require more elaborate treatment than matters of lesser consequence.

Maintaining Competence

[6] To maintain the requisite knowledge and skill, a lawyer should engage in continuing study and education. If a system of peer review has been established, the lawyer should consider making use of it in appropriate circumstances.

MODEL CODE COMPARISON:

DR 6–101(A)(1) provided that a lawyer shall not handle a matter "which he knows or should know that he is not competent to handle, without associating himself with a lawyer who is competent to handle it"; DR 6–101(A)(2) requires "preparation adequate in the circumstances." Rule 1.1 more fully particularizes the elements of competence. Whereas DR 6–101(A)(3) prohibited the "[N]eglect of a legal matter," Rule 1.1 does not contain such a prohibition. Instead, Rule 1.1 affirmatively requires the lawyer to be competent.

RULE 1.2 Scope of Representation

(a) A lawyer shall abide by a client's decisions concerning the objectives of representation, subject to paragraphs (c), (d) and (e), and shall consult with the client as to the means by which they are to be pursued. A lawyer shall abide by a client's decision whether to accept an offer of settlement of a matter. In a criminal case, the lawyer shall abide by the client's decision, after consultation with the lawyer, as to a plea to be entered, whether to waive jury trial and whether the client will testify.

(b) A lawyer's representation of a client, including representation by appointment, does not constitute an endorsement of the client's political, economic, social or moral views or activities.

(c) A lawyer may limit the objectives of the representation if the client consents after consultation.

(d) A lawyer shall not counsel a client to engage, or assist a client, in conduct that the lawyer knows is criminal or fraudulent, but a lawyer may discuss the legal consequences of any proposed course of conduct with a client and may counsel or assist a client to make a good faith effort to determine the validity, scope, meaning or application of the law.

(e) When a lawyer knows that a client expects assistance not permitted by the rules of professional conduct or other law, the lawyer shall consult with the client regarding the relevant limitations on the lawyer's conduct.

COMMENT:

Scope of Representation

[1] Both lawyer and client have authority and responsibility in the objectives and means of representation. The client has ultimate authority to determine the purposes to be served by legal representation, within the limits imposed by law and the lawyer's professional obligations. Within those limits, a client also has a right to consult with the lawyer about the means to be used in pursuing those objectives. At the same time, a lawyer is not required to pursue objectives or employ means simply because a client may wish that the lawyer do so. A clear distinction between objectives and means sometimes cannot be drawn, and in many cases the client-lawyer relationship partakes of a joint undertaking. In questions of means, the lawyer should assume responsibility for technical and legal tactical issues, but should defer to the client regarding such questions as the expense to be incurred and concern for third persons who might be adversely affected. Law defining the lawyer's scope of authority in litigation varies among jurisdictions.

[2] In a case in which the client appears to be suffering mental disability, the lawyer's duty to abide by the client's decisions is to be guided by reference to Rule 1.14.

Independence From Client's Views or Activities

[3] Legal representation should not be denied to people who are unable to afford legal services, or whose cause is controversial or the subject of popular disapproval. By the same token, representing

a client does not constitute approval of the client's views or activities.

Services Limited in Objectives or Means

[4] The objectives or scope of services provided by a lawyer may be limited by agreement with the client or by the terms under which the lawyer's services are made available to the client. For example, a retainer may be for a specifically defined purpose. Representation provided through a legal aid agency may be subject to limitations on the types of cases the agency handles. When a lawyer has been retained by an insurer to represent an insured, the representation may be limited to matters related to the insurance coverage. The terms upon which representation is undertaken may exclude specific objectives or means. Such limitations may exclude objectives or means that the lawyer regards as repugnant or imprudent.

[5] An agreement concerning the scope of representation must accord with the Rules of Professional Conduct and other law. Thus, the client may not be asked to agree to representation so limited in scope as to violate Rule 1.1, or to surrender the right to terminate the lawyer's services or the right to settle litigation that the lawyer might wish to continue.

Criminal, Fraudulent and Prohibited Transactions

[6] A lawyer is required to give an honest opinion about the actual consequences that appear likely to result from a client's conduct. The fact that a client uses advice in a course of action that is criminal or fraudulent does not, of itself, make a lawyer a party to the course of action. However, a lawyer may not knowingly assist a client in criminal or fraudulent conduct. There is a critical distinction between presenting an analysis of legal aspects of questionable conduct and recommending the means by which a crime or fraud might be committed with impunity.

[7] When the client's course of action has already begun and is continuing, the lawyer's responsibility is especially delicate. The lawyer is not permitted to reveal the client's wrongdoing, except where permitted by Rule 1.6. However, the lawyer is required to avoid furthering the purpose, for example, by suggesting how it might be concealed. A lawyer may not continue assisting a client in conduct that the lawyer originally supposes is legally proper but then discovers is criminal or fraudulent. Withdrawal from the representation, therefore, may be required.

[8] Where the client is a fiduciary, the lawyer may be charged with special obligations in dealings with a beneficiary.

[9] Paragraph (d) applies whether or not the defrauded party is a party to the transaction. Hence, a lawyer should not participate in a sham transaction; for example, a transaction to effectuate criminal or fraudulent escape of tax liability. Paragraph (d) does not preclude undertaking a criminal defense incident to a general retainer for legal services to a lawful enterprise. The last clause of paragraph (d) recognizes that determining the validity or interpretation of a statute or regulation may require a course of action involving disobedience of the statute or regulation or of the interpretation placed upon it by governmental authorities.

MODEL CODE COMPARISON

[1] Paragraph (a) has no counterpart in the Disciplinary Rules of the Model Code. EC 7–7 stated: "In certain areas of legal representation not affecting the merits of the cause or substantially prejudicing the rights of a client, a lawyer is entitled to make decisions on his own. But otherwise the authority to make decisions is exclusively that of the client. . . ." EC 7–8 stated that "[I]n the final analysis, however, the . . . decision whether to forego legally available objectives or methods because of nonlegal factors is ultimately for the client. . . . In the event that the client in a nonadjudicatory matter insists upon a course of conduct that is contrary to the judgment and advice of the lawyer but not prohibited by Disciplinary Rules, the lawyer may withdraw from the employment." DR 7–101(A)(1) provided that a lawyer "shall not intentionally . . . fail to seek the lawful objectives of his client through reasonably available means permitted by law. . . . A lawyer does not violate this Disciplinary Rule, however, by . . . avoiding offensive tactics. . . ."

[2] Paragraph (b) has no counterpart in the Model Code.

[3] With regard to paragraph (c), DR 7–101(B)(1) provided that a lawyer may, "where permissible, exercise his professional judgment to waive or fail to assert a right or position of his client."

[4] With regard to paragraph (d), DR 7–102(A)(7) provided that a lawyer shall not "counsel or assist his client in conduct that the lawyer knows to be illegal or fraudulent." DR 7–102(A)(6) provided that a lawyer shall not "participate in the creation or preservation of evidence when he knows or it is obvious that the evidence is false." DR 7–106 provided that a lawyer shall not "advise his client to disregard a standing rule of a tribunal or a ruling of a tribunal . . . but he may take appropriate steps in good faith to test the validity of such rule or ruling." EC 7–5 stated that a lawyer "should never encourage or aid his client to commit criminal acts or counsel his client on how to violate the law and avoid punishment therefor."

[5] With regard to Rule 1.2(e), DR 2–110(C)(1)(c) provided that a lawyer may withdraw from representation if a client "insists" that the lawyer engage in "conduct that is illegal or that is prohibited under the Disciplinary Rules." DR 9–101(C) provided that "a lawyer shall not state or imply that he is able to influence improperly . . . any tribunal, legislative body or public official."

RULE 1.3 Diligence

A lawyer shall act with reasonable diligence and promptness in representing a client.

COMMENT:

[1] A lawyer should pursue a matter on behalf of a client despite opposition, obstruction or personal inconvenience to the lawyer, and may take whatever lawful and ethical measures are required to vindicate a client's cause or endeavor. A lawyer should act with commitment and dedication to the interests of the client and with zeal in advocacy upon the client's behalf. However, a lawyer is not bound to press for every advantage that might be realized for a client. A lawyer has professional discretion in determining the means by which a matter should be pursued. See Rule 1.2. A lawyer's workload should be controlled so that each matter can be handled adequately.

[2] Perhaps no professional shortcoming is more widely resented than procrastination. A client's interests often can be adversely affected by the passage of time or the change of conditions; in extreme instances, as when a lawyer overlooks a statute of limitations, the client's legal position may be destroyed. Even when the client's interests are not affected in substance, however, unreasonable delay can cause a client needless anxiety and undermine confidence in the lawyer's trustworthiness.

[3] Unless the relationship is terminated as provided in Rule 1.16, a lawyer should carry through to conclusion all matters undertaken for a client. If a lawyer's employment is limited to a specific matter, the relationship terminates when the matter has been resolved. If a lawyer has served a client over a substantial period in a variety of matters, the client sometimes may assume that the lawyer will continue to serve on a continuing basis unless the lawyer gives notice of withdrawal. Doubt about whether a client-lawyer relationship still exists should be clarified by the lawyer, preferably in writing, so that the client will not mistakenly suppose the lawyer is looking after the client's affairs when the lawyer has ceased to do so. For example, if a lawyer has handled a judicial or administrative proceeding that produced a result adverse to the client but has not been specifically instructed concerning pursuit of an appeal, the lawyer should advise the client of the possibility of appeal before relinquishing responsibility for the matter.

MODEL CODE COMPARISON:

DR 6–101(A)(3) required that a lawyer not "[n]eglect a legal matter entrusted to him." EC 6–4 stated that a lawyer should "give appropriate attention to his legal work." Canon 7 stated that "a lawyer should represent a client zealously within the bounds of the law." DR 7–101(A)(1) provided that a lawyer "shall not intentionally . . . fail to seek the lawful objectives of his client through reasonably available means permitted by law and the Disciplinary Rules. . . ." DR 7–101(A)(3) provided that a lawyer "shall not intentionally . . . [p]rejudice or damage his client during the course of the relationship. . . ."

RULE 1.4 Communication

(a) A lawyer shall keep a client reasonably informed about the status of a matter and promptly comply with reasonable requests for information.

(b) A lawyer shall explain a matter to the extent reasonably necessary to permit the client to make informed decisions regarding the representation.

COMMENT:

[1] The client should have sufficient information to participate intelligently in decisions concerning the objectives of the representation and the means by which they are to be pursued, to the extent the client is willing and able to do so. For example, a lawyer negotiating on behalf of a client should provide the client with facts relevant to the matter, inform the client of communications from another party and take other reasonable steps that permit the client to make a decision regarding a serious offer from another party. A lawyer who receives from opposing counsel an offer of settlement in a civil controversy or a proffered plea bargain in a criminal case should promptly inform the client of its substance unless prior discussions with the client have left it clear that the proposal will be unacceptable. See Rule 1.2(a). Even when a client delegates authority to the lawyer, the client should be kept advised of the status of the matter.

[2] Adequacy of communication depends in part on the kind of advice or assistance involved. For example, in negotiations where there is time to explain a proposal the lawyer should review all important provisions with the client before proceeding to an agreement. In litigation a lawyer should explain the general strategy and prospects of success and ordinarily should consult the client on tactics that might injure or coerce others. On the other hand, a lawyer ordinarily cannot be expected to describe trial or negotiation strategy in detail. The guiding principle is that the lawyer should fulfill reasonable client expectations for information consistent with the duty to act in the client's best interests, and the client's overall requirements as to the character of representation.

[3] Ordinarily, the information to be provided is that appropriate for a client who is a comprehending and responsible adult. However, fully informing the client according to this standard may be impracticable, for example, where the client is a child or suffers from mental disability. See Rule 1.14. When the client is an organization or group, it is often impossible or inappropriate to inform every one of its members about its legal affairs; ordinarily, the lawyer should address communications to the appropriate officials of the organization. See Rule 1.13. Where many routine matters are involved, a system of limited or occasional reporting may be arranged with the client. Practical exigency may also require a lawyer to act for a client without prior consultation.

Withholding Information

[4] In some circumstances, a lawyer may be justified in delaying transmission of information when the client would be likely to react imprudently to an immediate communication. Thus, a lawyer might withhold a psychiatric diagnosis of a

client when the examining psychiatrist indicates that disclosure would harm the client. A lawyer may not withhold information to serve the lawyer's own interest or convenience. Rules or court orders governing litigation may provide that information supplied to a lawyer may not be disclosed to the client. Rule 3.4(c) directs compliance with such rules or orders.

MODEL CODE COMPARISON:

Rule 1.4 has no direct counterpart in the Disciplinary Rules of the Model Code. DR 6–101(A)(3) provided that a lawyer shall not "[n]eglect a legal matter entrusted to him." DR 9–102(B)(1) provided that a lawyer shall "[p]romptly notify a client of the receipt of his funds, securities, or other properties." EC 7–8 stated that a lawyer "should exert his best efforts to insure that decisions of his client are made only after the client has been informed of relevant considerations." EC 9–2 stated that "a lawyer should fully and promptly inform his client of material developments in the matters being handled for the client."

RULE 1.5   Fees

(a) A lawyer's fee shall be reasonable. The factors to be considered in determining the reasonableness of a fee include the following:

(1) the time and labor required, the novelty and difficulty of the questions involved, and the skill requisite to perform the legal service properly;

(2) the likelihood, if apparent to the client, that the acceptance of the particular employment will preclude other employment by the lawyer;

(3) the fee customarily charged in the locality for similar legal services;

(4) the amount involved and the results obtained;

(5) the time limitations imposed by the client or by the circumstances;

(6) the nature and length of the professional relationship with the client;

(7) the experience, reputation, and ability of the lawyer or lawyers performing the services; and

(8) whether the fee is fixed or contingent.

(b) When the lawyer has not regularly represented the client, the basis or rate of the fee shall be communicated to the client, preferably in writing, before or within a reasonable time after commencing the representation.

(c) A fee may be contingent on the outcome of the matter for which the service is rendered, except in a matter in which a contingent fee is prohibited by paragraph (d) or other law. A contingent fee agreement shall be in writing and shall state the method by which the fee is to be determined, including the percentage or percentages that shall accrue to the lawyer in the event of settlement, trial or appeal, litigation and other expenses to be deducted from the recovery, and whether such expenses are to be deducted before or after the contingent fee is calculated. Upon conclusion of a contingent fee matter, the lawyer shall provide the client with a written statement stating the outcome of the matter and, if there is a recovery, showing the remittance to the client and the method of its determination.

(d) A lawyer shall not enter into an arrangement for, charge, or collect:

(1) any fee in a domestic relations matter, the payment or amount of which is contingent upon the securing of a divorce or upon the amount of alimony or support, or property settlement in lieu thereof; or

(2) a contingent fee for representing a defendant in a criminal case.

(e) a division of fee between lawyers who are not in the same firm may be made only if:

(1) the division is in proportion to the services performed by each lawyer or, by written agreement with the client, each lawyer assumes joint responsibility for the representation;

(2) the client is advised of and does not object to the participation of all the lawyers involved; and

(3) the total fee is reasonable.

COMMENT:

Basis or Rate of Fee

[1] When the lawyer has regularly represented a client, they ordinarily will have evolved an understanding concerning the basis or rate of the fee. In a new client-lawyer relationship, however, an understanding as to the fee should be promptly established. It is not necessary to recite all the factors that underlie the basis of the fee, but only

those that are directly involved in its computation. It is sufficient, for example, to state that the basic rate is an hourly charge or a fixed amount or an estimated amount, or to identify the factors that may be taken into account in finally fixing the fee. When developments occur during the representation that render an earlier estimate substantially inaccurate, a revised estimate should be provided to the client. A written statement concerning the fee reduces the possibility of misunderstanding. Furnishing the client with a simple memorandum or a copy of the lawyer's customary fee schedule is sufficient if the basis or rate of the fee is set forth.

Terms of Payment

[2] A lawyer may require advance payment of a fee, but is obliged to return any unearned portion. See Rule 1.16(d). A lawyer may accept property in payment for services, such as an ownership interest in an enterprise, providing this does not involve acquisition of a proprietary interest in the cause of action or subject matter of the litigation contrary to Rule 1.8(j).* However, a fee paid in property instead of money may be subject to special scrutiny because it involves questions concerning both the value of the services and the lawyer's special knowledge of the value of the property.

[3] An agreement may not be made whose terms might induce the lawyer improperly to curtail services for the client or perform them in a way contrary to the client's interest. For example, a lawyer should not enter into an agreement whereby services are to be provided only up to a stated amount when it is foreseeable that more extensive services probably will be required, unless the situation is adequately explained to the client. Otherwise, the client might have to bargain for further assistance in the midst of a proceeding or transaction. However, it is proper to define the extent of services in light of the client's ability to pay. A lawyer should not exploit a fee arrangement based primarily on hourly charges by using wasteful procedures. When there is doubt whether a contingent fee is consistent with the client's best interest, the lawyer should offer the client alternative bases for the fee and explain their implications. Applicable law may impose limitations on contingent fees, such as a ceiling on the percentage.

Division of Fee

[4] A division of fee is a single billing to a client covering the fee of two or more lawyers who are not in the same firm. A division of fee facilitates association of more than one lawyer in a matter in which neither alone could serve the client as well, and most often is used when the fee is contingent and the division is between a referring lawyer and a trial specialist. Paragraph (e) permits the lawyers to divide a fee on either the basis of the proportion of services they render or by agreement between the participating lawyers if all assume responsibility for the representation as a whole and the client is advised and does not object. It does not require disclosure to the client of the share that each lawyer is to receive. Joint responsibility for the representation entails the obligations stated in Rule 5.1 for purposes of the matter involved.

Disputes Over Fees

[5] If a procedure has been established for resolution of fee disputes, such as an arbitration or mediation procedure established by the bar, the lawyer should conscientiously consider submitting to it. Law may prescribe a procedure for determining a lawyer's fee, for example, in representation of an executor or administrator, a class or a person entitled to a reasonable fee as part of the measure of damages. The lawyer entitled to such a fee and a lawyer representing another party concerned with the fee should comply with the prescribed procedure.

MODEL CODE COMPARISON:

[1] DR 2–106(A) provided that a lawyer "shall not enter into an agreeement for, charge, or collect an illegal or clearly excessive fee." DR 2–106(B) provided that a fee is "clearly excessive when, after a review of the facts, a lawyer of ordinary prudence would be left with a definite and firm conviction that the fee is in excess of a reasonable fee." The factors of a reasonable fee in Rule 1.5(a) are substantially identical to those listed in DR 2–106(B). EC 2–17 states that a lawyer "should not charge more than a reasonable fee . . . ."

[2] There was no counterpart to Rule 1.5(b) in the Disciplinary Rules of the Model Code. EC 2–19 stated that it is "usually bene-

---

* In 1987, the ABA added the following clause to the 1983 version of the Model Rules: "providing this does not involve acquisition of a proprietary interest in the cause of action or subject matter of the litigation contrary to Rule 1.8(j)."

ficial to reduce to writing the understanding of the parties regarding the fee, particularly when it is contingent."

[3] There was no counterpart to paragraph (c) in the Disciplinary Rules of the Model Code. EC 2–20 provided that "[c]ontingent fee arrangements in civil cases have long been commonly accepted in the United States," but that "a lawyer generally should decline to accept employment on a contingent fee basis by one who is able to pay a reasonable fixed fee . . . ."

[4] With regard to paragraph (d), DR 2–106(C) prohibited "a contingent fee in a criminal case." EC 2–20 provided that "contingent fee arrangements in domestic relation cases are rarely justified."

[5] With regard to paragraph (e), DR 2–107(A) permitted division of fees only if: "(1) The client consents to employment of the other lawyer after a full disclosure that a division of fees will be made. (2) The division is in proportion to the services performed and responsibility assumed by each. (3) The total fee does not exceed clearly reasonable compensation . . . ." Paragraph (e) permits division without regard to the services rendered by each lawyer if they assume joint responsibility for the representation.

RULE 1.6 Confidentiality of Information *

(a) A lawyer shall not reveal information relating to representation of a client unless the client consents after consultation, except for disclosures that are impliedly authorized in order to carry out the representation, and except as stated in paragraph (b).

(b) A lawyer may reveal such information to the extent the lawyer reasonably believes necessary:

(1) to prevent the client from committing a criminal act that the lawyer believes is likely to result in imminent death or substantial bodily harm; or

(2) to establish a claim or defense on behalf of the lawyer in a controversy between the lawyer and the client, to establish a defense to a criminal charge or civil claim against the lawyer based upon conduct in which the client was involved, or to respond to allegations in any proceeding concerning the lawyer's representation of the client.

COMMENT:

[1] The lawyer is part of a judicial system charged with upholding the law. One of the lawyer's functions is to advise clients so that they avoid any violation of the law in the proper exercise of their rights.

[2] The observance of the ethical obligation of a lawyer to hold inviolate confidential information of the client not only facilitates the full development of facts essential to proper representation of the client but also encourages people to seek early legal assistance.

[3] Almost without exception, clients come to lawyers in order to determine what their rights are and what is, in the maze of laws and regulations, deemed to be legal and correct. The common law recognizes that the client's confidences must be

---

* Editors' Note: As previously proposed by the Kutak Commission, Rule 1.6 (Revised Final Draft, June 30, 1982) read as follows:

RULE 1.6 Confidentiality of Information

(a) A lawyer shall not reveal information relating to representation of a client unless the client consents after consultation, except for disclosures that are impliedly authorized in order to carry out the representation, and except as stated in paragraph (b).

(b) A lawyer may reveal such information to the extent the lawyer reasonably believes necessary:

(1) to prevent the client from committing a criminal or fraudulent act that the lawyer reasonably believes is likely to result in death or substantial bodily harm, or in substantial injury to the financial interests or property of another;

(2) to rectify the consequences of a client's criminal or fraudulent act in the furtherance of which the lawyer's services had been used;

(3) to establish a claim or defense on behalf of the lawyer in a controversy between the lawyer and the client, or to establish a defense to a criminal charge, civil claim or disciplinary complaint against the lawyer based upon conduct in which the client was involved; or

(4) to comply with other law.

protected from disclosure. Based upon experience, lawyers know that almost all clients follow the advice given, and the law is upheld.

[4] A fundamental principle in the client-lawyer relationship is that the lawyer maintain confidentiality of information relating to the representation. The client is thereby encouraged to communicate fully and frankly with the lawyer even as to embarrassing or legally damaging subject matter.

[5] The principle of confidentiality is given effect in two related bodies of law, the attorney-client privilege (which includes the work product doctrine) in the law of evidence and the rule of confidentiality established in professional ethics. The attorney-client privilege applies in judicial and other proceedings in which a lawyer may be called as a witness or otherwise required to produce evidence concerning a client. The rule of client-lawyer confidentiality applies in situations other than those where evidence is sought from the lawyer through compulsion of law. The confidentiality rule applies not merely to matters communicated in confidence by the client but also to all information relating to the representation, whatever its source. A lawyer may not disclose such information except as authorized or required by the Rules of Professional Conduct or other law. See also Scope.

[6] The requirement of maintaining confidentiality of information relating to representation applies to government lawyers who may disagree with the policy goals that their representation is designed to advance.

Authorized Disclosure

[7] A lawyer is impliedly authorized to make disclosures about a client when appropriate in carrying out the representation, except to the extent that the client's instructions or special circumstances limit that authority. In litigation, for example, a lawyer may disclose information by admitting a fact that cannot properly be disputed, or in negotiation by making a disclosure that facilitates a satisfactory conclusion.

[8] Lawyers in a firm may, in the course of the firm's practice, disclose to each other information relating to a client of the firm, unless the client has instructed that particular information be confined to specified lawyers.

Disclosure Adverse to Client

[9] The confidentiality rule is subject to limited exceptions. In becoming privy to information about a client, a lawyer may foresee that the client intends serious harm to another person. However, to the extent a lawyer is required or permitted to disclose a client's purposes, the client will be inhibited from revealing facts which would enable the lawyer to counsel against a wrongful course of action. The public is better protected if full and open communication by the client is encouraged than if it is inhibited.

Several situations must be distinguished.

[10] First, the lawyer may not counsel or assist a client in conduct that is criminal or fraudulent. See Rule 1.2(d). Similarly, a lawyer has a duty under Rule 3.3(a)(4) not to use false evidence. This duty is essentially a special instance of the duty prescribed in Rule 1.2(d) to avoid assisting a client in criminal or fraudulent conduct.

[11] Second, the lawyer may have been innocently involved in past conduct by the client that was criminal or fraudulent. In such a situation the lawyer has not violated Rule 1.2(d), because to "counsel or assist" criminal or fraudulent conduct requires knowing that the conduct is of that character.

[12] Third, the lawyer may learn that a client intends prospective conduct that is criminal and likely to result in imminent death or substantial bodily harm. As stated in paragraph (b)(1), the lawyer has professional discretion to reveal information in order to prevent such consequences. The lawyer may make a disclosure in order to prevent homicide or serious bodily injury which the lawyer reasonable believes is intended by a client. It is very difficult for a lawyer to "know" when such a heinous purpose will actually be carried out, for the client may have a change of mind.

[13] The lawyer's exercise of discretion requires consideration of such factors as the nature of the lawyer's relationship with the client and with those who might be injured by the client, the lawyer's own involvement in the transaction and factors that may extenuate the conduct in question. Where practical, the lawyer should seek to persuade the client to take suitable action. In any case, a disclosure adverse to the client's interest should be no greater than the lawyer reasonably believes necessary to the purpose. A lawyer's decision not to take preventive action permitted by paragraph (b)(1) does not violate this Rule.

Withdrawal

[14] If the lawyer's services will be used by the client in materially furthering a course of

criminal or fraudulent conduct, the lawyer must withdraw, as stated in Rule 1.16(a)(1).

[15] After withdrawal the lawyer is required to refrain from making disclosure of the clients' confidences, except as otherwise provided in Rule 1.6. Neither this Rule nor Rule 1.8(b) nor Rule 1.16(d) prevents the lawyer from giving notice of the fact of withdrawal, and the lawyer may also withdraw or disaffirm any opinion, document, affirmation, or the like.

[16] Where the client is an organization, the lawyer may be in doubt whether contemplated conduct will actually be carried out by the organization. Where necessary to guide conduct in connection with this Rule, the lawyer may make inquiry within the organization as indicated in Rule 1.13(b).

Dispute Concerning Lawyer's Conduct

[17] Where a legal claim or disciplinary charge alleges complicity of the lawyer in a client's conduct or other misconduct of the lawyer involving representation of the client, the lawyer may respond to the extent the lawyer reasonably believes necessary to establish a defense. The same is true with respect to a claim involving the conduct or representation of a former client. The lawyer's right to respond arises when an assertion of such complicity has been made. Paragraph (b)(2) does not require the lawyer to await the commencement of an action or proceeding that charges such complicity, so that the defense may be established by responding directly to a third party who has made such an assertion. The right to defend, of course, applies where a proceeding has been commenced. Where practicable and not prejudicial to the lawyer's ability to establish the defense, the lawyer should advise the client of the third party's assertion and request that the client respond appropriately. In any event, disclosure should be no greater than the lawyer reasonably believes is necessary to vindicate innocence, the disclosure should be made in a manner which limits access to the information to the tribunal or other persons having a need to know it, and appropriate protective orders or other arrangements should be sought by the lawyer to the fullest extent practicable.

[18] If the lawyer is charged with wrongdoing in which the client's conduct is implicated, the rule of confidentiality should not prevent the lawyer from defending against the charge. Such a charge can arise in a civil, criminal or professional disciplinary proceeding, and can be based on a wrong allegedly committed by the lawyer against the client, or on a wrong alleged by a third person; for example, a person claiming to have been defrauded by the lawyer and client acting together. A lawyer entitled to a fee is permitted by paragraph (b)(2) to prove the services rendered in an action to collect it. This aspect of the rule expresses the principle that the beneficiary of a fiduciary relationship may not exploit it to the detriment of the fiduciary. As stated above, the lawyer must make every effort practicable to avoid unnecessary disclosure of information relating to a representation, to limit disclosure to those having the need to know it, and to obtain protective orders or make other arrangements minimizing the risk of disclosure.

Disclosures Otherwise Required or Authorized

[19] The attorney-client privilege is differently defined in various jurisdictions. If a lawyer is called as a witness to give testimony concerning a client, absent waiver by the client, Rule 1.6(a) requires the lawyer to invoke the privilege when it is applicable. The lawyer must comply with the final orders of a court or other tribunal of competent jurisdiction requiring the lawyer to give information about the client.

[20] The Rules of Professional Conduct in various circumstances permit or require a lawyer to disclose information relating to the representation. See Rules 2.2, 2.3, 3.3 and 4.1. In addition to these provisions, a lawyer may be obligated or permitted by other provisions of law to give information about a client. Whether another provision of law supersedes Rule 1.6 is a matter of interpretation beyond the scope of these Rules, but a presumption should exist against such a supersession.

Former Client

[21] The duty of confidentiality continues after the client-lawyer relationship has terminated.

MODEL CODE COMPARISON:

[1] Rule 1.6 eliminates the two-pronged duty under the Model Code in favor of a single standard protecting all information about a client "relating to the representation." Under DR 4–101, the requirement applied only to information protected by the attorney-client privilege and to information "gained in" the professional relationship that "the client has requested be held inviolate or the disclosure of which would be embarrassing or would be likely to be detrimental to the client." EC 4–4 added that the duty differed from the evidentiary privilege in that it existed "without re-

gard to the nature or source of information or the fact that others share the knowledge." Rule 1.6 imposes confidentiality on information relating to the representation even if it is acquired before or after the relationship existed. It does not require the client to indicate information that is to be confidential, or permit the lawyer to speculate whether particular information might be embarrassing or detrimental.

[2] Paragraph (a) permits a lawyer to disclose information where impliedly authorized to do so in order to carry out the representation. Under DR 4–101(B) and (C), a lawyer was not permitted to reveal "confidences" unless the client first consented after disclosure.

[3] Paragraph (b) redefines the exceptions to the requirement of confidentiality. Regarding paragraph (b)(1), DR 4–101(C)(3) provided that a lawyer "may reveal . . . [t]he intention of his client to commit a crime and the information necessary to prevent the crime." This option existed regardless of the seriousness of the proposed crime.

[4] With regard to paragraph (b)(2), DR 4–101(C)(4) provided that a lawyer may reveal "[c]onfidences or secrets necessary to establish or collect his fee or to defend himself or his employers or associates against an accusation of wrongful conduct." Paragraph (b)(2) enlarges the exception to include disclosure of information relating to claims by the lawyer other than for the lawyer's fee; for example, recovery of property from the client.

RULE 1.7 Conflict of Interest: General Rule

(a) A lawyer shall not represent a client if the representation of that client will be directly adverse to another client, unless:

(1) the lawyer reasonably believes the representation will not adversely affect the relationship with the other client; and

(2) each client consents after consultation.

(b) A lawyer shall not represent a client if the representation of that client may be materially limited by the lawyer's responsibilities to another client or to a third person, or by the lawyer's own interests, unless:

(1) the lawyer reasonably believes the representation will not be adversely affected; and

(2) the client consents after consultation. When representation of multiple clients in a single matter is undertaken, the consultation shall include explanation of the implications of the common representation and the advantages and risks involved.

COMMENT:

Loyalty to a Client

[1] Loyalty is an essential element in the lawyer's relationship to a client. An impermissible conflict of interest may exist before representation is undertaken, in which event the representation should be declined. The lawyer should adopt reasonable procedures, appropriate for the size and type of firm and practice, to determine in both litigation and non-litigation matters the parties and issues involved and to determine whether there are actual or potential conflicts of interest.*

[2] If such a conflict arises after representation has been undertaken, the lawyer should withdraw from the representation. See Rule 1.16. Where more than one client is involved and the lawyer withdraws because a conflict arises after representation, whether the lawyer may continue to represent any of the clients is determined by Rule 1.9. See also Rule 2.2(c). As to whether a client-lawyer relationship exists or, having once been established, is continuing, see Comment to Rule 1.3 and Scope.

[3] As a general proposition, loyalty to a client prohibits undertaking representation directly adverse to that client without that client's consent. Paragraph (a) expresses that general rule. Thus, a lawyer ordinarily may not act as advocate against a person the lawyer represents in some other matter, even if it is wholly unrelated. On the other hand, simultaneous representation in unrelated matters of clients whose interests are only generally adverse, such as competing economic enterprises, does not require consent of the respective clients. Paragraph (a) applies only when the representation of one client would be directly adverse to the other.

[4] Loyalty to a client is also impaired when a lawyer cannot consider, recommend or carry out an appropriate course of action for the client be-

---

* The ABA added this sentence in the comments to the Model Rules in 1987. The remainder of paragraph 1 in the original version of this comment now appears in the current paragraph 2.

cause of the lawyer's other responsibilities or interests. The conflict in effect forecloses alternatives that would otherwise be available to the client. Paragraph (b) addresses such situations. A possible conflict does not itself preclude the representation. The critical questions are the likelihood that a conflict will eventuate and, if it does, whether it will materially interfere with the lawyer's independent professional judgment in considering alternatives or foreclose courses of action that reasonably should be pursued on behalf of the client. Consideration should be given to whether the client wishes to accommodate the other interest involved.

Consultation and Consent

[5] A client may consent to representation notwithstanding a conflict. However, as indicated in paragraph (a)(1) with respect to representation directly adverse to a client, and paragraph (b)(1) with respect to material limitations on representation of a client, when a disinterested lawyer would conclude that the client should not agree to the representation under the circumstances, the lawyer involved cannot properly ask for such agreement or provide representation on the basis of the client's consent. When more than once client is involved, the question of conflict must be resolved as to each client. Moreover, there may be circumstances where it is impossible to make the disclosure necessary to obtain consent. For example, when the lawyer represents different clients in related matters and one of the clients refuses to consent to the dislcosure necessary to permit the other client to make an informed decision, the lawyer cannot properly ask the latter to consent.

Lawyer's Interests

[6] The lawyer's own interests should not be permitted to have adverse effect on representation of a client. For example, a lawyer's need for income should not lead the lawyer to undertake matters that cannot be handled competently and at a reasonable fee. See Rules 1.1 and 1.5. If the probity of a lawyer's own conduct in a transaction is in serious question, it may be difficult or impossible for the lawyer to give a client detached advice. A lawyer may not allow related business interests to affect representation, for example, by referring clients to an enterprise in which the lawyer has an undisclosed interest.

Conflicts in Litigation

[7] Paragraph (a) prohibits representation of opposing parties in litigation. Simultaneous representation of parties whose interests in litigation may conflict, such as co-plaintiffs or co-defendants, is governed by paragraph (b). An impermissible conflict may exist by reason of substantial discrepancy in the parties' testimony, incompatibility in positions in relation to an opposing party or the fact that there are substantially different possibilities of settlement of the claims or liabilities in question. Such conflicts can arise in criminal cases as well as civil. The potential for conflict of interest in representing multiple defendants in a criminal case is so grave that ordinarily a lawyer should decline to represent more than one codefendant. On the other hand, common representation of persons having similar interests is proper if the risk of adverse effect is minimal and the requirements of paragraph (b) are met. Compare Rule 2.2 involving intermediation between clients.

[8] Ordinarily, a lawyer may not act as advocate against a client the lawyer represents in some other matter, even if the other matter is wholly unrelated. However, there are circumstances in which a lawyer may act as advocate against a client. For example, a lawyer representing an enterprise with diverse operations may accept employment as an advocate against the enterprise in an unrelated matter if doing so will not adversely affect the lawyer's relationship with the enterprise or conduct of the suit and if both clients consent upon consultation. By the same token, government lawyers in some circumstances may represent government employees in proceedings in which a government agency is the opposing party. The propriety of concurrent representation can depend on the nature of the litigation. For example, a suit charging fraud entails conflict to a degree not involved in a suit for a declaratory judgment concerning statutory interpretation.

[9] A lawyer may represent parties having antagonistic positions on a legal question that has arisen in different cases, unless representation of either client would be adversely affected. Thus, it is ordinarily not improper to assert such positions in cases pending in different trial courts, but it may be improper to do so in cases pending at the same time in an appellate court.

Interest of Person Paying for a Lawyer's Service

[10] A lawyer may be paid from a source other than the client, if the client is informed of that fact and consents and the arrangement does not compromise the lawyer's duty of loyalty to the client. See Rule 1.8(f). For example, when an insurer and its insured have conflicting interests in a matter arising from a liability insurance agree-

ment, and the insurer is required to provide special counsel for the insured, the arrangement should assure the special counsel's professional independence. So also, when a corporation and its directors or employees are involved in a controversy in which they have conflicting interests, the corporation may provide funds for separate legal representation of the directors or employees, if the clients consent after consultation and the arrangement ensures the lawyer's professional independence.

Other Conflict Situations

[11] Conflicts of interest in contexts other than litigation sometimes may be difficult to assess. Relevant factors in determining whether there is potential for adverse effect include the duration and intimacy of the lawyer's relationship with the client or clients involved, the functions being performed by the lawyer, the likelihood that actual conflict will arise and the likely prejudice to the client from the conflict if it does arise. The question is often one of proximity and degree.

[12] For example, a lawyer may not represent multiple parties to a negotiation whose interests are fundamentally antagonistic to each other, but common representation is permissible where the clients are generally aligned in interest even though there is some difference of interest among them.

[13] Conflict questions may also arise in estate planning and estate administration. A lawyer may be called upon to prepare wills for several family members, such as husband and wife, and, depending upon the circumstances, a conflict of interest may arise. In estate administration the identity of the client may be unclear under the law of a particular jurisdiction. Under one view, the client is the fiduciary; under another view the client is the estate or trust, including its beneficiaries. The lawyer should make clear the relationship to the parties involved.

[14] A lawyer for a corporation or other organization who is also a member of its board of directors should determine whether the responsibilities of the two roles may conflict. The lawyer may be called on to advise the corporation in matters involving actions of the directors. Consideration should be given to the frequency with which such situations may arise, the potential intensity of the conflict, the effect of the lawyer's resignation from the board and the possibility of the corporation's obtaining legal advice from another lawyer in such situations. If there is material risk that the dual role will compromise the lawyer's independence of professional judgment, the lawyer should not serve as a director.

Conflict Charged by an Opposing Party

[15] Resolving questions of conflict of interest is primarily the responsibility of the lawyer undertaking the representation. In litigation, a court may raise the question when there is reason to infer that the lawyer has neglected the responsibility. In a criminal case, inquiry by the court is generally required when a lawyer represents multiple defendants. Where the conflict is such as clearly to call in question the fair or efficient administration of justice, opposing counsel may properly raise the question. Such an objection should be viewed with caution, however, for it can be misused as a technique of harassment. See Scope.

MODEL CODE COMPARISON:

[1] DR 5–101(A) provided that "[e]xcept with the consent of his client after full disclosure, a lawyer shall not accept employment if the exercise of his professional judgment on behalf of the client will be or reasonably may be affected by his own financial, business, property, or personal interests." DR 5–105(A) provided that a lawyer "shall decline proffered employment if the exercise of his independent professional judgment in behalf of a client will be or is likely to be adversely affected by the acceptance of the proffered employment, or if it would be likely to involve him in representing differing interests, except to the extent permitted under DR 5–105(C)." DR 5–105(C) provided that "a lawyer may represent multiple clients if it is obvious that he can adequately represent the interest of each and if each consents to the representation after full disclosure of the possible effect of such representation on the exercise of his independent professional judgment on behalf of each." DR 5–107(B) provided that a lawyer "shall not permit a person who recommends, employs, or pays him to render legal services for another to direct or regulate his professional judgment in rendering such services."

[2] Rule 1.7 clarifies DR 5–105(A) by requiring that, when the lawyer's other interests are involved, not only must the client consent after consultation but also that, independent of such consent, the representation reasonably appears not to be adversely affected by the lawyer's other interests. This requirement appears to be the intended meaning of the provi-

sion in DR 5–105(C) that "it is obvious that he can adequately represent" the client, and was implicit in EC 5–2, which stated that a lawyer "should not accept proffered employment if his personal interests or desires will, or there is a reasonable probability that they will, affect adversely the advice to be given or services to be rendered the prospective client."

RULE 1.8 Conflict of Interest: Prohibited Transactions

(a) A lawyer shall not enter into a business transaction with a client or knowingly acquire an ownership, possessory, security or other pecuniary interest adverse to a client unless:

(1) the transaction and terms on which the lawyer acquires the interest are fair and reasonable to the client and are fully disclosed and transmitted in writing to the client in a manner which can be reasonably understood by the client;

(2) the client is given a reasonable opportunity to seek the advice of independent counsel in the transaction; and

(3) the client consents in writing thereto.

(b) A lawyer shall not use information relating to representation of a client to the disadvantage of the client unless the client consents after consultation, except as permitted or required by Rule 1.6 or Rule 3.3.

(c) A lawyer shall not prepare an instrument giving the lawyer or a person related to the lawyer as parent, child, sibling, or spouse any substantial gift from a client, including a testamentary gift, except where the client is related to the donee.

(d) Prior to the conclusion of representation of a client, a lawyer shall not make or negotiate an agreement giving the lawyer literary or media rights to a portrayal or account based in substantial part on information relating to the representation.

(e) A lawyer shall not provide financial assistance to a client in connection with pending or contemplated litigation, except that:

(1) a lawyer may advance court costs and expenses of litigation, the repayment of which may be contingent on the outcome of the matter; and

(2) a lawyer representing an indigent client may pay court costs and expenses of litigation on behalf of the client.

(f) A lawyer shall not accept compensation for representing a client from one other than the client unless:

(1) the client consents after consultation;

(2) there is no interference with the lawyer's independence of professional judgment or with the client–lawyer relationship; and

(3) Information relating to representation of a client is protected as required by rule 1.6.

(g) A lawyer who represents two or more clients shall not participate in making an aggregate settlement of the claims of or against the clients, or in a criminal case an aggregated agreement as to guilty or nolo contendere pleas, unless each client consents after consultation, including disclosure of the existence and nature of all the claims or pleas involved and of the participation of each person in the settlement.

(h) A lawyer shall not make an agreement prospectively limiting the lawyer's liability to a client for malpractice unless permitted by law and the client is independently represented in making the agreement, or settle a claim for such liability with an unrepresented client or former client without first advising that person in writing that independent representation is appropriate in connection therewith.

(i) A lawyer related to another lawyer as parent, child, sibling or spouse shall not represent a client in a representation directly adverse to a person who the lawyer knows is represented by the other lawyer except upon consent by the client after consultation regarding the relationship.

(j) A lawyer shall not acquire a proprietary interest in the cause of action or subject matter of litigation the lawyer is conducting for a client, except that the lawyer may:

(1) acquire a lien granted by law to secure the lawyer's fee or expenses; and

(2) contract with a client for a reasonable contingent fee in a civil case.

COMMENT:

Transactions Between Client and Lawyer

[1] As a general principle, all transactions between client and lawyer should be fair and reasonable to the client. In such transactions a review by independent counsel on behalf of the client is often advisable. Furthermore, a lawyer may not exploit information relating to the representation to the client's disadvantage. For example, a lawyer who has learned that the client is investing in specific real estate may not, without the client's consent, seek to acquire nearby property where doing so would adversely affect the client's plan for investment. Paragraph (a) does not, however, apply to standard commercial transactions between the lawyer and the client for products or services that the client generally markets to others, for example, banking or brokerage services, medical services, products manufactured or distributed by the client, and utilities services. In such transactions, the lawyer has no advantage in dealing with the client, and the restrictions in paragraph (a) are unnecessary and impracticable.

[2] A lawyer may accept a gift from a client, if the transaction meets general standards of fairness. For example, a simple gift such as a present given at a holiday or as a token of appreciation is permitted. If effectuation of a substantial gift requires preparing a legal instrument such as a will or conveyance, however, the client should have the detached advice that another lawyer can provide. Paragraph (c) recognizes an exception where the client is a relative of the donee or the gift is not substantial.

Literary Rights

[3] An agreement by which a lawyer acquires literary or media rights concerning the conduct of the representation creates a conflict between the interests of the client and the personal interests of the lawyer. Measures suitable in the representation of the client may detract from the publication value of an account of the representation. Paragraph (d) does not prohibit a lawyer representing a client in a transaction concerning literary property from agreeing that the lawyer's fee shall consist of a share in ownership in the property, if the arrangement conforms to Rule 1.5 and paragraph (j).

Person Paying for Lawyer's Services

[4] Rule 1.8(f) requires disclosure of the fact that the lawyer's services are being paid for by a third party. Such an arrangement must also conform to the requirements of Rule 1.6 concerning confidentiality and Rule 1.7 concerning conflict of interest. Where the client is a class, consent may be obtained on behalf of the class by court-supervised procedure.

Family Relationships Between Lawyers

[5] Rule 1.8(i) applies to related lawyers who are in different firms. Related lawyers in the same firm are governed by Rules 1.7, 1.9, and 1.10. The disqualification stated in Rule 1.8(i) is personal and is not imputed to members of firms with whom the lawyers are associated.

Acquisition of Interest in Litigation

[6] Paragraph (j) states the traditional general rule that lawyers are prohibited from acquiring a proprietary interest in litigation. This general rule, which has its basis in common law champerty and maintenance, is subject to specific exceptions developed in decisional law and continued in these Rules, such as the exception for reasonable contingent fees set forth in Rule 1.5 and the exception for certain advances of the costs of litigation set forth in paragraph (e).

[7] This Rule is not intended to apply to customary qualification and limitations in legal opinions and memoranda.

MODEL CODE COMPARISON:

[1] With regard to paragraph (a), DR 5-104(A) provided that a lawyer "shall not enter into a business transaction with a client if they have differing interests therein and if the client expects the lawyer to exercise his professional judgment therein for the protection of the client, unless the client has consented after full disclosure." EC 5-3 stated that a lawyer "should not seek to persuade his client to permit him to invest in an undertaking of his client nor make improper use of his professional relationship to influence his client to invest in an enterprise in which the lawyer is interested."

[2] With regard to paragraph (b), DR 4-101(B)(3) provided that a lawyer should not use "a confidence or secret of his client for the advantage of himself, or of a third person, unless the client consents after full disclosure."

[3] There was no counterpart to paragraph (c) in the Disciplinary Rules of the Model Code. EC 5-5 stated that a lawyer "should not suggest to his client that a gift be made to himself or for his benefit. If a lawyer accepts a gift from his client, he is peculiarly

susceptible to the charge that he unduly influenced or overreached the client. If a client voluntarily offers to make a gift to his lawyer, the lawyer may accept the gift, but before doing so, he should urge that the client secure disinterested advice from an independent, competent person who is cognizant of all the circumstances. Other than in exceptional circumstances, a lawyer should insist that an instrument in which his client desires to name him beneficially be prepared by another lawyer selected by the client."

[4] Paragraph (d) is substantially similar to DR 5–104(B), but refers to "literary or media" rights, a more generally inclusive term than "publication" rights.

[5] Paragraph (e)(1) is similar to DR 5–103(B), but eliminates the requirement that "the client remains ultimately liable for such expenses."

[6] Paragraph (e)(2) has no counterpart in the Model Code.

[7] Paragraph (f) is substantially identical to DR 5–107(A)(1).

[8] Paragraph (g) is substantially identical to DR 5–106.

[9] The first clause of paragraph (h) is similar to DR 6–102(A). There was no counterpart in the Model Code to the second clause of paragraph (h).

[10] Paragraph (i) has no counterpart in the Model Code.

[11] Paragraph (j) is substantially identical to DR 5–103(A).

RULE 1.9 Conflict of Interest: Former Client *

(a) A lawyer who has formerly represented a client in a matter shall not thereafter represent another person in the same or a substantially related matter in which that person's interests are materially adverse to the interests of the former client unless the former client consents after consultation.

(b) A lawyer shall not knowingly represent a person in the same or a substantially related matter in which a firm with which the lawyer formerly was associated had previously represented a client,

(1) whose interests are materially adverse to that person; and

(2) about whom the lawyer had acquired information protected by Rules 1.6 and 1.9(c) that is material to the matter;

unless the former client consents after consultation.

(c) A lawyer who has formerly represented a client in a matter or whose present or former firm has formerly represented a client in a matter shall not thereafter:

(1) use information relating to the representation to the disadvantage of the former client except as Rule 1.6 or Rule 3.3 would permit or require with respect to a client, or when the information has become generally known; or

(2) reveal information relating to the representation except as Rule 1.6 or Rule 3.3 would permit or require with respect to a client.

COMMENT:

[1] After termination of a client-lawyer relationship, a lawyer may not represent another client except in conformity with this Rule. The principles in Rule 1.7 determine whether the interests of the present and former client are adverse. Thus, a lawyer could not properly seek to rescind on behalf of a new client a contract drafted on

---

* In 1989, the ABA amended Model Rule 1.9 by moving some of the text in original Model Rule 1.10(b) into current Model Rule 1.9(b). The original Model Rule 1.9(b) was moved to Model Rule 1.9(c). The impetus behind this change was to clarify an overlap between Model Rule 1.9 and 1.10 and to address the question of duties to former clients when a lawyer changes firms and did not represent the former client but may have acquired confidential information about a former client of the old firm. The following represents Model Rule 1.9 as adopted in 1983:

RULE 1.9 Conflict of Interest: Former Client

A Lawyer who has formerly represented a client in a matter shall not thereafter:

(a) Represent another person in the same or a substantially related matter in which that person's interests are materially adverse to the interests of the former client unless the former client consents after consultation; or

(b) Use information relating to the representation to the disadvantage of the former client except as Rule 1.6 would permit with respect to a client or when the information has become generally known.

behalf of the former client. So also a lawyer who has prosecuted an accused person could not properly represent the accused in a subsequent civil action against the government concerning the same transaction.

[2] The scope of a "matter" for purposes of this Rule may depend on the facts of a particular situation or transaction. The lawyer's involvement in a matter can also be a question of degree. When a lawyer has been directly involved in a specific transaction, subsequent representation of other clients with materially adverse interests clearly is prohibited. On the other hand, a lawyer who recurrently handled a type of problem for a former client is not precluded from later representing another client in a wholly distinct problem of that type even though the subsequent representation involves a position adverse to the prior client. Similar considerations can apply to the reassignment of military lawyers between defense and prosecution functions within the same military jurisdiction. The underlying question is whether the lawyer was so involved in the matter that the subsequent representation can be justly regarded as a changing of sides in the matter in question.

Lawyers Moving Between Firms*

[3] When lawyers have been associated within a firm but then end their association, the question of whether a lawyer should undertake representation is more complicated. There are several competing considerations. First, the client previously represented by the former firm must be reasonably assured that the principle of loyalty to the client is not compromised. Second, the rule should not be so broadly cast as to preclude other persons from having reasonable choice of legal counsel. Third, the rule should not unreasonably hamper lawyers from forming new associations and taking on new clients after having left a previous association. In this connection, it should be recognized that today many lawyers practice in firms, that many lawyers to some degree limit their practice to one field or another, and that many move from one association to another several times in their careers. If the concept of imputation were applied with unqualified rigor, the result would be radical curtailment of the opportunity of lawyers to move from one practice setting to another and of the opportunity of clients to change counsel.

[4] Reconciliation of these competing principles in the past has been attempted under two rubrics. One approach has been to seek per se rules of disqualification. For example, it has been held that a partner in a law firm is conclusively presumed to have access to all confidences concerning all clients of the firm. Under this analysis, if a lawyer has been a partner in one law firm and then becomes a partner in another law firm, there may be a presumption that all confidences known by the partner in the first firm are known to all partners in the second firm. This presumption might properly be applied in some circumstances, especially where the client has been extensively represented, but may be unrealistic where the client was represented only for limited purposes. Furthermore, such a rigid rule exaggerates the difference between a partner and an associate in modern law firms.

[5] The other rubric formerly used for dealing with disqualification is the appearance of impropriety proscribed in Canon 9 of the ABA Model Code of Professional Responsibility. This rubric has a two fold problem. First, the appearance of impropriety can be taken to include any new client-lawyer relationship that might make a former client feel anxious. If that meaning were adopted, disqualification would become little more than a question of subjective judgment by the former client. Second, since "impropriety" is undefined, the term "appearance of impropriety" is question-begging. It therefore has to be recognized that the problem of disqualification cannot be properly resolved either by simple analogy to a lawyer practicing alone or by the very general concept of appearance of impropriety.

[6] A rule based on a functional analysis is more appropriate for determining the question of disqualification. Two functions are involved: preserving confidentiality and avoiding positions adverse to a client.

Confidentiality**

[7] Preserving confidentiality is a question of access to information. Access to information, in turn, is essentially a question of fact in particular circumstances, aided by inferences, deductions or

---

* The comments under this topic originally appeared under Model Rule 1.10. With the modification of Model Rule 1.9, the ABA moved these comments under Model Rule 1.9 without significant change.

** The comments under this topic originally appeared under Model Rule 1.10. With the modification of Model Rule 1.9, the ABA moved these comments under Model Rule 1.9 without significant change.

working presumptions that reasonably may be made about the way in which lawyers work together. A lawyer may have general access to files of all clients of a law firm and may regularly participate in discussions of their affairs; it should be inferred that such a lawyer in fact is privy to all information about all the firm's clients. In contrast, another lawyer may have access to the files of only a limited number of clients and participate in discussions of the affairs of no other clients; inthe absence of information to the contrary, it should be inferred that such a lawyer in fact is privy to information about the clients actually served but not those of other clients.

[8] Application of paragraph (b) depends on a situation's particular facts. In such an inquiry, the burden of proof should rest upon the firm whose disqualification is sought.

[9] Paragraph (b) operates to disqualify the lawyer only when the lawyer involved has actual knowledge of information protected by Rules 1.6 and 1.9(b). Thus, if a lawyer while with one firm acquired no knowledge or information relating to a particular client of the firm, and that lawyer later joined another firm, neither the lawyer individually nor the second firm is disqualified from representing another client in the same or a related matter even though the interests of the two clients conflict. See Rule 1.10(b) for the restrictions on a firm once a lawyer has terminated association with the firm.

[10] Independent of the question of disqualification of a firm, a lawyer changing professional association has a continuing duty to preserve confidentiality of information about a client formerly represented. See Rules 1.6 and 1.9.

Adverse Positions*

[11] The second aspect of loyalty to a client is the lawyer's obligation to decline subsequent representations involving positions adverse to a former client arising in substantially related matters. This obligation requires abstention from adverse representation by the individual lawyer involved, but does not properly entail abstention of other lawyers through imputed disqualification. Hence, this aspect of the problem is governed by Rule

1.9(a). Thus, if a lawyer left one firm for another, the new affiliation would not preclude the firms involved from continuing to represent clients with adverse interests in the same or related matters, so long as the conditions of paragraphs (b) and (c) concerning confidentiality have been met.

[12] Information acquired by the lawyer in the course of representing a client may not subsequently be used or revealed by the lawyer to the disadvantage of the client. However, the fact that a lawyer has once served a client does not preclude the lawyer from using generally known information about that client when later representing another client.

[13] Disqualification from subsequent representation is for the protection of former clients and can be waived by them. A waiver is effective only if there is disclosure of the circumstances, including the lawyer's intended role in behalf of the new client.

[14] With regard to an opposing party's raising a question of conflict of interest, see Comment to Rule 1.7. With regard to disqualification of a firm with which a lawyer is or was formerly associated, see Rule 1.10.

MODEL CODE COMPARISON: **

[1] There was no counterpart to this Rule in the Disciplinary Rules of the Model Code. Representation adverse to a former client was sometimes dealt with under the rubric of Canon 9 of the Model Code, which provided: "A lawyer should avoid even the appearance of impropriety." Also applicable were EC 4–6 which stated that the "obligation of a lawyer to preserve the confidences and secrets of his client continues after the termination of his employment" and Canon 5 which stated that "[a] lawyer should exercise independent professional judgment on behalf of a client."

[2] The provision in paragraph (a) for waiver by the former client is similar to DR 5–105(C).

[3] The exception in the last clause of paragraph (c)(1) permits a lawyer to use information relating to a former client that is in the

---

* The comments under this topic originally appeared under Model Rule 1.10. With the modification of Model Rule 1.9, the ABA moved these comments under Model Rule 1.9 without significant change.

** When ABA modified Model Rule 1.9 in 1989, it did not change the text of the Model Code Comparison. Thus, the current Model Code Comparison only refers to the Model Rule 1.9 as originally enacted. To understand the amended Model Rule 1.9, one must read the following text quoted from the Code Comparison to Model Rule 1.10: "DR 5–105(D) provided that '[i]f a lawyer is required to decline or to withdraw from employment under a Disciplinary Rule, no partner, or associate, or any other lawyer affiliated with him or his firm, may accept or continue such employment.' "

"public domain," a use that was also not prohibited by the Model Code, which protected only "confidences and secrets." Since the scope of paragraph (a) is much broader than "confidences and secrets," it is necessary to define when a lawyer may make use of information about a client after the client-lawyer relationship has terminated.

RULE 1.10   Imputed Disqualification: General Rule*

(a) While lawyers are associated in a firm, none of them shall knowingly represent a client when any one of them practicing alone would be prohibited from doing so by Rules 1.7, 1.8(c), 1.9 or 2.2.

(b) When a lawyer has terminated an association with a firm, the firm is not prohibited from thereafter representing a person with in-terests materially adverse to those of a client represented by the formerly associated lawyer and not currently represented by the firm, unless:

(1) the matter is the same or substantially related to that in which the formerly associated lawyer represented the client; and

(2) any lawyer remaining in the firm has information protected by Rules 1.6 and 1.9(c) that is material to the matter.

(c) A disqualification prescribed by this rule may be waived by the affected client under the conditions stated in Rule 1.7.

COMMENT: **

Definition of "Firm"

[1]   For purposes of the Rules of Professional Conduct, the term "firm" includes lawyers in a

---

* In 1989, the ABA amended Model Rule 1.10 to remove original Rule 1.10(b) and move it to Model Rule 1.9(b). The ABA thus renumbered original Model Rule 1.10(c) and 1.10(d) as new Model Rule 1.10(b) and 1.10(c). The impetus behind this change was to clarify an overlap between Model Rule 1.9 and 1.10 and to address the question of duties to former clients when a lawyer changes firms and did not represent the former client but may have acquired confidential information about a former client of the old firm. Also, the ABA added the words "and, not currently represented by the firm" to current Model Rule 1.10(b). This was added to clarify the problem that when a lawyer leaves a firm, Model Rule 1.7's general prohibition of a directly adverse conflict still applies to the situation. The original version of Model Rule 1.10 is reproduced below:

RULE 1.10   Imputed Disqualification: General Rule

(a) While lawyers are associated in a firm, none of them shall knowingly represent a client when any one of them practicing alone would be prohibited from doing so by Rules 1.7, 1.8(c), 1.9 or 2.2.

(b) When a lawyer becomes associated with a firm, the firm may not knowingly represent a person in the same or a substantially related matter in which that lawyer, or a firm with which the lawyer was associated, had previously represented a client whose interests are materially adverse to that person and about whom the lawyer had acquired information protected by Rules 1.6 and 1.9(b) that is material to the matter.

(c) When a lawyer has terminated an association with a firm, the firm is not prohibited from thereafter representing a person with interests materially adverse to those of a client represented by the formerly associated lawyer unless:

(1) the matter is the same or substantially related to that in which the formerly associated lawyer represented the client; and

(2) any lawyer remaining in the firm has information protected by Rules 1.6 and 1.9(b) that is material to the matter.

(d) A disqualification prescribed by this rule may be waived by the affected client under the conditions stated in Rule 1.7.

** When the ABA amended Model Rule 1.10 in 1989, it moved several paragraphs of comments from Model Rule 1.10 to Model Rule 1.9. The paragraphs which appeared in the original version of the Model Rules are reproduced below:

Lawyers Moving Between Firms

When lawyers have been associated in a firm but then end their association, however, the problem is more complicated. The fiction that the law firm is the same as a single lawyer is no longer wholly realistic. There are several competing considerations. First, the client previously represented must be reasonably assured that the principle of loyalty to the client is not compromised. Second, the rule of disqualification should not be so broadly cast as to preclude other persons from having reasonable choice of legal counsel. Third, the rule of disqualification should not unreasonably hamper lawyers from forming new associations and taking on new clients after having left a private firm, and lawyers in the legal department of a corporation or other organization, or in a legal services organization. Whether two or more lawyers constitute a firm within this definition can depend on the specific facts. For example, two

practitioners who share office space and occasionally consult or assist each other ordinarily would not be regarded as constituting a firm. However, if they present themselves to the public in a way suggesting that they are a firm or conduct them-

---

previous association. In this connection, it should be recognized that today many lawyers practice in firms, that many to some degree limit their practice to one field or another, and that many move from one association to another several times in their careers. If the concept of imputed disqualification were defined with unqualified rigor, the result would be radical curtailment of the opportunity of lawyers to move from one practice setting to another and of the opportunity of clients to change counsel.

Reconciliation of these competing principles in the past has been attempted under two rubrics. One approach has been to seek per se rules of disqualification. For example, it has been held that a partner in a law firm is conclusively presumed to have access to all confidences concerning all clients of the firm. Under this analysis, if a lawyer has been a partner in one law firm and then becomes a partner in another law firm, there is a presumption that all confidences known by a partner in the first firm are known to all partners in the second firm. This presumption might properly be applied in some circumstances, especially where the client has been extensively represented, but may be unrealistic where the client was represented only for limited purposes. Furthermore, such a rigid rule exaggerates the difference between a partner and an associate in modern law firms.

The other rubric formerly used for dealing with vicarious disqualification is the appearance of impropriety proscribed in Canon 9 of the ABA Model Code of Professional Responsibility. This rubric has a twofold problem. First, the appearance of impropriety can be taken to include any new client-lawyer relationship that might make a former client feel anxious. If that meaning were adopted, disqualification would become little more than a question of subjective judgment by the former client. Second, since "impropriety" is undefined, the term "appearance of impropriety" is question-begging. It therefore has to be recognized that the problem of imputed disqualification cannot be properly resolved either by simple analogy to a lawyer practicing alone or by the very general concept of appearance of impropriety.

A rule based on a functional analysis is more appropriate for determining the question of vicarious disqualification. Two functions are involved: preserving confidentiality and avoiding positions adverse to a client.

Confidentiality

Preserving confidentiality is a question of access to information. Access to information, in turn, is essentially a question of fact in particular circumstances, aided by inferences, deductions or working presumptions that reasonably may be made about the way in which lawyers work together. A lawyer may have general access to files of all clients of a law firm and may regularly participate in discussions of their affairs; it should be inferred that such a lawyer in fact is privy to all information about all the firm's clients. In contrast, another lawyer may have access to the files of only a limited number of clients and participate in discussion of the affairs of no other clients; in the absence of information to the contrary, it should be inferred that such a lawyer in fact is privy to information about the clients actually served but not those of other clients.

Application of paragraphs (b) and (c) depends on a situation's particular facts. In any such inquiry, the burden of proof should rest upon the firm whose disqualification is sought.

Paragraphs (b) and (c) operate to disqualify the firm only when the lawyer involved has actual knowledge of information protected by Rules 1.6 and 1.9(b). Thus, if a lawyer while with one firm acquired no knowledge of information relating to a particular client of the firm, and that lawyer later joined another firm, neither the lawyer individually nor the second firm is disqualified from representing another client in the same or a related matter even though the interests of the two clients conflict.

Independent of the question of disqualification of a firm, a lawyer changing professional association has a continuing duty to preserve confidentiality of information about a client formerly represented. See Rules 1.6 and 1.9.

Adverse Positions

The second aspect of loyalty to client is the lawyer's obligation to decline subsequent representations involving positions adverse to a former client arising in substantially related matters. This obligation requires abstention from adverse representation by the individual lawyer involved, but does not properly entail abstention of other lawyers through imputed disqualification. Hence, this aspect of the problem is governed by Rule 1.9(a). Thus, if a lawyer left one firm for another, the new affiliation would not preclude the firms involved from continuing to represent clients with adverse interests in the same or related matters, so long as the conditions of Rule 1.10(b) and (c) concerning confidentiality have been met.

selves as a firm, they should be regarded as a firm for the purposes of the Rules. The terms of any formal agreement between associated lawyers are relevant in determining whether they are a firm, as is the fact that they have mutual access to information concerning the clients they serve. Furthermore, it is relevant in doubtful cases to consider the underlying purpose of the Rule that is involved. A group of lawyers could be regarded as a firm for purposes of the rule that the same lawyer should not represent opposing parties in litigation, while it might not be so regarded for purposes of the rule that information acquired by one lawyer is attributed to the other.

[2] With respect to the law department of an organization, there is ordinarily no question that the members of the department constitute a firm within the meaning of the Rules of Professional Conduct. However, there can be uncertainty as to the identity of the client. For example, it may not be clear whether the law department of a corporation represents a subsidiary or an affiliated corporation, as well as the corporation by which the members of the department are directly employed. A similar question can arise concerning an unincorporated association and its local affiliates.

[3] Similar questions can also arise with respect to lawyers in legal aid. Lawyers employed in the same unit of a legal service organization constitute a firm, but not necessarily those employed in separate units. As in the case of independent practitioners, whether the lawyers should be treated as associated with each other can depend on the particular rule that is involved, and on the specific facts of the situation.

[4] Where a lawyer has joined a private firm after having represented the government, the situation is governed by Rule 1.11(a) and (b); where a lawyer represents the government after having served private clients, the situation is governed by Rule 1.11(c)(1). The individual lawyer involved is bound by the Rules generally, including Rules 1.6, 1.7 and 1.9.

[5] Different provisions are thus made for movement of a lawyer from one private firm to another and for movement of a lawyer between a private firm and the government. The government is entitled to protection of its client confidences and, therefore, to the protections provided in Rules 1.6, 1.9 and 1.11. However, if the more

extensive disqualification in Rule 1.10 were applied to former government lawyers, the potential effect on the government would be unduly burdensome. The government deals with all private citizens and organizations and, thus, has a much wider circle of adverse legal interests than does any private law firm. In these circumstances, the government's recruitment of lawyers would be seriously impaired if Rule 1.10 were applied to the government. On balance, therefore, the government is better served in the long run by the protections stated in Rule 1.11.

Principles of Imputed Disqualification

[6] The rule of imputed disqualification stated in paragraph (a) gives effect to the principle of loyalty to the client as it applies to lawyers who practice in a law firm. Such situations can be considered from the premise that a firm of lawyers is essentially one lawyer for purposes of the rules governing loyalty to the client, or from the premise that each lawyer is vicariously bound by the obligation of loyalty owed by each lawyer with whom the lawyer is associated. Paragraph (a) operates only among the lawyers currently associated in a firm. When a lawyer moves from one firm to another, the situation is governed by Rules 1.9(b) and 1.10(b).

[7] * Rule 1.10(b) operates to permit a law firm, under certain circumstances, to represent a person with interests directly adverse to those of a client represented by a lawyer who formerly was associated with the firm. The Rule applies regardless of when the formerly associated lawyer represented the client. However, the law firm may not represent a person with interests adverse to those of a present client of the firm, which would violate Rule 1.7. Moreover, the firm may not represent the person where the matter is the same or substantially related to that in which the formerly associated lawyer represented the client and any other lawyer currently in the firm has material information protected by Rules 1.6 and 1.9(c).

MODEL CODE COMPARISON:

DR 5–105(D) provided that "[i]f a lawyer is required to decline or to withdraw from employment under a Disciplinary Rule, no partner, or associate, or any other lawyer affiliated with him or his firm, may accept or continue such employment."

---

* The ABA added this entire paragraph to the comments to Model Rule 1.10 in 1989. Thus, this language does not appear in the original version of the Model Rules.

RULE 1.11 Successive Government and Private Employment

(a) Except as law may otherwise expressly permit, a lawyer shall not represent a private client in connection with a matter in which the lawyer participated personally and substantially as a public officer or employee, unless the appropriate government agency consents after consultation. No lawyer in a firm with which that lawyer is associated may knowingly undertake or continue representation in such a matter unless:

(1) the disqualified lawyer is screened from any participation in the matter and is apportioned no part of the fee therefrom; and

(2) written notice is promptly given to the appropriate government agency to enable it to ascertain compliance with the provisions of this rule.

(b) Except as law may otherwise expressly permit, a lawyer having information that the lawyer knows is confidential government information about a person acquired when the lawyer was a public officer or employee, may not represent a private client whose interests are adverse to that person in a matter in which the information could be used to the material disadvantage of that person. A firm with which that lawyer is associated may undertake or continue representation in the matter only if the disqualified lawyer is screened from any participation in the matter and is apportioned no part of the fee therefrom.

(c) Except as law may otherwise expressly permit, a lawyer serving as a public officer or employee shall not:

(1) participate in a matter in which the lawyer participated personally and substantially while in private practice or non-governmental employment, unless under applicable law no one is, or by lawful delegation may be, authorized to act in the lawyer's stead in the matter; or

(2) negotiate for private employment with any person who is involved as a party or as attorney for a party in a matter in which the lawyer is participating personally and substantially, except that a lawyer serving as a law clerk to a judge, other adjudicative officer or arbitrator may negotiate for private employment as permit-

ted by Rule 1.12(b) and subject to the conditions stated in Rule 1.12(b).

(d) As used in this rule, the term "matter" includes:

(1) any judicial or other proceeding, application, request for a ruling or other determination, contract, claim, controversy, investigation, charge, accusation, arrest or other particular matter involving a specific party or parties; and

(2) any other matter covered by the conflict of interest rules of the appropriate government agency.

(e) As used in this rule, the term "confidential government information" means information which has been obtained under governmental authority and which, at the time this rule is applied, the government is prohibited by law from disclosing to the public or has a legal privilege not to disclose, and which is not otherwise available to the public.

COMMENT:

[1] This Rule prevents a lawyer from exploiting public office for the advantage of a private client. It is a counterpart of Rule 1.10(b), which applies to lawyers moving from one firm to another.

[2] A lawyer representing a government agency, whether employed or specially retained by the government, is subject to the Rules of Professional Conduct, including the prohibition against representing adverse interests stated in Rule 1.7 and the protections afforded former clients in Rule 1.9. In addition, such a lawyer is subject to Rule 1.11 and to statutes and government regulations regarding conflict of interest. Such statutes and regulations may circumscribe the extent to which the government agency may give consent under this Rule.

[3] Where the successive clients are a public agency and a private client, the risk exists that power or discretion vested in public authority might be used for the special benefit of a private client. A lawyer should not be in a position where benefit to a private client might affect performance of the lawyer's professional functions on behalf of public authority. Also, unfair advantage could accrue to the private client by reason of access to confidential government information about the client's adversary obtainable only through the lawyer's government service. However, the rules governing lawyers presently or formerly employed by

a government agency should not be so restrictive as to inhibit transfer of employment to and from the government. The government has a legitimate need to attract qualified lawyers as well as to maintain high ethical standards. The provisions for screening and waiver are necessary to prevent the disqualification rule from imposing too severe a deterrent against entering public service.

[4] When the client is an agency of one government, that agency should be treated as a private client for purposes of this Rule if the lawyer thereafter represents an agency of another government, as when a lawyer represents a city and subsequently is employed by a federal agency.

[5] Paragraphs (a)(1) and (b) do not prohibit a lawyer from receiving a salary or partnership share established by prior independent agreement. They prohibit directly relating the attorney's compensation to the fee in the matter in which the lawyer is disqualified.

[6] Paragraph (a)(2) does not require that a lawyer give notice to the government agency at a time when premature disclosure would injure the client; a requirement for premature disclosure might preclude engagement of the lawyer. Such notice is, however, required to be given as soon as practicable in order that the government agency will have a reasonable opportunity to ascertain that the lawyer is complying with Rule 1.11 and to take appropriate action if it believes the lawyer is not complying.

[7] Paragaph (b) operates only when the lawyer in question has knowledge of the information, which means actual knowledge; it does not operate with respect to information that merely could be imputed to the lawyer.

[8] Paragraphs (a) and (c) do not prohibit a lawyer from jointly representing a private party and a government agency when doing so is permitted by Rule 1.7 and is not otherwise prohibited by law.

[9] Paragraph (c) does not disqualify other lawyers in the agency with which the lawyer in question has become associated.

MODEL CODE COMPARISON:

[1] Paragraph (a) is similar to DR 9–101(B), except that the latter used the terms "in which he had substantial responsibility while he was a public employee."

[2] Paragraphs (b), (c), (d) and (e) have no counterparts in the Model Code.

RULE 1.12 Former Judge or Arbitrator

(a) Except as stated in paragraph (d), a lawyer shall not represent anyone in connection with a matter in which the lawyer participated personally and substantially as a judge or other adjudicative officer, arbitrator or law clerk to such a person, unless all parties to the proceeding consent after consultation.

(b) A lawyer shall not negotiate for employment with any person who is involved as a party or as attorney for a party in a matter in which the lawyer is participating personally and substantially as a judge or other adjudicative officer, or arbitrator. A lawyer serving as a law clerk to a judge, other adjudicative officer or arbitrator may negotiate for employment with a party or attorney involved in a matter in which the clerk is participating personally and substantially, but only after the lawyer has notified the judge, other adjudicative officer or arbitrator.

(c) If a lawyer is disqualified by paragraph (a), no lawyer in a firm with which that lawyer is associated may knowingly undertake or continue representation in the matter unless:

(1) the disqualified lawyer is screened from any participation in the matter and is apportioned no part of the fee therefrom; and

(2) written notice is promptly given to the appropriate tribunal to enable it to ascertain compliance with the provisions of this rule.

(d) An arbitrator selected as a partisan of a party in a multi-member arbitration panel is not prohibited from subsequently representing that party.

COMMENT:

[1] This Rule generally parallels Rule 1.11. The term "personally and substantially" signifies that a judge who was a member of a multi-member court, and thereafter left judicial office to practice law, is not prohibited from representing a client in a matter pending in the court, but in which the former judge did not participate. So also the fact that a former judge exercised administrative responsibility in a court does not prevent the former judge from acting as a lawyer in a matter where the judge had previously exercised remote or incidental administrative responsibility that did not affect the merits. Compare the Comment to Rule 1.11. The term "adjudicative officer" includes

such officials as judges pro tempore, referees, special masters, hearing officers and other parajudicial officers, and also lawyers who serve as part-time judges. Compliance Canons A(2), B(2) and C of the Model Code of Judicial Conduct provide that a part-time judge, judge pro tempore or retired judge recalled to active service, may not "act as a lawyer in any proceeding in which he served as a judge or in any other proceeding related thereto." Although phrased differently from this Rule, those Rules correspond in meaning.

MODEL CODE COMPARISON:

[1] Paragaph (a) is substantially similar to DR 9–101(A), which provided that a lawyer "shall not accept private employment in a matter upon the merits of which he has acted in a judicial capacity." Paragraph (a) differs, however, in that it is broader in scope and states more specifically the persons to whom it applies. There was no counterpart in the Model Code to paragraphs (b), (c) or (d).

[2] With regard to arbitrators, EC 5–20 stated that "a lawyer [who] has undertaken to act as an impartial arbitrator or mediator, . . . should not thereafter represent in the dispute any of the parties involved." DR 9–101(A) did not permit a waiver of the disqualification applied to former judges by consent of the parties. However, DR 5–105(C) was similar in effect and could be construed to permit waiver.

RULE 1.13   Organization as Client *

(a) A lawyer employed or retained by an organization represents the organization acting through its duly authorized constituents.

---

* Editors' Note: As previously proposed by the Kutak Commission, Rule 1.13 (Revised Final Draft, June 30, 1982) read as follows:

RULE 1.13   Organization as the Client

(a) A lawyer employed or retained to represent an organization represents the organization as distinct from its directors, officers, employees, members, shareholders or other constituents.

(b) If a lawyer for an organization knows that an officer, employee or other person associated with the organization is engaged in action, intends to act or refuses to act in a matter related to the representation that is a violation of a legal obligation to the organization, or a violation of law which reasonably might be imputed to the organization, and is likely to result in substantial injury to the organization, the lawyer shall proceed as is reasonably necessary in the best interest of the organization. In determining how to proceed, the lawyer shall give due consideration to the seriousness of the violation and its consequences, the scope and nature of the lawyer's representation, the responsibility in the organization and the apparent motivation of the person involved, the policies of the organization concerning such matters and any other relevant considerations. Any measures taken shall be designed to minimize disruption of the organization and the risk of revealing information relating to the representation to persons outside the organization. Such measures may include among others:

(1) asking reconsideration of the matter;

(2) advising that a separate legal opinion on the matter be sought for presentation to appropriate authority in the organization; and

(3) referring the matter to higher authority in the organization, including, if warranted by the seriousness of the matter, referral to the highest authority that can act in behalf of the organization as determined by applicable law.

(c) When the organization's highest authority insists upon action, or refuses to take action, that is clearly a violation of a legal obligation to the organization, or a violation of law which reasonably might be imputed to the organization, and is likely to result in substantial injury to the organization, the lawyer may take further remedial action that the lawyer reasonably believes to be in the best interest of the organization. Such action may include revealing information otherwise protected by Rule 1.6 only if the lawyer reasonably believes that:

(1) the highest authority in the organization has acted to further the personal or financial interests of members of that authority which are in conflict with the interest of the organization; and

(2) revealing the informaiton is necessary in the best interest of the organization.

(d) In dealing with an organization's directors, officers, employees, members, shareholders or other constituents, a lawyer shall explain the identity of the client when the lawyer believes that such explanation is necessary to avoid misunderstandings on their part.

(e) A lawyer representing an organization may also represent any of its directors, officers, employees, members, shareholders or other constituents, subject to the provisions of Rule 1.7. If the organization's consent to the dual representation is required by Rule 1.7, the consent shall be given by an appropriate official of the organization other than the individual who is to be represented or by the shareholders.

(b) If a lawyer for an organization knows that an officer, employee or other person associated with the organization is engaged in action, intends to act or refuses to act in a matter related to the representation that is a violation of a legal obligation to the organization, or a violation of law which reasonably might be imputed to the organization, and is likely to result in substantial injury to the organization, the lawyer shall proceed as is reasonably necessary in the best interest of the organization. In determining how to proceed, the lawyer shall give due consideration to the seriousness of the violation and its consequences, the scope and nature of the lawyer's representation, the responsibility in the organization and the apparent motivation of the person involved, the policies of the organization concerning such matters and any other relevant considerations. Any measures taken shall be designed to minimize disruption of the organization and the risk of revealing information relating to the representation to persons outside the organization. Such measures may include among others:

(1) asking reconsideration of the matter;

(2) advising that a separate legal opinion on the matter be sought for presentation to appropriate authority in the organization; and

(3) referring the matter to higher authority in the organization, including, if warranted by the seriousness of the matter, referral to the highest authority that can act in behalf of the organization as determined by applicable law.

(c) If, despite the lawyer's efforts in accordance with paragraph (b), the highest authority that can act on behalf of the organization insists upon action, or a refusal to act, that is clearly a violation of law and is likely to result in substantial injury to the organization, the lawyer may resign in accordance with rule 1.16.

(d) In dealing with an organization's directors, officers, employees, members, shareholders or other constituents, a lawyer shall explain the identity of the client when it is apparent that the organization's interests are adverse to those of the constituents with whom the lawyer is dealing.

(e) A lawyer representing an organization may also represent any of its directors, officers, employees, members, shareholders or other constituents, subject to the provisions of rule 1.7. If the organization's consent to the dual representation is required by rule 1.7, the consent shall be given by an appropriate official of the organization other than the individual who is to be represented, or by the shareholders.

COMMENT:

The Entity as the Client

[1] An organizational client is a legal entity, but it cannot act except through its officers, directors, employees, shareholders and other constituents.

[2] Officers, directors, employees and shareholders are the constituents of the corporate organizational client. The duties defined in this Comment apply equally to unincorporated associations. "Other constituents" as used in this Comment means the positions equivalent to officers, directors, employees and shareholders held by persons acting for organizational clients that are not corporations.

[3] When one of the constituents of an organizational client communicates with the organization's lawyer in that person's organizational capacity, the communication is protected by Rule 1.6. Thus, by way of example, if an organizational client requests its lawyer to investigate allegations of wrongdoing, interviews made in the course of that investigation between the lawyer and the client's employees or other constituents are covered by Rule 1.6. This does not mean, however, that constituents of an organizational client are the clients of the lawyer. The lawyer may not disclose to such constituents information relating to the representation except for disclosures explicitly or impliedly authorized by the organizational client in order to carry out the representation or as otherwise permitted by Rule 1.6.

[4] When constituents of the organization make decisions for it, the decisions ordinarily must be accepted by the lawyer even if their utility or prudence is doubtful. Decisions concerning policy and operations, including ones entailing serious risk, are not as such in the lawyer's province. However, different considerations arise when the lawyer knows that the organization may be substantially injured by action of [a] constituent that is in violation of law. In such a circumstance, it may be reasonably necessary for the lawyer to ask

the constituent to reconsider the matter. If that fails, or if the matter is of sufficient seriousness and importance to the organization, it may be reasonably necessary for the lawyer to take steps to have the matter reviewed by a higher authority in the organization. Clear justification should exist for seeking review over the head of the constituent normally responsible for it. The stated policy of the organization may define circumstances and prescribe channels for such review, and a lawyer should encourage the formulation of such a policy. Even in the absence of organization policy, however, the lawyer may have an obligation to refer a matter to higher authority, depending on the seriousness of the matter and whether the constituent in question has apparent motives to act at variance with the organization's interest. Review by the chief executive officer or by the board of directors may be required when the matter is of importance commensurate with their authority. At some point it may be useful or essential to obtain an independent legal opinion.

[5] In an extreme case, it may be reasonably necessary for the lawyer to refer the matter to the organization's highest authority. Ordinarily, that is the board of directors or similar governing body. However, applicable law may prescribe that under certain conditions highest authority reposes elsewhere; for example, in the independent directors of a corporation.

Relation to Other Rules

[6] The authority and responsibility provided in paragraph (b) are concurrent with the authority and responsibility provided in other Rules. In particular, this Rule does not limit or expand the lawyer's responsibility under Rules 1.6, 1.8, and 1.16, 3.3 or 4.1. If the lawyer's services are being used by an organization to further a crime or fraud by the organization, Rule 1.2(d) can be applicable.

Government Agency

[7] The duty defined in this Rule applies to governmental organizations. However, when the client is a governmental organization, a different balance may be appropriate between maintaining confidentiality and assuring that the wrongful official act is prevented or rectified, for public business is involved. In addition, duties of lawyers employed by the government or lawyers in military service may be defined by statutes and regulation. Therefore, defining precisely the identity of the client and prescribing the resulting obligations of such lawyers may be more difficult in the government context. Although in some circmstances the

client may be a specific agency, it is generally the government as a whole. For example, if the action or failure to act involves the head of a bureau, either the department of which the bureau is a part or the government as a whole may be the client for purpose of this Rule. Moreover, in a matter involving the conduct of government officials, a government lawyer may have authority to question such conduct more extensively than that of a lawyer for a private organization in similar circumstances. This Rule does not limit that authority. See note on Scope.

Clarifying the Lawyer's Role

[8] There are times when the organization's interest may be or become adverse to those of one or more of its constituents. In such circumstances the lawyer should advise any constituent, whose interest the lawyer finds adverse to that of the organization of the conflict or potential conflict of interest, that the lawyer cannot represent such constituent, and that such person may wish to obtain independent representation. Care must be taken to assure that the individual understands that, when there is such adversity of interest, the lawyer for the organization cannot provide legal representation for that constituent individual, and that discussions between the lawyer for the organization and the individual may not be privileged.

[9] Whether such a warning should be given by the lawyer for the organization to any constituent individual may turn on the facts of each case.

Dual Representation

[10] Paragraph (e) recognizes that a lawyer for an organization may also represent a principal officer or major shareholder.

Derivative Actions

[11] Under generally prevailing law, the shareholders or members of a corporation may bring suit to compel the directors to perform their legal obligations in the supervision of the organization. Members of unincorporated associations have essentially the same right. Such an action may be brought nominally by the organization, but usually is, in fact, a legal controversy over management of the organization.

[12] The question can arise whether counsel for the organization may defend such an action. The proposition that the organization is the lawyer's client does not alone resolve the issue. Most derivative actions are a normal incident of an organization's affairs, to be defended by the organization's lawyer like any other suit. However, if

the claim involves serious charges of wrongdoing by those in control of the organization, a conflict may arise between the lawyer's duty to the organization and the lawyer's relationship with the board. In those circumstances, Rule 1.7 governs who should represent the directors and the organization.

MODEL CODE COMPARISON:

There was no counterpart to this Rule in the Disciplinary Rules of the Model Code. EC 5–18 stated that a "lawyer employed or retained by a corporation or similar entity owes his allegiance to the entity and not to a stockholder, director, officer, employee, representative, or other person connected with the entity. In advising the entity, a lawyer should keep paramount its interests and his professional judgment should not be influenced by the personal desires of any person or organization. Occasionally, a lawyer for an entity is requested by a stockholder, director, officer, employee, representative, or other person connected with the entity to represent him in an individual capacity; in such case the lawyer may serve the individual only if the lawyer is convinced that differing interests are not present." EC 5–24 stated that although a lawyer "may be employed by a business corporation with non-lawyers serving as directors or officers, and they necessarily have the right to make decisions of business policy, a lawyer must decline to accept direction of his professional judgment from any layman." DR 5–107(B) provided that a lawyer "shall not permit a person who . . . employs . . . him to render legal services for another to direct or regulate his professional judgment in rendering such legal services."

RULE 1.14 Client Under a Disability

(a) When a client's ability to make adequately considered decisions in connection with the representation is impaired, whether because of minority, mental disability or for some other reason, the lawyer shall, as far as reasonably possible, maintain a normal client–lawyer relationship with the client.

(b) A lawyer may seek the appointment of a guardian or take other protective action with respect to a client, only when the lawyer reasonably believes that the client cannot adequately act in the client's own interest.

COMMENT:

[1] The normal client-lawyer relationship is based on the assumption that the client, when properly advised and assisted, is capable of making decisions about important matters. When the client is a minor or suffers from a mental disorder or disability, however, maintaining the ordinary client-lawyer relationship may not be possible in all respects. In particular, an incapacitated person may have no power to make legally binding decisions. Nevertheless, a client lacking legal competence often has the ability to understand, deliberate upon, and reach conclusions about matters affecting the client's own well-being. Furthermore, to an increasing extent the law recognizes intermediate degrees of competence. For example, children as young as five or six years of age, and certainly those of ten or twelve, are regarded as having opinions that are entitled to weight in legal proceedings concerning their custody. So also, it is recognized that some persons of advanced age can be quite capable of handling routine financial matters while needing special legal protection concerning major transactions.

[2] The fact that a client suffers a disability does not diminish the lawyer's obligation to treat the client with attention and respect. If the person has no guardian or legal representative, the lawyer often must act as de facto guardian. Even if the person does have a legal representative, the lawyer should as far as possible accord the represented person the status of client, particularly in maintaining communication.

[3] If a legal representative has already been appointed for the client, the lawyer should ordinarily look to the representative for decisions on behalf of the client. If a legal representative has not been appointed, the lawyer should see to such an appointment where it would serve the client's best interests. Thus, if a disabled client has substantial property that should be sold for the client's benefit, effective completion of the transaction ordinarily requires appointment of a legal representative. In many circumstances, however, appointment of a legal representative may be expensive or traumatic for the client. Evaluation of these considerations is a matter of professional judgment on the lawyer's part.

[4] If the lawyer represents the guardian as distinct from the ward, and is aware that the guardian is acting adversely to the ward's interest, the lawyer may have an obligation to prevent or rectify the guardian's misconduct. See Rule 1.2(d).

Disclosure of the Client's Condition

[5] Rules of procedure in litigation generally provide that minors or persons suffering mental disability shall be represented by a guardian or next friend if they do not have a general guardian. However, disclosure of the client's disability can adversely affect the client's interests. For example, raising the question of disability could, in some circumstances, lead to proceedings for involuntary commitment. The lawyer's position in such cases is an unavoidably difficult one. The lawyer may seek guidance from an appropriate diagnostician.

MODEL CODE COMPARISON:

There was no counterpart to this Rule in the Disciplinary Rules of the Model Code. EC 7-11 stated that the "responsibilities of a lawyer may vary according to the intelligence, experience, mental condition or age of a client. . . . Examples include the representation of an illiterate or an incompetent." EC 7-12 stated that "[a]ny mental or physical condition of a client that renders him incapable of making a considered judgment on his own behalf casts additional responsibilities upon his lawyer. Where an incompetent is acting through a guardian or other legal representative, a lawyer must look to such representative for those decisions which are normally the prerogative of the client to make. If a client under disability has no legal representative, his lawyer may be compelled in court proceedings to make decisions on behalf of the client. If the client is capable of understanding the matter in question or of contributing to the advancement of his interests, regardless of whether he is legally disqualified from performing certain acts, the lawyer should obtain from him all possible aid. If the disability of a client and the lack of a legal representative compel the lawyer to make decisions for his client, the lawyer should consider all circumstances then prevailing and act with care to safeguard and advance the interests of his client. But obviously a lawyer cannot perform any act or make any decision which the law requires his client to perform or make, either acting for himself if competent, or by a duly constituted representative if legally incompetent."

RULE 1.15 Safekeeping Property

(a) A lawyer shall hold property of clients or third persons that is in a lawyer's possession in connection with a representation separate from the lawyer's own property. Funds shall be kept in a separate account maintained in the state where the lawyer's office is situated, or elsewhere with the consent of the client or third person. Other property shall be identified as such and appropriately safeguarded. Complete records of such account funds and other property shall be kept by the lawyer and shall be preserved for a period of [five years] after termination of the representation.

(b) Upon receiving funds or other property in which a client or third person has an interest, a lawyer shall promptly notify the client or third person. Except as stated in this rule or otherwise permitted by law or by agreement with the client, a lawyer shall promptly deliver to the client or third person any funds or other property that the client or third person is entitled to receive and, upon request by the client or third person, shall promptly render a full accounting regarding such property.

(c) When in the course of representation a lawyer is in possession of property in which both the lawyer and another person claim interests, the property shall be kept separate by the lawyer until there is an accounting and severance of their interest. If a dispute arises concerning their respective interests, the portion in dispute shall be kept separate by the lawyer until the dispute is resolved.

COMMENT:

[1] A lawyer should hold property of others with the care required of a professional fiduciary. Securities should be kept in a safe deposit box, except when some other form of safekeeping is warranted by special circumstances. All property which is the property of clients or third persons should be kept separate from the lawyer's business and personal property and, if monies, in one or more trust accounts. Separate trust accounts may be warranted when administering estate monies or acting in similar fiduciary capacities.

[2] Lawyers often receive funds from third parties from which the lawyer's fee will be paid. If there is risk that the client may divert the funds without paying the fee, the lawyer is not required to remit the portion from which the fee is to be paid. However, a lawyer may not hold funds to coerce a client into accepting the lawyer's contention. The disputed portion of the funds should be kept in trust and the lawyer should suggest means for prompt resolution of the dispute, such as arbi-

tration. The undisputed portion of the funds shall be promptly distributed.

[3] Third parties, such as a client's creditors, may have just claims against funds or other property in a lawyer's custody. A lawyer may have a duty under applicable law to protect such third-party claims against wrongful interference by the client, and accordingly may refuse to surrender the property to the client. However, a lawyer should not unilaterally assume to arbitrate a dispute between the client and the third party.

[4] The obligations of a lawyer under this Rule are independent of those arising from activity other than rendering legal services. For example, a lawyer who serves as an escrow agent is governed by the applicable law relating to fiduciaries even though the lawyer does not render legal services in the transaction.

[5] A "client's security fund" provides a means through the collective efforts of the bar to reimburse persons who have lost money or property as a result of dishonest conduct of a lawyer. Where such a fund has been established, a lawyer should participate.

MODEL CODE COMPARISON:

[1] With regard to paragraph (a), DR 9–102(A) provided that "funds of clients" are to be kept in an identifiable bank account in the state in which the lawyer's office is situated. DR 9–102(B)(2) provided that a lawyer shall "identify and label securities and properties of a client . . . and place them in . . . safekeeping. . . ." DR 9–102(B)(3) required that a lawyer "[m]aintain complete records of all funds, securities, and other properties of a client. . . ." Paragraph (a) extends these requirements to property of a third person that is in the lawyer's possession in connection with the representation.

[2] Paragraph (b) is substantially similar to DR 9–102(B)(1), (3) and (4).

[3] Paragraph (c) is similar to DR 9–102(A)(2), except that the requirement regarding disputes applies to property concerning which an interest is claimed by a third person as well as by a client.

RULE 1.16 Declining or Terminating Representation

(a) Except as stated in paragraph (c), a lawyer shall not represent a client or, where representation has commenced, shall withdraw from the representation of a client if:

(1) the representation will result in violation of the rules of professional conduct or other law;

(2) the lawyer's physical or mental condition materially impairs the lawyer's ability to represent the client; or

(3) the lawyer is discharged.

(b) Except as stated in paragraph (c), a lawyer may withdraw from representing a client if withdrawal can be accomplished without material adverse effect on the interests of the client, or if:

(1) the client persists in a course of action involving the lawyer's services that the lawyer reasonably believes is criminal or fraudulent;

(2) the client has used the lawyer's services to perpetrate a crime or fraud;

(3) a client insists upon pursuing an objective that the lawyer considers repugnant or imprudent;

(4) the client fails substantially to fulfill an obligation to the lawyer regarding the lawyer's services and has been given reasonable warning that the lawyer will withdraw unless the obligation is fulfilled;

(5) the representation will result in an unreasonable financial burden on the lawyer or has been rendered unreasonably difficult by the client; or

(6) other good cause for withdrawal exists.

(c) When ordered to do so by a tribunal, a lawyer shall continue representation notwithstanding good cause for terminating the representation.

(d) Upon termination of representation, a lawyer shall take steps to the extent reasonably practicable to protect a client's interests, such as giving reasonable notice to the client, allowing time for employment of other counsel, surrendering papers and property to which the client is entitled and refunding any advance payment of fee that has not been earned. The lawyer may retain papers relating to the client to the extent permitted by other law.

COMMENT:

[1] A lawyer should not accept representation in a matter unless it can be performed competent-

ly, promptly, without improper conflict of interest and to completion.

Mandatory Withdrawal

[2] A lawyer ordinarily must decline or withdraw from representation if the client demands that the lawyer engage in conduct that is illegal or violates the Rules of Professional Conduct or other law. The lawyer is not obliged to decline or withdraw simply because the client suggests such a course of conduct; a client may make such a suggestion in the hope that a lawyer will not be constrained by a professional obligation.

[3] When a lawyer has been appointed to represent a client, withdrawal ordinarily requires approval of the appointing authority. See also Rule 6.2. Difficulty may be encountered if withdrawal is based on the client's demand that the lawyer engage in unprofessional conduct. The court may wish an explanation for the withdrawal, while the lawyer may be bound to keep confidential the facts that would constitute such an explanation. The lawyer's statement that professional considerations require termination of the representation ordinarily should be accepted as sufficient.

Discharge

[4] A client has a right to discharge a lawyer at any time, with or without cause, subject to liability for payment for the lawyer's services. Where future dispute about the withdrawal may be anticipated, it may be advisable to prepare a written statement reciting the circumstances.

[5] Whether a client can discharge appointed counsel may depend on applicable law. A client seeking to do so should be given a full explanation of the consequences. These consequences may include a decision by the appointing authority that appointment of successor counsel is unjustified, thus requiring the client to represent himself.

[6] If the client is mentally incompetent, the client may lack the legal capacity to discharge the lawyer, and in any event the discharge may be seriously adverse to the client's interests. The lawyer should make special effort to help the client consider the consequences and, in an extreme case, may initiate proceedings for a conservatorship or similar protection of the client. See Rule 1.14.

Optional Withdrawal

[7] A lawyer may withdraw from representation in some circumstances. The lawyer has the option to withdraw if it can be accomplished without material adverse effect on the client's interests. Withdrawal is also justified if the client persists in a course of action that the lawyer reasonably believes is criminal or fraudulent, for a lawyer is not required to be associated with such conduct even if the lawyer does not further it. Withdrawal is also permitted if the lawyer's services were misused in the past even if that would materially prejudice the client. The lawyer also may withdraw where the client insists on a repugnant or imprudent objective.

[8] A lawyer may withdraw if the client refuses to abide by the terms of an agreement relating to the representation, such as an agreement concerning fees or court costs or an agreement limiting the objectives of the representation.

Assisting the Client Upon Withdrawal

[9] Even if the lawyer has been unfairly discharged by the client, a lawyer must take all reasonable steps to mitigate the consequences to the client. The lawyer may retain papers as security for a fee only to the extent permitted by law.

[10] Whether or not a lawyer for an organization may under certain unusual circumstances have a legal obligation to the organization after withdrawing or being discharged by the organization's highest authority is beyond the scope of these Rules.

MODEL CODE COMPARISON:

[1] With regard to paragraph (a), DR 2-109(A) provided that a lawyer "shall not accept employment . . . if he knows or it is obvious that [the prospective client] wishes to . . . [b]ring a legal action . . . or otherwise have steps taken for him, merely for the purpose of harassing or maliciously injuring any person. . . ." Nor may a lawyer accept employment if the lawyer is aware that the prospective client wishes to "[p]resent a claim or defense . . . that is not warranted under existing law, unless it can be supported by good faith argument for an extension, modification, or reversal of existing law." DR 2-110(B) provided that a lawyer "shall withdraw from employment . . . if:

"(1) He knows or it is obvious that his client is bringing the legal action . . . or is otherwise having steps taken for him, merely for the purpose of harassing or maliciously injuring any person.

"(2) He knows or it is obvious that his continued employment will result in violation of a Disciplinary Rule.

"(3) His mental or physical condition renders it unreasonably difficult for him to carry out the employment effectively.

"(4) He is discharged by his client."

[2] With regard to paragraph (b), DR 2–110(C) permitted withdrawal regardless of the effect on the client if:

"(1) His client: (a) Insists upon presenting a claim or defense that is not warranted under existing law and cannot be supported by good faith argument for an extension, modification, or reversal of existing law; (b) Personally seeks to pursue an illegal course of conduct; (c) Insists that the lawyer pursue a course of conduct that is illegal or that is prohibited under the Disciplinary Rules; (d) By other conduct renders it unreasonably difficult for the lawyer to carry out his employment effectively; (e) Insists, in a matter not pending before a tribunal, that the lawyer engage in conduct that is contrary to the judgment and advice of the lawyer but not prohibited under the Disciplinary Rules; (f) Deliberately disregards an agreement or obligation to the lawyer as to expenses and fees.

"(2) His continued employment is likely to result in a violation of a Disciplinary Rule.

"(3) His inability to work with cocounsel indicates that the best interest of the client likely will be served by withdrawal.

"(4) His mental or physical condition renders it difficult for him to carry out the employment effectively.

"(5) His client knowingly and freely assents to termination of his employment.

"(6) He believes in good faith, in a proceeding pending before a tribunal, that the tribunal will find the existence of other good cause for withdrawal."

[3] With regard to paragraph (c), DR 2–110(A)(1) provided: "If permission for withdrawal from employment is required by the rules of a tribunal, the lawyer shall not withdraw . . . without its permission."

[4] The provisions of paragraph (d) are substantially identical to DR 2–110(A)(2) and (3).

RULE 1.17 Sale of Law Practice*

A lawyer or a law firm may sell or purchase a law practice, including good will, if the following conditions are satisfied:

(a) The seller ceases to engage in the private practice of law [in the geographic area] [in the jurisdiction] (a jurisdiction may elect either version) in which the practice has been conducted;

(b) The practice is sold as an entirety to another lawyer or law firm;

(c) Actual written notice is given to each of the seller's clients regarding:

(1) the proposed sale;

(2) the terms of any proposed change in the fee arrangement authorized by paragraph (d);

(3) the client's right to retain other counsel or to take possession of the file; and

(4) the fact that the client's consent to the sale will be presumed if the client does not take any action or does not otherwise object within niney (90) days of receipt of the notice.

If a client cannot be given notice, the representation of that client may be transferred to the purchaser only upon entry of an order so authorizing by a court having jurisdiction. The seller may disclose to the court *in camera* information relating to the representation only to the extent necessary to obtain an order authorizing the transfer of a file.

(d) The fees charged clients shall not be increased by reason of the sale. The purchaser may, however, refuse to undertake the representation unless the client consents to pay the purchaser fees at a rate not exceeding the fees charged by the purchaser for rendering substantially similar services prior to the initiation of the purchase negotiations.

COMMENT:

[1] The practice of law is a profession, not merely a business. Clients are not commodities

---

* Model Rule 1.17 did not appear in the original version of the Model Rules. This provision and its comments were added by the ABA in 1990.

that can be purchased and sold at will. Pursuant to this Rule, when a lawyer or an entire firm ceases to practice and another lawyer or firm takes over the representation, the selling lawyer or firm may obtain compensation for the reasonable value of the practice as may withdrawing partners of law firms. See Rules 5.4 and 5.6.

Termination of Practice by the Seller

[2] The requirement that all of the private practice be sold is satisfied if the seller in good faith makes the entire practice available for sale to the purchaser. The fact that a number of the seller's clients decide not to be represented by the purchaser but take their matters elsewhere, therefore, does not result in a violation. Neither does a return to private practice as a result of an unanticipated change in circumstances result in a violation. For example, a lawyer who has sold the practice to accept an appointment to judicial office does not violate the requirement that the sale be attendant to cessation of practice if the lawyer later resumes private practice upon being defeated in a contested or a retention election for the office.

[3] The requirement that the seller cease to engage in the private practice of law does not prohibit employment as a lawyer on the staff of a public agency or a legal services entity which provides legal services to the poor, or as in-house counsel to a business.

[4] The Rule permits a sale attendant upon retirement from the private practice of law within the jurisdiction. Its provisions, therefore, accommodate the lawyer who sells the practice upon the occasion of moving to another state. Some states are so large that a move from one locale therein to another is tantamount to leaving the jurisdiction in which the lawyer has engaged in the practice of law. To also accommodate lawyers so situated, states may permit the sale of the practice when the lawyer leaves the geographic area rather than the jurisdiction. The alternative desired should be indicated by selecting one of the two provided for in Rule 1.17(a).

Single Purchaser

[5] The Rule requires a single purchaser. The prohibition against piecemeal sale of a practice protects those clients whose matters are less lucrative and who might find it difficult to secure other counsel if a sale could be limited to substantial fee-generating matters. The purchaser is required to undertake all client matters in the practice, subject to client consent. If, however, the purchaser is unable to undertake all client matters because of a conflict of interest in a specific matter respecting which the purchaser is not permitted by Rule 1.7 or another rule to represent the client, the requirement that there be a single purchaser is nevertheless satisfied.

Client Confidences, Consent and Notice

[6] Negotiations between seller and prospective purchaser prior to disclosure of information relating to a specific representation of an identifiable client no more violate the confidentiality provisions of Model Rule 1.6 than do preliminary discussions concerning the possible association of another lawyer or mergers between firms, with respect to which client consent is not required. Providing the purchaser access to client-specific information relating to the representation and to the file, however, requires client consent. The Rule provides that before such information can be disclosed by the seller to the purchaser the client must be given actual written notice of the contemplated sale, including the identity of the purchaser and any proposed change in the terms of future representation, and must be told that the decision to consent or make other arrangements must be made within 90 days. If nothing is heard from the client within that time, consent to the sale is presumed.

[7] A lawyer or law firm ceasing to practice cannot be required to remain in practice because some clients cannot be given actual notice of the proposed purchase. Since these clients cannot themselves consent to the purchase or direct any other disposition of their files, the Rule requires an order from a court having jurisdiction authorizing their transfer or other disposition. The Court can be expected to determine whether reasonable efforts to locate the client have been exhausted, and whether the absent client's legitimate interests will be served by authorizing the transfer of the file so that the purchaser may continue the representation. Preservation of client confidences requires that the petition for a court order be considered *in camera*. (A procedure by which such an order can be obtained needs to be established in jurisdictions in which it presently does not exist.)

[8] All the elements of client autonomy, including the client's absolute right to discharge a lawyer and transfer the representation to another, survive the sale of the practice.

Fee Arrangements Between Client and Purchaser

[9] The sale may not be financed by increases in fees charged the clients of the practice. Ex-

isting agreements between the seller and the client as to fees and the scope of the work must be honored by the purchaser, unless the client consents after consultation. The purchaser may, however, advise the client that the purchaser will not undertake the representation unless the client consents to pay the higher fees the purchaser usually charges. To prevent client financing of the sale, the higher fee the purchaser may charge must not exceed the fees charged by the purchaser for substantially similar service rendered prior to the initiation of the purchase negotiations.

[10] The purchaser may not intentionally fragment the practice which is the subject of the sale by charging significantly different fees in substantially similar matters. Doing so would make it possible for the purchaser to avoid the obligation to take over the entire practice by charging arbitrarily higher fees for less lucrative matters, thereby increasing the likelihood that those clients would not consent to the new representation.

Other Applicable Ethical Standards

[11] Lawyers participating in the sale of a law practice are subject to the ethical standards applicable to involving another lawyer in the representation of a client. These include, for example, the seller's obligation to exercise competence in identifying a purchaser qualified to assume the practice and the purchaser's obligation to undertake the representation competently (see Rule 1.1); the obligation to avoid disqualifying conflicts, and to secure client consent after consultation for those conflicts which can be agreed to (see Rule 1.7); and the obligation to protect information relating to the representation (see Rules 1.6 and 1.9).

[12] If approval of the substitution of the purchasing attorney for the selling attorney is required by the rules of any tribunal in which a matter is pending, such approval must be obtained before the matter can be included in the sale (see Rule 1.16).

Applicability of the Rule

[13] This Rule applies to the sale of a law practice by representatives of a deceased, disabled or disappeared lawyer. Thus, the seller may be represented by a non-lawyer representative not subject to these Rules. Since, however, no lawyer may participate in a sale of a law practice which does not conform to the requirements of this Rule, the representatives of the seller as well as the purchasing lawyer can be expected to see to it that they are met.

[14] Admission to or retirement from a law partnership or professional association, retirement plans and similar arrangements, and a sale of tangible assets of a law practice, do not constitute a sale or purchase governed by this Rule.

[15] This Rule does not apply to the transfers of legal representation between lawyers when such transfers are unrelated to the sale of a practice.

MODEL CODE COMPARISON:

There was no counterpart to this Rule in the Model Code.

COUNSELOR

RULE 2.1 Advisor

In representing a client, a lawyer shall exercise independent professional judgment and render candid advice. In rendering advice, a lawyer may refer not only to law but to other considerations such as moral, economic, social and political factors, that may be relevant to the client's situation.

COMMENT:

Scope of Advice

[1] A client is entitled to straightforward advice expressing the lawyer's honest assessment. Legal advice often involves unpleasant facts and alternatives that a client may be disinclined to confront. In presenting advice, a lawyer endeavors to sustain the client's morale and may put advice in as acceptable a form as honesty permits. However, a lawyer should not be deterred from giving candid advice by the prospect that the advice will be unpalatable to the client.

[2] Advice couched in narrowly legal terms may be of little value to a client, especially where practical considerations, such as cost or effects on other people, are predominant. Purely technical legal advice, therefore, can sometimes be inadequate. It is proper for a lawyer to refer to relevant moral and ethical considerations in giving advice. Although a lawyer is not a moral advisor as such, moral and ethical considerations impinge upon most legal questions and may decisively influence how the law will be applied.

[3] A client may expressly or impliedly ask the lawyer for purely technical advice. When such a request is made by a client experienced in legal matters, the lawyer may accept it at face value. When such a request is made by a client inexperienced in legal matters, however, the lawyer's re-

sponsibility as advisor may include indicating that more may be involved than strictly legal considerations.

[4] Matters that go beyond strictly legal questions may also be in the domain of another profession. Family matters can involve problems within the professional competence of psychiatry, clinical psychology or social work; business matters can involve problems within the competence of the accounting profession or of financial specialists. Where consultation with a professional in another field is itself something a competent lawyer would recommend, the lawyer should make such a recommendation. At the same time, a lawyer's advice at its best often consists of recommending a course of action in the face of conflicting recommendations of experts.

Offering Advice

[5] In general, a lawyer is not expected to give advice until asked by the client. However, when a lawyer knows that a client proposes a course of action that is likely to result in substantial adverse legal consequences to the client, duty to the client under Rule 1.4 may require that the lawyer act if the client's course of action is related to the representation. A lawyer ordinarily has no duty to initiate investigation of a client's affairs or to give advice that the client has indicated is unwanted, but a lawyer may initiate advice to a client when doing so appears to be in the client's interest.

MODEL CODE COMPARISON:

There was no direct counterpart to this Rule in the Disciplinary Rules of the Model Code. DR 5–107(B) provided that a lawyer "shall not permit a person who recommends, employs, or pays him to render legal services for another to direct or regulate his professional judgment in rendering such legal services." EC 7–8 stated that "[a]dvice of a lawyer to his client need not be confined to purely legal considerations. . . . In assisting his client to reach a proper decision, it is often desirable for a lawyer to point out those factors which may lead to a decision that is morally just as well as legally permissible. . . . In the final analysis, however, . . . the decision whether to forego legally available objectives or methods because of nonlegal factors is ultimately for the client. . . ."

RULE 2.2 Intermediary

(a) A lawyer may act as intermediary between clients if:

(1) the lawyer consults with each client concerning the implications of the common representation, including the advantages and risks involved, and the effect on the attorney–client privileges, and obtains each client's consent to the common representation;

(2) the lawyer reasonably believes that the matter can be resolved on terms compatible with the clients' best interests, that each client will be able to make adequately informed decisions in the matter and that there is little risk of material prejudice to the interest of any of the clients if the contemplated resolution is unsuccessful; and

(3) the lawyer reasonably believes that the common representation can be undertaken impartially and without improper effect on other responsibilities the lawyer has to any of the clients.

(b) While acting as intermediary, the lawyer shall consult with each client concerning the decisions to be made and the considerations relevant in making them, so that each client can make adequately informed decisions.

(c) A lawyer shall withdraw as intermediary if any of the clients so request, or if any of the conditions stated in paragraph (a) is no longer satisfied. Upon withdrawal, the lawyer shall not continue to represent any of the clients in the matter that was the subject of the intermediation.

COMMENT:

[1] A lawyer acts as intermediary under this Rule when the lawyer represents two or more parties with potentially conflicting interests. A key factor in defining the relationship is whether the parties share responsibility for the lawyer's fee, but the common representation may be inferred from other circumstances. Because confusion can arise as to the lawyer's role where each party is not separately represented, it is important that the lawyer make clear the relationship.

[2] The Rule does not apply to a lawyer acting as arbitrator or mediator between or among parties who are not clients of the lawyer, even where the lawyer has been appointed with the

concurrence of the parties. In performing such a role the lawyer may be subject to applicable codes of ethics, such as the Code of Ethics for Arbitration in Commercial Disputes prepared by a joint Committee of the American Bar Association and the American Arbitration Association.

[3] A lawyer acts as intermediary in seeking to establish or adjust a relationship between clients on an amicable and mutually advantageous basis; for example, in helping to organize a business in which two or more clients are entrepreneurs, working out the financial reorganization of an enterprise in which two or more clients have an interest, arranging a property distribution in settlement of an estate or mediating a dispute between clients. The lawyer seeks to resolve potentially conflicting interests by developing the parties' mutual interests. The alternative can be that each party may have to obtain separate representation, with the possibility in some situations of incurring additional cost, complication or even litigation. Given these and other relevant factors, all the clients may prefer that the lawyer act as intermediary.

[4] In considering whether to act as intermediary between clients, a lawyer should be mindful that if the intermediation fails the result can be additional cost, embarrassment and recrimination. In some situations the risk of failure is so great that intermediation is plainly impossible. For example, a lawyer cannot undertake common representation of clients between whom contentious litigation is imminent or who contemplate contentious negotiations. More generally, if the relationship between the parties has already assumed definite antagonism, the possibility that the clients' interests can be adjusted by intermediation ordinarily is not very good.

[5] The appropriateness of intermediation can depend on its form. Forms of intermediation range from informal arbitration, where each client's case is presented by the respective client and the lawyer decides the outcome, to mediation, to common representation where the clients' interests are substantially though not entirely compatible. One form may be appropriate in circumstances where another would not. Other relevant factors are whether the lawyer subsequently will represent both parties on a continuing basis and whether the situation involves creating a relationship between the parties or terminating one.

Confidentiality and Privilege

[6] A particularly important factor in determining the appropriateness of intermediation is the effect on client-lawyer confidentiality and the attorney-client privilege. In a common representation, the lawyer is still required both to keep each client adequately informed and to maintain confidentiality of information relating to the representation. See Rules 1.4 and 1.6. Complying with both requirements while acting as intermediary requires a delicate balance. If the balance cannot be maintained, the common representation is improper. With regard to the attorney-client privilege, the prevailing rule is that as between commonly represented clients the privilege does not attach. Hence, it must be assumed that if litigation eventuates between the clients, the privilege will not protect any such communications, and the clients should be so advised.

[7] Since the lawyer is required to be impartial between commonly represented clients, intermediation is improper when that impartiality cannot be maintained. For example, a lawyer who has represented one of the clients for a long period and in a variety of matters might have diffculty being impartial between that client and one to whom the lawyer has only recently been introduced.

Consultation

[8] In acting as intermediary between clients, the lawyer is required to consult with the clients on the implications of doing so, and proceed only upon consent based on such a consultation. The consultation should make clear that the lawyer's role is not that of partisanship normally expected in other circumstances.

[9] Paragraph (b) is an application of the principle expressed in Rule 1.4. Where the lawyer is intermediary, the clients ordinarily must assume greater responsibility for decisions than when each client is independently represented.

Withdrawal

[10] Common representation does not diminish the rights of each client in the client-lawyer relationship. Each has the right to loyal and diligent representation, the right to discharge the lawyer as stated in Rule 1.16, and the protection of Rule 1.9 concerning obligations to a former client.

MODEL CODE COMPARISON:

There was no direct counterpart to this Rule in the Disciplinary Rules of the Model Code. EC 5–20 stated that a "lawyer is often asked to serve as an impartial arbitrator or mediator in matters which involve present or former clients. He may serve in either capacity if he first discloses such present or former relationships." DR 5–105(B) provided that a lawyer "shall not continue multiple employment if the exercise of his independent judgment in behalf of a client will be or is likely to be adversely affected by his representation of another client, or if it would be likely to involve him in representation of differing interests, except to the extent permitted under DR 5–105(C)." DR 5–105(C) provided that "a lawyer may represent multiple clients if it is obvious that he can adequately represent the interests of each and if each consents to the representation after full disclosure of the possible effect of such representation on the exercise of his independent professional judgment on behalf of each."

RULE 2.3 Evaluation for Use by Third Persons

(a) A lawyer may undertake an evaluation of a matter affecting a client for the use of someone other than the client if:

(1) the lawyer reasonably believes that making the evaluation is compatible with other aspects of the lawyer's relationship with the client; and

(2) the client consents after consultation.

(b) Except as disclosure is required in connection with a report of an evaluation, information relating to the evaluation is otherwise protected by rule 1.6.

COMMENT:

Definition

[1] An evaluation may be performed at the client's direction but for the primary purpose of establishing information for the benefit of third parties; for example, an opinion concerning the title of property rendered at the behest of a vendor for the information of a prospective purchaser, or at the behest of a borrower for the information of a prospective lender. In some situations, the evaluation may be required by a government agency; for example, an opinion concerning the legality of the securities registered for sale under the securities laws. In other instances, the evaluation may be required by a third person, such as a purchaser of a business.

[2] Lawyers for the government may be called upon to give a formal opinion on the legality of contemplated government agency action. In making such an evaluation, the government lawyer acts at the behest of the government as the client but for the purpose of establishing the limits of the agency's authorized activity. Such an opinion is to be distinguished from confidential legal advice given agency officials. The critical question is whether the opinion is to be made public.

[3] A legal evaluation should be distinguished from an investigation of a person with whom the lawyer does not have a client-lawyer relationship. For example, a lawyer retained by a purchaser to analyze a vendor's title to property does not have a client-lawyer relationship with the vendor. So also, an investigation into a person's affairs by a government lawyer, or by special counsel employed by the government, is not an evaluation as that term is used in this Rule. The question is whether the lawyer is retained by the person whose affairs are being examined. When the lawyer is retained by that person, the general rules concerning loyalty to client and preservation of confidences apply, which is not the case if the lawyer is retained by someone else. For this reason, it is essential to identify the person by whom the lawyer is retained. This should be made clear not only to the person under examination, but also to others to whom the results are to be made available.

Duty to Third Person

[4] When the evaluation is intended for the information or use of a third person, a legal duty to that person may or may not arise. That legal question is beyond the scope of this Rule. However, since such an evaluation involves a departure from the normal client-lawyer relationship, careful analysis of the situation is required. The lawyer must be satisfied as a matter of professional judgment that making the evaluation is compatible with other functions undertaken in behalf of the client. For example, if the lawyer is acting as advocate in defending the client against charges of fraud, it would normally be incompatible with that responsibility for the lawyer to perform an evaluation for others concerning the same or a related transaction. Assuming no such impediment is apparent, however, the lawyer should advise the client of the implications of the evaluation, particularly the lawyer's responsibilities to third persons and the duty to disseminate the findings.

Access to and Disclosure of Information

[5] The quality of an evaluation depends on the freedom and extent of the investigation upon which it is based. Ordinarily a lawyer should have whatever latitude of investigation seems necessary

as a matter of professional judgment. Under some circumstances, however, the terms of the evaluation may be limited. For example, certain issues or sources may be categorically excluded, or the scope of search may be limited by time constraints or the noncooperation of persons having relevant information. Any such limitations which are material to the evaluation should be described in the report. If after a lawyer has commenced an evaluation, the client refuses to comply with the terms upon which it was understood the evaluation was to have been made, the lawyer's obligations are determined by law, having reference to the terms of the client's agreement and the surrounding circumstances.

Financial Auditors' Requests for Information

[6] When a question concerning the legal situation of a client arises at the instance of the client's financial auditor and the question is referred to the lawyer, the lawyer's response may be made in accordance with procedures recognized in the legal profession. Such a procedure is set forth in the American Bar Association Statement of Policy Regarding Lawyers' Responses to Auditors' Requests for Information, adopted in 1975.

MODEL CODE COMPARISON:

There was no counterpart to this Rule in the Model Code.

ADVOCATE

RULE 3.1 Meritorious Claims and Contentions

A lawyer shall not bring or defend a proceeding, or assert or controvert an issue therein, unless there is a basis for doing so that is not frivolous, which includes a good faith argument for an extension, modification or reversal of existing law. A lawyer for the defendant in a criminal proceeding, or the respondent in a proceeding that could result in incarceration, may nevertheless so defend the proceeding as to require that every element of the case be established.

COMMENT:

[1] The advocate has a duty to use legal procedure for the fullest benefit of the client's cause, but also a duty not to abuse legal procedure. The law, both procedural and substantive, establishes the limits within which an advocate may proceed. However, the law is not always clear and never is static. Accordingly, in determining the proper scope of advocacy, account must be taken of the law's ambiguities and potential for change.

[2] The filing of an action or defense or similar action taken for a client is not frivolous merely because the facts have not first been fully substantiated or because the lawyer expects to develop vital evidence only by discovery. Such action is not frivolous even though the lawyer believes that the client's position ultimately will not prevail. The action is frivolous, however, if the client desires to have the action taken primarily for the purpose of harassing or maliciously injuring a person or if the lawyer is unable either to make a good faith argument on the merits of the action taken or to support the action taken by a good faith argument for an extension, modification or reversal of existing law.

MODEL CODE COMPARISON:

DR 7-102(A)(1) provided that a lawyer may not "[f]ile a suit, assert a position, conduct a defense, delay a trial, or take other action on behalf of his client when he knows or when it is obvious that such action would serve merely to harass or maliciously injure another." Rule 3.1 is to the same general effect as DR 7-102(A)(1), with three qualifications. First, the test of improper conduct is changed from "merely to harass or maliciously injure another" to the requirement that there be a basis for the litigation measure involved that is "not frivolous." This includes the concept stated in DR 7-102(A)(2) that a lawyer may advance a claim or defense unwarranted by existing law if "it can be supported by good faith argument for an extension, modification, or reversal of existing law." Second, the test in Rule 3.1 is an objective test, whereas DR 7-102(A)(1) applied only if the lawyer "knows or when it is obvious" that the litigation is frivolous. Third, Rule 3.1 has an exception that in a criminal case, or a case in which incarceration of the client may result (for example, certain juvenile proceedings), the lawyer may put the prosecution to its proof even if there is no nonfrivolous basis for defense.

RULE 3.2 Expediting Litigation

A lawyer shall make reasonable efforts to expedite litigation consistent with the interests of the client.

COMMENT:

[1] Dilatory practices bring the administration of justice into disrepute. Delay should not be indulged merely for the convenience of the advocates, or for the purpose of frustrating an opposing party's attempt to obtain rightful redress or repose. It is not a justification that similar conduct is often tolerated by the bench and bar. The question is whether a competent lawyer acting in good faith would regard the course of action as having some substantial purpose other than delay. Realizing financial or other benefit from otherwise improper delay in litigation it not a legitimate interest of the client.

MODEL CODE COMPARISON:

DR 7–101(A)(1) stated that a lawyer does not violate the duty to represent a client zealously "by being punctual in fulfilling all professional commitments." DR 7–102(A)(1) provided that a lawyer "shall not . . . file a suit, assert a position, conduct a defense [or] delay a trial . . . when he knows or when it is obvious that such action would serve merely to harass or maliciously injure another."

RULE 3.3   Candor Toward the Tribunal

(a) A lawyer shall not knowingly:

(1) make a false statement of material fact or law to a tribunal;

(2) fail to disclose a material fact to a tribunal when disclosure is necessary to avoid assisting a criminal or fraudulent act by the client;

(3) fail to disclose to the tribunal legal authority in the controlling jurisdiction known to the lawyer to be directly adverse to the position of the client and not disclosed by opposing counsel; or

(4) offer evidence that the lawyer knows to be false. If a lawyer has offered material evidence and comes to know of its falsity, the lawyer shall take reasonable remedial measures.

(b) The duties stated in paragraph (a) continue to the conclusion of the proceeding, and apply even if compliance requires disclosure of information otherwise protected by rule 1.6.

(c) A lawyer may refuse to offer evidence that the lawyer reasonably believes is false.

(d) In an ex parte proceeding, a lawyer shall inform the tribunal of all material facts known to the lawyer which will enable the tribunal to make an informed decision, whether or not the facts are adverse.

COMMENT:

[1] The advocate's task is to present the client's case with persuasive force. Performance of that duty while maintaining confidences of the client is qualified by the advocate's duty of candor to the tribunal. However, an advocate does not vouch for the evidence submitted in a cause; the tribunal is responsible for assessing its probative value.

Representations by a Lawyer

[2] An advocate is responsible for pleadings and other documents prepared for litigation, but is usually not required to have personal knowledge of matters asserted therein, for litigation documents ordinarily present assertions by the client, or by someone on the client's behalf, and not assertions by the lawyer. Compare Rule 3.1. However, an assertion purporting to be on the lawyer's own knowledge, as in an affidavit by the lawyer or in a statement in open court, may properly be made only when the lawyer knows the assertion is true or believes it to be true on the basis of a reasonably diligent inquiry. There are circumstances where failure to make a disclosure is the equivalent of an affirmative misrepresentation. The obligation prescribed in Rule 1.2(d) not to counsel a client to commit or assist the client in committing a fraud applies in litigation. Regarding compliance with Rule 1.2(d), see the Comment to that Rule. See also the Comment to Rule 8.4(b).

Misleading Legal Argument

[3] Legal argument based on a knowingly false representation of law constitutes dishonesty toward the tribunal. A lawyer is not required to make a disinterested exposition of the law, but must recognize the existence of pertinent legal authorities. Furthermore, as stated in paragraph (a)(3), an advocate has a duty to disclose directly adverse authority in the controlling jurisdiction which has not been disclosed by the opposing party. The underlying concept is that legal argument is a discussion seeking to determine the legal premises properly applicable to the case.

False Evidence

[4] When evidence that a lawyer knows to be false is provided by a person who is not the client,

the lawyer must refuse to offer it regardless of the client's wishes.

[5]   When false evidence is offered by the client, however, a conflict may arise between the lawyer's duty to keep the client's revelations confidential and the duty of candor to the court. Upon ascertaining that material evidence is false, the lawyer should seek to persuade the client that the evidence should not be offered or, if it has been offered, that its false character should immediately be disclosed. If the persuasion is ineffective, the lawyer must take reasonable remedial measures.

[6]   Except in the defense of a criminal accused, the rule generally recognized is that, if necessary to rectify the situation, an advocate must disclose the existence of the client's deception to the court or to the other party. Such a disclosure can result in grave consequences to the client, including not only a sense of betrayal but also loss of the case and perhaps a prosecution for perjury. But the alternative is that the lawyer cooperate in deceiving the court, thereby subverting the truth-finding process which the adversary system is designed to implement. See Rule 1.2(d). Furthermore, unless it is clearly understood that the lawyer will act upon the duty to disclose the existence of false evidence, the client can simply reject the lawyer's advice to reveal the false evidence and insist that the lawyer keep silent. Thus the client could in effect coerce the lawyer into being a party to fraud on the court.

Perjury by a Criminal Defendant

[7]   Whether an advocate for a criminally accused has the same duty of disclosure has been intensely debated. While it is agreed that the lawyer should seek to persuade the client to refrain from perjurious testimony, there has been dispute concerning the lawyer's duty when that persuasion fails. If the confrontation with the client occurs before trial, the lawyer ordinarily can withdraw. Withdrawal before trial may not be possible, however, either because trial is imminent, or because the confrontation with the client does not take place until the trial itself, or because no other counsel is available.

[8]   The most difficult situation, therefore, arises in a criminal case where the accused insists on testifying when the lawyer knows that the testimony is perjurious. The lawyer's effort to rectify the situation can increase the likelihood of the client's being convicted as well as opening the possibility of a prosecution for perjury. On the other hand, if the lawyer does not exercise control over the proof, the lawyer participates, although in a merely passive way, in deception of the court.

[9]   Three resolutions of this dilemma have been proposed. One is to permit the accused to testify by a narrative without guidance through the lawyer's questioning. This compromises both contending principles; it exempts the lawyer from the duty to disclose false evidence but subjects the client to an implicit disclosure of information imparted to counsel. Another suggested resolution, of relatively recent origin, is that the advocate be entirely excused from the duty to reveal perjury if the perjury is that of the client. This is a coherent solution but makes the advocate a knowing instrument of perjury.

[10]   The other resolution of the dilemma is that the lawyer must reveal the client's perjury if necessary to rectify the situation. A criminal accused has a right to the assistance of an advocate, a right to testify and a right of confidential communication with counsel. However, an accused should not have a right to assistance of counsel in committing perjury. Furthermore, an advocate has an obligation, not only in professional ethics but under the law as well, to avoid implication in the commission of perjury or other falsification of evidence. See Rule 1.2(d).

Remedial Measures

[11]   If perjured testimony or false evidence has been offered, the advocate's proper course ordinarily is to remonstrate with the client confidentially. If that fails, the advocate should seek to withdraw if that will remedy the situation. If withdrawal will not remedy the situation or is impossible, the advocate should make disclosure to the court. It is for the court then to determine what should be done—making a statement about the matter to the trier of fact, ordering a mistrial or perhaps nothing. If the false testimony was that of the client, the client may controvert the lawyer's version of their communication when the lawyer discloses the situation to the court. If there is an issue whether the client has committed perjury, the lawyer cannot represent the client in resolution of the issue and a mistrial may be unavoidable. An unscrupulous client might in this way attempt to produce a series of mistrials and thus escape prosecution. However, a second such encounter could be construed as a deliberate abuse of the right to counsel and as such a waiver of the right to further representation.

Constitutional Requirements

[12] The general rule—that an advocate must disclose the existence of perjury with respect to a material fact, even that of a client—applies to defense counsel in criminal cases, as well as in other instances. However, the definition of the lawyer's ethical duty in such a situation may be qualified by constitutional provisions for due process and the right to counsel in criminal cases. In some jurisdictions these provisions have been construed to require that counsel present an accused as a witness if the accused wishes to testify, even if counsel knows the testimony will be false. The obligation of the advocate under these Rules is subordinate to such a constitutional requirement.

Duration of Obligation

[13] A practical time limit on the obligation to rectify the presentation of false evidence has to be established. The conclusion of the proceeding is a reasonably definite point for the termination of the obligation.

Refusing to Offer Proof Believed to Be False

[14] Generally speaking, a lawyer has authority to refuse to offer testimony or other proof that the lawyer believes is untrustworthy. Offering such proof may reflect adversely on the lawyer's ability to discriminate in the quality of evidence and thus impair the lawyer's effectiveness as an advocate. In criminal cases, however, a lawyer may, in some jurisdictions, be denied this authority by constitutional requirements governing the right to counsel.

Ex Parte Proceedings

[15] Ordinarily, an advocate has the limited responsibility of presenting one side of the matters that a tribunal should consider in reaching a decision; the conflicting position is expected to be presented by the opposing party. However, in an ex parte proceeding, such as an application for a temporary restraining order, there is no balance of presentation by opposing advocates. The object of an ex parte proceeding is nevertheless to yield a substantially just result. The judge has an affirmative responsibility to accord the absent party just consideration. The lawyer for the represented party has the correlative duty to make disclosures of material facts known to the lawyer and that the lawyer reasonably believes are necessary to an informed decision.

MODEL CODE COMPARISON:

[1] Paragraph (a)(1) is substantially identical to DR 7–102(A)(5), which provided that a lawyer shall not "knowingly make a false statement of law or fact."

[2] Paragraph (a)(2) is implicit in DR 7–102(A)(3), which provided that "a lawyer shall not . . . knowingly fail to disclose that which he is required by law to reveal."

[3] Paragraph (a)(3) is substantially identical to DR 7–106(B)(1).

[4] With regard to paragraph (a)(4), the first sentence of this subparagraph is similar to DR 7–102(A)(4), which provided that a lawyer shall not "knowingly use" perjured testimony or false evidence. The second sentence of paragraph (a)(4) resolves an ambiguity in the Model Code concerning the action required of a lawyer who discovers that the lawyer has offered perjured testimony or false evidence. DR 7–102(A)(4), quoted above, did not expressly deal with this situation, but the prohibition against "use" of false evidence can be construed to preclude carrying through with a case based on such evidence when that fact has become known during the trial. DR 7–102(B)(1), also noted in connection with Rule 1.6, provided that a lawyer "who receives information clearly establishing that . . . [h]is client has . . . perpetrated a fraud upon . . . a tribunal shall [if the client does not rectify the situation] . . . reveal the fraud to the . . . tribunal. . . ." Since use of perjured testimony or false evidence is usually regarded as "fraud" upon the court, DR 7–102(B)(1) apparently required disclosure by the lawyer in such circumstances. However, some states have amended DR 7–102(B)(1) in conformity with an ABA-recommended amendment to provide that the duty of disclosure does not apply when the "information is protected as a privileged communication." This qualification may be empty, for the rule of attorney-client privilege has been construed to exclude communications that further a crime, including the crime of perjury. On this interpretation of DR 7–102(B)(1), the lawyer has a duty to disclose the perjury.

[5] Paragraph (c) confers discretion on the lawyer to refuse to offer evidence that the lawyer "reasonably believes" is false. This gives the lawyer more latitude than DR 7–102(A)(4), which prohibited the lawyer from offering evidence the lawyer "knows" is false.

[6] There was no counterpart in the Model Code to paragraph (d).

RULE 3.4 Fairness to Opposing Party and Counsel

A lawyer shall not:

(a) unlawfully obstruct another party's access to evidence or unlawfully alter, destroy or conceal a document or other material having potential evidentiary value. A lawyer shall not counsel or assist another person to do any such act;

(b) falsify evidence, counsel or assist a witness to testify falsely, or offer an inducement to a witness that is prohibited by law;

(c) knowingly disobey an obligation under the rules of a tribunal except for an open refusal based on an assertion that no valid obligation exists;

(d) in pretrial procedure, make a frivolous discovery request or fail to make reasonably diligent effort to comply with a legally proper discovery request by an opposing party;

(e) in trial, allude to any matter that the lawyer does not reasonably believe is relevant or that will not be supported by admissible evidence, assert personal knowledge of facts in issue except when testifying as a witness, or state a personal opinion as to the justness of a cause, the credibility of a witness, the culpability of a civil litigant or the guilt or innocence of an accused; or

(f) request a person other than a client to refrain from voluntarily giving relevant information to another party unless:

(1) the person is a relative or an employee or other agent of a client; and

(2) the lawyer reasonably believes that the person's interests will not be adversely affected by refraining from giving such information.

COMMENT:

[1] The procedure of the adversary system contemplates that the evidence in a case is to be marshalled competitively by the contending parties. Fair competition in the adversary system is secured by prohibitions against destruction or concealment of evidence, improperly influencing witnesses, obstructive tactics in discovery procedure, and the like.

[2] Documents and other items of evidence are often essential to establish a claim or defense. Subject to evidentiary privileges, the right of an opposing party, including the government, to obtain evidence through discovery or subpoena is an important procedural right. The exercise of that right can be frustrated if relevant material is altered, concealed or destroyed. Applicable law in many jurisdictions makes it an offense to destroy material for purpose of impairing its availability in a pending proceeding or one whose commencement can be foreseen. Falsifying evidence is also generally a criminal offense. Paragraph (a) applies to evidentiary material generally, including computerized information.

[3] With regard to paragrah (b), it is not improper to pay a witness's expenses or to compensate an expert witness on terms permitted by law. The common law rule in most jurisdictions is that it is improper to pay an occurrence witness any fee for testifying and that it is improper to pay an expert witness a contingent fee.

[4] Paragraph (f) permits a lawyer to advise employees of a client to refrain from giving information to another party, for the employees may identify their interests with those of the client. See also Rule 4.2.

MODEL CODE COMPARISON:

[1] With regard to paragraph (a), DR 7-109(A) provided that a lawyer "shall not suppress any evidence that he or his client has a legal obligation to reveal." DR 7-109(B) provided that a lawyer "shall not advise or cause a person to secrete himself . . . for the purpose of making him unavailable as a witness. . . ." DR 7-106(C)(7) provided that a lawyer shall not "[i]ntentionally or habitually violate any established rule of procedure or of evidence."

[2] With regard to paragraph (b), DR 7-102(A)(6) provided that a lawyer shall not participate "in the creation or preservation of evidence when he knows or it is obvious that the evidence is false." DR 7-109(C) provided that a lawyer "shall not pay, offer to pay, or acquiesce in the payment of compensation to a witness contingent upon the content of his testimony or the outcome of the case. But a lawyer may advance, guarantee or acquiesce in the payment of: (1) Expenses reasonably incurred by a witness in attending or testifying; (2) Reasonable compensation to a witness for his loss of time in attending or testifying; [or]

(3) A reasonable fee for the professional services of an expert witness." EC 7–28 stated that witnesses "should always testify truthfully and should be free from any financial inducements that might tempt them to do otherwise."

[3] Paragraph (c) is substantially similar to DR 7–106(A), which provided that "A lawyer shall not disregard . . . a standing rule of a tribunal or a ruling of a tribunal made in the course of a proceeding, but he may take appropriate steps in good faith to test the validity of such rule or ruling."

[4] Paragraph (d) has no counterpart in the Model Code.

[5] Paragraph (e) substantially incorporates DR 7–106(C)(1), (2), (3) and (4). DR 7–106(C)(2) proscribed asking a question "intended to degrade a witness or other person," a matter dealt with in Rule 4.4. DR 7–106(C)(5), providing that a lawyer shall not "fail to comply with known local customs of courtesy or practice," was too vague to be a rule of conduct enforceable as law.

[6] With regard to paragraph (f), DR 7–104(A)(2) provided that a lawyer shall not "give advice to a person who is not represented . . . other than the advice to secure counsel, if the interests of such person are or have a reasonable possibility of being in conflict with the interests of his client."

RULE 3.5 Impartiality and Decorum of the Tribunal

A lawyer shall not:

(a) seek to influence a judge, juror, prospective juror or other official by means prohibited by law;

(b) communicate ex parte with such a person except as permitted by law; or

(c) engage in conduct intended to disrupt a tribunal.

COMMENT:

[1] Many forms of improper influence upon a tribunal are proscribed by criminal law. Others are specified in the ABA Model Code of Judicial Conduct, with which an advocate should be familiar. A lawyer is required to avoid contributing to a violation of such provisions.

[2] The advocate's function is to present evidence and argument so that the cause may be decided according to law. Refraining from abusive or obstreperous conduct is a corollary of the advocate's right to speak on behalf of litigants. A lawyer may stand firm against abuse by a judge but should avoid reciprocation; the judge's default is no justification for similar dereliction by an advocate. An advocate can present the cause, protect the record for subsequent review and preserve professional integrity by patient firmness no less effectively than by belligerence or theatrics.

MODEL CODE COMPARISON:

[1] With regard to paragraphs (a) and (b), DR 7–108(A) provided that "[b]efore the trial of a case a lawyer . . . shall not communicate with . . . anyone he knows to be a member of the venire. . . ." DR 7–108(B) provided that during the trial of a case a lawyer "shall not communicate with . . . any member of the jury." DR 7–110(B) provided that a lawyer shall not "communicate . . . as to the merits of the cause with a judge or an official before whom the proceeding is pending, except . . . upon adequate notice to opposing counsel," or as "otherwise authorized by law."

[2] With regard to paragraph (c), DR 7–106(C)(6) provided that a lawyer shall not engage in "undignified or discourteous conduct which is degrading to a tribunal."

RULE 3.6 Trial Publicity

(a) A lawyer shall not make an extrajudicial statement that a reasonable person would expect to be disseminated by means of public communication if the lawyer knows or reasonably should know that it will have a substantial likelihood of materially prejudicing an adjudicative proceeding.

(b) A statement referred to in paragraph (a) ordinarily is likely to have such an effect when it refers to a civil matter triable to a jury, a criminal matter, or any other proceeding that could result in incarceration, and the statement relates to:

(1) the character, credibility, reputation or criminal record of a party, suspect in a criminal investigation or witness, or the identity of a witness, or the expected testimony of a party or witness;

(2) in a criminal case or proceeding that could result in incarceration, the possibility of a plea of guilty to the offense or the existence or contents of any confession,

admission, or statement given by a defendant or suspect or that person's refusal or failure to make a statement;

(3) the performance or results of any examination or test or the refusal or failure of a person to submit to an examination or test, or the identity or nature of physical evidence expected to be presented;

(4) any opinion as to the guilt or innocence of a defendant or suspect in a criminal case or proceeding that could result in incarceration;

(5) information the lawyer knows or reasonably should know is likely to be inadmissible as evidence in a trial and would if disclosed create a substantial risk of prejudicing an impartial trial; or

(6) the fact that a defendant has been charged with a crime, unless there is included therein a statement explaining that the charge is merely an accusation and that the defendant is presumed innocent until and unless proven guilty.

(c) Notwithstanding paragraph (a) and (b) (1–5), a lawyer involved in the investigation or litigation of a matter may state without elaboration:

(1) the general nature of the claim or defense;

(2) the information contained in a public record;

(3) that an investigation of the matter is in progress, including the general scope of the investigation, the offense or claim or defense involved and, except when prohibited by law, the identity of the persons involved;

(4) the scheduling or result of any step in litigation;

(5) a request for assistance in obtaining evidence and information necessary thereto;

(6) a warning of danger concerning the behavior of a person involved, when there is reason to believe that there exists the likelihood of substantial harm to an individual or to the public interest; and

(7) in a criminal case:

(i) the identity, residence, occupation and family status of the accused;

(ii) if the accused has not been apprehended, information necessary to aid in apprehension of that person;

(iii) the fact, time and place of arrest; and

(iv) the identity of investigating and arresting officers or agencies and the length of the investigation.

COMMENT:

[1] It is difficult to strike a balance between protecting the right to a fair trial and safeguarding the right of free expression. Preserving the right to a fair trial necessarily entails some curtailment of the information that may be disseminated about a party prior to trial, particularly where trial by jury is involved. If there were no such limits, the result would be the practical nullification of the protective effect of the rules of forensic decorum and the exclusionary rules of evidence. On the other hand, there are vital social interests served by the free dissemination of information about events having legal consequences and about legal proceedings themselves. The public has a right to know about threats to its safety and measures aimed at assuring its security. It also has a legitimate interest in the conduct of judicial proceedings, particularly in matters of general public concern. Furthermore, the subject matter of legal proceedings is often of direct significance in debate and deliberation over questions of public policy.

[2] No body of rules can simultaneously satisfy all interests of fair trial and all those of free expression. The formula in this Rule is based upon the ABA Model Code of Professional Responsibility and the ABA Standards Relating to Fair Trial and Free Press, as amended in 1978.

[3] Special rules of confidentiality may validly govern proceedings in juvenile, domestic relations and mental disability proceedings, and perhaps other types of litigation. Rule 3.4(c) requires compliance with such Rules.

MODEL CODE COMPARISON:

[1] Rule 3.6 is similar to DR 7–107, except as follows: First, Rule 3.6 adopts the general criteria of "substantial likelihood of materially prejudicing an adjudicative proceeding" to describe impermissible conduct. Second, Rule 3.6 transforms the particulars in DR 7–107 into an illustrative compilation that gives fair notice of conduct ordinarily posing unacceptable dangers to the fair administration of justice. Finally, Rule 3.6 omits DR 7–

107(C)(7), which provided that a lawyer may reveal "[a]t the time of seizure, a description of the physical evidence seized, other than a confession, admission or statement." Such revelations may be substantially prejudicial and are frequently the subject of pretrial suppression motions, which, if successful, may be circumvented by prior disclosure to the press.

RULE 3.7 Lawyer as Witness

(a) A lawyer shall not act as advocate at a trial in which the lawyer is likely to be a necessary witness except where:

(1) the testimony relates to an uncontested issue;

(2) the testimony relates to the nature and value of legal services rendered in the case; or

(3) disqualification of the lawyer would work substantial hardship on the client.

(b) A lawyer may act as advocate in a trial in which another lawyer in the lawyer's firm is likely to be called as a witness unless precluded from doing so by rule 1.7 or rule 1.9.

COMMENT:

[1] Combining the roles of advocate and witness can prejudice the opposing party and can involve a conflict of interest between the lawyer and client.

[2] The opposing party has proper objection where the combination of roles may prejudice that party's rights in the litigation. A witness is required to testify on the basis of personal knowledge, while an advocate is expected to explain and comment on evidence given by others. It may not be clear whether a statement by an advocate-witness should be taken as proof or as an analysis of the proof.

[3] Paragraph (a)(1) recognizes that if the testimony will be uncontested, the ambiguities in the dual role are purely theoretical. Paragraph (a)(2) recognizes that where the testimony concerns the extent and value of legal services rendered in the action in which the testimony is offered, permitting the lawyers to testify avoids the need for a second trial with new counsel to resolve that issue. Moreover, in such a situation the judge has first hand knowledge of the matter in issue; hence, there is less dependence on the adversary process to test the credibility of the testimony.

[4] Apart from these two exceptions, paragraph (a)(3) recognizes that a balancing is required between the interests of the client and those of the opposing party. Whether the opposing party is likely to suffer prejudice depends on the nature of the case, the importance and probable tenor of the lawyer's testimony, and the probability that the lawyer's testimony will conflict with that of other witnesses. Even if there is risk of such prejudice, in determining whether the lawyer should be disqualified due regard must be given to the effect of disqualification on the lawyer's client. It is relevant that one or both parties could reasonably foresee that the lawyer would probably be a witness. The principle of imputed disqualification stated in Rule 1.10 has no application to this aspect of the problem.

[5] Whether the combination of roles involves an improper conflict of interest with respect to the client is determined by Rule 1.7 or 1.9. For example, if there is likely to be substantial conflict between the testimony of the client and that of the lawyer or a member of the lawyer's firm, the representation is improper. The problem can arise whether the lawyer is called as a witness on behalf of the client or is called by the opposing party. Determining whether or not such a conflict exists is primarily the responsibility of the lawyer involved. See Comment to Rule 1.7. If a lawyer who is a member of a firm may not act as both advocate and witness by reason of conflict of interest, Rule 1.10 disqualifies the firm also.

MODEL CODE COMPARISON:

DR 5–102(A) prohibited a lawyer, or the lawyer's firm, from serving as advocate if the lawyer "learns or it is obvious that he or a lawyer in his firm ought to be called as a witness on behalf of his client." DR 5–102(B) provided that a lawyer, and the lawyer's firm, may continue representation if the "lawyer learns or it is obvious that he or a lawyer in his firm may be called as a witness other than on behalf of his client . . . until it is apparent that his testimony is or may be prejudicial to his client." DR 5–101(B) permitted a lawyer to testify while representing a client: "(1) If the testimony will relate solely to an uncontested matter; (2) If the testimony will relate solely to a matter of formality and there is no reason to believe that substantial evidence will be offered in opposition to the testimony; (3) If the testimony will relate solely to the nature and value of legal services rendered in the case by the lawyer or his firm to the client; (4) As to any matter if refusal would work a substantial hardship on the client because of the distinctive value of the lawyer or his firm as counsel in the particular case."

The exception stated in paragraph (a)(1) consolidates provisions of DR 5–101(B)(1) and (2). Testimony relating to a formality, referred to in DR 5–101(B)(2), in effect defines the phrase "uncontested issue," and is redundant.

RULE 3.8   Special Responsibilities of a Prosecutor*

The prosecutor in a criminal case shall:

(a) refrain from prosecuting a charge that the prosecutor knows is not supported by probable cause;

(b) make reasonable efforts to assure that the accused has been advised of the right to, and the procedure for obtaining, counsel and has been given reasonable opportunity to obtain counsel;

(c) not seek to obtain from an unrepresented accused a waiver of important pretrial rights, such as the right to a preliminary hearing;

(d) make timely disclosure to the defense of all evidence or information known to the prosecutor that tends to negate the guilt of the accused or mitigates the offense, and, in connection with sentencing, disclose to the defense and to the tribunal all unprivileged mitigating information known to the prosecutor, except when the prosecutor is relieved of this responsibility by a protective order of the tribunal; and

(e) exercise reasonable care to prevent investigators, law enforcement personnel, employees or other persons assisting or associated with the prosecutor in a criminal case from making an extrajudicial statement that the prosecutor would be prohibited from making under rule 3.6.

(f) not subpoena a lawyer in a grand jury or other criminal proceeding to present evidence about a past or present client unless:

(1) the prosecutor reasonably believes:

(i) the information sought is not protected from disclosure by any applicable privilege;

(ii) the evidence sought is essential to the successful completion of an ongoing investigation or prosecution;

(iii) there is no other feasible alternative to obtain the information; and

(2) the prosecutor obtains prior judicial approval after an opportunity for an adversarial proceeding.

COMMENT:

[1] A prosecutor has the responsibility of a minister of justice and not simply that of an advocate. This responsibility carries with it specific obligations to see that the defendant is accorded procedural justice and that guilt is decided upon the basis of sufficient evidence. Precisely how far the prosecutor is required to go in this direction is a matter of debate and varies in different jurisdictions. Many jurisdictions have adopted the ABA Standards of Criminal Justice Relating to Prosecution Function, which in turn are the product of prolonged and careful deliberation by lawyers experienced in both criminal prosecution and defense. See also Rule 3.3(d), governing ex parte proceedings, among which grand jury proceedings are included. Applicable law may require other measures by the prosecutor and knowing disregard of those obligations or a systematic abuse of prosecutorial discretion could constitute a violation of Rule 8.4.

[2] Paragraph (c) does not apply to an accused appearing pro se with the approval of the tribunal. Nor does it forbid the lawful questioning of a suspect who has knowingly waived the rights to counsel and silence.

[3] The exception in paragraph (d) recognizes that a prosecutor may seek an appropriate protective order from the tribunal if disclosure of information to the defense could result in substantial harm to an individual or to the public interest.

---

* In 1990, the ABA added the text in subparagraph (f) to original Model Rule 3.8. This amendment seeks to address the profession's concerns over the increased use of subpoenas that are directed towards attorneys for information about their clients. The adopted rule seeks to limit the use of such subpoenas because of their potential to disrupt the attorney-client relationship.

[4] * Paragraph (f) is intended to limit the issuance of lawyer subpoenas in grand jury and other criminal proceedings to those situations in which there is a genuine need to intrude into the client-lawyer relationship. The prosecutor is required to obtain court approval for the issuance of the subpoena after an opportunity for an adversarial hearing is afforded in order to assure an independent determination that the applicable standards are met.

MODEL CODE COMPARISON:

[1] DR 7–103(A) provided that a "public prosecutor . . . shall not institute . . . criminal charges when he knows or it is obvious that the charges are not supported by probable cause." DR 7–103(B) provided that "[a] public prosecutor . . . shall make timely disclosure . . . of the existence of evidence, known to the prosecutor . . . that tends to negate the guilt of the accused, mitigate the degree of the offense, or reduce the punishment."

RULE 3.9 Advocate in Nonadjudicative Proceedings

A lawyer representing a client before a legislative or administrative tribunal in a nonadjudicative proceeding shall disclose that the appearance is in a representative capacity and shall conform to the provisions of rules 3.3(a) through (c), 3.4(a) through (c), and 3.5.

COMMENT:

[1] In representation before bodies such as legislatures, municipal councils, and executive and administrative agencies acting in a rule-making or policy-making capacity, lawyers present facts, formulate issues and advance argument in the matters under consideration. The decision-making body, like a court, should be able to rely on the integrity of the submissions made to it. A lawyer appearing before such a body should deal with the tribunal honestly and in conformity with applicable rules of procedure.

[2] Lawyers have no exclusive right to appear before nonadjudicative bodies, as they do before a court. The requirements of this Rule therefore may subject lawyers to regulations inapplicable to advocates who are not lawyers. However, legislatures and administrative agencies have a right to expect lawyers to deal with them as they deal with courts.

[3] This Rule does not apply to representation of a client in a negotiation or other bilateral transaction with a governmental agency; representation in such a transaction is governed by Rules 4.1 through 4.4.

MODEL CODE COMPARISON:

[1] EC 7–15 stated that a lawyer "appearing before an administrative agency, regardless of the nature of the proceeding it is conducting, has the continuing duty to advance the cause of his client within the bounds of the law." EC 7–16 stated that "[w]hen a lawyer appears in connection with proposed legislation, he . . . should comply with applicable laws and legislative rules." EC 8–5 stated that "[f]raudulent, deceptive, or otherwise illegal conduct by a participant in a proceeding before a . . . legislative body . . . should never be participated in . . . by lawyers." DR 7–106(B)(1) provided that "[i]n presenting a matter to a tribunal, a lawyer shall disclose . . . [u]nless privileged or irrelevant, the identity of the clients he represents and of the persons who employed him."

TRANSACTIONS WITH PERSONS OTHER THAN CLIENTS

RULE 4.1 Truthfulness in Statements to Others

In the course of representing a client a lawyer shall not knowingly:

(a) make a false statement of material fact or law to a third person; or

(b) fail to disclose a material fact to a third person when disclosure is necessary to avoid assisting a criminal or fraudulent act by a client, unless disclosure is prohibited by rule 1.6.

COMMENT:

Misrepresentation

[1] A lawyer is required to be truthful when dealing with others on a client's behalf, but generally has no affirmative duty to inform an opposing party of relevant facts. A misrepresentation can occur if the lawyer incorporates or affirms a statement of another person that the lawyer knows is false. Misrepresentations can also occur by failure to act.

---

* The ABA added this paragraph in 1990 when it amended Model Rule 3.8 by adding subparagraph (f).

Statements of Fact

[2] This Rule refers to statements of fact. Whether a particular statement should be regarded as one of fact can depend on the circumstances. Under generally accepted conventions in negotiation, certain types of statements ordinarily are not taken as statements of material fact. Estimates of price or value placed on the subject of a transaction and a party's intentions as to an acceptable settlement of a claim are in this category, and so is the existence of an undisclosed principal except where nondisclosure of the principal would constitute fraud.

Fraud by Client

[3] Paragraph (b) recognizes that substantive law may require a lawyer to disclose certain information to avoid being deemed to have assisted the client's crime or fraud. The requirement of disclosure created by this paragraph is, however, subject to the obligations created by Rule 1.6.

MODEL CODE COMPARISON:

[1] Paragraph (a) is substantially similar to DR 7–102(A)(5), which stated that "[i]n his representation of a client, a lawyer shall not . . . [k]nowingly make a false statement of law or fact."

[2] With regard to paragraph (b), DR 7–102(A)(3) provided that a lawyer shall not "[c]onceal or knowingly fail to disclose that which he is required by law to reveal."

RULE 4.2 Communication With Person Represented by Counsel

In representing a client, a lawyer shall not communicate about the subject of the representation with a party the lawyer knows to be represented by another lawyer in the matter, unless the lawyer has the consent of the other lawyer or is authorized by law to do so.

COMMENT:

[1] This Rule does not prohibit communication with a party, or an employee or agent of a party, concerning matters outside the representation. For example, the existence of a controversy between a government agency and a private party, or between two organizations, does not prohibit a lawyer for either from communicating with non-lawyer representatives of the other regarding a separate matter. Also, parties to a matter may communicate directly with each other and a lawyer having independent justification for communicating with the other party is permitted to do so. Communications authorized by law include, for example, the right of a party to a controversy with a government agency to speak with government officials about the matter.

[2] In the case of an organization, this Rule prohibits communications by a lawyer for one party concerning the matter in representation with persons having a managerial responsibility on behalf of the organization, and with any other person whose act or omission in connection with that matter may be imputed to the organization for purposes of civil or criminal liability or whose statement may constitute an admission on the part of the organization. If an agent or employee of the organization is represented in the matter by his or her own counsel, the consent by that counsel to a communication will be sufficient for purposes of this Rule. Compare Rule 3.4(f).

[3] This Rule also covers any person, whether or not a party to a formal proceeding, who is represented by counsel concerning the matter in question.

MODEL CODE COMPARISON:

[1] This Rule is substantially identical to DR 7–104(A)(1).

RULE 4.3 Dealing With Unrepresented Person

In dealing on behalf of a client with a person who is not represented by counsel, a lawyer shall not state or imply that the lawyer is disinterested. When the lawyer knows or reasonably should know that the unrepresented person misunderstands the lawyer's role in the matter, the lawyer shall make reasonable efforts to correct the misunderstanding.

COMMENT:

[1] An unrepresented person, particularly one not experienced in dealing with legal matters, might assume that a lawyer is disinterested in loyalties or is a disinterested authority on the law even when the lawyer represents a client. During the course of a lawyer's representation of a client, the lawyer should not give advice to an unrepresented person other than the advice to obtain counsel.

MODEL CODE COMPARISON:

[1] There was no direct counterpart to this Rule in the Model Code. DR 7–104(A)(2) provided that a lawyer shall not "[g]ive advice

to a person who is not represented by a lawyer, other than the advice to secure counsel. . . ."

RULE 4.4 Respect for Rights of Third Persons

In representing a client, a lawyer shall not use means that have no substantial purpose other than to embarrass, delay, or burden a third person, or use methods of obtaining evidence that violate the legal rights of such a person.

COMMENT:

[1] Responsibility to a client requires a lawyer to subordinate the interests of others to those of the client, but that responsibility does not imply that a lawyer may disregard the rights of third persons. It is impractical to catalogue all such rights, but they include legal restrictions on methods of obtaining evidence from third persons.

MODEL CODE COMPARISON:

[1] DR 7–106(C)(2) provided that a lawyer shall not "[a]sk any question that he has no reasonable basis to believe is relevant to the case and that is intended to degrade a witness or other person." DR 7–102(A)(1) provided that a lawyer shall not "take . . . action on behalf of his client when he knows or when it is obvious that such action would serve merely to harass or maliciously injure another." DR 7–108(D) provided that "[a]fter discharge of the jury . . . the lawyer shall not ask questions or make comments to a member of that jury that are calculated merely to harass or embarrass the juror. . . ." DR 7–108(E) provided that a lawyer "shall not conduct . . . a vexatious or harassing investigation of either a venireman or a juror."

LAW FIRMS AND ASSOCIATIONS

RULE 5.1 Responsibilities of a Partner or Supervisory Lawyer

(a) A partner in a law firm shall make reasonable efforts to ensure that the firm has in effect measures giving reasonable assurance that all lawyers in the firm conform to the rules of professional conduct.

(b) A lawyer having direct supervisory authority over another lawyer shall make reasonable efforts to ensure that the other lawyer conforms to the rules of professional conduct.

(c) A lawyer shall be responsible for another lawyer's violation of the rules of professional conduct if:

(1) the lawyer orders or, with knowledge of the specific conduct, ratifies the conduct involved; or

(2) the lawyer is a partner in the law firm in which the other lawyer practices, or has direct supervisory authority over the other lawyer, and knows of the conduct at a time when its consequences can be avoided or mitigated but fails to take reasonable remedial action.

COMMENT:

[1] Paragraphs (a) and (b) refer to lawyers who have supervisory authority over the professional work of a firm or legal department of a government agency. This includes members of a partnership and the shareholders in a law firm organized as a professional corporation; lawyers having supervisory authority in the law department of an enterprise or government agency; and lawyers who have intermediate managerial responsibilities in a firm.

[2] The measures required to fulfill the responsibility prescribed in paragraphs (a) and (b) can depend on the firm's structure and the nature of its practice. In a small firm, informal supervision and occasional admonition ordinarily might be sufficient. In a large firm, or in practice situations in which intensely difficult ethical problems frequently arise, more elaborate procedures may be necessary. Some firms, for example, have a procedure whereby junior lawyers can make confidential referral of ethical problems directly to a designated senior partner or special committee. See Rule 5.2. Firms, whether large or small, may also rely on continuing legal education in professional ethics. In any event, the ethical atmosphere of a firm can influence the conduct of all its members and a lawyer having authority over the work of another may not assume that the subordinate lawyer will inevitably conform to the Rules.

[3] Paragraph (c)(1) expresses a general principle of responsibility for acts of another. See also Rule 8.4(a).

[4] Paragraph (c)(2) defines the duty of a lawyer having direct supervisory authority over performance of specific legal work by another lawyer. Whether a lawyer has such supervisory authority in particular circumstances is a question of fact. Partners of a private firm have at least indirect responsibility for all work being done by the firm,

while a partner in charge of a particular matter ordinarily has direct authority over other firm lawyers engaged in the matter. Appropriate remedial action by a partner would depend on the immediacy of the partner's involvement and the seriousness of the misconduct. The supervisor is required to intervene to prevent avoidable consequences of misconduct if the supervisor knows that the misconduct occurred. Thus, if a supervising lawyer knows that a subordinate misrepresented a matter to an opposing party in negotiation, the supervisor as well as the subordinate has a duty to correct the resulting misapprehension.

[5] Professional misconduct by a lawyer under supervision could reveal a violation of paragraph (b) on the part of the supervisory lawyer even though it does not entail a violation of paragraph (c) because there was no direction, ratification or knowledge or the violation.

[6] Apart from this Rule and Rule 8.4(a), a lawyer does not have disciplinary liability for the conduct of a partner, associate or subordinate. Whether a lawyer may be liable civilly or criminally for another lawyer's conduct is a question of law beyond the scope of these Rules.

MODEL CODE COMPARISON:

There was no direct counterpart to this Rule in the Model Code. DR 1–103(A) provided that a lawyer "possessing unprivileged knowledge of a violation of DR 1–102 shall report such knowledge to . . . authority empowered to investigate or act upon such violation."

RULE 5.2 Responsibilities of a Subordinate Lawyer

(a) A lawyer is bound by the rules of professional conduct notwithstanding that the lawyer acted at the direction of another person.

(b) A subordinate lawyer does not violate the rules of professional conduct if that lawyer acts in accordance with a supervisory lawyer's reasonable resolution of an arguable question of professional duty.

COMMENT:

[1] Although a lawyer is not relieved of responsibility for a violation by the fact that the lawyer acted at the direction of a supervisor, that fact may be relevant in determining whether a lawyer had the knowledge required to render conduct a violation of the Rules. For example, if a

subordinate filed a frivolous pleading at the direction of a supervisor, the subordinate would not be guilty of a professional violation unless the subordinate knew of the document's frivolous character.

[2] When lawyers in a supervisor-subordinate relationship encounter a matter involving professional judgment as to ethical duty, the supervisor may assume responsibility for making the judgment. Otherwise a consistent course of action or position could not be taken. If the question can reasonably be answered only one way, the duty of both lawyers is clear and they are equally responsible for fulfilling it. However, if the question is reasonably arguable, someone has to decide upon the course of action. That authority ordinarily reposes in the supervisor, and a subordinate may be guided accordingly. For example, if a question arises whether the interests of two clients conflict under Rule 1.7, the supervisor's reasonable resolution of the question should protect the subordinate professionally if the resolution is subsequently challenged.

MODEL CODE COMPARISON:

[1] There was no counterpart to this Rule in the Model Code.

RULE 5.3 Responsibilities Regarding Nonlawyer Assistants

With respect to a nonlawyer employed or retained by or associated with a lawyer:

(a) a partner in a law firm shall make reasonable efforts to ensure that the firm has in effect measures giving reasonable assurance that the person's conduct is compatible with the professional obligations of the lawyer;

(b) a lawyer having direct supervisory authority over the nonlawyer shall make reasonable efforts to ensure that the person's conduct is compatible with the professional obligations of the lawyer; and

(c) a lawyer shall be responsible for conduct of such a person that would be a violation of the rules of professional conduct if engaged in by a lawyer if:

(1) the lawyer orders or, with the knowledge of the specific conduct, ratifies the conduct involved; or

(2) the lawyer is a partner in the law firm in which the person is employed, or has direct supervisory authority over the person, and knows of the conduct at a time when its consequences can be avoided or

mitigated but fails to take reasonable remedial action.

COMMENT:

[1] Lawyers generally employ assistants in their practice, including secretaries, investigators, law student interns, and paraprofessionals. Such assistants, whether employees or independent contractors, act for the lawyer in rendition of the lawyer's professional services. A lawyer should give such assistants appropriate instruction and supervision concerning the ethical aspects of their employment, particularly regarding the obligation not to disclose information relating to representation of the client, and should be responsible for their work product. The measures employed in supervising nonlawyers should take account of the fact that they do not have legal training and are not subject to professional discipline.

MODEL CODE COMPARISON:

[1] There was no direct counterpart to this Rule in the Model Code. DR 4–101(D) provided that a lawyer "shall exercise reasonable care to prevent his employees, associates, and others whose services are utilized by him from disclosing or using confidences or secrets of a client. . . ." DR 7–107(J) provided that "[a] lawyer shall exercise reasonable care to prevent his employees and associates from making an extrajudicial statement that he would be prohibited from making under DR 7–107."

RULE 5.4 Professional Independence of a Lawyer *

(a) A lawyer or law firm shall not share legal fees with a nonlawyer, except that:

(1) an agreement by a lawyer with the lawyer's firm, partner, or associate may provide for the payment of money, over a reasonable period of time after the lawyer's death, to the lawyer's estate or to one or more specified persons;

(2) a lawyer who purchases the practice of a deceased, disabled, or disappeared lawyer may, pursuant to the provisions of Rule 1.17, pay to the estate or other representative of that lawyer the agreed-upon purchase price; and

(3) a lawyer or law firm may include nonlawyer employees in a compensation or retirement plan, even though the plan is based in whole or in part on a profit-sharing arrangement.

(b) A lawyer shall not form a partnership with a nonlawyer if any of the activities of the partnership consist of the practice of law.

(c) A lawyer shall not permit a person who recommends, employs, or pays the lawyer to render legal services for another to direct or regulate the lawyer's professional judgment in rendering such legal services.

(d) A lawyer shall not practice with or in the form of a professional corporation or association authorized to practice law for a profit, if:

(1) a nonlawyer owns any interest therein, except that a fiduciary representative of the estate of a lawyer may hold the stock or interest of the lawyer for a reasonable time during administration;

(2) a nonlawyer is a corporate director or officer thereof; or

(3) a nonlawyer has the right to direct or control the professional judgment of a lawyer.

COMMENT:

[1] The provisions of this Rule express traditional limitations on sharing fees. These limitations are to protect the lawyer's professional independence of judgment. Where someone other than the client pays the lawyer's fee or salary, or recommends employment of the lawyer, that arrangement does not modify the lawyer's obligation to the client. As stated in paragraph (c), such arrange-

---

* In 1990, the ABA amended the text of Model Rule 5.4(a)(2) to recognize the addition of Model Rule 1.17 on the sale of a law practice. The original Model Rule 5.4(a)(2) read as follows:

RULE 5.4 Professional Independence of a Lawyer

(a) A lawyer or law firm shall not share legal fees with a nonlawyer, except that:

* * *

(2) a lawyer who undertakes to complete unfinished legal business of a deceased lawyer may pay to the estate of the deceased lawyer that proportion of the total compensation which fairly represents the services rendered by the deceased lawyer; and

* * *

ments should not interfere with the lawyer's professional judgment.

MODEL CODE COMPARISON:

[1] Paragraph (a) is substantially identical to DR 3–102(A).

[2] Paragraph (b) is substantially identical to DR 3–103(A).

[3] Paragraph (c) is substantially identical to DR 5–107(B).

[4] Paragraph (d) is substantially identical to DR 5–107(C).

RULE 5.5 Unauthorized Practice of Law

A lawyer shall not:

(a) practice law in a jurisdiction where doing so violates the regulation of the legal profession in that jurisdiction; or

(b) assist a person who is not a member of the bar in the performance of activity that constitutes the unauthorized practice of law.

COMMENT:

[1] The definition of the practice of law is established by law and varies from one jurisdiction to another. Whatever the definition, limiting the practice of law to members of the bar protects the public against rendition of legal services by unqualified persons. Paragraph (b) does not prohibit a lawyer from employing the services of paraprofessionals and delegating functions to them, so long as the lawyer supervises the delegated work and retains responsibility for their work. See Rule 5.3. Likewise, it does not prohibit lawyers from providing professional advice and instruction to nonlawyers whose employment requires knowledge of law; for example, claims adjusters, employees of financial or commercial institutions, social workers, accountants and persons employed in government agencies. In addition, a lawyer may counsel nonlawyers who wish to proceed pro se.

MODEL CODE COMPARISON:

[1] With regard to paragraph (a), DR 3–101(B) of the Model Code provided that "[a] lawyer shall not practice law in a jurisdiction where to do so would be in violation of regulations of the profession in that jurisdiction."

[2] With regard to paragraph (b), DR 3–101(A) of the Model Code provided that "[a] lawyer shall not aid a non-lawyer in the unauthorized practice of law."

RULE 5.6 Restrictions on Right to Practice

A lawyer shall not participate in offering or making:

(a) a partnership or employment agreement that restricts the rights of a lawyer to practice after termination of the relationship, except an agreement concerning benefits upon retirement; or

(b) an agreement in which a restriction on the lawyer's right to practice is part of the settlement of a controversy between private parties.

COMMENT:

[1] An agreement restricting the right of partners or associates to practice after leaving a firm not only limits their professional autonomy but also limits the freedom of clients to choose a lawyer. Paragraph (a) prohibits such agreements except for restrictions incident to provisions concerning retirement benefits for service with the firm.

[2] Paragraph (b) prohibits a lawyer from agreeing not to represent other persons in connection with settling a claim on behalf of a client.

[3] * This Rule does not apply to prohibit restrictions that may be included in the terms of the sale of a law practice pursuant to Rule 1.17.

MODEL CODE COMPARISON:

[1] This Rule is substantially similar to DR 2–108.

RULE 5.7 Provision of Ancillary Services**

(a) A lawyer shall not practice law in a law firm which owns a controlling interest in, or operates, an entity which provides non-legal services which are ancillary to the practice of law, or otherwise provides such ancillary non-legal services, except as provided in paragraph (b).

---

* This paragraph was added by the ABA in 1990 to resolve the potential overlap between this provision and the restrictions placed in Model Rule 1.17 regarding the sale of a law practice.

** The A.B.A. House of Delegates adopted this Rule and Comments on August 13, 1991.

(b) A lawyer may practice law in a law firm wich provides non-legal services which are ancillary to the practice of law if:

(1) The ancillary services are provided solely to clients of the law firm and are incidental to, in connection with and concurrent to, the provision of legal services by the law firm to such clients;

(2) Such ancillary services are provided solely by employees of the law firm itself and not by a subsidiary or other affiliate of the law firm;

(3) The law firm makes appropriate disclosure in writing to its clients; and

(4) The law firm does not hold itself out as engaging in any non-legal activities except in conjunction with the provision of legal services, as provided in this rule.

(c) One or more lawyers who engage in the practice of law in a law firm shall neither own a controlling interest in, nor operate, an entity which provides non-legal services which are ancillary to the practice of law, nor otherwise provide such ancillary non-legal services, except that their firms may provide such services as provided in paragraph (b).

(d) Two or more lawyers who engage in the practice of law in separate law firms shall neither own a controlling interest in, nor operate, an entity which provides non-legal services which are ancillary to the practice of law, nor otherwise provide such ancillary non-legal services.

COMMENT

General

[1] For many years, lawyers have provided to their clients non-legal services which are ancillary to the practice of law. Such services included title insurance, trust services and patent consulting. In most instances, these ancillary non-legal services were provided to law firm clients in connection with, and concurrent to, the provision of legal services by the lawyer or law firm. The provision of such services afforded benefits to clients, including making available a greater range of services from one source and maintaining technical expertise in various fields within a law firm. However, the provision of both legal and ancillary non-legal services raises ethical concerns, including conflicts of interest, confusion on the part of clients and possible loss (or inapplicability) of the attorney-client privilege, which may not have been ad-

dressed adequately by the other Model Rules of Professional Conduct.

[2] Eventually, law firms began to form affiliates, largely staffed by nonlawyers, to provide ancillary non-legal services to both clients and customers who were not clients for legal services. In addition to exacerbating the ethical problems of conflicts of interest, confusion and threats to confidentiality, the large-scale movement of law firms into ancillary non-legal businesses raised serious professionalism concerns, including compromising lawyers' independent judgment, the loss of the bar's right to self regulation and the provision of legal services by entities controlled by nonlawyers.

[3] Rule 5.7 addresses both the ethical and professionalism concerns implicated by the provision of ancillary non-legal services by lawyers and law firms. It preserves the ability of lawyers to provide additional services to their clients and maintain within the law firm a broad range of technical expertise. However, Rule 5.7 restricts the ability of law firms to provide ancillary non-legal services through affiliates to non-client customers and clients alike, the rendition of which raises serious ethical and professionalism concerns.

Limitations on the Provision of Non-legal Services Which Are Ancillary to the Practice of Law

[4] Paragraph (a) attempts to forestall the ethical and professional concerns which are raised when law firms own or operate non-legal businesses which are ancillary to the practice of law or otherwise provide such services. The provision of such ancillary services by law firms has the potential of compromising a lawyer's independent professional judgment and othewise causing harm to law firm clients (e.g., creating conflicts of interest, jeopardizing clients' expectations of confidentiality and causing confusion on the part of clients). Additionally, serious threats to lawyers' professionalism are also posed when law firms own or operate ancillary businesses which provide services to persons who are not concurrently seeking legal services from the law firm.

[5] Paragraph (a) prohibits lawyers from practicing in a law firm which owns a controlling interest in, or operates, an entity which provides non-legal services which are ancillary to the practice of law, or which provides such ancillary services from within the law firm, unless such services are incidental to the law firm's provision of legal services as set forth in Paragraph (b).

[6] The term "non-legal services which are ancillary to the practice of law" refers to those services which satisfy all or most of the following indicia: (1) are provided to clients of a law firm (or customers of a business owned or controlled by a law firm); (2) clearly do not constitute the practice of law; (3) are readily available from those not licensed to practice law; (4) are functionally connected to the provision of legal services, i.e., services which are often sought or needed in connection with (and in addition to) legal services; (5) involve intellectual ability or learning; and (6) have the potential for creating serious ethical problems in the lawyer client realtionship, such as compromising the independent professional judgment of lawyers; creating conflicts of interest; threatening the clients' (or customers') expectations of confidentiality and/or causing confusion on the part of clients or customers.

[7] Among those activities which are not included in the term "non-legal services which are ancillary to the practice of law" because they do not pose serious ethical problems in the lawyer client relationship are:

(1) law firms or lawyers owning, for example, restaurants, shops or taxi services (since these services are not functionally connected to the practice of law);

(2) law firms providing copying services or other clerical services incidental to the practice of law;

(3) law firms owning and managing the buildings in which their offices are located or other property (since owning and managing property—even though a subsidiary or affiliate—is not functionally connected to the provision of legal services to clients);

(4) a law firm priividing services or products intended for use by other lawyers, such as publications, software programs, or legal malpractice insurance (since such services or products are not functionally connected to the provision of legal services to clients);

(5) lawyers serving as fiduciaries of trusts or corporate directors or lawyers serving in quasi-judicial positions such as mediators or arbitrators.

[8] When services provided by a law firm are performed by nonlawyers, there should be an initial presumption that the services do not constitute the practice of law and may be a "non-legal service which is ancillary to the practice of law." In addition, a presumption that a service is "ancillary"

to the practice of law" should exist if the service is normally provided by nonlawyers in discrete professions or occupations, e.g., doctors, architects, engineers, real estate brokers, investment bankers, or financial consultants.

[9] Note that Paragraph (a) does not prohibit a lawyer from practicing in a law firm which acquires a passive financial interest in an entity which provides non-legal ancillary services (i.e., purchasing shares of an investment banking firm or a consulting company), provided that the interest is not a controlling one. This rule does not define the concept of control, which is generally a fact based inquiry dependent on the particular facts and circumstances. However, the existence of an ownership interest by lawyers in other entities (especially clients) may implicate conflict of interest concerns (see Model Rules of Professional Conduct 1.7 and 1.8) and may require disclosure by the lawyers pursuant to these rules.

Connection Between the Provision of Legal and Ancillary Non-legal Services

[10] Paragraph (b) preserves the ability of law firms to provide non-legal services which are ancillary to the practice of law, but under conditions designed to ensure that such services are closely related to the firms' provision of legal services and not independent of, and unrelated to, such legal services.

[11] Subsection (1) of Paragraph (b) requires that ancillary non-legal services be provided solely to law firm clients (as opposed to persons who are not currently seeking legal services from a law firm) and be incidental to, in connection with, and concurrent to, the provision of legal services by the law firm. The requirement that ancillary services be "incidental to" and "in connection with" the firm's provision of legal services seeks to ensure that any non-legal services be secondary to, strictly related to, and under the supervision of those responsible for, the provision of legal services.

[12] Paragraph (b) permits law firms to employ the services of other professionals if their services are connected to the firm's provision of legal services. For example, an architect on staff at a law firm would be permitted to help clients and lawyers understand the technical issues in a construction contract negotiation, a building accident litigation or the like. However, the requirement in Paragraph (b) that such services be "incidental to" and "in connection with" the provision of legal services would proscribe a law firm from employing architects to design buildings for law firm

clients or for non-client customers who do not use the law firm's legal services. Similarly, an investment banker on staff at a law firm would be permitted to assist lawyers in the negotiation of a transaction or the litigation of valuation issues or the like, as well as to consult with law firm clients when the firm is providing legal services to them, but a law firm would be prohibited from employing investment bankers to seek out acquisitions, sell securities (or otherwise secure financing) or perform other investment banking services unrelated to a pending legal representation. Likewise, a corporation pursuing an acquisition might need the assistance of non-lawyer lobbyists before a state legislature considering anti-takeover legislation. Such lobbying designed to forestall (or attain) a change in the law, if provided by nonlawyers within a law firm, could reasonably be construed to be incidental to the firm's provision of legal services.

[13] Paragraph (b) also requires that the provision of non-legal services be concurrent with the provision of legal services. In essence, law firm clients (like non-legal services customers generally) may not obtain ancillary non-legal services from the law firm (e.g., investment banking services or medical tests), and the firm may not provide them, at a time when the client is not obtaining legal services from the law firm on a related matter.

Provision of Ancillary Non-legal Services by Employees of Law Firms

[14] Subsection (2) of Paragraph (b), in an effort to vitiate risks of compromise to lawyers' professional judgment, conflicts of interest, client confusion and potential loss of confidentiality, provides that any ancillary services provided by a law firm must be performed within the law firm by employees of the law firm itself (who work together with, and are supervised by, the firm's lawyers), and not through a subsidiary or affiliate of the law firm. This requirement closely unites the provision of legal and non-legal services under the supervision of lawyers and thereby affords lawyers the opportunity to ensure that their non-lawyer employees are acting responsibly and in accordance with the rules of legal ethics. Such a requirement minimizes the risks of non-legal employees either providing advice with which the firm's lawyers will disagree and/or engaging in improper behavior for which the firm's lawyers would be responsible. In addition, structuring the provision of non-legal services in such a way forestalls confusion on the part of clients as to whether the non-legal services are provided subject to the limitations of the Model Rules (and will prevent lawyers

from seeking to provide services outside of the protections afforded to clients by the Model Rules). Finally, if lawyers are present (or otherwise involved) in the provision of non-legal services ancillary to the practice of law, there is a greater likelihood that client confidences will be protected and a client will be able to maintain evidentiary privileges with respect to communications made by the client to the providers of non-legal ancillary services. Paragraph (b)(2) is not designed to limit the ability of lawyers to retain outside (i.e., non-affiliated) consultants such as experts, private investigators or accountants to help them provide legal services to clients.

Disclosure Requirements Relating to the Provision of Ancillary Non-legal Services

[15] Subsection (3) of Paragraph (b) requires that before providing ancillary services to a client, a law firm must comply with appropriate disclosure requirements (as mandated in Model Rule of Professional Conduct 1.8, relevant case law and other authorities) and fully disclose in writing the firm's interest in the providers of non-legal services employed by the firm and the potential conflicts of interest inherent in the provision of such services. The law firm should also consider, in appropriate circumstances, recommending that the client seek the advice of independent counsel (or independent providers of non-legal services) before obtaining non-legal services from the firm.

Representations Concerning Ancillary and Non-legal Services

[16] Subsection (4) of Paragraph (b) ensures that when law firms deal with clients (whether prospective or actual) or the public, they do not represent themselves as providing any ancillary non-legal services independent of the firm's provision of legal services. This proscription attempts to obviate the risks of confusion on the part of clients and the public, actual or apparent overreaching by attorneys and improper solicitation. It ensures that clients and the public are aware that they are dealing with a law firm and can therefore assume that representatives of the firm are bound by the rules of legal ethics; prospective or actual clients do not feel compelled to use the firm's ancillary services; and law firms do not engage in improper solicitation by seeking business for the firm's non-legal services with an expectation that these non-legal services will serve as a "feeder" for the firm's legal services. Paragraph (b)(4) also seeks to preserve the unique and independent status of the legal profession in the pub-

lic's perception by preventing law firms from representing themselves to clients and the public as multidisciplinary conglomerates or otherwise emphasizing their non-legal acivities.

[17] Paragraph (b)(4) is not intended to preclude law firms from making the existence of their non-legal businesses known to clients who have retained the firm for legal services, and who, in the attorney's opinion, might have a need for the firm's ancillary services in addition to legal services (subject to appropriate disclosure requirements). In addition, Paragraph (b)(4) is not intended to prevent individual lawyers from indicating that they are qualified or licensed in other professions, e.g., accounting, where relevant jurisdictions so permit.

Provision of Ancillary Non-legal Services by One or More Lawyers in a Law Firm

[18] Paragraph (c) prevents one or more lawyers in a single law firm from owning or operating an entity which provides non-legal services which are ancillary to the practice of law. Paragraph (c) attempts to prevent lawyers or law firms from circumventing the restrictions on law firm ownership and operation of ancillary businesses by vesting ownership not in the entire law firm, but in one or more of the attorneys in a law firm. The ethical and professional concerns inherent in the ownership of ancillary businesses are not vitiated when ownership or operation is vested in several partners in a law firm (as opposed to an entire law firm). However, a law firm itself may provide such ancillary non-legal services in accordance with Paragraph (b).

Provision of Ancillary Non-legal Services by Lawyers From Different Law Firms

[19] Paragraph (d) addresses the concerns which may result when lawyers in separate law firms own or operate an entity which provides non-legal services which are ancillary to the practice of law. The ethical and professional concerns inherent in the ownership and operation of such ancillary businesses by law firms (or one or more lawyers in a firm) are also present (or may be exacerbated) when lawyers in different firms own or operate such businesses.

MODEL CODE COMPARISON

[1] There was no counterpart to this Rule in the Model Code.

PUBLIC SERVICE

RULE 6.1 *Pro Bono Publico* Service

A lawyer should render public interest legal service. A lawyer may discharge this responsibility by providing professional services at no fee or a reduced fee to persons of limited means or to public service or charitable groups or organizations, by service in activities for improving the law, the legal system or the legal profession, and by financial support for organizations that provide legal services to persons of limited means.

COMMENT:

[1] The ABA House of Delegates has formally acknowledged "the basic responsibility of each lawyer engaged in the practice of law to provide public interest legal services" without fee, or at a substantially reduced fee, in one or more of the following areas: poverty law, civil rights law, public rights law, charitable organization representation and the administration of justice. This Rule expresses that policy but is not intended to be enforced through disciplinary process.

[2] The rights and responsibilities of individuals and organizations in the United States are increasingly defined in legal terms. As a consequence, legal assistance in coping with the web of statutes, rules and regulations is imperative for persons of modest and limited means, as well as for the relatively well-to-do.

[3] The basic responsibility for providing legal services for those unable to pay ultimately rests upon the individual lawyer, and personal involvement in the problems of the disadvantaged can be one of the most rewarding experiences in the life of a lawyer. Every lawyer, regardless of professional prominence or professional workload, should find time to participate in or otherwise support the provision of legal services to the disadvantaged. The provision of free legal services to those unable to pay reasonable fees continues to be an obligation of each lawyer as well as the profession generally, but the efforts of individual lawyers are often not enough to meet the need. Thus, it has been necessary for the profession and government to institute additional programs to provide legal services. Accordingly, legal aid offices, lawyer referral services and other related programs have been developed, and others will be developed by the profession and government. Every lawyer should support all proper efforts to meet this need for legal services.

MODEL CODE COMPARISON:

[1] There was no counterpart of this Rule in the Disciplinary Rules of the Model Code. EC 2–25 stated that the "basic responsibility for providing legal services for those unable to pay ultimately rests upon the individual lawyer. . . . Every lawyer, regardless of professional prominence or professional work load, should find time to participate in serving the disadvantaged." EC 8–9 stated that "[t]he advancement of our legal system is of vital importance in maintaining the rule of law . . . [and] lawyers should encourage, and should aid in making, needed changes and improvements." EC 8–3 stated that "[t]hose persons unable to pay for legal services should be provided needed services."

RULE 6.2 Accepting Appointments

A lawyer shall not seek to avoid appointment by a tribunal to represent a person except for good cause, such as:

(a) representing the client is likely to result in violation of the rules of professional conduct or other law;

(b) representing the client is likely to result in an unreasonable financial burden on the lawyer; or

(c) the client or the cause is so repugnant to the lawyer as to be likely to impair the client-lawyer relationship or the lawyer's ability to represent the client.

COMMENT:

[1] A lawyer ordinarily is not obliged to accept a client whose character or cause the lawyer regards as repugnant. The lawyer's freedom to select clients is, however, qualified. All lawyers have a responsibility to assist in providing pro bono publico service. See Rule 6.1. An individual lawyer fulfills this responsibility by accepting a fair share of unpopular matters or indigent or unpopular clients. A lawyer may also be subject to appointment by a court to serve unpopular clients or persons unable to afford legal services.

Appointed Counsel

[2] For good cause a lawyer may seek to decline an appointment to represent a person who cannot afford to retain counsel or whose cause is unpopular. Good cause exists if the lawyer could not handle the matter competently, see Rule 1.1, or if undertaking the representation would result in an improper conflict of interest, for example, when

the client or the cause is so repugnant to the lawyer as to be likely to impair the client-lawyer relationship or the lawyer's ability to represent the client. A lawyer may also seek to decline an appointment if acceptance would be unreasonably burdensome, for example, when it would impose a financial sacrifice so great as to be unjust.

[3] An appointed lawyer has the same obligations to the client as retained counsel, including the obligations of loyalty and confidentiality, and is subject to the same limitations on the client-lawyer relationship, such as the obligation to refrain from assisting the client in violation of the Rules.

MODEL CODE COMPARISON:

[1] There was no counterpart to this Rule in the Disciplinary Rules of the Model Code. EC 2–29 stated that when a lawyer is "appointed by a court or requested by a bar association to undertake representation of a person unable to obtain counsel, whether for financial or other reasons, he should not seek to be excused from undertaking the representation except for compelling reasons. Compelling reasons do not include such factors as the repugnance of the subject matter of the proceeding, the identity or position of a person involved in the case, the belief of the lawyer that the defendant in a criminal proceeding is guilty, or the belief of the lawyer regarding the merits of the civil case." EC 2–30 stated that "a lawyer should decline employment if the intensity of his personal feelings, as distinguished from a community attitude, may impair his effective representation of a prospective client."

RULE 6.3 Membership in Legal Services Organization

A lawyer may serve as a director, officer or member of a legal services organization, apart from the law firm in which the lawyer practices, notwithstanding that the organization serves persons having interests adverse to a client of the lawyer. The lawyer shall not knowingly participate in a decision or action of the organization:

(a) if participating in the decision or action would be incompatible with the lawyer's obligations to a client under rule 1.7; or

(b) where the decision or action could have a material adverse effect on the representation of a client of the organization whose interests are adverse to a client of the lawyer.

COMMENT:

[1] Lawyers should be encouraged to support and participate in legal service organizations. A lawyer who is an officer or a member of such an organization does not thereby have a client-lawyer relationship with persons served by the organization. However, there is potential conflict between the interests of such persons and the interests of the lawyer's clients. If the possibility of such conflict disqualified a lawyer from serving on the board of a legal services organization, the profession's involvement in such organizations would be severely curtailed.

[2] It may be necessary in appropriate cases to reassure a client of the organization that the representation will not be affected by conflicting loyalties of a member of the board. Established, written policies in this respect can enhance the credibility of such assurances.

MODEL CODE COMPARISON:

[1] There was no counterpart to this Rule in the Model Code.

RULE 6.4 Law Reform Activities Affecting Client Interests

A lawyer may serve as a director, officer or member of an organization involved in reform of the law or its administration notwithstanding that the reform may affect the interests of a client of the lawyer. When the lawyer knows that the interests of a client may be materially benefitted by a decision in which the lawyer participates, the lawyer shall disclose that fact but need not identify the client.

COMMENT:

[1] Lawyers involved in organizations seeking law reform generally do not have a client-lawyer relationship with the organization. Otherwise, it might follow that a lawyer could not be involved in a bar association law reform program that might indirectly affect a client. See also Rule 1.2(b). For example, a lawyer specializing in antitrust litigation might be regarded as disqualified from participating in drafting revisions of rules governing that subject. In determining the nature and scope of participation in such activities, a lawyer should be mindful of obligations to clients under other Rules, particularly Rule 1.7. A lawyer is professionally obligated to protect the integrity of the program by making an appropriate disclosure within the organization when the lawyer knows a private client might be materially benefitted.

MODEL CODE COMPARISON:

[1] There was no counterpart to this Rule in the Model Code.

INFORMATION ABOUT LEGAL SERVICES

RULE 7.1 Communications Concerning a Lawyer's Services

A lawyer shall not make a false or misleading communication about the lawyer or the lawyer's services. A communication is false or misleading if it:

(a) contains a material misrepresentation of fact or law, or omits a fact necessary to make the statement considered as a whole not materially misleading;

(b) is likely to create an unjustified expectation about results the lawyer can achieve, or states or implies that the lawyer can achieve results by means that violate the rules of professional conduct or other law; or

(c) compares the lawyer's services with other lawyers' services, unless the comparison can be factually substantiated.

COMMENT:

[1] This Rule governs all communications about a lawyer's services, including advertising permitted by Rule 7.2. Whatever means are used to make known a lawyer's services, statements about them should be truthful. The prohibition in paragraph (b) of statements that may create "unjustified expectations" would ordinarily preclude advertisements about results obtained on behalf of a client, such as the amount of a damage award or the lawyer's record in obtaining favorable verdicts, and advertisements containing client endorsements. Such information may create the unjustified expectation that similar results can be obtained for others without reference to the specific factual and legal circumstances.

MODEL CODE COMPARISON:

[1] DR 2–101 provided that "[a] lawyer shall not . . . use . . . any form of public communication containing a false, fraudulent, misleading, deceptive, self-laudatory or unfair statement or claim." DR 2–101(B) provided that a lawyer "may publish or broadcast . . . the following information . . . in the geographic area or areas in which the lawyer resides or maintains offices or in which a significant part of the lawyer's clientele re-

sides, provided that the information . . . complies with DR 2–101(A), and is presented in a dignified manner. . . ." DR 2–101(B) then specified twenty-five categories of information that may be disseminated. DR 2–101(C) provided that "[a]ny person desiring to expand the information authorized for disclosure in DR 2–101(B), or to provide for its dissemination through other forums may apply to [the agency having jurisdiction under state law]. . . . The relief granted in response to any such application shall be promulgated as an amendment to DR 2–101(B), universally applicable to all lawyers."

RULE 7.2 Advertising*

(a) Subject to the requirements of rule 7.1 and 7.3, a lawyer may advertise services through public media, such as a telephone directory, legal directory, newspaper or other periodical, outdoor advertising, radio or television, or through written or recorded communication.

(b) A copy or recording of an advertisement or written communication shall be kept for two years after its last dissemination along with a record of when and where it was used.

(c) A lawyer shall not give anything of value to a person for recommending the lawyer's services, except that a lawyer may

(1) pay the reasonable costs of advertisements or communications permitted by this Rule;

(2) pay the usual charges of a not-for-profit lawyer referral service or legal service organization; and

(3) pay for a law practice in accordance with Rule 1.17.

(d) Any communication made pursuant to this rule shall include the name of at least one lawyer responsible for its content.

COMMENT:

[1] To assist the public in obtaining legal services, lawyers should be allowed to make known their services not only through reputation but also through organized information campaigns in the form of advertising. Advertising involves an active quest for clients, contrary to the tradition that a lawyer should not seek clientele. However, the public's need to know about legal services can be fulfilled in part through advertising. This need is particularly acute in the case of persons of moderate means who have not made extensive use of legal services. The interest in expanding public information about legal services ought to prevail over considerations of tradition. Nevertheless, advertising by lawyers entails the risk of practices that are misleading or overreaching.

[2] This Rule permits public dissemination of information concerning a lawyer's name or firm name, address and telephone number; the kinds of services the lawyer will undertake; the basis on which the lawyer's fees are determined, including prices for specific services and payment and credit arrangements; a lawyer's foreign language ability; names of references and, with their consent, names of clients regularly represented; and other information that might invite the attention of those seeking legal assistance.

[3] Questions of effectiveness and taste in advertising are matters of speculation and subjective judgment. Some jurisdictions have had extensive prohibitions against television advertising, against advertising going beyond specified facts about a lawyer, or against "undignified" advertising. Television is now one of the most powerful media for

---

* The ABA amended Model Rule 7.2 in 1989 to conform to the holding in Shapero v. Kentucky Bar Ass'n, 486 U.S. 466, 108 S.Ct. 1916, 100 L.Ed.2d 475 (1988) and in 1990 to reflect the addition of Model Rule 1.17 on the sale of a law practice. The original version of Model Rule 7.2 read as follows:

RULE 7.2 Advertising

(a) Subject to the requirements of Rules 7.1, a lawyer may advertise services through public media, such as a telephone directory, legal directory, newspaper or other periodical, outdoor, radio or television, or through written communication not involving solicitation as defined in Rule 7.3.

(b) A copy or recording of an advertisement or written communication shall be kept for two years after its last dissemination along with a record of when and where it was used.

(c) A lawyer shall not give anything of value to a person for recommending the lawyer's services, except that a lawyer may pay the reasonable cost of advertising or written communication permitted by this rule and may pay the usual charges of a not-for-profit lawyer referral service or other legal service organization.

(d) Any communication made pursuant to this rule shall include the name of at least one lawyer responsible for its content.

getting information to the public, particularly persons of low and moderate income; prohibiting television advertising, therefore, would impede the flow of information about legal services to many sectors of the public. Limiting the information that may be advertised has a similar effect and assumes that the bar can accurately forecast the kind of information that the public would regard as relevant.

[4] Neither this Rule nor Rule 7.3 prohibits communications authorized by law, such as notice to members of a class in class action litigation.

Record of Advertising

[5] Paragraph (b) requires that a record of the content and use of advertising be kept in order to facilitate enforcement of this Rule. It does not require that advertising be subject to review prior to dissemination. Such a requirement would be burdensome and expensive relative to its possible benefits, and may be of doubtful constitutionality.

Paying Others to Recommend a Lawyer*

[6] A lawyer is allowed to pay for advertising permitted by this Rule and for the purchase of a law practice in accordance with the provisions of Rule 1.17, but otherwise is not permitted to pay another person for channeling professional work. This restriction does not prevent an organization or person other than the lawyer from advertising or recommending the lawyer's services. Thus, a legal aid agency or prepaid legal services plan may pay to advertise legal services provided under its auspices. Likewise, a lawyer may participate in not-for-profit lawyer referral programs and pay the usual fees charged by such programs. Paragraph (c) does not prohibit paying regular compensation to an assistant, such as a secretary, to prepare communications permitted by this Rule.

MODEL CODE COMPARISON:

[1] With regard to paragraph (a), DR 2–101(B) provided that a lawyer "may publish or broadcast, subject to DR 2–103, . . . in print media . . . or television or radio. . . ."

[2] With regard to paragraph (b), DR 2–101(D) provided that if the advertisement is "communicated to the public over television or radio, . . . a recording of the actual transmission shall be retained by the lawyer."

[3] With regard to paragraph (c), DR 2–103(B) provided that a lawyer "shall not compensate or give anything of value to a person or organization to recommend or secure his employment . . . except that he may pay the usual and reasonable fees or dues charged by any of the organizations listed in DR 2–103(D)." (DR 2–103(D) referred to legal aid and other legal services organizations.) DR 2–101(I) provided that a lawyer "shall not compensate or give anything of value to representatives of the press, radio, television, or other communication medium in anticipation of or in return for professional publicity in a news item."

[4] There was no counterpart to paragraph (d) in the Model Code.

RULE 7.3 Direct Contact With Prospective Clients **

(a) A lawyer shall not by in-person or live telephone contact solicit professional employment from a prospective client with whom the lawyer has no family or prior professional relationship when a significant motive for the lawyer's doing so is the lawyer's pecuniary gain.

---

* In 1990, the ABA added the clause "and for the purchase of a law practice in accordance with the provisions of Rule 1.17" to reflect to addition of this provision to the Model Rules.

** The ABA amended the original version of Model Rule 7.3 in 1989 because in 1988 the Supreme Court had declared a blanket restriction on targeted mailings unconstitutional under the First Amendment. See Shapero v. Kentucky Bar Ass'n, 486 U.S. 466 (1988). The Kentucky rule which was the subject of the Supreme Court decision was identical to the original Model Rule 7.3. This provision read as follows:

RULE 7.3 Direct Contact With Prospective Clients

A lawyer may not solicit professional employment from a prospective client with whom the lawyer has no family or prior professional relationship, by mail, in-person or otherwise, when a significant motive for the lawyer's doing so is the lawyer's pecuniary gain. The term "solicit" includes contact in person, by telephone or telegraph, by letter or other writing or by other communication directed to a specific recipient, but does not include letters addressed or advertising circulars distributed generally to persons not known to need legal services of the kind provided by the lawyer in a particular matter, but who are so situated that they might in general find such services useful.

(b) A lawyer shall not solicit professional employment from a prospective client by written or recorded communication or by in-person or telephone contact even when not otherwise prohibited by paragraph (a), if:

(1) the prospective client has made known to the lawyer a desire not to be solicited by the lawyer; or

(2) the solicitation involves coercion, duress or harassment.

(c) Every written or recorded communication from a lawyer soliciting professional employment from a prospective client known to be in need of legal services in a particular matter, and with whom the lawyer has no family or prior professional relationship, shall

include the words "Advertising Material" on the outside envelope and at the beginning and ending of any recorded communication.

(d) Notwithstanding the prohibitions in paragraph (a), a lawyer may participate with a prepaid or group legal service plan operated by an organization not owned or directed by the lawyer which uses in-person or telephone contact to solicit memberships or subscriptions for the plan from persons who are not known to need legal services in a particular matter covered by the plan.

COMMENT: *

[1] There is a potential for abuse inherent in direct in-person or live telephone contact by a

---

* The ABA amended the comments to Model Rule 7.3 in 1989 to reflect changes made in the text of the Rule brought about by the *Shapero* decision. The text of the original comment reads as follows:

COMMENT:

There is a potential for abuse inherent in direct solicitation by a lawyer of prospective clients known to need legal services. It subjects the lay person to the private importuning of a trained advocate, in a direct interpersonal encounter. A prospective client often feels overwhelmed by the situation giving rise to the need for legal services, and may have an impaired capacity for reason, judgment and protective self-interest. Furthermore, the lawyer seeking the retainer is faced with a conflict stemming from the lawyer's own interest, which may color the advice and representation offered the vulnerable prospect.

The situation is therefore fraught with the possibility of undue influence, intimidation, and over-reaching. This potential for abuse inherent in direct solicitation of prospective clients justifies its prohibition, particularly since lawyer advertising permitted under Rule 7.2 offers an alternative means of communicating necessary information to those who may be in need of legal services.

Advertising makes it possible for a prospective client to be informed about the need for legal services, and about the qualifications of available lawyers and law firms, without subjecting the prospective client to direct personal persuasion that may overwhelm the client's judgment.

The use of general advertising to transmit information from lawyer to prospective client, rather than direct private contact, will help to assure that the information flows cleanly as well as freely. Advertising is out in public view, thus subject to scrutiny by those who know the lawyer. This informal review is itself likely to help guard against statements and claims that might constitute false or misleading communications, in violation of Rule 7.1. Direct, private communications from a lawyer to a prospective client are not subject to such third-scrutiny and consequently are much more likely to approach (and occasionally cross) the dividing line between accurate representations and those that are false and misleading.

These dangers attend direct solicitation whether in-person or by mail. Direct mail solicitation cannot be effectively regulated by means less drastic than outright prohibition. One proposed safeguard is to require that the designation "Advertising" be stamped on any envelope containing a solicitation letter. This would do nothing to assure the accuracy and reliability of the contents. Another suggestion is that solicitation letters be filed with a state regulatory agency. This would be ineffective as a practical matter. State lawyer discipline agencies struggle for resources to investigate specific complaints, much less for those necessary to screen lawyers' mail solicitation material. Even if they could examine such materials, agency staff members are unlikely to know anything about the lawyer or about the prospective client's underlying problem. Without such knowledge they cannot determine whether the lawyer's representations are misleading. In any event, such review would be after the fact, potentially too late to avert the undesirable consequences of disseminating false and misleading material.

General mailings not speaking to a specific matter do not pose the same danger of abuse as targeted mailings, and therefore are not prohibited by this Rule. The representations made in such mailings are necessarily general rather than tailored, less importuning than informative. They are addressed to recipients unlikely to be specially vulnerable at the time, hence who are likely to be more skeptical about unsubstantiated claims. General mailings not addressed to recipients involved in a specific legal matter or incident, therefore, more closely resemble permissible advertising rather than prohibited solicitation.

lawyer with a prospective client known to need legal services. These forms of contact between a lawyer and a prospective client subject the layperson to the private importuning of the trained advocate in a direct interpersonal encounter. The prospective client, who may already feel overwhelmed by the circumstances giving rise to the need for legal services, may find it difficult fully to evaluate all available alternatives with reasoned judgment and appropriate self-interest in the face of the lawyer's presence and insistence upon being retained immediately. The situation is fraught with the possibility of undue influence, intimidation, and over-reaching.

[2] This potential for abuse inherent in direct in-person or live telephone solicitation of prospective clients justifies its prohibition, particularly since lawyer advertising and written and recorded communication permitted under Rule 7.2 offer alternative means of conveying necessary information to those who may be in need of legal services. Advertising and written and recorded communications which may be mailed or autodialed make it possible for a prospective client to be informed about the need for legal services, and about the qualifications of available lawyers and law firms, without subjecting the prospective client to direct in-person or telephone persuasion that may overwhelm the client's judgment.

[3] The use of general advertising and written and recorded communications to transmit information from lawyer to prospective client, rather than direct in-person or live telephone contact, will help to assure that the information flows cleanly as well as freely. The contents of advertisements and communications permitted under Rule 7.2 are permanently recorded so that they cannot be disputed and may be shared with others who know the lawyer. This potential for informal review is itself likely to help guard against statements and claims that might constitute false and misleading communications, in violation of Rule 7.1. The contents of direct in-person or live telephone conversations between a lawyer to a prospective client can be disputed and are not subject to third-party scruti-

ny. Consequently, they are much more likely to approach (and occasionally cross) the dividing line between accurate representations and those that are false and misleading.

[4] There is far less likelihood that a lawyer would engage in abusive practices against an individual with whom the lawyer has a prior personal or professional relationship or where the lawyer is motivated by considerations other than the lawyer's pecuniary gain. Consequently, the general prohibition in Rule 7.3(a) and the requirements of Rule 7.3(c) are not applicable in those situations.

[5] But even permitted forms of solicitation can be abused. Thus, any solicitation which contains information which is false or misleading within the meaning of Rule 7.1, which involves coercion, duress or harassment within the meaning of Rule 7.3(b)(2), or which involves contact with a prospective client who has made known to the lawyer a desire not to be solicited by the lawyer within the meaning of Rule 7.3(b)(1) is prohibited. Moreover, if after sending a letter or other communication to a client as permitted by Rule 7.2 the lawyer receives no response, any further effort to communicate with the prospective client may violate the provisions of Rule 7.3(b).

[6] This Rule is not intended to prohibit a lawyer from contacting representatives of organizations or groups that may be interested in establishing a group or prepaid legal plan for their members, insureds, beneficiaries or other third parties for the purpose of informing such entities of the availability of and details concerning the plan or arrangement which the lawyer or lawyer's firm is willing to offer. This form of communication is not directed to a prospective client. Rather, it is usually addressed to an individual acting in a fiduciary capacity seeking a supplier of legal services for others who may, if they choose, become prospective clients of the lawyer. Under these circumstances, the activity which the lawyer undertakes in communicating with such representatives and the type of information transmitted to the individual are functionally similar to and serve

---

Similarly, this Rule would not prohibit a lawyer from contacting representatives of organizations or groups that may be interested in establishing a group or prepaid legal plan for its members, insureds, beneficiaries or other third parties for the purpose of informing such entities of the availability of and details concerning the plan or arrangement which he or his firm is willing to offer. This form of communication is not directed to a specific prospective client known to need legal services related to a particular matter. Rather, it is usually addressed to an individual acting in a fiduciary capacity seeking a supplier of legal services for others who may, if they choose, become prospective clients of the lawyer. Under these circumstances, the activity which the lawyer undertakes in communicating with such representatives and the type of information transmitted to the individual are functionally similar to and serve the same purpose as advertising permitted under Rule 7.2.

the same purpose as advertising permitted under Rule 7.2.

[7] The requirement in Rule 7.3(c) that certain communications be marked "Advertising Material" does not apply to communications sent in response to requests of potential clients or their spokespersons or sponsors. General announcements by lawyers, including changes in personnel or office location, do not constitute communications soliciting professional employment from a client known to be in need of legal services within the meaning of this Rule.

[8] Paragraph (d) of this Rule would permit an attorney to participate with an organization which uses personal contact to solicit members for its group or prepaid legal service plan, provided that the personal contact is not undertaken by any lawyer who would be a provider of legal services through the plan. The organization referred to in paragraph (d) must not be owned by or directed (whether as manager or otherwise) by any lawyer or law firm that participates in the plan. For example, paragraph (d) would not permit a lawyer to create an organization controlled directly or indirectly by the lawyer and use the organization for the in-person or telephone solicitation of legal employment of the lawyer through memberships in the plan or otherwise. The communication permitted by these organizations also must not be directed to a person known to need legal services in a particular matter, but is to be designed to inform potential plan members gnerally of another means of affordable legal services. Lawyers who participate in a legal service plan must reasonably assure that the plan sponsors are in compliance with Rules 7.1, 7.2 and 7.3(a). See 8.4(a).

MODEL CODE COMPARISON:

[1] DR 2–104(A) provided with certain exceptions that "[a] lawyer who has given in-person unsolicited advice to a layperson that he should obtain counsel or take legal action shall not accept employment resulting from that advice. . . ." The exceptions include

DR 2–104(A)(1), which provided that a lawyer "may accept employment by a close friend, relative, former client (if the advice is germane to the former employment), or one whom the lawyer reasonably believes to be a client." DR 2–104(A)(2) through DR 2–104(A)(5) provided other exceptions relating, respectively, to employment resulting from public educational programs, recommendation by a legal assistance organization, public speaking or writing and representing members of a class in class action litigation.

RULE 7.4   Communication of Fields of Practice

A lawyer may communicate the fact that the lawyer does or does not practice in particular fields of law. A lawyer shall not state or imply that the lawyer is a specialist except as follows:

(a) a lawyer admitted to engage in patent practice before the United States Patent and Trademark Office may use the designation "Patent Attorney" or a substantially similar designation;

(b) a lawyer engaged in admiralty practice may use the designation "Admiralty," "Proctor in Admiralty" or a substantially similar designation; and

(c) (provisions on designation of specialization of the particular state).

COMMENT: *

[1] This Rule permits a lawyer to indicate areas of practice in communications about the lawyer's services; for example, in a telephone directory or other advertising. If a lawyer practices only in certain fields, or will not accept matters except in such fields, the lawyer is permitted so to indicate. However, a lawyer is not permitted to state that the lawyer is a "specialist," practices a "specialty," or "specializes in" particular fields. These terms have acquired a secondary meaning imply-

---

* In 1989, the ABA amended the comment to Model Rule 7.3 to reflect concerns that the language in the original comment may violate the Supreme Court's legal advertising decisions. The original language read as follows:

COMMENT:

This Rule permits a lawyer to indicate areas of practice in communications about the lawyer's services; for example, in a telephone directory or other advertising. If a lawyer practices only in certain fields, or will not accept matters except in such fields, the lawyer is permitted so to indicate. However, stating that the lawyer is a "specialist" or that the lawyer's practice "is limited to" or "concentrated in" particular fields is not permitted. These terms have acquired a secondary meaning implying formal recognition as a specialist. Hence, use of these terms may be misleading unless the lawyer is certified or recognized in accordance with procedures in the state where the lawyer is licensed to practice.

ing formal recognition as a specialist and therefore, use of these terms is misleading. [An exception would apply in those states which provide procedures for certification or recognition of specialization and the lawyer has complied with such procedures.]

[2] Recognition of specialization in patent matters is a matter of long-established policy of the Patent and Trademark Office. Designation of admiralty practice has a long historical tradition associated with maritime commerce and the federal courts.

MODEL CODE COMPARISON:

[1] DR 2–105(A) provided that a lawyer "shall not hold himself out publicly as a specialist, as practicing in certain areas of law or as limiting his practice . . . except as follows:

"(1) A lawyer admitted to practice before the United States Patent and Trademark Office may use the designation 'Patents,' 'Patent Attorney,' 'Patent Lawyer,' or 'Registered Patent Attorney' or any combination of those terms, on his letterhead and office sign.

"(2) A lawyer who publicly discloses fields of law in which the lawyer . . . practices or states that his practice is limited to one or more fields of law shall do so by using designations and definitions authorized and approved by [the agency having jurisdiction of the subject under state law].

"(3) A lawyer who is certified as a specialist in a particular field of law or law practice by [the authority having jurisdiction under state law over the subject of specialization by lawyers] may hold himself out as such, but only in accordance with the rules prescribed by that authority."

[2] EC 2–14 stated that "In the absence of state controls to insure the existence of special competence, a lawyer should not be permitted to hold himself out as a specialist, . . . other than in the fields of admiralty, trademark, and patent law where a holding out as a specialist historically has been permitted."

RULE 7.5 Firm Names and Letterheads

(a) A lawyer shall not use a firm name, letterhead or other professional designation that violates rule 7.1. A trade name may be used by a lawyer in private practice if it does not imply a connection with a government agency or with a public or charitable legal services organization and is not otherwise in violation of rule 7.1.

(b) A law firm with offices in more than one jurisdiction may use the same name in each jurisdiction, but identification of the lawyers in an office of the firm shall indicate the jurisdictional limitations on those not licensed to practice in the jurisdiction where the office is located.

(c) The name of a lawyer holding a public office shall not be used in the name of a law firm, or in communications on its behalf, during any substantial period in which the lawyer is not actively and regularly practicing with the firm.

(d) Lawyers may state or imply that they practice in a partnership or other organization only when that is the fact.

COMMENT:

[1] A firm may be designated by the names of all or some of its members, by the names of deceased members where there has been a continuing succession in the firm's identity or by a trade name such as the "ABC Legal Clinic." Although the United States Supreme Court has held that legislation may prohibit the use of trade names in professional practice, use of such names in law practice is acceptable so long as it is not misleading. If a private firm uses a trade name that includes a geographical name such as "Springfield Legal Clinic," an express disclaimer that it is a public legal aid agency may be required to avoid a misleading implication. It may be observed that any firm name including the name of a deceased partner is, strictly speaking, a trade name. The use of such names to designate law firms has proven a useful means of identification. However, it is misleading to use the name of a lawyer not associated with the firm or a predecessor of the firm.

[2] With regard to paragraph (d), lawyers sharing office facilities, but who are not in fact partners, may not denominate themselves as, for example, "Smith and Jones," for that title suggests partnership in the practice of law.

MODEL CODE COMPARISON:

[1] With regard to paragraph (a), DR 2–102(A) provided that "[a] lawyer . . . shall not use . . . professional announcement cards . . . letterheads, or similar professional notices or devices, except . . . if they are in dignified form. . . ." DR 2–102(B) provided that "[a] lawyer in private practice shall not practice under a trade name, a name that is misleading as to the identity of the lawyer or lawyers practicing under such name, or a firm name containing names other than those of one or more of the lawyers in the firm, except that . . . a firm may use as . . . its name the name or names of one or more deceased or retired members of the firm or of a predecessor firm in a continuing line of succession."

[2] With regard to paragraph (b), DR 2–102(D) provided that a partnership "shall not be formed or continued between or among lawyers licensed in different jurisdictions unless all enumerations of the members and associates of the firm on its letterhead and in other permissible listings make clear the jurisdictional limitations on those members and associates of the firm not licensed to practice in all listed jurisdictions; however, the same firm name may be used in each jurisdiction."

[3] With regard to paragraph (c), DR 2–102(B) provided that "[a] lawyer who assumes a judicial, legislative, or public executive or administrative post or office shall not permit his name to remain in the name of a law firm . . . during any significant period in which he is not actively and regularly practicing law as a member of the firm. . . ."

[4] Paragraph (d) is substantially identical to DR 2–102(C).

MAINTAINING THE INTEGRITY OF THE PROFESSION

RULE 8.1 Bar Admission and Disciplinary Matters

An applicant for admission to the bar, or a lawyer in connection with a bar admission application or in connection with a disciplinary matter, shall not:

(a) knowingly make a false statement of material fact; or

(b) fail to disclose a fact necessary to correct a misapprehension known by the person to have arisen in the matter, or knowingly fail to respond to a lawful demand for information from an admission or disciplinary authority, except that this rule does not require disclosure of information otherwise protected by rule 1.6.

COMMENT:

[1] The duty imposed by this Rule extends to persons seeking admission to the bar as well as to lawyers. Hence, if a person makes a material false statement in connection with an application for admission, it may be the basis for subsequent disciplinary action if the person is admitted, and in any event may be relevant in a subsequent admission application. The duty imposed by this Rule applies to a lawyer's own admission or discipline as well as that of others. Thus, it is a separate professional offense for a lawyer to knowingly make a misrepresentation or omission in connection with a disciplinary investigation of the lawyer's own conduct. This Rule also requires affirmative clarification of any misunderstanding on the part of the admissions or disciplinary authority of which the person involved becomes aware.

[2] This Rule is subject to the provisions of the Fifth Amendment of the United States Constitution and corresponding provisions of state constitutions. A person relying on such a provision in response to a question, however, should do so openly and not use the right of nondisclosure as a justification for failure to comply with this Rule.

[3] A lawyer representing an applicant for admission to the bar, or representing a lawyer who is the subject of a disciplinary inquiry or proceeding, is governed by the rules applicable to the client-lawyer relationship.

MODEL CODE COMPARISON:

[1] DR 1–101(A) provided that a lawyer is "subject to discipline if he has made a materially false statement in, or if he has deliberately failed to disclose a material fact requested in connection with, his application for admission to the bar." DR 1–101(B) provided that a lawyer "shall not further the application for admission to the bar of another person known by him to be unqualified in respect to character, education, or other relevant attribute." With respect to paragraph (b), DR 1–102(A)(5) provided that a lawyer shall not engage in "conduct that is prejudicial to the administration of justice."

RULE 8.2 Judicial and Legal Officials

(a) A lawyer shall not make a statement that the lawyer knows to be false or with reckless disregard as to its truth or falsity concerning the qualifications or integrity of a judge, adjudicatory officer or public legal officer, or of a candidate for election or appointment to judicial or legal office.

(b) A lawyer who is a candidate for judicial office shall comply with the applicable provisions of the code of judicial conduct.

COMMENT:

[1] Assessments by lawyers are relied on in evaluating the professional or personal fitness of persons being considered for election or appointment to judicial office and to public legal offices, such as attorney general, prosecuting attorney and public defender. Expressing honest and candid opinions on such matters contributes to improving the administration of justice. Conversely, false statements by a lawyer can unfairly undermine public confidence in the administration of justice.

[2] When a lawyer seeks judicial office, the lawyer should be bound by applicable limitations on political activity.

[3] To maintain the fair and independent administration of justice, lawyers are encouraged to continue traditional efforts to defend judges and courts unjustly criticized.

MODEL CODE COMPARISON:

[1] With regard to paragraph (a), DR 8–102(A) provided that a lawyer "shall not knowingly make false statements of fact concerning the qualifications of a candidate for election or appointment to a judicial office." DR 8–102(B) provided that a lawyer "shall not knowingly make false accusations against a judge or other adjudicatory officer."

[2] Paragraph (b) is substantially identical to DR 8–103.

RULE 8.3 Reporting Professional Misconduct

(a) A lawyer having knowledge that another lawyer has committed a violation of the rules of professional conduct that raises a substantial question as to that lawyer's honesty, trustworthiness or fitness as a lawyer in other respects, shall inform the appropriate professional authority.

(b) A lawyer having knowledge that a judge has committed a violation of applicable rules of judicial conduct that raises a substantial question as to the judge's fitness for office shall inform the appropriate authority.

(c) This rule does not require disclosure of information otherwise protected by Rule 1.6 or information gained by a lawyer or judge while serving as a member of an approved lawyers assistance program to the extent that such information would be confidential if it were communicated subject to the attorney-client privilege.*

COMMENT:

[1] Self-regulation of the legal profession requires that members of the profession initiate disciplinary investigation when they know of a violation of the Rules of Professional Conduct. Lawyers have a similar obligation with respect to judicial misconduct. An apparently isolated violation may indicate a pattern of misconduct that only a disciplinary investigation can uncover. Reporting a violation is especially important where the victim is unlikely to discover the offense.

[2] A report about misconduct is not required where it would involve violation of Rule 1.6. However, a lawyer should encourage a client to consent to disclosure where prosecution would not substantially prejudice the client's interests.

[3] If a lawyer were obliged to report every violation of the Rules, the failure to report any violation would itself be a professional offense. Such a requirement existed in many jurisdictions but proved to be unenforceable. This Rule limits the reporting obligation to those offenses that a self-regulating profession must vigorously endeavor to prevent. A measure of judgment is, therefore, required in complying with the provisions of this Rule. The term "substantial" refers to the seriousness of the possible offense and not the quantum of evidence of which the lawyer is aware. A report should be made to the bar disciplinary agency unless some other agency, such as a peer review agency, is more appropriate in the circumstances. Similar considerations apply to the reporting of judicial misconduct.

[4] The duty to report professional misconduct does not apply to a lawyer retained to repre-

---

* The A.B.A. House of Delegates added the clause following the phrase "by Rule 1.6," at its August, 1991 Annual Meeting. At the same time it added Comment 5.

sent a lawyer whose professional conduct is in question. Such a situation is governed by the rules applicable to the client-lawyer relationship.

[5]** Information about a lawyer's or judge's misconduct or fitness may be received by a lawyer in the course of that lawyer's participation in an approved lawyers' or judges' assistance program. In that circumstance, providing for the confidentiality of such information encourages lawyers and judges to seek treatment throught such program. Conversely, without such confidentiality, lawyers and judges may hesitate to seek assistance from these programs, which may then result in additional harm to their professional careers and additional injury to the welfare of clients and the public. The Rule therefore exempts the lawyer from the reporting requirements of Paragraphs (a) and (b) with respect to information that would be privileged if the relationship between the impaired lawyer or judge and the recipient of the information were that of a client and a lawyer. On the other hand, a lawyer who receives such information would nevertheless be required to comply with the Rule 8.3 reporting provisions to report misconduct if the impaired lawyer or judge indicates an intent to engage in illegal activity, for example, the conversion of client funds to his or her use.

MODEL CODE COMPARISON:

[1] DR 1–103(A) provided that "[a] lawyer possessing unprivileged knowledge of a violation of [a Disciplinary Rule] shall report such knowledge to . . . authority empowered to investigate or act upon such violation."

RULE 8.4 Misconduct

It is professional misconduct for a lawyer to:

(a) violate or attempt to violate the rules of professional conduct, knowingly assist or induce another to do so, or do so through the acts of another;

(b) commit a criminal act that reflects adversely on the lawyer's honesty, trustworthiness or fitness as a lawyer in other respects;

(c) engage in conduct involving dishonesty, fraud, deceit or misrepresentation;

(d) engage in conduct that is prejudicial to the administration of justice;

(e) state or imply an ability to influence improperly a government agency or official; or

(f) knowingly assist a judge or judicial officer in conduct that is a violation of applicable rules of judicial conduct or other law.

COMMENT:

[1] Many kinds of illegal conduct reflect adversely on fitness to practice law, such as offenses involving fraud and the offense of willful failure to file an income tax return. However, some kinds of offense carry no such implication. Traditionally, the distinction was drawn in terms of offenses involving "moral turpitude." That concept can be construed to include offenses concerning some matters of personal morality, such as adultery and comparable offenses, that have no specific connection to fitness for the practice of law. Although a lawyer is personally answerable to the entire criminal law, a lawyer should be professionally answerable only for offenses that indicate lack of those characteristics relevant to law practice. Offenses involving violence, dishonesty or breach of trust, or serious interference with the administration of justice are in that category. A pattern of repeated offenses, even ones of minor significance when considered separately, can indicate indifference to legal obligation.

[2] A lawyer may refuse to comply with an obligation imposed by law upon a good faith belief that no valid obligation exists. The provisions of Rule 1.2(d) concerning a good faith challenge to the validity, scope, meaning or application of the law apply to challenges of legal regulation of the practice of law.

[3] Lawyers holding public office assume legal responsibilities going beyond those of other citizens. A lawyer's abuse of public office can suggest an inability to fulfill the professional role of attorney. The same is true of abuse of positions of private trust such as trustee, executor, administrator, guardian, agent and officer, director or manager of a corporation or other organization.

MODEL CODE COMPARISON:

[1] With regard to paragraphs (a) through (d) DR 1–102(A) provided that a lawyer shall not:

"(1) Violate a Disciplinary Rule.

** The A.B.A. House of Delegates added this Comment when it amended Model Rule 8.3(c), at its August, 1991 Annual Meeting.

"(2) Circumvent a Disciplinary Rule through actions of another.

"(3) Engage in illegal conduct involving moral turpitude.

"(4) Engage in conduct involving dishonesty, fraud, deceit, or misrepresentation.

"(5) Engage in conduct that is prejudicial to the administration of justice.

"(6) Engage in any other conduct that adversely reflects on his fitness to practice law."

[2] Paragraph (e) is substantially similar to DR 9–101(C).

[3] There was no direct counterpart to paragraph (f) in the Disciplinary Rules of the Model Code. EC 7–34 stated in part that "[a] lawyer . . . is never justified in making a gift or a loan to a [judicial officer] except as permitted by . . . the Code of Judicial Conduct." EC 9–1 stated that a lawyer "should promote public confidence in our [legal] system and in the legal profession."

RULE 8.5 Jurisdiction

A lawyer admitted to practice in this jurisdiction is subject to the disciplinary authority of this jurisdiction although engaged in practice elsewhere.

COMMENT:

[1] In modern practice lawyers frequently act outside the territorial limits of the jurisdiction in which they are licensed to practice, either in another state or outside the United States. In doing so, they remain subject to the governing authority of the jurisdiction in which they are licensed to practice. If their activity in another jurisdiction is substantial and continuous, it may constitute practice of law in that jurisdiction. See Rule 5.5.

[2] If the rules of professional conduct in the two jurisdictions differ, principles of conflict of laws may apply. Similar problems can arise when a lawyer is licensed to practice in more than one jurisdiction.

[3] Where the lawyer is licensed to practice law in two jurisdictions which impose conflicting obligations, applicable rules of choice of law may govern the situation. A related problem arises with respect to practice before a federal tribunal, where the general authority of the states to regulate the practice of law must be reconciled with such authority as federal tribunals may have to regulate practice before them.

MODEL CODE COMPARISON:

[1] There was no counterpart to this Rule in the Model Code.

*

INDEX TO ABA MODEL RULES

*

APPENDIX E

MODEL CODE OF JUDICIAL CONDUCT (1990) †

Table of Contents

Preamble
Terminology

PREAMBLE

[1] Our legal system is based on the principle that an independent, fair and competent judiciary will interpret and apply the laws that govern us. The role of the judiciary is central to American concepts of justice and the rule of law. Intrinsic to all sections of this Code are the precepts that judges, individually and collectively, must respect and honor the judicial office as a public trust and strive to enhance and maintain confidence in our legal system. The judge is an arbiter of facts and law for the resolution of disputes and a highly visible symbol of government under the rule of law.

[2] The Code of Judicial Conduct is intended to establish standards for ethical conduct of judges. It consists of broad statements called Canons, specific rules set forth in Sections under each Canon, a Terminology Section, an Application Section and Commentary. The text of the Canons and the Sections, including the Terminology and Application Sections, is authoritative. The Commentary, by explanation and example, provides guidance with respect to the purpose and meaning of the Canons and Sections. The Commentary is not intended as a statement of additional rules. When the text uses "shall" or "shall not," it is intended to impose binding obligations the violation of which can result in disciplinary action. When "should" or "should not" is used, the text is intended as hortatory and as a statement of what is or is not appropriate conduct but not as a binding rule under which a judge may be disciplined. When "may" is used, it denotes permissible discretion or, depending on the context, it refers to action that is not covered by specific proscriptions.

[3] The Canons and Sections are rules of reason. They should be applied consistent with constitutional requirements, statutes, other court rules and decisional law and in the context of all relevant circumstances. The Code is to be construed so as not to impinge on the essential independence of judges in making judicial decisions.

[4] The Code is designed to provide guidance to judges and candidates for judicial office and to provide a structure for regulating conduct through disciplinary agencies. It is not designed or intended as a basis for civil liability or criminal prosecution. Furthermore, the purpose of the Code would be subverted if the Code were invoked by lawyers for mere tactical advantage in a proceeding.

[5] The text of the Canons and Sections is intended to govern conduct of judges and to be binding upon them. It is not intended, however, that every transgression will result in disciplinary action. Whether disciplinary action is appropriate, and the degree of discipline to be imposed, should be determined through a reasonable and reasoned application of the text and should depend on such factors as the seriousness of the transgression, whether there is a pattern of improper activity and the effect of the improper activity on others or on the judicial system. See ABA Standards Relating to Judicial Discipline and Disability Retirement.†

[6] The Code of Judicial Conduct is not intended as an exhaustive guide for the conduct of judges. They should also be governed in their judicial and personal conduct by general ethical standards. The Code is intended, however, to state basic standards which should govern the conduct of all judges and to provide guidance to assist judges in establishing and maintaining high standards of judicial and personal conduct.

TERMINOLOGY

Terms explained below are noted with an asterisk (*) in the Sections where they appear. In addition, the Sections where terms appear are referred to after the explanation of each term below.

[1] **"Appropriate authority"** denotes the authority with responsibility for initiation of disciplinary process with respect to the violation to be reported. See Sections 3D(1) and 3D(2).

[2] **"Candidate."** A candidate is a person seeking selection for or retention in judicial office by election or appointment. A person becomes a candidate for judicial office as soon as he or she makes a public announcement of candidacy, declares or files as a candidate with the election or appointment authority, or authorizes solicitation or acceptance of contributions or support. The term "candidate" has the same meaning when applied to a judge seeking election or appointment to non-judicial office. See Preamble and Sections 5A, 5B, 5C and 5E.

---

† Judicial disciplinary procedures adopted in the jurisdictions should comport with the requirements of due process. The ABA Standards Relating to Judicial Discipline and Disability Retirement are cited as an example of how these due process requirements may be satisfied.

[3] **"Continuing part-time judge."** A continuing part-time judge is a judge who serves repeatedly on a part-time basis by election or under a continuing appointment, including a retired judge subject to recall who is permitted to practice law. See Application Section C.

[4] **"Court personnel"** does not include the lawyers in a proceeding before a judge. See Sections 3B(7)(c) and 3B(9).

[5] **"De minimis"** denotes an insignificant interest that could not raise reasonable question as to a judge's impartiality. See Sections 3E(1)(c) and 3E(1)(d).

[6] **"Economic interest"** denotes ownership of a more than de minimis legal or equitable interest, or a relationship as officer, director, advisor or other active participant in the affairs of a party, except that:

(i) ownership of an interest in a mutual or common investment fund that holds securities is not an economic interest in such securities unless the judge participates in the management of the fund or a proceeding pending or impending before the judge could substantially affect the value of the interest;

(ii) service by a judge as an officer, director, advisor or other active participant in an educational, religious, charitable, fraternal or civic organization, or service by a judge's spouse, parent or child as an officer, director, advisor or other active participant in any organization does not create an economic interest in securities held by that organization;

(iii) a deposit in a financial institution, the proprietary interest of a policy holder in a mutual insurance company, of a depositor in a mutual savings association or of a member in a credit union, or a similar proprietary interest, is not an economic interest in the organization unless a proceeding pending or impending before the judge could substantially affect the value of the interest;

(iv) ownership of government securities is not an economic interest in the issuer unless a proceeding pending or impending before the judge could substantially affect the value of the securities.

See Sections 3E(1)(c) and 3E(2).

[7] **"Fiduciary"** includes such relationships as executor, administrator, trustee, and guardian. See Sections 3E(2) and 4E.

[8] **"Knowingly,"** "knowledge," "known" or "knows" denotes actual knowledge of the fact in question. A person's knowledge may be inferred from circumstances. See Sections 3D, 3E(1), and 5A(3).

[9] **"Law"** denotes court rules as well as statutes, constitutional provisions and decisional law. See Sections 2A, 3A, 3B(2), 3B(6), 4B, 4C, 4D(5), 4F, 4I, 5A(2), 5A(3), 5B(2), 5C(1), 5C(3) and 5D.

[10] **"Member of the candidate's family"** denotes a spouse, child, grandchild, parent, grandparent or other relative or person with whom the candidate maintains a close familial relationship. See Section 5A(3)(a).

[11] **"Member of the judge's family"** denotes a spouse, child, grandchild, parent, grandparent, or other relative or person with whom the judge maintains a close familial relationship. See Sections 4D(3), 4E and 4G.

[12] **"Member of the judge's family residing in the judge's household"** denotes any relative of a judge by blood or marriage, or a person treated by a judge as a member of the judge's family, who resides in the judge's household. See Sections 3E(1) and 4D(5).

[13] **"Nonpublic information"** denotes information that, by law, is not available to the public. Nonpublic information may include but is not limited to: information that is sealed by statute or court order, impounded or communicated in camera; and information offered in grand jury proceedings, presentencing reports, dependency cases or psychiatric reports. See Section 3B(11).

[14] **"Periodic part-time judge."** A periodic part-time judge is a judge who serves or expects to serve repeatedly on a part-time basis but under a separate appointment for each limited period of service or for each matter. See Application Section D.

[15] **"Political organization"** denotes a political party or other group, the principal purpose of which is to further the election or appointment of candidates to political office. See Sections 5A(1), 5B(2) and 5C(1).

[16] **"Pro tempore part-time judge."** A pro tempore part-time judge is a judge who serves or expects to serve once or only sporadically on a part-time basis under a separate appointment for each period of service or for each case heard. See Application Section E.

[17] **"Public election."** This term includes primary and general elections; it includes partisan

elections, nonpartisan elections and retention elections. See Section 5C.

[18] **"Require."** The rules prescribing that a judge "require" certain conduct of others are, like all of the rules in this Code, rules of reason. The use of the term "require" in that context means a judge is to exercise reasonable direction and control over the conduct of those persons subject to the judge's direction and control. See Sections 3B(3), 3B(4), 3B(6), 3B(9) and 3C(2).

[19] **"Third degree of relationship."** The following persons are relatives within the third degree of relationship: great-grandparent, grandparent, parent, uncle, aunt, brother, sister, child, grandchild, great-grandchild, nephew or niece. See Section 3E(1)(d).

CANON 1

A Judge Shall Uphold the Integrity and Independence of the Judiciary

A. An independent and honorable judiciary is indispensable to justice in our society. A judge should participate in establishing, maintaining and enforcing high standards of conduct, and shall personally observe those standards so that the integrity and independence of the judiciary will be preserved. The provisions of this Code are to be construed and applied to further that objective.

Commentary

[1] Deference to the judgments and rulings of courts depends upon public confidence in the integrity and independence of judges. The integrity and independence of judges depends in turn upon their acting without fear or favor. Although judges should be independent, they must comply with the law, including the provisions of this Code. Public confidence in the impartiality of the judiciary is maintained by the adherence of each judge to this responsibility. Conversely, violation of this Code diminishes public confidence in the judiciary and thereby does injury to the system of government under law.

CANON 2

A Judge Shall Avoid Impropriety and the Appearance of Impropriety in All of the Judge's Activities

A. A judge shall respect and comply with the law * and shall act at all times in a manner that promotes public confidence in the integrity and impartiality of the judiciary.

Commentary

[1] Public confidence in the judiciary is eroded by irresponsible or improper conduct by judges. A judge must avoid all impropriety and appearance of impropriety. A judge must expect to be the subject of constant public scrutiny. A judge must therefore accept restrictions on the judge's conduct that might be viewed as burdensome by the ordinary citizen and should do so freely and willingly.

[2] The prohibition against behaving with impropriety or the appearance of impropriety applies to both the professional and personal conduct of a judge. Because it is not practicable to list all prohibited acts, the proscription is necessarily cast in general terms that extend to conduct by judges that is harmful although not specifically mentioned in the Code. Actual improprieties under this standard include violations of law, court rules or other specific provisions of this Code. The test for appearance of impropriety is whether the conduct would create in reasonable minds a perception that the judge's ability to carry out judicial responsibilities with integrity, impartiality and competence is impaired.

[3] See also Commentary under Section 2C.

B. A judge shall not allow family, social, political or other relationships to influence the judge's judicial conduct or judgment. A judge shall not lend the prestige of judicial office to advance the private interests of the judge or others; nor shall a judge convey or permit others to convey the impression that they are in a special position to influence the judge. A judge shall not testify voluntarily as a character witness.

Commentary

[1] Maintaining the prestige of judicial office is essential to a system of government in which the judiciary functions independently of

---

* See Terminology, "law."

the executive and legislative branches. Respect for the judicial office facilitates the orderly conduct of legitimate judicial functions. Judges should distinguish between proper and improper use of the prestige of office in all of their activities. For example, it would be improper for a judge to allude to his or her judgeship to gain a personal advantage such as deferential treatment when stopped by a police officer for a traffic offense. Similarly, judicial letterhead must not be used for conducting a judge's personal business.

[2] A judge must avoid lending the prestige of judicial office for the advancement of the private interests of others. For example, a judge must not use the judge's judicial position to gain advantage in a civil suit involving a member of the judge's family. In contracts for publication of a judge's writings, a judge should retain control over the advertising to avoid exploitation of the judge's office. As to the acceptance of awards, see Section 4D(5)(a) and Commentary.

[3] Although a judge should be sensitive to possible abuse of the prestige of office, a judge may, based on the judge's personal knowledge, serve as a reference or provide a letter of recommendation. However, a judge must not initiate the communication of information to a sentencing judge or a probation or corrections officer but may provide to such persons information for the record in response to a formal request.

[4] Judges may participate in the process of judicial selection by cooperating with appointing authorities and screening committees seeking names for consideration, and by responding to official inquiries concerning a person being considered for a judgeship. See also Canon 5 regarding use of a judge's name in political activities.

[5] A judge must not testify voluntarily as a character witness because to do so may lend the prestige of the judicial office in support of the party for whom the judge testifies. Moreover, when a judge testifies as a witness, a lawyer who regularly appears before the judge may be placed in the awkward position of cross-examining the judge. A judge may, however, testify when properly summoned. Except in unusual circumstances where the demands of justice require, a judge should discourage a party from requiring the judge to testify as a character witness.

C. A judge shall not hold membership in any organization that practices invidious discrimination on the basis of race, sex, religion or national origin.

Commentary

[1] Membership of a judge in an organization that practices invidious discrimination gives rise to perceptions that the judge's impartiality is impaired. Section 2C refers to the current practices of the organization. Whether an organization practices invidious discrimination is often a complex question to which judges should be sensitive. The answer cannot be determined from a mere examination of an organization's current membership rolls but rather depends on how the organization selects members and other relevant factors, such as that the organization is dedicated to the preservation of religious, ethnic or cultural values of legitimate common interest to its members, or that it is in fact and effect an intimate, purely private organization whose membership limitations could not be constitutionally prohibited. Absent such factors, an organization is generally said to discriminate invidiously if it arbitrarily excludes from membership on the basis of race, religion, sex or national origin persons who would otherwise be admitted to membership. *See New York State Club Ass'n. Inc. v. City of New York,* 108 S.Ct. 2225, 101 L.Ed.2d 1 (1988); *Board of Directors of Rotary International v. Rotary Club of Duarte,* 481 U.S. 537, 107 S.Ct. 1940, 95 L.Ed.2d 474 (1987); *Roberts v. United States Jaycees,* 468 U.S. 609, 104 S.Ct. 3244, 82 L.Ed.2d 462 (1984).

[2] Although Section 2C relates only to membership in organizations that invidiously discriminate on the basis of race, sex, religion or national origin, a judge's membership in an organization that engages in any discriminatory membership practices prohibited by the law of the jurisdiction also violates Canon 2 and Section 2A and gives the appearance of impropriety. In addition, it would be a violation of Canon 2 and Section 2A for a judge to arrange a meeting at a club that the judge knows practices invidious discrimination on the basis of race, sex, religion or national origin in its membership or other policies, or for the judge to regularly use such a club. Moreover, public manifestation by a judge of the judge's knowing approval of invidious discrimination on any basis gives the appearance of impropriety under Canon 2 and diminishes public confi-

dence in the integrity and impartiality of the judiciary, in violation of Section 2A.

[3] When a person who is a judge on the date this Code becomes effective [in the jurisdiction in which the person is a judge][1] learns that an organization to which the judge belongs engages in invidious discrimination that would preclude membership under Section 2C or under Canon 2 and Section 2A, the judge is permitted, in lieu of resigning, to make immediate efforts to have the organization discontinue its invidiously discriminatory practices, but is required to suspend participation in any other activities of the organization. If the organization fails to discontinue its invidiously discriminatory practices as promptly as possible (and in all events within a year of the judge's first learning of the practices), the judge is required to resign immediately from the organization.

CANON 3

A Judge Shall Perform the Duties of Judicial Office Impartially and Diligently

A. JUDICIAL DUTIES IN GENERAL. The judicial duties of a judge take precedence over all the judge's other activities. The judge's judicial duties include all the duties of the judge's office prescribed by law.* In the performance of these duties, the following standards apply.

B. ADJUDICATIVE RESPONSIBILITIES.

(1) A judge shall hear and decide matters assigned to the judge except those in which disqualification is required.

(2) A judge shall be faithful to the law* and maintain professional competence in it. A judge shall not be swayed by partisan interests, public clamor or fear of criticism.

(3) A judge shall require* order and decorum in proceedings before the judge.

(4) A judge shall be patient, dignified and courteous to litigants, jurors, witnesses, lawyers and others with whom the judge deals in an official capacity, and shall require* similar conduct of lawyers, and of staff, court officials

and others subject to the judge's direction and control.

Commentary

[1] The duty to hear all proceedings fairly and with patience is not inconsistent with the duty to dispose promptly of the business of the court. Judges can be efficient and businesslike while being patient and deliberate.

(5) A judge shall perform judicial duties without bias or prejudice. A judge shall not, in the performance of judicial duties, by words or conduct manifest bias or prejudice, including but not limited to bias or prejudice based upon race, sex, religion, national origin, disability, age, sexual orientation or socioeconomic status, and shall not permit staff, court officials and others subject to the judge's direction and control to do so.

Commentary

[1] A judge must refrain from speech, gestures or other conduct that could reasonably be perceived as sexual harassment and must require the same standard of conduct of others subject to the judge's direction and control.

[2] A judge must perform judicial duties impartially and fairly. A judge who manifests bias on any basis in a proceeding impairs the fairness of the proceeding and brings the judiciary into disrepute. Facial expression and body language, in addition to oral communication, can give to parties or lawyers in the proceeding, jurors, the media and others an appearance of judicial bias. A judge must be alert to avoid behavior that may be perceived as prejudicial.

(6) A judge shall require* lawyers in proceedings before the judge to refrain from manifesting, by words or conduct, bias or prejudice based upon race, sex, religion, national origin, disability, age, sexual orientation or socioeconomic status, against parties, witnesses, counsel or others. This Section 3B(6) does not preclude legitimate advocacy when race, sex, religion, national origin, disability, age, sexual orientation or socioeconomic status, or other similar factors, are issues in the proceeding.

---

1. The language within the brackets should be deleted when the jurisdiction adopts this provision.

* See Terminology, "law."

* See Terminology, "require."

(7) A judge shall accord to every person who has a legal interest in a proceeding, or that person's lawyer, the right to be heard according to law.* A judge shall not initiate, permit, or consider ex parte communications, or consider other communications made to the judge outside the presence of the parties concerning a pending or impending proceeding except that:

(a) Where circumstances require, ex parte communications for scheduling, administrative purposes or emergencies that do not deal with substantive matters or issues on the merits are authorized; provided:

(i) the judge reasonably believes that no party will gain a procedural or tactical advantage as a result of the ex parte communication, and

(ii) the judge makes provision promptly to notify all other parties of the substance of the ex parte communication and allows an opportunity to respond.

(b) A judge may obtain the advice of a disinterested expert on the law * applicable to a proceeding before the judge if the judge gives notice to the parties of the person consulted and the substance of the advice, and affords the parties reasonable opportunity to respond.

(c) A judge may consult with court personnel * whose function is to aid the judge in carrying out the judge's adjudicative responsibilities or with other judges.

(d) A judge may, with the consent of the parties, confer separately with the parties and their lawyers in an effort to mediate or settle matters pending before the judge.

(e) A judge may initiate or consider any ex parte communications when expressly authorized by law * to do so.

Commentary

[1] The proscription against communications concerning a proceeding includes communications from lawyers, law teachers, and other persons who are not participants in the proceeding, except to the limited extent permitted.

[2] To the extent reasonably possible, all parties or their lawyers shall be included in communications with a judge.

[3] Whenever presence of a party or notice to a party is required by Section 3B(7), it is the party's lawyer, or if the party is unrepresented the party, who is to be present or to whom notice is to be given.

[4] An appropriate and often desirable procedure for a court to obtain the advice of a disinterested expert on legal issues is to invite the expert to file a brief amicus curiae.

[5] Certain ex parte communication is approved by Section 3B(7) to facilitate scheduling and other administrative purposes and to accommodate emergencies. In general, however, a judge must discourage ex parte communication and allow it only if all the criteria stated in Section 3B(7) are clearly met. A judge must disclose to all parties all ex parte communications described in Sections 3B(7)(a) and 3B(7)(b) regarding a proceeding pending or impending before the judge.

[6] A judge must not independently investigate facts in a case and must consider only the evidence presented.

[7] A judge may request a party to submit proposed findings of fact and conclusions of law, so long as the other parties are apprised of the request and are given an opportunity to respond to the proposed findings and conclusions.

[8] A judge must make reasonable efforts, including the provision of appropriate supervision, to ensure that Section 3B(7) is not violated through law clerks or other personnel on the judge's staff.

[9] If communication between the trial judge and the appellate court with respect to a proceeding is permitted, a copy of any written communication or the substance of any oral communication should be provided to all parties.

(8) A judge shall dispose of all judicial matters promptly, efficiently and fairly.

---

* See Terminology, "law."

* See Terminology, "court personnel."

Commentary

[1] In disposing of matters promptly, efficiently and fairly, a judge must demonstrate due regard for the rights of the parties to be heard and to have issues resolved without unnecessary cost or delay. Containing costs while preserving fundamental rights of parties also protects the interests of witnesses and the general public. A judge should monitor and supervise cases so as to reduce or eliminate dilatory practices, avoidable delays and unnecessary costs. A judge should encourage and seek to facilitate settlement, but parties should not feel coerced into surrendering the right to have their controversy resolved by the courts.

[2] Prompt disposition of the court's business requires a judge to devote adequate time to judicial duties, to be punctual in attending court and expeditious in determining matters under submission, and to insist that court officials, litigants and their lawyers cooperate with the judge to that end.

(9) A judge shall not, while a proceeding is pending or impending in any court, make any public comment that might reasonably be expected to affect its outcome or impair its fairness or make any nonpublic comment that might substantially interfere with a fair trial or hearing. The judge shall require * similar abstention on the part of court personnel * subject to the judge's direction and control. This Section does not prohibit judges from making public statements in the course of their official duties or from explaining for public information the procedures of the court. This Section does not apply to proceedings in which the judge is a litigant in a personal capacity.

Commentary

[1] The requirement that judges abstain from public comment regarding a pending or impending proceeding continues during any appellate process and until final disposition. This Section does not prohibit a judge from commenting on proceedings in which the judge is a litigant in a personal capacity, but in cases such as a writ of mandamus where the judge is a litigant in an official capacity, the judge must not comment publicly. The conduct of lawyers relating to trial publicity is governed by [Rule 3.6 of the ABA Model Rules of Professional Conduct]. (Each jurisdiction should substitute an appropriate reference to its rule.)

(10) A judge shall not commend or criticize jurors for their verdict other than in a court order or opinion in a proceeding, but may express appreciation to jurors for their service to the judicial system and the community.

Commentary

[1] Commending or criticizing jurors for their verdict may imply a judicial expectation in future cases and may impair a juror's ability to be fair and impartial in a subsequent case.

(11) A judge shall not disclose or use, for any purpose unrelated to judicial duties, nonpublic information * acquired in a judicial capacity.

C. ADMINISTRATIVE RESPONSIBILITIES.

(1) A judge shall diligently discharge the judge's administrative responsibilities without bias or prejudice and maintain professional competence in judicial administration, and should cooperate with other judges and court officials in the administration of court business.

(2) A judge shall require * staff, court officials and others subject to the judge's direction and control to observe the standards of fidelity and diligence that apply to the judge and to refrain from manifesting bias or prejudice in the performance of their official duties.

(3) A judge with supervisory authority for the judicial performance of other judges shall take reasonable measures to assure the prompt disposition of matters before them and the proper performance of their other judicial responsibilities.

(4) A judge shall not make unnecessary appointments. A judge shall exercise the power of appointment impartially and on the basis of merit. A judge shall avoid nepotism and favoritism. A judge shall not approve compensation of appointees beyond the fair value of services rendered.

* See Terminology, "require."

* See Terminology, "court personnel."

* See Terminology, "nonpublic information."

Commentary

[1] Appointees of a judge include assigned counsel, officials such as referees, commissioners, special masters, receivers and guardians and personnel such as clerks, secretaries and bailiffs. Consent by the parties to an appointment or an award of compensation does not relieve the judge of the obligation prescribed by Section 3C(4).

D. DISCIPLINARY RESPONSIBILITIES.

(1) A judge who receives information indicating a substantial likelihood that another judge has committed a violation of this Code should take appropriate action. A judge having knowledge * that another judge has committed a violation of this Code that raises a substantial question as to the other judge's fitness for office shall inform the appropriate authority.*

(2) A judge who receives information indicating a substantial likelihood that a lawyer has committed a violation of the Rules of Professional Conduct [substitute correct title if the applicable rules of lawyer conduct have a different title] should take appropriate action. A judge having knowledge * that a lawyer has committed a violation of the Rules of Professional Conduct [substitute correct title if the applicable rules of lawyer conduct have a different title] that raises a substantial question as to the lawyer's honesty, trustworthiness or fitness as a lawyer in other respects shall inform the appropriate authority.*

(3) Acts of a judge, in the discharge of disciplinary responsibilities, required or permitted by Sections 3D(1) and 3D(2) are part of a judge's judicial duties and shall be absolutely privileged, and no civil action predicated thereon may be instituted against the judge.

Commentary

[1] Appropriate action may include direct communication with the judge or lawyer who has committed the violation, other direct action if available, and reporting the violation to the appropriate authority or other agency or body.

E. DISQUALIFICATION.

(1) A judge shall disqualify himself or herself in a proceeding in which the judge's im-partiality might reasonably be questioned, including but not limited to instances where:

Commentary

[1] Under this rule, a judge is disqualified whenever the judge's impartiality might reasonably be questioned, regardless whether any of the specific rules in Section 3E(1) apply. For example, if a judge were in the process of negotiating for employment with a law firm, the judge would be disqualified from any matters in which that law firm appeared, unless the disqualification was waived by the parties after disclosure by the judge.

[2] A judge should disclose on the record information that the judge believes the parties or their lawyers might consider relevant to the question of disqualification, even if the judge believes there is no real basis for disqualification.

[3] By decisional law, the rule of necessity may override the rule of disqualification. For example, a judge might be required to participate in judicial review of a judicial salary statute, or might be the only judge available in a matter requiring immediate judicial action, such as a hearing on probable cause or a temporary restraining order. In the latter case, the judge must disclose on the record the basis for possible disqualification and use reasonable efforts to transfer the matter to another judge as soon as practicable.

(a) the judge has a personal bias or prejudice concerning a party or a party's lawyer, or personal knowledge * of disputed evidentiary facts concerning the proceeding;

(b) the judge served as a lawyer in the matter in controversy, or a lawyer with whom the judge previously practiced law served during such association as a lawyer concerning the matter, or the judge has been a material witness concerning it;

Commentary

[1] A lawyer in a government agency does not ordinarily have an association with other lawyers employed by that agency within the meaning of Section 3E(1)(b); a judge formerly employed by a government agency, however, should disqualify himself or herself in a proceeding if the judge's impartiality might

* See Terminology, "knowingly," "knowledge," "known" and "knows."

* See Terminology, "appropriate authority."

reasonably be questioned because of such association.

(c) the judge knows* that he or she, individually or as a fiduciary*, or the judge's spouse, parent or child wherever residing, or any other member of the judge's family residing in the judge's household,* has an economic interest* in the subject matter in controversy or in a party to the proceeding or has any other more than de minimis* interest that could be substantially affected by the proceeding;

(d) the judge or the judge's spouse, or a person within the third degree of relationship* to either of them, or the spouse of such a person:

(i) is a party to the proceeding, or an officer, director or trustee of a party;

(ii) is acting as a lawyer in the proceeding;

(iii) is known* by the judge to have a more than de minimis* interest that could be substantially affected by the proceeding;

(iv) is to the judge's knowledge* likely to be a material witness in the proceeding.

Commentary

[1] The fact that a lawyer in a proceeding is affiliated with a law firm with which a relative of the judge is affiliated does not of itself disqualify the judge. Under appropriate circumstances, the fact that "the judge's impartiality might reasonably be questioned" under Section 3E(1), or that the relative is known by the judge to have an interest in the law firm that could be "substantially affected by

the outcome of the proceeding" under Section 3E(1)(d)(iii) may require the judge's disqualification.

(2) A judge shall keep informed about the judge's personal and fiduciary* economic interests,* and make a reasonable effort to keep informed about the personal economic interests of the judge's spouse and minor children residing in the judge's household.

F. REMITTAL OF DISQUALIFICATION. A judge disqualified by the terms of Section 3E may disclose on the record the basis of the judge's disqualification and may ask the parties and their lawyers to consider, out of the presence of the judge, whether to waive disqualification. If following disclosure of any basis for disqualification other than personal bias or prejudice concerning a party, the parties and lawyers, without participation by the judge, all agree that the judge should not be disqualified, and the judge is then willing to participate, the judge may participate in the proceeding. The agreement shall be incorporated in the record of the proceeding.

Commentary

[1] A remittal procedure provides the parties an opportunity to proceed without delay if they wish to waive the disqualification. To assure that consideration of the question of remittal is made independently of the judge, a judge must not solicit, seek or hear comment on possible remittal or waiver of the disqualification unless the lawyers jointly propose remittal after consultation as provided in the rule. A party may act through counsel if counsel represents on the record that the party has been consulted and consents. As a practical matter, a judge may wish to have all parties and their lawyers sign the remittal agreement.

---

* See Terminology, "knowingly," "knowledge," "known" and "knows."

* See Terminology, "fiduciary."

* See Terminology, "member of the judge's family residing in the judge's household."

* See Terminology, "economic interest."

* See Terminology, "de minimis."

* See Terminology, "third degree of relationship."

CANON 4

A Judge Shall So Conduct the Judge's Extra–Judicial Activities as to Minimize the Risk of Conflict With Judicial Obligations

A. EXTRA–JUDICIAL ACTIVITIES IN GENERAL. A judge shall conduct all of the judge's extra-judicial activities so that they do not:

(1) cast reasonable doubt on the judge's capacity to act impartially as a judge;

(2) demean the judicial office; or

(3) interfere with the proper performance of judicial duties.

Commentary

[1] Complete separation of a judge from extra-judicial activities is neither possible nor wise; a judge should not become isolated from the community in which the judge lives.

[2] Expressions of bias or prejudice by a judge, even outside the judge's judicial activities, may cast reasonable doubt on the judge's capacity to act impartially as a judge. Expressions which may do so include jokes or other remarks demeaning individuals on the basis of their race, sex, religion, national origin, disability, age, sexual orientation or socioeconomic status. See Section 2C and accompanying Commentary.

B. AVOCATIONAL ACTIVITIES. A judge may speak, write, lecture, teach and participate in other extra-judicial activities concerning the law,* the legal system, the administration of justice and non-legal subjects, subject to the requirements of this Code.

Commentary

[1] As a judicial officer and person specially learned in the law, a judge is in a unique position to contribute to the improvement of the law, the legal system, and the administration of justice, including revision of substantive and procedural law and improvement of criminal and juvenile justice. To the extent that time permits, a judge is encouraged to do so, either independently or through a bar association, judicial conference or other organization dedicated to the improvement of the law. Judges may participate in efforts to promote the fair administration of justice, the indepen-

dence of the judiciary and the integrity of the legal profession and may express opposition to the persecution of lawyers and judges in other countries because of their professional activities.

[2] In this and other Sections of Canon 4, the phrase "subject to the requirements of this Code" is used, notably in connection with a judge's governmental, civic or charitable activities. This phrase is included to remind judges that the use of permissive language in various Sections of the Code does not relieve a judge from the other requirements of the Code that apply to the specific conduct.

C. GOVERNMENTAL, CIVIC OR CHARITABLE ACTIVITIES.

(1) A judge shall not appear at a public hearing before, or otherwise consult with, an executive or legislative body or official except on matters concerning the law,* the legal system or the administration of justice or except when acting pro se in a matter involving the judge or the judge's interests.

Commentary

[1] See Section 2B regarding the obligation to avoid improper influence.

(2) A judge shall not accept appointment to a governmental committee or commission or other governmental position that is concerned with issues of fact or policy on matters other than the improvement of the law,* the legal system or the administration of justice. A judge may, however, represent a country, state or locality on ceremonial occasions or in connection with historical, educational or cultural activities.

Commentary

[1] Section 4C(2) prohibits a judge from accepting any governmental position except one relating to the law, legal system or administration of justice as authorized by Section 4C(3). The appropriateness of accepting extra-judicial assignments must be assessed in light of the demands on judicial resources created by crowded dockets and the need to protect the courts from involvement in extra-judicial matters that may prove to be controversial. Judges should not accept governmental appointments that are likely to interfere with the

effectiveness and independence of the judiciary.

[2] Section 4C(2) does not govern a judge's service in a nongovernmental position. See Section 4C(3) permitting service by a judge with organizations devoted to the improvement of the law, the legal system or the administration of justice and with educational, religious, charitable, fraternal or civic organizations not conducted for profit. For example, service on the board of a public educational institution, unless it were a law school, would be prohibited under Section 4C(2), but service on the board of a public law school or any private educational institution would generally be permitted under Section 4C(3).

(3) A judge may serve as an officer, director, trustee or non-legal advisor of an organization or governmental agency devoted to the improvement of the law,* the legal system or the administration of justice or of an educational, religious, charitable, fraternal or civic organization not conducted for profit, subject to the following limitations and the other requirements of this Code.

Commentary

[1] Section 4C(3) does not apply to a judge's service in a governmental position unconnected with the improvement of the law, the legal system or the administration of justice; see Section 4C(2).

[2] See Commentary to Section 4B regarding use of the phrase "subject to the following limitations and the other requirements of this Code." As an example of the meaning of the phrase, a judge permitted by Section 4C(3) to serve on the board of a fraternal institution may be prohibited from such service by Sections 2C or 4A if the institution practices invidious discrimination or if service on the board otherwise casts reasonable doubt on the judge's capacity to act impartially as a judge.

[3] Service by a judge on behalf of a civic or charitable organization may be governed by other provisions of Canon 4 in addition to Section 4C. For example, a judge is prohibited by Section 4G from serving as a legal advisor to a civic or charitable organization.

* See Terminology, "law."

(a) A judge shall not serve as an officer, director, trustee or non-legal advisor if it is likely that the organization

(i) will be engaged in proceedings that would ordinarily come before the judge, or

(ii) will be engaged frequently in adversary proceedings in the court of which the judge is a member or in any court subject to the appellate jurisdiction of the court of which the judge is a member.

Commentary

[1] The changing nature of some organizations and of their relationship to the law makes it necessary for a judge regularly to reexamine the activities of each organization with which the judge is affiliated to determine if it is proper for the judge to continue the affiliation. For example, in many jurisdictions charitable hospitals are now more frequently in court than in the past. Similarly, the boards of some legal aid organizations now make policy decisions that may have political significance or imply commitment to causes that may come before the courts for adjudication.

(b) A judge as an officer, director, trustee or non-legal advisor, or as a member or otherwise:

(i) may assist such an organization in planning fund-raising and may participate in the management and investment of the organization's funds, but shall not personally participate in the solicitation of funds or other fund-raising activities, except that a judge may solicit funds from other judges over whom the judge does not exercise supervisory or appellate authority;

(ii) may make recommendations to public and private fund-granting organizations on projects and programs concerning the law,* the legal system or the administration of justice;

(iii) shall not personally participate in membership solicitation if the solicitation might reasonably be perceived as coercive or, except as permitted in Section 4C(3)(b)(i), if the member-

ship solicitation is essentially a fund-raising mechanism;

(iv) shall not use or permit the use of the prestige of judicial office for fund-raising or membership solicitation.

Commentary

[1] A judge may solicit membership or endorse or encourage membership efforts for an organization devoted to the improvement of the law, the legal system or the administration of justice or a nonprofit educational, religious, charitable, fraternal or civic organization as long as the solicitation cannot reasonably be perceived as coercive and is not essentially a fund-raising mechanism. Solicitation of funds for an organization and solicitation of memberships similarly involve the danger that the person solicited will feel obligated to respond favorably to the solicitor if the solicitor is in a position of influence or control. A judge must not engage in direct, individual solicitation of funds or memberships in person, in writing or by telephone except in the following cases: 1) a judge may solicit for funds or memberships other judges over whom the judge does not exercise supervisory or appellate authority, 2) a judge may solicit other persons for membership in the organizations described above if neither those persons nor persons with whom they are affiliated are likely ever to appear before the court on which the judge serves and 3) a judge who is an officer of such an organization may send a general membership solicitation mailing over the judge's signature.

[2] Use of an organization letterhead for fund-raising or membership solicitation does not violate Section 4C(3)(b) provided the letterhead lists only the judge's name and office or other position in the organization, and, if comparable designations are listed for other persons, the judge's judicial designation. In addition, a judge must also make reasonable efforts to ensure that the judge's staff, court officials and others subject to the judge's direction and control do not solicit funds on the judge's behalf for any purpose, charitable or otherwise.

[3] A judge must not be a speaker or guest of honor at an organization's fund-raising event, but mere attendance at such an event is permissible if otherwise consistent with this Code.

D. FINANCIAL ACTIVITIES.

(1) A judge shall not engage in financial and business dealings that:

(a) may reasonably be perceived to exploit the judge's judicial position, or

(b) involve the judge in frequent transactions or continuing business relationships with those lawyers or other persons likely to come before the court on which the judge serves.

Commentary

[1] The Time for Compliance provision of this Code (Application, Section F) postpones the time for compliance with certain provisions of this Section in some cases.

[2] When a judge acquires in a judicial capacity information, such as material contained in filings with the court, that is not yet generally known, the judge must not use the information for private gain. See Section 2B; see also Section 3B(11).

[3] A judge must avoid financial and business dealings that involve the judge in frequent transactions or continuing business relationships with persons likely to come either before the judge personally or before other judges on the judge's court. In addition, a judge should discourage members of the judge's family from engaging in dealings that would reasonably appear to exploit the judge's judicial position. This rule is necessary to avoid creating an appearance of exploitation of office or favoritism and to minimize the potential for disqualification. With respect to affiliation of relatives of judge with law firms appearing before the judge, see Commentary to Section 3E(1) relating to disqualification.

[4] Participation by a judge in financial and business dealings is subject to the general prohibitions in Section 4A against activities that tend to reflect adversely on impartiality, demean the judicial office, or interfere with the proper performance of judicial duties. Such participation is also subject to the general prohibition in Canon 2 against activities involving impropriety or the appearance of impropriety and the prohibition in Section 2B against the misuse of the prestige of judicial office. In addition, a judge must maintain high standards of conduct in all of the judge's activities, as set forth in Canon 1. See Commentary for Section 4B regarding use of the

phrase "subject to the requirements of this Code."

(2) A judge may, subject to the requirements of this Code, hold and manage investments of the judge and members of the judge's family,* including real estate, and engage in other remunerative activity.

Commentary

[1] This Section provides that, subject to the requirements of this Code, a judge may hold and manage investments owned solely by the judge, investments owned solely by a member or members of the judge's family, and investments owned jointly by the judge and members of the judge's family.

(3) A judge shall not serve as an officer, director, manager, general partner, advisor or employee of any business entity except that a judge may, subject to the requirements of this Code, manage and participate in:

(a) a business closely held by the judge or members of the judge's family,* or

(b) a business entity primarily engaged in investment of the financial resources of the judge or members of the judge's family.

Commentary

[1] Subject to the requirements of this Code, a judge may participate in a business that is closely held either by the judge alone, by members of the judge's family, or by the judge and members of the judge's family.

[2] Although participation by a judge in a closely-held family business might otherwise be permitted by Section 4D(3), a judge may be prohibited from participation by other provisions of this Code when, for example, the business entity frequently appears before the judge's court or the participation requires significant time away from judicial duties. Similarly, a judge must avoid participating in a closely-held family business if the judge's participation would involve misuse of the prestige of judicial office.

(4) A judge shall manage the judge's investments and other financial interests to minimize the number of cases in which the judge is disqualified. As soon as the judge can do so

without serious financial detriment, the judge shall divest himself or herself of investments and other financial interests that might require frequent disqualification.

(5) A judge shall not accept, and shall urge members of the judge's family residing in the judge's household,* not to accept, a gift, bequest, favor or loan from anyone except for:

Commentary

[1] Section 4D(5) does not apply to contributions to a judge's campaign for judicial office, a matter governed by Canon 5.

[2] Because a gift, bequest, favor or loan to a member of the judge's family residing in the judge's household might be viewed as intended to influence the judge, a judge must inform those family members of the relevant ethical constraints upon the judge in this regard and discourage those family members from violating them. A judge cannot, however, reasonably be expected to know or control all of the financial or business activities of all family members residing in the judge's household.

(a) a gift incident to a public testimonial, books, tapes and other resource materials supplied by publishers on a complimentary basis for official use, or an invitation to the judge and the judge's spouse or guest to attend a bar-related function or an activity devoted to the improvement of the law,* the legal system or the administration of justice;

Commentary

[1] Acceptance of an invitation to a law-related function is governed by Section 4D(5) (a); acceptance of an invitation paid for by an individual lawyer or group of lawyers is governed by Section 4D(5)(h).

[2] A judge may accept a public testimonial or a gift incident thereto only if the donor organization is not an organization whose members comprise or frequently represent the same side in litigation, and the testimonial and gift are otherwise in compliance with other provisions of this Code. See Sections 4A(1) and 2B.

---

* See Terminology, "member of the judge's family."

* See Terminology, "member of the judge's family residing in the judge's household."

* See Terminology, "law."

(b) a gift, award or benefit incident to the business, profession or other separate activity of a spouse or other family member of a judge residing in the judge's household, including gifts, awards and benefits for the use of both the spouse or other family member and the judge (as spouse or family member), provided the gift, award or benefit could not reasonably be perceived as intended to influence the judge in the performance of judicial duties;

(c) ordinary social hospitality;

(d) a gift from a relative or friend, for a special occasion, such as a wedding, anniversary or birthday, if the gift is fairly commensurate with the occasion and the relationship;

Commentary

[1] A gift to a judge, or to a member of the judge's family living in the judge's household, that is excessive in value raises questions about the judge's impartiality and the integrity of the judicial office and might require disqualification of the judge where disqualification would not otherwise be required. See, however, Section 4D(5)(e).

(e) a gift, bequest, favor or loan from a relative or close personal friend whose appearance or interest in a case would in any event require disqualification under Section 3E;

(f) a loan from a lending institution in its regular course of business on the same terms generally available to persons who are not judges;

(g) a scholarship or fellowship awarded on the same terms and based on the same criteria applied to other applicants; or

(h) any other gift, bequest, favor or loan, only if: the donor is not a party or other person who has come or is likely to come or whose interests have come or are likely to come before the judge; and, if its value exceeds $150.00, the judge reports it in the same manner as the judge reports compensation in Section 4H.

Commentary

[1] Section 4D(5)(h) prohibits judges from accepting gifts, favors, bequests or loans from lawyers or their firms if they have come or are likely to come before the judge; it also prohibits gifts, favors, bequests or loans from clients of lawyers or their firms when the clients' interests have come or are likely to come before the judge.

E. FIDUCIARY ACTIVITIES.

(1) A judge shall not serve as executor, administrator or other personal representative, trustee, guardian, attorney in fact or other fiduciary,* except for the estate, trust or person of a member of the judge's family,* and then only if such service will not interfere with the proper performance of judicial duties.

(2) A judge shall not serve as a fiduciary * if it is likely that the judge as a fiduciary will be engaged in proceedings that would ordinarily come before the judge, or if the estate, trust or ward becomes involved in adversary proceedings in the court on which the judge serves or one under its appellate jurisdiction.

(3) The same restrictions on financial activities that apply to a judge personally also apply to the judge while acting in a fiduciary * capacity.

Commentary

[1] The Time for Compliance provision of this Code (Application, Section F) postpones the time for compliance with certain provisions of this Section in some cases.

[2] The restrictions imposed by this Canon may conflict with the judge's obligation as a fiduciary. For example, a judge should resign as trustee if detriment to the trust would result from divestiture of holdings the retention of which would place the judge in violation of Section 4D(4).

F. SERVICE AS ARBITRATOR OR MEDIATOR. A judge shall not act as an arbitrator or mediator or otherwise perform judicial functions in a private capacity unless expressly authorized by law.*

---

* See Terminology, "fiduciary."

* See Terminology, "member of the judge's family."

* See Terminology, "law."

Commentary

[1] Section 4F does not prohibit a judge from participating in arbitration, mediation or settlement conferences performed as part of judicial duties.

G. PRACTICE OF LAW. A judge shall not practice law. Notwithstanding this prohibition, a judge may act pro se and may, without compensation, give legal advice to and draft or review documents for a member of the judge's family.*

Commentary

[1] This prohibition refers to the practice of law in a representative capacity and not in a pro se capacity. A judge may act for himself or herself in all legal matters, including matters involving litigation and matters involving appearances before or other dealings with legislative and other governmental bodies. However, in so doing, a judge must not abuse the prestige of office to advance the interests of the judge or the judge's family. See Section 2(B).

[2] The Code allows a judge to give legal advice to and draft legal documents for members of the judge's family, so long as the judge receives no compensation. A judge must not, however, act as an advocate or negotiator for a member of the judge's family in a legal matter.

* * *

[3] Canon 6, new in the 1972 Code, reflected concerns about conflicts of interest and appearances of impropriety arising from compensation for off-the-bench activities. Since 1972, however, reporting requirements that are much more comprehensive with respect to what must be reported and with whom reports must be filed have been adopted by many jurisdictions. The Committee believes that although reports of compensation for extra-judicial activities should be required, reporting requirements preferably should be developed to suit the respective jurisdictions, not simply adopted as set forth in a national model code of judicial conduct. Because of the Committee's concern that deletion of this Canon might lead to the misconception that reporting compensation for extra-judicial activities is no longer important, the substance of Canon 6 is carried forward as Section 4H in this Code for

adoption in those jurisdictions that do not have other reporting requirements. In jurisdictions that have separately established reporting requirements, Section 4H(2) (Public Reporting) may be deleted and the caption for Section 4H modified appropriately.

* * *

H. COMPENSATION,   REIMBURSEMENT AND REPORTING.

(1) COMPENSATION AND REIMBURSEMENT. A judge may receive compensation and reimbursement of expenses for the extra-judicial activities permitted by this Code, if the source of such payments does not give the appearance of influencing the judge's performance of judicial duties or otherwise give the appearance of impropriety.

(a) Compensation shall not exceed a reasonable amount nor shall it exceed what a person who is not a judge would receive for the same activity.

(b) Expense reimbursement shall be limited to the actual cost of travel, food and lodging reasonably incurred by the judge and, where appropriate to the occasion, by the judge's spouse or guest. Any payment in excess of such an amount is compensation.

(2) PUBLIC REPORTS. A judge shall report the date, place and nature of any activity for which the judge received compensation, and the name of the payor and the amount of compensation so received. Compensation or income of a spouse attributed to the judge by operation of a community property law is not extra-judicial compensation to the judge. The judge's report shall be made at least annually and shall be filed as a public document in the office of the clerk of the court on which the judge serves or other office designated by law.*

Commentary

[1] See Section 4D(5) regarding reporting of gifts, bequests and loans.

[2] The Code does not prohibit a judge from accepting honoraria or speaking fees provided that the compensation is reasonable and commensurate with the task performed. A judge should ensure, however, that no conflicts are created by the arrangement. A judge

---

* See Terminology, "member of the judge's family."

* See Terminology, "law."

must not appear to trade on the judicial position for personal advantage. Nor should a judge spend significant time away from court duties to meet speaking or writing commitments for compensation. In addition, the source of the payment must not raise any question of undue influence or the judge's ability or willingness to be impartial.

I. Disclosure of a judge's income, debts, investments or other assets is required only to the extent provided in this Canon and in Sections 3E and 3F, or as otherwise required by law.*

Commentary

[1] Section 3E requires a judge to disqualify himself or herself in any proceeding in which the judge has an economic interest. See "economic interest" as explained in the Terminology Section. Section 4D requires a judge to refrain from engaging in business and from financial activities that might interfere with the impartial performance of judicial duties; Section 4H requires a judge to report all compensation the judge received for activities outside judicial office. A judge has the rights of any other citizen, including the right to privacy of the judge's financial affairs, except to the extent that limitations established by law are required to safeguard the proper performance of the judge's duties.

CANON 5 [2]

A Judge or Judicial Candidate Shall Refrain From Inappropriate Political Activity

A. ALL JUDGES AND CANDIDATES.

(1) Except as authorized in Sections 5B(2), 5C(1) and 5C(3), a judge or a candidate * for election or appointment to judicial office shall not:

(a) act as a leader or hold an office in a political organization *;

(b) publicly endorse or publicly oppose another candidate for public office;

(c) make speeches on behalf of a political organization;

(d) attend political gatherings; or

(e) solicit funds for, pay an assessment to or make a contribution to a political organization or candidate, or purchase tickets for political party dinners or other functions.

Commentary

[1] A judge or candidate for judicial office retains the right to participate in the political process as a voter.

[2] Where false information concerning a judicial candidate is made public, a judge or another judicial candidate having knowledge of the facts is not prohibited by Section 5A(1) from making the facts public.

---

2. Introductory Note to Canon 5: There is wide variation in the methods of judicial selection used, both among jurisdictions and within the jurisdictions themselves. In a given state, judges may be selected by one method initially, retained by a different method, and selected by still another method to fill interim vacancies.

According to figures compiled in 1987 by the National Center for State Courts, 32 states and the District of Columbia use a merit selection method (in which an executive such as a governor appoints a judge from a group of nominees selected by a judicial nominating commission) to select judges in the state either initially or to fill an interim vacancy. Of those 33 jurisdictions, a merit selection method is used in 18 jurisdictions to choose judges of courts of last resort, in 13 jurisdictions to choose judges of intermediate appellate courts, in 12 jurisdictions to choose judges of general jurisdiction courts and in 5 jurisdictions to choose judges of limited jurisdiction courts.

Methods of judicial selection other than merit selection include nonpartisan election (10 states use it for initial selection at all court levels, another 10 states use it for initial selection for at least one court level) and partisan election (8 states use it for initial selection at all court levels, another 7 states use it for initial selection for at least one level). In a small minority of the states, judicial selection methods include executive or legislative appointment (without nomination of a group of potential appointees by a judicial nominating commission) and court selection. In addition, the federal judicial system utilizes an executive appointment method. See State Court Organization 1987 (National Center for State Courts, 1988).

* See Terminology, "law."

* See Terminology, "candidate."

* See Terminology, "political organization."

[3] Section 5A(1)(a) does not prohibit a candidate for elective judicial office from retaining during candidacy a public office such as county prosecutor, which is not "an office in a political organization."

[4] Section 5A(1)(b) does not prohibit a judge or judicial candidate from privately expressing his or her views on judicial candidates or other candidates for public office.

[5] A candidate does not publicly endorse another candidate for public office by having that candidate's name on the same ticket.

(2) A judge shall resign from judicial office upon becoming a candidate * for a non-judicial office either in a primary or in a general election, except that the judge may continue to hold judicial office while being a candidate for election to or serving as a delegate in a state constitutional convention if the judge is otherwise permitted by law * to do so.

(3) A candidate * for a judicial office:

(a) shall maintain the dignity appropriate to judicial office and act in a manner consistent with the integrity and independence of the judiciary, and shall encourage members of the candidate's family * to adhere to the same standards of political conduct in support of the candidate as apply to the candidate;

Commentary

[1] Although a judicial candidate must encourage members of his or her family to adhere to the same standards of political conduct in support of the candidate that apply to the candidate, family members are free to participate in other political activity.

(b) shall prohibit employees and officials who serve at the pleasure of the candidate,* and shall discourage other employees and officials subject to the candidate's direction and control from doing on the candidate's behalf what the candidate is prohibited from doing under the Sections of this Canon;

(c) except to the extent permitted by Section 5C(2), shall not authorize or knowingly * permit any other person to do for the candidate * what the candidate is pro-

hibited from doing under the Sections of this Canon;

(d) shall not:

(i) make pledges or promises of conduct in office other than the faithful and impartial performance of the duties of the office;

(ii) make statements that commit or appear to commit the candidate with respect to cases, controversies or issues that are likely to come before the court; or

(iii) knowingly * misrepresent the identity, qualifications, present position or other fact concerning the candidate or an opponent;

Commentary

[1] Section 5A(3)(d) prohibits a candidate for judicial office from making statements that appear to commit the candidate regarding cases, controversies or issues likely to come before the court. As a corollary, a candidate should emphasize in any public statement the candidate's duty to uphold the law regardless of his or her personal views. See also Section 3B(9), the general rule on public comment by judges. Section 5A(3)(d) does not prohibit a candidate from making pledges or promises respecting improvements in court administration. Nor does this Section prohibit an incumbent judge from making private statements to other judges or court personnel in the performance of judicial duties. This Section applies to any statement made in the process of securing judicial office, such as statements to commissions charged with judicial selection and tenure and legislative bodies confirming appointment. See also Rule 8.2 of the ABA Model Rules of Professional Conduct.

(e) may respond to personal attacks or attacks on the candidate's record as long as the response does not violate Section 5A(3)(d).

B. CANDIDATES SEEKING APPOINTMENT TO JUDICIAL OR OTHER GOVERNMENTAL OFFICE.

(1) A candidate * for appointment to judicial office or a judge seeking other governmen-

---

* See Terminology, "member of the candidate's family."

* See Terminology, "candidate."

* See Terminology, "knowingly."

tal office shall not solicit or accept funds, personally or through a committee or otherwise, to support his or her candidacy.

(2) A candidate * for appointment to judicial office or a judge seeking other governmental office shall not engage in any political activity to secure the appointment except that:

(a) such persons may:

(i) communicate with the appointing authority, including any selection or nominating commission or other agency designated to screen candidates;

(ii) seek support or endorsement for the appointment from organizations that regularly make recommendations for reappointment or appointment to the office, and from individuals to the extent requested or required by those specified in Section 5B(2)(a); and

(iii) provide to those specified in Sections 5B(2)(a)(i) and 5B(2)(a)(ii) information as to his or her qualifications for the office;

(b) a non-judge candidate * for appointment to judicial office may, in addition, unless otherwise prohibited by law *;

(i) retain an office in a political organization,*

(ii) attend political gatherings, and

(iii) continue to pay ordinary assessments and ordinary contributions to a political organization or candidate and purchase tickets for political party dinners or other functions.

Commentary

[1] Section 5B(2) provides a limited exception to the restrictions imposed by Sections 5A(1) and 5D. Under Section 5B(2), candidates seeking reappointment to the same judicial office or appointment to another judicial office or other governmental office may apply for the appointment and seek appropriate support.

[2] Although under Section 5B(2) non-judge candidates seeking appointment to judi-

cial office are permitted during candidacy to retain office in a political organization, attend political gatherings and pay ordinary dues and assessments, they remain subject to other provisions of this Code during candidacy. See Sections 5B(1), 5B(2)(a), 5E and Application Section.

C. JUDGES AND CANDIDATES SUBJECT TO PUBLIC ELECTION.

(1) A judge or a candidate * subject to public election * may, except as prohibited by law *:

(a) at any time

(i) purchase tickets for and attend political gatherings;

(ii) identify himself or herself as a member of a political party; and

(iii) contribute to a political organization *;

(b) when a candidate for election

(i) speak to gatherings on his or her own behalf;

(ii) appear in newspaper, television and other media advertisements supporting his or her candidacy;

(iii) distribute pamphlets and other promotional campaign literature supporting his or her candidacy; and

(iv) publicly endorse or publicly oppose other candidates for the same judicial office in a public election in which the judge or judicial candidate is running.

Commentary

[1] Section 5C(1) permits judges subject to election at any time to be involved in limited political activity. Section 5D, applicable solely to incumbent judges, would otherwise bar this activity.

(2) A candidate * shall not personally solicit or accept campaign contributions or personally solicit publicly stated support. A candidate may, however, establish committees of responsible persons to conduct campaigns for the candidate through media advertisements,

---

* See Terminology, "candidate."

* See Terminology, "law."

* See Terminology, "political organization."

* See Terminology, "public election."

brochures, mailings, candidate forums and other means not prohibited by law. Such committees may solicit and accept reasonable campaign contributions, manage the expenditure of funds for the candidate's campaign and obtain public statements of support for his or her candidacy. Such committees are not prohibited from soliciting and accepting reasonable campaign contributions and public support from lawyers. A candidate's committees may solicit contributions and public support for the candidate's campaign no earlier than [one year] before an election and no later than [90] days after the last election in which the candidate participates during the election year. A candidate shall not use or permit the use of campaign contributions for the private benefit of the candidate or others.

Commentary

[1] Section 5C(2) permits a candidate, other than a candidate for appointment, to establish campaign committees to solicit and accept public support and reasonable financial contributions. At the start of the campaign, the candidate must instruct his or her campaign committees to solicit or accept only contributions that are reasonable under the circumstances. Though not prohibited, campaign contributions of which a judge has knowledge, made by lawyers or others who appear before the judge, may be relevant to disqualification under Section 3E.

[2] Campaign committees established under Section 5C(2) should manage campaign finances responsibly, avoiding deficits that might necessitate post-election fund-raising, to the extent possible.

[3] Section 5C(2) does not prohibit a candidate from initiating an evaluation by a judicial selection commission or bar association, or, subject to the requirements of this Code, from responding to a request for information from any organization.

(3) Except as prohibited by law,* a candidate * for judicial office in a public election *

may permit the candidate's name: (a) to be listed on election materials along with the names of other candidates for elective public office, and (b) to appear in promotions of the ticket.

Commentary

[1] Section 5C(3) provides a limited exception to the restrictions imposed by Section 5A(1).

D. INCUMBENT JUDGES. A judge shall not engage in any political activity except (i) as authorized under any other Section of this Code, (ii) on behalf of measures to improve the law,* the legal system or the administration of justice, or (iii) as expressly authorized by law.

Commentary

[1] Neither Section 5D nor any other section of the Code prohibits a judge in the exercise of administrative functions from engaging in planning and other official activities with members of the executive and legislative branches of government. With respect to a judge's activity on behalf of measures to improve the law, the legal system and the administration of justice, see Commentary to Section 4B and Section 4C(1) and its Commentary.

E. APPLICABILITY. Canon 5 generally applies to all incumbent judges and judicial candidates.* A successful candidate, whether or not an incumbent, is subject to judicial discipline for his or her campaign conduct; an unsuccessful candidate who is a lawyer is subject to lawyer discipline for his or her campaign conduct. A lawyer who is a candidate for judicial office is subject to [Rule 8.2(b) of the ABA Model Rules of Professional Conduct]. (An adopting jurisdiction should substitute a reference to its applicable rule.)

APPLICATION OF THE CODE OF JUDICIAL CONDUCT

A. Anyone, whether or not a lawyer, who is an officer of a judicial system [3] and who performs judicial functions, including an of-

---

* See Terminology, "law."

* See Terminology, "candidate."

* See Terminology, "public election."

3. Applicability of this Code to administrative law judges should be determined by each adopting jurisdiction. Administrative law judges generally are affiliated with the executive branch of government rather than the judicial branch and each adopting jurisdiction should consider the unique characteristics of particular administrative law judge positions in adopting and adapting the Code for administrative law judges. See, e.g., Model Code of Judicial Conduct for

ficer such as a magistrate, court commissioner, special master or referee, is a judge within the meaning of this Code. All judges shall comply with this Code except as provided below.

Commentary

[1] The four categories of judicial service in other than a full-time capacity are necessarily defined in general terms because of the widely varying forms of judicial service. For the purposes of this Section, as long as a retired judge is subject to recall the judge is considered to "perform judicial functions." The determination of which category and, accordingly, which specific Code provisions apply to an individual judicial officer, depend upon the facts of the particular judicial service.

B. RETIRED JUDGE SUBJECT TO RECALL. A retired judge subject to recall who by law is not permitted to practice law is not required to comply:

(1) except while serving as a judge, with Section 4F; and

(2) at any time with Section 4E.

C. CONTINUING PART–TIME JUDGE. A continuing part-time judge *:

(1) is not required to comply:

(a) except while serving as a judge, with Section 3B(9); and

(b) at any time with Sections 4C(2), 4D(3), 4E(1), 4F, 4G, 4H, 5A(1), 5B(2) and 5D.

(2) shall not practice law in the court on which the judge serves or in any court subject to the appellate jurisdiction of the court on which the judge serves, and shall not act as a lawyer in a proceeding in which the judge has served as a judge or in any other proceeding related thereto.

Commentary

[1] When a person who has been a continuing part-time judge is no longer a continuing part-time judge, including a retired judge no longer subject to recall, that person may act as a lawyer in a proceeding in which he or she has served as a judge or in any other proceeding related thereto only with the express con-

sent of all parties pursuant to [Rule 1.12(a) of the ABA Model Rules of Professional Conduct]. (An adopting jurisdiction should substitute a reference to its applicable rule).

D. PERIODIC PART–TIME JUDGE. A periodic part-time judge *:

(1) is not required to comply

(a) except while serving as a judge, with Section 3B(9);

(b) at any time, with Sections 4C(2), 4C(3)(a), 4D(1)(b), 4D(3), 4D(4), 4D(5), 4E, 4F, 4G, 4H, 5A(1), 5B(2) and 5D.

(2) shall not practice law in the court on which the judge serves or in any court subject to the appellate jurisdiction of the court on which the judge serves, and shall not act as a lawyer in a proceeding in which the judge has served as a judge or in any other proceeding related thereto.

Commentary

[1] When a person who has been a periodic part-time judge is no longer a periodic part-time judge (no longer accepts appointments), that person may act as a lawyer in a proceeding in which he or she has served as a judge or in any other proceeding related thereto only with the express consent of all parties pursuant to [Rule 1.12(a) of the ABA Model Rules of Professional Conduct]. (An adopting jurisdiction should substitute a reference to its applicable rule).

E. PRO TEMPORE PART–TIME JUDGE. A pro tempore part-time judge *:

(1) is not required to comply:

(a) except while serving as a judge, with Sections 2A, 2B, 3B(9) and 4C(1);

(b) at any time with Sections 2C, 4C(2), 4C(3)(a), 4C(3)(b), 4D(1)(b), 4D(3), 4D(4), 4D(5), 4E, 4F, 4G, 4H, 5A(1), 5A(2), 5B(2) and 5D.

(2) A person who has been a pro tempore part-time judge * shall not act as a lawyer in a proceeding in which the judge has served as a judge or in any other proceeding related thereto except as otherwise permitted by [Rule 1.12(a) of the ABA Model Rules of Professional

---

Federal Administrative Law Judges, endorsed by the National Conference of Administrative Law Judges in February 1989.

* See Terminology, "continuing part-time judge."

* See Terminology, "periodic part-time judge."

* See Terminology, "pro tempore part-time judge."

Conduct]. (An adopting jurisdiction should substitute a reference to its applicable rule.)

F. TIME FOR COMPLIANCE. A person to whom this Code becomes applicable shall comply immediately with all provisions of this Code except Sections 4D(2), 4D(3) and 4E and shall comply with these Sections as soon as reasonably possible and shall do so in any event within the period of one year.

Commentary

[1] If serving as a fiduciary when selected as judge, a new judge may, notwithstanding the prohibitions in Section 4E, continue to serve as fiduciary but only for that period of time necessary to avoid serious adverse consequences to the beneficiary of the fiduciary relationship and in no event longer than one year. Similarly, if engaged at the time of judicial selection in a business activity, a new judge may, notwithstanding the prohibitions in Section 4D(3), continue in that activity for a reasonable period but in no event longer than one year.

28 U.S.C.A. § 455
DISQUALIFICATION OF JUSTICE, JUDGE, OR MAGISTRATE

§ 455. Disqualification of justice, judge, or magistrate

(a) Any justice, judge, or magistrate of the United States shall disqualify himself in any proceeding in which his impartiality might reasonably be questioned.

(b) He shall also disqualify himself in the following circumstances:

(1) Where he has a personal bias or prejudice concerning a party, or personal knowledge of disputed evidentiary facts concerning the proceeding;

(2) Where in private practice he served as lawyer in the matter in controversy, or a lawyer with whom he previously practiced law served during such association as a lawyer concerning the matter, or the judge or such lawyer has been a material witness concerning it;

(3) Where he has served in governmental employment and in such capacity participated as counsel, adviser or material witness concerning the proceeding or expressed an opinion concerning the merits of the particular case in controversy;

(4) He knows that he, individually or as a fiduciary, or his spouse or minor child residing in his household, has a financial interest in the subject matter in controversy or in a party to the proceeding, or any other interest that could be substantially affected by the outcome of the proceeding;

(5) He or his spouse, or a person within the third degree of relationship to either of them, or the spouse of such a person:

(i) Is a party to the proceeding, or an officer, director, or trustee of a party;

(ii) Is acting as a lawyer in the proceeding;

(iii) Is known by the judge to have an interest that could be substantially affected by the outcome of the proceeding;

(iv) Is to the judge's knowledge likely to be a material witness in the proceeding.

(c) A judge should inform himself about his personal and fiduciary financial interests, and make a reasonable effort to inform himself about the personal financial interests of his spouse and minor children residing in his household.

(d) For the purposes of this section the following words or phrases shall have the meaning indicated:

(1) "proceeding" includes pretrial, trial, appellate review, or other stages of litigation;

(2) the degree of relationship is calculated according to the civil law system;

(3) "fiduciary" includes such relationships as executor, administrator, trustee, and guardian;

(4) "financial interest" means ownership of a legal or equitable interest, however small, or a relationship as director, adviser, or other active participant in the affairs of a party, except that:

(i) Ownership in a mutual or common investment fund that holds securities is not a "financial interest" in such securities unless the judge participates in the management of the fund;

(ii) An office in an educational, religious, charitable, fraternal, or civic organization is not a "financial interest" in securities held by the organization;

(iii) The proprietary interest of a policyholder in a mutual insurance company, of a depositor in a mutual savings association, or a similar proprietary interest, is a "financial interest" in the organization only if the outcome of the proceeding could substantially affect the value of the interest;

(iv) Ownership of government securities is a "financial interest" in the issuer only if the outcome of the proceeding could substantially affect the value of the securities.

(e) No justice, judge, or magistrate shall accept from the parties to the proceeding a waiver of any ground for disqualification enumerated in subsection (b). Where the ground for disqualification arises only under subsection (a), waiver may be accepted provided it is preceded by a full disclosure on the record of the basis for disqualification.

(f) Notwithstanding the preceding provisions of this section, if any justice, judge, magistrate, or bankruptcy judge to whom a matter has been assigned would be disqualified, after substantial judicial time has been devoted to the matter, because of the appearance or discovery, after the matter was assigned to him or her, that he or she individually or as a fiduciary, or his or her spouse or minor child residing in his or her household, has a financial interest in a party (other than an interest that could be substantially affected by the outcome), disqualification is not required if the justice, judge, magistrate, bankruptcy judge, spouse or minor child, as the case may be, divests himself or herself of the interest that provides the grounds for the disqualification.

APPENDIX G

MPRE SAMPLE QUESTIONS I

Multistate Professional Responsibility Examination

DESCRIPTION OF THE MULTISTATE PROFESSIONAL RESPONSIBILITY EXAMINATION

The purpose of the NCBE Multistate Professional Responsibility Examination (MPRE) is to measure the examinee's knowledge of the ethical standards of the legal profession as those standards are set forth in the American Bar Association's Code of Professional Responsibility, Model Rules of Professional Conduct, and the Code of Judicial Conduct. The MPRE is not a test to determine an individual's ethical standards; rather, it is intended to measure knowledge and understanding of established ethical standards.

The MPRE is developed by a six-member Drafting Committee composed of recognized experts in the area of professional responsibility. Before a question is selected for inclusion in the MPRE, it undergoes a multistage review process that occurs over the course of one to two years. Besides intensive reviews by the Drafting Committee and testing specialists, each question is reviewed by national and state experts. All items must successfully pass all reviews before they are included in the MPRE. In addition to the multistage review process, the statistical performance of each item is reviewed and evaluated by content and testing experts before the items are included in the computation of examinees' scores. This review process is conducted as a further check to ensure that each item is accurate and psychometrically sound.

The MPRE consists of 50 multiple-choice test questions. These questions are followed by 10 Test Center Review questions that request the examinee's reactions to the testing conditions. The examination is two hours and five minutes in length.

Approximately ten to fifteen percent of the questions contained in the MPRE measure aspects of the American Bar Association's Code of Judicial Conduct (CJC). The remaining questions contained in the MPREs that have been administered since 1984 are designed so that the correct answer will be the same under both the American Bar Association's prior Code of Professional Responsibility (CPR) and the American Bar Association's presently recommended Model Rules of Professional Conduct (MRPC), including the Preamble to and the Comments accompanying the MRPC. All questions are to be answered according to the provisions of these codes and rules. Local statutes or rules of court are not to be considered.

SAMPLE QUESTIONS FROM THE MULTISTATE PROFESSIONAL RESPONSIBILITY EXAMINATION

This booklet contains fifty (50) test questions, some of which appear in the MPRE Information Booklet, which is provided as part of the MPRE application packet. The questions contained herein have been selected from previous forms of the MPRE administered since 1984.

Each question contained in this booklet uses one of the following four key words or phrases, each of which is provided below with its intended meaning.

1. *Must* or *subject to discipline* asks whether the conduct referred to or described in the question subjects the attorney to discipline under the provisions of the Disciplinary Rules of the CPR and the MRPC.

2. *Should* asks whether the conduct referred to or described in the question at least conforms to the level of conduct expected of the attorney pursuant to the CPR and the MRPC, regardless of whether the obligation arises under the ethical considerations, comments, or disciplinary rules.

3. *May* or *proper* asks whether the conduct referred to or described in the question is professionally appropriate in that it:

   a. would not subject the attorney to discipline.

   b. is not inconsistent with the Ethical Considerations of the CPR and the Preamble and Comments to the MRPC.

   c. is not inconsistent with the ABA CJC.

4. *Subject to liability for malpractice* asks whether the conduct referred to or described in the question subjects the attorney to liability for damages for harm to the client resulting from that conduct. If a question refers to liability for malpractice, it should be answered according to generally accepted principles of law, and the relationship, if any, between liability for malpractice and subjection to discipline.

When a question refers to discipline by the "bar" or "state bar," it refers to whatever agency in the jurisdiction has the authority to administer the standards for admission to practice and for maintenance of professional competence and integrity. Whenever a lawyer is identified as a "certified specialist," that lawyer has been so certified by the appropriate agency in the jurisdiction in which the lawyer practices.

The questions in the MPRE may include qualifications as part of the alternative responses. These qualifications may be essential to the selection of the best response to the question. Consequently, each question should be read through thoroughly before a response is selected. Sample questions 2, 3, 6, 8, 9, 10, 11, 12, 15, 18, 20, 21, 24, 26, 27, 28, 29, 31, 32, 33, 34, 35, 37, 38, 39, 41, 42, 43, 44, 45, 46, 47, 48, and 50 in this booklet illustrate the types of conditions that may appear in questions in the MPRE.

The questions in this test are numbered, and the four suggested answers for each question are lettered. For each question first decide which answer is best. Then on the sample answer sheet on page 25 of this booklet, find the row of ovals with the same number as the question. Then find the oval in the row with the same letter as your answer. Blacken the oval completely. For example, if you choose response B for question 3, blacken oval B in the row of ovals next to the number 3 on the sample answer sheet. Choose only one answer for each question. Once you have answered the questions in this booklet, you may check your answers with the key provided [at the end of this Appendix G].

The Multistate Professional Responsibility Examination is part of the bar examination requirement of participating jurisdictions, and the same standards of conduct by the applicants apply as if the examination were being administered by a board of bar examiners. Any misconduct in connection with the MPRE will be reported to the appropriate board of bar examiners.

Question 1.

Attorney, while working in her office, overheard a conversation between two law students, who were summer interns, about a third intern, Stu. At the time, all three students were about to enter their last year of law study. The conversation indicated that Stu had used some law school student bar association funds for his own purposes. Attorney later discussed the matter with Stu, who admitted having used the funds but explained that he did so because of an emergency illness. Stu indicated that he had repaid the student bar association in full. Stu is now applying for admission to the bar. The admitting authority has asked Attorney for an evaluation of Stu's fitness for admission to the bar, including any knowledge of facts material to his moral character.

Which of the following correctly states Attorney's professional responsibility?

A. Attorney *should* inform the bar admission authority about Stu's past conduct and *may* make whatever recommendation Attorney believes is justified.

B. Attorney *should* recommend Stu for admission without disclosing Attorney's knowledge of Stu's past conduct if Attorney believes Stu is of good moral character.

C. Attorney *should* decline to reply because Attorney acquired some of her information in a discussion with Stu.

D. Attorney *should* decline to reply because Stu has not asked her for a recommendation.

Question 2.

Attorney is representing Seller in a civil suit for breach of a contract in which Seller agreed to sell a racehorse to Buyer for $25,000. Buyer refused to accept the horse when it was delivered after a three-hour trip because the horse had a condition that made it unfit for racing. The horse had been placed in Buyer's trailer by Seller. If the horse was injured during transit in the trailer, Seller will recover.

Seller asserts that the horse was in good condition and fit for racing when placed in the trailer and insists that Attorney file a motion for summary judgment supported by Seller's affidavit to that effect. Attorney's investigation has disclosed that the horse's condition is one that ordinarily is caused by prolonged neglect. Attorney has advised Seller that there is a disputed issue of fact, and, therefore, the motion will almost certainly be denied.

Is Attorney *subject to discipline* if Attorney does not withdraw from the case?

A. Yes, if Attorney believes the motion for summary judgment will be denied.

B. Yes, because Seller refuses to follow Attorney's advice.

C. No, because Attorney must accept Seller's version of the facts.

D. No, unless Attorney knows that Seller's affidavit will contain false statements.

Question 3.

Attorney employs Baker as an office assistant. Baker has studied law extensively but has never been admitted to practice. Attorney has several corporations as clients. If a corporate client is sued and the matter involves more than the jurisdictional limit of the small claims court but is less than $10,000, Attorney has the corporate client execute a power of attorney authorizing Baker to act on its behalf. Baker then represents the corporate client in the trial of the matter.

Is Attorney *subject to discipline?*

A. Yes, because Attorney is employing Baker in the unauthorized practice of law.

B. Yes, because a corporation may not confer a power of attorney on a person who is not an officer or employee.

C. No, if, in each matter, Attorney obtains the client's informed consent to representation by Baker.

D. No, if Baker competently represents the client.

Question 4.

Four years ago, Mafco, represented by Attorney, purchased a parcel of land and took title in the name of Trust Company. Mafco's president had informed Attorney that Mafco intended to build a large manufacturing plant on the property but did not wish its ownership of the land or its building plans to be public. After the purchase was completed, Attorney did not represent Mafco in any other matter. Because of financial problems, Mafco postponed construction of the plant.

One year ago, Investor, a client of Attorney, consulted Attorney about the tax consequences of acquiring the local electric utility company. Attorney, without revealing the name of Mafco, told Investor that a company was planning to build a large manufacturing plant in the area and that if the company went ahead with its plans, Investor's investment in the electric utility should be very profitable. Investor acquired the utility company.

Mafco is now building the manufacturing plant.

Is Attorney *subject to discipline?*

A. Yes, because Attorney accepted representation of Investor, knowing that Investor's financial interests might be adverse to those of Mafco.

B. Yes, because Attorney revealed to Investor information Attorney acquired during the representation of Mafco.

C. No, because Attorney did not personally profit from Investor's acquisition of the utility company.

D. No, because Investor initiated the discussion with Attorney with regard to acquiring the utility company.

Question 5.

Attorney, an experienced trademark litigator, represents Publisher in an action seeking damages from Bookco for an alleged trademark violation. Attorney believes the services of an expert witness are essential to proper presentation of the case.

Wit, a competent expert witness, was available to testify on Publisher's behalf, but Wit demanded a fee of $8,000. Publisher was unable to pay a fee of that size. Expert, an equally competent expert witness, offered to testify for Publisher for a fee of $1,000 plus 10% of any damages recovered. Publisher is willing to agree to Expert's requested fee.

Which of the following would be *proper* for Attorney?

I. Withdraw from representation of Publisher if the inability to obtain an expert witness will make the suit difficult to win

II. Guarantee to Wit the requested fee of $8,000 upon Publisher's agreeing to reimburse Attorney when Publisher is able to do so

III. Employ Expert on the terms requested by Expert

A. I only

B. II only

C. I and II, but not III

D. II and III, but not I

Question 6.

Attorney Alpha was retained by Passenger, a passenger on a bus, who had been injured in a collision between the bus and a truck. Passenger paid Alpha a retainer of $1,000 and agreed further that Alpha should have a fee of 25% of any recovery before filing suit, 30% of any recovery after suit was filed but before judgment, and 35% of any recovery after trial and judgment. Alpha promptly called the lawyer for the bus company and told him she was representing Passenger and would like to talk about a settlement. Alpha made an appointment to talk to the lawyer for the bus company but did not keep the appointment. Alpha continued to put off talking to the lawyer for the bus company. Meanwhile, Passenger became concerned because she had heard nothing from Alpha. Passenger called Alpha's office but was told Alpha was not in and would not call back. Passenger was told not to worry because Alpha would look after her interests. After ten months had passed, Passenger went to Attorney Beta for advice. Beta advised Passenger that the statute of limitations would run out in one week and immediately filed suit for Passenger. Alpha, upon Passenger's demand, refunded the $1,000 Passenger had paid.

Is Alpha *subject to discipline?*

A. Yes, unless Alpha's time was completely occupied with work for other clients.

B. Yes, because Alpha neglected the representation of Passenger.

C. No, because Passenger's suit was filed before the statute of limitations ran.

D. No, because Alpha returned the $1,000 retainer to Passenger.

Question 7.

Attorney Alpha filed a personal injury suit on behalf of Plaintiff against Defendant. Defendant was personally served with process. Alpha knows that Defendant is insured by Insco and that Attorney Beta has been retained by Insco to represent Defendant. No responsive pleading has been filed on behalf of Defendant, and the time for filing expired over ten days ago.

Is Alpha *subject to discipline* if Alpha proceeds to have a default judgment entered?

A. Yes, because Alpha knew that Beta had been retained by Insco to represent Defendant.

B. Yes, because Alpha failed to extend professional courtesy to another lawyer.

C. No, because Alpha is properly representing her client's interests.

D. No, because any judgment will be satisfied by Insco.

Question 8.

Attorney is a candidate in a contested election for judicial office. Her opponent, Judge, is the incumbent and has occupied the bench for many years. The director of the state commission on judicial conduct, upon inquiry by Attorney, erroneously told Attorney that Judge had been reprimanded by the commission for misconduct in office. Attorney, who had confidence in the director, believed him. In fact, Judge had not been reprimanded by the commission; the commission had conducted hearings on Judge's alleged misconduct in office and, by a three to two vote, declined to reprimand Judge.

Decisions of the commission, including reprimands, are not confidential.

Is Attorney *subject to discipline* for publicly stating that Judge had been reprimanded for misconduct?

A. Yes, because the official records of the commission would have disclosed the truth.

B. Yes, because Judge had not been reprimanded.

C. No, if Attorney reasonably relied on the director's information.

D. No, because Judge was a candidate in a contested election.

Question 9.

Attorney is a well-known, highly skilled litigator. Attorney's practice is in an area of law in which the trial proceedings are heard by the court without a jury.

In an interview with a prospective client, Attorney said, "I make certain that I give the campaign committee of every candidate for elective judicial office more money than any other lawyer gives, whether it's $500 or $5,000. Judges know who help them get elected." The prospective client did not retain Attorney.

Is Attorney *subject to discipline?*

A. Yes, if Attorney's contributions are made without consideration of candidates' merits.

B. Yes, because Attorney implied that Attorney receives favored treatment by judges.

C. No, if Attorney's statements were true.

D. No, because the prospective client did not retain Attorney.

Questions 10–11 are based on the following fact situation.

Judge is presiding in a case that has, as its main issue, a complicated point of commercial law. The lawyers have not presented the case to Judge's satisfaction, and Judge believes she needs additional legal advice. Judge's former partner in law practice, Attorney, is an expert in the field of law that is at issue. Attorney has no interest in the case.

Question 10.

Is it *proper* for Attorney to advise Judge in the matter?

A. Yes, because Judge was not satisfied with the presentation by the lawyers in the case.

B. Yes, if Judge requests Attorney's legal advice.

C. No, because Attorney may not participate in the case unless retained by a party to the proceeding.

D. No, unless Attorney first gives notice to the parties of the intent to advise Judge.

Question 11.

Is it *proper* for Judge to consult Attorney?

A. Yes, because Attorney has no interest in the case.

B. Yes, if Judge believes that Attorney's advice is needed to serve the interests of justice.

C. No, unless all parties in the case first give their written consent to Judge's consultation with Attorney.

D. No, unless Judge informs the parties of Attorney's identity and the substance of Attorney's advice, and asks for their responses.

Question 12.

Attorney is a lawyer employed by State's Industrial Safety Agency (ISA). ISA is authorized, after investigation and hearing, to make administrative determinations requiring employers to install industrial safety devices. Attorney is considering a career change and has submitted his application for employment as chief counsel of Union, a large industrial labor union. Attorney has directed ISA's investigation of the need for smoke and toxic fume detectors at Giant's steel mill. Giant is State's largest private employer.

At a public hearing conducted by ISA pursuant to statute, Attorney presented the case for ISA. Attorney made an opening statement in which he said that the evidence to be produced would show that Giant had failed to install safety devices "in callous, willful, and total disregard for the safety and welfare of Giant's employees." Attorney made his opening statement with knowledge that members of Union's Executive Committee, to whom his application for employment with Union had been sent, were in attendance at the hearing.

Was it *proper* for Attorney to make the quoted statement?

A. Yes, because opening statements are not evidence in a proceeding.

B. Yes, if Attorney believed the statement would be supported by the evidence.

C. No, because the statement was made in the presence of representatives of Attorney's prospective employer.

D. No, because the statement exceeded the bounds of justifiable advocacy.

Question 13.

Attorney's advertisement in the local newspaper includes the following information, all of which is true:

I. Attorney, B.A., magna cum laude, Eastern College; J.D., summa cum laude, State Law School; LL.M., Eastern Law School.

II. My offices are open Monday through Friday from 9:00 a.m. to 5:00 p.m., but you may call my answering service twenty-four hours a day, seven days a week.

III. I speak modern Greek fluently.

For which, if any, of these statements is Attorney *subject to discipline?*

A. III only

B. I and II, but not III

C. I, II, and III

D. Neither I, nor II, nor III

Question 14.

Trustco, a trust company, entered into the following arrangement with Attorney, a lawyer newly admitted to the bar.

Trustco would provide Attorney with free office space in the building in which Trustco had its offices. If a customer of Trustco contacted Trustco about a trust or will, an officer of Trustco, who is not a lawyer, would advise the customer and help the customer work out the details of the trust or will. The customer would be informed that the necessary documents would be prepared by Trustco's staff. The completed documents would be submitted by an officer of Trustco to the customer for execution.

Attorney, in accordance with a memorandum from Trustco's trust officer detailing the plan, would prepare the necessary documents. Attorney would never meet with the customer and would not charge the customer for these services. Attorney would be free to engage in private practice, subject only to the limitation that Attorney could not accept employment adverse to Trustco.

Is Attorney *subject to discipline* for entering into the arrangement with Trustco?

A. Yes, because Attorney is restricting his right to practice.

B. Yes, because Attorney is aiding Trustco in the practice of law.

C. No, because Attorney is not charging the customer for his services.

D. No, because Attorney is not giving advice to Trustco's customers.

Question 15.

Attorney represented Husband and Wife in the purchase of a business financed by contributions from their respective separate funds. The business was jointly operated by Husband and Wife after acquisition. After several years, a dispute arose over the management of the business. Husband and Wife sought Attorney's advice, and the matter was settled on the basis of an agreement drawn by Attorney and signed by Husband and Wife. Later, Wife asked Attorney to represent her in litigation against Husband based on the claim that Husband was guilty of fraud and misrepresentation in the negotiations for the prior settlement agreement.

Is it *proper* for Attorney to represent Wife in this matter?

A. Yes, if all information relevant to the litigation was received by Attorney in the presence of both Husband and Wife.

B. Yes, if there is reason to believe Husband misled both Wife and Attorney at the time of the prior agreement.

C. No, because Attorney had previously acted for both parties in reaching the agreement now in dispute.

D. No, unless Husband is now represented by independent counsel.

Question 16.

Attorney represents Deft, the defendant in a criminal prosecution that has attracted widespread publicity. After the indictment was returned, but before arraignment, Attorney was interviewed and, in response to reporters' questions, stated:

I. where Deft was arrested.

II. the nature of the specific charges contained in the indictment.

III. that Deft denied the charges against him and would plead not guilty at his arraignment.

Is Attorney *subject to discipline* for making any of the above statements?

A. No.

B. Yes, for statement III only.

C. Yes, for statements I and II, but not III.

D. Yes, for statements II and III, but not I.

Question 17.

Alpha and Beta are members of the bar in the same community but have never practiced together. Beta is a candidate in a contested election for judicial office. Beta is opposed by Delta, another lawyer in the community. Alpha believes Beta is better qualified than Delta for the judiciary and is supporting Beta's candidacy.

Which of the following would be *proper* for Alpha?

I. Solicit public endorsements for Beta's candidacy by other attorneys in the community who know Beta and are likely to appear before Beta if Beta becomes a judge

II. Solicit contributions to Beta's campaign committee from other attorneys in the community who are likely to appear before Beta if Beta becomes a judge

III. Publicly oppose the candidacy of Delta

A. I only

B. I and II, but not III

C. I and III, but not II

D. I, II, and III

Question 18.

Attorney advertises on the local television station. In the advertisements, a professional actor says:

> "Do you need a lawyer? Call Attorney—her telephone number is area code 555-555-5555. Her fees might be lower than you think."

Attorney approved the prerecorded advertisement and is keeping in her office files a copy of the recording of the actual transmission and a record of when each transmission was made.

Is the advertisement *proper*?

A. Yes.

B. No, unless Attorney's fees are lower than those generally charged in the area where she practices.

C. No, because she used a professional actor for the television advertisement.

D. No, if she makes a charge for the initial consultation.

Questions 19–20 are based on the following fact situation.

Deft, who has been indicted for auto theft, is represented by Attorney. Prosecutor reasonably believes that Deft committed the offense, but, because of Deft's youth, it is in the interest of justice to permit Deft to plead guilty to the lesser offense of "joy-riding" in return for an agreement by Prosecutor to recommend probation. Prosecutor has so advised Attorney, but Attorney told Prosecutor she would not plea bargain and would insist on a jury trial. Attorney informed Deft of Prosecutor's offer and advised Deft not to accept it. Deft followed

Attorney's advice. Attorney is a candidate for public office, and Prosecutor suspects that Attorney is insisting on a trial of the case to secure publicity for herself.

Question 19.

Which of the following would be *proper* for Prosecutor?

  I. Send a member of his staff who is not a lawyer to consult with Deft

 II. Move the trial court to dismiss the indictment and accept a new complaint charging the offense of "joy-riding"

III. Proceed to trial on the indictment and prosecute the case vigorously

A. II only

B. III only

C. I and II, but not III

D. II and III, but not I

Question 20.

Assume for the purposes of this question ONLY that Deft was tried, convicted, and sentenced to prison for two years.

Should Prosecutor report to the disciplinary authority his suspicions about Attorney's conduct of the case?

A. Yes, because Deft suffered a detriment from Attorney's refusal to plea bargain.

B. Yes, if Attorney in fact received widespread publicity as a result of the trial.

C. No, unless Prosecutor has knowledge that Attorney's refusal to plea bargain was due to personal motives.

D. No, if Attorney zealously and competently represented Deft at the trial.

Question 21.

Driver consulted Attorney and asked Attorney to represent Driver, who was being prosecuted for driving while intoxicated in a jurisdiction in which there is an increased penalty for a second offense. Driver told Attorney that his driver's license had been obtained under an assumed name because his prior license had been suspended for driving while under the influence of alcohol. Driver asked Attorney not to disclose Driver's true name during the course of the representation and told Attorney that, if called as a witness, he would give his assumed name. Attorney informed Driver that, in order properly to defend the case, Attorney must call Driver as a witness.

Attorney called Driver as a witness and, in response to Attorney's question "What is your name?", Driver gave his assumed name and not his true name.

Is Attorney *subject to discipline?*

A. Yes, because Attorney knowingly used false testimony.

B. Yes, if Driver committed a felony when he obtained the driver's license under an assumed name.

C. No, because Attorney's knowledge of Driver's true name was obtained during the course of representation.

D. No, unless Driver's true name is an issue in the proceeding.

Question 22.

Attorney represents Client, a plaintiff in a personal injury action. Wit was an eyewitness to the accident. Wit lives about 500 miles distant from the city where the case will be tried. Attorney interviewed Wit and determined that Wit's testimony would be favorable for Client. Wit asked Attorney to pay Wit, in addition to the statutory witness fees while attending the trial, the following:

  I. Reimbursement for actual travel expenses while attending the trial

 II. Reimbursement for lost wages while present at the trial

III. An amount equal to 5% of any recovery in the matter

If Attorney agrees to pay Wit the above, for which, if any, is Attorney *subject to discipline?*

A. III only

B. II and III, but not I

C. I, II, and III

D. Neither I, nor II, nor III

Question 23.

Judge is a judge of the trial court in City. Judge has served for many years as a director of a charitable organization that maintains a camp for disadvantaged children. The organization has never been involved in litigation. Judge has not received any compensation for her services. The charity has decided to sponsor a public testimonial dinner in Judge's honor. As part of the occasion, the local bar association intends to commission and present to Judge her portrait at a cost of $4,000.

The money to pay for the portrait will come from a "public testimonial fund" that will be raised by the City Bar Association from contributions of lawyers who are members of the association and who practice in the courts of City.

Is it *proper* for Judge to accept the gift of the portrait?

A. Yes, because the gift is incident to a public testimonial for Judge.

B. Yes, because Judge did not receive compensation for her services to the charitable organization.

C. No, because the cost of the gift exceeds $1,000.

D. No, because the funds for the gift are contributed by lawyers who practice in the courts of City.

Question 24.

Three lawyers, Alpha, Beta, and Delta, formed a partnership to practice law with offices in both State First and State Second. Alpha is admitted to practice only in State First, Beta is admitted to practice only in State Second, and Delta is admitted to practice in both States First and Second. The following letterhead is on stationery used by their offices in both states:

**Alpha, Beta, and Delta
Attorneys at Law**

100 State Street
City, State First
(200)555–5555

200 Bank Building
City, State Second
(202)555–5555

Attorney Alpha
Admitted to practice only
in State First

Attorney Beta
Admitted to practice only
in State Second

Attorney Delta
Admitted to practice
in States First and Second

Are the members of the partnership *subject to discipline?*

A. No, because the letterhead states the jurisdictions in which each partner is admitted.

B. Yes, because there is no jurisdiction in which both Alpha and Beta are admitted to practice.

C. Yes, because the firm name used by each office contains the name of a lawyer not admitted to practice in that jurisdiction.

D. Yes, unless Delta actively practices law in both States First and Second.

Question 25.

Attorney, who had represented Testator for many years, prepared Testator's will and acted as one of the two subscribing witnesses to its execution. The will gave 90% of Testator's estate to Testator's housekeeper and 10% to Testator's son and sole heir, Son. Upon Testator's death one year later, Executor, the executor named in the will, asked Attorney to represent him in probating the will and administering the estate. At that time Executor informed Attorney that Son had notified him that he would contest the probate of the will on the grounds that Testator lacked the required mental capacity at the time the will was executed. Attorney believes that Testator was fully competent at all times and will so testify, if called as a witness. The other subscribing witness to Testator's will predeceased Testator.

Is it *proper* for Attorney to represent Executor in the probate of the will?

A. Yes, because Attorney is the sole surviving witness to the execution of the will.

B. Yes, because Attorney's testimony will support the validity of the will.

C. No, because Attorney will be called to testify on a contested issue of fact.

D. No, because Attorney will be representing an interest adverse to Testator's heir at law.

Question 26.

Attorney, after being sued groundlessly for malpractice by a disgruntled former client, instituted the practice of conducting a final interview with each client whose work Attorney had completed. Attorney informed the client that the purpose of the interview was to explain to the client's satisfaction all action taken on the client's behalf. After Attorney obtained the client's consent to do so, the interview was recorded on tape, and the tape was placed in the client's closed file. At the interview, Attorney reviewed all matters in the client's file, explained each item, answered the client's questions, and described the choices Attorney had made in the case and the reasons for each of the decisions. At the end of the interview, Attorney asked these questions: "Do you fully understand the work I have done for you? Do you have any questions you want to ask me?"

Is Attorney *subject to discipline* for this practice?

A. Yes, if Attorney is attempting to preserve evidence relevant to a possible malpractice claim.

B. Yes, because Attorney is acting adversely to the client before the lawyer-client relationship has been terminated.

C. No, because the interview was conducted after Attorney had completed the client's work.

D. No, if Attorney fully explained in good faith all items in the file.

Question 27.

Plaintiff and Defendant are next-door neighbors and bitter personal enemies. Plaintiff is suing Defendant over an alleged trespass. Each party believes, in good faith, in the correctness of his position. Plaintiff is represented by Attorney Alpha, and Defendant is represented by Attorney Beta. After Plaintiff had retained Alpha, he told Alpha: "I do not want you to grant any delays or courtesies to Defendant or his lawyer. I want you to insist on every technicality."

Alpha has served Beta with a demand to answer written interrogatories. Beta, because of the illness of his secretary, has asked Alpha for a five-day extension of time within which to answer them.

Is Alpha *subject to discipline* if she grants Beta's request for a five-day extension?

A. Yes, because Alpha is acting contrary to her client's instructions.

B. Yes, unless Alpha first informs Plaintiff of the request and obtains Plaintiff's consent to grant it.

C. No, unless granting the extension would prejudice Plaintiff's rights.

D. No, because Beta was not at fault in causing the delay.

Question 28.

Attorneys Alpha and Beta had been political opponents. Alpha was elected to the state legislature after a bitter race in which Beta had managed the campaign of Alpha's opponent. Alpha had publicly blamed Beta at that time for what Alpha reasonably believed were illegal and unethical campaign practices and later had publicly objected to Beta's appointment as a judge.

Alpha represented Client in a widely publicized case tried in Judge Beta's court. At the conclusion of the trial, Beta ruled against Alpha's client. Alpha then held a press conference and said: "All that you reporters have to do is check your files

and you will know what I think about Judge Beta's character and fitness."

Is Alpha *subject to discipline* for making this statement?

A. Yes, if Alpha's statement might lessen confidence in the legal system.

B. Yes, because Alpha's past accusations were unrelated to Beta's legal knowledge.

C. No, because Alpha reasonably believed that the statements about Beta were true.

D. No, if Beta had equal access to the press.

Question 29.

Judge and Attorney were formerly law partners and during their partnership acquired several parcels of real property as co-tenants. After Judge was elected to the trial court in County, she remained a co-tenant with Attorney, but left the management of the properties to Attorney.

Judge's term of office will expire soon and she is opposed for re-election by two members of the bar. Attorney, who has not discussed the matter with Judge, intends to make a substantial contribution to Judge's campaign for re-election.

Judge is one of fifteen judges sitting as trial court judges in County.

Is Attorney *subject to discipline* if Attorney contributes $10,000 to Judge's re-election campaign?

A. Yes, if Attorney frequently represents clients in cases tried in the trial court of County.

B. Yes, because Judge and Attorney have not discussed the matter of a campaign contribution.

C. No, if the contribution is made to a campaign committee organized to support Judge's re-election.

D. No, because Attorney and Judge have a long-standing personal and business relationship.

Question 30.

Alpha, a member of the bar, placed a printed flyer in the booth of each artist exhibiting works at a county fair. The face of the flyer contained the following information:

"I, Alpha, am an attorney, with offices in 800 Bank Building, telephone (555)555–5555. I have a J.D. degree from State Law School and an M.A. degree in fine arts from State University. My practice includes representing artists in negotiating contracts between artists and dealers and protecting artists' interests. You can find me in the van parked at the fair entrance."

All factual information on the face of the flyer was correct. There was a retainer agreement on the back of the flyer. At the entrance to the fair, Alpha parked a van with a sign that read "Alpha—Attorney at Law."

For which, if any, of the following is Alpha *subject to discipline?*

I. Placing copies of the flyer in the booth of each artist

II. Including a retainer agreement on the back of the flyer

III. Parking the van with the sign on it at the fair entrance

A. III only

B. I and II, but not III

C. I, II, and III

D. Neither I, nor II, nor III

Question 31.

Witness was subpoenaed to appear and testify at a state legislative committee hearing. Witness retained Attorney to represent her at the hearing. During the hearing, Attorney, reasonably believing that it was in Witness's best interest not to answer, advised Witness not to answer certain questions on the grounds that Witness had a constitutional right not to answer. The committee chairperson directed Witness to answer and cautioned her that refusal to answer was a misdemeanor and that criminal prosecution would be instituted if she did not answer.

Upon Attorney's advice, Witness persisted in her refusal to answer. Witness was subsequently convicted for her refusal to answer.

Is Attorney *subject to discipline?*

A. Yes, because his advice to Witness was not legally sound.

B. Yes, because Witness, in acting on Attorney's advice, committed a crime.

C. No, if the offense Witness committed did not involve moral turpitude.

D. No, if Attorney reasonably believed Witness had a legal right to refuse to answer the questions.

Question 32.

Attorney had been representing Client for several months in a matter involving the ownership of some antique jewelry. Client claimed he purchased the jewelry for his wife with his own funds. Partner, Client's business partner, claimed the jewelry was a partnership purchase in which he, Partner, had a one-half interest. While the matter was pending, Client brought a valuable antique jewelry box to Attorney's office and said:

"Keep this in your vault for me. I bought it before I went into business with Partner. Don't tell him or anyone else about it until my matter with Partner is settled."

Later that same day, a police officer, who was in Attorney's office on another matter, saw the jewelry box when a clerk opened the vault to put in some papers. The police officer recognized it as one that had recently been stolen from a collector. Attorney was arrested and later charged with receiving stolen property.

Is Attorney *subject to discipline* if Attorney reveals that Client brought the box to her office?

A. Yes, because Client instructed Attorney not to tell anyone about the jewelry box.

B. Yes, if the disclosure would be detrimental to Client's interests.

C. No, because the jewelry box was not involved in the dispute between Client and Partner.

D. No, if the disclosure is necessary to enable Attorney to defend against a criminal charge.

Question 33.

Attorney Alpha currently represents Builder, a building contractor and the plaintiff in a suit to recover for breach of a contract to build a house. Builder also has pending before the zoning commission a petition to rezone property Builder owns. Builder is represented by Attorney Beta in the zoning matter.

Neighbor, who owns property adjoining that of Builder, has asked Alpha to represent Neighbor in opposing Builder's petition for rezoning. Neighbor knows that Alpha represents Builder in the contract action.

Is it *proper* for Alpha to represent Neighbor in the zoning matter?

A. Yes, if there is no common issue of law or fact between the two matters.

B. Yes, because one matter is a judicial proceeding and the other is an administrative proceeding.

C. No, because Alpha is currently representing Builder in the contract action.

D. No, if there is a possibility that both matters will be appealed to the same court.

Question 34.

Attorney represented Plaintiff, the plaintiff in an automobile accident case against Defendant. The accident occurred at the intersection of two rural roads; the intersection was marked by four-way stop signs. Plaintiff had told Attorney that he arrived at the intersection before Defendant and that Plaintiff came to a full stop before entering the intersection. Plaintiff said that Defendant did not slow down but proceeded into the intersection without stopping and hit the side of Plaintiff's car.

Attorney learned from highway patrol records that Wit, who was a disinterested witness, had called the patrol and reported that she had seen the collision between Plaintiff and Defendant. The highway patrol records did not disclose the substance of Wit's observations. In fact, Wit's testimony would support Plaintiff's version of the accident.

Attorney believed that Plaintiff's testimony would be persuasive and did not interview Wit. At the trial, Defendant testified that he had entered the intersection first and that Plaintiff ran the stop sign. The jury believed Defendant and returned a verdict in his favor.

Is Attorney *subject to discipline?*

A. Yes, because Attorney's preparation for trial was inadequate.

B. Yes, unless Wit was not subject to subpoena.

C. No, because the highway patrol records did not disclose the substance of Wit's testimony.

D. No, if Attorney believed that Plaintiff's testimony would be sufficient to establish Plaintiff's case.

Question 35.

Client consulted Attorney and asked Attorney to represent him on a claim for damages for personal injuries. Attorney told Client that she would not accept employment unless Client executed a retainer agreement containing the following provision:

> "Attorney has full authority to reject any settlement offer if, in Attorney's opinion, it is inadequate and to accept a settlement offer, provided the net recovery to Client, after payment of Attorney's fee and all costs and expenses of litigation, appears reasonable to Attorney."

Was it *proper* for Attorney to require execution of the retainer agreement as a condition to employment?

A. Yes, if Client was fully advised of the effect of the provision.

B. Yes, because Attorney is in a better position than Client to evaluate a settlement offer.

C. No, because Client was asked to surrender his right to accept or reject the settlement offer.

D. No, unless Attorney's fee is a determined amount and not contingent on the amount of recovery.

Question 36.

Alpha and Beta practiced law under the firm name of Alpha and Beta. When Beta died, Alpha did not change the firm name. Thereafter, Alpha entered into an arrangement with another attorney, Gamma. Gamma pays Alpha a certain sum each month for office space and use of Alpha's law library and for secretarial services, but Alpha and Gamma each has his own clients, and neither participates in the representation of the other's clients or shares in fees paid. On the entrance to the suite of offices shared by Alpha and Gamma are the words "Law Firm of Alpha, Beta, and Gamma."

Is Alpha *subject to discipline?*

A. Yes, because Beta was deceased when Alpha made the arrangement with Gamma.

B. Yes, because Gamma is not a partner of Alpha.

C. No, because Alpha and Beta were partners at the time of Beta's death.

D. No, because Gamma is paying a share of the rent and office expenses.

Question 37.

Attorney was employed as a lawyer by the state Environmental Control Commission (ECC) for ten years. During the last two years of her employment, Attorney spent most of her time in the preparation, trial, and appeal of a case involving the discharge by Deftco of industrial effluent into a river in the state. The judgment in the case, which is now final, contained a finding of a continuing and knowing discharge of a dangerous substance into a major stream by Deftco and assessed a penalty of $25,000.

The governing statute also provides for private actions for damages by persons injured by the discharge of the effluent.

Attorney recently left the employment of ECC and went into private practice. Three landowners have brought private damage actions against Deftco. They claim their truck farms were contaminated because they irrigated them with water that contained effluent from dangerous chemicals discharged by Deftco. Deftco has asked Attorney to represent it in defense of the three pending actions.

Is Attorney *subject to discipline* if she represents Deftco in these actions?

A. Yes, unless the judgment in the prior case is determinative of Deftco's liability.

B. Yes, because Attorney had substantial responsibility in the matter while employed by ECC.

C. No, because Attorney has acquired special competence in the matter.

D. No, if all information acquired by Attorney while representing ECC is now a matter of public record.

Question 38.

Attorney Alpha is skilled in trying personal injury cases. Alpha accepted the representation of Plaintiff in a personal injury case on a contingent fee basis. While preparing the case for trial, Alpha realized that the direct examination and cross-examination of the medical experts would involve medical issues with which Alpha was not familiar and, as a consequence, Alpha might not be able to represent Plaintiff competently.

Without informing Plaintiff, Alpha consulted Beta, who is both a lawyer and a medical doctor and who is a recognized specialist in the care and treatment of injuries of the type sustained by Plaintiff. Alpha and Beta agreed that Beta would participate in the trial to the limited extent of conducting the direct examination and cross-examination of the medical experts and that Alpha would divide the fee in proportion to the services performed and the responsibility assumed by each.

Was the arrangement between Alpha and Beta *proper?*

A. Yes, because the fee to be paid by Plaintiff was not increased by reason of Beta's association.

B. Yes, because the fee would be divided in proportion to the services performed and the responsibility assumed by each.

C. No, because Plaintiff was not informed of the association of Beta.

D. No, unless, upon conclusion of the matter, Alpha provides Plaintiff with a written statement setting forth the method of determining both the fee and the division of the fee with Beta.

Question 39.

Attorney was retained by Defendant to represent him in a paternity suit. Aunt, Defendant's aunt, believed the suit was unfounded and motivated by malice. Aunt sent Attorney a check for $1,000 and asked Attorney to apply it to the payment of Defendant's fee. Aunt told Attorney not to tell Defendant of the payment because "Defendant is too proud to accept gifts, but I know he really needs the money."

Is it *proper* for Attorney to accept Aunt's check?

A. Yes, if Aunt does not attempt to influence Attorney's conduct of the case.

B. Yes, if Attorney's charges to Defendant are reduced accordingly.

C. No, because Aunt is attempting to finance litigation to which she is not a party.

D. No, unless Attorney first informs Defendant and obtains Defendant's consent to retain the payment.

Question 40.

Attorney represents Client, a famous politician, in an action against Newspaper for libel. The case has attracted much publicity, and a jury trial has been demanded. After one of the pretrial hearings, as Attorney left the courthouse, news reporters interviewed Attorney. In responding to questions, Attorney truthfully stated:

> "The judge has upheld our right to subpoena the reporter involved, identified in our motion as Repo, and question her on her mental impressions when she prepared the article."

Is Attorney *subject to discipline* for making this statement?

A. Yes, because Attorney identified a prospective witness in the case.

B. Yes, because prospective jurors might learn of Attorney's remarks.

C. No, because the statement relates to a matter of public record.

D. No, because the trial has not commenced.

Question 41.

Attorney Alpha has been employed as an assistant prosecutor in the district attorney's office during the time that an investigation of Deft was being conducted by that office. Alpha took no part in the investigation and had no knowledge of the facts other than those disclosed in the press. Two months ago, Alpha left the district attorney's office and formed a partnership with Attorney Beta.

Last week, Deft was indicted for offenses allegedly disclosed by the prior investigation. Deft asked Alpha to represent him. Alpha declined to do so, but suggested Beta.

Is Beta *subject to discipline* if Beta represents Deft?

A. Yes, because Alpha was employed in the district attorney's office while the investigation of Deft was being conducted.

B. Yes, unless the district attorney's office is promptly notified and consents to the representation.

C. No, unless Alpha participates in the representation or shares in the fee.

D. No, because Alpha had no responsibility for or knowledge of the facts of the investigation of Deft.

Question 42.

The following advertisement appeared in daily newspapers published in City, where Legal Associates Group (LAG) maintains its offices. The use of the trade name Legal Associates Group is permitted in the jurisdiction. City is located in a jurisdiction that certifies legal specialists.

> Do you need a lawyer who specializes in handling the kind of problem you face?
>
> Legal Associates Group (LAG) will put you in touch with the right lawyer. We can furnish you with a lawyer on our staff who is a specialist in your kind of legal problem. And, the fee for our first consultation is only $15.

Consumer Law	Negligence
Criminal	Wills
Family	Real Estate

LAG

Telephone: 555–5555 (24 hours—day or night)

Is this advertisement *proper?*

A. Yes, if each of the lawyers on the staff of LAG limits his or her practice to one of the named areas of law.

B. Yes, if a prospective client, during the first consultation, is given an estimate of the fee to be charged.

C. No, because the advertisement does not contain any fee schedule for services rendered after the first consultation.

D. No, unless there are lawyers on the staff of LAG who are certified as specialists in the listed areas by the appropriate authority in the jurisdiction.

Question 43.

Attorney limits her practice to criminal defense. When she is consulted by a prospective client who is not indigent, Attorney informs the prospective client, in advance of accepting employment, of the amount of her fee. Her fee is fixed and is based on the difficulty of the case and a reasonable hourly charge for the estimated time that she will spend in the preparation for trial and actual trial of the case. Attorney will not accept the employment unless the prospective client agrees to the fee set by Attorney, pays at least 50% of the fee in advance, and gives a negotiable promissory note with full collateral to secure payment of the balance of the fee.

Is Attorney's conduct *proper?*

A. Yes, because there is no attorney-client relationship at the time Attorney sets her fee.

B. Yes, if the amount of the fee fixed by Attorney is reasonable.

C. No, because Attorney required at least 50% of the fee in advance of rendering service.

D. No, because Attorney will be acquiring a security interest in the property of a client in a criminal matter.

Question 44.

Deft was on trial for the murder of Victim, who was killed during a barroom brawl. In the course of closing arguments to the jury, Prosecutor said, "Deft's whole defense is based on the testimony of Wit, who said that Victim attacked Deft with a knife before Deft struck him. No other witness testified to such an attack by Victim. I don't believe Wit was telling the truth, and I don't think you believe him either."

Was Prosecutor's statement *proper?*

A. Yes, if Prosecutor accurately stated the testimony in the case.

B. Yes, if Prosecutor, in fact, believed Wit was lying.

C. No, because Prosecutor alluded to the beliefs of the jurors.

D. No, because Prosecutor asserted his personal opinion about Wit's credibility.

Question 45.

Attorney, representing Plaintiff, failed to appear at the hearing of a motion to set the case for trial. At the request of Defendant's lawyer, Judge dismissed the case for failure to proceed in a timely manner. Six months later, Attorney filed a motion to set aside the dismissal, which was denied.

Should Judge report to the disciplinary authority Attorney's failure to appear at the motion to set the case for trial?

A. Yes, if Judge believes that Attorney's failure to appear was due to incompetence.

B. Yes, because Attorney's failure to appear resulted in Plaintiff's case being dismissed.

C. No, unless Judge is reasonably certain Plaintiff would have prevailed at a trial.

D. No, unless Attorney's conduct was a contempt of court.

Question 46.

Commission, the State Waterways Commission, announced that it would conduct a hearing to consider a proposed plan for straightening a small river. Several landowners, whose lands abut the river, objected to the plan. At a meeting of the landowners, Baker, one of the landowners, offered to have her lawyer, Attorney, appear on behalf of all the landowners and agreed to pay Attorney's fee. All the landowners present agreed to Baker's proposal.

Attorney appeared at the hearing. At that time, Commission proposed a modification in the plan. This modification would reduce the risk of flooding Baker's land, while increasing the risk for the other landowners who had been present at the previous meeting. Attorney supported the modified plan, and it was approved by Commission.

Was Attorney's conduct *proper?*

A. Yes, if, in Attorney's professional judgment, the modified plan was in the public interest.

B. Yes, because the modified plan was proposed by Commission and not by Attorney.

C. No, because Attorney did not adequately represent the interests of all the landowners.

D. No, unless failure to support the modified plan would cause Baker substantial hardship.

Question 47.

Attorney represented Deft, who was charged with arson, at Deft's trial. Deft was convicted. Thereafter, Attorney received information which, if true, established that the key prosecution witness had given perjured testimony. Attorney, with Deft's

knowledge but using Attorney's own funds, employed a private investigator. Attorney instructed the investigator to gain the confidence of the prosecution witness in an attempt to get that witness to admit that he had given perjured testimony at Deft's trial.

Is Attorney *subject to discipline* for so employing and instructing the investigator?

A. Yes, unless Attorney first advises the court of the information received.

B. Yes, because Attorney is arranging to have a prosecution witness interviewed.

C. No, because Attorney is properly representing the interests of his client.

D. No, unless Attorney personally communicated with the witness.

Question 48.

Attorney represents Client, plaintiff in a civil action that was filed a year ago and is about to be set for trial. Client informed Attorney that he could be available at any time during the months of October, November, and December. In discussing possible trial dates with opposing counsel and the court clerk, Attorney was advised that a trial date on October 5 was available and that the next available trial date would be December 10. Without first consulting Client, Attorney requested the December 10 trial date because she was representing Deft, the defendant in a felony criminal trial that was set for October 20 and she wanted as much time as possible to prepare for that trial.

Was it *proper* for Attorney to agree to the December trial date without obtaining Client's consent?

A. Yes, unless Client will be prejudiced by the delay.

B. Yes, because a criminal trial takes precedence over a civil trial.

C. No, because Attorney should manage her calendar so that her cases can be tried promptly.

D. No, unless Attorney was court-appointed counsel in the criminal case.

Question 49.

Able, Baker, and Carter had been indicted for the armed robbery of the cashier of a grocery store. Together, Able and Baker met with Attorney and asked Attorney to represent them. Attorney then interviewed Able and Baker separately. Each told Attorney that the robbery had been committed by Carter while Able and Baker sat in Carter's car outside the store, that Carter had said he needed some cigarettes, and that each knew nothing of

Carter's plan to rob the cashier. Attorney agreed to represent both Able and Baker. One week prior to the trial date, Able told Attorney that he wanted to plea bargain and that he was prepared to turn state's evidence and testify that Baker had loaned Carter the gun Carter used in the robbery. Able also said that he and Baker had shared in the proceeds of the robbery with Carter.

It is *proper* for Attorney to:

A. request court approval to withdraw as lawyer for both Able and Baker.

B. continue to represent Baker and, with Able's consent and court approval, withdraw as Able's lawyer.

C. continue to represent Able and, with Baker's consent and court approval, withdraw as Baker's lawyer.

D. continue to represent Able and Baker, but not call Able as a witness.

Question 50.

While presiding over the trial of a highly publicized antitrust case, *ABCO v. DEFO,* Judge received in the mail a lengthy letter from Attorney, a local lawyer. The letter discussed the law applicable to *ABCO v. DEFO.* Judge knew that Attorney did not represent either party. Judge read the letter and, without mentioning its receipt to the lawyers in the pending case, filed the letter in his general file on antitrust litigation.

Later, after reading the trial briefs in *ABCO v. DEFO,* Judge concluded that Attorney's letter better explained the law applicable to the case pending before him than either of the trial briefs. Judge followed Attorney's reasoning in formulating his decision.

Was it *proper* for Judge to consider Attorney's letter?

A. Yes, because Judge did not initiate the communication with Attorney.

B. Yes, if Attorney did not represent any client whose interests could be affected by the outcome.

C. No, unless Judge, prior to rendering his decision, communicated its contents to all counsel and gave them an opportunity to respond.

D. No, because Attorney is not of record as counsel in the case.

MPRE SAMPLE ANSWER SHEET

1 Ⓐ Ⓑ Ⓒ Ⓓ	15 Ⓐ Ⓑ Ⓒ Ⓓ	29 Ⓐ Ⓑ Ⓒ Ⓓ	43 Ⓐ Ⓑ Ⓒ Ⓓ
2 Ⓐ Ⓑ Ⓒ Ⓓ	16 Ⓐ Ⓑ Ⓒ Ⓓ	30 Ⓐ Ⓑ Ⓒ Ⓓ	44 Ⓐ Ⓑ Ⓒ Ⓓ
3 Ⓐ Ⓑ Ⓒ Ⓓ	17 Ⓐ Ⓑ Ⓒ Ⓓ	31 Ⓐ Ⓑ Ⓒ Ⓓ	45 Ⓐ Ⓑ Ⓒ Ⓓ
4 Ⓐ Ⓑ Ⓒ Ⓓ	18 Ⓐ Ⓑ Ⓒ Ⓓ	32 Ⓐ Ⓑ Ⓒ Ⓓ	46 Ⓐ Ⓑ Ⓒ Ⓓ
5 Ⓐ Ⓑ Ⓒ Ⓓ	19 Ⓐ Ⓑ Ⓒ Ⓓ	33 Ⓐ Ⓑ Ⓒ Ⓓ	47 Ⓐ Ⓑ Ⓒ Ⓓ
6 Ⓐ Ⓑ Ⓒ Ⓓ	20 Ⓐ Ⓑ Ⓒ Ⓓ	34 Ⓐ Ⓑ Ⓒ Ⓓ	48 Ⓐ Ⓑ Ⓒ Ⓓ
7 Ⓐ Ⓑ Ⓒ Ⓓ	21 Ⓐ Ⓑ Ⓒ Ⓓ	35 Ⓐ Ⓑ Ⓒ Ⓓ	49 Ⓐ Ⓑ Ⓒ Ⓓ
8 Ⓐ Ⓑ Ⓒ Ⓓ	22 Ⓐ Ⓑ Ⓒ Ⓓ	36 Ⓐ Ⓑ Ⓒ Ⓓ	50 Ⓐ Ⓑ Ⓒ Ⓓ
9 Ⓐ Ⓑ Ⓒ Ⓓ	23 Ⓐ Ⓑ Ⓒ Ⓓ	37 Ⓐ Ⓑ Ⓒ Ⓓ	
10 Ⓐ Ⓑ Ⓒ Ⓓ	24 Ⓐ Ⓑ Ⓒ Ⓓ	38 Ⓐ Ⓑ Ⓒ Ⓓ	
11 Ⓐ Ⓑ Ⓒ Ⓓ	25 Ⓐ Ⓑ Ⓒ Ⓓ	39 Ⓐ Ⓑ Ⓒ Ⓓ	
12 Ⓐ Ⓑ Ⓒ Ⓓ	26 Ⓐ Ⓑ Ⓒ Ⓓ	40 Ⓐ Ⓑ Ⓒ Ⓓ	
13 Ⓐ Ⓑ Ⓒ Ⓓ	27 Ⓐ Ⓑ Ⓒ Ⓓ	41 Ⓐ Ⓑ Ⓒ Ⓓ	
14 Ⓐ Ⓑ Ⓒ Ⓓ	28 Ⓐ Ⓑ Ⓒ Ⓓ	42 Ⓐ Ⓑ Ⓒ Ⓓ	

[G7402]

ANSWER KEY
FOR MPRE SAMPLE QUESTIONS

1. A	14. B	27. C	39. D
2. D	15. C	28. C	40. C
3. A	16. A	29. C	41. D
4. B	17. D	30. D	42. D
5. B	18. A	31. D	43. B
6. B	19. D	32. D	44. D
7. C	20. C	33. C	45. A
8. C	21. A	34. A	46. C
9. B	22. A	35. C	47. C
10. B	23. A	36. B	48. A
11. D	24. A	37. B	49. A
12. B	25. C	38. C	50. C
13. D	26. D		

GUIDELINES FOR TAKING THE EXAMINATION

Please read the following guidelines carefully. They are designed to help you do your best on the Multistate Professional Responsibility Examination.

1. Listen closely to all directions. Do not hesitate to ask questions if you do not understand what you are to do.

2. Be very precise in marking your answer sheet. Be sure that you blacken the appropriate ovals and that you completely erase any incorrect marks.

3. Your responses must be marked on the answer sheet if you are to receive credit for them.

4. Keep your answer sheet near your test booklet so you can mark answers quickly without moving either the booklet or the answer sheet.

5. Read each question carefully. Pay special attention to such key words or phrases as *must, subject to discipline, should, may, proper,* and *subject to liability for malpractice.* They are crucial in determining the correct answer.

6. Answer every question. There is no penalty for guessing, so use any clues you have in choosing an answer.

7. When you are unsure of the correct answer to a question, first eliminate every wrong answer you can. Each wrong answer eliminated improves your chances of selecting the correct answer.

8. Do not spend too much time on one question. If a question is too hard for you, choose a reasonable answer and go on to the next question. Work quickly but carefully.

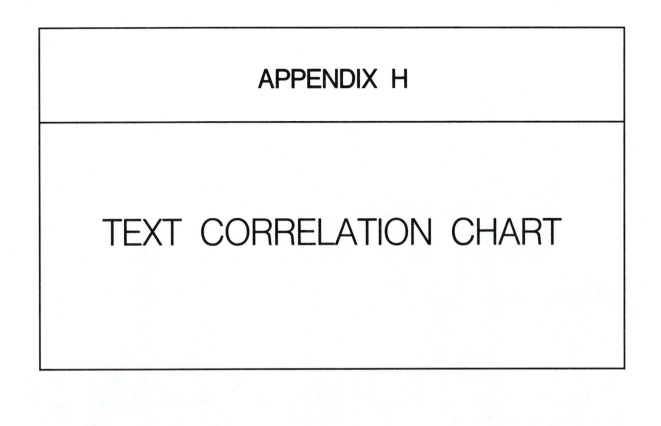

APPENDIX H

TEXT CORRELATION CHART

Topic in Outline	Aronson, Devine & Fisch, Problems, Cases and Materials in Professional Responsibility	Brown & Dauer, Planning by Lawyers	Countryman, Finman & Schneyer, The Lawyer in Modern Society (2d ed.)	Gillers & Dorsen, Regulation of Lawyers: Problems of Law and Ethics (2d ed.)	Hazard & Koniak, The Law and Ethics of Lawyering	Kaufman, Problems in Professional Responsibility (2d ed.)
One: Defining Disciplinable Conduct	Ch. 1, 2A		Ch. 1, 9, § B	Ch. 1	Ch. X	Ch. 1, 10
Two: The Lawyer's Obligation to Support Bar Admissions and the Disciplinary System	Ch. 2C, 2D		Ch. 8, §§ A–D; 9	Ch. 4A, 5D, 13B	Ch. X(A); (B)	Ch. 7D, 10, 11
Three: The Lawyer's Obligation to the Client						
I Confidentiality	Ch. 4	Passim	Ch. 2	Ch. 8A	Ch. IV	Ch. 3, 4
II Conflicts	Ch. 5		Ch. 2	Ch. 11, 12, 13D, 13E	Ch. VII, VIII, IX	Ch. 2, 5A
III Competence	Ch. 3E		Ch. 2, § A	Ch. 4C, 4D, 5A, 5B, 5C, 5E	Ch. III	Ch. 11
IV Fees	Ch. 3D	Ch. 4, § B	Ch. 2, § C	Ch. 3	Ch. VI(B)	Ch. 8A
V Acceptance & Termination	Ch. 3A, 3B, 3F		Ch. 2	Ch. 8B, 8C	Ch. VI(A); (E)	Ch. 7A
VI Trust Funds	Ch. 3C		Ch. 2		Ch. VI(D)	
Four: The Lawyer's Obligations as a Member of a Firm	Ch. 2B	Ch. 4, §§ C, D	Ch. 5, § B	Ch. 4B, 4E	Ch. X(C)	Ch. 10B
Five: The Lawyer's Obligations Regarding Advertising and Solicitation	Ch. 6	Ch. 5	Ch. 5, § A; 8, § E	Ch. 2, 4F, 6	Ch. VIII(C)	Ch. 8B, 9
Six: The Lawyer's Obligation not to Misuse the Office of Government	Ch. 7A(2)			Ch. 8D, 10A, 10E, 10F, 10G	Ch. VIII(C); IX(C)	Ch. 5B, 6A
Seven: The Lawyer's Obligations as an Advocate	Ch. 7		Ch. 3, § B	Ch. 8D, 9, 10	Ch. V	Ch. 6, 7

Topic in Outline	Aronson, Devine & Fisch, Problems, Cases and Materials in Professional Responsibility	Brown & Dauer, Planning by Lawyers	Countryman, Finman & Schneyer, The Lawyer in Modern Society (2d ed.)	Gillers & Dorsen, Regulation of Lawyers: Problems of Law and Ethics (2d ed.)	Hazard & Koniak, The Law and Ethics of Lawyering	Kaufman, Problems in Professional Responsibility (2d ed.)
Eight: The Lawyer's Obligations as Adviser	Ch. 7B	Ch. 3, 5	Ch. 3, §§ C, D	Ch. 13A	Ch. VII(B)	Ch. 5C, 5D, 6F, 7B
Nine: The Lawyer's Obligations Regarding Pro Bono Activities	Ch. 6B		Ch. 6, 7, § A	Ch. 13C	Ch. X(D)	Ch. 9
Ten: The Lawyer's Obligation as a Judge	Ch. 8		Ch. 7, § B	Ch. 7B, 13F	Ch. X(E)	Ch. 12

Topic in Outline	Mellinkoff, Lawyers and the System of Justice	Morgan & Rotunda Problems and Materials on Professional Responsibility (5th ed.)	Patterson, Legal Ethics (2d ed.)	Persig & Kirwin, Professional Responsibility (4th ed.)	Redlich, Professional Responsibility (2d ed.)
One: Defining Disciplinable Conduct	Ch. 1	Ch. I	Ch. 1, 2	Ch. 1	
Two: The Lawyer's Obligation to Support Bar Admissions and the Disciplinary System	Ch. 10, § 1; 13	Ch. II	Ch. 17	Ch. 1, 2, § B, 2	
Three: The Lawyer's Obligation to the Client					
I Confidentiality	Ch. 14	Ch. III	Ch. 6	Ch. 3	Problems 2, 4
II Conflicts	Ch. 15	Ch. III, VI, Problem 29; VII, Problems 40, 41	Ch. 5, 20	Ch. 4	Problems 12, 13, 14
III Competence	Ch. 3, 16	Ch. 2	Ch. 4	Ch. 7, § E	
IV Fees	Ch. 5, §§ 1, 2	Ch. III, Problems 7, 8; VII, Problems 37, 39	Ch. 16	Ch. 7, § A	
V Acceptance & Termination	Ch. 5, § 1	Ch. III	Ch. 3	Ch. 7, § B	Problems 1, 3
VI Trust Funds		Ch. III, Problem 9		Ch. 7, § C	
Four: The Lawyer's Obligations as a Member of a Firm	Ch. 5, §§ 4, 6	Ch. VII, Problems 38, 42	Ch. 2	Ch. 2, § C, Ch. 7, § A, 3	
Five: The Lawyer's Obligations Regarding Advertising and Solicitation	Ch. 5, § 3	Ch. VII	Ch. 16	Ch. 8	
Six: The Lawyer's Obligation not to Misuse the Office of Government	Ch. 9	Ch. IV, Problem 17; V, Problem 26	Ch. 13	Ch. 5, § B; 6, § F	Problems 15, 16, 17
Seven: The Lawyer's Obligations as an Advocate	Ch. 6, 7, 12	Ch. V	Ch. 6, 7, 8, 12	Ch. 6	Problems 4, 5, 6, 7

Topic in Outline	Mellinkoff, Lawyers and the System of Justice	Morgan & Rotunda Problems and Materials on Professional Responsibility (5th ed.)	Patterson, Legal Ethics (2d ed.)	Persig & Kirwin, Professional Responsibility (4th ed.)	Redlich, Professional Responsibility (2d ed.)
Eight: The Lawyer's Obligations as Adviser	Ch. 8	Ch. VI	Ch. 10, 11	Ch. 6, §§ A, B, C, E, J	Problems 8, 9, 10, 11
Nine: The Lawyer's Obligations Regarding Pro Bono Activities	Ch. 5, § 5	Ch. VII, Problem 39	Ch. 15	Ch. 8, § A	Problem 1
Ten: The Lawyer's Obligation as a Judge	Ch. 10, § 1	Ch. VIII	Ch. 14		

Topic in Outline	Schwartz, Lawyers and the Legal Profession (2d ed.)	Schwartz & Wydick, Problems in Legal Ethics (2d ed.)	Shaffer, American Legal Ethics: Text Readings, and Discussion Topics	Sutton & Dzienkowski, Professional Responsibility of Lawyers	Thurman, Phillips & Cheatham, The Legal Profession
One: Defining Disciplinable Conduct		Ch. 2	Ch. 1, 2	Ch. I, II	Ch. 1
Two: The Lawyer's Obligation to Support Bar Admissions and the Disciplinary System		Ch. 2	Ch. 10	Ch. II	Ch. III, XIII
Three: The Lawyer's Obligation to the Client					
I Confidentiality		Ch. 7		Ch. IVB	Ch. XI, XII
II Conflicts	Ch. 6, 7	Ch. 9, 10, 11	Ch. 3, 4	Ch. IVB	Ch. XI, XII
III Competence	Ch. 6	Ch. 6		Ch. IVC	Ch. XI, XII
IV Fees	Ch. 10	Ch. 5		Ch. IVC	Ch. XI, XII
V Acceptance & Termination		Ch. 3		Ch. IIIA; B; IVA; V	Ch. XI, XII
VI Trust Funds		Ch. 5		Ch. IVA	Ch. XI, XII
Four: The Lawyer's Obligations as a Member of a Firm	Ch. 8	Ch. 3(IV), 5	Ch. 6, 7	Ch. IIH	Ch. II, § 2
Five: The Lawyer's Obligations Regarding Advertising and Solicitation	Ch. 9	Ch. 4		Ch. IIIA	Ch. II, § 6
Six: The Lawyer's Obligation not to Misuse the Office of Government	Ch. 6B	Ch. 11, 13(I)(A)		Ch. IVA(4)	Ch. VIII, IX
Seven: The Lawyer's Obligations as an Advocate	Ch. 1, 2, 3	Ch. 8, 12, 13	Ch. 1, 2, 11	Ch. IVC	Ch. VII
Eight: The Lawyer's Obligations as Adviser	Ch. 4, 5		Ch. 5	Ch. IVC	Ch. V, VI

Topic in Outline	Schwartz, Lawyers and the Legal Profession (2d ed.)	Schwartz & Wydick, Problems in Legal Ethics (2d ed.)	Shaffer, American Legal Ethics: Text Readings, and Discussion Topics	Sutton & Dzienkowski, Professional Responsibility of Lawyers	Thurman, Phillips & Cheatham, The Legal Profession
Nine: The Lawyer's Obligations Regarding Pro Bono Activities	Ch. 11, 12, 13	Ch. 3(IV)	Ch. 11	Ch. IIG	Ch. X
Ten: The Lawyer's Obligation as a Judge		Ch. 14		Ch. VII	Ch. XIV

*

APPENDIX I

GLOSSARY

A

ABA Commission on Evaluation of Professional Standards (See, *Kutak Commission*).

ABA Formal Opinion If an ethics opinion written by the ABA Committee on Professional Ethics is called a *Formal Opinion*, it overrules any earlier opinions either Formal or Informal, with which it is necessarily in conflict, whether or not the earlier opinion is specifically mentioned in the later opinion. In contrast, if an opinion is called an *Informal Opinion*, it only overrules earlier Informal Opinions that necessarily conflict with it, whether or not they are specifically mentioned. An Informal Opinion cannot overrule a Formal Opinion. See ABA Formal Opinion 317 (May 23, 1967).

ABA Informal Opinion (See, *ABA Formal Opinion*).

Active Lien (See, *Lien*).

Admonition A term used in the ABA Model Standards for Lawyer Discipline and Disability Proceedings to refer to a "form of private discipline which declares the respondent's conduct to have been improper but does not limit his right to practice."

American Lawyer's Code of Conduct The title of an alternative to the ABA Model Code of Professional Responsibility or the ABA Model Rules of Professional Conduct. This alternative code was prepared under the auspices of the Roscoe Pound–American Trial Lawyers Foundation.

Attorney On a very general level, an attorney is one person (an agent) authorized to act for, or represent, another (the principal). In order for the attorney to practice law, the attorney must be a licensed member of the bar. An attorney is a lawyer.

The word "attorney" is derived from the law-French and means a person to whom one can *turn* for help.

Attorney's Lien (See, *Lien*).

B

Bar Association An association of lawyers admitted to the bar. A bar association may be limited to specialists. Model Code, Definitions (7).

Bar, Integrated (See, *Integrated Bar*).

Bar, Unified (See, *Integrated Bar*).

Belief A term used in the Model Rules to mean that the "person involved actually supposed the fact in question to be true. A person's belief may be inferred from circumstances." See Model Rules, Terminology 1.

Believes (see, *Belief*).

C

Canons When used in connection with the ABA Model Code of Professional Responsibility, they refer to the titles of the nine divisions of the Model Code. They "are statements of axiomatic norms. . . ." Model Code, Preliminary Statement.

The term "Canons" may also refer to the seven divisions of the ABA Model Code of Judicial Conduct (1972), the ABA Model Code of Judicial Conduct (1990), the ABA Canons of Professional Ethics (1908), or a similar body of ethical guidance.

Charging Lien (See, *Lien*).

Comment (See, *Rules of Professional Conduct*).

Commission, Kutak (See, *Kutak Commission*).

Commission on Evaluation of Professional Standards (See, *Kutak Commission*).

Common Law Lien (See, *Lien*).

Confidence As defined in the Model Code, a confidence is information protected by the attorney-client evidentiary privilege under local law. (See, *Secret*).

Consult A term used in the Model Rules to refer to the "communication of information reasonably sufficient to permit the client to appreciate the significance of the matter in question." See Model Rules, Terminology 2.

Consultation (See, *Consult*).

Continuing Part-time Judge A judge who serves repeatedly on a part-time basis by election or under a continuing appointment, including a retired judge subject to recall who is permitted to practice law. ABA Model Code of Judicial Conduct (1990), Terminology [3]

Counsel, Of (See, *Of Counsel*).

D

De minimis A term used in the ABA Model Code of Judicial Conduct (1990), in, Terminology [5], to signify an "insignificant interest that could not raise reasonable question as to a judge's impartiality."

Differing Interests A term used in the ABA Model Code of Professional Responsibility to include "every interest that will adversely affect either the judgment or the loyalty of a lawyer to a client, whether it be a conflicting, inconsistent, diverse, or other interest." Model Codes, Definitions (1).

Discipline The sanction imposed on a lawyer after a finding or admission of misconduct is referred to as the lawyer's discipline.

Disciplinary Matter A term used in the ABA Model Standards for Lawyer Discipline and Disability Proceedings to refer to "anything involving a lawyer admitted in a jurisdiction under consideration within the discipline and disability system, e.g., complaint, reinstatement proceedings, formal charges."

Disciplinary Rules Those regulations of the ABA Model Code of Professional Responsibility that are called Disciplinary Rules are mandatory in character. They "state the minimum level of conduct below which no lawyer can fall without being subject to disciplinary action." See ABA Model Code, Preliminary Statement. See also, DR 1–102(A) (1).

See, *Rules of Professional Conduct.*

Division of Fee A division of fee is "a single billing to a client covering the fee of two or more lawyers who are not in the same firm." See Rule 1.5, Comment 4.

E

Economic Interest A term used in the ABA Model Code of Judicial Conduct (1990), in Terminology [5], to denote ownership of a more than *de minimis* legal or equitable interest, or a relationship as officer, director, advisor, or other active participant in the affairs of a party, subject to various exceptions.

Esquire Often abbreviated, Esq., it is often used as a title signifying that the holder is a lawyer as in: John Doe, Esq.

Ethical Consideration A term used in the ABA Model Code of Professional Responsibility to refer to statements in the Model Code what are aspirational rather than mandatory. They also "constitute a body of principles upon which the lawyer can rely for guidance in many specific circumstances." See ABA Model Code, Preliminary Statement.

See, *Disciplinary Rules* and *Canons.*

F

Fiduciary A term to refer to a person having duties involving good faith, trust, special confidence, and candor towards another. A fiduciary "includes such relationships as executor, administrator, trustee, and guardian." ABA Code of Judicial Conduct (1972), Canon 3C(3) (b); ABA Model Code of Judicial Conduct (1990), Terminology [7].

A lawyer is also in a fiduciary relationship with the client.

Firm (See, *Law Firm*).

Formal Opinion (See, *ABA Formal Opinion*).

Fraud A term used in the Model Rules to refer to "conduct having a purpose to deceive and not merely negligent misrepresentation or failure to apprise another of relevant information." See Model Rules, Terminology 4.

Fraudulent (See, *Fraud*).

G

General Retainer (See, *Retainer*).

General Counsel A term defined in the Model Code of Professional Responsibility as applying to a lawyer or law firm who is general counsel to a given client only "if he or the firm devotes a substantial amount of professional time in the representation of that client." DR 2–102(A)(4).

H

House Counsel An attorney working full time for one client is typically called the house counsel.

House of Delegates When used in connection with the American Bar Association, the House of Delegates is the body in which is vested the control and administration of the ABA. See ABA Constitution, Art. VI. It was the House of Delegates that approved the final draft of the ABA Model Code and Model Rules.

I

Informal Opinion (See, *ABA Formal Opinion*).

In Propria Persona A Latin term meaning, literally, in one's own proper person. It is often abbreviated as p.p. See also, *pro se.*

Integrated Bar A term used to refer to mandatory bar membership as a prerequisite—by either legislative enactment or order of the court—to the practice of law in a given geographic area. See, e.g., *Integration of Bar Case,* 244 Wisc. 8, 11 N.W.2d 604 (1943). The term "integrated" is derived from the Latin "integer," meaning whole, untouched, one.

Interests, Differing (See, *Differing Interests*).

J

Judge, Continuing Part-time (See, *Continuing Part-time Judge*)

Judge, Lay (See, *Lay Judge*).

Judge, Part-time (See, *Part-time Judge).*

Judge, Periodic Part-time (See, *Periodic Part-time Judge*).

Judge Pro Tempore A term used in the ABA Model Code of Judicial Conduct (1972), Compliance (B), to refer to a person who is appointed to act as a judge only for a time, temporarily. (See also, *Pro tempore part-time judge,* a slightly different term that the ABA Model Code of Judicial Conduct (1990), Terminology [16], uses).

K

Knowingly A term used in the ABA Model Rules of Professional Conduct to mean "actu-

al knowledge of the fact in question. A person's knowledge may be inferred from circumstances." See Model Rules, Terminology 5. The ABA Model Code of Judicial Conduct (1990), Terminology [8] uses the same definition.

Known (See, *Knowingly*).

Knows (See, *Knowingly*).

Kutak Commission The popular name to refer to the ABA Commission on Evaluation of Professional Standards, the body that drafted the ABA Model Rules of Professional Conduct. The Commission was called the Kutak Commission after its first chairman, the late Robert J. Kutak.

L

Law Firm A term used in the Model Rules to refer to "a lawyer or lawyers in a private firm, lawyers employed in the legal department of a corporation or other organization and lawyers employed in a legal services organization." See Model Rules, Terminology 3. See also Model Rule 1.10, Comments 1–3. A law firm, as used in either the Model Rules or Model Code, includes a professional legal corporation. See Model Code, Definitions (2); cf. Model Rules, Terminology [6].

Law Partner (See, *Partner*).

Lawyer (See, *Attorney*).

Lay Judge A judge who is not a lawyer.

Lien A lien in general is an encumbrance, a charge, imposed on specific property.

An attorney's lien is generally divided into two types: a charging lien, and a retaining lien. See, e.g., Tuite, *Something to Lien On,* 76 A.B.A.J. 92 (Dec. 1990).

A retaining lien, or a common law lien, is "a general lien resting wholly upon possession, which is a [lawyer's] mere right to *retain,* until his whole bill is paid, all papers, deeds, vouchers, etc., in his possession upon which, or in connection with which, he has expended money or given his professional services. This 'retaining lien' is a general one for whatever may be due to him; and though a client may change his attorney at will, if the latter is without fault and willing to proceed in pending causes, none of the papers or vouchers can ordinarily be withdrawn from him except upon payment of his entire bill for professional services. This lien, like other mere possessory liens, is however, purely passive, being a base right to hold possession till payment. The articles cannot be sold or parted without the loss of the lien, nor can any active proceedings be taken at law or in equity to procure payment of the debt out of the articles so held." *In re Wilson*, 12 F. 235, 238 (S.D.N.Y.1882) (internal citations and paragraphing omitted). The retaining lien does not apply to property, such as escrow funds, that the client conveys to the lawyer unrelated to the lien. E.g., *State Bar v. Bratton,* 413 S.2d 754 (Fla. 1982).

In contrast, a *charging lien* is a specific lien, which is often governed by statute. It exists on the judgment that the attorney has recovered for the client, or the money payable on the judgment or upon some fund in court. "This lien, so far as it extends, is not merely a passive lien, but entitles the attorney to take active steps to secure payment. It did not exist at common law [and] does not depend upon possession, but upon the favor of the court in protecting attorneys, as its own officers, by taking care . . . that a 'party should not run away with the fruits of the cause without satisfying the legal demands of the attorney by whose industry, and expense those fruits were obtained.' " 12 F. at 239 (internal citations omitted).

M

Malum in Se A Latin term meaning, literally, a wrong in itself. It is often used to refer to acts generally recognized as serious immoral wrongs in the nature of things, such as

murder, rather than acts recognized as wrongs only because a statute so provides. Compare *malum prohibitum.*

Malum Prohibitum A Latin term meaning, literally, a wrong prohibited. It is often used to refer to acts that are not inherently immoral but wrong only because a statute so provides. Compare *malum in se.*

Model Rules of Professional Conduct (See, *Rules of Professional Conduct*).

N

Neglect DR 6–101(a)(3) provides that a lawyer shall not "[n]eglect a legal matter entrusted to him." ABA Informal Opinion 1273 (1973) explains: "Neglect involves indifference and a consistent failure to carry out the obligations which the lawyer has assumed to his clients or a conscious disregard for the responsibility owed to the client. . . . Neglect usually involves more than a single act or omission. Neglect cannot be found if the acts or omissions complained of were inadvertent or the result of an error of judgment made in good faith." The Model Rules do not contain a prohibition of "neglect." Instead, Rule 1.1 affirmatively requires the lawyer to be competent, and Rule 1.3 affirmatively mandates "reasonable diligence and promptness in representing a client."

Nonpublic Information A term used in the Model Code of Judicial Conduct (1990), Terminology [13], to denote information not available to the public, including (but not limited to) information sealed by statute or court order; information impounded or communicated in camera; and information offered in grand jury proceedings, presentencing reports, dependency cases, or psychiatric reports.

Notice of Withdrawal A concept, used in the Model Rules, to refer to a lawyer informing third parties that the lawyer no longer represents a given client. This notice may also inform those third parties that they no longer should rely on the lawyer's participation in the case or that the lawyer is withdrawing any previously issued opinion, document, or other affirmation. A client cannot prevent a lawyer from issuing a Notice of Withdrawal, or require the lawyer to keep secret the fact of withdrawal. See Rule 1.6, Comment 15.

O

Of Counsel This term is often used in *court pleadings* to refer to a lawyer representing a party in a particular case. In briefs it is usually used to refer to the lawyer who is not the main lawyer of record but rather is assisting, or associated with, the main counsel of record.

When *law firm stationery* lists an attorney as of counsel, it typically indicates that the lawyer listed is neither a partner nor associate of the firm but has a special contractual relationship with the firm and may not be practicing law full time.

The Model Rules include a specific reference to "of counsel in DR 2–102(A)(4), which provides that a lawyer who has a continuing relationship with a lawyer or law firm, other than as a partner or associate, may be designated "of counsel" on the firm's letterhead. The Model Rules have no specific reference, but ABA Formal Opinion 90–357 (May 10, 1990) discusses the term extensively. It concluded that it is permissible to use the title "of counsel" on the filings in a particular case even though the attorneys have only collaborated in that one case. However, when the term is used on legal stationery,, professional cards, office signs and the like, it is proper to use the term only as long as the relationship between the two is close and regular (the relationship must exist for more than a single case) and the use of the title is not otherwise misleading. The Formal Opinion also concluded that not only an individual but also a law firm can be "of counsel" to another firm; that a lawyer may be "of counsel" to more than one firm, as long as the controlling criterion of a "close and regular" relationship is

met; and that it is not ethically permissible to use the "of counsel" term on firm stationery and the like to designate a relationship involving only a single case (but one can use the term on court filings in a particular case), a relationship of forwarder or receiver of a legal business, a relationship involving only collaborative efforts among otherwise unrelated lawyers, and the relationship of outside consultant.

If two or more firms share the same of counsel lawyer, the law firms are treated as a single firm for purposes of attribution of disqualifications. ABA Formal Opinion 90–357.

If a lawyer who is a named partner in a law firm subsequently retires from active practice and assumed the status of "of counsel," the firm can continue to use the retired lawyer's name in the firm name. However, if a new lawyer joins a firm as "of counsel" it would be misleading for that lawyer to lend his or her name to the name of the firm when that lawyer is not undertaking the responsibilities of a partner or principle. ABA Formal Opinion 90–357.

P

Partner A term used in the Model Rules to refer to "a member of a partnership" or "a shareholder in a law firm organized as a professional legal corporation." See Model Rules, Terminology [6].

Part-time Judge A term specifically defined in the ABA Code of Judicial Conduct (1972) to refer to a judge "who serves on a continuing or periodic basis, but is permitted by law to devote time to some other profession or occupation and whose compensation for that reason is less than that of a full time judge." ABA Code of Judicial Conduct (1972), Compliance with the Code of Judicial Conduct, A. (See also, *Continuing Part-time Judge, Periodic Part-time judge,* and *Pro Tempore Part-time judge.*

Passive Lien (See, *Lien*).

Periodic Part-time Judge A term used in the Model Code of Judicial Conduct (1990), Terminology [14], to denote a judge "who serves or expects to serve repeatedly on a part-time basis but under a separate appointment for each limited period of service or for each matter."

Person A term specifically defined in the ABA Model Code of Professional Responsibility to include "a corporation, an association, a trust, a partnership, and any other organization or legal entity." See Model Code, Definitions (3).

Pro Bono Publico A Latin term meaning, literally for the public good. Often it is used to refer to lawyer giving uncompensated legal advice, or advice for which less than the usual fee is charged.

Professional Legal Corporation A term used to refer to "a corporation or an association treated as a corporation, authorized by law to practice law for profit." Model Code, Definitions (4).

Pro Hac Vice A Latin term meaning, literally, for this turn, or for this particular occasion. Often it is used to refer to a lawyer who, while not a member of the bar of a particular jurisdiction, is admitted by the court for that particular case only.

Propria Persona, In (See, *In Propria Persona*).

Pro Se A Latin term meaning, literally, for himself, or, in his own behalf. Often it is used to refer to a litigant who has no attorney and is representing himself.

See, *In Propria Persona*.

Pro Tempore, Judge (See, *Judge Pro Tempore*, and *Pro Tempore Part-time Judge*).

Pro Tempore Part-time Judge A term used in the Model Code of Judicial Conduct (1990), Terminology [16], to denote a judge "who serves or expects to serve once or only sporadically on a part-time basis under a separate appointment for each period of service or for each case heard."

Q

Qualified Legal Assistance Organization A term specifically defined in the ABA Model Code of Professional Responsibility to mean "an office or organization of one of the four types listed in DR 2–103(D)(1)–(4), inclusive that meets all of the requirements thereof." Model Code, Definitions (8).

R

Reasonable A term used in the Model Rules to mean, when used to refer to a lawyer's conduct, "the conduct of a reasonably prudent and competent lawyer." See, Model Rules, Terminology [7].

Reasonable Belief A term used in the Model Rules that, when used with reference to a lawyer, means "that the lawyer believes the matter in question and that the circumstances are such that the belief is reasonable." See Model Rules, Terminology [8].

Reasonably (See, *Reasonable*).

Reasonably Believes (See, *Reasonable Belief*).

Reasonably Should Know A phrase used in the Model Rules that, when used to refer to a lawyer, means "that a lawyer of reasonable prudence and competence would ascertain the matter in question." See Model Rules, Terminology [9].

Reprimand A term defined in the ABA Model Standards for Lawyer Discipline and Disability Proceedings to refer to a "form of public discipline imposed after trial or formal charges, which declares the respondent's conduct to have been improper but does not limit his right to practice."

Require A term that the ABA Model Code of Judicial Conduct (1990, Terminology [18], uses to mean that the judge is to exercise reasonable direction and control over the conduct of those persons subject to the judge's direction and control. "Require" is a rule of reason.

Restatement (third) of the Law Governing Lawyers A proposed Restatement of the Law of Lawyering, prepared by the American Law Institute. The project is now in tentative draft form. There is no Restatement First, or Restatement Second.

Retainer In the practice of law, when a client hires an attorney to represent him, the client is said to have retained the attorney. This act of employment is called the retainer. The fee agreed upon is also called the retainer. (If the client employs the attorney for a specific case, that is called a *special retainer*. In contrast, if a client hires a lawyer for a specific length of time (e.g., a year) rather than for a specific project, that is called a *general retainer*. The lawyer, during the period of the general retainer, may not accept any conflicting employment. And, the attorney is to perform legal services that the client requests, and none that is not requested. Since the client is hiring the lawyer to stand ready to deliver the services requested, the lawyer is entitled to be paid for the general retainer whether or not the client actually calls upon the lawyer. See *Rhode Island Exchange Bank v. Hawkins*, 6 R.I. 198, 206 (1859). A *nonrefundable retainer* is earned when paid. It is "an agreement between lawyer and client providing for the payment of part or all of the fee in advance of the lawyer's performance. The payment is designated in the retainer agreement as nonrefundable. The dispute regarding the validity of these agreements usually arises when the client terminates the lawyer's employment without just cause before completion of the task and demands return of the unearned part of the advance fee." Nonrefundable retainers are "contractual forfeiture provisions." Brickman & Cunningham, *Nonrefundable Retainers: Impermissible Under Fiduciary, Statutory*

and Contract Law, 57 Ford.L.Rev. 149, 150 n.1 & 151 (1988).

Retaining Lien (See, *Lien*).

Rules, Disciplinary (See, *Disciplinary Rules* and *Canons*).

Rules of Professional Conduct A model code developed by the ABA Commission on Evaluation of Professional Standards. The ABA House of Delegates adopted these rules on August 2, 1983. They are not positive law unless enacted into law, usually as a court rule.

The black letter *Rules* of the Rules of Professional Conduct, when cast as imperative, using the terms "shall" or "shall not," "define proper conduct for purposes of professional discipline." See ABA Model Rules, Scope 1; Rule 8.4(a).

See *Disciplinary Rules*.

The *Comment* accompanying each of these black letter Rules is intended to explain and illustrate the purpose of the Rule. "The Comments are intended as guides to interpretation, but the text of each Rule is authoritative." Model Rules, Scope 9.

S

Secret As defined in the Model Code, a secret refers to information gained in the attorney-client relationship that is not privileged under the laws of evidence but which the client has requested be held inviolate or which would be embarrassing or is likely to be detrimental to the client if disclosed. DR 4–101(A). See *Confidence*.

Special Retainer (See *Retainer*).

Specific Lien (See, *Lien*).

State A term specifically defined in the ABA Model Code of Professional Responsibility to include the District of Columbia, Puerto Rico, and all other federal territories and possessions. Model Code, Definitions (5).

Substantial A term used in the Model Rules to refer to "a material matter of clear and weighty importance when used to refer to extent or degree." See Model Rules, Terminology [10].

T

Third Degree of Relationship A term used in the ABA Model Code of Judicial Conduct (1990), Terminology [19], to mean great-grandparent, grandparent, parent, uncle, aunt, brother, sister, child, grandchild, great-grandchild, nephew, or niece.

Tribunal A term specifically defined in the ABA Model Code of Professional Responsibility to include "all courts and all other adjudicatory bodies." Model Code, Definitions (5).

U

Unified Bar (See, *Integrated Bar*).

*

APPENDIX J

TABLE OF CASES

Table of Cases

APPENDIX L

INDEX

†